CHINESE CIVILIZATION
A Sourcebook

SECOND EDITION, REVISED AND EXPANDED

Edited by

Patricia Buckley Ebrey

THE FREE PRESS
New York   London   Toronto   Sydney   Tokyo   Singapore

The Free Press
A Division of Simon & Schuster Inc.
1230 Avenue of the Americas
New York, N.Y. 10020

Printed in the United States of America

printing number

     6 7 8 9 10

Library of Congress Cataloging-in-Publication Data

Chinese civilization : a sourcebook / edited by Patricia Buckley
  Ebrey.—2nd ed., rev. and expanded.
     p. cm.
    Rev. and expanded ed. of: Chinese civilization and society.
    Includes bibliographical references and index.
    ISBN 0-02-908752-X
    1. China—Civilization—Sources. 2. China—History—Sources.
I. Ebrey, Patricia Buckley II. Chinese civilization and
society.
DS721.C517 1993
951—dc20   92-47017
                                    CIP

CONTENTS

III. THE ERA OF DIVISION AND THE TANG DYNASTY   87

IV. THE SONG AND YUAN DYNASTIES   137

V. THE MING DYNASTY 203

VI. THE QING DYNASTY 267

VIII. THE PEOPLE'S REPUBLIC / 407

PREFACE TO THE SECOND EDITION

Over the years I have had the pleasure of meeting and talking with many students and teachers who used *Chinese Civilization and Society: A Sourcebook* in their classes. Repeatedly they told me that what they liked most about it was its liveliness—the variety in the kinds of sources, the abundance of ones about ordinary life, the sprinkling of humor and glimpses of personal life. For their sakes I have long been thinking I should update it to bring it up to the 1990s and take into account reevaluations of the Mao years.

When I finally found the time to tackle revisions, I decided to do a more thorough rethinking of the overall purposes of this sourcebook and how it actually gets used. My original goal fifteen years ago was to get into print lots of new translations of the sorts of documents that had been neglected in other sourcebooks: popular stories, descriptions of local customs, texts like tenancy contracts, essays that would reveal how relatively ordinary people thought, and so on. There were already many good translations of philosophical and religious texts, of standard historical accounts of great events, and of China's relations with foreign peoples, so I did not give these topics as much space as texts about daily life or the mental world of ordinary people. From my conversations with colleagues around the country who have been assigning this book to their students, I have come to realize that few of them assign any other sourcebook or any other original texts. Chinese history is commonly taught in a rapid survey lasting only one or two semesters, with never enough time to read widely in the avail-

able translations. The *Sourcebook* would better meet classroom needs, I now realized, if it gave balanced coverage to all aspects of Chinese civilization, regardless of whether a source had also been translated elsewhere.

Consequently I have made revisions throughout this book. The selection of sources for China since 1949 has been extensively revised and the coverage of the earliest periods expanded. Sometimes I have substituted an earlier piece for a later one on the same subject; for instance, I added a selection from the Tang code in place of one from the Ming code and some fourth-century ghost stories instead of some seventeenth-century ones. I have also expanded coverage of philosophy and religion in general, with new selections on Confucianism, Taoism, Legalism, and Buddhism. In addition, I have added quite a few pieces that relate to political ideas and practices and to China's contacts with foreign peoples. Altogether there are thirty-nine new selections, bringing the total to one hundred. To make room for these new pieces, I have had to make cuts, sometimes shortening pieces, sometimes eliminating ones that seemed, on balance, to contribute less to the overall understanding of Chinese civilization. Although the final selection is still rich in sources for social and cultural history, I now believe that it is sufficiently well rounded to serve as the sole sourcebook in a course on Chinese history or civilization. To bring attention to the change in the focus of this book, I decided to change the title as well, to *Chinese Civilization: A Sourcebook*.

Several people have helped me prepare this new

edition. My colleagues Kai-wing Chow, Peter Gregory, and Kenneth Klinker offered advice on new selections. Chiu-yueh Lai did the conversions from Wade-Giles to pinyin romanization. She and Chunyu Wang each translated one of the new pieces. Susan Harum helped with the final preparation of the manuscript. Two scholars at other universities generously provided translations in areas of their expertise, David Keightley of the University of California at Berkeley and Ruth Dunnell of Kenyon College. The remainder of the new translations I did myself.

P.B.E.

September 1992

PREFACE TO THE FIRST EDITION

This sourcebook came into being because of my belief that listening to what the Chinese themselves have had to say is the best way to learn about China. In teaching Chinese history and culture, however, I found that available translations were of limited use for the kinds of questions students were asking: How different were ordinary Chinese from ordinary Westerners? Did their different religions or philosophies lead to major differences in daily life? Did the Chinese have the same kinds of personal, social, and political problems as we do, or different ones? To help students find answers to these questions, I had to search for sources that could tell us more about the lives, outlooks, and habits of the full range of the Chinese population, not merely philosophers and scholars, but also women, peasants, townsmen, and undistinguished local officials. Since such people seldom wrote essays or autobiographies, I had to look for different kinds of sources—folk songs, plays, moral primers, descriptions, contracts, newspaper articles, and so on.

My efforts to make a sourcebook out of this material could never have succeeded without the generous help of others. Acknowledgment for funding must be made to the National Endowment for the Humanities for an Education Project Grant. This grant allowed me to employ several graduate-student research assistants. Jane Chen, Lucie Clark, Mark Coyle, Nancy Gibbs, Lily Hwa, Jeh-hang Lai, Barbara Matthies, and Clara Yu helped prepare, correct, and polish the translations in this book. Although all the trans-

lations we did are attributed to specific translators, they are in fact joint efforts, since in all cases either I as editor or one of the assistants extensively revised the translation to improve accuracy or style. Clara Yu's contribution to this book deserves particular note; she worked with me from the inception of the project to its completion and is responsible for thirty of the eighty-nine selections.

Over the past five years, I have also regularly profited from the advice and criticisms of colleagues. Robert Crawford and Howard Wechsler helped test the translations in courses at the University of Illinois. Several other faculty members at Illinois have been ready to answer my questions on subjects about which they knew more than I, including Richard Chang, Lloyd Eastman, James Hart, Richard Kraus, Whalen Lai, and William MacDonald. I have also benefited greatly from the reactions and suggestions of professors at other colleges who saw earlier versions of this sourcebook in whole or part. These include Suzanne Barnett (University of Puget Sound), David Buck (University of Wisconsin–Milwaukee), Parks Coble (University of Nebraska), Wolfram Eberhard (University of California, Berkeley), Edward Farmer (University of Minnesota), Charlotte Furth (California State University at Long Beach), Peter Golas (University of Denver), John Langlois (Bowdoin College), Susan Mann Jones (University of Chicago), Susan Naquin (University of Pennsylvania), John Meskill (Barnard College), Keith Schoppa (Valparaiso University), Jonathan Spence (Yale University), Philip West (Indiana

University), and Arthur Wolf (Stanford University).

Finally, I was fortunate to have excellent clerical assistance from Mary Mann, who typed several versions of this manuscript, and Sandy Price, who helped with the final typing. Christina Pheley conscientiously corrected the page proofs and galleys.

P.B.E.

CONTENTS ACCORDING TO TOPICS

RELIGION AND COSMOLOGY

CONFUCIANISM

GOVERNMENT

HISTORY WRITING AND HISTORICAL GENRE

CONTACTS WITH OUTSIDE PEOPLES

FAMILY, KINSHIP, AND GENDER

LOCAL SOCIAL AND ECONOMIC ACTIVITIES

UPPER CLASS AND INTELLECTUALS

TALES AND FICTION

A NOTE ON THE SELECTION AND TRANSLATION OF SOURCES

In selecting sources for inclusion in this book, I had to balance many goals. Each source had to reveal something important about Chinese civilization, but at the same time I wanted each to be intrinsically interesting to read. I also tried to balance the needs of topical and chronological coverage and my desire to show something of the life of people in different stations in society. I have drawn from many well-known works but have also made a concerted effort to find sources about the lives of the kinds of people who did not ordinarily write, such as women, peasants, soldiers, artisans, and merchants.

Translating the sources was as challenging as selecting them. Fully capturing meaning, style, and mood is never possible. If we transpose other peoples' common ways of expression into ways of expression common to us, important elements of the culture are lost to us, for much of culture is communicated in the metaphors and imagery people use. On the other hand, to convey all of the meanings in a text usually results in such bad English that the intelligence, grace, or humor of the original is lost. And even when the style is satisfactory, bringing out too many subtleties from texts, especially popular works, can distort their real meaning. For instance, Buddhist monks certainly read more into technical Buddhist terms than lay persons do; to bring out all possible meanings for such terms in a popular moral tract or fictional story would be to misrepresent what it meant to much of the audience that actually read it. Unfortunately, judging how much an audience understood is nearly impossible. Did most people who invoked the phrase "the tyrant Xia Jie" know anything about Xia Jie except that he was a famous tyrant? If they did know more, was it very close to the Xia Jie of the historical accounts, or was it based on the portrayal of him in popular plays or operas?

Thus a number of compromises have been made in the translations in this sourcebook. To make extensive reading more inviting, we have translated into standard, easily intelligible English, often eliminating redundancies but trying to preserve much of the imagery and style of the original. Many selections have been abridged, but omissions are marked with ellipsis points (. . .). To avoid cluttering the text, footnotes and interpolations have been kept to an absolute minimum. When authors mention specific people, they are not identified when the point can be understood without it. Allusions and philosophical terms are translated simply, generally with little explanation. It is hoped that wide reading will give readers a surer sense of what authors and audiences understood by such terms than footnotes ever could.

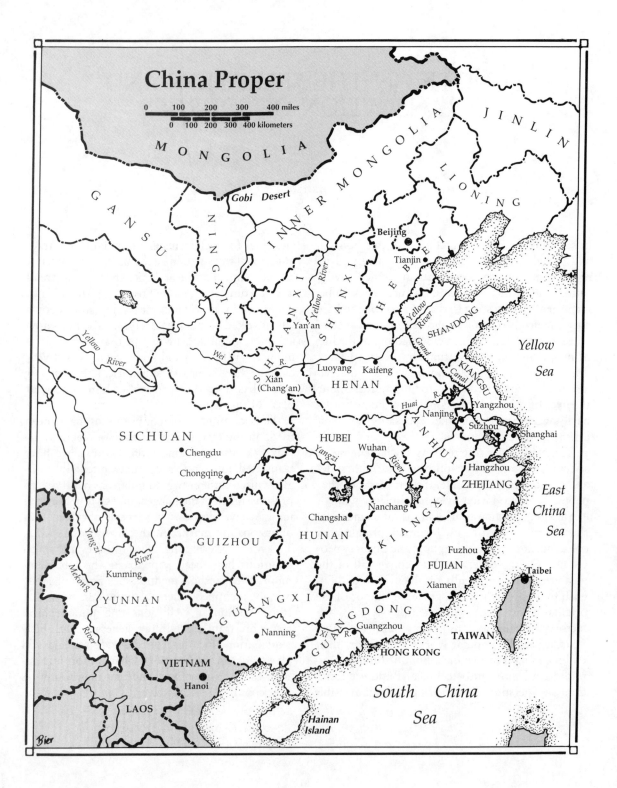

China Proper

0 100 200 300 400 miles

0 100 200 300 400 kilometers

MONGOLIA

INNER MONGOLIA

JINLIN

LIONING

Gobi Desert

GANSU

NINGXIA

SHAANXI

Yellow River

SHANXI

HEBEI

Beijing

Tianjin

Yellow River

SHANDONG

Grand Canal

Yellow Sea

Yellow River

Wei R.

Yan'an

Luoyang

Kaifeng

Xian (Chang'an)

HENAN

Huai R.

KIANGSU

Yangzhou

Suzhou

Shanghai

SICHUAN

Chengdu

HUBEI

Yangzi

Wuhan

Nanjing

ANHUI

Hangzhou

Chongqing

River

ZHEJIANG

East China Sea

Yangzi

Changsha

HUNAN

Nanchang

KIANGXI

Fuzhou

FUJIAN

Xiamen

Taibei

GUIZHOU

River

Mekong

Kunming

YUNNAN

GUANGXI

Nanning

GUANGDONG

Xi R.

Guangzhou

HONG KONG

TAIWAN

River

VIETNAM

Hanoi

LAOS

Hainan Island

South China Sea

Bier

PART I

THE CLASSICAL PERIOD

The archaeological record of human existence in China goes back to the remote past. By the fifth millennium B.C. neolithic cultures flourished in several parts of the country. Archaeologists have found village settlements, finely decorated pottery, carved and polished jades, and evidence of ancestor worship. With the Shang dynasty (ca. 1600–ca. 1050 B.C.), the historical and archaeological records begin to coincide; the Chinese accounts of the Shang rulers match the diviners' inscriptions on animal bones and tortoise shells found during the past century at the city of Anyang in the Yellow River valley. The Shang had built a strong state on the basis of bronze technology, chariot warfare, and elaborate social differentiation. Shang kings could mobilize large armies for warfare and huge numbers of workers to construct defensive walls or elaborate tombs.

Much fuller historical records survive for the next dynasty, the Zhou (ca. 1050–256 B.C.). The Zhou house originated in what is now Shaanxi province in northwestern China, moving eastward to conquer the Shang and establish their rule over much of northern China. The early Zhou rulers secured their position by enfeoffing loyal supporters and relatives in different regions, thus establishing a social order somewhat like the feudal system in medieval Europe. The early Zhou dynasty was an age when blood kinship was honored and social status distinctions were stressed. Members of the nobility were linked both to each other and to their ancestors by bonds of obligation based on kinship. Ancestors were seen as having great influence over the living, with powers similar to but far surpassing those of the living elders of the clan. Even the relationship between lord and peasant was supposed to be a paternalistic one, the peasant serving the lord and the lord concerned about his welfare.

The Zhou kingdom remained strong for over two centuries, but its position gradually weakened, until finally in 771 B.C., the capital was sacked by non-Chinese tribes. The Zhou rulers then established a new capital further east in the Yellow River valley, marking the beginning of the Eastern Zhou. In this period real political power lay with the feudal states. The Zhou king continued to reign only because of the prestige of his house and the fact that no one feudal state was strong enough to dominate the others.

The Eastern Zhou is divided into two major eras, the Spring and Autumn period (722–481 B.C.) and the Warring States period (403–221 B.C.). During these centuries the states attacked and absorbed each other until only a half-dozen powerful ones survived. This period of political strife witnessed social and economic advances of all sorts, including the introduction of iron, the development of infantry armies, the circulation of money, the beginning of private ownership of land, the growth of cities, and the breakdown of class barriers. During this period also there was a gradual expansion of the culture of the North southward into the Yangzi River region, and at the same time elements of the indigenous culture of the lusher southern region were incorporated into the culture of the North.

The political disruption and social change of the late Zhou drew many men's attention to the problem of how to achieve stability. Those who responded to this challenge included not only military and political leaders but also many philosophers. The foremost philosophers were Confucius (551–479 B.C.) and his followers Mencius (ca. 370–ca. 300 B.C.) and Xunzi (ca. 310–ca. 215 B.C.), who emphasized the preservation of tradition and moral cultivation. They were closely rivaled at the time by the Mohists and Legalists, the former emphasizing frugality, discipline, and universal love, the latter law and statecraft. Opposed to all of these proposed methods of reform were the Daoists, who preached a return to the Dao or Way, the true condition of man, which had been lost through the process of civilization and could be regained only if people were allowed to return to naturalness. The proliferation of philosophy in this period was so great that it came to be known as the period of the "one hundred schools." Without doubt it was one of the most intellectually creative eras in Chinese history.

The major sources for the Classical period are the oracle bones and bronze inscriptions, the *Book of Documents*, the *Book of Changes*, the *Book of Songs*, the ritual classics, several historical texts, and the essays and recorded sayings of the philosophers. Passages from these texts have been selected for inclusion here first of all to illuminate the Classical period. A second, complementary goal, is to introduce the classics themselves, important because they were studied by so many generations of students and thus profoundly shaped the thinking of the educated.

I

占卜，预测）

LATE SHANG DIVINATION RECORDS

3/30

预言

The kings of the late Shang (ca. 1200–1050 B.C.) attempted to communicate with the spiritual forces that ruled their world by reading the stress cracks in cattle bones and turtle plastrons. They and their diviners produced these cracks by applying a heated brand or poker to the consecrated bones or shells, intoning as they did so a charge that conveyed their intentions, wishes, or need to know. After the divination ritual was over, a record of the topic and, sometimes, of the prognostication and the result, was engraved into the bone. Those inscriptions, only recovered in the twentieth century by archaeologists and painstakingly deciphered by paleographers, provide direct contact with many of the Shang kings' daily activities and concerns. Some 150,000 oracle-bone fragments, mainly excavated at the late Shang cult center near modern Anyang, have been preserved, of which 50,000 have been thought worth reproduction. The following inscriptions—most of them from the reign of the twenty-first king, Wu Ding (ca. 1200–1181 B.C.), the heyday of Shang divination as it is recorded in the bone inscriptions—cover the topics that were of major concern to the Shang diviners. As in the first example, many of the early charges were paired, being expressed in both the positive and negative mode and placed in matching opposition on the bone. The inscriptions, as can be seen below, include references to Di, the high god of the Shang. The offering of cult to Di, however, was rarely divined, perhaps because, unlike the ancestors, Di was virtually beyond human comprehension and influence.

Sacrifices and Rituals

[A] [Preface:] Divined: [Charge:] "[We] should offer to Xiang Jia, Father Geng, and Father Xin [the seventeenth, eighteenth, and nineteenth kings], one cow."

[B] [Preface:] Divined: [Charge:] "[We] should not offer to Xiang Jia, Father Geng, and Father Xin, one cow."

Mobilizations

[Preface:] Crack-making on *dingyou* [day 34], Que divined: [Charge:] "This season, the king

3

raises five thousand men to campaign against the Tufang; he will receive assistance in this case." [Postface:] Third moon.

Military Campaigns

[A] Divined: "It should be Zhi Guo whom the king joins to attack the Bafang, [for if he does] Di will [confer assistance] on us."

[B] "It should not be Zhi Guo whom the king joins to attack the Bafang [for if he does] Di may not [confer assistance] on us."

Meteorological Phenomena

[A] [Preface:] Crack-making on *bingshen* [day 33], Que divined: [Charge:] "On the coming *yisi* [day 42], [we] will perform the *you*-ritual to Xia Yi [the twelfth king]." [Prognostication:] The king read the cracks and said: "When [we] perform the *you*-ritual there will be occasion for calamities; there may be thunder." [Verification:] On *yisi* [day 42], [we] performed the *you*-ritual. At dawn it rained; at the beheading sacrifice it stopped raining; when the beheading sacrifice was all done, it likewise rained; when [we] displayed [the victims] and split them open, it suddenly cleared.

[B] [Verification:] In the night of *yisi* [day 42] there was thunder in the west.

Agriculture

[A] [Preface:] Crack-making on [*bing-*]*chen* [day 53], Que divined: [Charge:] "We will receive millet harvest."

[B] [Preface:] Crack-making on *bingchen* [day 53], Que divined: [Charge:] "We may not receive millet harvest." (Postface:) Fourth moon.

[C] [Prognostication:] The king read the cracks and said: "Auspicious. We will receive this harvest."

Sickness

Divined: "There is a sick tooth; it is not Father Yi [the twentieth king, Wu Ding's father] who is harming [it]."

Childbirth

[A] [Preface:] Crack-making on *jiashen* [day 21], Que divined: [Charge:] "Lady Hao [a consort of Wu Ding] will give birth and it will be good." [Prognostication:] The king read the cracks and said: "If it be on a *ding* day that she give birth, it will be good. If it be on a *geng* day that she give birth, it will be prolonged auspiciousness." [Verification:] [After] thirty-one days, on *jiayin* [day 51], she gave birth. It was not good. It was a girl.

[B] [Preface:] Crack-making on *jiashen* [day 21], Que divined: [Charge:] "Lady Hao will give birth and it may not be good." [Verification:] [After] thirty-one days, on *jiayin* [day 51], she gave birth. It really was not good. It was a girl.

Disaster, Distress, or Trouble

[A] Crack-making on *jiashen* [day 21], Zheng divined: "This rain will be disastrous for us."

[B] Divined: "This rain will not be disastrous for us."

Dreams

[A] Crack-making on *jichou* [day 26], Que divined: "The king's dream was due to Ancestor Yi."

[B] Divined: "The king's dream was not due to Ancestor Yi."

Settlement Building

[A] Crack-making on *renzi* [day 49], Zheng divined: "If we build a settlement, Di will not obstruct [but] approve." Third moon.

[B] Crack-making on *guichou* [day 50], Zheng divined: "If we do not build a settlement, Di will approve."

Orders

Crack-making on [*jia*]*wu* [day 31], Bin divined: "It should be Lady Hao whom the king orders to campaign against the Yi."

Tribute Payments

[Marginal notation:] Wo brought in one thousand [shells]; Lady Jing [a consort of Wu Ding] ritually prepared forty of them. [Recorded by the diviner] Bin.

Divine Assistance or Approval

[A] Crack-making on *xinchou* [day 38], Que divined: "Di approves the king."
[B] Divined: "Di does not approve the king."

Requests to Ancestral or Nature Powers

Crack-making on *xinhai* [day 48], Gu divined: "In praying for harvest to Yue [a mountain spirit], [we] make a burnt offering of three small penned sheep [and] split open three cattle." Second moon.

The Night or the Day

[A] Crack-making on *renshen* [day 9], Shi divined: "This night there will be no disasters."
[B] Divined: "This night it will not rain." Ninth moon.

Hunting Expeditions and Excursions

On *renzi* [day 49] the king made cracks and divined: "[We] hunt at Zhi; going and coming back there will be no harm." [Prognostication:] The king read the cracks and said: "Prolonged auspiciousness." [Verification:] This was used. [We] caught forty-one foxes, eight *mi*-deer, one rhinoceros.

The Ten-Day Week

[A] On *guichou* [day 50], the king made cracks and divined: "In the [next] ten days, there will be no disasters." [Prognostication:] The king read the cracks and said: "Auspicious."
[B] On *guihai* [day 60], the king made cracks and divined: "In the [next] ten days, there will be no disasters." [Prognostication:] The king read the cracks and said: "Auspicious."

Translated by David N. Keightley

2

THE METAL BOUND BOX

The cult of the ancestors and the practice of divination as a means of learning the wishes of the ancestors remained important in the early Zhou period. This is shown in the story below concerning the Duke of Zhou, brother of the founder of the Zhou dynasty, King Wu. When King Wu died, his son, King Cheng, was still a child. The Duke of Zhou acted as regent for him for seven years but never attempted to take the throne himself. The story here, which begins while King Wu is still alive, shows the duke's assumptions about the needs, desires, and powers of ancestors.

This selection is from the Book of Documents, *a collection of purported speeches, pronouncements, and arguments of the early kings and their advisers. The oldest of these documents date from the beginning of the Zhou dynasty, although the one included here is probably of later date. This book became one of the Five Classics, held sacred by the Confucians. Even though each document deals with a particular political situation, as a group they have been taken to provide an ideal statement of how government should be conducted.*

Two years after he had conquered the Shang dynasty, King Wu became ill and grew despondent. The two ducal councillors advised making a reverent divination on behalf of the king. However, the Duke of Zhou said, "We must not upset our royal ancestors."

The duke then took the burden upon himself. He constructed three altars on a single lot of cleared ground. Then he constructed another altar to the south, facing north. Standing there, he arranged the jade disc and grasped the jade baton. Then he addressed his ancestors, King Tai, King Ji, and King Wen. The scribe recorded his prayer.

It read, "Your principal descendant, whose name I dare not utter, has contracted a terrible and cruel illness. Heaven has made you three kings responsible for your distinguished son. Take me as a substitute for the king. I was kind and obedient to my father. I have many talents and skills, and can serve the ghosts and spirits. Your principal descendant is not as talented or skilled as I, nor can he serve the ghosts and spirits as well. Furthermore, he was given a mandate by the imperial ancestor to lend assistance to the four quarters that he might firmly establish your sons and grandsons here on the earth below. There are no people from the four quarters who do not stand in awe of him. Alas! Do not let the precious mandate which Heaven has conferred on him fail. With him, our royal ancestors will always have a refuge. I now seek a decree from the great tortoise. If you grant my request, I shall take the jade disc and baton and return to await your decree."

He divined with three tortoises, and they all indicated good fortune. He then opened the lock and looked at the writing; it too indicated good fortune. The duke said, "The configuration shows that the king will not suffer harm, and that I, the small child, have obtained a renewed mandate from the three kings. It is the long range that must be considered, and so I await my fate. They will take care of our king." The duke returned and put the scribe's record in a metal bound box. By the next day the king had improved.

After King Wu died, the Duke of Zhou's older brother, Guan Shu, along with his younger brothers, spread rumors around the country that the duke was not benefiting the young king. The Duke of Zhou informed the two ducal councillors, "Unless I flee from my brothers, I will not be able to report to our royal ancestors." The duke then lived in the east for two years, until the criminals were caught. Afterwards, he composed a poem, called "The Owl," which he presented to the young king. King Cheng, for his part, did not blame the duke at all.

In the autumn when the grain was full and ripe but not yet harvested, Heaven sent down a wind accompanied by great thunder and lightning. The grain was completely flattened. Even great trees were uprooted, and the citizens were very much afraid. King Cheng and his officers all put on their ceremonial caps and went to open the great writings in the metal bound box. Then they discovered the burden that the Duke of Zhou had taken on himself, how he had wished to substitute himself for King Wu. The two ducal councillors and the king then asked the scribe and all of the officers whether this had in fact happened. They replied, "It is true, but, oh, the duke commanded us not to utter a word about it."

The king took up the writing and cried, saying, "We need not reverently divine. Formerly the duke worked diligently for the royal family, but I was only a child and did not realize it. Now Heaven has stirred its awesome power to reveal the virtue of the Duke of Zhou. I, a small child, must greet him anew, in accordance with the ritual of our state and clan."

King Cheng then went out to the suburbs, and Heaven sent down rain and a wind from the opposite direction, so that all the grain stood up straight again. The two ducal councillors ordered the citizens to raise up and replant all of the trees which had been flattened. In that year there was a great harvest.

Translated by James Hart

3

HEXAGRAMS IN THE *BOOK OF CHANGES*

By early Zhou the interpretation of hexagrams gained favor as a method of divination. To obtain advice a person would randomly draw six milfoil stalks, long or short, to form a hexagram of six lines, broken or unbroken. A diviner would then interpret the hexagram according to traditional meanings associated with each of its lines. These meanings and interpretations became the Book of Changes.

As befits a fortunetellers' handbook, many of the passages in the Book of Changes *are brief, even cryptic, susceptible to varying interpretations. Nevertheless, the* Changes *came to be revered as one of the* Five Classics, *and over the centuries thousands of scholars have tried to reconstruct its philosophical meanings. The selection below consists of the first hexagram, all whole lines and therefore the strongest, most creative or assertive hexagram, used to represent Heaven; and the second hexagram, all broken lines, therefore the most receptive and yielding hexagram, used to represent earth. The dualistic principles found in these hexagrams also underlie the theories of Yin (female, receptive, dark) and Yang (male, assertive, bright), which were more fully developed during the late Zhou period.*

1. QIAN (THE CREATIVE, HEAVEN)

Qian above

Qian below

The Judgment: *Qian* is the ultimate source. There is great success. There is benefit in perseverance.

Nine at the beginning: There is a hidden dragon. Do not use.

Nine in the second place: See the dragon in the field. It is beneficial to see a great man.

Nine in the third place: The gentleman strives to be creative all day. At night he acts with caution and restraint. There is no fault.

Nine in the fourth place: There is an uncertain leap at the abyss. There is no fault.

Nine in the fifth place: There is a flying dragon in Heaven. It is beneficial to see a great man.

Nine in the sixth place: The overbearing dragon is cause for regret.

Nine in all the lines: There appears a myriad of dragons without heads. This is good fortune.

Commentary: Great indeed is *qian* the ultimate source. The ten thousand things receive their beginnings from it. It governs Heaven. The clouds drift by and the rain falls. All things flow into their forms. The ends and the beginnings are greatly illuminated. The six lines of the hexagram take shape at their own times.

In timely fashion they ride the six dragons and so rule over the heavens. The way of *qian* is change and transformation. Each thing thereby achieves its true nature and destiny and assures that it is in accord with great harmony. There is great benefit and constancy. It stands out from all the things of the world, and the nations of the earth enjoy peace.

The Image: The movements of Heaven have great force. The gentleman invigorates himself and does not become jaded. There is a hidden dragon. Do not use it. The Yang still is buried below. See the dragon in the field. Virtue is everywhere. The gentleman strives to be creative all day. He always follows the correct way. There is an uncertain leap at the abyss. There is no fault in going forward. There is a flying dragon in the heavens. The great man is creative. The overbearing dragon is cause for regret. Nine in all the lines. The virtue of Heaven is not to act as head.

2. *KUN* (THE RECEPTIVE, EARTH)

Kun above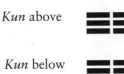

Kun below

The Judgment: *Kun* is the ultimate of receptivity. There is great success. There is benefit in the per-

severance of a mare. If the gentleman has a particular goal and attempts to attain it, at first he may lose his way, but ultimately he will achieve it. It is beneficial to make friends in the west and the south, but avoid friends in the east and north. Peaceful perseverance will yield good fortune.

Commentary: Great indeed is that originating in *kun.* The ten thousand things all receive life from it when it is in harmonious union with Heaven. *Kun* contains everything in abundance. Its virtue is in harmony with the infinite. It encompasses all things and illuminates the universe. Each individual thing achieves perfect success. The mare is an animal of the land. It wanders freely over the land. It is gentle and obedient and symbolizes great benefit through perseverance. The gentleman should conduct himself in a like manner. At first he may lose his way, but later by being humbly obedient he will achieve it forever. In the west and south there are friends. One may associate with people of a sympathetic nature. In the east and north there are no friends, but in the end one may gain benefit from this. The good fortune of peaceful perseverance will result from being in harmony with the forces of the earth.

The Image: The power of the earth lies in receptivity. The gentleman with great virtue encompasses all things.

Six at the beginning: When one steps on hoarfrost, one knows that solid ice will soon appear.

Comment: When one steps on hoarfrost, one knows that solid ice will appear soon. When the forces of Yin begin to congeal and follow this way, the time of solid ice is about to arrive.

Six in the second place: It is straight, square, and great. Without hustle and bustle there is nothing that does not prosper.

Comment: The movement of six in the second place is straight by means of being square. Without hustle and bustle there is nothing that does not prosper. There is brilliance in the Way of the earth.

Six in the third place: One's badges are hidden. One can persevere. If in the service of a king, do not try to force affairs but rather bring them to completion.

Comment: One's badges are hidden. One can persevere. At the proper time come forth. If you are in the service of a king, you should have the wisdom to spread greatness.

Six in the fourth place: To be closemouthed like a tied-up sack is neither blameworthy nor praiseworthy.

Comment: To be closemouthed like a tied-up sack is neither blameworthy nor praiseworthy. If one is careful there will be no trouble.

Six in the fifth place: There is great fortune in yellow clothing.

Comment: There is great fortune in yellow clothing. Brilliance lies within.

Six at the top: Dragons do battle in the fields. Their blood is black and yellow.

Comment: Dragons do battle in the fields. Their Way has run its course.

Six in all the lines: There is benefit in steadfast perseverance.

Comment: When all six lines yield six, it shows steadfast perseverance. In this way one can achieve great ends.

Translated by Mark Coyle

4

SONGS AND POEMS

The best source for the daily lives, hopes, complaints, and beliefs of ordinary people in the early Zhou period is the Book of Songs. *Over half of the 305 poems in this classic are said to have originally been popular songs and concern basic human problems such as love, marriage, work, and war. The remainder are court poems, including legendary accounts in praise of the founders of the Zhou dynasty, complaints about the decay of royal power, and hymns used in sacrificial rites. The four poems given below show something of this range of topics.*

In several ways the Book of Songs *set the pattern for later Chinese poetry: Its poems have fairly strict patterns in both rhyme and rhythm, they make great use of imagery, and they tend to be short. As one of the most revered of the Confucian classics, this collection of poems has been studied and memorized by centuries of scholars. The popular songs were regarded as good keys to understanding the troubles of the common people and were often read allegorically, so that complaints against faithless lovers were seen as complaints against faithless rulers.*

Please, Zhongzi,
Do not climb into our hamlet,
Do not break our willow trees.
It's not that I begrudge the willows,
But I fear my father and mother.
You I would embrace,
But my parents' words—
Those I dread.

Please, Zhongzi,
Do not leap over our wall,
Do not break our mulberry trees.
It's not that I begrudge the mulberries,
But I fear my brothers.
You I would embrace,
But my brother's words—
Those I dread.

Please, Zhongzi,
Do not climb into our yard,
Do not break our rosewood tree.
It's not that I begrudge the rosewood,
But I fear gossip.
You I would embrace,
But people's words—
Those I dread.

*   *   *

In the seventh month the Fire star declines.
In the ninth month we give out the clothes.
In the days of the first, rushing winds.
In the days of the second, bitter cold.
Without coats or garments,
How could we finish the year?

11

In the days of the third, we plow.
In the days of the fourth, we step out.
Our wives and children
Bring food to us in the southern field,
And the inspector of the fields is pleased.

In the seventh month the Fire star declines.
In the ninth month we give out the clothes.
Spring days are sunny
And the oriole sings.
The girls take their fine baskets,
And walk down the little paths
To collect the tender mulberry leaves.
Spring days get longer,
In groups they go to pick the Artemesia.
A young girl is heart-sick,
Waiting to go home with the lord's son.

In the seventh month the Fire star declines.
In the eighth month the rushes are ready.
In the silkworm month, we prune the mulberry
    trees.
We take axes and hachet
To cut off the far and high branches
And make the small mulberry luxuriant.
In the seventh month the shrike cries.
In the eighth month we splice the thread,
Both black and yellow.
With red dye very bright
We make a robe for the lord's son.

In the fourth month the grasses mature.
In the fifth month the cicada sings.
In the eighth month the crops are gathered,
In the tenth month the leaves fall.
In the days of the first we hunt badgers.
We catch foxes and wildcats.
We make furs for the lord's son.
In the days of the second we assemble
To practice the military arts.
We keep for ourselves the young boars
And give to the lord the old ones.

In the fifth month the locusts move their legs.
In the sixth month the grasshoppers shake their
    wings.
In the seventh month, the insects are out in the
    meadows.
In the eighth month, they are under the roof.
In the ninth month, they are at the door.
In the tenth month, the crickets are under our
    beds.

We stop up the holes to smoke out the rats.
We seal the northern window and plaster shut the
    door.
Come, wife and children,
The new year is starting,
Let's move into this house.

In the sixth month we eat fruits and berries.
In the seventh month we cook vegetables and
    beans.
In the eighth month we pick dates.
In the tenth month we harvest rice.
We use it to make spring wine
As a tonic for long life.
In the seventh month we eat melons.
In the eighth month we split the gourds.
In the ninth month we harvest the hemp seed.
We gather herbs and firewood.
And we feed our farm workers.

In the ninth month we make the garden into a
    threshing ground.
In the tenth month we bring in the harvest.
Millet of all varieties,
Rice and hemp, beans and wheat.
Oh, farmworkers,
The harvest is collected;
Come up to work in the house.
In the daytime you can gather grasses,
In the evening make them into rope.
Let us get quickly to the house.
Sowing grain starts again soon.

In the days of the second we cut the ice, ding-ding.
In the days of the third we take it to the ice house.
In the days of the fourth we get up early.
We make offerings of lamb and scallions.
In the ninth month the plants wither from the
    frost.
In the tenth month we clear the threshing ground.
We set out a feast with a pair of wine jars,
We slaughter lambs and sheep
And go up to the public hall.
Raising our cups of rhinocerous horn,
May you live forever!

*   *   *

We were harvesting
At the new field,
At the newly cleared acre,

When Fangshu arrived
With three thousand chariots
And a well-tested army.
Fangshu led them here,
Driving four dappled grey horses,
Such well-trained horses.
His chariot was red,
The canopy of bamboo mat, the quiver of fish
    skin.
He had breast plates with hooks and metal-
    rimmed reins.

We were harvesting
At the new field
In the central district
When Fangshu arrived
With his three thousand chariots
And emblazoned banners.
Fangshu led them here,
His wheel hubs wrapped, the yokes ornamented.
Eight bells tinkled on the bits.
He wore his official garb
With brilliant red knee-covers
And green pendants at his waist.

Swift flies the hawk,
Straight up to heaven.
Yet it stops here to roost.
Fangshu arrived
With three thousand chariots
And a well-tested army.
Fangshu led them here,
The musicians beating the drums.
He marshalled the army and lectured the troops.
Illustrious and faithful is Fangshu.
The drums sound,
And the troops move.

Foolish were you, tribes of Jing,
To make enemies of a great state.
Fangshu is an old man
Strong in his ability to plan.
Fangshu led them here,
Taking captives, capturing chiefs.
His war chariots rumble,
Rumble and crash,
Like thunder and lightning.
Illustrious and faithful is Fangshu.
He has already conquered the Xianyun
And now overawes the Jing tribes.

*   *   *

Which plant is not yellow?
Which day don't we march?
Which man does not go
To bring peace to the four quarters?

Which plant is not brown?
Which man is not sad?
Have pity on us soldiers,
Treated as though we were not men!

We are neither rhinos nor tigers,
Yet are led through the wilds.
Have pity on us soldiers,
Never resting morn or night.

A thick-furred fox
Scurries through the dark grass.
Our loaded carts
Proceed along the Zhou road.

Translated by Patricia Ebrey

5

THE BATTLE BETWEEN JIN AND CHU

To early historians, probably no activity better illustrated human greatness and human foibles than warfare. In the Spring and Autumn period, when China was divided among competing states but warfare was not yet incessant, battles were conceived of as dramas or rituals, with the various actors performing their assigned roles and being judged by how well they fulfilled them.

The following account of a major battle is from the Zuo Chronicle, *a late Zhou history that survived in the form of a commentary to the* Spring and Autumn Annals. *The* Annals *is a terse, dry, month-by-month record of items of interest to the court in the state of Lu, the home state of Confucius, during the years 722 to 481 B.C. It came to be included among the Confucian classics, but its entries are so brief as to be practically meaningless. The* Zuo Chronicle, *by contrast, provides detailed narrative of people and events, full of violence, intrigue, treachery, and heroism.*

The battle recounted here occurred in 597 B.C. The army of Jin had set out to save the besieged state of Zheng from conquest by Chu. When Zheng made peace with Chu, the Jin officers debated whether to return home and were ready to do so when two of their soldiers, eager to provoke a battle, managed to taunt some Chu soldiers into fighting.

The soldiers of Jin, afraid that Wei Yi and Zhao Zhan would anger the army of Chu, had sent out their war chariots to the Chu forces. When Pan Tang saw their dust in the distance he sent a horseman to race back with the message, "The Jin army is coming!"

The soldiers of Chu, fearful that their king might find himself surrounded by the Jin army, drew up in battle formation. Their prime minister, Wei Ao, cried, "Advance! It is better for us to

hit them than for them to hit us. The poem says, 'Ten great chariots went first to open the way.' Let us move first! The *Art of War* says, 'Move first, and rob your opponent of his will.' Let us attack them!"

Then they advanced rapidly. With the chariot horses galloping and the foot soldiers on the run, they fell upon the Jin army. Jin Commander Xun Linfu did not know what to do, so he beat the signal drum in the midst of the army and shouted,

14

"The first to cross the river will receive a reward!" The Middle and Lower Armies fought for the boats until the severed fingers could be scooped up in handfuls from the bottoms of the boats. The whole Jin army shifted to the right, except for the Upper Army, which did not move. With the Minister of Works Chi in command, the right wing of the Chu infantry pursued the Lower Army of Jin. . . .

When asked what to do, Commander Shi Hui replied, "Chu's army is now at the peak of its strength. If they gather their forces against us, our army will be annihilated. We had better regroup and leave. Then at least we can share the blame and save our men." Acting as rearguard for their infantry, they retreated and were thus not defeated. . . .

A chariot from Jin became stuck and could not move, whereupon a Chu soldier told the charioteer to remove the brace-bar. After that the chariot advanced only a little before the horses wheeled around. The Chu soldier told him to pull out the flagstaff and lay it crosswise, and this time the chariot came free. The charioteer turned back and said, "We are not as experienced at fleeing as are the soldiers of your great state."

Zhao Zhan of Jin saved his older brother and uncle by giving them his two best horses. Then he turned back with other horses but met the enemy and was not able to escape. He abandoned his chariot and ran into the woods. Just then the Great Officer Feng rode by with his two sons. He told them not to look back, but they did anyway and said, "Venerable Zhao is being left behind us." Their father became angry at them and ordered them to dismount. Then he pointed to a tree and said, "Leave your corpses there." He then gave the chariot to Zhao Zhan, who made his escape. The next day Feng found the corpses of his sons piled beneath the tree to which he had pointed.

Xiong Fuji of Chu captured Zhi Ying, whose father, Great Officer Xun Shou, set off in pursuit along with his clansmen. Wei Yi drove the chariot, and many officers of the Lower Army accompanied them. Every time Xun Shou wished to shoot, he would select the best arrows but then put them back in Wei Yi's quiver. Wei Yi became angry and said, "If you want to save your son, why are you so stingy with these willow sticks? Are you afraid of using up all the willows of Dong Marsh?"

Xun Shou replied, "Unless I capture other men's sons, how can I get my own son back? I act as I do because I cannot afford to shoot carelessly." He then shot the Officer Xiang Lao, captured his body, and took it with him in his chariot. Then he shot Gongzi Guchen and took him prisoner. He then turned back with these two prizes in his chariot.

At dusk the army of Chu set up a defensive position at Bi. Jin did not have enough troops left to set up a counter position of their own, so they retreated across the Yellow River under cover of darkness. All night long the sounds of their crossing could be heard.

The next day, the Chu supply wagons reached Bi, and so the army camped at Hengyong. Pan Dang said to the king of Chu, "My Lord, we should erect a fortress and collect the bodies of the Jin soldiers in it as a war memorial. Your subject has heard that when one conquers an enemy, he should display that fact to his sons and grandsons, so that they will not forget his military achievements."

The king of Chu replied, "You do not understand this. In writing, the characters 'stop' and 'spear' fit together to make 'military.' After King Wu conquered Shang, a hymn was written which says, 'Store the shields and spears, / Encase the arrows and bows. / We seek admirable virtue, / To extend throughout this great land. / May the king genuinely preserve it.' They also wrote the 'Military' Poem. Its last stanza states, 'You have made your achievement secure.' The third stanza says, 'May we extend this continuously; / What we seek now is to make it secure.' The sixth stanza says, 'There is peace in ten thousand states, / And repeated years of plenty.' "

" 'Military' means to prevent violence, store weapons, preserve greatness, secure achievements, pacify the people, harmonize groups, and increase wealth. Thus King Wu wanted to make sure that his sons and grandsons did not forget these stanzas. Now I have caused the bones of the soldiers from two states to lie exposed on the battlefield; this is violence. I have made a show of weapons to coerce the feudal lords; this is not storing weapons. Since I have caused violence and have not placed the weapons in storage, how could I have preserved greatness? Furthermore, the enemy state of Jin still exists; so how could my achievement be secure? In many ways I have gone against the people's wishes; so how could they be pacified? I have not been virtuous but have used force against the feudal lords; so how could the groups be harmonized? I have found profit in other men's crises and peace in their disorders. This has given me glory, but how has it increased wealth? There are seven military virtues, but I have not attained a single one of them. What do I have to display to my sons and grandsons? Let us set up an altar to our Ancestral Rulers and announce to them what we have done. Then we should stop there, for what I have done is not a military achievement.

"In ancient times when the enlightened kings chastised the disrespectful, they took the most monstrous offenders and buried them in mounds as a punishment of supreme disgrace. This is the origin of war memorials, and they were used to warn the evil and corrupt. But in the present conflict, there were no criminals. All of the people have been completely loyal, fighting to the death to carry out their rulers' decrees. So what reason is there to build a war memorial?"

So, the king of Chu conducted sacrifices to the Spirit of the Yellow River. Then he built an altar for his Ancestral Rulers and announced to them his accomplishment. After this he returned home. . . .

In the autumn, when the army of Jin arrived home, the defeated Commander Xun Linfu requested to be put to death. The Duke of Jin wished to grant his request, but Shi Zhenzi admonished him, "This must not be allowed. Remember that after the battle of Chengbu, the army of Jin celebrated with three days of feasting, and yet Duke Wen still had a sad countenance. His advisers said, 'In this time of happiness you are sad. Must there be a time of sadness for you to be happy?' The duke replied, 'As long as De Chen of Chu is still alive, my sadness cannot be alleviated. A caged beast will still fight; how much more so will the chief minister of a state!' But after De Chen had been put to death, the duke's happiness was apparent, and he said, 'Now there is no one left to poison my joy.' This was a double victory for Jin and a double defeat for Chu. Because of this, for the next two generations Chu was out of contention. At the present time it may be that Heaven is sending a great warning to us; if we would kill our commander Xun Linfu and compound Chu's victory, then would we not also be out of contention for a long time? Xun Linfu in serving his ruler has always tried to be completely loyal when in office and to mend his faults when out of office. He is the guardian of the altars to our Gods of Soil and Grain. Why should we kill him? His defeat is like an eclipse of the sun or moon, which does not diminish their brilliance."

The Duke of Jin then restored Xun Linfu to his position.

Translated by James Hart

6

CONFUCIAN TEACHINGS

Confucius (traditional dates, 551–479 B.C.) was a man of no particular distinction in his own day who exerted a profound influence on the development of Chinese culture through his teachings. He tried in vain to gain a high office, traveling from state to state with his disciples in search of a ruler who would listen to him. He talked repeatedly of an ideal age in the early Zhou, revealing his vision of a more perfect society, in which rulers and subjects, nobles and commoners, parents and children, men and women would all wholeheartedly accept the parts assigned to them, devoting themselves to their responsibilities to others. Confucius revered tradition and taught his disciples the traditional arts—music, rituals, the Book of Songs *and* Book of Documents—*while continually holding up for them high moral standards.*

Confucius's ideas are known to us primarily through the sayings recorded by his disciples in the Analects. *This book does not provide carefully organized or argued philosophical discourses, and the sayings seem to have been haphazardly arranged. Yet this short text became a sacred book, memorized by beginning students and known to all educated people. As such it influenced the values and habits of thought of Chinese for centuries. Many of its passages became proverbial sayings, unknowingly cited by illiterate peasants. In the selection that follows, sayings have been reorganized and grouped under four of the topics he most frequently discussed.*

The eventual success of Confucian ideas owes much to Confucius's followers in the two centuries following his death, the most important of whom were Mencius (ca. 370–ca. 300 B.C.) and Xunzi (ca. 310–ca. 215 B.C.). The Mencius, *like the* Analects, *is a collection of the philosopher's conversations, presented in no particular order, but unlike the* Analects, *specific points are often analyzed at length, perhaps because Mencius himself had a hand in recording them. Mencius, like Confucius, traveled around offering advice to rulers of various states. Over and over he tried to convert them to the view that the ruler who wins over the people through benevolent government would be the one to unify the realm. He proposed concrete political and financial measures for easing tax burdens and otherwise improving the people's lot. With his disciples and fellow philosophers, he discussed other issues in moral philosophy, particularly ones related to the goodness of human nature.*

17

Xunzi, a half century later, had much more actual political and administrative experience than either Confucius or Mencius and was less committed to the precedents set in the early Zhou. He wrote fully argued essays on many of the issues in social, political, and moral philosophy that engaged thinkers of his age. He carried further than either Confucius or Mencius the tendency in Confucianism toward a humanistic and rationalistic view of the cosmos. Divination was to him fine as a social ritual but did not reveal Heaven's desires or tell anything about the future. He directly attacked Mencius's argument that human nature is inherently good, claiming to the contrary that men's inborn tendencies are bad and therefore education is essential.

SELECTIONS FROM THE *ANALECTS*

The Gentleman

Confucius said, "The gentleman concerns himself with the Way; he does not worry about his salary. Hunger may be found in plowing; wealth may be found in studying. The gentleman worries about the Way, not about poverty."

Confucius said, "When he eats, the gentleman does not seek to stuff himself. In his home he does not seek luxury. He is diligent in his work and cautious in his speech. He associates with those who possess the Way, and thereby rectifies himself. He may be considered a lover of learning."

Zigong inquired about being a gentleman. Confucius said, "First he behaves properly and then he speaks, so that his words follow his actions."

Sima Niu asked about the nature of the gentleman. Confucius replied, "The gentleman does not worry and is not fearful." Si asked, "Then, can not fearing and not worrying be considered the essence of being a gentleman?" Confucius responded, "If you can look into yourself and find no cause for dissatisfaction, how can you worry and how can you fear?"

Confucius said, "The gentleman reveres three things. He reveres the mandate of Heaven; he reveres great people; and he reveres the words of the sages. Petty people do not know the mandate of Heaven and so do not revere it. They are disrespectful to great people and they ridicule the words of the sages."

Confucius said, "The gentleman must exert caution in three areas. When he is a youth and his blood and spirit have not yet settled down, he must be on his guard lest he fall into lusting. When he reaches the full vigor of his manhood in his thirties and his blood and spirit are strong, he must guard against getting into quarrels. When he reaches old age and his blood and spirit have begun to weaken, he must guard against envy."

Confucius said, "The gentleman understands integrity; the petty person knows about profit."

Confucius said, "For the gentleman integrity is the essence; the rules of decorum are the way he puts it into effect; humility is the way he brings it forth; sincerity is the way he develops it. Such indeed is what it means to be a gentleman."

Confucius said that Zichan possessed the way of the gentleman in four areas. In his personal conduct he was respectful; in serving his superiors he was reverent; in nourishing the people he was kind; in governing the people he was righteous.

Confucius said, "The gentleman has nine concerns. In seeing he is concerned with clarity. In hearing he is concerned with acuity. In his expression he wishes to be warm. In his bearing he wishes to be respectful. In his words he is concerned with sincerity. In his service he is concerned with reverence. When he is in doubt, he wants to ask questions. When he is angry, he is wary of the pitfalls. When he sees the chance for profit, he keeps in mind the need for integrity."

Confucius said, "The gentleman is easy to serve but difficult to please. When you try to please him, if your manner of pleasing is not in accord with the Way, then he will not be pleased. On the other hand, he does not expect more from people than their capacities warrant. The petty individual is hard to serve and easy to please. When you try to please him, even if your method of pleasing him is not in accord with the Way, he will be pleased. But in employing people he expects them to be perfectly accomplished in everything."

Confucius said, "The gentleman is in harmony with those around him but not on their level. The small man is on the level of those around him but not in harmony with them."

Confucius said, "The gentleman aspires to things lofty; the petty person aspires to things base."

Confucius said, "The gentleman looks to himself; the petty person looks to other people."

Confucius said, "The gentleman feels bad when his capabilities fall short of some task. He does not feel bad if people fail to recognize him."

Confucius said, "The gentleman fears that after his death his name will not be honored."

Confucius said, "The gentleman does not promote people merely on the basis of their words, nor does he reject words merely because of the person who uttered them."

Confucius said, "The gentleman is exalted and yet not proud. The petty person is proud and yet not exalted."

Zixia said, "The gentleman has three transformations. Seen from afar he appears majestic. Upon approaching him you see he is amiable. Upon hearing his words you find they are serious."

Confucius said, "If the gentleman is not dignified, he will not command respect and his teachings will not be considered solid. He emphasizes sincerity and honesty. He has no friends who are not his equals. If he finds a fault in himself, he does not shirk from reforming himself."

Zigong said, "When the gentleman falls into error, it is like the eclipse of the sun and moon: everyone sees it. When he corrects it, everyone will look up to him again."

Zigong said, "Does not the gentleman also have his hatreds?" Confucius replied, "Yes, he has his hatreds. He hates those who harp on the weak points of others. He hates those who are base and yet slander those who are exalted. He hates those who are bold but do not observe the proprieties. He hates those who are brash and daring and yet have limited outlook." Confucius then asked, "You too have your hatreds, do you not?" Zigong replied, "I hate those who pry into things and consider it wisdom. I hate those who are imprudent and consider it courage. I hate those who leak out secrets and consider it honesty."

Zengzi said, "The gentleman knows enough not to exceed his position."

Confucius said, "The gentleman is not a tool."

Humanity

Zizhang asked Confucius about humanity. Confucius said, "If an individual can practice five things anywhere in the world, he is a man of humanity." "May I ask what these things are?" said Zizhang. Confucius replied, "Reverence, generosity, truthfulness, diligence, and kindness. If a person acts with reverence, he will not be insulted. If he is generous, he will win over the people. If he is truthful, he will be trusted by people. If he is diligent, he will have great achievements. If he is kind, he will be able to influence others."

Zhonggong asked about humanity. Confucius said, "When you go out, treat everyone as if you were welcoming a great guest. Employ people as if you were conducting a great sacrifice. Do not do unto others what you would not have them do unto you. Then neither in your country nor in your family will there be complaints against you." Zhonggong said, "Although I am not intelligent, please allow me to practice your teachings."

Sima Niu asked about humanity. Confucius said, "The man of humanity is cautious in his speech." Sima Niu replied, "If a man is cautious in his speech, may it be said that he has achieved the virtue of humanity?" Confucius said, "When a man realizes that accomplishing things is difficult, can his use of words be anything but cautious?"

Confucius said, "A person with honeyed words and pious gestures is seldom a man of humanity."

Confucius said, "The individual who is forceful, resolute, simple, and cautious of speech is near to humanity."

Confucius said, "The man of wisdom takes pleasure in water; the man of humanity delights in the mountains. The man of wisdom desires action; the man of humanity wishes for quietude. The man of wisdom seeks happiness; the man of humanity looks for long life."

Confucius said, "If a man does not have humanity, how can he have propriety? If a man does not have humanity, how can he be in tune with the rites or music?"

Confucius said, "The humanity of a village makes it beautiful. If you choose a village where humanity does not dwell, how can you gain wisdom?"

Confucius said, "Humanity is more important for people than water or fire. I have seen people walk through water and fire and die. I have never seen someone tread the path of humanity and perish."

Confucius said, "Riches and honors are the things people desire; but if one obtains them by not following the Way, then one will not be able to hold them. Poverty and low position in society are the things that people hate; but if one can avoid them only by not following the Way, then one should not avoid them. If the gentleman abandons humanity, how can he live up to his name? The gentleman must not forget about humanity for even the space of time it takes him to finish a meal. When hurried, he must act according to it. Even when confronted with a crisis, he must follow its tenets."

Confucius said, "The strong-minded scholar and the man of humanity do not seek to live by violating the virtue of humanity. They will suffer death if necessary to achieve humanity."

Confucius said, "In practicing the virtue of humanity, one should not defer even to one's teacher."

Confucius said, "Is humanity far away? Whenever I want the virtue of humanity, it comes at once."

Zigong asked about the virtue of humanity. Confucius said, "The artisan who wants to do his work well must first of all sharpen his tools. When you reside in a given state, enter the service of the best of the officials and make friends with the most humane of the scholars."

Confucius said, "Only the man of humanity can rightly love some people and rightly despise some people."

Confucius said, "People can be classified according to their faults. By observing an individual's faults, you will know if he is a person of humanity."

Confucius said, "Those who possess virtue will be sure to speak out; but those who speak out do not necessarily have virtue. Those who possess the virtue of humanity certainly have strength; but those who are strong do not necessarily have the virtue of humanity."

Confucius said, "Although there have been gentlemen who did not possess the virtue of humanity, there have never been petty men who did possess it."

Filial Piety

Ziyou inquired about filial piety. Confucius said, "Nowadays, filial piety is considered to be the ability to nourish one's parents. But this obligation to nourish even extends down to the dogs and horses. Unless we have reverence for our parents, what makes us any different?"

Confucius said, "When your father is alive observe his intentions. When he is deceased, model yourself on the memory of his behavior. If in three years after his death you have not deviated from your father's ways, then you may be considered a filial child."

Zengzi said, "I have heard from Confucius that

the filial piety of Meng Zhuangzi is such that it could also be attained by others, but his not changing his father's ministers and his father's government is a virtue difficult indeed to match."

Meng Yizi inquired about filial piety. Confucius said, "Do not offend your parents." Fan Zhi was giving Confucius a ride in a wagon, and Confucius told him, "Meng Sun questioned me about filial piety and I told him, 'Do not offend your parents.'" Fan Zhi said, "What are you driving at?" Confucius replied, "When your parents are alive, serve them according to the rules of ritual and decorum. When they are deceased, give them a funeral and offer sacrifices to them according to the rules of ritual and decorum."

Confucius said, "When your father and mother are alive, do not go rambling around far away. If you must travel, make sure you have a set destination."

Confucius said, "It is unacceptable not to be aware of your parents' ages. Their advancing years are a cause for joy and at the same time a cause for sorrow."

Confucius said, "You can be of service to your father and mother by remonstrating with them tactfully. If you perceive that they do not wish to follow your advice, then continue to be reverent toward them without offending or disobeying them; work hard and do not murmur against them."

The Duke of She said to Confucius, "In my land there is an upright man. His father stole a sheep, and the man turned him in to the authorities." Confucius replied, "The upright men of my land are different. The father will shelter the son and the son will shelter the father. Righteousness lies precisely in this."

On Governing

The Master said, "Lead them by means of government policies and regulate them through punishments, and the people will be evasive and have no sense of shame. Lead them by means of virtue and regulate them through rituals and they will have a sense of shame and moreover have standards."

Duke Ding asked about how rulers should direct their ministers and ministers serve their rulers. Confucius responded, "A ruler directs his ministers through established ritual protocols. A minister serves his ruler with loyalty."

Zigong inquired about governing. The Master said, "Make food supplies sufficient, provide an adequate army, and give the people reason to have faith." Zigong asked, "If one had no choice but to dispense with one of these three, which should it be?" "Eliminate the army." Zigong continued, "If one had no choice but to get rid of one of the two remaining, which should it be?" "Dispense with food," Confucius said. "Since ancient times, death has always occurred, but people without faith cannot stand."

Jikangzi asked Confucius about governing, posing the question, "What would you think of my killing those without principles to help those with principles?" Confucius responded, "You are the government. Why employ killing? If you want what is good, the people will be good. The virtue of a gentleman is like the wind, the virtue of a small person like the grass. When the wind blows over it, the grass must bend."

When Zhonggong was serving as chief minister to the Ji family, he asked for advice on governing. The Master said, "Put priority on your subordinate officials. Pardon their minor mistakes and promote those who are worthy and talented." "How can I recognize those who are talented and worthy to promote them?" Confucius replied, "Promote those you know. Will others neglect those you do not know?"

The Master said, "If one has corrected himself, what problem would he have in governing? But if he is unable to correct himself, how can he govern others?"

Duke Ding asked, "Is there a single saying that can bring about the success of a country?" Confucius responded, "One cannot expect so much from a saying, but the people do have this maxim: 'To be a ruler is difficult; to be a minister is not easy.' If you recognize the difficulty of being a ruler, that may come close to furthering your state through a single maxim." The Duke asked again, "Can a single saying lead to the ruin of a state?" Confucius responded, "One cannot expect so much from a saying, but the people do have this maxim, 'I get no pleasure from being ruler other than that no one can contradict what I say.' If what he says is good and no one contradicts it, that is fine. But if what he says is not good and no one contradicts it, isn't that almost a case of one maxim bringing about the ruin of the state?"

The Master said, "When superiors love ritual the people are easy to direct."

The Master said, "Shun was the one who governed effectively without activism. What was there for him to do? He simply made himself respectful and took up his position facing south."

SELECTIONS FROM THE *MENCIUS*

On Government

Mencius had an audience with King Hui of Liang. The king said, "Sir, you did not consider a thousand *li* too far to come. You must have some ideas about how to benefit my state." Mencius replied, "Why must Your Majesty use the word 'benefit'? All I am concerned with are the benevolent and the right. If Your Majesty says, 'How can I benefit my state?' your officials will say, 'How can I benefit my family,' and officers and common people will say, 'How can I benefit myself.' Once superiors and inferiors are competing for benefit, the state will be in danger. When the head of a state of ten thousand chariots is murdered, the assassin is invariably a noble with a fief of a thousand chariots. When the head of a fief of a thousand chariots is murdered, the assassin is invariably head of a subfief of a hundred chariots. Those with a thousand out of ten thousand, or a hundred out of a thousand, had quite a bit. But when benefit is put before what is right, they are not satisfied without snatching it all. By contrast, there has never been a benevolent person who neglected his parents or a righteous person who put his lord last. Your Majesty perhaps will now also say, 'All I am concerned with are the benevolent and the right. Why mention 'benefit?' "

After seeing King Xiang of Liang, Mencius said to someone, "When I saw him from a distance, he did not look like a ruler, and when I got closer, I saw nothing to command respect. But he asked, 'How can the realm be settled?' I answered, 'It can be settled through unity.' 'Who can unify it?' he asked. I answered, 'Someone not fond of killing people.' 'Who could give it to him?' I answered, 'Everyone in the world will give it to him. Your Majesty knows what rice plants are? If there is a drought in the seventh and eighth months, the plants wither, but if moisture collects in the sky and forms clouds and rain falls in torrents, the plants suddenly revive. This is the way it is; no one can stop the process. In the world today there are no rulers disinclined toward killing. If there were a ruler who did not like to kill people, everyone in the world would crane their necks to catch sight of him. This is really true. The people would flow toward him the way water flows down. No one would be able to repress them.' "

King Xuan of Qi asked, "Is it true that King Wen's park was seventy *li* square?" Mencius answered, "That is what the records say." The King said, "Isn't that large?" Mencius responded, "The people considered it small." "Why then do the people consider my park large when it is forty *li* square?" "In the forty square *li* of King Wen's park, people could collect firewood and catch birds and rabbits. Since he shared it with the people, isn't it fitting that they considered it small? When I arrived at the border, I asked about the main rules of the state before daring to enter. I learned that there was a forty-*li* park within the outskirts of the capital where killing a deer was punished like killing a person. Thus these forty *li* are a trap in the center of the state. Isn't it appropriate that the people consider it too large?"

After an incident between Zou and Lu, Duke Mu asked, "Thirty-three of my officials died but no common people died. I could punish them, but I could not punish them all. I could refrain from punishing them, but they did angrily watch their superiors die without saving them. What would be the best course for me to follow?" Mencius answered, "When the harvest failed, even though your granaries were full, nearly a thousand of your subjects were lost—the old and weak among them dying in the gutters, the able-bodied scattering in all directions. Your officials never reported the situation, a case of superiors callously inflicting suffering on their subordinates. Zengzi said, 'Watch out, watch out! What you do will be done to you.' This was the first chance the people had to pay them back. You should not resent them. If Your Highness practices benevolent government, the common people will love their superiors and die for those in charge of them."

King Xuan of Qi asked, "Is it true that Tang banished Jie and King Wu took up arms against Zhou?" Mencius replied, "That is what the records say." "Then is it permissible for a subject to assassinate his lord?" Mencius said, "Someone who does violence to the good we call a villain; someone who does violence to the right we call a criminal. A person who is both a villain and a criminal we call a scoundrel. I have heard that the scoundrel Zhou was killed, but have not heard that a lord was killed."

King Xuan of Qi asked about ministers. Mencius said, "What sort of ministers does Your Majesty mean?" The king said, "Are there different kinds of ministers?" "There are. There are noble ministers related to the ruler and ministers of other surnames." The king said, "I'd like to hear about noble ministers." Mencius replied, "When the ruler makes a major error, they point it out. If he does not listen to their repeated remonstrations, then they put someone else on the throne." The king blanched. Mencius continued, "Your Majesty should not be surprised at this. Since you asked me, I had to tell you truthfully." After the king regained his composure, he asked about unrelated ministers. Mencius said, "When the king makes an error, they point it out. If he does not heed their repeated remonstrations, they quit their posts."

Bo Gui said, "I'd like a tax of one part in twenty. What do you think?" Mencius said, "Your way is that of the northern tribes. Is one potter enough for a state with ten thousand households?" "No, there would not be enough wares." "The northern tribes do not grow all the five grains, only millet. They have no cities or houses, no ritual sacrifices. They do not provide gifts or banquets for feudal lords, and do not have a full array of officials. Therefore, for them, one part in twenty is enough. But we live in the central states. How could we abolish social roles and do without gentlemen? If a state cannot do without potters, how much less can it do without gentlemen. Those who want to make government lighter than it was under Yao and Shun are to some degree barbarians. Those who wish to make government heavier than it was under Yao and Shun are to some degree [tyrants like] Jie."

On Human Nature

Mencius said, "Everyone has a heart that is sensitive to the sufferings of others. The great kings of the past had this sort of sensitive heart and thus adopted compassionate policies. Bringing order to the realm is as easy as moving an object in your palm when you have a sensitive heart and put into practice compassionate policies. Let me give an example of what I mean when I say everyone has a heart that is sensitive to the sufferings of others. Anyone today who suddenly saw a baby about to fall into a well would feel alarmed and concerned. It would not be because he wanted to improve his relations with the child's parents, nor because he wanted a good reputation among his friends and neighbors, nor because he disliked hearing the child cry. From this it follows that anyone who lacks feelings of commiseration, shame, and courtesy or a sense of right and wrong is not a human being. From the feeling of commiseration benevolence grows; from the feeling of shame righteousness grows; from the feeling of courtesy ritual grows; from a sense of right and wrong wisdom grows. People have these four germs, just as they have four limbs. For someone with these four potentials to claim incompetence is to cripple himself; to say his ruler is incapable of them is to cripple his ruler. Those who know how to develop the four potentials within themselves will take off like a fire or burst forth like a spring. Those who can fully develop them can protect the entire land, while those unable to develop them cannot even take care of their parents."

Gaozi said, "Human nature is like whirling water. When an outlet is opened to the east, it flows east; when an outlet is opened to the west, it flows west. Human nature is no more inclined to good or bad than water is inclined to east or west." Mencius responded, "Water, it is true, is not inclined to either east or west, but does it have no preference for high or low? Goodness is to human nature like flowing downward is to water. There are no people who are not good and no water that does not flow down. Still, water, if splashed, can go higher than your head; if forced, it can be brought up a hill. This isn't the nature of water; it is the specific circumstances. Although people can be made to be bad, their natures are not changed."

SELECTIONS FROM *XUNZI*

A Discussion of Heaven

Constant principles underlie Heaven's behavior. Heaven does not prevail because you are the sage Yao or disappear because you are the tyrant Jie. Blessings result when you respond to Heaven by creating order; misfortune results when you respond to it with disorder. When you concentrate on agriculture and industry and are frugal in expenditures, Heaven cannot impoverish your state. When you store provisions and act quickly in emergencies, Heaven cannot afflict illness on your people. When you are singleminded in your cultivation of the Way, Heaven cannot send disasters. Thus, even if they come, droughts and floods will not bring starvation, extremes of temperature will not bring illness, uncanny phenomena will not prove unlucky.

On the other hand, if you ignore agriculture and industry and spend extravagantly, then Heaven cannot make your country rich. If you are negligent concerning provisions and slow to respond to crises, Heaven cannot keep your country whole. If you renounce the Way and act recklessly, Heaven cannot make you lucky. In such a case, starvation will result even without flood or drought; illness will occur even without severe weather; misfortunes will occur without any uncanny phenomena. Even though the seasons are identical to those of an orderly age, the resulting fortune or misfortune is different. But you should not resent Heaven. It is your Way that is responsible. Thus those who can distinguish what is in the realm of Heaven and what is in the realm of man are men of the highest order. . . .

Are order and disorder the product of Heaven? I say, the sun and the moon, the stars and the constellations are the same as they were in the time of Yu and Jie. Yu brought order, Jie created disorder, so order and disorder do not come from Heaven. Are they a product of the seasons? I say, plants sprout and grow in spring and summer, and are harvested and stored in fall and winter, just the way they were during the reigns of Yu and Jie. Yet Yu brought order, Jie disorder, so order and disorder are not the product of seasons. Is it land then? I say, obtaining land leads to life, losing it leads to death, just as in the time of Yu and Jie. Yet Yu brought order, Jie disorder, so order and disorder are not a product of land. . . .

Why does it rain after a prayer for rain? I say, for no reason. It is the same as raining when you had not prayed. When there is an eclipse of the sun or moon, you "save" it; when there is a drought, you pray for rain; when an important decision is to be made, you divine. It is not that you can get anything by doing so. It is just decoration. Hence, the gentleman considers them ornament, but the common people think spirits are involved. To consider them ornament is auspicious; to consider them as spiritual acts is inauspicious.

A Discussion of Ritual

Where does ritual come from? I say, people have desires from the time they are born. When they want something they do not get, they inevitably try to get it. When there are no limits imposed on how they can try to get it, they inevitably struggle for it. Struggles lead to disorder, disorder to exhaustion. The ancient kings detested disorder and so instituted ritual and moral principles to set shares, thus satisfying people's desires and supplying their wants. They saw to it that desires and the supply of goods were kept in balance. This is how ritual began. . . .

Sacrifices are concerned with the feelings of devotion and longing. Feelings of depression and melancholy cannot be prevented from occasionally arising. Thus, even when enjoying himself in pleasant company, a loyal official or a filial son will occasionally be overcome by grief. If he is greatly moved by his feelings, but he restrains himself and does not express them, he will be incomplete in ritual. Therefore the ancient kings established ways to fulfill the principle of honoring those deserving honor and expressing closeness to relatives. Hence, sacrifices are concerned with the feelings of devotion and longing. They fulfill loyalty, faith, love, and respect. Ritual conduct is the perfection of decorum. Only sages can fully understand this. Sages comprehend it, gentlemen comfortably carry them out, officials preserve them, and the common people consider them the custom. Gentlemen consider them to be part of the way of man; common people think they have something to do with ghosts. . . .

Human Nature Is Bad

Human nature is bad. Good is a human product. Human nature is such that people are born with a love of profit. If they follow these inclinations, they will struggle and snatch from each other, and inclinations to defer or yield will die. They are born with fears and hatreds. If they follow them, they will become violent and tendencies toward good faith will die. They are born with sensory desires for pleasing sounds and sights. If they indulge them, the disorder of sexual license will result and ritual and moral principles will be lost. In other words, if people accord with human nature and follow their desires, they inevitably end up struggling, snatching, violating norms, and acting with violent abandon. Consequently, only after men are transformed by teachers and by ritual and moral principles do they defer, conform to culture, and abide in good order. Viewed this way, it is obvious that human nature is bad and good is a human product.

A warped piece of wood must be steamed and forced before it is made straight; a metal blade must be put to the whetstone before it becomes sharp. Since the nature of people is bad, to become corrected they must be taught by teachers and to be orderly they must acquire ritual and moral principles. When people lack teachers, their tendencies are not corrected; when they do not have ritual and moral principles, then their lawlessness is not controlled. In antiquity the sage kings recognized that men's nature is bad and that their tendencies were not being corrected and their lawlessness controlled. Consequently, they created rituals and moral principles and instituted laws and limitations to give shape to people's feelings while correcting them, to transform people's emotional nature while guiding it. Thus all became orderly and conformed to the Way. Those people today who are transformed by teachers, accumulate learning, and follow ritual and moral principles are gentlemen. Those who indulge their instincts, act impulsively, and violate ritual and moral principles are inferior people. Seen from this perspective, it is obvious that human nature is bad, and good is a human product.

Mencius said that people's capacity to learn is evidence that their nature is good. I disagree. His statement shows he does not know what human nature is and has not pondered the distinction between what is human nature and what is created by man. Human nature is what Heaven supplies. It cannot be learned or worked at. Ritual and moral principles were produced by the sages; they

People get the consequences from what they do not because of heaven.

are things people can master by study and effort. Human nature refers to what is in people but which they cannot study or work at achieving. Human products refers to what people acquire through study and effort. . . .

Now, it is human nature to want to eat to one's fill when hungry, to want to warm up when cold, to want to rest when tired. These all are a part of people's emotional nature. When a man is hungry and yet on seeing an elder lets him eat first, it is because he knows he should yield. When he is tired but does not dare rest, it is because he knows it is his turn. When a son yields to his father, or a younger brother yields to his elder brother, or when a son takes on the work for his father or a younger brother for his elder brother, their actions go against their natures and run counter to their feelings. And yet these are the way of the filial son and the principles of ritual and morality. Thus, if people followed their feelings and nature, they would not defer or yield, for deferring and yielding run counter to their emotional nature. Viewed from this perspective, it is obvious that man's nature is bad and good is a human product. . . .

Fanruo and Jushu were great bows of ancient times, but they could not on their own have become accurate without being pressed and straightened. The great swords of ancient times—Duke Huan's Cong, King Wen's Lu, Lord Zhuang's Hu, and King Helü's Ganjiang, Moyeh, Juque, and Bilü—would never have become sharp without being put to the grindstone. Nor could they have cut without men using their strength. The great horses of ancient times—Hualiu, Qiji, Xianli, and Luer—could never have run a thousand *li* in a day if they had not first been restrained by the bit and bridle, taught to respond to the whip, and driven by someone like Zaofu. Similarly, a man may have a fine temperament and a discriminating mind, but he must first seek a wise teacher to study under and good friends to associate with. If he studies with a wise teacher, what he hears will concern the way of Yao, Shun, Yü, and Tang. If he finds good friends to associate with, what he observes will be loyalty, good faith, respect, and deference. Each day he will come closer to humanity and morality without realizing it, all because of their influence. But if he lives with bad people, what he will hear will be deceit and lies, and what he will observe will be wild, undisciplined, greedy behavior. Without knowing it, he will end up a criminal, all because of their influence. It has been said, "If you do not know the man, observe his friends. If you do not know the lord, look at his attendants." Influence affects everyone.

Translated by Mark Coyle and Patricia Ebrey

7

DAOIST TEACHINGS

Amid the intellectual ferment of the three centuries after Confucius, a bewildering array of new ideas were propounded. Two strands that proved particularly long-lasting are those generally labeled "Daoist" and "Legalist." The two key texts of Daoism are the Laozi, *also called the* Classic of the Way and Its Power, *traditionally ascribed to Lao Dan (sixth century* B.C.*) but probably written in the third century, and the* Zhuangzi, *a good portion of which was probably written by the philosopher Zhuang Zhou (369–286* B.C.*). These two works share disapproval of the unnatural and artificial. Whereas plants and animals act spontaneously in the ways appropriate to them, humans have separated themselves from the Way by plotting and planning, analyzing and organizing. Both texts reject social conventions for an ecstatic surrender to the spontaneity of cosmic processes. The two books, nevertheless, differ in many regards as well. The* Laozi *is a long philosophical poem, so elliptical that it can be read in many ways. The* Zhuangzi *is more like a collection of tall tales; it is full of flights of fancy, parables, and fictional encounters between historical figures. Whereas Laozi seems concerned with protecting each person's life, Zhuangzi searches for a view of man's place in the cosmos which will reconcile him to death.*

These two works are of interest not only for what they reveal of the intellectual ferment of the late Zhou, but also because they were among the favorite books of Chinese readers throughout history, enriching the Chinese imagination and giving pleasure to people who accepted most social conventions. Both books were also granted canonical status in the literature of the Daoist religion which developed after the second century A.D.

PASSAGES FROM THE *LAOZI*

The Way that can be discussed
Is not the constant Way.
The name that can be named
Is not the invariant name.
The nameless is the source of Heaven and earth.

The named is the mother of all creatures.
Ever without desires, one can observe its secrets.
Ever possessed of desires, one can observe its manifestations.
These two truths are the same, but appear under different names.
Their identity can be called a mystery.

Mystery upon mystery—the gate of the many secrets.

When everyone in the world sees beauty in the beautiful,
Ugliness is already there.
When everyone sees good in the good,
Bad is already there.
Thus existence and nonexistence give birth to each other,
The hard and the easy complement each other,
The long and the short stand in comparison to each other,
The high and the low incline toward each other,
Sounds and notes harmonize with each other,
And before and after follow each other.
Thus the sage takes on the task of doing nothing
And teaches without speaking.
All things arise from him, and he does not reject them.
He produces them but does not own them.
He acts on their behalf but does not depend on them.
He succeeds but does not stay.
Because he does not stay,
Nothing leaves.

Do not honor the worthy,
And the people will not compete.
Do not value rare treasures,
And the people will not steal.
Do not display what others want,
And the people will not have their hearts confused.
A sage governs this way:
He empties people's minds and fills their bellies.
He weakens their wills and strengthens their bones.
Keep the people always without knowledge and without desires,
For then the clever will not dare act.
Engage in no action and order will prevail.

Heaven and earth are ruthless.
They treat all creatures like straw dogs [to be discarded after the sacrifice].
The sage is ruthless and treats the common people like straw dogs.
Isn't the realm of Heaven and earth like a bellows?
Empty, it does not collapse,
But the more it is moved, the more that comes out.
But too much talking leads to depletion.
It is better to preserve what is within.

The spirit of the valley never dies.
Call it the mysterious female.

The gateway to the mysterious female
Is called the root of Heaven and earth.
Hard to perceive,
It cannot be used up.

Heaven persists and earth endures.
The reason they can do this is that they do not generate themselves.
Therefore the sage puts his own person behind and yet is ahead.
He puts his own person outside and yet survives.
Isn't it because he is without selfishness that he is able to be successfully selfish?

The highest good is like water. Water benefits all creatures but does not compete. It occupies the places people disdain. Thus it comes near to the Way.
For dwelling, the earth is good,
For minds, depth is good,
In social relations, human-heartedness is good,
In speaking, trustworthiness is good,
In governing, order is good.
For tasks, ability is good,
For action, timeliness is good.
Simply by not contending,
Blame is avoided.

The Way is eternally nameless.
The uncarved block may be small,
But no one in the world can subordinate it.
If lords and kings could preserve it,
All creatures would pay homage of their own accord,
Heaven and earth would join to send down sweet dew,
And without any decrees being issued, the people would be equitable.
As soon as cuts are made names appear.
Once there are names, one should sense it is time to stop.
Knowing when to stop is the means of avoiding danger.
The Way functions in the world
Much like the rivers flow into the sea.

If you want to shrink something,
Be sure to stretch it.
If you want to weaken something,
Be sure to strengthen it.
If you want to discard something,
Be sure to promote it.

If you want to take from something,
Be sure to give to it.
This is called the brilliance of the minute.
The soft and weak overcomes the hard and strong.
Fish should not be taken from the water;
The tools of statecraft should not be shown to
people.

In ancient times, those who excelled in the Way
Did not use it to enlighten the people but to keep
them ignorant.
When people are hard to govern, it is because they
know too much.
Thus those who use knowledge to rule a state
Are a plague on the country.
Those who do not use knowledge to rule the state
Are the country's blessing.
Understand these two—they are the standard.
Constant recognition of the standard is called mys-
terious virtue.
Mysterious virtue is deep and far-reaching;
It returns with things all the way to the great con-
formity.

Make the state small and its people few.
Let the people give up use of their tools.
Let them take death seriously and desist from distant
campaigns.
Then even if they have boats and wagons, they will
not travel in them.
Even though they have weapons and armor, they
will not form ranks with them.
Let people revert to the practice of rope-tying [in-
stead of writing].
Then they will find their food sweet,
Their clothes beautiful,
Their houses comfortable,
Their customs enjoyable.
  People from neighboring states so close that they
  can see each other and hear the sounds of each
  other's dogs and chickens will then grow old
  without ever visiting each other.

SELECTIONS FROM THE *ZHUANGZI*

Hui Shi said to Zhuangzi, "I have a large tree, of
the sort people call a shu tree. Its trunk is too
gnarled for measuring lines to be applied to it, its
branches are too twisted for use with compasses
or T-squares. If you stood it on the road, no carpenter would pay any attention to it. Now your
talk is similarly vast but useless; people are unanimous in rejecting it."

Zhuangzi replied, "Haven't you ever seen a
wildcat or a weasel? It crouches down to wait for
something to pass, ready to pounce east or west,
high or low, only to end by falling into a trap and
dying in a net. But then there is the yak. It is as big
as a cloud hanging in the sky. It has an ability to
be big, but hardly an ability to catch mice. Now
you have a large tree but fret over its uselessness.
Why not plant it in Nothing At All town or Vast
Nothing wilds? Then you could roam about doing nothing by its side or sleep beneath it. Axes
will never shorten its life and nothing will ever
harm it. If you are of no use at all, who will make
trouble for you?"

*   *   *

How do I know that enjoying life is not a delusion? How do I know that in hating death we
are not like people who got lost in early childhood and do not know the way home? Lady Li
was the child of a border guard in Ai. When first
captured by the state of Jin, she wept so much
her clothes were soaked. But after she entered
the palace, shared the king's bed, and dined on
the finest meats, she regretted her tears. How do
I know that the dead do not regret their previous
longing for life? One who dreams of drinking
wine may in the morning weep; one who dreams
of weeping may in the morning go out to hunt.
During our dreams we do not know we are
dreaming. We may even dream of interpreting a
dream. Only on waking do we know it was a
dream. Only after the great awakening will we
realize that this is the great dream. And yet fools
think they are awake, presuming to know that
they are rulers or herdsmen. How dense! You
and Confucius are both dreaming, and I who say
you are a dream am also a dream. Such is my
tale. It will probably be called preposterous, but
after ten thousand generations there may be a
great sage who will be able to explain it, a trivial
interval equivalent to the passage from morning
to night.

* * *

Once Zhuang Zhou dreamed he was a butterfly, a fluttering butterfly. What fun he had, doing as he pleased! He did not know he was Zhou. Suddenly he woke up and found himself to be Zhou. He did not know whether Zhou had dreamed he was a butterfly, or a butterfly had dreamed he was Zhou. Between Zhou and the butterfly there must be some distinction. This is what is meant by the transformation of things.

* * *

Cook Ding was cutting up a cow for Duke Wenhui. With a touch of his hand, a lunge of his shoulder, a stamp of his foot, a bend of his knee, zip, his knife slithered, never missing a beat, in time to "the dance of the mulberry forest," or the "Jingshou suite." Lord Wenhui exclaimed, "How amazing that your skill has reached such heights!"

Cook Ding put down his knife and replied, "What I love is the Way, which goes beyond skill. When I first butchered cows, I saw nothing but cows. After three years, I never saw a cow as a whole. At present, I deal with it through my spirit rather than looking at it with my eyes. My perception stops and my spirit runs its course. I rely on the natural patterning, striking at the big openings, leading into the main cavities. By following what is inherently so I never cut a ligament or tendon, not to mention a bone. A good cook changes his knife once a year, because he cuts. An ordinary cook changes his knife every month, because he hacks. This knife of mine is nineteen years old. It has carved several thousand cows, yet its blade looks like it had just come from the grindstone. There are spaces in the joints, and the blade has no thickness. So when something with no thickness enters something with space, it has plenty of room to move about. This is why after nineteen years it seems fresh from the grindstone.

However, when I come to something complicated, I inspect it closely to prepare myself. I keep my eyes on what I am doing and proceed deliberately, moving my knife imperceptibly. Then with a stroke it all comes apart like a clod of earth crumbling. I stand there, my knife in my hand, look all around, enjoying my success. Then I clean the knife and put it away."

Lord Wenhui said, "Excellent! By listening to Cook Ding I learned how to nurture life."

* * *

Consider Cripple Shu. His chin is down by his navel. His shoulders stick up above his head. The bones at the base of his neck point to the sky. The five pipes of his spine are on top; his two thighs form ribs. Yet by sewing and washing he is able to fill his mouth; by shaking the fortune-telling sticks he earns enough to feed ten. When the authorities draft soldiers, a cripple can walk among them confidently flapping his sleeves; when they are conscripting work gangs, cripples are excused because of their infirmity. When the authorities give relief grain to the ailing, a criple gets three measures, along with ten bundles of firewood. Thus one whose form is crippled can nurture his body and live out the years Heaven grants him. Think what he could do if his virtue was crippled too!

* * *

Root of Heaven roamed on the south side of Mount Vast. When he came to the bank of Clear Stream, he met Nameless Man and asked him, "Please tell me how to manage the world."

"Go away, you dunce," Nameless Man said. "Such questions are no fun. I was just about to join the Creator of Things. If I get bored with that, I'll climb on the bird Merges with the Sky and soar beyond the six directions. I'll visit Nothing Whatever town and stay in Boundless country. Why do you bring up managing the world to disturb my thoughts?"

Still Root of Heaven repeated his question and Nameless Man responded, "Let your mind wander among the insipid, blend your energies with the featureless, spontaneously accord with things, and you will have no room for selfishness. Then the world will be in order."

* * *

Duke Huan was reading a book in the hall. Wheelwright Pian, who had been chiseling a wheel in the courtyard below, set down his tools and climbed the stairs to ask Duke Huan, "May I ask what words are in the book Your Grace is reading?"

"The words of the sages," the duke responded.

"Are these sages alive?"

"They are already dead."

"That means you are reading the dregs of long gone men, doesn't it?"

Duke Huan said, "How does a wheelwright get to have opinions on the books I read? If you can explain yourself, I'll let it pass; otherwise, it's death."

Wheelwright Pian said, "In my case, I see things in terms of my own work. When I chisel at a wheel, if I go slow, the chisel slides and does not stay put; if I hurry, it jams and doesn't move properly. When it is neither too slow nor too fast, I can feel it in my hand and respond to it from my heart. My mouth cannot describe it in words, but there is something there. I cannot teach it to my son, and my son cannot learn it from me. So I have gone on for seventy years, growing old chiseling wheels. The men of old died in possession of what they could not transmit. So it follows that what you are reading is their dregs."

*　　*　　*

When Zhuangzi's wife died and Hui Shi came to convey his condolences, he found Zhuangzi squatting with his knees out, drumming on a pan and singing. "You lived with her, she raised your children, and you grew old together," Hui Shi said. "Not weeping when she died would have been bad enough. Aren't you going too far by drumming on a pan and singing?"

"No," Zhuangzi said, "when she first died, how could I have escaped feeling the loss? Then I looked back to the beginning before she had life. Not only before she had life, but before she had form. Not only before she had form, but before she had vital energy. In this confused amorphous realm, something changed and vital energy appeared; when the vital energy was changed, form appeared; with changes in form, life began. Now there is another change bringing death. This is like the progression of the four seasons of spring and fall, winter and summer. Here she was lying down to sleep in a huge room and I followed her, sobbing and wailing. When I realized my actions showed I hadn't understood destiny, I stopped."

*　　*　　*

When Zhuangzi was about to die, his disciples wanted to bury him in a well-appointed tomb. Zhuangzi said, "I have the sky and the earth for inner and outer coffins, the sun and the moon for jade disks, the stars for pearls, and the ten thousand things for farewell gifts. Isn't the paraphernalia for my burial adequate without adding anything?"

"We are afraid the crows and kites will eat you, master," a disciple said.

"Above ground, I will be eaten by crows and kites; below ground by ants. You are robbing from the one to give to the other. Why play favorites?"

Translated by Patricia Ebrey

8

LEGALIST TEACHINGS

By the third century B.C., *as small states one after another were conquered by large ones and the number of surviving states dwindled, those rulers still in contention were receptive to political theorists who claimed to understand power and the techniques that would allow rulers to strengthen control over officials and subjects. These advisors argued that strong government depended not on the moral qualities of the ruler and his officials, as Confucians claimed, but on establishing effective institutional structures. Because of their emphasis on laws, these thinkers are usually labeled the Legalists.*

Below are selections from the two fullest Legalist treatises. The first has traditionally been ascribed to Lord Shang (Gongsun Yang, died in 338 B.C.), *long chief minister of the state of Qin, the state most fully to adopt legalist policies. The second is from the major synthesizer of Legalist thought, Han Feizi. Han Feizi once studied with Xunzi and eventually traveled to Qin, where he had access to high court politics. Slandered by his former fellow student Li Si, then in power, he was forced to commit suicide in 233* B.C.

SELECTIONS FROM *THE BOOK OF LORD SHANG*

Changing the Laws

Duke Xiao was discussing policies. Three great officers, Gongsun Yang, Gan Long, and Du Zhi, were assisting him. They considered changes in social practices, debated the basis for laws, and searched for ways to lead the people.

The ruler said, "The proper course for the ruler is to keep in mind the sacrifices to the soil and grain from the time he first succeeds to his posi-

tion. The job of the minister is to shape the laws and devote himself to the lord of the people. Now I wish to change the laws in order to govern better and reform the rituals in order to instruct the common people. I am afraid that everyone will criticize me."

Gongsun Yang said, "I have heard that those who hesitate to act accomplish nothing. Your Highness should quickly make up your mind about reforming the laws, ignoring everyone's criticisms. After all, those who excel in what they do or have independent thoughts are always condemned by their contemporaries. There is a saying, 'The dull cannot even see what has already happened, but the intelligent can see what is yet to sprout. The people should not be consulted in the beginning; but they should join in in enjoying the results. The laws of Guo Yan said, 'Those who discuss the highest virtues do not accord with common sentiments; those who attain the greatest feats do not ask ordinary people for advice.' Laws exist to love the people; rites exist to make affairs go smoothly. Therefore, the sage does not stick to ancient laws if he can strengthen his state by changing them and does not keep ancient rituals if he can benefit the people by altering them."

Duke Xiao said, "Good."

Gan Long objected, "I disagree. I have heard that a sage teaches the people without changing them and a wise man governs without altering the laws. One can attain success without much effort when one teaches on the basis of the people's ways. When one governs on the basis of the established laws, the officials will have experience and the common people will feel secure. If you now change the laws, abandoning the old practices of the state of Qin, and alter the rituals to instruct the people, I fear that everyone will criticize Your Highness. Please give the matter careful consideration."

Gongsun Yang responded, "You have expressed the conventional wisdom. Ordinary people feel secure with old habits and scholars are mired in what they have heard. Both may be all right for occupying offices and enforcing laws, but they cannot be brought into discussion of matters outside the law. The founders of the three dynasties became kings using different rituals; the five hegemons established their supremacy using different laws. Therefore the wise person creates laws while the ignorant are controlled by them; the worthy alter the rites while the unworthy are held fast by them. Those held fast by rituals or controlled by laws are not the people with whom to discuss policies. Your Highness, have no doubts."

Du Zhi countered, "I have heard that unless the advantage is a hundredfold, one does not change the laws, and unless the success will be up tenfold, one does not alter the equipment. I have also heard that modeling on the past eliminates errors and preserving rituals eliminates deviance. Let Your Highness plan that way."

Gongsun Yang said, "Former ages did not all have the same teachings. Which past will you use as a model? The great kings did not repeat each other. Which rituals will you follow? Fu Xi and Shen Nong taught but did not punish; the Yellow Emperor, Yao, and Shun punished but not in anger. More recently, Kings Wen and Wu each created laws suited to their time and rituals suited to the circumstances. Rituals and laws should be established according to the times, rules and regulations according to what is right, and military equipment according to what is needed. Therefore I say, 'There is more than one way to bring peace to the world and no need to follow the past.' The kings Tang and Wu flourished without copying the past; the Shang and Xia dynasties fell despite preserving their rituals. Consequently opposing the past is not necessarily wrong; following conventions is not worth much praise. Your Highness, have no doubts."

Duke Xiao said, "Good. I have heard that poor villagers are easily alarmed and pedantic scholars love to argue. What amuses the ignorant grieves the wise; what gives joy to the foolish gives grief to the wise. I will not worry about what people say." Thereupon he issued the law on reclaiming wastelands.

SELECTIONS FROM *HAN FEIZI*

Precautions with Regard to the Inner Quarters

The ruler gets into difficulties through placing his trust in others. When he trusts someone, he falls under the person's control. Ministers are not attached to their ruler through kinship, but serve only because they suit his needs. Therefore ministers observe their ruler's moods constantly while the ruler gets to take his ease. This is the reason some rulers are deposed or assassinated.

When a ruler puts great confidence in his son, treacherous ministers will make use of the son to achieve their private ends. Li Dai, for instance, helped the King of Zhao starve his father. When a ruler places great trust in his wife, then treacherous ministers will make use of her to achieve their private ends. The actor Shi, for instance, helped Lady Li kill [the heir apparent] Shensheng and set up Xiqi in his stead. Since one cannot trust even someone as close as a wife or child, there is no one who should be trusted.

Among the wives, concubines, and sons of a ruler of a state, large or small, there will probably be someone who would like to see the ruler die early. How do I know this? A wife is not tied by flesh and blood. When the ruler loves her, they are close; when he does not love her, they are distant. It is like the saying, "The child whose mother is loved is cherished." The opposite also holds true: The child whose mother is hated is cast aside. A man of fifty has not lost his interest in women, but a woman begins to lose her looks before thirty. When a woman whose looks are deteriorating serves a man who still loves sex, she will be despised and her son is not likely to be made heir. This is the reason queens, consorts, and concubines plot the death of the ruler. When the mother of the ruler is the queen, all orders are carried out and all prohibitions are effective. She enjoys male-female relations as much as when the previous ruler lived and can control all the powers of a large state without raising suspicions. [To preserve this situation she may well] poison (her son) the ruler or hang him in secret. It is for these reasons that Tao Zuo, in the *Spring and Autumn Annals*, said, "Not even half of all rulers die of illness." When a ruler does not realize this, his troubles will worsen. Hence the saying, "When many people will profit from his death, a ruler is in danger."

Lords

Lords' lives are endangered and their states perish when the high ministers are too honored and the rulers' attendants are too influential. Those too highly honored will act on their own authority, disregarding the law and manipulating the organs of the state for their selfish ends. Those too influential will take advantage of the situation and act arbitrarily. One must be on guard for both of these.

The strength of their muscles is what makes it possible for horses to carry heavy loads and pull carriages long distances. The power of position is what makes it possible for lords of large or small states to control the world and subjugate the feudal lords. The power of position is a ruler's muscular strength. Now for senior officials to get influence and attendants to get power reduces the ruler's strength. Not one ruler in a thousand can keep his state if he loses his power. Tigers and leopards can win over men and catch other animals because of their claws and fangs, without which they would be dominated by men. Now, superior power constitutes the lords's claws and fangs, loss of it is comparable to tigers and leopards losing their claws and fangs. The ruler of Song lost his claws and fangs to Zihan, and Duke Jian lost his to Tian Chang. Because they could not get them back quickly enough, they lost their lives and their states were destroyed. Today, even rulers with no knowledge of techniques of control understand Song Jian's error. Still, they do not see their own failings and how similar they are.

Men of law and techniques of control [i.e., Legalists] do not get along with these sorts of ministers. How can I show this? When the ruler has men who know techniques of control, then the high ministers are not able to act arbitrarily and the close attendants will not dare to sell favors. When the influence of the ministers and attendants ceases, the ruler's way will be bright. This is not the case today. These sorts of ministers have the power to protect their private interests and the attendants and intimates form factions and control access in order to keep out those more distant from the ruler. When, then, can men of law and techniques of control get the chance to be employed? When can the lord get to discuss strategy and make decisions? It is for these reasons that techniques of control are not always employed and legalists cannot coexist with these ministers and attendants.

Six Examples of Having It Backwards

The sort of person who out of fear of death avoids trouble and surrenders or retreats is honored by the world as a man who values life. The sort of person who studies the Way and proposes plans but distances himself from the law is honored by the world as a man of learning. The sort of person who travels around letting others support him is honored by the world as a man of talent. The sort of person who twists words, pretends to have knowledge, and practices deception, the world honors as a skilled debater. The sort of person who wields a sword to kill or intimidate is honored by the world as a man of courage. The sort of person who deserves to die because he has harbored criminals is honored by the world as a man of chivalry. The world praises these six sorts of people.

By contrast, the sort of person who will risk his life for matters of principle, the world belittles as a person who cannot calculate the odds. The sort of person who knows little but obeys the law, the world belittles as a simple rustic. The sort of person who does productive work, feeding himself through his own efforts, the world belittles as a fellow of little ability. The sort of person who is generous, honest, and good, the world belittles as silly. The sort of person who obeys orders and respects authority, the world belittles as timid. The sort of person who resists criminals and informs the authorities about them, the world belittles as a slanderer. The world belittles these six sorts of people.

The six sorts who plot, deceive, and do nothing of value the world honors; the six sorts who farm, wage war, and prove of use the world disparages. These are the six examples of having it backwards. Ordinary people, out of partiality, praise someone; then the ruler, hearing of his undeserved reputation, treats him with courtesy. Those who are treated courteously always end up gaining profit as well. Ordinary people, because of a private grudge, slander someone; then the ruler, following convention, despises him. Those who are despised always come to harm. Thus rewards go to selfish and evil people who ought to be punished and harm comes to public-minded men who ought to be rewarded. Consequently there is no hope of enriching and strengthening the state.

The ancients had a saying, "Governing is like washing hair. Even if some hairs fall out, it must be done." Anyone who begrudges the loss of some hair and forgets the advantage to the growing hair has no understanding of expediency. Lancing boils hurts, drinking medicine tastes bitter. But if on that account one does not lance them or drink them, one will not recover.

Now, the relationship between superior and subordinate is not based on affection like that between father and son. So if one wishes to curb subordinates by acting righteously, the relationship will be flawed. Think of parents' relations to their children. They congratulate each other when a son is born, but complain to each other when a daughter is born. Why do parents have these divergent responses when both are equally their offspring? It is because they calculate their long-term advantage. Since even parents deal with their children in this calculating way, what can one expect where there are no parent-child bonds? When present-day scholars counsel rulers, they all tell them to rid themselves of thoughts of profit and follow the path of mutual love. This is expecting rulers to go further than parents. These are immature ideas, false and deceptive. Therefore the intelligent ruler does not accept them.

The sage's method of governing is as follows. He scrutinizes the laws and prohibitions, and once they are made clear, his officials are orderly. He defines the rewards and punishments, and when they are fair, the people can be employed by the officials. When the officials are orderly and the people are employed, the state will get rich and from that the army will be strong. Then it is possible to succeed in establishing hegemony over other states. For rulers, becoming hegemon or king is the ultimate benefit. A ruler must keep this ultimate benefit in mind in governing. Therefore he must employ officials according to their talents and give rewards and punishments impartially so that all can see. When men work hard and risk their lives, military campaigns can succeed and rewards of rank and salary are deserved. Thus one succeeds in gaining wealth and high rank. For subjects, wealth and high rank are the ultimate benefit. When subjects attend to their work with these goals in mind, they will face danger and risk their lives, putting out every last bit of effort. This is what is meant by the saying that unless the ruler is generous and the subjects loyal hegemony cannot be achieved.

Criminals are careful if they are likely to be discovered and stop if they are likely to be executed. But they are reckless if they will not be discovered and carry out their plans if they will not be punished. If goods of little value are left in a deserted place, even Zeng and Shi could be tempted. But if a hundred pieces of gold are hung up in the marketplace, even great robbers will not take them. When no one will know, even Zeng and Shi can be suspected. When sure to be discovered, then even great robbers do not take the gold hung in the marketplace. Therefore the enlightened ruler, in ruling his country, increases the guards and makes the penalties heavier; he depends on laws and prohibitions to control the people, not on their sense of decency. A mother loves her son twice as much as a father does, but a father's orders are ten times more effective than a mother's. The relationship between officials and the people is not based on love and their orders are ten thousand times more effective than parents'. Parents pile up love, but their orders fail; officials are strict and the people obey. Such is the basis for choosing between severity and love.

Furthermore, parents make every effort to keep their children safe and far from trouble, but a ruler's relation to his people is different. In times of difficulty he needs them to risk death and in times of peace he needs them to exhaust their strength for him. Parents, who lovingly consider their children's comfort and benefit, are not obeyed. Rulers, who with no concern for their benefit demand that they risk their lives or work hard, have their orders followed. The intelligent ruler recognizes this and so does not cultivate feelings of empathy but builds up awe for his power. Indulgent mothers generally spoil their sons through their love. Harsh fathers generally rear good sons through their strictness.

Esteemed Scholars

When a sage rules a state he does not count on people doing good on their own but rather takes measures to keep them from doing wrong. If he depended on people who do good of themselves, he could hardly find a few dozen in the whole realm. But if he uses methods to keep them from doing wrong, then everyone in the state can be made to act the same. In governing it is better to disregard the small minority to make use of the bulk of the population. Thus the ruler should concentrate on laws rather than on moral influence. After all, if one had to depend on shafts that were naturally straight, a hundred generations would go by before one could make an arrow, and if one had to depend on wood that was naturally curved, a thousand generations would go by without a wheel. Naturally straight shafts and naturally curved wood appear not even once in a hundred generations yet people ride carriages and shoot birds in every generation. How do they accomplish this? They use the techniques for straightening and bending. A skilled craftsman places no particular value on shafts that are straight or boards that are round of themselves even before straightening or bending. Why? Because there isn't only one person who wants to ride or shoot. In the same way, a ruler does not value people who are good of themselves even without rewards and punishments. Why? Because the state's laws should not be ignored and it is not enough to govern just one man. Therefore a ruler who knows the techniques is not swayed by accidental goodness but carries out policies that will assure success. . . .

Those who do not understand how to govern

all say: "Obtain the hearts of the people." . . . The people are no more intelligent than an infant. If an infant's head is not shaved, his sores will not heal; if his boils are not lanced, his illness will worsen. Even when someone holds him and his loving mother does the shaving or lancing, he will howl without stop, for a baby cannot see that a small discomfort will result in a major improvement. Now the ruler wants to people to till land and maintain pastures to increase their production, but they think he is cruel. He imposes heavy penalties to prevent wickedness, but they think he is harsh. He levies taxes in cash and grain to fill the storehouses and thus relieve them in time of famine and have funds for the army, but they consider him greedy. He imposes military training on everyone in the land and makes his forces fight hard in order to capture the enemy, but they consider him violent. In all four cases, he uses means that will lead to peace, but the people are not happy.

Translated by Patricia Ebrey

9

TWO AVENGERS

As the states fought ruthlessly against one another, old hierarchies and old loyalties were repeatedly put to the test. When a state was conquered, its nobles lost their aristocratic ranks and fell to the level of ordinary gentlemen (shi). At the same time, ambitious rulers were recruiting men of humble background to serve them, thus adding further social diversity to the ranks of gentlemen. This social movement was compounded by the practice of ambitious men moving from one state or one lord to another. Some men opportunistically served under one lord after another, even moving to a former lord's opponent. Such disloyalty, however, also evoked its opposite: a cult of personal devotion to one's lord and his honor.

Below are accounts of two men who undertook to avenge slights to a patron who had honored them. The stories were recorded in the Intrigues of the Warring States, *a collection of records of events in the Warring States period, often highly dramatized or even fictionalized, dating from the third century* B.C. *and edited in the Han.*

YURANG

Yurang, grandson of Bi Yang of Jin, had served the Fan and Zhonghang families but, discontented, took up service under Earl Zhi, who favored him. When the Three Jin states conquered and divided Zhi's land, Viscount Xiang of Zhao hated Earl Zhi so much he lacquered his skull and used it as a wine cup.

Yurang, having escaped to the mountains, sighed and said, "A man of valor dies for the one who appreciates him, just as a woman makes herself beautiful for the man who loves her. I must avenge Earl Zhi." He changed his name and disguised himself as a convict laborer. He got into the palace of the ruler of Zhao to plaster the privy, hoping for a chance to stab Viscount Xiang. But as Viscount Xiang was entering the privy he acted on a premonition and checked on the plasterer. Yurang, with his sharpened trowel, admitted he had planned to avenge Earl Zhi.

The attendants wanted to kill him but Viscount Xiang of Zhao said, "This is a man of honor. I shall just keep out of his way. Earl Zhi died and his descendants were all killed, yet his officer feels called on to avenge him. He is one of the most worthy men in the land." With that he released him.

Yurang disguised himself by painting his skin with lacquer to cause sores, shaving off his hair and eyebrows, and mutilating his face. When he went and his begged, his wife did not recognize him. "You don't look like my husband," she said, "but your voice is identical to his." So Yurang drank lye to hoarsen his voice.

A friend said to him, "Your way is so difficult and it may not succeed. Your determination is apparent, but you are hardly being intelligent. A man of your talent could gain Viscount Xiang's patronage by serving him well. Once you gained his favor, you could easily carry out your plan. Such a strategy would be easy to implement and sure to work."

Yurang laughed, "This would be taking vengeance on someone who appreciated me later for the sake of someone who appreciated me first, and harming my new lord for the sake of my old lord. Nothing could more confuse the proper duty of lord and subordinate. My goal in what I am doing is to illustrate these duties, not to find an easy out. To take an oath of fealty to a man one is seeking to assassinate would be to serve a lord duplicitously. I have taken the hard way to shame all those who in the future are guilty of such duplicity."

Sometime later Yurang heard that Viscount Xiang was going on an excursion. Yurang hid under a bridge the lord would cross. When Viscount Xiang reached the bridge his horse shied and he said, "Yurang must be here!" He sent men to investigate and discovered him.

Viscount Xiang of Zhao reproached Yurang to his face, "Formerly you served the houses of Fan and Zhonghang, yet when Earl Zhi destroyed them, instead of avenging them you took service under him. Why are you so determined now to avenge Lord Zhi's death?"

Yurang replied, "When I served the houses of Fan and Zhonghang, they treated me as an ordinary man and I repaid them as an ordinary men would. But Earl Zhi treated me as the finest man in the state, and that is how I must treat him in return."

"Ah, Yurang," sighed Viscount Xiang, with tears in his eyes. "You have made a name by your loyalty to Earl Zhi, and I have been as tolerant as I can. You must realize I can't let you off again." He ordered his troops to surround him.

"I have heard that a wise ruler does not conceal other men's good deeds," Yurang said, "and a loyal subject will die for honor. Already the whole world is praising your generosity for sparing me. Now I am ready to take my punishment. But I beg you first to give me your coat so that I can stab it to express my desire for vengeance. I know this is more than I deserve, but I dare to tell you what is in my heart."

Viscount Xiang, greatly moved by Yurang's sense of loyalty, had someone give his coat to him. Yurang unsheathed his sword and leaped three times into the air, slashing at it. "I am repaying Earl Zhi!" he cried. With that he fell upon his sword and died. News of his death made all valiant men of Zhao shed tears.

NIE ZHENG

Han Kui, the minister of Han, and Yan Sui, favored by the ruler, hated each other. Once in a discussion of government policies, Yan Sui explicitly brought up Han Kui's faults, and Han Kui yelled at him right in the court. Yan Sui drew his sword and lunged at him, but others saved him. Fearful of being punished, Yan Sui fled to search for someone who would avenge Han Kui for him.

When he got to Qi someone there told him, "Nie Zheng of Shenjing Village in Zhi is a brave and daring man living as a butcher to escape his enemies." Yan Sui secretly tried to make friends with Nie Zheng, lavishing gifts on him.

Nie Zheng asked, "What service is it you wish me to perform?"

Yan Sui said, "I haven't been able to help you very long, so even if I had something pressing, how would I dare make a request?"

Yan Sui then prepared wine and lifted a cup in honor of Nie Zheng's mother. Yan presented her with a hundred pieces of gold and wishes for her long life. Astonished by such munificence, Nie Zheng firmly declined the gift. When Yan Sui just as persistently insisted he take it, Nie Zheng explained, "I am lucky to have my old mother living with me. I may be poor and a stranger here, but I am able to take care of her, supplying her food and clothing by selling dog meat. Since I can provide for her, I do not dare accept your gift."

Yan Sui asked the others to leave and told Nie Zheng privately, "I have an enemy. I traveled through many states before I got to Qi and learned about you and your high sense of honor. I am offering you a hundred gold pieces to help you supply food and clothing for your mother. I hope to win your friendship, but am asking for nothing else in return."

Nie Zheng replied, "I have lowered my ambitions and humbled myself to sell meat in the market solely to let me take care of my aged mother. While she survives, I cannot promise my services to anyone." Yan Sui tried to persuade him, but could not prevail upon him to accept. Yan Sui then took leave of him, careful to do so with full courtesy.

In due time Nie Zheng's mother died. After she was buried and the mourning over, Nie Zheng said to himself, "I work in the market wielding a butcher's knife, while Yan Sui is a minister to a feudal lord. Yet he drove a thousand *li* to seek my friendship. I didn't treat him very well. I have never done anything to deserve his favor, yet he offered my mother a hundred pieces of gold. Even though I didn't accept, his act shows his appreciation of me. A worthy gentleman burning with the desire for revenge placed his faith in a humble and obscure man like me. How, then, can I remain silent? Previously I ignored his overtures because of my mother. Now that my mother has passed away, I must serve this man who appreciates me."

So he went west to Puyang to see Yan Sui. He told him, "Before I refused you because my mother was still alive, but now she has passed away. Who is it you want to take vengeance on? I am at your service."

Yan Sui then told him the whole story, "My enemy is Han Kui, chief minister of Han and uncle of the marquis of Han. He has many clansmen and is always closely guarded. All my attempts to have him assassinated have failed. Since you are so kind as to consent to help me, let me supply you with chariots, horses, and men."

"Han is not far from Wei, and our plan is to kill a man who is not only the chief minister but also the ruler's relative," said Nie Zheng. "In these circumstances, too many men would be a hindrance. With a lot of people, something will go wrong, then word will leak out. When word gets to Han, that whole state will take up arms against you. It would be disastrous."

So refusing all assistance, Nie Zheng bid farewell. He set out alone, his hand on the hilt of his sword, eventually reaching the capital of Han. At that time, there was a meeting at Dongmeng which the king and all his ministers were attending, surrounded by guards and armed attendants. Yet Nie Zheng marched straight in and up the steps and stabbed Han Kui. Han Kui ran to Marquis Ai and wrapped his arms around him. Nie Zheng stabbed him and cut Marquis Ai as well. Everyone was in total confusion. Shouting loudly, Nie Zheng then attacked the attendants, killing several dozen. Then he slashed his face, gouged out his eyes, and disemboweled himself the way he had often disemboweled animals. In this way he died.

Nie Zheng's corpse was exposed in the market place in Han. A reward of a thousand gold pieces was offered to anyone who could identify him but no one knew who he was.

Meanwhile Nie Zheng's sister heard of these events and said, "My brother was an exceptional man. I should not let his name be lost out of fear for my own body. It would not be his wish."

She set off for Han and when she saw his body said, "What courage! He surpassed Ben and Yu and even Cheng Qing. Today he is dead and nameless. His parents are dead and he has no brothers. It is up to me. I could not bear to fail to broadcast his name out of fear for my own person." So she embraced the body and wept over it. "This is my brother, Nie Zheng of Shenjing village in Zhi." Then she killed herself at his side.

When word of this reached Jin, Chu, Qi and Wei, everyone commented, "Not only was Nie Zheng able, but his sister was a woman of valor as well." The reason Nie Zheng's name has been preserved is that his sister made it known, not afraid that she would be hacked into little pieces [as an assassin's relative].

Translated by Patricia Ebrey

10

3/30 SOCIAL RITUALS

Manners and everyday rituals serve to mold interpersonal relations and orient people in everyday affairs. Although people may not consider such gestures as bowing, shaking hands, or motioning for others to go first as anything more than politeness, the habits of deference and respect they ingrain cannot help but extend into other realms of social life.

Confucius attributed great power to ritual, once stating that "The whole world would respond to the true goodness of [a ruler] who could for one day restrain himself and return to ritual." Xunzi, as seen in Selection 6, also had high regard for the power of ritual to mold behavior. Highly precise rules for the performance of rituals were compiled in the late Zhou, with different rules for different ranks of society: rulers, nobles, high officials, low officials, and gentlemen (shi). The Book of Etiquette and Ritual *preserves many of the rules for gentlemen. The chapter given below contains the procedures to be followed when one gentleman calls on another. Even though some of the specific rules given in this selection, such as the kinds of gifts to be given, quickly became outdated, the general outline remained influential for many centuries.*

THE CEREMONIES FOR VISITS BETWEEN GENTLEMEN

In winter one presents a freshly killed pheasant and in summer a dried one. The bird is held up in both hands, the head to the left.

THE VISITOR: I have desired an interview for some time, but have had no justification for asking for one. Now his honor So-and-so has commanded me to visit.

THE HOST: The gentleman who introduced us has ordered me to grant you an interview. But you, sir, are demeaning yourself by coming. Please return home, and I shall hasten to present myself before you.

THE GUEST: I cannot disgrace you by obeying this command. Be good enough to end by granting me this interview.

THE HOST: I do not dare to set an example of how a reception of this kind should be conducted, and so I persist in asking you to return home, and I shall call on you without delay.

THE GUEST: It is I who do not dare to show that

example, and so I persist in asking you for an interview.

THE HOST: Since I have failed to receive permission to decline this honor, I shall not press it further. But I hear that you are offering me a gift, and this I must decline.

THE GUEST: Without a gift I cannot dare to come into your presence.

THE HOST: I am not worthy of these ceremonies, and so I must persist in declining.

THE GUEST: If I cannot have the support of my gift, I dare not pay you this visit; so I persist in my request.

THE HOST: I also am decided in declining; but as I cannot secure your consent, how dare I refuse?

Then the host goes to meet the guest outside the gate, and there bows twice, answered by two bows from the guest. Then the host, with a salute, invites him to enter. The host goes in by the right side of the door, the guest holding up the present and entering by the left. When they enter the courtyard the host bows twice and accepts the present, the guest bows twice as he hands it to him, and then starts going out. Then the host invites him to carry out the visit, and the guest returns and complies. When the guest leaves, the host escorts him outside the gate and bows twice.

When the former host pays his return visit, he takes the other's present with him. He says: "Recently when your honor demeaned himself by visiting me, you commanded me to an interview. I now ask permission to return your gift to the attendant."

THE HOST: Since I have already secured an interview, how could I now refuse to grant one?

THE GUEST: I do not dare to ask for an interview; I only presume to request permission to return the gift by your attendant.

THE HOST: Since I have already obtained an interview by the help of this gift, I must persist in declining to receive it back.

THE GUEST: I dare not listen to such a speech, so I will press my request through your attendant.

THE HOST: Since I cannot secure your consent to my declining, I dare not but obey.

Then the guest enters, carrying the present. The host bows twice and receives it, the guest bowing twice as he gives it. On departure, the host escorts him outside the gate and bows twice.

When a gentleman visits an official, the latter declines altogether to receive his present. At his entrance the host bows once, acknowledging their difference in rank. When the guest withdraws, he escorts him and bows twice.

When a gentleman calls on his former superior, the host formally declines the visitor's gift: "As I have not been able to receive your consent to my declining, I dare not persist in it."

Then the guest enters, lays down his gift, and bows twice. The host replies with a single bow. When the guest leaves, the host sends the attendant to return the gift outside the gate.

THE ATTENDANT: So-and-so sends me to hand back your gift.

THE GUEST: Since I have already obtained an interview, I venture to decline to receive the gift.

THE ATTENDANT: So-and-so has issued his commands to me, and I cannot myself take the initiative in this matter. I must press his request on you.

THE GUEST: I am the humble servant of his excellency, and am not capable of observing the ceremonies of a visitor with his host; so I venture to persist in declining.

THE ATTENDANT: Since So-and-do has ordered me, I dare not take it upon myself to make decisions in this matter, but persist in this request.

THE GUEST: I have repeatedly declined, without receiving his honor's permission to do so. How then dare I not obey? [He thus bows twice and receives the present back.]

The lower officials, in visiting one another, use a live wild goose as a present. It is wrapped in a cloth, its feet bound with a cord, and is carried like the pheasant. In visits among the higher officials, a live lamb is presented. It is wrapped in a cloth, with the four legs bound in front. The head is held to the left as a fawn is held. The ceremonial is the same as that observed in visits exchanged between gentlemen.

At their first interview with the ruler, visitors carry a gift, holding it on a level with the girdle. Their deportment shows a respectful uneasiness. When commoners have an interview with their ruler, they do not assume dignified carriage, but hurry along both in advancing and retreating. Gentlemen and officials lay down their present and kowtow twice. To this the ruler responds with a single bow.

If the visitor is from another state, the usher is sent to hand him back his gift, saying: "My unworthy ruler has sent me to return your present."

The visitor replies: "A ruler has no ministers beyond his own borders, and therefore I dare not refuse to do as he commands." Then kowtowing twice, he receives it back.

Anyone who sees his ruler on business stands directly in front of him when he faces south. If that is impossible, then the minister faces squarely east or west, and not in whatever direction the ruler happens to face. If the ruler is in the hall, the minister goes up the steps nearest the ruler, without making any distinction between direction.

Except to answer questions, in addressing the ruler a person composes himself before speaking. In speaking with the ruler, one talks of official business; with an official, of service to the ruler; with older men, of the control of children; with young people, of their filial and brotherly duties; with the common man, of loyalty and geniality; with those in minor offices, of loyalty.

In speaking to an official, one begins by looking him in the face; toward the middle of the interview one looks at his breast, and at the end of the interview one's eyes are again directed to his face. The order is never changed, and is used in all cases. In talking to one's father, the eyes are allowed to wander, but not higher than the face, nor lower than the girdle. If one is not speaking when the other is standing, one looks at his feet, and, if he sits, at his knees.

When one is sitting in attendance on a great man, should he yawn, stretch himself, ask the time of day, order his dinner, or change his position, then one must ask permission to retire. When one is sitting in attendance at night, if the great man should ask the time of night or start eating pungent things to prevent sleepiness, one may ask permission to retire.

If the ruler invites a guest to dinner, after the ruler makes an offering, the guest begins the meal by first tasting all the foods. He then drinks and awaits the ruler's command before beginning to eat. If there is anyone in charge of tasting the food, then the guest waits until the ruler has eaten before he eats. If the ruler gives him a cup of wine, he gets off his mat, kowtows twice, and then receives the cup. He then returns to his mat, sits down, and pours a libation. When he has emptied the cup, he waits until the ruler has emptied his, and then hands back his empty cup.

When he is leaving, the guest takes his shoes, goes quietly to one side, and puts them on. If the ruler rises on his account, the gentleman says: "There is no reason why you, ruler, should get up, but your servant does not dare presume to decline the honor." If by any chance the ruler should escort him to the gate, he does not dare to look at him, but goes away immediately after taking his leave. In the case of an official, he declines the honor of being escorted. When he goes down the steps, and the ruler follows, he declines again. When he is escorted to the door, he declines for the third time.

Should a retired official call on a gentleman and ask to see him, the gentleman requests permission to decline. Not receiving it, he says: "I am not in a position to be visited by his honor, but not being able to secure permission to decline, I hurry to wait on him." Then he anticipates the visitor by going out and bowing to him first.

Unless a man is sent on a mission by his ruler, he does not call himself an official of his ruler. A gentleman calls himself the "old one" of his ruler.

When bearing a present of silk, one does not walk with great strides but deports himself with an anxious uneasiness. A person carrying jade steps carefully, lifting his toes and dragging his heels.

In speaking of himself to his ruler, a gentleman or official calls himself "Your servant." A speaker residing at home within the capital calls himself "Your servant of the marketplace well"; and if in the country, "Your servant of the grass and fields." A commoner calls himself "Your servant the grass-cutter." A man from another state calls himself "Your servant from outside."

Translated by Patricia Ebrey

PART II

THE QIN AND HAN DYNASTIES

In 221 B.C., following centuries of warfare between the competing states, China was finally unified by Qin, the westernmost of the states. For more than a century this state had been organized along Legalist principles; that is, every effort had been made to strengthen the power of the government through uniformly enforced laws and punishments and through more efficient bureaucratic procedures. Attempts were made to undermine both the old nobility and the patriarchal family and clan and to create in their stead a direct relationship between the ruler and his subjects. With the unification of China these imperial policies were extended throughout the country. Currency and weights and measures were standardized, and attempts were made to eliminate the non-Legalist schools of thought by the famous "burning of the books." The position of ruler was elevated and given the new title "emperor."

The harshness of Qin rule led to an uprising in 209 B.C., and by 207 the second Qin emperor had surrendered. The eventual victor was Liu Bang, a man who had served the Qin as a local official and who proved to be an excellent general. He established the Han dynasty, and his descendants ruled for the next four centuries except for an interregnum (A.D. 9–23) when Wang Mang (a maternal relative of the imperial family) usurped the throne and declared his own dynasty. The period before Wang Mang (206 B.C.–A.D. 9) is generally referred to as the Western or Former Han and the period following him (A.D. 25–220) as the Eastern or Later Han. Western and Eastern refer to the shift in the capital from Changan (in modern Shaanxi) to Luoyang (in Henan).

The Han government, while publicly repudiating the severity of Qin rule, nevertheless built on its heritage of unified control. Despite a brief experiment with giving out large and nearly autonomous fiefs to relatives of the emperor, the overall trend of the Former Han was toward strengthening the central government. The major difference from the previous Qin administration was in the choice of men to staff the government offices. By the first century B.C. it became widely accepted that officials should be men trained in the classics. Thus officials had to reconcile their roles as agents of the emperor and the court with their Confucian values of integrity and proper behavior. The prestige and influence of government posts steadily rose, and men of wealth and local standing throughout the country began to compete to gain recognition for their learning and character so that they could gain access to office.

Under the stability of Han rule, the population of China increased to over fifty million. The centuries of peace also facilitated the growth of trade and industry and led to improved communication and transportation, all of which helped tie Chinese society more closely together. Cities flourished and the capitals became important cultural centers attracting men of education and wealth from all over the country. Extensive migrations from areas of hardship to the fertile South also contributed to integrating Chinese society. Thus, while great regional variation in customs and ideas continued to exist, people in different parts of the country were brought into greater contact with each other than ever before.

One of the aims of Legalism under the Qin was direct rule by the emperor of everyone in the society. The Han government retained this policy in its tax and labor service obligations, which were imposed directly on each subject according to age, sex, and imperially granted rank, instead of on families, plots of land, or communities. This governmental policy ran counter to some strongly entrenched particularistic forces in Chinese society. With the revival of Confucianism in the Han, family values were reasserted, as was emphasis on personal loyalty to friends and neighbors. Forms of social organization based on private relations (kinship, landlord-tenant, teacher-student, patron-client) gained in importance. Thus, whatever the theory, Han China was not a society of independent peasants subject only to the demands of the emperor and his delegated officials. Rather it was a highly complex society in which individuals were obligated to a wide variety of superiors and subordinates, and a government official might find it impossible to draft peasants who had the protection of powerful landlords.

Because of the loss of most books in the centuries of warfare following the Han, the sources for studying Han society and civilization are not much more abundant than they were for the pre-Han period. Yet there are new kinds of sources. A major intellectual achievement of the Han was the creation of the standard or dynastic history by Sima Qian (145–ca. 85 B.C.) and Ban Gu (A.D. 32–92). The three standard histories written about the Han give biographies of important men, recount political events, and describe institutional measures. Other sources useful for perceiving the structure and organization of Han society are the essays of writers, collections of popular or inspirational tales and stories, and a few contemporary documents written on wood or carved in stone and fortuitously preserved until today.

II

PENAL SERVITUDE IN QIN LAW

The Qin state, which unified China in 221 B.C., was remembered in later China above all for its harsh laws and extensive use of unfree labor. People were rewarded for denouncing those who broke the law, and the lawbreakers, once convicted, were punished severely by execution, mutilation, or penal labor.

Very little was known of the exact provisions of Qin law until 1975 when 625 bamboo strips inscribed with Qin laws were found in a tomb in central Hubei. The laws inscribed on these strips (the normal sort of "book" of the period) mostly concern provisions of interest to an official who had to prepare reports and impose penalties and keep track of money, grain, and various sorts of laborers. Below are some of the scattered laws relevant to the four grades of penal servitude. The least oppressive, termed here "debt worker," was a form of penal servitude imposed to pay off debts, including debts arising from fines and commutation of other sentences. The next three levels, from lightest to heaviest, are called here convict servant, convict worker, and convict laborer. The last category could either be "mutilated" or intact, the mutilations varying from tattooing to cutting off one or both feet. Male convict laborers usually were put to work on projects such as building roads or defensive walls or digging canals or imperial tombs. Women were usually assigned other tasks, such as sifting or pounding grain.

SOME OFFENSES LEADING TO PENAL SERVITUDE

Criminals who owe fines or redemption fees and others who have debts to the government are told to pay immediately. Those unable to pay must work off their debt from the day the order is given. Each day they work off eight cash, or six cash if they are fed by the government.

When five men jointly rob something worth one cash or more, they should have their left foot amputated, be tattooed, and made convict laborers. If fewer than five men were involved but what they robbed was worth more than 660 cash, they should be tattooed, their noses cut off, and made convict laborers. When the value falls between 220 and 660 cash, they should be tattooed and made convict laborers. Under 220 cash, they are banished.

Suppose a slave gets his master's female slave

to steal the master's ox, then they sell it, take the money, and flee the country, only to be caught at the border. How should they each be sentenced? They should be made convict laborers and tattooed. [At the end of their term] they should be returned to their master.

Suppose A stole an ox when he was only 1.4 meters tall, but after being in detention for a year, he was measured at 1.57 meters [i.e. adult height]. How is A to be sentenced? He should be left intact and made a convict laborer [the lower penalty].

Suppose the holder of a low rank [granting some privileges] stole a sheep. Before the case was judged, he falsely accused someone else of stealing a pig. How should he be sentenced? He should be left intact and made a convict laborer.

Anyone who kills a child without authorization is to be made a convict laborer. This does not apply to killing a deformed or abnormal newborn. Suppose a child is born whole and normal, and a person kills it merely because he or she already has too many children. What is the sentence? It counts as killing a child.

Suppose someone arresting a person charged with a crime punishable with a fine stabs him on purpose with a sword or sharp weapon. What is the sentence? If he killed him, he is left intact and made a convict laborer. If he wounded him, he has his beard shaved off and is made a convict servant.

Suppose A ran away from her husband and married B, who had also run away, without telling him [that she had a husband]. Two years later, after she had borne children, she told him, but he did not repudiate her. After they are caught, what should the sentence be? They should be tattooed and made convict laborers.

When commoners need to pay fines, commutation fees, or debts, they may have their male or female slave, horse, or ox work it off for them.

Prisoners of war are made convict servants.

TREATMENT OF CONVICTS

Male convict servants and convict laborers who are not 1.5 meters and female convict servants and convict laborers who are not 1.43 meters are classed as undersized. When convicts reach 1.2 meters they are all put to work.

Convict laborers are to wear red clothes and red head cloths. They are to be manacled and fettered. They are not to be supervised by capable convict laborers, but only by those assigned the task. Convict laborers sent out to work are not to enter the market and must stay outside the outer gate of buildings. If they have to go past a market, they should make a detour, not pass through it.

When working for the government, male convict servants are given two bushels of grain a month, female convict servants one and a half. Those not engaged in work are not given anything. When working, undersized convict laborers and convict servants are given one and a half bushels of grain a month; those still too young to work get one bushel. Working undersized female convict servants and convict laborers get one bushel and two and a half pecks a month; those still too young to work get one bushel. Infants, whether in the care of their mother or not, get a half bushel a month. Male convict servants doing agricultural work get two and a half bushels from the second to the ninth month, when rations stop.

Overseers who increase the rations for convict laborers performing easy tasks will be judged according to the rules on infringing the ordinances.

Convict servants, convict supervisors, and debt workers detained among the convict laborers must not be charged for their food and clothing. Anyone who works with the convict laborers should be clothed and fed like them. But a convict servant with a wife with only periodic duty or on the outside has to pay for his clothing.

Male convict servants without wives and all male convict laborers get money to cover their clothing: 110 cash in winter and 55 in summer; undersized ones get 77 in winter and 44 in summer. Women convict laborers get 55 cash in winter and 44 in summer; undersized ones get 44 in winter and 33 in summer. Women convict servants, if old or undersized and thus unable to provide their own clothes, are clothed like the women convict laborers.

Officials need not petition to use convict laborers to enlarge or repair government buildings and storehouses.

When convict laborers break pottery vessels or iron or wooden tools or break the rims of cart wheels, they should be beaten ten strokes for each cash of value, up to twenty cash, and the object is to be written off. An official who does not immediately beat them is to be charged half the value.

A commoner not guilty of any crime who has a mother or sister serving as a convict servant may if he wishes be assigned to the frontier for five years without pay to free her.

In exchange for two degrees of aristocratic rank a person may free a father or mother who has been made a convict servant.

If a convict servant lets a convict laborer escape, he will be made an intact convict laborer himself and his wife and children outside will be confiscated.

Debt workers may return home for ten days when it is time to plow or weed.

Translated by Patricia Ebrey

12

THE WORLD BEYOND CHINA

From early times the Chinese had traded, negotiated, and fought with neighboring peoples. As the Han dynasty consolidated its power, the emperors looked for ways to strengthen their border defenses and extend the territory under their control. Emperor Wu (r. 140–87 B.C.) in particular pursued expansionist policies; he asserted control over the southeast down to Northern Vietnam, set up colonies in Korea, and waged several campaigns against the Xiongnu tribes who had established a strong confederation along China's north and northwest borders. He sent the explorer-diplomat Zhang Qian far into Inner Asia to look for possible allies against the Xiongnu, and while he did not succeed in finding allies he did bring back new knowledge of the societies of central and west Asia.

Below are Sima Qian's (ca. 145–ca. 90 B.C.) descriptions of some of the peoples beyond China proper in his monumental history of China from earliest times to his own day. From it we can see the cultural traits that Chinese saw as distinguishing them from other peoples and their particular concern with traits that made some such people formidable military opponents. A fine stylist and gifted raconteur, Sima Qian was also a serious student of history who carefully mined court documents and attempted to separate his opinions from what he took as the facts. His composite history, with annals, biographies, treatises, and tables, proved extremely influential, setting the model for the later histories of each dynasty.

THE SOUTHWESTERN BARBARIANS

Among the dozens of chieftains of the southwestern barbarians, Yelang is the greatest. To the west of his tribe live the Mimo; of the dozens of chiefs, the greatest is Dian. Of the dozens of chiefs north of Dian, the most important is Qiongdu. All of these peoples wear their hair tied up in mallet-shaped hairknots, cultivate the land, and live in towns. Beyond them to the west, east of Tongshi and north to Yeyu, are the Sui and Kunming who braid their hair and move about following their flocks, without permanent settlements or chiefs. Their territory extends several thousand *li* in each direction. Northeast of the Sui are several dozen chieftains, the most important of whom are Xi and Zuodu. Northeast of Zuo are several dozen chiefs, the greatest of whom are Ran and Mang. Their customs vary, some settling on the land, others moving about. They live west of Shu [i.e., Sichuan]. Northeast of Ran and Mang are several dozen chieftains, of whom the Baima are the most important. All of these tribes are Di. They constitute the barbarians living outside China's borders to the southwest of Ba and Shu.

DAYUAN

Dayuan is southwest of the Xiongnu, about ten thousand *li* directly west of the Han. Their customs are to stay in one place, cultivate the land, and grow rice and wheat. They make wine from grapes. They have many fine horses. These horses sweat blood, perhaps being descended from Heavenly horses. They have city walls and houses. With some seventy or more cities of various sizes, their population is probably several hundred thousand. Their soldiers use bows and spears, shooting while on horseback.

THE XIONGNU

The Xiongnu are descended from the rulers of the Xia dynasty. . . . They live among the northern barbarians, moving to follow their flocks. They primarly raise horses, oxen, and sheep, but also keep unusual animals like camels, asses, mules, and wild horses. They move about in search of water and grass, having no cities, permanent dwellings, or agriculture. Still, they divide their territory into regions. They have no written language, so make oral agreements. Little boys are able to ride sheep and shoot birds and mice with bows and arrows. When they are somewhat older they shoot foxes and rabbits for food. Thus all the men can shoot and serve as cavalry.

It is the custom of the Xiongnu to support themselves in ordinary times by following their flocks and hunting, but in times of hardship they take up arms to raid. This would appear to be their nature. Bows and arrows are the weapons they use for distant targets; swords and spears the ones they use at close range. When it is to their advantage, they advance; when not they retreat, as they see no shame in retreat. Concern for propriety or duty does not inhibit their pursuit of advantage. Everyone, from the ruler on down, eats meat and dresses in leather or felt. The strongest eat the best food; the old eat the leftovers. They honor the young and strong and despise the old and weak. A man whose father has died marries his stepmother; a man whose brother has died marries his brother's wife. They only have personal names, no family names or polite names, and observe no name taboos. . . .

Over a thousand years elapsed from the time of [their founder] Shunwei to Modun. Sometimes they expanded, sometimes they shrunk; they split up and scattered. Thus it is impossible to give an orderly genealogy for them. Under Modun the Xiongnu reached their apogee, subjugating all the other northern barbarians and coming into conflict with China to the south. Their political organization since that time can be described as follows. The top leaders are the left and right wise kings, Luli kings, generals, commandants, administrators, and Gudu lords. . . . These leaders have under them from a few thousand to ten thousand horsemen. There are twenty-four chiefs altogether, each titled a "ten thousand horsemen." All of the major offices are hereditary. The three clans of the Huyan, Lan, and later the Xubu are the nobility. . . .

Each year in the first month all the chiefs, large and small, assemble at the Shanyu's court to make sacrifices. In the fifth month there is a great assembly at Long Fort, where they make sacrifices to their ancestors, to heaven and earth, and to gods and spirits. In the fall, when the horses are fat, there is a major assembly at Dai Forest, where the people and animals are assessed and counted.

According to their laws, anyone who draws his sword a foot is killed. Those who commit robbery have their property confiscated. For minor offenses people are flogged and for major ones executed. No one stays in jail awaiting sentence more than ten days, and there are never more than a few prisoners in the whole country.

Every morning the Shanyu leaves the camp and bows to the sun as it rises; in the evening he bows to the moon. At a feast, the honored seat is the one to the left or the one facing north. They favor the days *wu* and *ji* in the ten-day week. In seeing off the dead, they use inner and outer coffins, gold and silver ornaments, and clothes and furs, but do not construct mounds or plant trees over the grave or put on mourning garments. Sometimes up to several hundred or several thousand favored subordinates or concubines follow their master in death.

In making decisions, the Xiongnu take note of the stars and moon; when the moon is full, they attack; when it wanes they retreat. In battles, those who decapitate an enemy are given a cup of wine and whatever booty they have seized. Captives are made into slaves. Consequently, when they fight, they all compete for profit. They are good at setting up decoys to deceive the enemy. When they see the enemy, eager for booty, they swoop down like a flock of birds. If surrounded or defeated, they break like tiles or scatter like mist. Anyone who is able to bring back the body of someone who died in battle gets all of the dead man's property.

Translated by Patricia Ebrey

13

HEAVEN, EARTH, AND MAN

The early Han rulers, although prudently avoiding the harsh policies of the repudiated Qin government, had no particular fondness for Confucianism or at least the Confucianists of their day. Yet under the most activist of the Han emperors, Emperor Wu (r.141–87 B.C.), Confucianism was given a privileged position. Emperor Wu pronounced Confucianism the ideological basis of imperial rule, decreed that only Confucians should serve as officials, and established a national university to train officials in a Confucian curriculum of the classics.

Credit for the political success of Confucianism belongs in large part to thinkers like Dong Zhongshu (ca. 179–104 B.C.) who developed Confucianism in ways that legitimated the new imperial state and elevated the role of emperor. Dong drew on ideas of diverse origins, especially strands of correlative thinking, to relate natural and human phenomena of all sorts. He joined Confucian ideas of human virtue and social order to notions of the workings of the cosmos in terms of Yin and Yang and the Five Agents (wood, metal, fire, water, and earth). Man still has a very major role in his cosmic scheme, and the ruler has a unique position because he can link the realms of Heaven, earth, and man through his actions. A corollary of Dong's conception of the cosmos was that a ruler who did not fulfil his role properly would directly cause disturbances of the balance of Heaven and earth such as floods, earthquakes, and other natural calamities. The selection below is from Dong's major treatise, the Chunqiu Fanlu.

Heaven, earth, and man are the source of all creatures. Heaven gives birth to them, earth nourishes them, and human beings complete them. Heaven endows creatures at birth with a sense of kinship loyalties; earth nourishes them with food and clothing; man completes them through ritual and music. These three aid each other like hands and feet; each is essential and together they make one body. . . .

Heaven has the power to cause proliferation; earth the power to cause transformation; and human beings the power to make moral distinctions. Heaven's vital energy (*qi*) rises, earth's vital energy descends, and man's is in the middle. When spring gives birth and summer nurtures, plant and animal life flourish. When fall cuts down and winter conserves, plant and animal life are stored. Hence nothing is more ethereal than vital energy, nothing richer than the earth, nothing more spiritual than Heaven.

Of the creatures born of the essence of Heaven and earth, human beings are the most noble. Human beings receive their destiny from Heaven and therefore are much above other creatures, which due to their flaws are not able to practice humanity and righteousness. Human beings alone are capable of acting humanely and on the basis of moral principles. Due to their defects, none of the other creatures can match Heaven and earth the way man alone can. Human beings have 360 joints, which is a heavenly number. With their bodies of flesh and bones, humans match the fullness of the earth. Above, the brightness of their ears and eyes correspond to the sun and moon. The cavities and veins of their bodies resemble the rivers and valleys. Their hearts feel grief, joy, and anger, much like divine entities.

Look at the human body. How superior it is to that of other creatures, and how much like Heaven! Other creatures gain life by taking from the Yin and Yang of Heaven in a bent and off-center way, but human beings brilliantly have their orderly patterns. Thus other creatures' bodies are bent and crouched as they move about in Heaven and on earth. Human beings alone stand erect and look forward, able to take an upright posture. Creatures that received little from Heaven and earth bend and crouch; those that receive much stand upright. From this we can see that human beings exceed other creatures and are on a level with Heaven and earth. Therefore in human bodies the head rises up and is round, shaped like Heaven, with the hair resembling the stars. The ears and eyes in their brilliance resemble the sun and moon; the nose and mouth, in their breathing, resemble the wind; the ability to comprehend which lies within the breast resembles the spiritual intelligence (of Heaven); the alternating fullness of bellies and wombs resembles animals. Animals are closest to earth so the part of the body below the waist has the characteristics of earth. The waist marks the division between Heavenly and earthly parts of the body. The part above the neck has a refined spirit and noble bearing, showing its resemblance to Heaven. The part below the neck has fullness and lowliness, comparable to the soil of the earth. The feet, when they step, are square, resembling the shape of the earth. Therefore when one wears ceremonial sashes and belts, the neck must be straight to distinguish it from the heart.

Everything above the belt is Yang, everything below it Yin, each with its own part to play. Yang is the vital energy of Heaven, Yin of earth. The movement of Yin and Yang causes a person to have a foot ailment or a sore throat and also causes the vital energy of the earth to rise and bring clouds and rain. The processes are comparable in each case. The matching of Heaven and earth and the correspondence of Yin and Yang are fully manifested in the human body.

The body is like Heaven, with matching numbers, so life spans are linked to Heaven. Heaven gives form to the human body through the numbers of the year. Thus the 366 small joints of the body match the number of days, the twelve large joints match the number of months; internally the five organs match the Five Agents [wood, fire, earth, metal, water]; externally the four limbs match the four seasons. The alternation of opening and shutting the eyes matches daylight and nighttime. The alternation of strength and weakness matches winter and summer. The alternation of grief and joy matches Yin and Yang. The mind can calculate and plan, which matches the measurements of the world. Conduct based on ethical principles resembles the relationship of Heaven and earth. . . .

Whoever invented writing in ancient times connected three lines through the middle and called it "king." The three lines stand for Heaven, earth, and man. The one who connects them through the middle joins their paths. Who else but a king could take the central place among Heaven, earth, and man and connect them all? . . .

Heaven's constant desire is to love and bring benefit, its task to nurture. Spring, fall, winter, and summer are the instruments it uses. The king also makes loving and bringing benefit his constant desire and his task is to bring peace and happiness to his age. Love and hate, joy and anger, are the instruments he uses. His love, hate, joy, and anger are like Heaven's seasons. It is through changes in temperature that things are transformed and completed. If Heaven produces these plants and animals in the right season, then the year will be one of abundance, but if at the wrong time, then the year will be a bad one. Similarly, if the ruler expresses his four emotions in accord with moral principles, then the world will be well governed, but if not, the age will be chaotic. Thus, an orderly age is like a good harvest, a disorderly age is like a bad harvest. Thus one can see that the principles of man match the way of Heaven.

Translated by Patricia Ebrey

14

THE DEBATE ON SALT AND IRON

Even if Confucians were given honored positions in the Han government from Emperor Wu's time on, they rarely were entirely satisfied with how the government was run. Emperor Wu, in particular, pursued activist policies which they believed deleterious. To generate revenue to pay for his military campaigns, he manipulated coinage, confiscated the lands of nobles, sold offices and titles, and increased taxes. He also established government monopolies in the production of iron, salt, and liquor, enterprises that had previously been sources of great profit for private entrepreneurs. Large-scale grain dealing had also been a profitable business, which the government now took over under the name of the system of equable marketing. Grain was to be bought where it was plentiful and its price low and either stored in granaries or transported to areas of scarcity. This procedure was supposed to eliminate speculation in grain, provide more constant prices, and bring profit to the government.

From the start these fiscal ventures were controversial. Confucians questioned their morality and their effect on the livelihood of the people. They thought that farming was an essential or "root" activity but that trade and crafts produced little of real value and were to be discouraged. Although the government claimed that it was protecting the people from the exploitation of merchants, its critics argued that it was teaching people mercantile tricks by setting itself up in commerce. In 81 B.C., after Emperor Wu's death, Confucian scholars who opposed the fiscal policies he had instituted were invited by the new emperor to argue their case with the chief minister, the man who had been instrumental in establishing them. A record was made of their debate in twenty-four chapters, the first of which is given below.

In 81 B.C. an imperial edict directed the chancellor and chief minister to confer with a group of wise and learned men about the people's hardships.

The learned men responded: We have heard that the way to rule lies in preventing frivolity while encouraging morality, in suppressing the pursuit of profit while opening the way for benevolence and duty. When profit is not emphasized, civilization flourishes and the customs of the people improve.

Recently, a system of salt and iron monopolies, a liquor excise tax, and an equable marketing system have been established throughout the country. These represent financial competition with the people which undermines their native honesty and promotes selfishness. As a result, few among the people take up the fundamental pursuits [agriculture] while many flock to the secondary [trade and industry]. When artificiality thrives, simplicity declines; when the secondary flourishes, the basic decays. Stress on the secondary makes the people decadent; emphasis on the basic keeps them unsophisticated. When the people are unsophisticated, wealth abounds; when they are extravagant, cold and hunger ensue.

We desire that the salt, iron, and liquor monopolies and the system of equable marketing be abolished. In that way the basic pursuits will be encouraged, and the people will be deterred from entering secondary occupations. Agriculture will then greatly prosper. This would be expedient.

The minister: The Xiongnu rebel against our authority and frequently raid the frontier settlements. To guard against this requires the effort of the nation's soldiers. If we take no action, these attacks and raids will never cease. The late emperor had sympathy for the long-suffering of the frontier settlers who live in fear of capture by the barbarians. As defensive measures, he therefore built forts and beacon relay stations and set up garrisons. When the revenue for the defense of the frontier fell short, he established the salt and iron monopolies, the liquor excise tax, and the system of equable marketing. Wealth increased and was used to furnish the frontier expenses.

Now our critics wish to abolish these measures. They would have the treasury depleted and the border deprived of funds for its defense. They would expose our soldiers who defend the frontier passes and walls to hunger and cold, since there is no other way to supply them. Abolition is not expedient.

The learned men: Confucius observed, "The ruler of a kingdom or head of a family does not worry about his people's being poor, only about their being unevenly distributed. He does not worry about their being few, only about their being dissatisfied." Thus, the emperor should not talk of much and little, nor the feudal lords of advantage and harm, nor the ministers of gain and loss. Instead they all should set examples of benevolence and duty and virtuously care for people, for then those nearby will flock to them and those far away will joyfully submit to their authority. Indeed, the master conqueror need not fight, the expert warrior needs no soldiers, and the great commander need not array his troops.

If you foster high standards in the temple and courtroom, you need only make a bold show and bring home your troops, for the king who practices benevolent government has no enemies anywhere. What need can he then have for expense funds?

The minister: The Xiongnu are savage and cunning. They brazenly push through the frontier passes and harass the interior, killing provincial officials and military officers at the border. Although they have long deserved punishment for their lawless rebellion, Your Majesty has taken pity on the financial exigencies of the people and has not wished to expose his officers to the wilderness. Still, we cherish the goal of raising a great army and driving the Xiongnu back north.

I again assert that to do away with the salt and iron monopolies and equable marketing system would bring havoc to our frontier military policies and would be heartless toward those on the frontier. Therefore this proposal is inexpedient.

The learned men: The ancients honored the use of virtue and discredited the use of arms. Confucius said, "If the people of far-off lands do not submit, then the ruler must attract them by enhancing his refinement and virtue. When they have been attracted, he gives them peace."

At present, morality is discarded and reliance is placed on military force. Troops are raised for campaigns and garrisons are stationed for defense. It is the long-drawn-out campaigns and the ceaseless transportation of provisions that burden our people at home and cause our frontier soldiers to suffer from hunger and cold.

The establishment of the salt and iron monopolies and the appointment of financial officers to supply the army were meant to be temporary measures. Therefore, it is expedient that they now be abolished.

The minister: The ancient founders of our country laid the groundwork for both basic and secondary occupations. They facilitated the circulation of goods and provided markets and courts to harmonize the various demands. People of all classes gathered and goods of all sorts were assembled, so that farmers, merchants, and workers could all obtain what they needed. When the exchange of goods was complete, everyone went home. The *Book of Changes* says, "Facilitate exchange so that the people will not be overworked." This is because farmers are deprived of tools, and without merchants, desired commodities are unavailable. When farmers lack tools, grain is not planted, just as when valued goods are unavailable, wealth is exhausted.

The salt and iron monopolies and the equable marketing system are intended to circulate accumulated wealth and to regulate consumption according to the urgency of need. It is inexpedient to abolish them.

The learned men: If virtue is used to lead the people, they will return to honesty, but if they are enticed with gain, they will become vulgar. Vulgar habits lead them to shun duty. Vulgar habits lead them to shun duty and chase profit; soon they throng the roads and markets. Laozi said, "A poor country will appear to have a surplus." It is not that it possesses abundance, but that when wishes multiply the people become restive. Hence, a true king promotes the basic and discourages the secondary. He restrains the people's desires through the principles of ritual and duty and arranges to have grain exchanged for other goods. In his mar-

kets merchants do not circulate worthless goods nor artisans make worthless implements.

The purpose of merchants is circulation and the purpose of artisans is making tools. These matters should not become a major concern of the government.

The minister: Guanzi* said: "If a country possesses fertile land and yet its people are underfed, the reason is that there are not enough tools. If it possesses rich natural resources in its mountains and seas and yet the people are poor, the reason is that there are not enough artisans and merchants." The scarlet lacquer and pennant feathers from the kingdoms of Long and Shu; the leather goods, bone, and ivory from Jing and Yang; the cedar, catalpa, bamboo, and reeds from Jiangnan; the fish, salt, felt, and furs from Yan and Qi; the silk yarn, linen, and hemp cloth from Yan and You—all are needed to maintain our lives or be used in our funerals. We depend upon merchants for their distribution and on artisans for their production. For such reasons the ancient sages built boats and bridges to cross rivers; they domesticated cattle and horses to travel over mountains and plains. By penetrating to remote areas, they were able to exchange all kinds of goods for the benefit of the people.

Thus, the former emperor set up iron officials to meet the farmers' needs and started the equable marketing system to assure the people adequate goods. The bulk of the people look to the salt and iron monopolies and the equable marketing system as their source of supply. To abolish them would not be expedient.

The learned men: If a country possesses a wealth of fertile land and yet its people are underfed, the reason is that merchants and workers have prospered while agriculture has been neglected. Likewise, if a country possesses rich natural resources in its mountains and seas and yet its people are poor, the reason is that the people's necessities

---

* I.e., Guan Zhong, a famous minister of the seventh century B.C. noted for his economic policies.

have not been attended to while luxuries have multiplied. A spring cannot fill a leaking cup; the mountains and seas cannot satisfy unlimited desires. This is why [the ancient emperor] Pan Geng practiced communal living, [the ancient emperor] Shun concealed the gold, and [the Han dynasty founder] Gaozu prohibited merchants and shopkeepers from becoming officials. Their purpose was to discourage habits of greed and to strengthen the spirit of sincerity. Now, even with all of the discriminations against commerce, people still do evil. How much worse it would be if the ruler himself were to pursue profit!

The *Zuo Chronicle* says: "When the feudal lords take delight in profit, the officers become petty; when the officers are petty, the gentlemen become greedy; when the gentlemen are greedy, the common people steal." Thus to open the way for profit is to provide a ladder for the people to become criminals!

The minister: Formerly the feudal lords in the commanderies and kingdoms sent in the products of their respective regions as tribute. Transportation was troublesome and disorganized and the goods often of such bad quality as not to be worth the transport cost. Therefore, transport officers were appointed in every commandery and kingdom to assist in speeding the delivery of tribute and taxes from distant regions. This was called the equable marketing system. A receiving bureau was established at the capital for all the commodities. Because goods were bought when prices were low and sold when prices were high, the government suffered no loss and the merchants could not speculate for profit. This was called the balancing standard.

The balancing standard safeguards the people from unemployment; the equable marketing system distributes their work fairly. Both of these measures are intended to even out goods and be a convenience for the people. They do not provide a ladder for the people to become criminals by opening the way to profit!

The learned men: The ancients in placing levies and taxes on the people would look for what they could provide. Thus farmers contributed their harvest and the weaving women the products of their skill. At present the government ignores what people have and exacts what they lack. The common people then must sell their products cheaply to satisfy the demands of the government. Recently, some commanderies and kingdoms ordered the people to weave cloth. The officials caused the producers various difficulties and then traded with them. They requisitioned not only the silk from Qi and Tao and the broadcloth from Shu and Han, but also the ordinary cloth people make. These were then nefariously sold at "equable" prices. Thus the farmers suffered twice over and the weavers were doubly taxed. Where is the equability in this marketing?

The government officers busy themselves with gaining control of the market and cornering commodities. With the commodities cornered, prices soar and merchants make private deals and speculate. The officers connive with the cunning merchants who are hoarding commodities against future need. Quick traders and unscrupulous officials buy when goods are cheap in order to make high profits. Where is the balance in this standard? The equable marketing system of antiquity aimed at bringing about fair division of labor and facilitating transportation of tribute. It was surely not for profit or commodity trade.

Translated by Patricia Ebrey

15

THE CLASSIC OF FILIAL PIETY

The family has always been considered by the Chinese as the fundamental unit of their society. Filial piety had been praised by Confucius, and thinkers of all schools took for granted that a well-run family was one in which parents looked out for the interests of their children and children obeyed their parents and supported them in their old age. In the Han dynasty, the exaltation of filial piety was carried to new heights. Men could be made officials if they were recommended as paragons of filial piety. The brief Classic of Filial Piety *was probably written in the early Han. Purporting to be the recorded conversations between Confucius and his disciple, Zeng Zi, it extolled the vast powers of wholehearted devotion to parents and superiors more generally. Filial piety was presented as a political virtue, tied to loyalty to political superiors up to the Son of Heaven (the emperor). The* Classic of Filial Piety *was widely used in the Han and later as a primer to teach children basic moral maxims while they were learning how to read.*

OPENING THE DISCUSSION

Confucius was at home and Zengzi was attending him. The Master said, "The former kings had the highest virtue and the essential Way. By using them they kept the world ordered and the people in harmony, and neither superiors nor inferiors resented each other. Do you understand this?"

Zengzi rose from his seat and replied, "Since I am not clever, how can I understand this?"

The Master said, "Filial piety is the root of virtue and the source of civilization. Sit down again and I will explain it to you. Since we receive our body, hair, and skin from our parents, we do not dare let it be injured in any way. This is the be-

ginning of filial piety. We establish ourselves and practice the Way, thereby perpetuating our name for future generations and bringing glory to our parents. This is the fulfillment of filial piety. Thus filial piety begins with serving our parents, continues with serving the ruler, and is completed by establishing one's character."

THE SON OF HEAVEN

The Master said, "Those who love their parents do not dare to hate others. Those who respect their parents do not dare to show contempt towards others. The filial piety of the Son of Heaven consists in serving his parents with complete love and respect so that his moral influence reaches the common people and he becomes a model for the distant regions in all directions."

THE FEUDAL LORDS

"Although in superior positions, they are not arrogant and thus can hold lofty positions without peril. By exercising restraint and caution they can have plenty without going overboard. Holding a lofty position without peril is the way to preserve high rank for a long time. Having plenty without going overboard is the way to preserve wealth for a long time. If they retain their wealth and rank they will later be able to protect their heritage and keep their people in peace. This is the filial piety of the feudal lords."

THE MINISTERS AND HIGH OFFICERS

"They do not dare wear garments not prescribed by the former kings; they do not dare use words not approved by the former kings; they do not dare to behave in any ways outside the virtuous ways of the former kings. Thus, they will not speak improper words and will not follow anything outside the Way. Their words are not arbitrary, nor their actions capricious. Their words reach all in the world, yet offend no one. Their words fill the world, yet give no one cause for complaint. When these three conditions are fulfilled, they are able to preserve their ancestral altars. This is the filial piety of the ministers and high officers."

SCHOLARS

"They serve their mothers as they serve their fathers; the love shown them is the same. They serve their rulers as they serve their fathers; the respect shown both is the same. Therefore mothers get love and rulers elicit respect, and fathers combine them both. To serve a ruler with filial piety is to be loyal. To serve an elder with filial piety is to be obedient. Never failing in loyalty or obedience in their service to superiors, they are able to preserve their offices and salaries and maintain their family line. This is the filial piety of the scholars."

THE COMMON PEOPLE

"They follow the laws of nature to utilize the earth to the best advantage. They take care of themselves and are cautious in expenditures in order to support their parents. This is the filial piety of the common people. Thus from the Son of Heaven to the common people, unless filial piety is pursued from beginning to end, calamities will surely result."

THE THREE POWERS

Zengzi said, "How exceedingly great is filial piety!"

The Master responded, "Filial piety is the pattern of Heaven, the standard of the earth, the norm of conduct for the people. When people follow the pattern of Heaven and earth, they model themselves on the brilliance of Heaven and make use of the resources of the earth and through these means comply with all under Heaven. Thus, [a ruler's] instruction succeeds without being stringent, and his policies are effective without being severe. The former kings, realizing that their instruction could transform the people, showed them an example of universal love. As a consequence, men did not neglect their parents. These kings set an example of rectitude and virtue, and as a consequence the people enthusiastically copied them. The kings showed an example of respectful yielding, and the people did not contend with each other. They taught through ritual and music, and the people lived in concord. They made clear to them the difference between good and evil, and as a consequence the people knew restraint."

GOVERNMENT BY FILIAL PIETY

The Master said, "Formerly the illustrious kings brought order to the world through filial piety. They did not dare neglect the ministers of small states—not to mention their own dukes, marquises, earls, counts, and barons. Therefore they gained the hearts of all the states and were able to serve their former kings. The rulers did not dare insult the widows and widowers—not to mention the upper class or the common people. Therefore they gained the hearts of all the people and were able to serve their former rulers. The heads of families did not dare mistreat their servants and concubines—not to mention their wives and children. Therefore they gained their hearts and were able to serve their parents. Accordingly, while living, parents were well taken care of; after their death, their ghosts received sacrifices. In this way the world was kept in peace and harmony. Calamities did not occur nor was disorder created. Such was the way the former illustrious kings brought order to the world through filial piety."

THE RULE OF THE SAGES

Zengzi said, "May I ask if there isn't anything in the virtue of the sages that surpasses filial piety?"

The Master replied, "Of all the creatures in Heaven and earth, man is the most important. Of all man's acts, none is greater than filial piety. In the practice of filial piety, nothing is greater than respecting one's father. For respecting one's father, nothing is greater than placing him on the level with Heaven. The person who did all this was the Duke of Zhou. In former times the Duke of Zhou sacrificed to the Spirit of Agriculture, placing him on a level with Heaven. He sacrificed to his father King Wen, in the Bright Hall, placing him on a level with the Supreme Lord. Therefore, within the four seas all of the lords, according to their stations, came to sacrifice. Thus, how can there be anything in the virtue of the sages that surpasses filial piety? From infancy a child's desire to care for his parents daily grows more re-

spectful. The sages used this natural reverence for parents to teach respect and used this natural affection to teach love. Thus, the teachings of the sages were effective though not severe and their rule was orderly though not harsh. This was because they relied on what was basic to human nature.

"The proper relation between father and son is a part of nature and forms the principles which regulate the conduct of rulers and ministers. Parents give life—no tie is stronger than this. Rulers personally watch over the people—no care is greater than this. Therefore to love others without first loving one's parents is to reject virtue. To reverence other men without first reverencing one's parents is to reject the rules of ritual. If one copies such perversity, the people will have no model to follow. Although a person who does not do good but only evil may gain a high position, a man of honor will not esteem him. The practice of a man of honor is different: his speech is praiseworthy, his behavior is pleasing, his standards are respected, his management of affairs can be taken as a model, his department is pleasant to observe, his movements are deliberate. When a man of honor deals with his people they look on him with awe and affection; they imitate and seek to resemble him. Thus he can carry out his moral instruction and put into effect his political directives."

FILIAL CONDUCT

The Master said, "In serving his parents a filial son renders the utmost reverence to them while at home. In supporting them he maximizes their pleasure. When they are sick he takes every care. At their death he expresses all his grief. Then he sacrifices to them with full solemnity. If he has fulfilled these five requirements, then he is truly able to serve his parents. He who really loves his parents will not be proud in high position. He will not be insubordinate in an inferior position. And among equals he will not be quarrelsome. If he were proud in high station he might be ruined. If he were insubordinate in an inferior position he might incur punishment. If he were quarrelsome among his equals, he might end up fighting. Thus, unless these three evils are eliminated, a son cannot be called filial—even if every day he supplies his parents the three choice meats."

THE FIVE PUNISHMENTS

The Master said, "There are three thousand offenses subject to the five punishments, but of these none is greater than lack of filial piety. To use force against the ruler is to defy authority. To deny the sages is to be unprincipled. And to decry filial piety is to renounce kinship ties. These are the road to chaos."

ELABORATING "THE ESSENTIAL WAY"

The Master said, "For teaching men to love one another there is nothing better than filial piety. For teaching men ceremonial behavior and obedience there is nothing better than fraternal love. For transforming their manners and habits there is nothing better than music. For giving security to the rulers and governing the people there is nothing better than ritual. Ritual is essentially reverence. The son is happy when his father is reverenced. The younger brother is happy when his elder brother is reverenced. The ministers are made happy when their ruler is reverenced. Everyone is happy when the One Man, the Son of Heaven, is reverenced. Only a few are revered but multitudes are made happy. This is said to be the essential Way."

ELABORATING "THE HIGHEST VIRTUE"

The Master said, "A man of honor in teaching the duties of filial piety does not need to go daily to the people's homes to observe them. He merely teaches the principles of filial piety and all the fathers in the world receive the filial respect due to them. He teaches the principles of fraternal love and all the elder brothers receive the respect due to them. He teaches the duties of subjects and all the rulers of the world receive the reverence due to them. The Odes say: 'The man of honor, affectionate, is the father and mother to the people.' Unless he possessed the highest virtue, who could educate the people to such an extent?"

ELABORATING "PERPETUATING ONE'S NAME"

The Master said, "The man of honor's service to his parents is filial; the fidelity involved in it can be transferred to his ruler. His service to his elder brothers is deferential; the obedience involved in it can be transferred to his superiors. Self-disciplined at home, he can transfer his good management to official life. Through these means when his conduct is perfect at home his name will be perpetuated to later generations."

REMONSTRATING

Zengzi remarked, "As regards kind affection, loving respect, comforting one's parents, and bringing glory to one's name, all this I have understood. May I ask if a son can be called filial if he obeys all of his father's commands?"

The Master replied, "What kind of talk is this? In ancient times if the Son of Heaven had seven ministers to remonstrate with him, he would not lose his empire, even if he were imperfect. If a feudal lord had five good ministers to advise him, he would not lose his state, even if he were imperfect. If a high officer had three officials to remonstrate with him, he would not lose his home, even if he were imperfect. If a gentleman had a friend to correct him, he would not lose his good name. And if a father had a son to advise him, he would not fall into doing wrong. Thus, when he might do something wrong, a son must not fail to warn his father against it, nor a minister fail to warn his ruler. In short, when it is a question of doing wrong, one must remonstrate. How can following a father's orders be considered fulfilling filial piety?"

MUTUAL INTERACTION

The Master said, "In ancient times the illustrious kings, because they were filial to their fathers were able to serve Heaven intelligently. Because they were filial to their mothers they were able to serve earth with circumspection. Superiors could govern inferiors because the young obeyed their elders. Thus, because Heaven and earth were served with intelligence and care the spirits manifested themselves brilliantly. Even the Son of Heaven had someone he paid reverence to, that is to say, his father. He had someone he deferred to, that is to say, his elder brothers. At the ancestral temple he was reverential, not forgetting his parents. He cultivated his character and acted prudently, for fear of disgracing his ancestors. When he paid reverence at the ancestral temple, the ghosts and spirits sent blessings. When his filial piety and fraternity were perfected, his influence reached the spirits. He illuminated the four seas; there was no place his virtue did not penetrate."

SERVING THE RULER

The Master said, "In serving his superior the man of honor makes every effort to be faithful when he is in office. In retirement he tries to make up for his shortcomings. He encourages his superior in his good inclinations and tries to keep him from doing wrong. In this way, the relations between superiors and inferiors can be cordial."

MOURNING FOR PARENTS

The Master said, "When mourning a parent a filial son cries without wailing loudly, he performs the rites without attention to his appearance, he speaks without attention to the beauty of his words, he feels uncomfortable in elegant clothes, he gets no joy from hearing music, he does not relish good food—all of this is the emotion of grief. After three days he eats again to show men that the dead should not hurt the living and that the suffering should not lead to the destruction of life. This was the regulation of the sages. The period of mourning is not allowed to exceed three years, thus showing the people that everything ends. [The filial son] prepares a double coffin and grave clothes. When he sets out the sacrificial vessels, he grieves. Beating the breast, jumping up and down, and crying, he bids a last sad farewell. He divines to choose the burial place where the body can be placed to rest. He prepares an ancestral altar, so that the ghost can receive sacrifices. Spring and autumn he offers sacrifices thus thinking of the dead once every season. When his parents were alive he served them with love and reverence; in death he grieves. With the man's fundamental duty fulfilled, relations between the living and the dead are complete, and the filial son's service to his parents is finished."

Translated by Patricia Ebrey

16

WANG FU ON FRIENDSHIP AND GETTING AHEAD

Service as a government official conferred great prestige in the Han, and educated men competed eagerly for posts. To enter the civil service, a man generally had to be recommended by either the official in charge of his local commandery or a high central government official. The rationale for this selection system was that moral character was what mattered most and only those personally acquainted with a candidate could judge it. From the beginning, critics of this system pointed out that officials often recommended friends, relatives, and men of wealth and influence rather than the most worthy.

In the following essay, Wang Fu (ca. 100–150) decries the effect this system of recruitment had on friendships within the educated class. He placed high demands on true friendship and believed that all talented men should have opportunities to gain office. Wang Fu himself never gained an official post, undoubtedly accounting for some of the bitterness of his complaints.

It is said, "With people, the old friends are best; with things, the new ones are best." In other words, brothers may drift apart as time goes by, but it is normal for friends to become closer with the passage of time.

Nowadays this is not so. People often seem to miss those they hardly know but forget close friends; they turn away from old friends as they seek new ones. Sometimes after several years friendships become weaker and weaker, and friendships of long standing break down. People not only discard the ancient sages' instruction to treasure old friends but also break oaths of enduring fidelity.

What are the reasons for this change in attitude toward friendship? Careful analysis makes them clear. There are common tendencies and normal ways of operating in the world. People compete to flatter and get close to those who are wealthy and prominent; this is a common tendency. People are also quick to snub those who are poor and humble; this is a normal way of operating. If a person makes friends with the rich and prominent, he will gain the benefits of influential recommendations for advancement in office and the advantages of generous presents and other emoluments. But if he makes friends with the poor and humble, he will lose money either from giving them handouts or from unrepaid loans.

A powerful official may be as evil as the tyrant

69

Jie and the bandit Dao Zhi, but if he rides in a magnificent carriage to summon scholars to him, they will take it as a great honor and flock to his service. How can a person avoid being drawn to those who can render him tangible benefits? A scholar may have the combined talents of Yan Hui and Bao Shangyan, yet if he wears poor clothing when he pays visits, others will feel insulted and will look with dread upon the prospect of further calls. How can a person not avoid those who will bring him disadvantage? Therefore, those who are rich and prosperous find it easy to get along in society, while those who are poor and humble find it difficult to secure a place in the world.

The poor, if they wear fine clothes, are regarded as extravagant and ostentatious, but if they wear coarse clothing, they are taken to be in dire straits and difficulties. If they walk slowly, people say they are weak from hunger, but if they walk fast, they are accused of trying to flee from debts. If the poor do not visit others, they are regarded as arrogant, but if they come around too often, they are suspected of trying to sponge free meals. If they come empty-handed, they are taken for insincere friends, but if they bring a gift, they are regarded as degenerate. If they are confident and self-assured, they are regarded as unvirtuous. All these are the woes of the unemployed scholar, poor and without rank.

The poor scholar, being in a humble position, has much to bear. At home he has to put up with his wife's complaints. Outside he must endure the cutting remarks of the scholar-officials. At banquets his gifts are small and considered inadequate. His own parties are simple and not up to others' standards. He is not rich enough to come to the aid of friends in need, and his power is too meager to save them. A friendship may have been long and cordial, but since the poor scholar is unable to save his friend in need, the relationship weakens. Once this occurs, the humble scholar becomes more and more aware of his own low status, while the other individual busies himself with cultivating relationships with more useful persons and forgets his old friend.

Since friendship is founded on mutual advantage, when disadvantage arises the friendship breaks down. An oath of friendship is meaningless and eventually will be discarded. Those who communicate often become close friends because they see advantage to themselves in the relationship. A commoner will act as follows. If a person can be useful, he will draw near to him. Being close to him, he will gradually develop a feeling of love for him. Because he thinks the friend is right, he will regard him as capable, and so he will turn his heart toward him and praise him happily. A commoner will keep his distance from those whom he regards as unable to render him benefits. Because they are distant, after a time he begins to feel hatred for them. Because he hates them, he always considers them in the wrong, and so feels disgust for them. Once he feels disgust for them, his heart naturally turns away from them and he slanders them. Therefore, even if one's friendship with a wealthy and prominent man is a new one, it will become closer and closer every day; and although one's friendship with a poor and humble man is of long standing, it will tend to become weaker and more distant. These are the reasons why a poor scholar cannot compete with officials for friends.

Rulers do not understand what causes people to form friendships, and so they readily believe the words of their high officials. This is why honest scholars are always excluded from court while crafty persons always get their way. In the past when Wei Qi lost his power, his retainers abandoned him to serve in another place. When the general Wei Qing lost imperial favor and was no longer able to shower his subordinates with rewards from the court, they left him to serve the newly powerful general Huo Quping. The retainers of the Zhao general Lian Po and of the Han general Di Gong came and went, depending on whether their benefactors were in power or not. These four gentlemen were all capable and all had illustrious pasts, yet the loyalty of their subordinates wavered with the amount of power they had. How much more would this happen to those who became really poor and humble!

Only those who have the heroic virtue of the

ancients will not desert their superiors and friends in such a fashion. When these people make commitments to friends, they do not abandon them their whole life long. If they love someone, their concern for him can only become greater as his situation worsens. The *Book of Songs* says, "The virtuous man, the princely one, is uniformly correct in his deportment. His heart is as if it were tied to what is correct." Only during the cold of winter, when all other trees have lost their leaves, do people realize that the pine trees resist the cold and do not shed their needles. Likewise, it is only when difficulties are encountered that a person's virtue can be noticed. You Ying and Yu Rang gave their lives to retain their master's good grace. Zhuan Zhu and Jing Ke sacrificed their lives to render service to their masters. It is easy to die, but to die for one's master willingly when he has encountered hard times is difficult indeed. . . .

Most scholars are very shortsighted, concerned only about the present moment. If they think that a powerful man will be of use to them, they rush to his service; but if they think that someone will be of no use, they are quick to avoid him. Those who burn for rapid promotion and advancement compete with one another to get close to persons of prominence but can find no time to associate with the humble. They scrape and claw to make their way to the front but have little time to concern themselves with those who have been left behind. When the Minister Han Anguo lost his official post, he sent some five hundred golden artifacts to the newly powerful Grand Commandant Dian Fen to seek a position. Yet not once did he give any assistance to a poor but capable scholar. Likewise the Minister Di Fangjin was eager to recommend Shun Youchang, a relative of the empress, for promotion, but was unable to recommend even one humble scholar. Now, both Han Anguo and Di Fangjin were good and loyal officials of the Han dynasty, and yet they still acted in such a snobbish way. How can one expect virtue from officials who are inferior to them? This is the reason that crafty, calculating individuals can worm their way up the official ladder while ordinary scholars slip ever more into obscurity. Unless the realm has a brilliant ruler, there may be no one to discern this. . . .

In this world there are three things which are loathsome indeed. These may be summed up as follows: first, to express in words extremely warm affections toward others while one's heart holds nothing but cold feelings; second, to express in writing dear thoughts toward others while in fact one's thoughts are rarely with them; third, to make appointments with others while having already decided not to show up at all. If people are always suspicious of others' words, they may fear that they will dismiss the genuine sentiments of a true worthy. But if people are quick to believe what they are told, they will be often fooled. This is why those disingenuous, mediocre people are so disgusting. . . .

Alas! The gentlemen of today speak nobly but act basely. Their words are upright, but their hearts are false. Their actions do not reflect their words, and their words are out of harmony with their thoughts. In talking of antiquity they always praise the conduct of Bo Yi, Shu Qi, Qu Yuan, and Yan Hui; but when it comes to the present, their only concern is the scramble for official ranks and positions. In their lofty speeches they refer to virtuous and righteous persons as being worthy. But when they actually recommend people for office, they consider only such requirements as influence and prominence. If a man is just an obscure scholar, even if he possesses the virtue of Yan Hui and Min Ziqian, even if he is modest and diligent, even if he has the ability of Yi Yin and Lu Shang, even if he is filled with the most devoted compassion for the people, he is clearly not going to be employed in this world.

Translated by Lily Hwa

17

WOMEN'S VIRTUES AND VICES

Pre-Han philosophers directed little of their writing to women, even women of the nobility. In the Han, however, the eminent scholar and bibliographer Liu Xiang (79–8 B.C.) wrote the Biographies of Heroic Women, *a collection of accounts of the gallant deeds and unselfish behavior of 125 women of antiquity. Many of these women epitomized a single virtue— for instance, loyalty to the ruler, self-sacrifice to help husband or father, or preservation of chastity under duress. As seen in the selection from this book given below, however, the mother of Mencius had several virtues. It is followed here by two of the seven sections of the* Admonitions for Women, *an equally famous Han text on women's virtues. It was written by Ban Zhao (ca. 45–116), sister of the famous historian Ban Gu (32–92), as a guide to the cultivation of virtues appropriate to women, such as humility, resignation, subservience, self-abasement, obedience, cleanliness, and industry. The selections from these two texts show what people admired in women, but not what women were like. To complement them, a description of a real but far-from-ideal woman is also included here. It is from a letter written by the woman's husband, Feng Yan, to her younger brother explaining his reasons for divorcing her.*

THE MOTHER OF MENCIUS

The mother of Mencius lived in Zou in a house near a cemetery. When Mencius was a little boy he liked to play burial rituals in the cemetery, happily building tombs and grave mounds. His mother said to herself, "This is no place to bring up my son."

She moved near the marketplace in town. Mencius then played merchant games of buying and selling. His mother again said, "This is no place to bring up my son."

So once again she moved, this time next to a school house. Mencius then played games of ancestor sacrifices and practiced the common courtesies between students and teachers. His mother said, "At last, this is the right place for my son!" There they remained.

When Mencius grew up he studied the six arts of propriety, music, archery, charioteering, writing, and mathematics. Later he became a famous Confucian scholar. Superior men commented that Mencius's mother knew the right influences for her sons. The *Book of Songs* says,

"That admirable lady, what will she do for them!"

When Mencius was young, he came home from school one day and found his mother was weaving at the loom. She asked him, "Is school out already?"

He replied, "I left because I felt like it."

His mother took her knife and cut the finished cloth on her loom. Mencius was startled and asked why. She replied, "Your neglecting your studies is very much like my cutting the cloth. The superior person studies to establish a reputation and gain wide knowledge. He is calm and poised and tries to do no wrong. If you do not study now, you will surely end up as a menial servant and will never be free from troubles. It would be just like a woman who supports herself by weaving to give it up. How long could such a person depend on her husband and son to stave off hunger? If a woman neglects her work or a man gives up the cultivation of his character, they may end up as common thieves if not slaves!"

Shaken, from then on Mencius studied hard from morning to night. He studied the philosophy of the master and eventually became a famous Confucian scholar. Superior men observed that Mencius's mother understood the way of motherhood. The *Book of Songs* says, "That admirable lady, what will she tell them!"

After Mencius was married, one day as he was going into his private quarters, he encountered his wife not fully dressed. Displeased, Mencius stopped going into his wife's room. She then went to his mother, begged to be sent home, and said, "I have heard that the etiquette between a man and a woman does not apply in their private room. But lately I have been too casual, and when my husband saw me improperly dressed, he was displeased. He is treating me like a stranger. It is not right for a woman to live as a guest; therefore, please send me back to my parents."

Mencius's mother called him to her and said, "It is polite to inquire before you enter a room. You should make some loud noise to warn anyone inside, and as you enter, you should keep your eyes low so that you will not embarrass anyone. Now, you have not behaved properly, yet you are quick to blame others for their impropriety. Isn't that going a little too far?"

Mencius apologized and took back his wife. Superior men said that his mother understood the way to be a mother-in-law.

When Mencius was living in Qi, he was feeling very depressed. His mother saw this and asked him, "Why are you looking so low?"

"It's nothing," he replied.

On another occasion when Mencius was not working, he leaned against the door and sighed. His mother saw him and said, "The other day I saw that you were troubled, but you answered that it was nothing. But why are you leaning against the door sighing?"

Mencius answered, "I have heard that the superior man judges his capabilities and then accepts a position. He neither seeks illicit gains nor covets glory or high salary. If the dukes and princes do not listen to his advice, then he does not talk to them. If they listen to him but do not use his ideas, then he no longer frequents their courts. Today my ideas are not being used in Qi, so I wish to go somewhere else. But I am worried because you are getting too old to travel about the country."

His mother answered, "A woman's duties are to cook the five grains, heat the wine, look after her parents-in-law, make clothes, and that is all! Therefore, she cultivates the skills required in the women's quarters and has no ambition to manage affairs outside of the house. The *Book of Changes* says, 'In her central place, she attends to the preparation of the food.' The *Book of Songs* says, 'It will be theirs neither to do wrong nor to do good, / Only about the spirits and the food will they have to think.' This means that a woman's duty is not to control or to take charge. Instead she must follow the 'three submissions.' When she is young, she must submit to her parents. After her marriage, she must submit to her husband. When she is widowed, she must submit to her son. These are the rules of propriety. Now you are an adult and I am old; therefore, whether you go depends on what you consider right, whether I follow depends on the rules of propriety."

Superior men observed that Mencius's mother knew the proper course for women. The *Book of Songs* says, "Serenely she looks and smiles, / Without any impatience she delivers her instructions."

Translated by Nancy Gibbs

LETTER FROM FENG YAN TO HIS BROTHER-IN-LAW

Man is a creature of emotion. Yet it is according to reason that husband and wife are joined together or put asunder. According to the rules of propriety which have been set down by the sage, a gentleman should have both a primary wife and concubines as well. Even men from poor and humble families long to possess concubines. I am old and approaching the end of my life, but I have never had a concubine. I will carry regret for this into my grave.

My wife is jealous and has destroyed the Way of a good family. Yet this mother of five children is still in my house. For the past five years her conduct has become worse and worse day after day. She sees white as black and wrong as right. I never err in the slightest, yet she lies about me and nags me without end. It is like falling among bandits on the road, for I constantly encounter unpredictable disasters through this woman. Those who slander us good officials seem to have no regard for the deleterious effects this has on the welfare of the country. Likewise, those who indulge their jealousy seem to have no concern for the unjust strain this puts on other people's lives.

Since antiquity it has always been considered a great disaster to have one's household be dominated by a woman. Now this disaster has befallen me. If I eat too much or too little or if I drink too much or too little, she jumps all over me like the tyrant Xia Jie. If I play some affectionate joke on her, she will gossip about it to everyone. She glowers with her eyes and clenches her fists tightly in anger over things which are purely the product of her imagination. I feel a severe pang in my heart, as though something is poisoning my five viscera. Anxiety cuts so deeply that I can hardly bear to go on living. My rage is so great that I often forget the calamities I might cause.

When she is at home, she is always lounging in bed. After she gave birth to my principal heir, she refused to have any more children. We have no female servants at our home who can do the work of weaving clothes and rugs. Our family is of modest means and we cannot afford a man-servant, so I have to work myself like a humble commoner. My old friends see my situation and feel very sorry for me, but this woman has not the slightest twinge of sympathy or pity.

Wu Da, you have seen our one and only female servant. She has no hairpins or hair ornaments. She has no make-up for her face, looks haggard, and is in bad shape. My wife does not extend the slightest pity to her, nor does she try to understand her. The woman flies into a rage, jumps around, and yells at her. Her screaming is so shrill that even a sugar peddler's concubine would be ashamed to behave in such a manner.

I should have sent this woman back long ago, but I was concerned by the fact that the children were still young and that there was no one else to do the work in our house. I feared that my children, Jiang and Bao, would end up doing servants' work. Therefore I retained her. But worry and anxiety plunge like a dagger into my heart and cause me great pain. The woman is always screaming fiercely. One can hardly bear to listen to it.

Since the servant was so mistreated, within half a year her body was covered with scabs and scars. Ever since the servant became ill, my daughter Jiang has had to hull the grain and do the cooking, and my son Bao has had to do all sorts of dirty work. Watching my children struggle under such labor gives me distress.

Food and clothing are scattered all over the house. Winter clothes which have become frayed are not patched. Even though the rest of us are very careful to be neat, she turns the house into a mess. She does not have the manner of a good wife, nor does she possess the virtue of a good mother. I despise her overbearing aggressiveness, and I hate to see our home turned into a sty.

She relies on the power of Magistrate Zheng to get what she wants. She is always threatening people, and her barbs are numerous. It seems as if she carries a sword and lance to the door. Never will she make a concession, and it feels as if there were a hundred bows around our house. How can we ever return to a happy family life?

When the respectable members of our family try to reason with her, she flings insults at them and makes sharp retorts. She never regrets her scandalous behavior and never allows her heart to be moved. I realize that I have placed myself in a difficult position, and so I have started to plan ahead. I write you this letter lest I be remiss in keeping you informed of what is happening. I believe that I have just cause, and I am not afraid of criticism. Unless I send this wife back, my family will have no peace. Unless I send this wife back, my house will never be clean. Unless I send this wife back, good fortune will not come to my family. Unless I send this wife back, I will never again get anything accomplished. I hate myself for not having made this decision while I was still young. The decision is now made, but I am old, humiliated, and poor. I hate myself for having allowed this ulcer to grow and spread its poison. I brought a great deal of trouble on myself.

Having suffered total ruin as a result of this family catastrophe, I am abandoning the gentry life to live as a recluse. I will sever relationships with my friends and give up my career as an official. I will stay at home all the time and concentrate on working my land to supply myself with food and clothing. How can I think of success and fame?

Translated by Lily Hwa

BAN ZHAO'S *ADMONITIONS FOR WOMEN*

Humility

In ancient times, on the third day after a girl was born, people placed her at the base of the bed, gave her a pot shard to play with, and made a sacrifice to announce her birth. She was put below the bed to show that she was lowly and weak and should concentrate on humbling herself before others. Playing with a shard showed that she should get accustomed to hard work and concentrate on being diligent. Announcing her birth to the ancestors showed that she should focus on continuing the sacrifices. These three customs convey the unchanging path for women and the ritual traditions.

Humility means yielding and acting respectful, putting others first and oneself last, never mentioning one's own good deeds or denying one's own faults, enduring insults and bearing with mistreatment, all with due trepidation. Industriousness means going to bed late, getting up early, never shirking work morning or night, never refusing to take on domestic work, and completing everything that needs to be done neatly and carefully. Continuing the sacrifices means serving one's husband-master with appropriate demeanor, keeping oneself clean and pure, never joking or laughing, and preparing pure wine and food to offer to the ancestors.

There has never been a woman who had these three traits and yet ruined her reputation or fell into disgrace. If a woman loses these three traits, she will have no name to preserve and will not be able to avoid shame.

Devotion

According to the rites, a man is obligated to take a second wife but nothing is written about a woman marrying twice. Hence the saying, "A husband is one's Heaven: one cannot flee Heaven; one cannot leave a husband." Heaven punishes those whose actions offend the spirits; a husband looks down on a wife who violates the rites and proprieties. Thus the *Model for Women* says, "To please one man is her goal; to displease one man ends her goal." It follows from this that a woman must seek her husband's love—not through such means as flattery, flirting, or false intimacy, but rather through devotion.

Devotion and proper demeanor entail propriety and purity, hearing nothing licentious, seeing nothing depraved, doing nothing likely to draw notice when outside the home; never neglecting one's appearance when at home; never gathering in groups or watching at the doorway. By contrast, those incapable of devotion and proper demeanor are careless in their actions, look at and listen to whatever they like, let their hair get messy when at home, put on an act of delicacy when away, speak of things they should not mention, and watch what they should not see.

Translated by Patricia Ebrey

18

YIN AND YANG IN MEDICAL THEORY

The concepts of Yin and Yang and the Five Agents provided the intellectual frame-work of much of Chinese scientific thinking, especially in fields like biology and medicine. The organs of the body were seen to be interrelated in the same sorts of ways as other natural phenomena, and best understood by looking for correlations and correspondences. Illness was seen as a disturbance in the balance of Yin and Yang or the Five Agents caused by emotions, heat or cold, or other influences. Therapy thus depended on accurate diagnosis of the source of the imbalance.

The earliest surviving medical texts are fragments of manuscripts unearthed from early Han tombs. Besides general theory, these texts cover drugs, gymnastics, minor surgery, and magic spells. The text which was to become the main source of medical theory also apparently dates from the Han. It is the Yellow Emperor's Classic of Medicine, *supposed to have been written during the third millennium B.C. by the mythical Yellow Emperor. A small portion of it is given below.*

The Yellow Emperor said: "The principle of Yin and Yang is the foundation of the entire universe. It underlies everything in creation. It brings about the development of parenthood; it is the root and source of life and death; it is found with the temples of the gods. In order to treat and cure diseases one must search for their origins.

"Heaven was created by the concentration of Yang, the force of light; earth was created by the concentration of Yin, the forces of darkness. Yang stands for peace and serenity; Yin stands for confusion and turmoil. Yang stands for destruction; Yin stands for conservation. Yang brings about disintegration; Yin gives shape to things. . . .

"The pure and lucid element of light is manifested in the upper orifices, and the turbid element of darkness is manifested in the lower orifices. Yang, the element of light, originates in the pores. Yin, the element of darkness, moves within the five viscera. Yang, the lucid force of light, truly is represented by the four extremities; and Yin, the turbid force of darkness, stores the power of the six treasures of nature. Water is an embodiment of Yin, as fire is an embodiment of Yang. Yang creates the air, while Yin creates the senses, which belong to the physical body. When the physical body dies, the spirit is restored to the air, its natural environment. The spirit receives its nourishment through the air, and the body receives its nourishment through the senses. . . .

"If Yang is overly powerful, then Yin may be too weak. If Yin is particularly strong, then Yang is apt to be defective. If the male force is overwhelming, then there will be excessive heat. If the female force is overwhelming, then there will be excessive cold. Exposure to repeated and severe heat will induce chills. Cold injures the body while heat injures the spirit. When the spirit is hurt, severe pain will ensue. When the body is hurt, there will be swelling. Thus, when severe pain occurs first and swelling comes on later, one may infer that a disharmony in the spirit has done harm to the body. Likewise, when swelling appears first and severe pain is felt later on, one can say that a dysfunction in the body has injured the spirit. . . .

"Nature has four seasons and five elements. To grant long life, these seasons and elements must store up the power of creation in cold, heat, dryness, moisture, and wind. Man has five viscera in which these five climates are transformed into joy, anger, sympathy, grief, and fear. The emotions of joy and anger are injurious to the spirit just as cold and heat are injurious to the body. Violent anger depletes Yin; violent joy depletes Yang. When rebellious emotions rise to Heaven, the pulse expires and leaves the body. When joy and anger are without moderation, then cold and heat exceed all measure, and life is no longer secure. Yin and Yang should be respected to an equal extent."

The Yellow Emperor asked, "Is there any alternative to the law of Ying and Yang?"

Qi Bo answered: "When Yang is the stronger, the body is hot, the pores are closed, and people begin to pant; they become boisterous and coarse and do not perspire. They become feverish, their mouths are dry and sore, their stomachs feel tight, and they die of constipation. When Yang is the stronger, people can endure winter but not summer. When Yin is the stronger, the body is cold and covered with perspiration. People realize they are ill; they tremble and feel chilly. When they feel chilled, their spirits

become rebellious. Their stomachs can no longer digest food and they die. When Yin is the stronger, people can endure summer but not winter. Thus Yin and Yang alternate. Their ebbs and surges vary, and so does the character of their diseases."

The Yellow Emperor asked, "Can anything be done to harmonize and adjust these two principles of nature?"

Qi Bo answered: "If one has the ability to know the seven injuries and the eight advantages, one can bring the two principles into harmony. If one does not know how to use this knowledge, his life will be doomed to early decay. By the age of forty the Yin force in the body has been reduced to one-half of its natural vigor, and an individual's youthful prowess has deteriorated. By the age of fifty the body has grown heavy. The ears no longer hear well. The eyes no longer see clearly. By the age of sixty the life-producing power of Yin has declined to a very low level. Impotence sets in. The nine orifices no longer benefit each other. . . .

Those who seek wisdom beyond the natural limits will retain good hearing and clear vision. Their bodies will remain light and strong. Although they grow old in years, they will stay able-bodied and vigorous and be capable of governing to great advantage. For this reason the ancient sages did not rush into the affairs of the world. In their pleasures and joys they were dignified and tranquil. They did what they thought best and did not bend their will or ambition to the achievement of empty ends. Thus their allotted span of life was without limit, like that of Heaven and earth. This is the way the ancient sages controlled and conducted themselves. . . .

"By observing myself I learn about others, and their diseases become apparent to me. By observing the external symptoms, I gather knowledge about the internal diseases. One should watch for things out of the ordinary. One should observe minute and trifling things and treat them as if they were big and important. When they are treated, the danger they pose will be dissipated. Experts in examining patients judge their general appearance; they feel their pulse and determine whether it is Yin or Yang that causes the disease. . . . To determine whether Yin or Yang predominates, one must be able to distinguish a light pulse of low tension from a hard, pounding one. With a disease of Yang, Yin predominates. With a disease of Yin, Yang predominates. When one is filled with vigor and strength, Yin and Yang are in proper harmony."

Translated by Mark Coyle

19

LOCAL CULTS

Throughout history, local cults played an important part in the religious lives of Chinese at all social levels. Shrines were dedicated to various kinds of spirits and deities, including the ghosts of local residents, the spirits of mountains or rivers, and mythical culture heroes and ancient rulers. Shrines were places where individuals could make offerings when asking the gods for help and also served as focal points for communal festivals. In the Han, when a shrine was constructed or repaired a stone was occasionally carved to record the deed. Below are the texts of three such inscriptions dating from the mid-second century A.D.

INSCRIPTION FOR PRINCE QIAO

Prince Qiao is an immortal from a past age whose divinity has been known for a long time. Not knowing his origins, I inquired widely of Daoist experts. Some said Yingchuan, some said Yanmeng. When this city was first built, this mound was here. The tradition passed down from former people was that it was the grave of a prince, but as his line of descent had not continued, no one had maintained it. How many years went by, no one could remember.

Then in the twelfth month of A.D. 136, on the night of the winter festival, there was a sound of crying at the top of the grave. Wang Bo, who lived nearby, heard it and marveled at it. At dawn he made an offering at the grave and looked around. Then Heaven sent a heavy snow, and athough there were no human tracks to be seen, he saw the traces of a large bird near the place of the sacrifice. Everyone thought it was the spirit.

Some time later, a person appeared in front of the grave. He was wearing a large hat and a single red gown and carried a bamboo pole. He shouted to a young woodcutter, Yin Yongchang, "I am Prince Qiao. Never again take the trees from the front of my grave!" In a moment he had disappeared.

The magistrate, Wan Xi of Taishan, looked into the sayings of the elders and learned that this was an auspicious response to some influence. He examined the evidence and believed that there was proof. Then he built a temple in order to give peace to the spirit. From that time on, ardent Daoists have come here from afar. Some would play lutes and sing of the "great unity." Some would meditate long in order to pass through Cinnabar Hill (home of immortals). The sick and emaciated would cleanse their bodies, pray for cures, and be blessed immediately. However, if they were not reverent, they would have a relapse. Therefore, it became known that this grave mound with its great power was really that of an immortal.

In the eighth month of A.D. 165 the emperor sent an emissary to offer sacrifices in order to honor this spirit. The solicitous dignity was just right. The administrator of the kingdom, Wang Zhang (styled Boyi) of Donglai, thought that since the spirit had been honored by the emperor, there should be an inscription to show to later generations. The common people were proud of the similarity to the recognition of Laozi by Yin Xi at the barrier.* Then with the help of Chief Aide Bian Qianfang and the gentlemen and clerks, the stone tablet was set up. On the black stone the spirit is praised and his merit recorded. People who search for the Way now have something to read.

INSCRIPTION FOR SANGONG MOUNTAIN

The people believed that a period of famine and hardship had occurred because the gods of the Sangong, Yuyu, and Santiao Mountains were on the west sides of the peaks, on the far side from them. Then when the officials and common people made offerings, clouds gathered and rains fell throughout the area. Later when the Tibetans raided and there were locusts, drought, and unseasonal weather, the people wandered away. As a consequence, sacrificial offerings became rare, and ever since, the weather has been intemperate.

Then there came a learned Daoist who traced the origins of these problems. He concluded that the divine power of the Sangong has been difficult to preserve because it is in a place difficult to reach. Therefore, a lucky piece of land to the east of the kingdom seat was selected by divination, and a shrine and altar raised near Heng Mountain. A pair of columns stand on either side of the gate. Sacrifices have been offered and wine presented in order to please the god. The god enjoys his position and sweet rain has repeatedly fallen,

the response as quick as a shadow or an echo. There is great abundance within the borders of the kingdom and grain sells for three cash a bushel. The common people have neither illness nor suffering and live into old age.

INSCRIPTION FOR THE SPIRIT TOWER AT CHENGYANG

This concerns the mother of Lord Yao.

In ancient times Qingdu lived in Qiongjing. Of the Yi lineage, she was endowed with the best virtue and behaved according to the most appropriate rites. She modeled herself on the interaction of Yin and Yang and attained to the brilliance of the sun, moon, and stars. On an excursion by the bank of the Yellow River, she was influenced by the red dragon and thus gave birth to [the mythical sage king] Yao. Later when Yao asked about his ancestry, Qingdu informed him of the river dragon. Yao went to three rivers and a dragon came and gave him the diagrams.† With these, he personally carried out sage government and took care of his people. His glory was like a fiery sun: at first dark but later brighter and brighter. Subsequently he went from being a noble to being ruler.

When Qingdu died, she was buried here. It was desired that no one know of the place, so it was named Spirit Tower. On top is a yellow room where Yao offered sacrifices. At the bottom he ran some water to please the dragon. Turtles played and fish jumped in the water there; flat fish with sleek scales appeared among the pebbles at the dark bottom; rushes grew along the edges of the tower. For a long time it was a center of worship, but dynasties changed, and it was abandoned and not repaired.

The five interacting forces went through their cycles and the Han dynasty received a long span. The people of Han revived what had been destroyed and continued what had been discarded. So, as Yao had done, they reinstated the sacrifices.

---

* That is, in both cases it was a commoner who had recognized the greatness of someone others had ignored.

† The "River diagrams" were revered by Confucians for their cosmological significance.

In a year the flat fish again appeared. Therefore the Spirit Tower's attendant and guard sent a messenger to offer the fish to the throne because they could prolong life. Later, the Way was in decline and blocked. Subsequently, under [the usurper] Wang Mang's rule, the offerings were stopped.

The former minister of punishments, Zhong Ding, began to ponder, "The great Han has flourished and its virtue has reached the four directions. Why has great peace not yet arrived, and the portents not yet appeared? Why, instead, have barbarians frequently encroached on us and our armies frequently been disturbed? Since the emperors are not inattentive, why does the sun decline and not reappear?" The minister examined the classics and checked the records and the secret diagrams of the Yellow and Luo rivers. He concluded that since the Han founder had been conceived through a red dragon, he was a descendant of Yao. Thus Yao's shrine ought to be restored to its original design, and in repairing the Yellow Hall the sage's intentions should be sought. At that time disasters occurred and the minister thought Heaven was making known its will. Several times he petitioned the throne, explaining these basic principles, proposing that one should draw forth the lucky omens and block unlucky ones for the future blessings of the Han dynasty. The court closely examined his proposals and the emperor accepted his plan that every year in the spring and fall a great animal sacrifice should be made.

At this time the minister of punishments was due for a new appointment. Repeatedly he asked to retire, and finally his wish was granted. He was given the title great palace grandee and returned home to repair the Yellow Hall. In a good month, on a lucky day, he drew up the plan and set up the boundaries. He assembled the workers and the area was leveled. Everything was in accord with both Heaven and earth, beautifully painted in five colors.

A column was set up which seemed to penetrate to Heaven. The gate faced the east, and in front there was a large hall for worship of the gods. The floor was made of stone slabs to keep it cool. It could be used for dances. . . .

At the time, the grand administrator of Qiyin, Shen Huang of Wei commandery, and the magistrate of Chengyang, Guan Zun of Boling, each sent a great officer to assist. Minister Zhong managed and directed it. Before long the project was completed. The essence of the gods relies on human beings; it will disappear if abandoned and flourish if preserved.

The minister led a group of his clan's poor and rich to buy a stone tablet, all contributing fairly. On it deeds and teachings were recorded, and it was set up outside the central gate.

By divination the minister selected a day and everyone came to worship sincerely. They first made reverent offerings, then prayed for blessings. They asked the spirits to enjoy the offerings, to send sweet rain, to let the grains ripen, to bring the foreign wastelands to submission, to bring prosperity to the ten thousand states and the multitudes of people.

Translated by Patricia Ebrey

20

UPRISINGS

The collapse of the Han was hastened by the outbreak in 184 of a large-scale rebellion staged by followers of the "Way of Great Peace." Although this uprising was suppressed within a year, other rebels, preaching similar doctrines and using similar principles of organization, appeared throughout the country and proved difficult for the government to defeat or control. Little is known about these rebels or the societies they formed except what was reported to the court by unsympathetic observers. We cannot therefore, even state for certain whether the leaders were religious prophets or anti-dynastic rebels.

Below are three slightly divergent accounts contained in three histories of the period, the History of the Later Han, *the* Chronicle of the Three Kingdoms, *and the* History of the State of Huayang. *The first account deals exclusively with Zhang Jue, the leader of the "Way of Great Peace." The second account discusses the doctrines and practices of four rebel religious leaders, with particular emphasis on Zhang Xiu, who gained control of Hanzhong in west-central China. The third account describes Zhang Lu, who was associated with Zhang Xiu, although these last two selections differ on who was leader and who was follower.*

ZHANG JUE

Zhang Jue of Julu called himself the "Great Worthy Leader" and devoted himself to the Way of the Yellow Emperor and Laozi. He accepted many disciples who would kneel, bow, and confess their faults to him. He cured illnesses with holy water and prayers, and when the sick recovered, the common people came to believe in him.

Zhang Jue sent eight disciples to different parts of the country to convert everyone to his faith, thereby propagating this delusion. After some ten years, he had several hundred thousand followers scattered through the commanderies and kingdoms. Everyone in the eight provinces of Jing, Xu, You, Ji, Qing, Yang, Yan, and Yu [that is, eastern and central China] followed him. Then he set up thirty-six directors, who were like generals. A great director had over ten thousand people under him, a lesser director six or seven thousand. Each had chiefs below him. Jue's followers falsely proclaimed, "Green Heaven is already dead. Yellow Heaven must be established. The year *jiazi* [184] will be a propitious one for the whole world." They wrote the characters *jiazi* in mud on the gates of government offices in the capital and the provinces.

In 184, the great director Ma Yuanyi and others gathered twenty or thirty thousand men in Qing and Yang provinces and planned an uprising to be staged in the city of Ye. Ma Yuanyi went back and forth from the capital several times, secretly plotting with several eunuch palace secretaries, including Feng Xu and Xu Feng. It was agreed that the uprising would begin on the 5th day of the third month in all parts of the country. But before the rebellion began, one of Zhang Jue's disciples, Tang Zhou of Ji'nan, reported it to the authorities. Ma Yuanyi was consequently executed by being drawn and quartered in the capital, Luoyang. Emperor Ling forwarded Zhou's report to the three ducal ministers and the capital area inspector, who ordered the imperial commissioner to direct the ducal ministers' subordinates in investigating who in the palace, government, guards, and among the common people were followers of Zhang Jue. In the end, over a thousand people were executed, and an emissary was sent to Ji province to arrest Jue and his men. When Jue learned that his plan had been exposed, he sent messengers galloping day and night to inform his followers in each region, who then all rebelled.

To distinguish themselves, the rebels wore yellow turbans, so people at the time referred to them as the "Yellow Turbans." They also called them the "Ant-like Bandits." These rebels killed people to sacrifice to Heaven. Zhang Jue called himself general, duke of Heaven. His younger brother Bao was called general, duke of earth, and his next younger brother Liang was called general, duke of man. Wherever they went, they burned government buildings and pillaged villages and towns. The local and regional governments collapsed, and most of the officials fled. Within ten days the whole country had risen up and the capital was trembling.

HETERODOX BANDITS

In the Xiping period [172–177] there were great uprisings of religious bandits, including Lu Yao in the Sanfu area [that is, around Chang'an]. In the Guanghe period [178–183] there was Zhang Jue in the east and Zhang Xiu in Hanzhong [Sichuan]. Luo Yao taught people the method of redemption; Jue had his Way of Great Peace; and Xiu had the Way of Five Pecks of Rice. In the Way of Great Peace a leader would hold a staff with nine joints while reciting spells and prayers and would instruct people to bow their heads and think of their faults, after which he would give them holy water to drink. Sick people who got better within a few days were said to have faith; those who did not were said to lack it.

Zhang Xiu's teaching was largely the same as Zhang Jue's, but he also set up quiet rooms where sick people would stay and think about their faults. He also had people serve as "debauchers" and "wine offerers." The "wine offerers" were in charge of the five thousand characters of the *Laozi* and the people who made everyone recite it were called "debauchers." The "demon clerks" were in charge of the prayers for the sick. These prayers were offered by writing the name of the sick person and explaining the crimes he had confessed to. Three copies would be made, one sent up to Heaven by being placed on top of a hill, one buried in the earth, and one immersed in water. These were called the "letters to the three officials." The families of sick people had to contribute five pecks of rice as a standard rule, and therefore the leaders were called "teachers of the five pecks of rice." In reality all this was merely wanton perversion, of no use in curing illness. Still, simple people were deceived by it and competed with each other to join.

Later Zhang Jue was executed and Zhang Xiu died. When Zhang Lu came to Hanzhong, he elaborated on the local populace's faith in Zhang Xiu's teaching. He instructed believers to set up "charity houses," which were stocked with grain and meat for the use of travelers. He taught personal redemption; those with minor faults would repair roads for a hundred paces to wipe out their offenses. He followed the "Ordinances of the Months" (in the *Book of Rites*), prohibiting killing in the spring and summer. He also prohibited alcohol. All those who strayed into his area had no choice but to accept his doctrines.

ZHANG LU

At the end of the Han period, Zhang Ling of Pei kingdom was studying the Way at Crane-Cry Mountain in Shu. He wrote the *Book of the Way* and called himself "Originator of the Great Purity," thus deluding the common people. After he died, his son Heng continued to propagate this religion, and in turn was succeeded by his son Lu. The governor of Yi province, Liu Yan, became a believer in this demonical religion; Lu's mother was somewhat attractive and became a frequent visitor to Liu Yan's house.

In the Chuping period [190–193], the governor appointed Lu a major and sent him to Hanzhong, which had been cut off from the rest of the country. When Lu arrived, he acted benevolently, teaching his religion and establishing charity houses stocked with meat and grain. Travelers were to take only enough to fill their bellies but no more. Those who took more could expect to be made sick by the demons. In the markets Lu had all prices standardized. Those who committed offenses would be forgiven three times and then punished. Those who learned of the religion but did not become believers were called "the demon's soldiers" and were later made "offerers of wine." In Ba commandery the common people, both Chinese and non-Chinese, largely found this a useful religion. Since contributions were specified as five pecks of rice, it was generally known as the "rice religion."

When Su Gu was made grand administrator of Hanzhong, Lu sent his associate Zhang Xiu to attack the city where Su Gu was stationed. . . . Lu then gained control of Hanzhong. One after another, he killed all the representatives sent by the central government. Governor Liu Yan had to inform the government that the "rice rebels" had cut the roads. When Liu Yan's son Zhang became governor, Lu became even more overbearing. This angered Zhang, who in the year 200 killed Lu's brother. Lu then led the non-Chinese Du Huo, Pu Hu, Yuan Yue, and others to rebel against the governor. Lu's representatives at court also became more arrogant. Once the court realized that Lu could not be controlled it gave him the titles of chief of the secretaries and grand administrator of Haining. No magistrates were appointed to serve under him. Instead, he governed his people through the "offerers of wine." . . .

In 215 [the de facto ruler of the North] Cao Cao went west to attack Lu, who fled to Bazhong where he was welcomed by [the de facto ruler of the Southwest] Liu Bei. . . . [In the end], Lu submitted to Cao Cao and sent a hostage. Cao Cao made him a general and enfeoffed him as the marquis of Xiangping; he also enfeoffed his five sons as feudal lords.

Translated by Patricia Ebrey

PART III

THE ERA OF DIVISION AND
THE TANG DYNASTY

The overthrow of the Han government, initiated in A.D. 184 by peasant rebels, was completed by the generals assigned to suppress them. By the early third century a stalemate had been reached with three warlords—one in the North, one in the Southeast, and one in the Southwest—each controlling distinct territories. With the abdication of the last Han emperor in 220, each of these warlords proclaimed himself ruler, beginning what is known as the Three Kingdoms Period (220–265). The northern state, Wei, was the strongest, but before it had succeeded in unifying the realm, it was overthrown by an internal coup. Its successor, the Jin (265–420), unified China in 280. Unity was only temporary, however, because the northern non-Chinese tribes—such as the Xiongnu, Jie, and Xianbei—now posed a threat. In 311 the Jin dynasty lost its capital and the court had to flee to the relatively undeveloped area south of the Yangzi River near modern Nanjing. Thus began a period of nearly three centuries (316–589) when the North and South were ruled independently. Both experienced a succession of dynasties, but in the North the rulers were ethnically non-Chinese.

The four centuries of division from the fall of the Han until the reunification of the Sui in 589 marked a serious setback to central government control and allowed the flourishing of all sorts of private social and political relations, with the concomitant growth of regionalism and greater class distinctions. In both North and South, aristocracy developed at the top and forms of personal bondage at the bottom. The new religion of

Buddhism found a receptive audience among many social groups in both regions and came to provide an entirely new world outlook, first to the upper class, but also by the end of the period to ordinary commoners, who could hear monks deliver sermons and could visit temples and other holy places.

The division of China into North and South, although largely following natural geographic divisions, was never stable. Attempts at conquest were regularly undertaken, and in 589 the Sui dynasty in the North finally succeeded in defeating the southern state of Chen. The Sui itself, however, lasted only two reigns, and was succeeded by the Tang dynasty (618–906), founded by a member of one of the Sui noble houses.

Elements of centralized, bureaucratic control had been gradually introduced in the North from the mid-fifth century on but under the Tang were more fully developed. The Tang proved generally successful in curbing private power and status, ruling and taxing peasants directly, and even in limiting the authority of the Buddhist church. Reunification and peace led to a cultural flowering, especially in literature. By the eighth and ninth centuries the opening up of wider trade and communication had stimulated the economy, which in many ways had stagnated since the Han. The capital cities of Chang'an and Luoyang became great metropolises, Chang'an and its suburbs growing to house over two million inhabitants.

Although stronger and more glorious than its predecessors, the Tang bore many structural similarities to them. When compared to the Song and later dynasties, the Tang was still "early imperial," not "late imperial." The martial aggressiveness and expansionist policies of the Han and Northern dynasties were retained through at least the first half of the Tang. The ruling class was still strongly shaped by aristocratic tendencies; men admired old families, and members of old families found the avenues to status and influence easily accessible. The nascent examination system had not yet come to determine the composition of more than a fraction of the upper class. And although the commercial economy grew in the Tang, it had not yet produced the great commercial cities of the Song.

The sources available for analyzing the content and organization of Chinese culture during the Era of Division and the Tang are much like those for the Han, with one fortuitous difference—the discovery by Aurel Stein in 1907 of a large cache of late Northern dynasty and Tang documents in a sealed cave temple in Dunhuang (a city on the northwest edge of China proper, sufficiently arid for paper to survive over a thousand years). These documents and ones discovered by subsequent expeditions are important for social and cultural history because they contain types of sources not normally published and preserved, such as bills of sale, contracts, guides to the composition of letters, elementary textbooks, moral and ritual primers, and popular ballads and tales. Several documents from Dunhuang are among the sources translated in Part III.

21

GE HONG'S AUTOBIOGRAPHY

In the third and fourth centuries, political life was exceptionally hazardous, marked by warfare between the separate kingdoms, internal coups, struggles among the aristocratic family, and finally invasion of North China by a series of non-Chinese tribes. Given this political turmoil, many educated men turned away from Confucian scholarship and political concerns, searching for spiritual and intellectual insight elsewhere, in poetry, Daoist philosophy, mysticism, and searches for immortality through drugs and alchemy.

Ge Hong (283–343), whose autobiographical account follows, was in many ways a typical figure of his period. From a well-established family, he was frequently asked to evaluate his friends and acquaintances as potential candidates for office. He was also called on to perform military service. Still, official life left him unsatisfied, and although he never rejected traditional Confucian virtues, he became interested in Daoist philosophy and the use of drugs to achieve the spiritual freedom of an immortal.

Ge Hong's account of his life was not published as a separate work, but as the last section of his collected writings. There was as yet no tradition in China of introspective autobiographies or of authors writing about their own moral or spiritual progress. But ever since Sima Qian had appended an account of his life to his magnum opus, some authors wrote about themselves in the third person, much as though they were writing about someone else. Here, since Ge Hong was the actual author, his narrative has been changed to the first person.

I was my father's third son. Because I was born late, my parents spoiled me and did not make me study. When I was thirteen my father passed away, so I was left without his guidance and had to endure the hardships of hunger and cold. I took on the farming chores myself. Having no inheritance whatsoever, I had only stars to look upon and the grass to tread on.

Since our family library had been completely lost in the repeated wars, there was nothing I could read in my leisure after farming. I was therefore forced to shoulder my satchel and walk long distances to borrow books. Because I could rarely get an entire book from one household, this task was rather time-consuming. Moreover, I had to cut firewood and sell it in order to buy paper and

91

writing brushes and do my copying by the light of fires amidst the fields and gardens. For these reasons, I was not introduced to literature at an early age. And because I constantly lacked paper, I would write on both sides of each sheet; as a result, no one could decipher my writing.

Not until I was sixteen did I start reading the *Classic of Filial Piety*, the *Analects*, the *Book of Songs*, and the *Book of Changes*. As I was too poor to travel far in search of teachers and learned friends, I was shallow in my knowledge and understanding. Although I could not understand the profundity of books, I was avid to read them; I would silently recite the texts and carefully memorize the key points. The books that I went through ranged from the classics, histories, and the various philosophical treatises to short, miscellaneous essays—altogether nearly ten thousand chapters. Because I was slow and forgetful by nature, because I did not have many ideas or a set goal, my knowledge was meager and I had doubts about many points. Nevertheless, in my writings I have found occasion to cite these sources. . . .

According to the *Imperial Library Catalog* and the *Treatise on Bibliography*, there were 13,299 volumes of books in all [in the Han], and since the Wei dynasty [220–265], all genres of literature have doubled in quantity. Realizing this made me aware of how many books I had never seen. Since so many books were not available in the area south of the Yangzi River, I decided to go to the capital to search for rare works. However, it so happened that there was a rebellion, and I had to turn back midway, much to my regret.

Now that I am approaching my fortieth year, my life-long ambitions are waning; I think only of further reducing my ambitions and converting my actions into nonaction. All that I do is till my fields to eke out a living, and my efforts to achieve broad learning diminish day by day. I am an unrefined person; my nature is dull, my speech slow, and my appearance ugly. I never try to hide my shortcomings. I wear a soiled hat, dirty shoes, and worn-out clothes but am not embarrassed by them. Clothing styles change quickly and frequently. Sometimes people all of a sudden wear broad collars and wide belts; at other times they dress up in tightly fitted clothes with long, narrow sleeves. Sometimes robes are so long that they sweep the ground, while at other times they are too short to cover the feet. I, however, stick with one style and do not follow the whims of the world.

When I speak I am straightforward and matter-of-fact, never sarcastic or playful. If I am not in the company of the right kind of people, I keep silent all day. This is why people call me "the scholar who embraces simplicity," a sobriquet which I have adopted for my writings.

I was born with a weak constitution and further was subjected to many illnesses. Thus, on top of being too poor to afford carriages or horses, I am too feeble to travel on foot. Anyway, travel is something that does not appeal to my nature; the corrupt custom of discarding the fundamental and pursuing the trivial, of placing too much emphasis on making friends and paying visits, makes me apprehensive. For these reasons, I have lived in quiet seclusion in my humble residence and have not rushed to visit others. I am not even acquainted with the rich and influential people who reside nearby.

My clothes do not protect me from the cold, my roof does not keep me from the rain, my food does not save me from being weak, and I am not known outside of my own house—yet none of this causes me worry. I am too poor to keep a servant, my bamboo fences have crumbled, thorny thistles grow thick in my yards, and weeds block the steps. To go out of my gate I have to push away the bushes; to get into my room I have to brush aside the tall grass. People unsympathetically criticize me for aiming at the faraway and ignoring the close-at-hand, when the truth of the matter is that I do not have anyone to do the housework.

Being ignorant of the etiquette for visiting superiors, I never pay visits to high officials. I do, however, make an effort to go and express my condolences to families who have lost an elderly member and to visit the seriously ill. Yet, though I intend to present myself on every such occasion, I often fail to do so because of my own frequent illnesses. I am often criticized on this account, and

I admit my own faults, but they do not worry me; I am fully sympathetic toward the bereaved and the ill, but my own illnesses prevent me from carrying out my intentions. As long as I do not have a bad conscience, why should I argue with those who do not understand me? Those who are discerning, nevertheless, do forgive me, for they know that I am not trying to cultivate an image of loftiness for myself. . . .

By nature I have a deep aversion to bothering officials and superiors. In the course of my life I have saved several good friends who were in distress, and in these cases I forced myself to speak with the officials in power. Yet I never let these friends know what I did for them, for it was because I could not bear to see them wronged that I secretly assisted them. Otherwise, even when my closest relatives, who would gladly do me favors, are in power, I never trouble them with written or oral requests. It is true that when I run out of food or desperately need medicine, I appeal to my friends and accept their help if they offer it. Whenever I have received favors from others, I have repaid them in subtle ways over a long period of time, so that they were not aware of it. Yet I do not lightly accept gifts from those who are not the right kind of people. When I have food for ten days, I share it with people who are in need; however, if I do not have enough for myself, I do not give away my own food—for I do not ostentatiously display little acts of virtue. Sometimes the good-natured common people of the village offer me wine and food. Even though they are not my equals, I do not decline their invitations, and later I repay them at my leisure. I once explained my motives by remarking that Shiyun's refusal to accept food from his own brothers and Master Hua's keeping himself aloof from his overfriendly company were but hypocritical acts performed to win a reputation and were not in accordance with the broad-mindedness required of people in high positions.

Those I abhor are the unprincipled men who do not work diligently at the principal occupations of farming and silk production but instead use unethical means to obtain undue profits. Such men control public opinion and sell their recommendations for gain. They use the power of their positions to extort money. Sometimes they accept bribes from the guilty and consequently wrong those who are in the right; at other times they harbor criminals fleeing for their lives. They appropriate corvée labor for their own purposes, thereby interfering with the public good; or they hoard currency or commodities to force the value up; or they dominate the markets to rob the commoners of their profit; or they encroach on others' land, destroying the livelihood of the orphaned and the weak; or they wander from one government office to another to look for profits to be made. In this way they impress their wives and concubines, angle for fame, and seek offices. I will have nothing to do with such people. For these reasons, the vulgar sort hate me since I dislike them, and it is only natural that we should become alienated. In my alley there are no traces of carriages and horses; in my living room there are no incompatible guests; my courtyard is so quiet one can set up bird nets; on my furniture dust accumulates.

Since the time I was old enough to understand things, I have never uttered a word concerning others' faults or private affairs. This comes naturally to me, for I do not even make fun of the defects of servants or little children. I never discuss my opinions of people's characters, nor do I like to criticize people on their selection of friends. When I am forced by my elders to give my evaluations, then I mention only a person's excellent qualities, or in evaluating his writing ability, raise only his good points. Because I never criticize others' shortcomings, I have never offended anyone through criticism. Occasionally I am asked by the higher-ups to give my opinion of officials, clerks, or common citizens. If the person is superior in morality and ability, I report on his achievements; if he is greedy, violent, stupid, or narrow-minded, I reply that I do not know him. As a result, I have been rather severely criticized for being overcautious and for failing to distinguish good from bad and black from white. However, I have never cared to change my ways. I have often observed that those who are fond of discussing others' personalities are not always fair in their comparisons and critiques. Those who are praised by them take it for granted and are not particularly grateful to them; whereas those who are offended regard them with a hatred more ferocious than that caused by a blood feud. I am therefore even more cautious and no longer talk about other people. I even leave the evaluation of the younger members of my own family and lineage to others. When people criticize me for this, I answer as follows: "It should be the easiest for me to evaluate myself. But if someone asks me to compare myself with other men, ancient and modern, I do not know who to consider my equal. How can I then take another person and give an evaluation of him?"

During the Taian period [302–303], Shi Bing led a revolt in six provinces which brought about the decline of the dynasty. The rightful rulers of the state were disobeyed and the loyalist army was opposed. The commander-in-chief asked me to take the position of commandant and lead troops. After repeated urgings, I agreed, taking into account that the country was endangered by the rebels, that the ancients saw it as one's obligation to act in emergencies, and also that martial law was not to be challenged freely. Thus, I drafted several hundred men and joined other regiments in an attack on a rebel general. On the day we broke into the rebel's city, money and silk were piled in heaps and valuables and curios covered the ground. All the other regiments set their soldiers loose upon the riches, and they loaded cart after cart, basket after basket. I alone gave orders that my soldiers were not to leave their positions. By beheading those who collected loot, I made sure no one else dared to set down their staffs. As expected, several hundred rebels burst forth to ambush us. As all the other brigades were out looting, there were no troops to speak of, and those there were were all so heavily laden with booty, they had no will to fight. Frightened and confused, many were killed or wounded, and defeat was imminent. Only my men maintained enough discipline to avoid casualties. I was thus instrumental in saving the other regiments from a disastrous defeat. Later, in another battle, we killed a minor commander of the rebels, seized large quantities of armor, and took many heads. When I reported our victory to headquarters, the commander-in-chief conferred on me the title of wave-conquering general. All the generals were awarded, according to custom, a hundred bolts of cloth, which they sealed up or sent home. I was the only one to distribute it among my officers, soldiers, and needy friends. I exchanged the last ten bolts for meat and wine and feasted my men, earning me much praise and attention.

When the rebellion was suppressed, I discarded my weapons and armor and set out for Luoyang in the hope of obtaining rare books. I did not at all intend to be rewarded for my military deeds, having long admired Lu Lian for not accepting gold from Liaocheng, and Baoxu for refusing a reward for saving Chu. Yet it so happened that while I was on my way, the capital was plagued by a major rebellion, blocking the route to the north. Furthermore, Chen Min staged an uprising in Jiangdong, cutting off my return route. Moreover, at that time an old friend of mine, Ji Jundao of Qiaoguo, was appointed as the governor of Guangzhou, and he petitioned the throne to appoint me as his military councillor. Although this position was not what I wanted, it provided a way to escape south, so I forced myself to accept it. I was ordered to leave early in order to draft soldiers. After I left, Ji Jundao was killed, so I stayed at Guangzhou, where I was frequently offered positions by the authorities. I declined them all, thinking that riches and high positions may be attained gradually but should not be amassed quickly. Besides, the trivialities one has to attend to in such posts are quite bothersome.

Honor, high posts, power, and profit are like sojourning guests: there is no way of keeping them when they are due to depart. Prosperity and glory will all come to an end, just like the spring flowers that quickly wither away. When I chance to have them, I do not rejoice; nor do I grieve when I lose them. They are not worth all the regret and blame, worry and anxiety they cause. Furthermore, I figure that I am by nature lazy and untalented. With these two characteristics, even if I could cringe, kneel, and rush about in the mundane world, I would certainly fail to obtain fame or high position—which is beside the fact since I could never bring myself to do so! It is better for me to cultivate the Way of the Daoists, Chi Songzi and Prince Qiao, and depend solely on myself.

I am hoping to ascend a famous mountain where I will regulate my diet and cultivate my nature. It is not that I wish to abandon worldly affairs, but unless I do so, how can I practice the abstruse and tranquil Way? Besides, to comprehend these matters is truly difficult, requiring considerable discussion and questioning. For these reasons, I neither visit nor send letters to powerful officials. However, even those scholars who refrain from visiting others cannot refuse to receive callers, who invariably become an obstacle to concentration. It is not that the Way is found in the mountains and forests; the reason the ancient practitioners of the Way always had to enter the mountains and forests was that they wished to be away from the noise of the world and keep their minds tranquil. Now I am about to fulfill an old wish; I will leave my hometown and go to Mount Song in order to walk in the paths of Fangping and Master Liang.

Fortunately, I have put my mind to it and completed my philosophical works, including the *Inner Chapters* and the *Outer Chapters*. Now I only need to finish the selection and rearrangement to make it ready for later readers. . . . They were written during a time of warfare and rebellion. As I wandered from place to place, homeless, some of my works were lost. Still, I never abandoned my writing brush. This continued for more than a decade, until 304, when my works were finally completed. They consisted of twenty chapters of the *Inner Chapters*, fifty chapters of the *Outer Chapters*, one hundred chapters of stone inscriptions, eulogies, poetry, and free verse, and thirty chapters of military strategies and proclamations, memorials, and commentaries. I also wrote ten chapters of *Biographies of Immortals*, ten dealing with those who are normally not recorded, and ten chapters of *Biographies of Recluses*, dealing

with those who are lofty-minded and seek no place in officialdom. In addition, I made selections from the Five Classics, seven histories, the philosophers, military treatises, esoteric skills, and miscellaneous strange events. These totaled 310 chapters. I also made a separate index of my anthology. My *Inner Chapters* belong to the Daoist school, as they discuss immortals, longevity medicines, ghosts and devils, transformations, the nurture and extension of human life. and the aversion of evil and misfortune. My *Outer Chapters*, which discuss the success and failure of men and the good and evil in the world, belong to the Confucian school.

At the end of the autobiographical notes to his *Records*, Emperor Wen of Wei [r. 220–227] mentioned such arts as playing chess and fencing. This gave me the idea to do something similar. But rather than boast of my own modest skills, I will give an account of what I do not know. I am physically clumsy and slow by nature and have few amusements or hobbies. As a child, I could not compete with other children in throwing tiles or wrestling. Throughout my life, I have never tried cockfighting, drake fighting, dog racing, or horse racing. Whenever I see people engaged in gambling, I try not to even glance at them; but if I have to watch, I do not pay close attention. Thus, to this day, I do not know how many rows there are on a chessboard, or the names of the chessmen. Another reason for my aversion is that I object to the way chess disturbs people's thoughts and wastes their time: this trivial art makes officials reduce their political undertakings, scholars ignore their studies, commoners forget their crops, and merchants lose their business. When engaged in a game at the marketplace, the players are fired up inside and worried in appearance. They lose their sense of righteousness and shame and become rivals; they take each other's money and develop hatreds and feuds. Long ago, the gaming of Duke Min of Song and the Crown Prince of Wu led to their violent deaths and rebellion; the seven feudal states were overthrown as a result and the dynasty nearly toppled. This example provides an obvious lesson for all later generations.

I have often observed the players in a chess game. Overwhelmed by shame and anger, they hit and kick each other and abuse each other with foul language, much to the detriment of their friendship. Since grudges can start from small matters, it is not worth doing things which can cause so many regrets. Confucius warned against sleeping during the day, a sentiment that I do not fully share. Sleeping during the day produces no benefit, but neither does it cause resentments or give rise to quarrels and lawsuits. Even the sage had to wear out the binding string of his books three times before he had completely familiarized himself with the classics. How then can an ordinary person of our time learn everything? I believe that playing all the games there are is less worthwhile than reading a short essay. Thus, finding no pleasure in games, I do not play them. Only the vulgar sort are attracted to them.

When I was young, I learned archery, but my strength was not up to drawing a bow as heavy as Yan Gao's. I studied it because archery is one of the six arts of a gentleman, and enables a person to defend himself against bandits and robbers and to hunt for birds and animals. When I was in the army, I myself shot at pursuing horsemen, who fell at the flicker of my bowstring. By killing two rebels and one horse, I escaped death myself. I also received instruction on sword-and-shield, single sword, and double lances. For all of these there are verbal formulae and essential skills needed to defeat the opponents. There are also secret methods that are as clever as magic and, used against the unknowing, guarantee victory every time. Later, I also learned the art of the seven-foot staff, which can be used to defeat people with daggers and lances. However, this is also a trivial art of no urgency; it does not have to be used any more than the unicorn's horn or the phoenix's spur. Besides the above-mentioned, I hardly know anything else. . . .

Because I am untalented and unlearned, whether I restrain myself or indulge freely, my practices are always ill-suited to the times, my actions against the ways of the world, my utterances out of tune with the customary, my steps out of line with the majority. At home, I do not have the advantage of being rich, like Jin and Zhang; out in the world, I do not have friends in high office. Although the road I have traveled is broad, I do not have the feet of a unicorn; although the universe is wide, I do not have the wings of the great roc. Thus, I have not been able to soar high like a hawk, helping to govern our country, nor have I been able to bring glory to my parents or to be remembered by posterity. My qualities are not entrusted to official historians to record; my words are not inscribed on bells and tripods. For these reasons, on finishing my writings, I composed this autobiographical chapter—although it will not make up for any failure on my part, at least it will be preserved for the future.

Translated by Clara Yu

22

BUDDHIST DOCTRINES AND PRACTICES

Buddhism was introduced into China in the late Han and flourished during the Age of Division and the Tang and Song dynasties. Buddhism differed markedly from earlier Chinese religions and philosophies. It was a universal religion appealing to individuals of all countries and all social stations. It had a founding figure, Shakyamuni Buddha (ca. 563–483 B.C.), and a body of scriptures called sutras said to be records of the sermons of the Buddha. Its most devoted followers became monks and nuns and formed a part of a complex organized church. As a set of ideas, it built on the Indian conviction that sentient beings transmigrate through endless series of lives as people, animals, gods, hungry ghosts, hell dwellers, or titans, moving up or down according to the karma, or good and bad deeds, that they have accumulated. The major insight of the Buddha was that life is inevitably unsatisfactory because beings become enmeshed in the web of their attachments. Yet he offered hope, teaching that it was possible to escape the cycle of rebirth by moral conduct, meditative discipline, and the development of wisdom.

To get at some of the complexities of the impact of Buddhism on Chinese civilization, four separate sources are given below. The first is a basic description of Buddhist teachings written by a Chinese historian of the sixth century, Wei Shou, as part of his account of Buddhism in his history of the Northern Wei dynasty. It shows how Buddhist ideas could be put into Chinese vocabulary by a reasonably well-informed scholar. The second piece consists of two biographies, both from the sixth century Lives of Eminent Monks. *These biographies illustrate different aspects of the spiritual life of the period, one showing an educated man caught between traditional social obligations and his religious calling, the other a charismatic figure who strongly influenced the religious life in the cities. The third selection consists in five colophons or notes appended to sutras that survived by chance at Dunhuang. Both lay persons and clergy would often commission the copying of sutras as a way to gain religious merit for themselves and their relatives, including deceased relatives. The colophons they wrote let us see how they understood Buddhist principles. The fourth piece, also from Dunhuang, is a popular song on the theme of how a woman's life changes as she grows older. By stressing how life inevitably leads to change and sorrow, it plays upon a familiar Buddhist theme of the transience of life but does not make explicit reference to Buddhist principles.*

WEI SHOU'S SUMMARY
OF BUDDHIST DOCTRINE

The words we use for Buddha (Fotu or Foto) are based on the sound of the words used in the western lands. The meaning of the word is "awakened." It refers to destroying impurities and gaining understanding, which lead to sagely enlightenment.

The general import of their scriptures is that everything in this and all other lives is a result of karma. Through the three ages of the past, the present, and the future, the conscious spirit is never destroyed. Any act of good or evil will be recompensed. By gradually accumulating good deeds, purifying vulgarities, passing through many forms, and refining the spirit, one can arrive at a level at which rebirth will not recur and thus attain buddhahood. There are many steps and mental activities to take, all proceeding from the simple to the profound, the imperceptible to the manifest. Through building up one's goodness and obedience, eliminating desires, and practicing serenity, one can break through.

The first step in cultivation of the mind is to take refuge in the Buddha, the dharma [Buddhist teachings], and the samgha [the community of Buddhists]. These are called the three refuges. These are comparable to the three things a man of virtue stands in awe of [in Confucianism]. There are also five prohibitions: one must not kill, rob, commit adultery, lie, or drink wine. The meaning is much like [the Confucian virtues of] benevolence, righteousness, propriety, wisdom, and trustworthiness, though the names are different. They say that those who adhere to these rules will be reborn among heavenly beings or humans, but those who violate them will end up suffering with demons and animals. Altogether there are six paths for rebirth according to how good or bad a person was.

Those who submit to these teachings shave their beards and hair, free themselves from obligations, and take leave of their homes. They attach themselves to a teacher, observe rules and regulations, and live together to bring their minds

under control and cultivate tranquility. They practice begging to support themselves. Individually, they are called by the foreign word sramana, or collectively by the term samgha. The word samgha means "group whose fate is harmonious," sramana means "quiet-hearted," bhiksu [another word for monk] means "beggar." Laymen who believe in the dharma are called upasaka, laywomen upasika.

Monks begin by cultivating the ten rules, which makes them beginners, and when they have mastered 250 they are ready to become senior monks. Women who enter the path are called nuns; they accept 500 rules. In each case the rules are gradually increased. They concern protecting one's mind, restraining one's person, and regulating one's speech. Their hearts must get rid of greed, anger, and folly; their bodies expunge killing, lust, and robbery; their mouths stop uttering false words. Taken together, these are called the ten good paths. Those who have mastered these are called triply accomplished and purified. Ordinary people's behavior is coarse in the extreme, but the Buddhists say that if they can comprehend the rewards for good and bad acts they can gradually climb to the level of sages. . . .

The one called the Buddha was originally named Shakyamuni, which can be translated "capable of benevolence" and means that when his virtue was perfected he was able to aid all creatures. Before Shakyamuni there were six buddhas; he succeeded to them and lived in the current eon. Their books say that the next buddha to enter the world in the future will be Maitreya Buddha.

Shakyamuni was the son of a king of the country of Kapilavastu in India. He was born from his mother's side at night on the eighth day of the fourth month. At his birth there were thirty-two unusual signs, and there were also thirty-two portents sent down by Heaven in response to him. The scripture on his origin describes them in detail. The year he was born was the ninth year of King Zhuang of Zhou [688 B.C]. In the *Spring and Autumn Annals*, under that year, the seventh year of the Duke Zhuang of Lu, it says, "the fixed stars were not visible but the sky was bright." From that time until the eighth year of the Wu-Ting period in Wei [650] is 1237 years.

When Shakyamuni was thirty he attained buddhahood, and he then spent forty-nine years preaching and converting others. Then on the fifteenth day of the second month, in the city of Kusinagara, between a pair of Sala trees, he entered nirvana. Nirvana means annihilation and crossing over. Another interpretation is that it means eternal joy; one is enlightened, free from change and suffering. . . . When the Buddha left the world, his body was burned with fragrant wood. His holy bones broke apart in pieces the size of grains. They could not be crushed by blows nor scorched by fire. Sometimes they would emit light as a sign of their spiritual power. In the foreign tongue these are called sarira, "relics." His followers took them and put them in jeweled jars and offered their respects to them with incense and flowers. They built buildings called stupas, another foreign word, which are like ancestral shrines, so that they are commonly called stupa-shrines. A hundred years later there was a King Asoka who with divine power divided the Buddha's relics and built 84,000 stupas all over the world for them, accomplishing it all in one day. Today Loyang, Pengcheng, Guzang, and Linzi all have Asokan temples where the traces can be seen. Even though the Buddha entered nirvana, he left footprints, nails, and teeth in India. Travelers to that land have mentioned seeing them.

Soon after he entered nirvana, five hundred disciples who had heard his teachings, such as Mahakasyapa and Ananda, recorded the teachings he had delivered orally. Ananda had received the teachings personally and understood much, and so was able to organize it all very thoroughly so that nothing got left out. This is the Tripitaka with its twelve categories of scriptures, which is comparable to the nine schools of thought [used by Chinese bibliographers]. All of them take the Three Vehicles as the basis. A few hundred years later, arhats and bodhisattvas, one after the other, discussed and elaborated on the meanings of the scriptures to combat heresies. Their books comment on the meanings in the Tripitaka, pose questions and answers, or elaborate in terms of inner teachings.

Translated by Patricia Ebrey

LIVES OF EMINENT MONKS

Zhu Seng Du was originally named Wang Xi (Xuanzong) and came from Donghuan, in Guangdong, South China. He came from a lesser literati family but was a very presentable young man. When he was sixteen his spirit soared high and his character stood out among his peers. His personality was mild and he was well loved by his neighbors. He lived with his mother and was a filial son to the last letter of the Confucian code. He courted the daughter of Mr. Yang Deshen in the same village. The Yang family was also respectable. Their daughter, Tiaohua, had a comely face and proper poise. She was versed in the apocryphal literature and was the same age as Du. The day he proposed to her, she accepted. However, not soon afterwards and before the marriage was set, Tiaohua's mother died. Tiaohua's father soon followed. Meanwhile, Du's mother also passed away. Suddenly realizing the transience of this world, Du left it behind and entered a monastic order, changing his name into Seng Du, Du, the follower of Sakyamuni. He left his trace beyond the world of dust and wandered, as a student, in faraway places. Tiaohua, after having tended to the mourning rites for her parents, realized that there was no place in society for a woman like her without anyone on whom to depend, neither parents, husband, nor child. Therefore she wrote to Du, "According to the Confucian norms of filial piety the hair and skin of one's body, being something one received from one's parents, should not be harmed [for example, by tonsure]. The ancestral temples should not be abandoned as you, Du, the monk, have done. Moreover, considering the teaching of Confucian society you should abandon your lofty hermit ideal, and arousing your talents make a name for yourself in the world. Through your success you should let shine the spirit and glory of your ancestors and be a comfort to those close to you, fulfilling the expectations of both man and the spirits." She also wrote five poems. . . .

Seng Du responded, "Serving the king, as demanded by Confucianism, is to assist in the ruling of one's country. That cannot be compared with pursuing the Buddhist path for all peoples. Serving one's parents means to establish a family of one's own; but that cannot be compared with following the Buddhist path for the sake of all beings in the three realms. The dictum 'Never to harm your body or hair' is the narrow advice of those committed to the world. I am ashamed that my present virtue has not extended itself to cover even that filial duty. However, small baskets of earth add up to a mountain: all beginnings are small. Thus I put on my monk's gown, drink the pure water, and laud the wisdom of the Buddhas. Although the dress of princes, the food of the eight rarities, the sound of music and the color of glories are all fine, I would not trade my lot for them. If our minds are in tune to one another, we will meet in nirvana. However, people's hearts are different, just as their faces are. Your distaste for the hermit's way is like my indifference to the world. Dear one, let this be the last parting and let all the karmic ties from ten thousand years past that brought us together end here. Time is running short. The student of the dharma must learn to daily eliminate his attachment to the world of action. Men and women of the world, however, should adapt themselves to the times. You are, in age and virtue, in your prime, so you should pursue what you desire and admire. Do not keep this man who is committed to Buddhism in your mind and thereby lose the best years of your life." Du further wrote five poems in reply. . . .

Du's mind was made up and, like a rock, it could not be swayed. Touched by his reply, Tiaohua also entered an order and became a nun.

* * *

Seng Baozhi, originally surnamed Zhu, came from Jincheng. He left home in his youth and entered the Daolin temple in the capital where he practiced meditation under the monk Jianwei. At the beginning of the Taishi period in Song (465–471), his behavior suddenly became extraordinary. He would regularly stop eating or sleeping, let his hair grow to several inches, and walk the streets bare-footed, holding a staff on which hung either a pair of scissors or a mirror, or sometimes a few strips of cloth.

During the Jianyuan period in Qi (479–482), Baozhi developed more extraordinary traits. He would go for days without food, showing no sign of hunger. He would talk to people in unintelligible enigmas that later turned out to be true. He composed poetry that was no less prophetic. As a result, the officials and the people in the capital became his followers. Emperor Wu of the Qi dynasty thought that Baozhi was bewitching the public and had him imprisoned in Jiankang. The next morning people saw him walking into the city again. When the matter was investigated, Baozhi was found to have been in jail all the time. Once he told the guards, "There are two carriages outside bringing rice in a golden alms-bowl. Accept it for me." Later, indeed Prince Hui and the Duke of Jingling, Wang Ziliang, sent food to Baozhi in the manner predicted.

The governor of Jiankang, Lu Wenxian, reported these events to Emperor Wu, who invited Baozhi to stay in the palace. Once when the emperor dismissed all courtiers during a private banquet, Baozhi left with the others. Soon it was learned that in the Jingyang mountain, another Baozhi was staying with seven renowned monks. The emperor, infuriated, sent people after him but they failed to find his whereabouts. Upon inquiry, it was reported that Baozhi had long since left the capital. The messengers were hoping to mark his body to prevent him from disappearing.

At another time, the eminent monk Faxian wanted to give Baozhi a robe. He sent a messenger to look for Baozhi in the two monasteries of Longguang and Jibin; and both places claimed that Baozhi had stayed there the previous night, leaving at daybreak. The messenger went to the residence of Bo, Count of Li, which Baozhi frequented. Bo said, "Baozhi was practicing devotions yesterday. He is still asleep now." The messenger returned and reported to Faxian. It was then clear that Baozhi could split himself into three persons and lodge at different places.

At one time Baozhi was walking in the cold winter without any upper garment. A monk, Baoliang, wanted to give Baozhi a monk's robe. Before Baoliang had uttered even a word, Baozhi appeared suddenly and took the robe. At another time, Baozhi asked someone for finely sliced pieces of fish. They were prepared for him. He dined to the full and left. Then the person turned around and saw the fish still alive and swimming in the bowl as before! . . .

The minister of war of Qi, Yin Qizhi, was to follow Chen Xianda to take up a post at Jiangzhou. When he took leave from Baozhi, Baozhi drew a picture of a tree with a crow in it, saying, "In case of an emergency, climb this tree." Later Xianda rebelled and left Qizhi to guard the state. When he was defeated, Qizhi also rebelled and then escaped into Lu Mountain. As the pursuers were drawing near, Qizhi saw a tree in the woods with a crow in it, just like the one Baozhi had drawn earlier. Realizing this, he climbed the tree and contrary to expectation, the crow did not fly away. The pursuers saw the bird and thought there was no one up in the tree. They turned back and thus Qizhi escaped death.

The general Sang Yan of Qi was planning a rebellion when he went to see Baozhi. When Baozhi saw him from afar, he ran away, crying: "Besieged city walls. Rebellions contemplated. Head chopped off. Chest rent." In less than ten days, the plot was exposed and Sang Yan, escaping to Zhufang, was captured. He was beheaded and his chest was rent as Baozhi had predicted.

Prince Zhonglie of Boyang in Liang asked Baozhi to stay at his place. One day, Baozhi suddenly ordered him to get bramble shrubs to be fixed to the gate. He did as he was told but could not figure out why. In a little while, the prince was made the governor of the state of Jin—literally "the bramble state." However, such cases of Baozhi's prophecies cannot all be fully documented.

Baozhi used to stay at the two monasteries of Xinghuang and Jingming. The previous emperor respected Baozhi highly, but did not allow Baozhi to come in and go out of the palace at will. When Emperor Wu came to the throne, he issued this decree, "Though the trace of Master Baozhi's body is within this world, his spirit roves in the mysteries. Fire cannot burn him; water cannot dampen him; snakes cannot bite him; tigers cannot frighten him. When he expounds the meaning of Buddhist doctrines, his voice rises to the heights above; when he discourses on the esoteric matters, he proves to be the highest of all withdrawn immortals. How can he be bound by the rules of common sentiments or by empty forms? How can the previous edicts be so narrow-minded? From now on, the master can come and go as he pleases. No one is to stop him." Since then, Baozhi has been in and out of the forbidden palace areas frequently.

In 506 there was a drought. All efforts at invocation and sacrifice were of no avail. Baozhi came to the emperor unexpectedly and said, "As I am ill, please ask an official to pray for a cure. If he fails, then the official should be whipped. I would hope to see the *Lion's Roar of Queen Srimala* read to pray for rain." The emperor then asked the monk, Fayun, to lecture on the sutra. When the lecture ended, heavy snow fell in that very night. Baozhi then demanded a basin of water and placed a knife on top of it. After a while, rain fell abundantly and the lands, high or low, had sufficient water.

The emperor once asked Baozhi, "I, your disciple, have not gotten rid of all defilements and delusions. What cure is there?" Baozhi answered cryptically, "Twelve." Those who knew interpreted that to mean the twelve-linked chain of causation, the medicine to cure delusions. The emperor then asked about the meaning of "Twelve." Baozhi answered, "The principle is to write characters according to the 'drip-clock' measure." Those who knew thought it meant writing within the twelve periods of time. The emperor then asked at what time he should quietly cultivate his mind. Baozhi answered, "Prohibiting ease and pleasure." Those who knew thought it meant stopping at the easy hours since the word "prohibit" could mean "stop."

Later the monk Fawen lectured on the *Lotus sutra* in the Hualin monastery. When he came to the passage on magically evoking the black winds, Baozhi suddenly asked whether there is wind or there is no wind. Fawen answered, "From the perspective of the conventional truth, there is. From the perspective of ultimate truth, there is not."

There was a captive slave of war from Chen, whose family followed Baozhi with reverence. Once Baozhi revealed his true form to them; and it shone forth like a bright image of a bodhisattva.

Baozhi was known to the world and performed miracles for more than forty years and attracted innumerable devout disciples. In 514 he revealed to the people in the Taihou Hall: "This bodhisattva will soon depart." Within ten days, he passed away without any illness, his body remaining soft and fragrant, his features serene and blissful. At his death bed he lit a candle which he gave to a palace attendant named Wu Qing. Qing reported it to the emperor who sighed, "This master is no longer with us. Does the candle (*zhu*) not indicate that he is entrusting (*zhu*) to me the matters of his funeral?" Thus he gave Baozhi an elaborate funeral and buried him at the Dulong hill on Zhong mountain. He erected a monastery at the tomb site and ordered Lu Chui to compose an eulogy to be engraved on the tomb, while Wang Yun wrote an inscription on the monument at the gate of the monastery. Baozhi's portrait was distributed all over the country to be preserved in reverence.

When Baozhi first showed his miraculous powers, he was already about fifty or sixty years old. He never seemed to age, though, and no one knew his age exactly. A man, Xu Jiedao, who lived to the north of Jiuri Terrace in the capital claimed to be the cousin of Baozhi. He was four years younger which would have made Baozhi ninety-seven when he passed away.

Translated by Walen Lai

DEDICATORY COLOPHONS

1.

Recorded on the 15th day of the fourth month of 531. The Buddhist lay disciple Yuanrong—having lived in this degenerate era for many years, fearful for his life, and yearning for home—now makes a donation of a thousand silver coins to the Three Jewels [the Buddha, the Dharma, and the Samgha]. This donation is made in the name of the Celestial King Vaisravana. In addition, as ransom money*, he makes a donation of a thousand to ransom himself and his wife and children, a thousand more to ransom his servants, and a thousand more to ransom his domestic animals. This money is to be used for copying sutras. It is accompanied by the prayer that the Celestial King may attain Buddhahood; that the disciple's family, servants, and animals may be blessed with long life, may attain enlightenment, and may all be permitted to return to the capital.

2.

Happiness is not fortuitous: pray for it and it will be found. Results are not born of thin air: pay heed to causes and results will follow. This explains how the Buddhist disciple and nun Daorong—because her conduct in her previous life was not correct—came to be born in her present form, a woman, vile and unclean.

Now if she does not honor the awesome decree of Buddha, how can future consequences be favorable for her? Therefore, having cut down her expenditures on food and clothing, she reverently has had the *Nirvana sutra* copied once. She prays that those who read it carefully will be exalted in mind to the highest realms and that those who communicate its meaning will cause others to be so enlightened.

She also prays that in her present existence she

* Ransom from their present existences

will have no further sickness or suffering, that her parents in seven other incarnations (who have already died or will die in the future) and her present family and close relatives may experience joy in the four elements [earth, water, fire, and air], and that whatever they seek may indeed come to pass. Finally, she prays that all those endowed with knowledge may be included within this prayer. Dated the 29th day of the fourth month of 550.

3.

Recorded on the 28th day of the fifth month of 583.

The army superintendent, Song Shao, having suffered the heavy sorrow of losing both his father and mother, made a vow on their behalf to read one section each of the following sutras: *The Sutra of the Great Assembly of Buddhas, The Nirvana sutra, The Lotus sutra, The Benevolent King sutra, The Golden Light sutra, The Sutra of the Daughter of Prasenajit,* and *The Master of Medicine sutra.* He prays that the spirits of his parents will someday reach the Pure Land [paradise of the Amitabha Buddha] and will thus be forever freed from the three unhappy states of existence and the eight calamities and that they may eternally listen to the Buddha's teachings.

He also prays that the members of his family, both great and small, may find happiness at will, that blessings may daily rain down upon them while hardships disperse like clouds. He prays that the imperial highways may be open and free of bandits, that the state may be preserved from pestilence, that wind and rain may obey their proper seasons, and that all suffering creatures may quickly find release. May all these prayers be granted!

4.

The preceding incantation has been translated and circulated.

If this incantation is recited seven, fourteen, or twenty-one times daily (after having cleansed the mouth in the morning with a willow twig, having scattered flowers and incense before the image of Buddha, having knelt and joined the palms of the hands), the four grave sins, the five wicked acts, and all other transgressions will be wiped away. The present body will not be afflicted by untimely calamities; one will at last be born into the realm of immeasurably long life; and reincarnation in the female form will be escaped forever.

Now, the Sanskrit text has been reexamined and the Indian Vinaya monk Buddhasangha and other monks have been consulted; thus we know that the awesome power of this incantation is beyond comprehension. If it is recited 100 times in the evening and again at noon, it will destroy the four grave sins and the five wicked acts. It will pluck out the very roots of sin and will ensure rebirth in the Western Regions. If, with sincerity of spirit, one is able to complete 200,000 recitations, perfect intelligence will be born and there will be no relapses. If 300,000 recitations are completed, one will see Amitabha Buddha face to face and will certainly be reborn into the Pure Land of tranquillity and bliss.

Copied by the disciple of pure faith Sun Sizhong on the 8th day of the fourth month of 720.

5.

The lay disciple Madame Duan (nee Zhang) has ever lamented that the fragrant orchid, like a bubble, blooms for but one day, and that separation from loved ones causes so much sorrow. She wonders how it can be that Heaven feels nothing for the calamities it inflicts, and causes the worthiest to be the first to be cut down, just as the young tree is the first to wither and the tallest blossoms are the first to fall.

Thus, on behalf of her deceased third son, Commissioner Duan, an officer of the local commandery, she has reverently had this section of the *Golden Light sutra* copied. Now that the transcription is completed, she prays that her son's spirit may visit the azure heavens, that he may mingle with the immortals, that he may travel in person to the Pure Land and listen to sutras being recited under the tree. She also prays that he may never pass through the three unhappy states of existence or the eight calamities, but will gather karma sufficient to enable him to proceed joyfully to the Lotus Palace and the Flowering Throne, that he will never again suffer a short life but enjoy longevity in the Pure Land and may be perpetually reborn only there.

His loving mother, thinking of him, prays that the karma for both of them may be good and that they may both enjoy the fruits of salvation.

Recorded on the 9th day of the sixth month of 900 in the Great Tang dynasty.

Translated by Lucie Clark and Lily Hwa

A Woman's Hundred Years

At ten, like a flowering branch in the rain,
She is slender, delicate, and full of grace.
Her parents are themselves as young as the rising
    moon
And do not allow her past the red curtain without a
    reason.

At twenty, receiving the hairpin, she is a spring bud.
Her parents arrange her betrothal; the matter's well
    done.
A fragrant carriage comes at evening to carry her to
    her lord.
Like Xioshi and his wife, at dawn they depart with
    the clouds.

At thirty, perfect as a pearl, full of the beauty of
    youth,
At her window, by the gauze curtain, she makes up
    in front of the mirror.
With her singing companions, in the waterlily sea-
    son,
She rows a boat and plucks the blue flowers.

At forty, she is mistress of a prosperous house and
    makes plans.
Three sons and five daughters give her some trouble.
With her lute not far away, she toils always at her
    loom,
Her only fear that the sun will set too soon.

At fifty, afraid of her husband's dislike,
She strains to please him with every charm.
Trying to remember the many tricks she had learned
    since the age of sixteen.
No longer is she afraid of mothers- and sisters-in-
    law.

At sixty, face wrinkled and hair like silk thread,
She walks unsteadily and speaks little.
Distressed that her sons can find no brides,
Grieved that her daughters have departed for their
    husband's homes.

At seventy, frail and thin, but not knowing what to
    do about it,
She is no longer able to learn the Buddhist Law even
    if she tries.
In the morning a light breeze.
Makes her joints crack like clanging gongs.

At eighty, eyes blinded and ears half-deaf,
When she goes out she cannot tell north from east.
Dreaming always of departed loves,
Who persuade her to chase the dying breeze.

At ninety, the glow fades like spent lightning.
Human affairs are no longer her concern.
Lying on a pillow, solitary on her high bed,
She resembles the dying leaves that fall in autumn.

At a hundred, like a cliff crumbling in the wind,
For her body it is the moment to become dust.
Children and grandchildren will perform sacrifices
    to her spirit,
And clear moonlight will forever illumine her patch
    of earth.

Translated by Patricia Ebrey and Lily Hwa

23

TALES OF GHOSTS AND DEMONS

Among the earliest Chinese narratives are stories that concern the interaction of human beings and nonhuman entities; gods, ghosts, demons, fox spirits, and the like. Ghosts who bore a grudge against the living—especially those who had been murdered—might come back to seek revenge. Fox spirits might turn themselves into beautiful women and seduce attractive young men. Demons might enjoy annoying people who had done nothing to provoke them. People who had done good deeds might receive supernatural rewards. Many of these stories probably began as folktales, and were retold innumerable times long before they were recorded. Others may well have been consciously invented by writers as literary art. These stories are thus interesting not only for what they reveal of people's understandings of spirits but also as examples of early narrative fiction.

The three stories below come from the earliest collection of these stories, the Record of Searches for Spirits, *traditionally said to be put together by Gan Bao in the fourth century from records of incidents that had not been included in the standard histories.*

In the Han dynasty, Ho Chang, of Jiujiang, while serving as the inspector of Jiao prefecture, went to Gaoan county, in Cangwu, on business. When night fell, he lodged at Snowgoose Flight Pavilion.

Sometime in the middle of the night a woman appeared at the base of the building and told this story:

"I am Su O from Xiu village in Guangxin county. I lost my parents at an early age and have no brothers. I married into the Shi family of my county, but ill-fated as I am, my husband died. I had one hundred twenty bolts of various sorts of silks and a maidservant named Zhifu.

"Alone and without resources, I could not support myself so decided to go to the neighboring county to sell the silks. I rented an oxcart from the man Wang Bo of my county, paying him 12,000 cash. I rode in the back with the silk and Zhifu held the reins. In this way, last year, on the tenth day of the fourth month, we arrived at this pavilion.

"At the time the sun was already setting, and there were no travelers about, so I did not dare go any further. Because Zhifu developed a violent stomach ache, I went to the home of the village head to ask for some porridge and fire.

"The village head, Gong Shou, grasped a dagger and halberd and came up to the cart. He demanded, 'Where do you come from? What is in your cart? Where is your husband? Why are you traveling alone?'

"I answered, 'Why are you so eager to know?'

"Shou then grabbed my arm and said, 'Young men like pretty girls. I was hoping to have some fun.'

"Terrified, I would not comply. Shou then stabbed me in the side with his knife, killing me with one blow. He then stabbed Zhifu, who also died. Shou dug a hole at the base of this building and buried us together, me on bottom, the maid on top. He took the goods, killed the ox, burned the cart, and tossed the ox's bones and the metal trim from the cart into an empty well east of the pavilion.

"Since my death has not been requited, I am angry enough to move Heaven. Having no one to report to, I have purposely returned here to tell my story to you."

Chang said, "I will need to dig up your body. What can serve as evidence?"

The woman responded, "I was wearing white upper and lower garments and had on green silk shoes. These have not yet decayed. I hope that you will travel to my hometown and return my bones to the side of my late husband's."

The excavation confirmed her story. Chang then raced back and sent an officer to arrest the headman Gong Shou. When he was questioned under torture, he confessed to everything. Chang went to Guangxin county for further inquiries, and Su O's story was corroborated. Gong Shou's parents and brothers were all arrested and put in jail.

Chang submitted a memorial arguing, "In ordinary cases of murder the punishment does not extend to the relatives. But Shou is truly vicious and managed to conceal his wrongdoing for over a year, escaping the royal law. Only once in a thousand years must the dead bring complaints. I request that the whole family be beheaded to prove the existence of ghosts and thereby assist the nether regions in dispensing justice."

The emperor approved the request.

* * *

Thirty *li* west of the home of Lu Chong, in Fanyang, was the tomb of Privy Treasurer Cui. When Chong was twenty, he went hunting for amusement the day before the winter solstice. Catching sight of a deer, he drew his bow and shot it. Hit, the deer fell but soon righted itself. Chong chased it, not noticing how far he was going. Suddenly he saw a tall gate and tile roofs, similar to a government office, a *li* or so north of the road. The deer was no where to be seen.

A guard at the gate sang out, "Enter."

Chong asked, "Whose office is this?" When told that it was the privy treasurer's, Chong said, "How could I see the privy treasurer in these awful clothes?" A man then gave him a bundle of fresh clothes, saying his master was making a gift of them.

Once Chong had changed his clothes, he went in to see the privy treasurer, giving his name. After several rounds of food and drink, the privy treasurer said to Chong, "Your father, not looking down on me, has recently sent me a letter asking for my young daughter as a wife for you. That is why I invited you in." He then showed Chong the letter. Although Chong had been young when his father died, he had learned to recognize his handwriting. He sobbed and made no more protests. The privy treasurer then informed the women's quarters that young Mr. Lu had arrived and to have the young mistress get made up. He also told Chong that he could go to the eastern wing.

That evening, word was sent from the inner quarters that the young mistress was ready. Chong was waiting in the eastern wing and saw the girl get down from her carriage. They stood at the head of a mat and bowed to each other. The feasting lasted three days.

At the conclusion of the third day Cui said to Chong, "You may go home. My daughter appears to be pregnant. If she gives birth to a boy, she will return it to you, have no doubt. If she gives birth to a girl, we will rear it ourselves." He ordered the outer quarters to send him home in a carriage. Chong then took his leave and left. His wife accompanied him to the middle gate, then took his hand and wept.

Once outside the gate, Chong saw an oxcart harnessed to a shiny ox. He also saw the clothes he had been wearing and his bow and arrows, all outside the gate. Someone gave him a bundle of clothes and relayed this message from the girl, "Parting after we were just married is very painful. I am now giving you another set of clothes and a set of quilts."

Chong got into the carriage and made his way home at the speed of lightning. Soon he was home, and his relatives were happy to see him. On making inquiries, he soon learned that Cui was dead. He felt sad on realizing that he had entered his grave.

Four years after Chong and Miss Cui had parted, on the third day of the third month, Chong was amusing himself near a river, when he suddenly saw two oxcarts near the bank bobbing around. When they got closer, Chong's companions all saw them too. Chong opened the back door of one, then saw the Cui girl with a three year old child inside. The girl handed the child to Chong and also gave him a golden bowl and this poem:

[He is] so bright and pure,
So beautiful and fine,
A flower that dazzles in its time,
Its brilliance demonstrating its amazing powers.
[I am] a bud that before it could bloom
A summer frost caused to wither;
My brilliance thus permanently obscured,
I will never again walk the paths of the world.

Not realizing the workings of Yin and Yang,
A wise man unexpectedly came to call.
Our time together was brief and our time apart long,
Due entirely to the spirits.
What can I give my beloved?
A gold bowl and an adorable child.
Our ties of love and obligation are here severed;
My heart is broken.

Once Chong had hold of the boy, the bowl, and the poem, the two carts disappeared.

Chong took the boy back. Everyone with him said he was a ghost or demon. They all spat on him from a distance, still his form did not change [proving he was human]. When they asked the boy, "Who is your father?" he climbed into Chong's lap. At first they found these events weird, but as they examined the poem, they became impressed by the mysterious connections between the dead and the living.

Sometime later, Chong took a carriage into the city to sell the bowl. He asked a high price, not actually wanting to sell it, but rather hoping someone would recognize it. An old maidservant recognized it and went back to tell her mistress, "In the market I saw a man in a carriage selling the bowl from Miss Cui's coffin." Her mistress was the sister of Miss Cui's mother. She sent her son to look at it, and it was indeed as the maid had reported.

This young man got into Chong's carriage, introduced himself, and said to Chong, "Formerly my mother's sister married the privy treasurer and gave birth to a girl who died before marrying. My mother was distressed by her death and gave a gold bowl to be placed in her coffin. Can you tell me how you got this bowl?" Chong told him the whole story, which moved the boy. He returned to tell his mother.

His mother immediately went to visit Chong and see the boy. All of Chong's relatives gathered round. The boy resembled Miss Cui, but also had something of Chong's demeanor. After examining both the boy and the bowl, the aunt said, "My niece was born at the end of the third month and her father gave her the name 'Warm-good' because in the spring it is warm and he wished her to be good. 'Warm-good' sounds like 'marriage among ghosts,' so we can see this was predicted."

The boy developed into a person of talent and served several times as prefect. His descendants up to the present have continued to serve as officials. Among them Lu Zhi is particularly famous.

* * *

In the time of the state of Wu, there was a man named Ni Yansi who lived to the west of the county seat of Jaixing. One day he discovered that a demon had entered his house. It would talk with people and ate and drank like a human, but no one could see it.

One of Yansi's servants was always cursing the mistress behind her back, and the demon said, "I'm going to tell on you this time." Yansi punished her, and no one in his house dared curse after that.

When the demon wanted Yansi's concubine, Yansi decided to invite a Daoist priest to exorcise it. After the priest had set out the sacrificial wine and food, the demon took some manure from the privy and spread it on top. The priest then struck the drum loudly, calling down the gods. The demon thereupon put a urinal on the altar where he played a tune on it. Shortly, the priest felt something cold on his back, and when he opened his robe, he discovered the urinal. With that, the priest quit.

In his bed at night, Yansi and his wife quietly talked about how the demon was making their life difficult. The demon then, from on top of the beam, told Yansi, "You and your wife are talking about me. I'm going to cut this beam in two." They could hear the sound of cutting. Yansi was afraid the beam would break, so took a torch to see better. The demon immediately extinguished the fire, and the sound of cutting resumed.

Yansi was afraid the house would collapse, so got everyone out, then took the torch to look again. The demon laughed and asked Yansi, "Are you going to talk about me any more?"

When the local superintendent of agriculture heard of these events he said, "This spirit must be a fox." The demon then went to the superintendent and said, "You took so-many bushels of government grain and stored them in such-and-such a place. As an official, you are corrupt, and yet you dare to talk about me! Now I will inform the authorities so that someone is sent to get the grain you stole." The superintendent, in fear, apologized. From this time on, no one dared to talk about the demon.

Three years later the demon left. Its current location is unknown.

Translated by Patricia Ebrey

24

CULTURAL DIFFERENCES BETWEEN
THE NORTH AND THE SOUTH

*In the aristocratic society that developed in both the northern and the southern
capitals, manners and deportment were very much stressed. Somewhat different
manners and customs developed in each region, and in both places there were
tendencies to label the customs of the other unrefined. The two pieces below
show something of these feelings. The first is from a description of the northern
capital of Luoyang, written in 547–50 by Yang Xuanzhi, a northerner. The second is from a book of advice addressed to his sons by Yan Zhitui (531–591+).
Yan's ancestors had lived in the South during the fourth and fifth centuries, and
he himself served at the Liang court, but in 556 when that dynasty was falling to
the Chen, he fled to the North, where he served at the Northern Qi court in the
city of Ye. Among the many topics Yan advised his son about was the differences
in the customs between polite society in the two regions.*

A NORTHERNER'S DEFENSE
OF NORTHERN CULTURE

In 529 [the southern ruler] Xiao Yan sent his
scribe Chen Qingzhi to escort the Prince of Beihai
to Luoyang and illegitimately set him on the
throne. Qingzhi was made the prince's chancellor. Zhang Jingren, who had known Qingzhi
while both were in the South, then invited Qingzhi to his house for a banquet. Two southerners,
Xiao Biao, the minister of agriculture, and Zhang
Sung, a deputy in the department of state affairs,
were also there, and Biao himself was a south-
erner. The only representatives of the eminent
families of the northern plain were Yang Yuan-

shen, the palace master, and Wang Xuan, the
grand secretary.

Drunk, Qingzhi said to [his fellow] southerners, "The Wei dynasty is at its height, but it is still
one of the five barbarians. The legitimate imperial
succession is in the South. The seals of the Qin
emperors are now at the Liang court."

Yuanshen, with a solemn expression, responded, "The South enjoys a respite of peace in
their remote corner, where it is hot and humid,
crawling with insects, and infected with malaria.
Like frogs and toads sharing the same hole, people live together with the birds. Your rulers wear
their hair short and never have long heads. The
people decorate their bodies. You float on the

three rivers or row in the five lakes, but have never been steeped in rites or music or reformed by laws. Even though some Qin and Han convicts brought the true Chinese pronunciation, the unpleasant tongues of Min and Chu have not been transformed. You may have a ruler and a court, but the ruler is overbearing and his subordinates violent. For instance, first Liu Shao murdered his father, then Xiulung committed incest with his mother. To commit such breaches of morality makes you no better than birds and beasts. On top of this, the princess of Shanyin asked to buy husbands to commit debauchery, caring nothing about how people ridiculed her. You, sirs, are still soaked in the old customs and have not yet been transformed by ritual. You can be compared to the people of Yangdi who did not realize that goiters were ugly. Our Wei dynasty has received the imperial regalia and set up its court in the region of Mount Sung and Luoyang. It controls the area of the five sacred mountains and makes its home in the area within the four seas. Our laws on reforming customs are comparable to those of the five ancient sage rulers. Ritual, music, and laws flourish to an extent not even matched by the hundred kings. You gentlemen, companions of fish and turtles, how can you be so disrespectful when you come to pay homage at our court, drink water from our ponds, and eat our rice and millet?"

When Shenzhi and the others heard how elegantly Yuanshen spoke, they were at a loss for how to respond. They broke into sweat and could utter no sound.

YAN ZHITUI'S ADVICE TO HIS SONS ON DIFFERENCES IN CUSTOMS

Southerners do not go out to greet a guest. When they meet, they clasp their hands but do not salute. When parting, they merely get down from their seat. Northerners, by contrast, greet their guests at the gate and also accompany them to that point on leaving. When they meet they salute. These are ancient ways, and I approve of them. . . .

Discussions of ancestors should be based on feelings of respect, something the ancients found easy but people today find hard. When Southerners cannot avoid discussing family affairs, they do it in writing, rarely in face-to-face discussions. Northerners would immediately get into such discussions and even ask each other questions about it. Do not inflict such matters on others. If someone else asks you such questions, give evasive answers. . . .

Parting is easy but meeting is difficult; the ancients stressed both. In the South, when parting, people shed tears when saying goodbye. There was a prince, a younger cousin of Emperor Wu of Liang, who before going to Dongjun took leave of Emperor Wu. The emperor said, "I am getting old and am desolate at parting from you." Tears streamed down his cheeks. The prince left looking sad but with dry cheeks, for which he was criticized. Although his boat drifted about by the pier for over a hundred days, he was never allowed to leave. The northern custom is not like this; they say goodbye at the crossroads with a happy expression. . . .

In the South, those wailing at a funeral sometimes express their grief in words addressed to the dead. In the North, at the death of a parent or husband, the mourners will call on Heaven. For the death of a brother or similar relative, they cry out that their suffering is deep. Thus they shout but do not wail.

In the South, when someone has lost a parent, he will sever his friendship with any of his acquaintances from the same city who do not come to condole within three days. After he is out of mourning, he will still avoid them when they meet, so bitter will he be about the lack of sympathy. Those who cannot call for a good reason like living far way are expected to send a letter. If they do not send a letter, they are treated the same way. The custom in the North is not like this.

In the South, those who come to condole do not grasp the hands of anyone they do not know, other than the chief mourner. Those who were acquainted with more distant relatives but not the chief mourner do not need to come to condole but can send a note to the family on another day. . . .

In the South, when people write essays, they like to get others' criticisms so that they can learn their failings and make improvements. Chen Wang received such advice from Ding Yi. The custom in the North is to avoid direct criticisms. When I first entered Ye, I once offended someone this way and still regret it. You boys should be careful not to give your opinions too freely.

Women in the South do not go out calling. Decades may go by without relatives through marriage seeing each other, keeping up their relations only through letters and gifts. By contrast, in the northern capital of Ye, women take charge of family affairs, entering into lawsuits, straightening out disagreements, and paying calls to seek favor. The streets are filled with their carriages, the government offices are filled with their fancy silks. They ask for offices for their sons and complain of injustices done their husbands. This may be the remnants of the customs of the Tuoba when they were in Heng and Dai. In the South, even the poor concentrated on external appearance; their clothes and carriages had to be expensive and smart even if that meant their wives and children suffered hunger and cold. Those in the North often let their wives manage the family; for them fine silks and jewels were essential but thin horses and decrepit manservants were satisfactory. Husbands and wives sometimes even addressed each other as "you." Women in the North are much better than those in the South with regard to weaving and sewing and all sorts of needlework. . . .

Translated by Patricia Ebrey

25

EMPEROR TAIZONG ON EFFECTIVE GOVERNMENT

One of the great achievements of the Tang was the strengthening of monarchical institutions after centuries in which dynasties seldom lasted long or controlled the whole country. The second Tang emperor, Taizong (600–649, r. 626–649), is given much of the credit for taking the vigorous measures needed. From his youth, Taizong was a man of action. He fought in the campaigns that put his father on the throne in 618 and during the next few years led armies against the Turks. He became embroiled in a struggle with his elder brother, the heir apparent, and eventually killed him and forced his father to abdicate in his favor. Reigning much longer than his father, he worked to rationalize the administrative structure and devise policies suited to his expanding state.

The brief text below sums up Taizong's views on the main principles of monarchical government. It was written in 648, near the end of his life, as advice for his heir.

HOW A RULER SHOULD ACT

A country cannot be a country without people and a ruler cannot be a ruler without a country. When the ruler looks as lofty and firm as a mountain peak and as pure, bright, and illuminating as the sun and the moon, the people will admire and respect him. He must broaden his will so as to be able to embrace both Heaven and earth and must regulate his heart so as to be able to make just decisions. He cannot expand his territory without majesty and virtue; he cannot soothe and protect his people without compassion and kindness. He comforts his relations with benevolence, treats his officials with courtesy, honors his ancestors with filial respect, and receives his subordinates with

thoughtfulness. Having disciplined himself, he practices virtue and righteousness diligently. This is how a ruler should act.

ESTABLISHING RELATIVES

The country is huge and the responsibility for it is heavy. A huge country cannot be evenly governed by the emperor alone; the responsibility is too great for one man. Thus, the emperor should enfeoff relatives to guard the outlying prefectures. Whether the country is at peace or in danger, they cooperate; whether the country is thriving or declining, they work together with one heart. Both distant and close relations are supported and employed; encroachment and rebellion are prevented.

Formerly when the Zhou dynasty was at its height, the empire was divided among the royal clan. Nearby there was Jin and Zheng to help; far off there was Lu and Wei. In this way, the dynasty was able to survive several centuries. Toward the end of the Qin dynasty, however, the emperor rejected Chunyu's scheme [of enfeoffing relatives] and accepted Li Si's plan [to enfeoff nonrelatives]. He thus detached himself from his relatives and valued only the wise. With no relatives to rely on, the dynasty fell after two generations. Isn't this all because of the fact that if a tree has a mass of branches and leaves, it is difficult to root up, but if the limbs are disabled, the trunk has nothing to depend on? Eager to avoid Qin's errors, the Han dynasty, upon stabilizing the land within the passes, enfeoffed the closest relatives generously. Outdoing the ancient system, the largest fiefs were as big as kingdoms, and the smallest had at least several prefectures. But a branch can get so heavy that it breaks the trunk; a tail can get too big to be wagged. Thus, the Six Kings harbored ambitions of overthrowing the throne and the Seven States were destroyed by arms, all because they had gained too much territory, military force, and power. When Emperor Wu established the Wei dynasty, being ignorant of past experience, he did not grant any titles to his descendants nor any fiefs to his kin. He had no one within or without the capital to protect him. Thus, his throne was usurped and his dynasty was overthrown by someone of a different surname. This is a good example of the old saying that a river does not run when its source dries up and branches wither when the root of the tree decays.

Subordinates granted too much power can develop into insurmountable problems for the throne. On the other hand, subordinates granted too little power will not be strong enough to protect the throne. Thus, the best way is to enfeoff many relatives to even up their power and to have them regulate one another and share one another's ups and downs. By so doing, the throne need not suspect its subordinates and the subordinates need not worry about being wronged or injured. These are the precautions one should take in granting fiefs. Neutralizing the power of subordinates so that none of them gets to be too strong or too weak is indeed the key to securing one's throne. . . .

EVALUATING OFFICIALS

Differentiation of the ranks and duties of officials is a means of improving customs. A wise emperor, therefore, knows how to choose the right person for the right task. He is like a skillful carpenter who knows to use straight timber to make shafts, curved timber to make wheels, long timber to make beams, and short timber to make posts. Wood of all shapes and lengths is thus fully utilized. The emperor should make use of personnel in the same way, using the wise for their resourcefulness, the ignorant for their strength, the brave for their daring, and the timid for their prudence. As a good carpenter does not discard any timber, so a wise emperor does not discard any gentleman. A mistake should not lead the emperor to ignore a gentleman's virtues, nor should a flaw overshadow his merits.

Government affairs should be departmentalized to make the best use of officials' abilities. A tripod large enough for an ox should not be used to cook a chicken, nor should a raccoon good only at catching rats be ordered to fight against huge beasts. . . . Those with low intelligence or capability should not be entrusted with heavy tasks or responsibilities. If the right person is given the right task or responsibility, the empire can be governed with ease. This is the proper way of utilizing people. Whether the emperor gets hold of the right person for the right task determines whether his empire will be well governed. . . .

WELCOMING ADVICE

The emperor, living in the palace, is blocked from direct access to information. For fear that faults might be left untold or defects unattended, he must set up various devices to elicit loyal suggestions and listen attentively to sincere advice. If what is said is right, he must not reject it even though it is offered by a low servant. On the other hand, if what is said is wrong, he must not accept it even though it is given by a high official. He should not find fault with the rhetoric of a comment that makes sense, nor cavil at the wording of a suggestion worth adopting. . . . If he acts these ways, the loyal will be devoted and the wise will fully employ their resourcefulness. Government officials will not keep any secrets from the emperor and the emperor, through his close ties to them, can thus gain access to the world.

A foolish emperor, in comparison, rebuffs remonstrations and punishes the critics. As a result, high officials do not give any advice lest they lose their salary and low officials do not make any comment lest they lose their lives. Being extremely tyrannical and dissipated, he blocks himself from any access to information. He considers himself more virtuous than the Three Lords and more talented than the Five Emperors. This eventually brings him and his empire to destruction. How sad it is! This is the evil consequence of rejecting remonstrations.

DISCOURAGING SLANDER

Slanderers and flatterers are as harmful to the country as grubs to seedlings. They devote all their time to getting ahead. At court they compete for power and out of court they compete for profit. They fawn to prevent the loyal and the worthy from outranking them; they cheat out of fear that others will acquire riches and honor before them. Acting in collusion and copying each other, they succeed all too often. They get close to their superiors by using fine words and pleasant manners; they please the emperor by anticipating and attending to his wishes. . . .

Advice that grates is difficult to take, but words that fall in with one's wishes are easy for one to follow. This is because while the former is like good medicine that tastes bitter, the latter is like poisoned wine that tastes sweet. A wise emperor accepts bitter criticisms that benefit his conduct; a foolish emperor takes sweet flattery that leads him to destruction. Beware!

AVOIDING EXTRAVAGANCE

The ruler cultivates his character through frugality and peacefulness. Restraining himself, he will not tire his people or disturb his subordinates. Thus, his people will not complain and his rule will not go off course. If the emperor indulges himself in curiosities, women, music, hunting, or travel, agriculture will be disturbed and labor service will have to be increased, leading to the exhaustion of the people and the neglect of farming. If the emperor indulges himself in magnificent dwelling, precious jewelry, or fine clothes, taxes will have to be increased, leading the people to flee and the country to be impoverished. A chaotic age is marked by a ruler who is arrogant and extravagant, indulging his desires. While his dwelling and garments are richly ornamented, his people are in need of simple clothes; while his dogs and horses are tired of grain, his people do not have enough husks and chaff. As a result, both the gods and the people become resentful and the ruler and the ruled become estranged. The dynasty is overthrown before the emperor has satisfied his wishes. Such is the fearsome cost of being arrogant and extravagant.

MAINTAINING MILITARY FORCES

Weapons and armor are a country's tools of violence. A warlike country, however huge and safe it may be, will end up declining and endangering its populace. Military force cannot be entirely eliminated nor used all the time. Teach people military arts when they are free from farming in order to equip them with a sense of military decorum and morale. Remember how Gou Jian, who paid respect to the fighting spirit of frogs, was able to achieve his supremacy, but Xu Yan, who disregarded military forces, lost his state. Why? Because Gou's troops were inspired and Xu was unprepared. Confucius said, "Not teaching people how to fight is the same as discarding them." Hence military might serves to benefit the realm. This is the gist of the art of war.

ESTEEMING CULTURE

Music should be played when a victory is gained; ritual should be established when the country is at peace. The ritual and music to be promulgated are rooted in Confucianism. Nothing is better than literature to spread manners and guide customs; nothing is better than schooling to propagate regulations and educate people. The Way is spread through culture; fame is gained through learning. Without visiting a deep ravine, one cannot understand how deep the earth is; without learning the arts, one cannot realize the source of wisdom. Just as the bamboos of the state of Wu cannot be made into arrows without feathers, so a clever man will not achieve any success without accumulating learning. Therefore, study halls and ritual halls should be built, books of various schools of thought should be widely read, and the six arts [propriety, music, archery, charioteering, writing, and mathematics] should be carefully studied. . . .

Literary arts and military arts should be employed by the state alternately. When the world is in an uproar and a battle will determine the fate of the country, military arts should be highlighted and schools given low priority. Reverse the two when the country is peaceful and prosperous; then slight the military and give weight to the classics. Neither military nor culture can the country do without; which to emphasize depends on circumstances. Neither soldiers nor scholars can be dispensed with.

Translated by Chiu-yueh Lai

26

THE TANG LEGAL CODE

Despite Confucian bias against law as a means of fostering good behavior, the Chinese state came to depend heavily on written rules of all sorts, both rules for the procedures officials should follow and rules for the penalties they should impose when dealing with crime. It became customary for each dynasty to issue a comprehensive set of laws, rules, and regulations, though these could still be amended by subsequent imperial decisions. The earliest of these to survive intact is the Tang code, issued in 653. This code contains laws on criminal matters like theft and murder, civil matters like inheritance and ownership of property, and bureaucratic procedures like transmittal of documents.

When Confucian officials codified laws, they infused them with their own view of moral order. The Legalists had wanted simple laws uniformly enforced, but Confucians thought not all murders or robberies were the same since the ethical basis of the relationship between the two parties made some offenses more heinous than others. Thus, in the laws on theft and robbery given below, the jurists took into account not only the degree to which force was used, but also any kinship relationship of the perpetrator and the victim.

For ordinary people, government laws on holding land probably had as big an impact on their lives as laws against crime. The second section below shows some of the legal consequences of the governments's "equal field" policies. The Tang government, continuing policies introduced by the Northern dynasties, allotted land and assessed taxes according to the age, sex, and marital status of the members of each household. Every male from eighteen to sixty was to get twenty mu *of "inheritable land" and eighty* mu *of "personal share land," the latter eventually to be redistributed. Widows and older men living in households with no adult men got smaller shares. As land was equalized, taxes were also equalized; thus the major taxes were imposed on adult men in equal amounts. To maintain the equity of this system, the government had to deal harshly with anyone who cultivated land not officially registered under his name.*

LAWS ON THEFT AND ROBBERY

1. In cases of robbery by force, when no property is obtained, the punishment is penal servitude for two years. When the stolen property is valued at up to a foot of silk, the punishment is penal servitude for three years. For each additional two lengths of silk, the punishment is one degree heavier. When the value has reached ten lengths or someone has been injured, the sentence is strangulation. When killing has occurred, the sentence is decapitation.

Commentary: Robbery by force means taking goods by intimidation or violence, and includes both first using force and then robbing and first robbing and then using force. Also included is giving a person drugged wine or food to make him confused and then taking his goods. Not included are such cases as taking something the owner negligently left, then fighting with the owner over giving it back; or the thief who when his robbery by stealth is discovered, discards the goods and runs, but uses force to resist arrest when the owner catches him.

Note: Killing or injuring a slave has the same penalty. Anyone killed or injured in a robbery is included, not just the owner of the goods.

2. In cases of robbery by stealth resulting in no gain, the punishment is fifty strokes of the light stick. When the stolen property is valued at up to a foot of silk, the punishment is sixty strokes of the heavy stick. For each additional bolt of silk, the punishment is one degree heavier. When the value has reached five bolts, the sentence is one year penal servitude. Thereafter for each five bolts add one degree. At fifty bolts, the sentence is exile with labor.

3. In cases of embezzlement, where the one left in charge of goods steals them, the sentence is two degrees higher than in ordinary robbery. When the value of the goods reaches thirty bolts of silk, the sentence is strangulation.

4. In cases of purposely setting fire to a person's house, to steal his goods, add the value of the damage caused by the fire to the value of the stolen goods in applying the law on robbery by force.

5. In cases of taking people's goods by threats or blackmail, the sentence is one degree heaver than in robbery. Even if the threats were not worth fearing, so long as the owner was frightened and gave over his goods, this law applies. If the goods were not received, the sentence is sixty strokes of the heavy stick. In cases involving blackmail of relatives within the mourning grades* offenses against seniors are sentenced at the same level as offenses against other people; offenses against juniors follow the usual rules [reducing penalties].

Commentary: Oral threats are included. Those who pass the word or receive the goods are sentenced as accessories. Not included under this law are such cases as a person who has suffered injury or damage and makes threats to try to get recompense.

6. In cases in which someone at first hit a person for some other reason, and then snatched his goods, calculate the value of the stolen goods to apply the law on robbery by force. When death resulted, the sentence is exile with labor. When he took the goods by stealth, use the law on robbery by stealth, but increase the penalties one degree. When killing or injuring resulted, apply the laws on intentional battery.

7. In cases of robbing a relative of the fourth or fifth mourning grades, the sentence is reduced one degree from what it would be for robbing a nonrelative; for robbing a relative of the third mourning grade, it is reduced two degrees; for robbing a relative of the second grade, it is re-

* The five grades of mourning included relatives as distant as second cousins, grandfather's brothers, and first cousins' children. The closest relatives were in the first grade, the most distant in the fifth.

duced three degrees. Cases involving killing or injuring have their own laws.

Commentary: The last point refers to accidentally killing in the course of robbery. If in the course of making demands one purposely kills a junior relative of the second degree or lower, the penalty is strangulation. The other specifications follow this pattern.

8. In cases in which a junior family member gets someone else to rob goods from his own family, apply the law on unauthorized use of property [with its lighter penalties] but increase the penalty two degrees. The other person is sentenced one degree lighter than in ordinary robbery. If killing or injury were involved, the appropriate laws apply.

Note: When the other person kills or injures, even if the junior knew nothing of it, he is still charged as an accessory according to the law on injuring and killing.

9. In cases of accidentally killing or injuring a person in the course of robbery, use the law on killing or injuring in a brawl. When death has resulted, the sentence is exile with labor. When several people jointly committed a robbery, and killing or injuring unintentionally occurred, apply the law on robbery with force. For those who were not involved in the killing or injuring, apply the law on robbery by stealth.

Note: This applies whether or not the robber got any goods. Not included are cases in which the owner pursued the robber and died for some other reason.

10. In cases of exchanging private goods, slaves, or animals for official property, compare the values in applying the laws on robbery.

Note: Even when the official property is worth less, this rule applies. In trading slaves, when the value exceeds that used in inducing them to flee, apply the laws for that offense.

11. In cases where someone on his own, without authorization, takes goods from a mountain or field that someone has cut or piled up, the laws on robbery apply.

12. In cases of abducting people or abducting and selling people as slaves, the sentence is strangulation. When those abducted are sold as retainers, the penalty is exile to three thousand *li*. When they are sold to be someone's wife, concubine, child, or grandchild, the penalty is three years penal servitude.

Note: Taking a person who did not want to leave is abduction. When the person is under ten, even if he or she goes voluntarily, the offense is classed as abduction. If death or injury results, the law on robbery with force applies.

LAWS ON LAND TENURE

1. Those who occupy more land than allowed will be beaten ten strokes for the first *mu*, increasing one degree for each additional ten *mu*. After the penalty reaches sixty strokes, it increases one degree for each twenty *mu*. The maximum penalty is one year of penal servitude. No charges are brought for occupying extra land in an area of ample land.

Commentary: The kings instituted the law that farmers have fields of one hundred *mu*, officials have permanent property according to rank, and the old, young, and widows each get graduated amounts. Except in areas of ample land, one cannot occupy more than these limits. . . .

2. Those who plant public or private land they do not have rights to are liable to a beating of thirty strokes for the first *mu* or less, increasing one degree for each five *mu*. After the penalty reaches one hundred strokes, it increases a degree for every ten *mu*. The maximum penalty is one and a half years penal servitude. The penalty is reduced one degree if the land had been unculti-

vated. If force was used, the penalty is increased one degree. The crops belong to the government or the owner.

Commentary: . . . In cases where these rules cannot be applied exactly, for instance where only part of the illicitly cultivated land had been uncultivated, or force had only been used in acquiring part, or where the parties were relatives, follow the rule that the more serious offense absorbs the lesser one. If the land of more than one family was illicitly cultivated, decide on the basis of one family. Do not add all the penalties together, but inflict the heaviest single one. In cases where relatives have plundered one another, the penalties are set according to the degree of kinship as in the rules on theft. . . .

Translated by Patricia Ebrey

27

THE ERRORS OF GEOMANCY

As seen in selections 1 and 3, "Late Shang Divination Texts" and "Hexagrams," divination had very old roots in China. Over time, however, the theories and uses of divination gradually evolved. During the Age of Division the practice of divining to choose auspicious grave sites took root. Credit for writing the first Burial Classic has traditionally been given to Guo Pu (276–324). By the early Tang people were commonly consulting geomancers for advice on when and where to bury their parents in the hope that they might find a site that would lead to them live longer, or get rich or powerful.

Below is the earliest detailed critique of the theories of grave geomancy. It was written by the official Lü Cai (d. 655) in response to Emperor Taizong's request that he evaluate the diverse divinatory manuals generally classed as writings on Yin-Yang. Geomancy remained popular in subsequent centuries, but there were almost always some scholars like Lü Cai who rejected its intellectual premises.

According to the *Book of Changes*, when the ancients buried their dead, they covered the body with pieces of wood but did not build mounds over the grave or plant trees around it. Nor did they have a fixed period of mourning. In subsequent ages the sages revised these customs by adding the use of inner and outer coffins. . . . The *Book of Rites* says that to bury is to hide; it is based on the desire to conceal the dead. The *Classic of Filial Piety* says, however, "Divine for a burial place before burying the dead." The reason for this is that the grave will be a place where the living can constantly go to think about the dead. Once the rituals are finished, it is the permanent home of the spirit. As change is constant, the future is always unpredictable. Because water keeps on eroding earth, people consequently have no way to know what is going on below the ground. So people turned to divination to feel safer, hoping to avoid future difficulties or damage by means of divination. Afterwards they conducted the funeral and burial, but all these practices had nothing to do with good or bad luck.

In recent times, however, grave geomancy has appeared. According to its doctrines, people need to choose a good day and mark out a good site for burial. If either choice is even slightly off, disasters befall both the living and the dead. Diviners, for the sake of profit, recklessly add new theories on how to avoid this or that. As a result, there are now about one hundred twenty schools of geomancy. They all have their own theories about what brings fortunes and misfortunes and what must be avoided. Now, cosmological theories are based on such principles as Heaven covering and the earth providing a base, and the alternation of hard and soft. Yin and Yang are also implicated in day and night, male and female relations, the sun, moon, and stars, and the seasons. There is no doubt about these matters. But it is distortion to apply Yin Yang ideas to the luck of burials.

According to the *Zuo Chronicle*, kings were encoffined on the seventh day after their deaths and interred after seven months. Feudal lords were encoffined on the fifth day and interred after five months. Great officers were buried after a season and officers and common people after a month. Rituals thus were graded by rank. These rules were intended to let allies and colleagues know when to attend the funeral and how to handle things properly; in time they became the convention. Once the rules were established, people were not supposed to break them. So if a person was buried earlier than proper, it was regarded as not cherishing the memory of the dead. If burial was delayed beyond the proper time, the living were criticized. Thus it is evident that there are rules on when to bury and there is no need to divine to choose a year or month. . . .

In addition, the *Book of Rites* records that in the Zhou dynasty people favored red, so chose sunrise for important ceremonies. In the Yin dynasty they favored white, so chose noon for important ceremonies. In the Xia they favored black, so chose dusk for important ceremonies. Zheng Xuan explained that "important ceremonies" means funerals and burials. Thus it is evident that the hour for burial depends on what is favored in an age and one should not select an earlier or later hour. The *Spring and Autumn Annals* mentions that when Zichan, minister of Zheng, and Zitaishu were preparing the burial of Duke Jian, the houses of the superintendent of graves were right on the way to the grave of the duke. If the houses were pulled down, the burial could be finished in the morning. If they were not destroyed, it would

be midday before the burial could take place. Zichan did not want to destroy the houses, preferring to wait till noon. Zitaishu replied, "If we wait till midday to inter the coffin, I am afraid that the long wait will tire the feudal lords who came to attend the burial." Zichan was a knowledgeable gentleman and Zitaishu was chosen from among the feudal lords. Furthermore, nothing is more important for a state than the burial of its ruler. If good or bad luck had been at stake, how could men like these two not mention it? They were not concerned about whether good or bad luck might result from the hour of burial but simply considered the benefits for human affairs. According to "Zengzi's Questions" [in the *Book of Rites*] if an eclipse of the sun occurs during a burial, the bier has to be stopped at the left of the road; people wait till the eclipse passes and it is light again before proceeding. This shows that people have to change plans sometimes so as to adjust to unpredictable conditions. Now if according to geomancy books, the hours close to midnight are perfect for a particular burial, then text and practice are in conflict. Thus an examination of the *Book of Rites* and the *Zuo Chronicle* shows that it is not necessary to select a particular hour for burial.

Geomancy books say that wealth and official position result from good burials. Longevity also is said to come from good burial sites. However, the *Classic of Filial Piety* says, "When we behave ourselves and follow the sages' way, then we can make our name famous in the future and thereby glorify our parents." The *Book of Changes* also says, "The most precious thing of the sages is called position, and the way to hold on to position is benevolence." These phrases mean that people who behave themselves receive limitless benefits, but those who do nothing good have no heirs. This again shows that fortunes and longevity have nothing to do with whether burials are held at good times or whether graves are in lucky sites. . . .

The fact is that official position and fame come and go; they are not permanent. There are cases of people who started humbly but later became prominent. Similarly there are cases of people who started smoothly but ended with disasters. Ziwen was dismissed from office three times, as was Zhan Qin. Neither had moved [their ancestors'] graves. Then why were their positions so unstable? This proves that high positions depend on human agency, not burial.

Ordinary, ignorant people all believe the geomancy books. The diviners cheat them by making up tales about fortunes or disasters they are going to experience, leading these ignorant folk to feel themselves lucky. As a result, even during the mourning period, they are eager to choose a good site for burial in the hope of an official position. They also select Indian summer as the date for burial in the hope of getting rich. Some mourners will smile when greeting funeral guests because the day of the burial is said to be improper for weeping. Some believe taboos on relatives attending the burial and so do not accompany their parents' bodies to the grave. No sage ever taught such ideas. Geomancy books have ruined customs.

Translated by Chunyu Wang

28

THE DANCING HORSES OF XUANZONG'S COURT

In the Tang capitals of Chang'an and Luoyang, and especially in the imperial courts, the unusual and the exotic were very popular. Foreign music and foreign musicians were much in demand. Horses from the north and west, areas more suited to horse raising than the dense agricultural lands of the Chinese heartland, were highly prized. The caravans that came from Central Asia were so welcome that pottery representations of camels and their non-Han grooms were among the objects people commonly placed in their tombs.

The selections below give a glimpse of this love of the exotic in the most splendid of the Tang courts, that of Emperor Xuanzong (r. 713–755). This emperor not only patronized poets, musicians, and dancers, but even arranged for a troops of dancing horses to perform at his court. The poems given below were written by a leading court official, Zhang Yue (667–731), to celebrate the wondrous performances of these horses. Following the poems is a note written over a century later concerning the fate of the horses after the destruction of Xuanzong's court during a rebellion led by An Lushan (703–757), a general who had been a favorite at this court himself.

VERSE BY ZHANG YUE ON THE DANCING HORSES

Our sage emperor's perfect virtue matches Heaven's.
Heavenly horses have come for the ceremony from
 far west of the sea.
They stride slowly with their feet arched, then kneel
 on both knees.
Though high-spirited, they stay in formation and
 stamp with a thousand hooves.

With colorful tails, eight rows form a column.
These dragons of our time—whose five colors match
 the directions.

With bent knees and wine cups in their mouths, and
 maintaining the rhythm,
Devotedly they make offerings for the sovereign's
 long life.
The emperor's dragon colts are well-trained.
These celestial thoroughbreds are amazing.
Nimbly prancing, they keep in step with the music.
High-spirited, they step together, never deviating.

THE FATE OF THE DANCING HORSES

Xuanzong once ordered that a hundred horses be trained to dance. They were divided into a right

123

and a left company and given names like Emperor's Favorite or Pride of the Household. From time to time fine horses were received as tribute from foreign states, and the emperor had these trained as well. Every one of them mastered the most marvelous skills.

By imperial order, the horses' cloths were of fine embroidery, their halters of gold and silver, and their manes and forelocks ornamented with pearls and jade. The tune they danced to was called "The Upturned Cup," and had several dozen stanzas. They shook their heads and drummed with their tails, moving this way and that, in time with the music. A wooden structure with three tiers was set out and the horses would ride to the top, turning around as though flying. Sometimes strong fellows were ordered to lift one of the platforms and a horse would dance on top of it. The musicians stood on all sides, front, back, left, and right, dressed in light yellow tunics with belts of patterned jade. Only good-looking young men were chosen for this job. Each year at the Thousand-Autumn celebration of the emperor's birthday, the emperor ordered the horses to perform by the Hall of Zealous Administration.

Later on, after [the rebellion of An Lushan and the flight of] the emperor to Sichuan, the horses were scattered, falling into private hands. An Lushan had often seen them dance and was entranced by them, and so had several sold to him when he was in Fanyang. Later these ended up in the possession of [the general] Tian Chengsi who knew nothing about their background. Confusing them with cavalry horses, he put them in the outer stables.

One day when the soldiers were having a celebration and musicians started to play, the horses began dancing and could not stop. The grooms thought evil spirits had possessed them and hit them with brooms. The horses, thinking this meant they were out of step with the music, stooped and reared, nodded and strained, trying to reproduce their old performances. When the stable master reported how weirdly the horses were acting, Tian Chengsi ordered them whipped. The more cruelly they were whipped, the more precise their dancing became. The whippings were increased until they fell dead in their stalls.

At the time there were in fact some men who knew that these were the dancing horses, but out of fear of Tian's violent temper, never dared speak up.

Translated by Patricia Ebrey

29

FAMILY BUSINESS

Among the documents that survived at Dunhuang are all sorts of everyday contracts, bills of sale, and government records. Included in this selection are three that relate to the organization and financial arrangements of ordinary families. The first is a household registration record. Such records were kept by the government to ensure that land allocations and tax obligations were correctly set. The one given here is for a family that had grown large because several brothers stayed together long after they had married and had children. The second document is a blank deed a family like this one could have used when they eventually split up. Family property was generally considered the property of all the male members of the household, and when brothers divided the property they normally did it according to the principle of each brother receiving an equal share (with sons of a deceased brother dividing his share). Since division changed legal ownership of property, it was important to have a written record of each party's agreement to the distribution. The third document given below is a bill of sale for a female slave being transferred from one owner to another. Through most of Chinese history a small fraction of the population had unfree or demeaned status, and in Tang times hereditary slavery was recognized. Not only was sale of slaves legal, but slaves had distinctly lower legal standing in many situations.

HOUSEHOLD REGISTRATION RECORD

HOUSEHOLD HEAD: Cao Sili, 56, deputy guard (rank conferred on the 16th day of the ninth month of 723 under He Zhitai. His great-grandfather was Gao, his grandfather Kuo, his father Jian. A rank 8 household, at present not taxed)

STEP-MOTHER: Sun, 60, widow (died this year)

WIFE: Zhang, 58, housewife

YOUNGER BROTHER: Lingxiu, 28, able-bodied man (died this year)

SON: Lingzhang, 18, youth (died in 745)

DECEASED YOUNGER BROTHER'S WIFE: Wang, 25, widow (omitted from record last year)

DAUGHTER: Niangniang, 31, woman

DAUGHTER: Miaoyin, 21, woman

DAUGHTER: Miaoxian, 17, girl

DAUGHTER: Jinjin, 15, girl

DAUGHTER: Shangzhen, 13, girl

YOUNGER BROTHER: Enqin, 42, able-bodied male (left in 727)

DECEASED ELDER BROTHER'S SON: Xiongzhang, 23, pillar of state (rank conferred in 710 by Yuanshuang, due to privilege inherited from his father Dejian. In 745 omitted from record. Great-grandfather Gao, grandfather Kuo, father Jian)

DECEASED ELDER BROTHER'S SON: Xiongyu, 17, boy (omitted from record in 745)

YOUNGER SISTER: Fa, 43, woman

Altogether they should receive 364 *mu* of fields. (They now have 62 *mu* and are owed 202 *mu*; 61 *mu* is inheritable land, one *mu* is personal share, and one *mu* is for house and garden)

PLOT 1: 15 *mu* of inheritable land 15 *li* west of the county seat. Elevated. Borders: east, a ditch; west, Cao Chi's property; south, Dian Xiangfu's property; north, the house.

PLOT 2: 6 *mu* of inheritable land 10 *li* west of the county seat. Clay. Borders: east, their own fields; west, ditch; south, ditch; north, ditch.

PLOT 3: 9 *mu* of inheritable land 7 *li* west of the county seat. Elevated. Borders: east, ditch; west, Cao Chi's property; south, ditch; north, Zhao Yi's property.

PLOT 4: 11 *mu* of inheritable land 7 *li* west of the county seat. Elevated. Borders: east, Zhang Congjiao's property; west, ditch; south, ditch; north, gully.

PLOT 5: 4 *mu* of inheritable land 10 *li* west of the county seat. Elevated. Borders: east, government lands; west, ditch; south, road; north, ditch.

PLOT 6: 4 *mu* of inheritable land 10 *li* west of the county seat. Elevated. Borders: east, ditch; west, Gao Shentong's property; south, same; north, ditch.

PLOT 7: 12 *mu*, 11 of which is inheritable land and 1 personal share land, 11 *li* west of the county seat. Elevated. Borders: east, own land; west, Gong Tuque's property; south, ditch; north, ditch.

PLOT 8: 1 *mu* of house and garden land.

RECORD OF FAMILY DIVISION

Brothers come from the same womb, share the same vital essences, and have strong affections toward each other. They complement each other like luxuriant leaves and stately boughs, and think that they will stay together forever. Little do they realize that one day they will part like birds that fly in different directions—each to a corner of the four seas. Just as winters and summers alternate, the bramble shrubs become withered and branches detach from each other, their time for parting eventually comes.

Elder brother, A, and younger brother, B, now have, in the presence of neighbors and relatives of various branches, meticulously divided into two parts their estate and fields outside of the city as well as their house, other property, miscellaneous objects, and livestock in the city. The details are clearly itemized below.

Afterwards, each brother is in charge of his own share of the family property, and there are to be no complaints or quarrels over it. Should either of them violate this agreement, he will be fined a bolt of fine silk for government use and fifteen bushels of wheat as ration for the military.

This document is drawn up as evidence of the agreement. From now on, each of the brothers has his own household. When the tree has grown too big, its branches will part. When the leaves become scattered, the attachment will be lost. Even the four black birds of the Heng Mountain have to fly their separate ways when their feathers turn dark. This agreement on the division of family property is based on the same principle.

DEED OF SALE OF A SLAVE

A contract executed on the 12th day of the eleventh month of 991.

On this day the functionary, Han Yuanding, having expenses to meet and lacking sufficient stores of silk, sells his household slave Jiansheng, aged about twenty-eight. The slave is being sold to the monastery dependent, Zhu Yuansong, then to Zhu's wife and sons, etc. The price of the slave has been fixed at a total of five bolts of silk, consisting of both finished and unfinished goods.* This day the buyer has remitted three bolts of unfinished silk. The fifth month of next year has been established as the deadline for the delivery of the remaining two bolts of finished silk.

After the woman and the goods have been exchanged and the sale completed, it is agreed that the sons and daughters of the Zhu family shall be masters of this slave forever and ever, from generation to generation. If in future a relative of the seller should reclaim this slave, it is ordered that Han Yuanding and his wife, Seventh Daughter, seek out an adequate slave as replacement. If an imperial amnesty should be declared subsequent to the sale, it may not be used to reopen discussions among the negotiants.

The two parties to the contract have met face to face and have reached their agreement after joint discussions. If one of the parties should default, he shall be fined one bolt of decorated silk and two large rams—all to be turned over to the non-defaulting party. In light of the chance of this contract's not being made in good faith, the following persons have witnessed it and will serve as its guarantors: (Note: In case this woman should prove to have a sickness, a waiting period of ten days has been agreed upon. Beyond this time withdrawal from the agreement will be impossible.)

The woman whose person is being sold, Jiansheng
The seller of the woman, her mistress,
Seventh Daughter
The seller of the woman, her master, Han Yuanding
A relative by marriage, who has participated in the
discussion, Fuzhen
A witness, Monk Chouda of Baoen Monastery
A witness, Monk Luo Xian of Longxing Monastery

(Additional note: In place of one of the bolts of finished silk it has been decided to furnish six lengths of Zhu serge and six lengths of white serge, making a total of twelve lengths, each measuring between ten and twenty feet. These goods are to be delivered by the fifth month of next year.)

Translated by Patricia Ebrey and Clara Yu

---

* Bolts of plain silk of standard size and quality were used as a unit of currency for larger transactions in the Tang and even formed a part of the standard tax payment.

30

THE EXAMINATION SYSTEM

The Tang was the first dynasty in which examinations came to play an important role in selecting men for office. With this change in the system of recruitment also came a change in the life of those who aspired to office. Although most such men were still from well-connected families, they now had to devote more effort and energy to preparing for the examinations by studying the classics and practicing literary composition. Those who passed became jinshi *(presented scholars) and were eligible for prestigious posts in the government.*

Whatever the seriousness of the examinations, men could also laugh at their distortions and excesses. The following anecdotes, supposedly based on true incidents, were included in an anthology of gossip and vignettes compiled in the late Tang. Some of these anecdotes were intended to poke fun at the way men acted, others to record noble aspirations and deeds.

Xiao Yingshi passed the imperial examination in 735. Proud of his talent, he was unequaled in conceit and arrogance. He often took a pot of wine and went out to visit rural scenic areas. Once during such an outing, he stayed at an inn, drinking and chanting poetry by himself. Suddenly a storm arose, and an old man dressed in a purple robe came in with a page boy to take shelter. Because of their informality, Xiao Yingshi treated them rather insolently. In a short while, the storm was over, the rain stopped, carriages and retinues came, and the old man was escorted away. Flustered, Xiao Yingshi inquired about the old man's identity, and the people around him said, "That was the minister of personnel."

Now, Xiao Yingshi had gone to see the minister many times, yet had not been received. When he heard that the old man was none other than the minister himself, he was flabbergasted.

The next day, Xiao brought a long letter with him and went to the minister's residence to apologize. The minister had him brought into the hallway and scolded him severely. "I regret that I am not related to you in any way, otherwise I would like to give you some good 'family discipline,' " said the minister. "You are reputed to be a literary talent, yet your arrogance and poor manners are such that it is perhaps better for you to remain a mere *jinshi* (presented scholar)."

Xiao Yingshi never got anywhere in officialdom, dying as a chief clerk in Yang prefecture.

*   *   *

Lu Zhao was from Yiqun of Yuanzhou. He and Huang Po, also from the same prefecture, were equally famous. When they were young, Huang Po was wealthy, but Lu Zhao was very poor. When they were ready for the imperial examination, the two of them decided to set out on the trip together. The prefect gave a farewell dinner at the Pavilion of Departure, but Huang Po alone was invited. When the party was at its peak, with lots of wine and music, Lu Zhao passed by the pavilion, riding on an old, weak horse. He traveled some ten *li* out of the city limits, then stopped to wait for Huang Po to join him.

The next year, Lu Zhao came back to his hometown, having been awarded the title of "number one." All the officials from the regional commander on down came out to welcome him, and the prefect of Yuanzhou was greatly embarrassed.

Once when the prefect invited him to watch the dragon boat race, Lu Zhao composed a poem during the banquet which read:

> "It is a dragon," I told you.
> But you had refused to believe.
> Now it returns with the trophy,
> Much in the way I predicted.

*   *   *

Lu Hui's mother's brother was Zheng Yu. As his parents died when he was small, Lu Hui was brought up in his mother's family, and Zheng Yu often encouraged him to take the imperial examination and become a *jinshi*. Lu Hui was recommended for the examinations for the "widely brilliant" in the early part of 870, but in 880 bandits encroached on the capital, forcing him to flee south. At that same time Zheng Yu's son Xu was stationed in Nanhai as a regional commander. Lu Hui and Zheng Xu had gone to school together, but when Xu was already a county official, Hui was still a commoner. The two of them, however, equally enjoyed the favor of Zheng Yu.

During the ten years in which Zheng Xu rose to become a governor-general, Lu Hui remained a destitute scholar. Once again he managed to escape an uprising and come to Zheng Xu, carrying but one sack of personal belongings. Zheng Xu still treated him kindly. At this time, the emperor was on the expedition to Shu, and the whole country was in turmoil. Zheng Xu encouraged Lu Hui to seize the opportunity to advance himself. "How long can a man live?" he said to Lu Hui. "If there is a shortcut to riches and fame, why insist on going through the examinations?"

But Lu Hui was adamant. Zheng Xu asked his friends and assistants to try to persuade Lu Hui to give up the exams; he even left the seat on his right-hand side vacant for Lu Hui to occupy. Lu Hui therefore said to him, "Our great nation has established the examination system for the outstanding and the talented. I do not have the ability and dare not dream of such honors. However, when he was alive, my uncle again and again encouraged me to take the examinations. Now with his study empty and quiet, I cannot bring myself to break our agreement. If I have to die as a mere student, it is my fate. But I will not change my mind for the sake of wealth. I would sooner die."

When Zheng Xu saw Lu Hui's determination, he respected him even more than before. Another ten years passed before Lu Hui finally passed the examination under the Lord of Hongnong, and he died as one of the highest officials in the whole empire.

*   *   *

Liu Xubo and Lord Pei of Taibing had once sat close to each other during the imperial examination. When Lord Pei became the administrator of the imperial examinations, Liu was still only an examination candidate. On the day when the examinees were tested on their "miscellaneous essays," Liu presented a poem to the chief examiner, his old classmate:

> I remember evenings like this twenty years ago:
> The candles were the same, so was the breeze.
> How many more years will I have, I wonder,
> To wear this gunny robe,
> And to wait to reach you.

* * *

The Chief Minister Wang Qi was appointed chief examiner in the imperial examinations during the Changqing period (821–824). He had Bai Minzhong in mind as the candidate for the "number one" but was displeased with Minzhong's close association with He Baji, a talented but eccentric man. Therefore, Wang Qi had a confidant reveal his displeasure to Minzhong, hinting to him to break off his friendship.

This messenger went to see Bai Minzhong and told him the chief minister's intentions. "I will do as you say," Minzhong readily agreed.

In a little while He Baji came to visit, as usual, and the servants lied to him, saying that Minzhong was not home. He waited a little, then left without saying a word. A moment later, Bai Minzhong rushed out and ordered the servants to send for He. When he arrived, Minzhong told him everything, and then said, "I can be a *jinshi* under any examiner. I can't, however, wrong my best friend for this reason." The two of them then merrily drank wine and took a nap.

This whole sequence took place right before the eyes of the messenger from the chief minister, and he left in a fury. When he returned to the chief minister, he told him the story and thought this was the end of Bai Minzhong. But Wang Qi said instead, "I only thought of taking Bai Minzhong; now I should also consider He Baji."

* * *

Xu Tang was from Jing county of Xuanzhou and had been taking the examinations since he was young. In the same village there was a man named Wang Zun, who had served as a minor government clerk when young. After Xu Tang had taken the examination more than twenty times, Wang Zun was still but a low functionary in the government. Yet Wang Zun wrote good poetry, although no one knew about it because he kept it a secret.

One day, Wang Zun resigned from his post and set out for the capital to take the imperial exam-

ination. As he was approaching the capital, he met Xu Tang, who was seeing some friends off at the outskirts of the city. "Eh," Xu Tang asked him, "what are you doing here in the capital?"

"I have come to take the imperial examination," answered the former functionary.

Upon hearing this, Xu Tang angrily declared, "How insolent you are, you lowly clerk!" Although they were now fellow candidates for the imperial examination, Xu Tang treated him with contempt. But in the end, Wang Zun passed the examination and became very famous. Xu Tang did not pass until five years later.

* * *

Peng Kan and Zhan Bi were both from Yiqun in Yuanzhou, and their wives were sisters. Peng Kan passed the imperial examination and became a *jinshi*, whereas Zhan Bi remained a mere functionary in the county.

At the celebration banquet given by Peng Kan's in-laws, all the guests were either high officials or renowned scholars. Peng Kan was seated at the head of the table, and the whole company was enchanted by his exuberant character. When Zhan Bi arrived at the banquet, he was told to eat his food in the back room.

Seeing that Zhan Bi was not even disturbed by this, his wife scolded him severely: "You are a man, yet you cannot push yourself ahead. Now that you are so humiliated, where is your sense of shame?" These words stimulated Zhan Bi, and he began to study very hard. Within a few years, he also passed the imperial examination.

Previously, Peng Kan used to insult Zhan Bi. On the day when the results of the imperial examination were announced, Peng Kan was out in the countryside, donkey riding for pleasure. Suddenly a servant boy came running and reported to him the good news about Zhan Bi. Peng Kan was so shocked that he fell off his saddle.

This is the origin of the lampoon that spread throughout Yuanzhou:

When Zhan Bi the exams did pass,
Peng Kan fell off his ass.

*   *   *

Zhang Shu and Cui Zhaowei were both sent up from Xichuan to take the examinations in the early years of Zhonghe [881–884]. While there the two of them went together to have their fortunes told.

At the time, Zhang Shu was reputed for his literary talent, and was generally known as the "number-one-to-be." Even Cui Zhaowei was regarded as inferior to him. However, the fortune-teller hardly paid any attention to Zhang Shu but looked Cui Zhaowei over and told him, "You will definitely pass the imperial examination and come out on top." Then, seeing that Zhang Shu was annoyed, the fortune-teller said to him, "As to you, sir, you will also pass, but not until Mr. Cui here becomes the minister and you pay homage to him."

When they were taking the examination that year, Zhang Shu had a death in the family and had to withdraw while Cui Zhaowei turned out to be the "number one." Frustrated, Zhang Shu vented his indignation in writing lines such as "I had followed you a thousand miles but only lost your tail during the morning's storm." Naturally, Cui Zhaowei was very disturbed. At a drinking party, Cui Zhaowei toasted Zhang Shu, asking him to drink a huge horn-shaped goblet of wine. When Zhang declined, Cui said to him, "Just drink it, and when I become the chief minister, I will let you be the number-one." Zhang walked out in a fury, and the two of them became foes.

Seven years later, Cui was appointed chief minister by the emperor, and Zhang Shu later passed the examination under the chief-examiner Lord Pei. As predicted, Zhang had to pay homage to Cui.

Translated by Clara Yu

31

A PILGRIM'S VISIT TO THE FIVE TERRACES MOUNTAINS

From very early times mountains were seen as points of access to heaven or places were deities dwelled. As Buddhism penetrated China more fully, this tradition was enriched. Monasteries were regularly built in mountains, and many came to attract pilgrims, including both laymen and clerics. The religious goal of a journey to a Buddhist mountain site was to make contact with the Buddha or bodhisattva enshrined at the temple and to gain religious merit. Among the many mountain temples, ones with special treasures—relics of the Buddha, magnificent paintings, or statues—were particularly likely to become major pilgrimage sites.

The monasteries of Five Terraces Mountains (Wutai Shan) near the northern border of China proper were among the first to develop as pilgrimage sites. As early as the sixth century there were two hundred temples in the mountains, and the region soon came to be identified with the great celestial bodhisattva Manjusri. By the ninth century thousands of monks lived in the monasteries on these mountains. In this period the pilgrims to Five Terraces Mountains seem to have been primarily Buddhist monks. These monks included not only Chinese from other parts of the country, but monks from elsewhere in East Asia, particularly Korea and Japan and even occasionally India. Below is an extract from the diary written in Chinese by the Japanese monk Ennin (793–864), who spent the years 838–847 in China. Ennin recorded his encounters with both holy men and holy places and was quick to notice the connections between important Buddhist establishments and the imperial government.

Twenty-eighth Day
[of the Fourth Month of 840]

We entered a broad valley and went west thirty *li* until 10 AM when we arrived at Stopping Point Common Cloister. Before entering the cloister we saw to the northwest the summit of the central terrace and prostrated ourselves to show our respect, for this is the region of Manjusri. . . .

First Day of the Fifth Month.

The weather was clear and we started out on our trip around the Five Terraces Mountains. We left our donkey at the Stopping Point Cloister, asking the monk in charge to feed it. From the cloister we traveled about seventeen *li* west, then turned north to cross the summit, going fifteen *li* until we stopped at Bamboo Grove Monastery. There we met several dozen novices who had come from various places to be ordained there.

After a meal we toured the monastery. It had a place for performing circumambulations. Formerly Priest Fazhao practiced calling the name of the Buddha in this hall. He was given the posthumous name of Priest Great Enlightenment by imperial edict when he died nearly two years ago. An image of him was made and placed in this hall. There is also a painting of Buddhapala meeting an old man when he arrived at Five Terraces in 676. In the Buddha Hall in the Garland Cloister there is a diamond mandala.

Second Day

We went to the Zhenyuan Commandment Cloister. On the second story we worshiped the mandala of the seventy-two sages and worthies made for the benefit of the nation, a marvelous painting. Next someone opened up the Ten Thousand Saints Ordination Platform for us to view. It was made entirely of white jade, three feet tall, and octagonal in shape. Its base is filled with incense ash, and it is covered with a multicolored carpet, also octagonal in shape, which fits it exactly. The pillars and beams are painted very beautifully.

We called on Linjue, the venerable monk in charge of the ordination platform. One hundred years old, he had been a monk for seventy-two years. His facial features were unusual, making him look like a veritable saint. He was affable on meeting his guests. We were told that the year before, in the sixth month, three monks from the Nalanda Monastery in India who came to the Five Terraces Mountains saw a multicolored cloud shining about his body. They have since returned to India.

The Bamboo Grove Monastery has six cloisters (the Rules Cloister, Living Quarters Cloister, Garland Cloister, Lotus Cloister, Balcony Cloister, and Buddha Hall Cloister) and forty monks. This monastery is not under the control of Five Terraces. . . .

Sixteenth Day

Early in the morning we left Bamboo Grove Monastery, following the valley east for ten *li*, then turning northeast for another ten *li*, until we got to Great Garland Monastery, where we lodged in the Living Quarters Cloister. After a meal we visited the Nirvana Cloister where we saw Abbot Faxian lecturing on the *Great Calming and Contemplation* in the upper story. Forty-odd monks were sitting and listening to his lecture. We recognized Priest Zhiyuan, the Tiantai Abbot, among the audience. The magnificence of the decoration of the hall is difficult to describe. The abbot announced that he had finished lecturing on chapter four and would proceed to the next part in his next lecture.

We went to Priest Zhiyuan's room to pay our respects to him. He expressed his kind concern for us. . . . The monks of the fifteen cloisters of Great Garland Monastery all regard Zhiyuan as their abbot. He receives no alms, is strict in observing rules, eats only once a day, and never misses any of the six daily worship services. He constantly practices the Lotus Repentance and is devoted to the concept of the three views [on unreality]. He is respected and honored by the venerable monks of the monasteries all over the mountains. His most deeply held ambition is to see the bodhisattva Samantabhadra (Puxian) and prove the worth of the Lotus Repentance.

After drinking tea we visited the Nirvana altar and worshiped the representation of the Buddha attaining nirvana. It showed him lying on his right side beneath two trees, sixteen feet long. His mother was on the ground, distraught. There were also the four heavenly kings, the eight gods, and the various saints, some wringing their hands and weeping, some with their eyes closed contemplating. It was exactly as described in the sutras. . . .

We also saw a portrait of Priest Big-shoe, who had practiced on this mountain. He made fifty pilgrimages around the mountains, once spending three years at the summit without coming down. Finally, with the aid of Manjusri, he put on a pair of large shoes, a foot five inches high, one twenty-five pounds, the other ten pounds. They are now on display in front of the portrait. The priest once made fifteen thousand robes to give to fifteen thousand monks. His portrait is now placed in the upper story where offerings are made to it. . . .

Seventeenth Day

. . . In the evening I went up to the Bodhisattva Hall Cloister with several other monks to see Priest Chinian. He is seventy years old, but to look at him you might think he was forty. People say that his robust appearance comes from the power of his devotions. The hall was opened for us, and we worshiped the incomparably magnificent image of the bodhisattva Manjusri riding a lion. The image fills the five-bay hall. The lifelike lion seems to be moving majestically with vapors coming out of its mouth. After we stared at it for a long time, it seemed to move.

The venerable monks told us that when they first tried to make this statue, it kept splitting, six times in a row. Vexed, the artist said, "Everyone in the world recognizes my unique skill. My whole life I have been casting Buddhist statues and never before have any split open. This time when I made this statue I prepared myself by observing abstinence and concentrated all my skill on making something that would move the people of the world to behold and worship it and thus turn their hearts [to Buddhism]. Now I have cast it six times and it has cracked six times. Clearly [my work] must displease Manjusri. If this is so, I humbly entreat the Great Sage Manjusri to show me his true appearance. If I personally gaze on his golden face, I will immediately copy it and make a statue."

As soon as he had made his prayer, he opened his eyes and saw before him the bodhisattva Manjusri riding on a golden-colored lion. After some time, Manjusri mounted a multicolored cloud and flew up into the sky. The artist wept for joy. He then realized that the statue he had made before had not been right. He changed his model to match what he had seen in size and appearance. Thus the seventh time he cast it, it did not crack; in fact, everything proved easy to do. Once the statue was finished it was placed in this hall. With tears in his eyes, the artist said, "What a miracle. I have seen what has never been seen before. I pray that in all my successive lives, age after age, I will be a disciple of Manjusri." Having said this, he died.

From then on this statue from time to time would emit light or manifest other signs of its marvelous powers. A record was made of each manifestation and sent to the emperor, who responded by sending a gift of Buddhist cloaks, one of which can be seen on the statue. Each year an imperial emissary sends five hundred cloaks for the monks of the monastery. This is in addition to the annual imperial gifts of incense, flowers, pearls, canopies, jades, jewels, crowns, chased metal incense burners, large and small mirrors, carpets with designs, white cloth, imitation fruit and flowers, all of which are already considerable. Not all of them can be displayed in the hall; the others have to be stored in the storehouse. Donations from official and private donors from around the country are too numerous to list.

When any of the monasteries at Five Terraces make statues of Manjusri, they always copy this one, but they never capture more than one percent of it.

Inside the hall a canopy with the seven treasures hangs over the bodhisattva. Brightly colored and decorated banners and crowns with rare jewels fill the hall, along with untold numbers of beautifully made mirrors of various sizes.

Exiting the hall to the north we could see the northern and eastern terraces with their entirely treeless high rounded summits. The short grasses were colorful, so seen from a distance, it looked like autumn, though it was the middle of summer. Returning to the front of the hall we gazed at the southern terrace, which is also treeless. Unlike the other mountains, its summit stands out by itself, touching the blue sky. The western terrace is cut off from the central terrace and was not visible.

In front of the Bodhisattva Hall on the end of a cliff there was a three-bay pavilion floored with boards and surrounded by a high railing on all four sides. Beneath it was a precipice going down ten thousand feet. The venerable monk told us that the Japanese monk Reisen saw ten thousand bodhisattvas from this pavilion.

After we had performed acts of worship at each place there, we went to Balcony Cloister to see Abbot Xuanliang, who, since the fourth month, has been lecturing on the *Garland sutra* and the Tiantai commentaries to over forty disciples of Priest Zhiyuan. In the morning he lectures on the *Garland sutra* in the Balcony Cloister, in the evening on the *Great Calming and Contemplation* in the Nirvana Cloister, with monks from both cloisters attending both. They are joined by many others from other cloisters [on the mountain]. . . .

With a group of monks we went to the upper story, where we worshiped. The interior and exterior were both impressive, and it had treasures similar to those in the Bodhisattva Hall. We saw the skull of a self-enlightened buddha. It was black and white, like pumice stones in our country. The bone inside was strong and as big as a two-pint bowl. It was the top of the skull, for on top was growing white hair about five inches long, which must have grown after being shaved. It was brought by a monk from the western regions during the Zhenguan period [627–650]. There was also a Sanskrit version of the *Lotus sutra* and a bone of the Buddha in a lapis lazuli bottle and two very fine copies of the *Lotus sutra*, one in gold characters, one in small characters.

In front of the building was a gorgeous two-story octagonal pagoda. At its base was an Asokan stupa, buried so no one could see it. It is one of the 84,000 stupas [the Indian] King Asoka made [to house relics of the Buddha].

Next we went to the Pavilion of Constancy and performed acts of adoration. More than fifty monks practice meditation there. They all have woolen robes and staves, having traveled from all over to come as pilgrims. By imperial command this temple has a place for performing rites for the protection of the country. A monk of the Tiantai tradition is lecturing there on the Rule of the Four Parts. He is also a disciple of Priest Zhiyuan. . . .

Sixth Day of the Sixth Month.

An imperial commissioner arrived, and all the monks in the monastery went out to welcome him. The regulations specify that each year the emperor sends such things as clothes, alms bowls, incense, and flowers to Five Terraces Mountains to be distributed to the twelve main monasteries. Included are five hundred fine robes, five hundred packages of silk floss, one thousand buddhist cloaks dyed blue, a thousand ounces of incense, a thousand pounds of tea, and a thousand towels. Vegetarian feasts are also provided at the twelve main monasteries.

Seventh Day

On this day the monastery held the maigre feast provided by imperial order. After it was completed, the monks performed a ritual recitation of the *Garland sutra*. In the evening the imperial emissary went to the Bodhisattva Hall with several dozen monks, hoping to see a manifestation [of Manjusri]. He also went to the Nirvana Cloister to pay his respects to Priest Zhiyuan.

Eighth Day

The imperial emissary provided a maigre feast for a thousand monks.

Ninth Day

After eating, the imperial emissary went to Golden Balcony Temple.

Eleventh Day

It was the birthday of the current emperor. On imperial instructions, the various monasteries at Five Terraces Mountains held birthday maigre feasts, all ringing their bells at the same time. The five or six most venerable monks got up from their seats to offer incense. I heard that the imperial emissary returned to the capital after offering incense at the Golden Balcony Temple.

Translated by Patricia Ebrey

PART IV

THE SONG AND YUAN DYNASTIES

From the mid-ninth century, the Tang government progressively lost control of the country and, like the Han before it, was finally destroyed by ambitious generals who seized control of the armies in the wake of peasant rebellions. After the official demise of the Tang in 906, no general was able to establish a long lasting dynasty until in 960 Zhao Kuangyin (r. 960–976) founded the Song dynasty (960–1279).

The Song was a brilliant and innovative age. Unprecedented wealth was created by a commercial revolution (begun in the mid-Tang), by technological improvements in industry, and by the great extensions of wet-field rice cultivation. In the new commercial cities, different social groups and classes were brought into greater contact with one another, contact based more on commercial relations and less on the paternalistic social relations of master and retainer or tenant (although such relations also persisted into modern times). Town and countryside became more closely integrated as extensive marketing networks developed. In the cities, storytellers could attract large audiences. Like Buddhist monks in earlier periods, they transmitted cultural ideals and principles to the illiterate, but by responding to popular demand, probably served as much to acquaint the educated with the attitudes and ways of thinking of commoners as the other way around.

An equally important development was the invention of printing. With books becoming more widely available and much less expensive, literacy and a familiarity with the works of the ancient and modern masters became less a preserve of the most privileged. Increased access to education thus served to undermine aristocratic ideals and reduce emphasis on birth.

Moreover, printing led to publishing more and more works addressed to those with a general, rather than a classical or literary education. These include popular moral tracts, guides for farming, handbooks for rituals, and books of moral, social, or economic advice. Several are included in Part IV.

Some of the warlords who briefly gained control of North China between the Tang and the Song had been ethnically non-Chinese, reflecting the growing strength of Turkic, Tibetan, Mongol, and Tungusic peoples in the dry region north of China proper. Considerable territory which the Tang had controlled in its heyday was never recovered by the Song, the Tanguts holding parts of the northwest (the Xia state) and the Khitans the northeast (the Liao state). Then in 1127 most of North China was lost to the Jurchen who had defeated the Liao and established the Jin dynasty. The Jurchen in turn succumbed in 1234 to the Mongols, then rapidly building up a pan-Asian empire. When the Song lost North China to the Jurchen, a "temporary" capital was established at modern Hangzhou, and a vigorous social, intellectual, and economic life was maintained in South China until it also fell to the Mongols in 1279.

The Mongol dynasty in China, called the Yuan (1234–1368), always remained an alien dynasty. Non-Chinese, including Marco Polo and many Central Asians, were assigned to governmental posts, and the Mongols themselves retained their identification as warriors. When the dynasty collapsed through internal weakness and rebellion, the Mongol nobility and armies largely withdrew to modern Mongolia. During the Yuan dynasty most of the economic advances of the Song slowed or were even temporarily reversed. Mongol oppression and mismanagement led to a setback in industrial innovation and commercial growth. Nevertheless, urban life remained vibrant, publishing continued, and popular drama in particular matured.

During the Song dynasty the culture and way of life of the scholarly gentleman acquired a characteristic style that lasted for centuries. The decline of aristocratic habits and ideals, the increase in wealth, the intellectual excitement caused by the revival of Confucian teachings, and the great growth in importance of the examination system for recruitment to office probably all influenced this development. From the Song to the end of imperial China, the way of life of educated men who aspired to hold office or move in cultivated circles involved years if not decades of intensive study, the formation of close student-teacher relationships that could last a lifetime, and often the cultivation of artistic, literary, or antiquarian interests. During the Yuan dynasty, although many upper-class men found political careers impossible or uninviting, their intellectual, literary, and artistic pursuits were not hampered and indeed seem to have thrived.

32

THE TANGUTS AND THEIR RELATIONS
WITH THE HAN CHINESE

*Through most of Chinese history the dry northern and northwestern fringes of
China proper were settled by nomadic or seminomadic people speaking a variety
of languages. Conquests, alliances, confederations, and migrations led to continually shifting political alignments and ethnic mixes. From late Tang times on the
Tanguts were dominant in the Gansu corridor and surrounding areas. Their ruling clan claimed descent from the rulers of the Northern Wei dynasty, one of the
non-Han states in the Northern and Southern dynasties. They helped the Tang
court suppress the Huang Chao rebellion in 881 and were able to consolidate
their power during the tenth century when China proper was fragmented. In
1038 the ambitious and forceful ruler Weiming Yuanhao (r. 1032–1048) proclaimed their state the Xia with himself as its third emperor, an act which led to
a brief war with the Song and a treaty of compromise in 1044. When the Jurchen
took North China in 1126, the Tanguts were able to preserve their independence
and the twelfth century witnessed a cultural flowering when many translations of
Chinese and Tibetan texts as well as original works were published in the Tangut
language. In 1227 the Xia state fell to the Mongols.*

*The three pieces below touch on different aspects of Tangut ethnic identity and
place in the larger Sino-centric world. The first is a collection of maxims, proverbs, and aphorisms, revealing something of the cultural ethos of the Tanguts.
The second is the letter sent from the Tangut ruler to the Song emperor in 1038
announcing his decision to take the title emperor. The third is the preface to a
bilingual aid for studying Tangut and Chinese written in 1190.*

TANGUT PROVERBS, MAXIMS, AND SAYINGS

Tanguts walk briskly and boldly ahead; Khitans step with a slow gait; Tibetans for the most part revere Buddha and monks; Chinese all love worldly literature; Tugu drink sour milk; Shanguo people adore buckwheat.

Mother's beauty is warmer than a thousand white suns, father's wisdom is brighter than ten thousand red moons.

Daughters from mother's clan are parted unfairly, sons from father's clan meet in full right.

Mother's clan was there in the past and will be there in the future; valor, beautiful birds, and sorrow all disappear.

There are no better intimates than father and mother, no meat tastier than meat off the bones.

To drink up the dregs after a friend is not offensive, to put on an ugly dress does not make you a monster.

Waiting for the dowry, the bride grows old; beginning to advance in office, death comes.

If you don't know proverbs well, you will be unable to converse; if you have few horses and yaks, you will not sing to your hearts' content.

You may eat ten bags of fruit, but will not escape from revenge; you may have ten daughters, but will not avoid being called childless.

If one person stands behind another, it does not make him weaker; if one member of the council sits behind another, his worth is not debased.

Having sold the goods and reaped the profits, do not neglect the accounts; closed eyes do not help the blind to fall asleep.

Even if you refrain from taking part in war, will you really live forever? Even if you are thrifty, will your cattle really not perish?

If the Tanguts lose their sense, Heaven and earth lose their sense.

Evil follows after good; ugliness stands behind beauty.

Beauty and vision are two sisters, wealth and reason two brothers.

Stupid children, even after growing up, argue with one another; a wild horse kicks even in the stall.

In the depths of the river the current is calm; broad learning does not overrate itself.

A good shaman does not heal himself; a bright lamp does not illumine its own interior.

Loving honesty and beauty will not make you a nobleman; gaining power will not bring you virtue.

Those families who love one another ally their households; the one with whom you desire to sleep—marry.

A man with a meager salary will be diligent in office; an unattractive woman will be true to her husband.

WEIMING YUANHAO'S LETTER TO THE SONG EMPEROR RENZONG, 1038

My ancestors were originally emperors of the Later Wei, for the old state of Helian is the legacy of the Tuoba. During the Tang, my distant ancestor Sigong led troops to rescue the court from peril and was granted the imperial surname. My grandfather Jiqian deeply grasped the requirements of strategy, held fast to Heaven's omen, grandly raised the righteous banner, and completely subdued all the tribes. The five districts by the Yellow River submitted at once; the seven prefectures along the border all surrendered. My father Deming inherited this great undertaking, perforce following the [Song] court's orders. The name of your great king made itself felt far and wide; our insignificant fief was explicitly received in an act of severing and sharing.

For my part, I, your servant, have managed to create a humble script for writing the Tangut language. I have also altered the great Han official dress, unified the five musical tones, and reduced the ritual bow from nine prostrations to three. Now that the dress regulations have been completed, the script put into effect, the rites and music made manifest, the vessels and implements prepared, the Tibetans, Tatars, Changye, and Jiaohe [Uighurs] have all recognized my sovereignty. Not satisfied with the title of king, these vassals insist that I be titled emperor. Converging without end until the mountains rang with their assembly, humbly they begged for a united land with one border, a "country of ten thousand chariots." I repeatedly declined, but the assembled crowd kept pressing, until I had no choice in the matter. Therefore on the eleventh day of the tenth month, an altar was erected and I was enthroned as Shizu, Originator of Literature, Rooted in

Might, Giver of Law, Founder of Ritual, Humane and Filial Emperor. My country is called Great Xia, and the reign era is called "Heaven-Conferred Rites, Law, and Protracted Blessings."

I humbly look to Your Majesty the emperor, in your profound wisdom and perfection, whose benevolence extends to all things, to permit me to be invested as the "ruler facing south" in this western land. I shall exert myself to maintain our good relations. As the fish come and the birds go, so will be transmitted the sounds of our neighboring states; as the earth is old and Heaven spacious, so long will I subdue disturbances along the border. In utmost sincerity I beseech you, humbly awaiting the imperial affirmation. I have respectfully sent the envoys Nushe Eji, Nisimen, Wopu Lingji, and Kuiyaini to submit this message.

PREFACE TO A TANGUT-CHINESE GLOSSARY, BY GULE MAOCAI (1190)

Gentlemen must all study if they are not to forget themselves in serving others' interests. Gentlemen must also all teach if they are not to abandon others for their own interests. By studying they complete themselves with wisdom; by teaching with benevolence they benefit others.

As for the Tangut and Chinese scripts, in their particulars they are different, but if you compare their roots, they are the same. Why? Because former and later sages always held to the same principles; thus, people of today should be able to master both the Tangut and Chinese languages. Not knowing Tangut, one cannot go among the Tanguts; likewise, if one does not study Chinese, then how can one get along with the Chinese people? So when a wise man appears among the Tanguts, the Chinese do not respect him, and when a sage appears among the Chinese, the Tanguts do not trust him. This is all because the languages are not the same.

Given this situation, how could I, Maocai, having studied both Tangut and Chinese, dare to remain silent and invite shame? Thus, I have compiled a book for studying the Tangut and Chinese languages, arranging it according to the three powers [of Heaven, earth, and man]. In every case the words and phrases have been recorded clearly; differences in pronunciation have been noted according to type. Where the pronunciation is missing, the instructor should correct it. The phrases given are commonplace ones so that students will easily comprehend them. I have named the book, "Timely Pearl in the Palm." When the wise see it, they may heap ridicule on it, but hopefully will not curse it.

Translated by Ruth Dunnell

33

BOOK OF REWARDS AND PUNISHMENTS

With the spread of printing came the frequent publication of moral and religious tracts, our surest sources for popular values and attitudes. From the Song through the Qing dynasties, the brief Book of Rewards and Punishments *was perhaps the most popular and widely circulated of these tracts. It is usually classified as a work of popular Daoism, probably because its text is anachronistically attributed to Laozi. In fact, like most other tracts, it is a highly eclectic product. The Buddhist concepts of karma and salvation run throughout the piece. The importance of retribution, immortality, nature, and cosmology stem largely from Daoist notions. Nevertheless, many of the virtues extolled are traditional Confucian ones.*

The grand elder [i.e., Laozi] has said that calamity and misfortune cannot gain entrance of their own into a person's life; it is the individual alone who calls them in. Good and evil are requited as automatically as shadow follows form. In keeping with this principle, Heaven and earth have spirits who judge transgressions. These spirits take into account the lightness or gravity of the evil deeds that human beings have committed and then deduct from those individuals' life spans correspondingly. After diminishing the culprits' life expectancy, they reduce them to poverty and visit upon them innumerable calamities. Everyone comes to hate them. Punishment and misfortune pursue them wherever they go; happiness and pleasure flee from them. An unlucky star torments them. When their allotted time is up, death claims them. There are also spirit rulers of the constella-tions of Three Towers and Northern Scoop, who reside far above the heads of people and who keep track of their foul deeds and wickedness. They may shorten an individual's life a hundred days or twelve years. There are also three spirits of the body, which reside within the human organism. On each gengshen day [once every sixty days] they ascend to the heavenly ruler and inform him of the transgressions and harmful deeds of the people over whom they watch. On the last day of the month the kitchen god does likewise. When individuals have been found guilty of a serious transgression, they are punished by a loss of twelve years from their allotted life span. For minor transgressions, they suffer the loss of one hundred days of life.

There are hundreds and hundreds of occasions for transgressions, large and small. People who want to achieve immortality must first of all avoid these occasions. They must recognize the path of righteousness and enter upon it; they must recognize the way of evil and stay clear of it. They do not tread the byways of depravity, nor do they poke into the private affairs of others. They accumulate virtue and gain merit and have compassion for all living things. They exhibit loyalty to their ruler, filial obedience to their parents, true friendship to their older brothers. By conducting themselves with propriety, they influence others. They take pity on orphans and are kindly toward widows; they venerate the elderly and are warmhearted toward the young. They will not permit themselves to do any harm even to an insect, a plant, or a tree. They consider it proper to feel sorry when others suffer misfortune and to rejoice when others enjoy good fortune, to aid those in need and to assist those in danger. They look upon the achievements of others as if they were their own achievements, and they regard the failures of others as if they were their own failures. They do not dwell on the shortcomings of others, nor do they brag about their own strong points. They put a stop to what is evil and praise what is good. They give much and seek little. They accept honors only with misgivings. They show favor to people without seeking anything in return. When they share things with others, they do not regret it later. They are called good people and everyone reveres them. The Way of Heaven protects them from harm. Happiness and good fortune follow them everywhere; the depravities of the world keep their distance from them. The spirits watch over them; whatever they undertake results in success. Thus, they can hope to become immortal. Individuals who desire to achieve heavenly immortality should establish in themselves the thirteen hundred good qualities, and those who aim for earthly immortality should establish within themselves the three hundred good qualities.

Evil persons, on the other hand, are devoid of righteousness, as their actions reflect. They turn their backs on the correct principle and equate wickedness with capability. They act heartlessly and do injury and harm. In stealth they rob the law-abiding. They insult their ruler and their parents behind their backs. They are rude to their teachers and rebellious toward those they are supposed to serve. They deceive the ignorant and slander their fellow students. They are treacherous and lying and bring charges against their ancestors. They are perverse, without humanheartedness, vicious, and selfish. Their priorities of right and wrong are out of place, and they turn their backs on their duties.

In office they are tyrannical toward their subordinates and take credit for their work, while at the same time being obsequious toward their superiors and currying their favor. If they receive some kindness, they show no gratitude. They brood over grievances incessantly. They are contemptuous of the common people and bring disorder and confusion into the state. They extend rewards to the unrighteous and dole out punishments to the innocent. They will have some people executed to get their hands on their wealth and will have other people fired from their jobs to grab their positions. In war they kill those they have captured and slaughter those who have surrendered. They dismiss the upright, dispose of the virtuous, mistreat orphans, and harass widows. They ignore the law and take bribes. They take straight for crooked and crooked for straight, treating light crimes as grave ones and watching the resultant executions with glee. They know that they are doing wrong but refuse to change; they know what is right but refuse to act upon it. They blame others for their own wickedness. They obstruct the arts and sciences. They slander wisdom and morality, insult the Way and virtue.

Evil persons shoot creatures that fly and hunt those that run, stirring up hibernating animals and rousing roosting fowl. They block up animals' dens and overturn birds' nests, injuring hens and breaking their eggs. They hope for others' ill-fortune and ruin in order to secure advantage for themselves. They let others bear risks to preserve their own safety and fleece people to enrich themselves. They present things of poor quality as good. They disregard the public good for their own private advantage. They take credit for others' achievements. Concealing others' good points, they exaggerate their bad points. They expose people's private affairs. They squander the wealth of the nation. They break up friends and families. They insult the things people love. They lure others into doing evil. They get their way by intimidating people to seek triumphs by ruining others. They destroy crops while they are just sprouting up and flowering. They break up marriages. If they have ill-gotten wealth, they bristle with pride over it. They shamelessly shirk the responsibility for their acts. Quick to claim credit, they are equally quick to deny fault. They are like marriage brokers who wed people to misfortune and like peddlers who sell people evil.

Evil people buy themselves false reputations. Their hearts are nests of wicked intentions. They deprecate the strong points of others while covering up their own shortcomings. They use power tyrannically to intimidate others, not hesitating to inflict cruel and even fatal injury on people. They cut up cloth without cause and cook animals they have slaughtered senselessly, waste the five grains, mistreat animals and other living creatures, wreck people's homes, confiscate their wealth, and destroy their homes by letting loose floods and starting fires. They throw the plans of others into confusion and thereby thwart their achievements. They break tools and make them worthless to workers. When they see others prosper, they desire to have them censured and exiled. If they encounter a rich and prosperous man, they hope he will be brought to ruin. At the sight of a beautiful woman, their hearts brim over with lust. Having borrowed, they wish their creditors would die to avoid repaying them. If their wishes are not met, they curse and burn with hatred. When they notice others having a bit of bad luck, they say it must be recompense for their transgressions. When they see persons who are deformed and crippled, they laugh at them. They play down any praiseworthy talents they observe in others. They resort to magic to get rid of their enemies and use poison to kill trees. They fly into a rage at their teachers and are obstinate toward their elders. They go to violent extremes to satisfy their lusts

and desires. They are more than happy to employ tricks and mischief to achieve their ends and gain wealth by plundering. Promotion they seek by cunning and deceit. They are unfair in rewarding and punishing. In indulging their pleasures they go beyond all moderation. They are cruel and severe to those below them, loving to instill fear in people.

Evil persons murmur against Heaven, blame others, curse the wind, and decry the rain. They engage in quarrels and lawsuits. Foolheartedly they become involved in cliques and factions. They use women to advise them and do not follow the teachings of their parents. As soon as they find something new, they abandon the old. They say "yes" with their mouths when their hearts say "no." They covet riches and take advantage of their superiors by deceiving them. They invent wicked stories to defame and ruin innocent people; and while defaming others, they praise their own straightforwardness. They slander the spirits and boast of their own rectitude. They reject virtue and adopt rebelliousness. They turn their backs on those who are close to them and embrace distant acquaintances. They call on Heaven and earth to witness their misdeeds. If they give something away, they soon regret it. They will borrow money with no intentions of repaying it. They crave those things they have no right to attain. They bend every effort to make an extravagant display.

Evil people's lustful desires go beyond all restraint. Although their hearts are poisonous, they put on a compassionate demeanor. They sell people contaminated food to eat; they deceive people by teaching falsehoods. They give a short foot, a narrow measure, a light pound, a small pint; they take the bad and mix it in with the good, trying to pass the whole lot off as top quality. In such ways they accumulate dishonest profits. They lure good people into disgraceful acts, deceiving and tricking the ignorant. Their avarice is insatiable. They curse those who seek rectitude. Their drunkenness leads them to sedition. They fight with their families.

A man with these evil traits is without loyalty

and virtue, a woman without kindness and obedience. Men like this do not live in harmony with their wives. Women of this sort do not respect their husbands. On every occasion such men love to brag, such women are moved by jealousy. Such men act badly toward their wives and children; such women show no sense of propriety before their fathers-in-law and mothers-in-law. These evil people treat the spirits of their ancestors with contempt. They disobey the orders of their superiors. Their activities benefit no one. They revel in duplicity. They curse themselves and others. Both their loves and their hatreds are based on prejudice.

These evil people skip over wells and hearths and jump over food and people [all of which exhibits a great disrespect for the spirits]. They commit infanticide and perform abortions. Many are their dark and depraved activities! On the sacred days at the end of the month and at the end of the year, they sing and dance with great frivolity. On the first of the month and in the mornings they shout and curse. They snivel, spit, and even urinate toward the north [which is the position of the emperor and the gods]. They hum, sing, and even cry in front of the hearth [which is the dwelling place of the kitchen god]. Moreover, they use the fire of the hearth to burn incense. They light filthy firewood to cook their food. They lounge around at night shamelessly naked. They inflict punishments during the eight prohibited periods of the year. They spit at shooting stars and point at the rainbow [by which they manifest their disdain for cosmological phenomena]. They point at the stars unceremoniously and regard the sun and the moon with disrespect. They go hunting and burn wood during the prohibited spring months, curse foully in the direction of the north, and without any reason kill tortoises and hack up snakes [which act as representatives of the gods].

For this sort of wickedness the judge of destiny shortens the culprit's life span twelve years or one hundred days, depending on the gravity of the of-

fenses. Should sentence be passed and death occur without the complete expiation of the crimes, then retribution is extended to the sons and grandsons. In cases in which a man has swindled another person out of his money, the burden of restitution is reckoned and passed on to his wife, his children, and all his household to be made good until sooner or later death devours them all. If death itself does not take them, then they are visited by such calamities as floods, fires, robberies, disinheritance, loss of property, disease, and slander in order to make restitution for the crime. In cases in which people kill others unjustly, it is as if they were to hand over their swords so that they themselves in turn could be slain. In cases in which people have acquired ill-gotten wealth, it is just as if they had gulped down rotting meat to satisfy their hunger or had drunk poisoned wine to quench their thirst: they derive a short-lived satisfaction, but death soon ensues. But if within their hearts people rise toward goodness, even if they have not yet achieved it, the spirits of good fortune will watch over them. On the other hand, if within their hearts people wink toward evil, even if they have not yet been totally debased, the spirits of misfortune will pursue them.

A person who has been guilty of doing evil but later changes, repents, ceases to indulge in wickedness, and follows the good completely can attain happiness and success little by little. This can be called changing disaster into blessing.

Therefore, good people are of virtuous speech, virtuous demeanor, and virtuous behavior. If they maintain these three modes of virtue every day, in three years' time Heaven will definitely shower them with its blessings. Wicked people are of evil speech, evil demeanor, and evil behavior. If they maintain these modes of evil every day, in three years' time Heaven will definitely rain down disaster upon them. How then can we not but endeavor to act properly!

Translated by Mark Coyle

34

PRECEPTS OF THE PERFECT TRUTH DAOIST SECT

Buddhist and Daoist monks were familiar figures in villages and towns through-out China. Even areas that had no monasteries nearby undoubtedly had a few temples or shrines taken care of by monks or priests, who could also perform religious ceremonies for the local residents. Monks, like doctors, geomancers, and merchants, were usually literate and educated in their specialty. Learned monks associated with leading scholars, but the typical monk would have been more likely to mix with townsmen and prosperous farmers.

The outlook and behavior of monks was shaped by their study of classical religious texts as well as the traditions and practices of the sect to which they belonged. The selection below sets forth the founding principles of the Perfect Truth (Quanzhen) Daoist sect. The twelfth and thirteenth centuries witnessed a Daoist reformation, which culminated in the formation of three reform Daoist sects. These sects preached a rejection of the alchemical and magical practices characteristic of the preceding centuries. Perfect Truth, the largest of the three, was founded by an eccentric ascetic, Wang Zhe (b. 1180), and represented a fusion of the "Three Teachings" (Daoism, Buddhism, and Confucianism). Al-though the Perfect Truth sect eventually reincorporated much of the popular beliefs and magic it had originally rejected, it outlived the other two sects and has remained the most prominent Daoist sect into the twentieth century. The found-ing principles given below were directed primarily at Daoist monks and concern matters of both doctrine and monastic practice.

ON THE CLOISTERED LIFE

All those who choose to leave their families and homes should join a Daoist monastery, for it is a place where the body may find rest. Where the body rests, the mind also will gradually find peace; the spirit and the vital energy will be harmonized, and entry into the Way (*Dao*) will be attained.

In all action there should be no overexertion, for when there is overexertion, the vital energy is damaged. On the other hand, when there is total inaction, the blood and vital energy become slug-gish. Thus a mean should be sought between ac-tivity and passivity, for only in this way can one

146

cherish what is permanent and be at ease with one's lot. This is the way to the correct cloistered life.

ON CLOUD-LIKE WANDERING

There are two kinds of wandering. One involves observing the wonders of mountains and waters; lingering over the colors of flowers and trees; admiring the splendor of cities and the architecture of temples; or simply enjoying a visit with relatives and friends. However, in this type of wandering the mind is constantly possessed by things, so this is merely an empty, outward wandering. In fact, one can travel the world over and see the myriad sights, walk millions of miles and exhaust one's body, only in the end to confuse one's mind and weaken one's vital energy without having gained a thing.

In contrast, the other type of wandering, cloud-like wandering, is like a pilgrimage into one's own nature and destiny in search of their darkest, innermost mysteries. To do this one may have to climb fearsome mountain heights to seek instruction from some knowledgeable teacher or cross tumultuous rivers to inquire tirelessly after the Way. Yet if one can find that solitary word which can trigger enlightenment, one will have awakened in oneself perfect illumination; then the great matters of life and death will become magnificent, and one will become a master of the Perfect Truth. This is true cloud-like wandering.

ON BOOK-LEARNING

In learning from books, one who merely grasps onto the literal sense of words will only confuse his eyes. If one can intuit the true meaning behind the words and bring one's heart into harmony with it, then the books themselves can be discarded. One must therefore first attain an understanding of meanings and locate the principles behind them; then one should discard the principle and internalize the meaning into one's heart. When the meaning is understood, then the mind will withdraw from externals, and in time will naturally become responsive to reality. The light of the mind will overflow, the spirit of wisdom will become active, and no problem will be insolvable.

Thus one should diligently cultivate the inner self, never letting one's mind run wild, lest one lose his nature and destiny. If one cannot fully comprehend the true meanings of books, and only tries to read more and more, one will end up merely jabbering away before others, seeking to show off one's meager talent. This will not only be detrimental to one's self-cultivation but it may do harm to one's spirit and vital energy. In short, no matter how many books one reads, they will be of no avail in attaining the Way. To understand fully the deep meaning of books, one must incorporate them into one's mind.

ON THE ART OF MEDICINE

Herbs are the treasures of the hills and the waters, the essence of the grass and the trees. Among the various herbs there are those which are warm and those which are cold; properly used, they can help in supplying elements to or eliminating them from the body. There are active and less active medicines, those that work externally and internally. Therefore people who know thoroughly the power of herbs can save lives, while those who do not will only do further harm to the body. Therefore the man of the Way must be expert in this art. But if he cannot be, he should not pursue it further because it will be of no use in the attainment of the Way and will even be detrimental to his accumulation of merits. This is because those who pride themselves in such knowledge crave after worldly goods, and do not cultivate the truth. They will pay for such transgression either in this life or the next. The Perfect Truth Daoist must pay heed to this.

ON RESIDENCE AND COVERING

Sleeping in the open air would violate the sun and the moon, therefore some simple thatched covering is necessary. However, it is not the habit of the superior man to live in great halls and lavish palaces, because to cut down the trees that would be necessary for the building of such grand residences would be like cutting the arteries of the earth or cutting the veins of a man. Such deeds would only add to one's superficial external merits while actually damaging one's inner credits. It would be like drawing a picture of a cake to ward off hunger or piling up snow for a meal—much ado and nothing gained. Thus the Perfect Truth Daoist will daily seek out the palace hall within his own body and avoid the mundane mind which seeks to build lavish external residences. The man of wisdom will scrutinize and comprehend this principle.

ON COMPANIONSHIP

A Daoist should find true friends who can help each other in times of illness and take care of each other's burials at death. However he must observe the character of a person before making friends with him. Do not commit oneself to friendship and then investigate the person's character. Love makes the heart cling to things and should therefore be avoided. On the other hand, if there is no love, human feelings will be strained. To love and yet not to become attached to love—this is the middle path one should follow.

There are three dimensions of compatibility and three of incompatibility. The three dimensions of compatibility are an understanding mind, the possession of wisdom, and an intensity of aspiration. Inability to understand the external world, lack of wisdom accompanied by foolish acts, and lack of high aspiration accompanied by a quarrelsome nature are the three dimensions of incompatibility. The principle of establishing oneself lies in the grand monastic community. The choice of a companion should be motivated by an appreciation of the loftiness of a person's mind and not by mere feelings of external appearance.

ON SITTING IN MEDITATION

Sitting in meditation which consists only of the act of closing the eyes and seating oneself in an upright position is only a pretense. The true way of sitting in meditation is to have the mind as immovable as Mount Tai all the hours of the day, whether walking, resting, sitting, or reclining. The four doors of the eyes, ears, mouth, and nose should be so pacified that no external sight can be let in to intrude upon the inner self. If ever an impure or wandering thought arises, it will no longer be true quiet sitting. For the person who is an accomplished meditator, even though his body may still reside within this dusty world, his name will already be registered in the ranks of the immortals or free spirits and there will be no need for him to travel to far-off places to seek them out; within his body the nature of the sage and the virtuous man will already be present. Through years of practice, a person by his own efforts can liberate his spirit from the shell of his body and send it soaring to the heights. A single session of meditation, when completed, will allow a person to rove through all the corners of the universe.

ON PACIFICATION OF THE MIND

There are two minds. One is quiet and unmoving, dark and silent, not reflecting on any of the myriad things. It is deep and subtle, makes no distinction between inner and outer, and contains not a single wandering thought. The other mind is that mind which, because it is in contact with external forms, will be dragged into all kinds of thoughts, pushed into seeking out beginnings and ends—a totally restless and confused mind. This confused mind must be eliminated. If one allows it to rule, then the Way and its power will be damaged, and one's nature and destiny will come to harm. Hearing, seeing, and conscious thoughts should be eliminated from all activities, from walking, resting, sitting, or reclining.

ON NURTURING ONE'S NATURE

The art of cultivating one's nature is like that of playing on the strings of a musical instrument: too great a force can break the string, while too weak a pull will not produce any sound; one must find the perfect mean to produce the perfect note. The art of nurturing one's nature is also like forging a sword: too much steel will make the sword too brittle while too much tin will make it too malleable. In training one's nature, this principle must be recognized. When it is properly implemented, one can master one's nature at will.

ON ALIGNING THE FIVE PRIMAL ENERGIES

The Five Primal Energies are found in the Middle Hall. The Three Primal Energies are located at the top of the head. If the two are harmonized, then, beginning with the Green Dragon and the White Tiger [the supreme Yin-Yang pair], the ten thousand gods in the body will be arranged in perfect harmony. When this is accomplished, then the energy in the hundred veins will flow smoothly. Cinnabar [symbol for nature] and mercury [symbol for destiny] will coalesce into a unity. The body of the adept may still be within the realm of men, but the spirit is already roving in the universe.

ON THE UNION OF NATURE AND DESTINY

Nature is spirit. Destiny is material energy. When nature is supported by destiny it is like a bird buoyed up and carried along by the wind—flying freely with little effort. Whatever one wills to be, one can be. This is the meaning in the line from the *Classic of the Shadowy Talismans*: "The bird is controlled by the air." The Perfect Truth Daoist must treasure this line and not reveal its message casually to the uninitiated. The gods themselves will chide the person who disobeys this instruction. The search for the hidden meaning of nature and mind is the basic motif of the art of self-cultivation. This must be remembered at all times.

ON THE PATH OF THE SAGE

In order to enter the path of the sage, one must accumulate patiently, over the course of many years, merit-actions and true practices. Men of high understanding, men of virtue, and men who have attained insight may all become sages. In attaining sagehood, the body of the person may still be in one room, but his nature will already be encompassing the world. The various sages in the various Heavens will protect him, and the free spirits and immortals in the highest realm of the nonultimate will be around him. His name will be registered in the Hall of the Immortals, and he will be ranked among the free spirits. Although his bodily form is in the world of dust, his mind will have transcended all corporal things.

ON TRANSCENDING THE THREE REALMS

The three realms refer to the realms of desire, form, and formlessness. The mind that has freed itself from all impure or random thoughts will have transcended the first realm of desire. The mind that is no longer tied to the perception of objects in the object-realm will have transcended the realm of form. The mind that no longer is fixed upon emptiness will further transcend the realm of formlessness. The spirit of the man who transcends all three of these realms will be in the realm of the immortals. His nature will abide forever in the realm of Jade-like Purity.

ON CULTIVATING THE BODY OF THE LAW

The body of the law is formless form. It is neither empty nor full. It has neither front nor back and is neither high nor low, long nor short. When it is functioning, there is nothing it does not penetrate. When it is withdrawn into itself, it is obscure and leaves no trace; it must be cultivated in order to attain the true Way. If the cultivation is great, the merit will be great; if the cultivation is small, the merit will be small. One should not wish to return to it, nor should one be attached to this world of things. One must allow nature to follow its own course.

ON LEAVING THE MUNDANE WORLD

Leaving the mundane world is not leaving the body; it is leaving behind the mundane mind. Consider the analogy of the lotus; although rooted in the mud, it blossoms pure and white into the clear air. The man who attains the Way, although corporally abiding in the world, may flourish through his mind in the realm of sages. Those people who presently seek after nondeath or escape from the world do not know this true principle and commit the greatest folly.

The words of these fifteen precepts are for our disciples of aspiration. Examine them carefully!

Translated by Whalen Lai and Lily Hwa

35

WANG ANSHI, SIMA GUANG, AND EMPEROR SHENZONG

The Song was in many ways the great age of the scholar-official. Economic growth, urbanization, and printing facilitated a flowering of poetry, painting, calligraphy, and appreciation of antiques. Opportunies for education increased, and the expanded civil service examination system brought scholars into government service in larger numbers than ever before. There was renewed interest in Confucian scholarship and renewed determination to use Confucian principles to reform the practice of government.

Scholars could, of course, disagree about which Confucian ideas were most relevant and how to apply them to current circumstances. When Emperor Shenzong (r. 1067–1085) took the throne at age twenty, he was impressed with the ideas of Wang Anshi (1021–1086), an experienced official admired also for his poetry and classical learning. Wang wanted thoroughgoing reform of fiscal administration down to the local level. Many other well-respected scholars and literati opposed his plans. The early stages of these disagreements are revealed in the three pieces below. The first is Sima Guang's (1019–1086) record of how he and Wang Anshi debated an issue of government expenditures in front of the emperor in 1067. It is followed by letters they exchanged in 1070 after the first of Wang's policies had been put into effect. The rift between these two continued to widen as Wang's opponents were forced out of office. For two generations, long after the deaths of the emperor, Wang, and Sima, scholar-officials were deeply divided on the appropriateness of these policies.

SIMA GUANG'S ACCOUNT
OF A DEBATE AT COURT

At the Yanhe Hall, Wang Kui, Wang Anshi, and I all presented petitions on the issue of the gifts granted to high officials at the occasion of the state sacrificial ceremonies. I said, "The country is currently short of funds and disasters occur repeatedly. Unnecessary expenses should be cut. The high statesmen who have access to the throne should set an example. Therefore, it is appropriate to let the two superior prefects have their wish in declining the gifts."

Wang Anshi countered, "Our country abounds

151

with resources. The gifts granted to high officials cost very little. To stop giving them out of stinginess will not help enrich the country but only damage the prestige of the government. Formerly, when Chang Gun declined a reward, his contemporaries assumed it was because he knew that his request would not be granted. The two superior prefects' declining the gifts granted them is exactly the same. The present shortage of funds is not particularly pressing."

I answered, "That Chang Gun resigned his post showed his humility. Wasn't he much better than those who keep their posts out of greed for salary? Our country has been short of funds since the end of Zhenzong's reign [997–1022]. The situation in recent years is particularly bad. How can you say it is not a pressing matter?"

Wang Anshi replied, "That the country is short of funds is because the government has not found someone good at finance."

"Financial experts," I said, "do nothing but impose heavy and annoying taxation on the people in order to drain their wealth. As a result, the common people are driven to poverty and end up refugees or bandits. How is this to the benefit of the country?"

"That does not describe a financial expert," he replied. "A financial expert raises more than enough revenue for the country without imposing heavy taxation on the people."

I countered, "These are exactly the words Sang Hongyang used to deceive Emperor Wu of the Han. Sima Qian only recorded them to show Emperor Wu's naivete. The things produced by Heaven or earth are finite. They are owned either by the people or by the government. The rich resources that Sang Hongyang got for the government must have been extracted from the people. Where else could he get them? If things had worked the way Sang Hongyang said, why near the end of Emperor's Wu reign were there so many uprisings that required troops to suppress? Wasn't it because the people had been so exhausted that they sank into banditry? How could you take Sang Hongyang's words as truth?"

"During the reign of Taizu," Wang Anshi responded, "men like Zhao Pu were the grand councillors. The gifts granted to them sometimes amounted to several tens of thousands of cash. Today the gifts granted to high officials come to no more than three thousand cash. This cannot be considered too much."

I answered, "Zhao Pu and his contemporaries devised the strategies that helped conquer the other states. Wasn't it appropriate to reward them with tens of thousands of cash? In the current case, the two superior prefects merely assisted in the sacrificial ceremonies. They did nothing but report to the throne, strictly carry out orders, prepare the water for hand washing, and offer towels. What service have they rendered? How could they be compared with men like Zhao Pu?"

My arguments with Wang Anshi went on and on. Wang Gui summed them up, "Sima Guang says that the policy of cutting expenses should start with the statesmen who have access to the throne. In this regard he is right. Wang Anshi says that the expenses for the gifts are slight and to save them might discredit the government. In this he is right. Only Your Majesty can make a final decision."

A LETTER FROM SIMA GUANG TO WANG ANSHI
dated 27th day of the second month of 1070

For a long time you and I have been debating issues at court and frequently disagreeing. I do not know whether you have given this much thought, but it has not changed my affection for you. You have enjoyed an excellent reputation for over thirty years. You are exceptionally talented and learned. . . .

The emperor selected you to participate in court councils because people had high expectations for you. But now that you have been in charge for nearly a year, scholars in and out of government all criticize you. Even poor villagers, petty clerks, and soldiers all resent you. . . . Scholars who are not your followers all say you have gotten control of the ruler and monopolized the government. They commonly think that opposing you would just invite trouble and so is not as good as simply waiting two or three months for you to defeat yourself. These sorts are not merely disloyal to you, they are disloyal to the emperor. If you in fact carry out your plans for two or three years, the harm to the dynasty will be so serious that it will be hard to salvage the situation. . . .

Those who most detest you repeat all sorts of slanders about you. I know that much of this is false. You may not be a great sage, but your fault lies in trying too hard and having too much confidence in yourself. How can I put it? Since antiquity the way sages have governed has been by delegating specific responsibilities to each office and holding each official accountable for fulfilling his duties. The sages looked after the interests of the common people simply by lightening taxes, imposts, and other burdens. In your opinion, this is conventional Confucian blather, not worthy of attention. You want to achieve what the ancients never achieved, and so you do not entrust finance to the finance commission but manage it yourself. You have even set up a new commission on regulations and selected literary scholars and men who understand finance to discuss making profit. Confucius said, "The man of virtue talks about moral principles. Inferior men talk about profit." . . . These men who talk of profit all clamor to be heard, each competing to see how cleverly they can change the inherited ways. In all probability the gains will not make up for the losses, nor what is added compensate for what is destroyed. They just want to come up with some original idea to get a reputation. This causes enough harm in and of itself.

You have also set up the ever-normal granaries and sent out more than forty commisioners to institute the New Policies throughout the country. First the commissioners distribute funds for the "green sprout" loans, then they want to get the ordinary households to pay cash to commute their labor service, then they want to seek ways to promote irrigation. Although you tried to select talented men to do this work, among them are some who are weak or careless, who offend the local

officials or disturb the common people. Thus the scholar-officials are alienated and the farmers and merchants go bankrupt. Criticisms pour forth and complainants fill the roads. . . . Confucius said that a man of virtue should seek the fault in himself. You also ought to think about how this happened. You cannot lay all the blame on everyone else.

Overstepping official duties and confusing the organization of the government are policies that you deliberately adopted. You insisted on having the government get into the vulgar business of lending money. Since ancient times labor service is something the people have supplied, but you, wanting to get more cash from the people, had them sell their labor. Ordinary people all see that these three policies will not work; you alone thought they were workable. It is not that you are less intelligent than the average person, but that you want to achieve something extraordinary and have contempt for the opinions of ordinary people. . . .

You have always been firm in your views. Whenever you have debated issues in front of the emperor, you act just as you do in arguing with friends in a private home. You do not mince words, but rather hammer home your ideas. When colleagues call on you to discuss issues, only rarely do you agree with them. Those who try to bend to your ways, you treat politely. But if there is the slightest difference, if the caller hints at inconvenient aspects of the New Policies, you fly into a rage and curse him to humiliate him. Sometimes you bring the case up to the emperor to get the person dismissed from office. You do not even let the man get a chance to express his opinion fully. The emperor is broadminded and forgiving, but you resist all remonstrances. . . .

I know very well that the emperor values you more than any of the other officials at court or in the provinces. In deciding on policies, promotions, or dismissals, he trusts in you alone. If you say the policies ought to be abolished, then everyone in the world will benefit. If you say they should be retained, then everyone in the world will suffer. Today the people's happiness and the security of the state all depend on a word from you. You must think of others. Is there anyone without fault? [As it says in the *Analects*], when a man of virtue is in error, it is as obvious as an eclipse: everyone sees it. When he changes, everyone looks up to him. How has his brilliance been damaged? If you could just suggest to the emperor that he abolish the commision on financial regulations and recall the ever-normal granary commissioners, the peace of the nation would be restored and your ability to correct your mistakes would shine forth. It would not hurt you at all.

I know that what I am proposing is directly counter to your aims. But although our directions are different we have the same goal. You wish to stay in office to carry out your plans to benefit the people. I wish to resign my post to carry out my goal of saving the people. This is what is called being in harmony while differing. Therefore I have dared to explain my concerns to you to fulfill the obligations of our friendship. Whether you accept them or not is up to you. . . .

WANG ANSHI'S LETTER OF REPLY TO SIMA GUANG

Yesterday I received your letter of advice. I see that although we have been on friendly terms for so long, our views on issues never coincide, probably because our approach to policy is so often different. Although I would like to reply at length, you probably would not want to read the whole thing, so I will be brief and not explain each and every one of my views. I hope you will read what I write carefully and thoughtfully and not be offended by it.

What Confucian scholars strive so hard to attain is a correspondence between what things are called and what they in fact are. If names and realities are both clear, the world can be managed. Now it is your opinion that I have overstepped my authority, caused trouble, pursued profit, and blocked criticism to the point where everyone in the world is enraged. In my view, I received my orders from the ruler, the policies were discussed in court, and executing them was delegated to the officials. This is not overstepping the authority of my post. I have adopted the policies of the ancient kings to bring about prosperity and relieve distress. This cannot be called causing trouble. To manage the nation's finances cannot be called pursuing profit. Putting an end to malicious slander cannot be called blocking criticism. As for the abundance of resentment, this is something I expected. Customs cannot be changed in a day. Scholar-officials often prefer not to worry about the nation and merely content themselves with the status quo. The emperor wanted to change this. I wished to help him, undaunted by how many might oppose me. When Pan Geng wanted to move the capital [in ancient times], both the common people and the officials objected. Pan Geng did not change his plan because of those who were annoyed by it. Since the plan had been adequately discussed, he saw no reason to reconsider.

You charge me with having served in office for a long time without succeeding in helping the emperor bring real benefit to the people. For this I must accept responsibility. But your argument that what we need today is a policy of doing nothing at all and merely preserving the old ways is something I cannot accept.

My regrets that we could not meet in person to discuss these issues.

Translated by Patricia Ebrey

36

RULES FOR THE FAN LINEAGE'S CHARITABLE ESTATE

From the Song dynasty until modern times many Chinese have belonged to organized patrilineal kinship groups called lineages. An important aspect of the strength and durability of these lineages has been the provision for common property handed down in perpetuity in the form of "charitable estates." The income from such property was used to cover lineage expenses and provide material benefits for lineage members. Usually the estates were started by successful men who donated land or money to the lineage.

Fan Zhongyan (989–1052), a famous statesman, was the first to establish such an estate. The rules he laid down for its use and management are given below. In later generations his descendants made many amendments to these rules to accommodate new situations as the lineage and its property grew, amendments that reflected the difficulty of preventing fraud, keeping competent managers, and maintaining a sense of common goals. Nevertheless, the basic provision set up by Fan Zhongyan survived several centuries.

1. One pint of rice per day may be granted for each person whom a branch has certified to be one of its members. (These quantities refer to polished rice. If hulled rice is used, the amount should be increased proportionately.)

2. Children of both sexes over five years of age are counted in the total.

3. Female servants may receive rice if they have borne children by men in the lineage and the children are over fifteen or they themselves are over fifty.

4. One bolt of silk for winter clothing may be granted for each individual, except children between five and ten years of age who may receive half a bolt.

5. Each branch may receive a rice ration for a single slave, but not any silk.

6. Every birth, marriage, death, or other change in the number of lineage members must immediately be recorded.

7. Each branch should make a list of those entitled to grain rations. At the end of the month the manager should examine these requests. He must not make any prior arrangements or exceed the stipulated monthly rations. The manager should also keep his own register in which he records the quantity due each branch based on the number of its members. If the manager spends money wastefully or makes advance payments to anyone, the branches have

the authority to require him to pay an indemnity.

8. For the expenses of marrying a daughter, thirty strings of cash may be granted, unless the marriage is a second one, in which case twenty strings may be granted.

9. For the expenses of taking a first wife, twenty strings may be granted (but nothing for a second wife).

10. Lineage members who become officials may receive the regular rice and silk grants and the special grants for weddings and funerals if they are living at home awaiting a post, awaiting selection, or mourning their parents. They may also receive the grants if they leave their families at home while they serve in Sichuan, Gwangdong, or Fujien, or for any other good reason.

11. For the expenses of mourning and funerals in the various branches, if the deceased is a senior member, when mourning begins, a grant of ten strings of cash may be made, and a further fifteen at the time of the burial. For more junior members, the figures are five and ten strings respectively. In the case of low-ranking members or youths under nineteen, seven strings for both expenses; for those under fifteen, three strings; for those under ten, two strings. No grant should be made for children who die before seven, or slaves or servants.

12. If any relatives through marriage living in the district face dire need or unexpected difficulties, the branches should jointly determine the facts and discuss ways to provide assistance from the income of the charitable estate.

13. A stock of rice should be stored by the charitable estate from year to year. The monthly rations and the grants of silk for winter clothing should start with the tenth month of 1050. Thereafter, during each year with a good harvest, two years' worth of grain rations should be hulled and stored. If a year of dearth occurs, no grants should be made except for the rice rations. Any surplus over and above the two years' reserve should be used first for funeral and mourning expenses, then marriage expenses. If there is still a remainder, winter clothes may be issued. However, if the surplus is not very large, the priorities should be discussed, and the amount available divided up and granted in equitable proportions. If grants cannot be made to all entitled to them, they should be made first to those who have suffered bereavement, next to those with weddings. In cases where more than one death has occurred at the same time, senior members take precedence over junior ones. Where the relative seniority of those concerned is the same, the grant should be made on the basis of which death or burial took place first. If, after paying out the rations and the allowances for marriages and burials, a surplus still remains, it must not be sold off, but hulled and put into storage for use as rations for three or more years. If there is a danger that the stored grain might go bad, it may be sold off and replaced with fresh rice after the autumn harvest. All members of the branches of the lineage will carefully comply with the above rules.

Tenth month, 1050. Academician of the Zizheng Hall, Vice-president of the Board of Rites, and Prefect of Hangzhou, Fan. Sealed.

Translated by Patricia Ebrey

37

ANCESTRAL RITES

The classical ritual texts, such as the Book of Rites *and the* Book of Etiquette and Ritual, *were based on the practices of an age with a social system very different from imperial China's. Hence, although always revered, these classics became less and less useful as practical guides to family rituals. More up-to-date handbooks were regularly written and circulated. Sima Guang (1019–1086) compiled a book with instructions on cappings, weddings, funerals, ancestor worship, forms of address to be used in letters, and other questions of etiquette. A century later Zhu Xi (1130–1200) built on Sima's work to write his* Family Rituals, *a manual that circulated for centuries and was widely considered the best book to turn to when one wished to perform the rituals correctly.*

Below are the instructions Zhu Xi gave for the rites honoring ancestors. As early as the Shang dynasty ancestor worship had been practiced by nobles. By the Han, at the latest, it had become an important part of the religious life of the common people, involving offerings to recent ancestors in home, at gravesites, or in specially constructed shrines. Domestic ancestral rites played an important part in fostering the solidarity of close relatives, and worship at graves or in temples became important to the formation and coherence of descent groups.

For the seasonal sacrifices, use the second month of the season. During the preceding ten-day period, divine to choose the day.

Three days before the event practice purification.

Three days before, the presiding man leads all the men to perform purification in the outer quarters, while the presiding woman leads the women to do the same in the inner quarters. They bathe and change their clothes. If they drink wine, they must not reach the point of disorder; if they eat meat, they must not use strong-smelling condiments (garlic, onions, scallions, and so on). During this period, they should not pay condolence visits to those in mourning, listen to music, or participate in anything inauspicious or unclean. One day before the event, set the places and arrange the utensils.

The men wear the long garment. The presiding man directs them and the attendants to dust and sweep the main room and wash the tables and armrests, making an effort to get everything sparkling clean. Places are set for the great-great-grandparents by the northwest corner of the room, facing south, the grandfather to the west and the grandmother to the east. Each has a table and armrest, but they are adjacent. The great-grandparents, the grandparents, and the parents are lined up in order going east, with places just like the great-great-grandparents. Each generation has a separate place setting; do not connect them. The places for the associated ancestors are all on the east side facing west, with the most senior at the north end. Alternatively, they can be on either side facing across to each other, the most senior on the west side.

The women from the wife down set the incense stand below the steps in the middle of the room. On it are put an incense burner and incense box. A bundle of reeds and pile of sand go in front of the incense table and on the ground in front of each of the ancestors' places. Set a wine rack at the top of the eastern steps and also set a table to the east of it, on which place a wine decanter, a cup for making the libation of wine, a plate, another plate for holding the meat offerings, a spoon, a cloth, a box of tea, a tea whisk, a tea cup, a salt saucer, and a bottle of vinegar. The brazier, hot water pitcher, incense spoon, and tongs go at the top of the western steps. Put a table to the west of them and set the prayer board on it. Set wash basins and towels on both the east and west sides of the base of the ceremonial steps, the western one with a rack. To the east also set up a large bench for laying out the cooked food.

Inspect the animal offerings, clean the utensils, and prepare the food.

The presiding man leads the men, dressed in the long garment, to inspect the animal offerings and oversee their slaughter. The presiding woman leads the women, wearing jackets, to clean the sacrificial vessels and prepare the foods for the sacrifice. At each place should be six kinds of fruit, three kinds each of vegetables and dried meat, a plate each of meat, fish, steamed buns, and cakes, a bowl each of soup and rice, a skewer each of liver, and two skewers each of meat. Work to ensure that they are pure and do not let anyone eat them or let cats, dogs, insects, or rodents defile them before the sacrifice takes place.

The next day get up at daybreak and set out the dishes of vegetables, fruit, wine, and meat.

The men from the presiding man on down wear the long garment. Along with the attendants, they all go to the place where the sacrifice will be held. They wash their hands and set fruit platters on the south end of the tables at each place, followed by the vegetables, then the dried meat. They set cups and saucers and plates for vinegar and salt at the north end, the cups to the west and the plates to the east. Spoons and chopsticks go in the middle. They set one bottle each of water and wine on the stand. The water first drawn from the well that day should be added to the water, and it goes west of the wine. Light the charcoal in the brazier, and fill the bottle with water. The presiding woman, in a jacket, warms up all the food for the sacrifice till it is very hot, then puts it into boxes and places them on the large bench at the base of the eastern steps.

When the sun is fully out, take the spirit tablets to their places.

Everyone, from the presiding man on down, in full attire, washes and dries his or her hands and goes to the front of the offering hall. The men all stand in order, as they did at the rite for reporting the day. The presiding woman stands at the base of the western steps facing north. If the presiding man's mother is alive, she has a special place in front of the presiding woman. Any uncle's wives or aunts come after her. Sisters-in-law and sisters are to the left of the presiding woman. Any of them senior to the presiding man's mother or the presiding woman stands a little forward. Daughters, granddaughters, the wives of sons and grandsons, and female attendants are behind the presiding woman in rows, facing north, in order with the most senior toward the east.

When everyone is standing in place, the presiding man goes up via the ceremonial steps. He puts his official plaque in his belt, lights the incense, then takes out his plaque and reports:

> Your filial grandson A, in the second month of spring, now serves your honor, our late great-great-grandfather, of such office, and our late great-great-grandmother, of such title and surname; your honor, our late great-grandfather, of such office, and our late great-grandmother, of such title and surname; your honor, our late grandfather, of such office, and our late grandmother, of such title and surname; your honor, our late father, of such office, and our late mother, of such title and surname. I am making associated offerings to our such-type relative, of such office, and the latter's wife, of such title, surname. I presume to ask the spirit tablets to go to the main room. I reverently extend to them these offerings.

When the report is finished, the presiding man puts his plaque in this belt. He arranges the cases and puts the regular and associated tablets in separate baskets, each basket carried by a different attendant. The presiding man, taking out his plaque, leads the way, with the presiding woman following, and the juniors in the rear. When they get to the main room, they put the baskets on the table by the western steps. The presiding man inserts his plaque, opens each case, and takes out the tablets of the ancestors and puts them by their places. The presiding woman washes, dries, and comes up. She takes the tablets for the ancestresses and does the same with them. For the associated spirits, a son or younger brother takes the tablets. When done, everyone from the presiding man on down comes down and returns to his or her place.

Greet the spirits.

Everyone from the presiding man on down stands in order, as in the rites at the offering hall. Once in

place, they bow twice. Any of the seniors who is too old or ill can rest elsewhere.

Invoke the spirits.

The presiding man goes up and inserts his plaque while he lights incense. He then takes out his plaque, steps back a little, and stands there. One attendant opens the wine and takes a cloth to wipe the mouth of the wine bottle, then fills the decanter with it. Another attendant takes the cup and saucer on the table at the eastern steps and stands to the presiding man's left. A third attendant takes the decanter and stands to the presiding man's right. The presiding man inserts the plaque and kneels. The one holding the cup and saucer also kneels and hands them to the presiding man. Then the one with the decanter also kneels and pours wine into the cup. The presiding man, taking the saucer in his left hand and the cup in his right, pours the wine onto the reeds. He passes the cup and saucer to the attendant, then takes out his plaque. After he prostrates himself, he rises, bows twice, comes down the steps, and resumes his place.

Present the food.

The presiding man goes up and the presiding woman follows. One attendant carries a tray of the meat and fish, another a tray of the grain and wheat-flour dishes, another a tray of the soup and rice. When they get to the front of the great-great-grandfather's place setting, the presiding man inserts his plaque and proffers the meat to the south of the cup and saucer while the presiding woman proffers the wheat-flour food to the west of the meat. He then proffers the fish to the south of the vinegar plate while she proffers the grain dishes to the east of the fish. He proffers the soup to the east of the vinegar saucer and she proffers the rice to the west of the cup and saucer. The presiding man then takes out his plaque and proceeds to lay out each of the other regular ancestors' places, but delegates a younger man and woman to lay out the food for the associated ancestors. Once all this is done, everyone from the presiding man on down goes down and back to his or her place.

Make the first offering.

The presiding man goes up to stand in front of the great-great-grandfather's place. An attendant takes the wine decanter to stand to his right (in winter, first warm it). The presiding man inserts his plaque, takes the cup and saucer for the great-great-grandfather, and stands in front of his place facing east. The attendant, facing west, pours the wine into the cup. The presiding man proffers it in the place used before. Next he takes the cup and saucer for the great-great-grandmother and does the same. Taking out his plaque, he stands facing north in front of the place setting. Two attendants, holding the cups and saucers for the great-great-grandfather and grandmother, stand on his left and right. The presiding man inserts his plaque and kneels, at which point the attendants also kneel. The presiding man accepts the cup and saucer for his great-great-grandfather. In his right hand he takes the cup and pours it in sacrifice onto the reeds, then passes the cup and saucer to the attendant, who puts them back where they were. He handles the cup and saucer of the great-great-grandmother in the same way. He takes out his plaque, prostrates himself, rises, and steps back a little. Meanwhile, the attendant grills the liver on the brazier and serves it up on a platter. The eldest of the brothers of the presiding man proffers it to the great-great-grandfather and grandmother to the south of the spoon and chopsticks.

The liturgist takes the board and stands to the left of the presiding man. He kneels and reads:

On the day of the new moon of this month of this year, such year cycle, I, filial great-great-grandson A, of such office, presume to report clearly to your honor, our late great-great-grandfather, of such office, and our late great-great-grandmother, of such title, such surname: "The succession of atmospheric

forces flows and changes. The time now is the middle of spring. When we think back with gratitude on the seasonal service, we cannot overcome our long-term longings. We presume to take this pure offering of a soft-haired animal, a vessel of millet, and sweet wine, and respectfully present them as our seasonal service. Please enjoy them along with the associated spirits, such-type relative, of such office, and such-type relative, of such title, such surname."

When finished, he rises.

The presiding man bows twice, steps back, and goes to each of the place settings to offer a prayer like this one. When a prayer has been read at each place setting, a younger male who is not making the second or third offerings goes to the associated seat and makes the same offerings but without reading a prayer. When these young men have finished they go back down to their places. The attendants, using separate utensils, clear away the wine and liver, putting the cups back where they were.

Make the second offering.

The presiding woman performs it. The women carry the grilled meat to the separate place settings as in the rite of the first offering, but they do not read prayers.

Make the final offering.

It is performed by the eldest of the presiding man's brothers, his eldest son, or a relative or guest. The younger men carry the grilled meat to the separate place settings, as in the second offering.

Urge the spirits to eat.

The presiding man goes up, inserts his plaque, takes the decanter, and pours wine for all of the place settings. When the cups are all full, he stands to the southeast of the incense table. At this point the presiding woman comes up. She sticks spoons into the cooked rice, their handles to the west, and straightens the chopsticks. Then she stands to the southwest of the incense table, where she and the presiding man both face north and bow twice, then go back down to their places.

Close the door.

Everyone, from the presiding man on down, exits. The liturgist closes the door. If there is no space for a door, lower a curtain. The presiding man stands to the east of the door facing west, the other men behind him. The presiding woman stands across from him, on the west of the door, facing east, with the other women behind her. If there are any relatives senior to the presiding man or presiding woman they take a short rest elsewhere. This is called "eating to repletion."

Open the door.

The liturgist coughs three times, then opens the door. Everyone from the presiding man on down enters, including the seniors who had been resting elsewhere. When they have taken their places, the presiding man and woman offer tea before each of the ancestors and ancestresses. They have a younger man and woman do the same for the associated spirits.

Receive the sacrificed foods.

The attendants set a mat in front of the incense table. The presiding man goes to the mat and faces north. The liturgist goes to the front of the great-great-grandfather's place, takes his wine cup and saucer, and brings them to the right of the presiding man. The presiding man and the liturgist kneel. The presiding man inserts his plaque and accepts the cup and saucer. He sacrifices the wine, then tastes it. The liturgist takes the spoon and

plate, dishes out a little of the rice from each place setting and takes it to the left of the presiding man. He blesses the presiding man, saying:

> The ancestors instruct me, the liturgist, to pass on abundant good luck to you filial descendants and to let you receive riches from Heaven, have good harvests from the fields, and live a long life forever, without interruption.

The presiding man sets the wine in front of the mat, takes out his plaque, and prostrates himself. After rising, he bows twice, inserts his plaque, and kneels to receive the rice. He tastes it, then puts it in his left sleeve, [keeping it from spilling by] hanging it on his little finger. He takes the wine and drinks it down. From his right an attendant takes the cup and puts it beside the decanter; from his left an attendant takes the rice and does the same with it. The presiding man, holding his tablet, prostrates himself. After rising he stands at the top of the eastern steps facing west. The liturgist stands at the top of the western steps, facing east, and announces that the nourishment of the spirits is over. He then goes back down to his place, and with those in line bows twice. The presiding man does not bow, but goes back down to his place.

Take leave of the spirits.

Everyone from the presiding man on down bows twice.

Put the tablets back.

The presiding man and presiding woman both go up and take each tablet and place it in its case. The presiding man arranges the cases in the basket and has them carried back to the offering hall, following the procedure used for bringing them out.

Clear away the remains.

The presiding woman returns to supervise the clean-up. All the wine that is in cups, decanters, or other vessels is poured into the bottle, then sealed. This is called "good luck wine." The fruit, vegetables, meat, and grain foods are all transferred to banquet dishes. The presiding woman supervises the cleaning and storage of the sacrificial vessels.

Eat the leftovers.

This day the presiding man supervises the division of the sacrificial foods. A small amount of each type is put in boxes, which are sealed along with wine. He sends a servant with letters to take these boxes to relatives and friends.

Next, feasts are laid out for the men and women in separate areas. For the men, the senior generation forms a single line, facing south, with the most honored place in the middle of the room and lower ones to the east and west. If there is only one man in the senior generation, he sits in the middle. Everyone else, in order, is across from each other, half facing east, the others west.

The most senior man takes his seat, then all the other men stand in order, each generation in a separate row, with the most senior of that generation to the east. These men all bow twice. A representative of the sons and younger brothers, the most senior of them, steps slightly forward. One attendant takes a decanter and stands on his right while another takes a cup and saucer and stands on his left. The representative inserts his plaque and kneels. (Original note: If the representative is a younger brother, the senior rises, if a son or nephew, then he remains seated.) He accepts the decanter, pours the wine, returns the decanter, and takes the cup. The liturgist says:

> The worship service is over. The ancestors had an excellent repast. I would wish such-type relative to receive fully the five blessings, preserve his agnates, and benefit his family.

The one holding the cup sets it in front of the elder. The representative takes out his plaque. When the elder is finished with the wine, the representative prostrates himself, rises, steps back, then returns to his place where he bows twice with all the other men. The most senior man instructs the attendant to take the decanter and the representative's cup to the latter's place and pour for him. The liturgist says:

> The worship service is over. The good fortune of the five blessings will be shared with all of you.

He instructs the attendants to go to each place and pour wine for everyone. The representative comes forward and kneels to receive it. When he has drunk it all he prostrates himself. On rising, he steps back. The other men come forward and salute. After they step back they drink the wine. Then the representative and the other men all bow twice.

The women make an offering to the most senior woman in the inner room following the same procedures as the men but without kneeling.

When these toasts are over, everyone sits and the meat and grain are brought forward. The women then go to the front of the hall to wish long life to the senior man; the senior toasts them in the same way he did the junior men. The men then go to the inner room to wish the senior woman long life; the senior woman toasts them in return in the same way.

When everyone is again seated, the food made of wheat flour is presented. This time, the male and female attendants all make a toast to the long life of the male and female seniors. The same procedure used before is followed, but they are not toasted back. Then they pour for all those sitting down, and when everyone has lifted his or her glass, they bow twice and step back.

Next the food made of grain is presented. From this point on wine is liberally served. For the feast, start with the sacrificed foods and wine. If they are insufficient, supplement them with other food and wine. When the end of the feast approaches, the presiding man distributes the remaining sacrificed food to the male servants, the presiding woman to the female attendants, in each case reaching to the very most lowly. Everything should be consumed that day. The recipients all bow twice, then clear away the feast.

*   *   *

In sacrifices, the emphasis is on fulfilling sincere feelings of love and respect. Before performing the rites, the poor should evaluate their resources and the ill their energy. Naturally those with the wealth and strength to conform to the rites should do so.

Translated by Patricia Ebrey

38

WOMEN AND THE PROBLEMS THEY CREATE

Getting beyond stereotyped descriptions of women's virtues to a fuller under-standing of the ideas, feelings, and conventions that shaped their lives is difficult because not nearly as many historical records survive concerning women's lives as men's. The sorts of sources included in selection 17, "Women's Virtues and Vices," survive in abundance for all periods. Following the conventions of Liu Xiang's Biographies of Heroic Women, *the standard dynastic histories regularly included brief accounts of women who achieved renown for some act of courage or principle, such as sacrificing themselves to save a parent or to prevent them-selves from being raped or forced to remarry. By Song times, however, with the explosion in the range and numbers of surviving books, it is possible to see other dimensions of women's lives and gender conceptions. Below are selections from two twelfth century authors who took fresh looks at women.*

First are three brief stories recorded by Hong Mai (1123–1202), a man at-tracted to the uncanny who collected stories wherever he went. Some of the stories he recorded probably began as folktales, others may be quite factual, altered little in the retelling. Either way, they reveal Song perceptions of women, their powers and weaknesses, and their relations with men.

These stories are followed by selections from Yuan Cai's (ca. 1140–ca. 1195) book of advice for family heads on how to handle both the financial and inter-personal problems commonly encountered by relatively well-off families. Yuan could not of course write from a woman's point of view, but he seems to have been a sensitive and sympathetic observer of the problems women faced and the problems they created for the men around them.

HONG MAI'S STORIES

Wang Balang's Wife

Wang Balang was a rich man from Biyang in Tangzhou. Every year he went to the Jianghuai area where he was a large merchant. While there he fell in love with a prostitute. Each time he went home, he would treat his wife badly, trying to drive her out. His wife was intelligent. She had borne four daughters, three of whom were already married, but since the youngest was only a few years old, she figured she could not leave. Consequently, she responded to her husband meekly, "I have been your wife for over twenty years. Our daughters are married and we have grandchildren. If you chase me out, where can I go?"

Wang left again, this time bringing the prostitute back with him and setting her up in an inn in a nearby street. The wife, at home, had to pawn or sell little by little everything she had stored in her cases, until there was not a thing left in the house. When Wang returned and saw this, he was even angrier. "You and I can never get together again. Let's settle things today." His wife, finally becoming agitated, said, "If that is how it is, we must go to court." She grabbed him by the sleeve and dragged him to the county court, where the magistrate granted the divorce and divided the property in two. Wang wanted to take the young girl, but his wife objected, "My husband is shameless. He abandoned his wife and took up with a prostitute. If this girl goes with him, she will certainly end up in degraded circumstances." The county magistrate agreed with her, and so she got custody of the girl.

The woman went to live in another village. She bought such things as jars and jugs and lined them up by her door the way shopkeepers do. One day her ex-husband passed her door, and spoke to her as though they were on the same familiar terms as before. "How much money can you make on these? Why not try something else?" She chased him away, railing at him, "Since we have broken our relationship, we are like strangers. How do you get to interfere in my family affairs?" Thereafter they never saw each other again.

When the daughter came of age, she was married into the Tian family of Fangcheng. By then the woman's property had grown to 100,000 strings, and the Tian family got it all. Mr. Wang lived with the prostitute and died away from home in Huainan. Several years later his ex-wife also died. When she was ready to be buried, the daughter, troubled that her father's body had not been brought back, sent someone to get it, wanting to bury him with her mother. After the two

bodies were washed and dressed, they were laid on the same table, and while those in charge were not paying attention, the two bodies turned their backs on each other. Thinking this a coincidence, the daughter cried and put them back in their original place, but before long it happened again. So she knew that this couple were as emotionally estranged in death as in life, and still hated each other. Nevertheless, she buried them in the same grave.

"Chaste Woman" Shi

Ning Six of South Meadow village, in the southern suburbs of Jianchang was a simple-minded man who concentrated on his farming. His younger brother's wife, Miss Shi, was a little sleeker than her peers. She was also ruthless and licentious, and had an adulterous affair with a youth who lived there. Whenever Ning looked askance at her she would scold him and there was not much he could do.

Once Miss Shi took a chicken, wanting to cook it. When Ning learned of it, he went into her room, demanded that she give it to him, then left with it. Miss Shi quickly cut her arm with a knife, then went to the neighbors screaming, "Because my husband is not home, brother-in-law offered me a chicken and tried to force me to have sex with him. I resisted, threatening to kill myself with the knife I was holding, and so just managed to escape."

Ning at that time had no wife, so the neighbors thought she might be telling the truth. They took them to the village headman, then the county jail. The clerks at the jail reviewed the evidence and demanded 10,000 cash to set things right. Ning was poor and stingy, and moreover, knew himself to be in the right, so stubbornly refused. The clerks sent up the dossier to the prefect Dai Qi. Dai was unable to examine it but noted that it involved an ordinary village wife who was able to protect her virtue and her body and not be violated. The administrative supervisor, Zhao Shiqing, concurred with Qi, and they sent up the case making Ning look guilty. Ning received the death penalty and Miss Shi was granted 100,000 cash, regular visits from the local officials, and a banner honoring her for her chastity. From this, she acquired a reputation as a chaste wife. The local people all realized Ning had been wronged and resented how overboard she had gone.

In the end Miss Shi had an affair with a monk at the nearly Lintian temple. Charges were brought and she received a beating and soon became ill. She saw Ning as a vengeful demon and then died. The date was the sixth month of 1177.

The Reward for Widow Wu

Miss Wu served her mother-in-law very filially. Her mother-in-law had an eye ailment and felt sorry for her daughter-in-law's solitary and poverty-stricken situation, so suggested that they call in a son-in-law for her and thereby get an adoptive heir. Miss Wu announced in tears, "A woman does not serve two husbands. I will support you. Don't talk this way." Her mother-in-law, seeing that she was determined, did not press her. Miss Wu did spinning, washing, sewing, cooking, and cleaning for her neighbors, earning perhaps a hundred cash a day, all of which she gave to her mother-in-law to cover the cost of firewood and food. If she was given any meat, she would wrap it up to take home.

Miss Wu was honest by nature. She did not chat idly, and even if other people's things were right in front of her, she did not look at them, wanting only what was her own. Thus neighbors often engaged her and they helped out her and her mother-in-law, so they managed to avoid dying of hunger or cold.

Once when her mother-in-law was cooking rice, a neighbor called to her, and to avoid overcooking the rice, she dumped it into a pan. Due to her bad eyes, however, she mistakenly put it in the dirty chamber pot. When Miss Wu returned and saw it, she did not say a word. She went to a neighbors to borrow some cooked rice for her mother-in-law and took the dirty rice and washed it to eat herself.

One day in the daytime neighbors saw Miss Wu ascending into the sky amid colored clouds. Startled, they told her mother-in-law, who said, "Don't be foolish. She just came back from pounding rice for someone, and is lying down on the bed. Go and look." They went to the room and peeked in and saw her sound asleep. Amazed, they left.

When Miss Wu woke up, her mother-in-law told her what happened, and she said, "I just dreamed of two young boys in blue clothes, holding documents, and riding on the clouds. They grabbed my clothes and said the Emperor of Heaven had summoned me. They took me to the gate of Heaven and I was brought in to see the emperor, who was seated beside a balustrade. He said, 'Although you are just a lowly ignorant village woman, you are able to serve your old mother-in-law sincerely and work hard. You really deserve respect.' He gave me a cup of aromatic wine and a string of cash, saying, 'I will supply you. From now on you will not need to work for others.' I bowed to thank him and came back, accompanied by the two boys. Then I woke up."

There was in fact a thousand cash on the bed and the room was filled with a fragrance. They then realized that the neighbors' vision had been a spirit journey. From this point on even more people asked her to work for them, and she never refused. But the money that had been given to her, she kept for her mother-in-law's use. Whatever they used promptly reappeared, so the thousand cash was never exhausted. The mother-in-law also regained her sight in both eyes.

YUAN CAI ON WOMEN'S PROBLEMS

Women Should Not Take Part in Affairs Outside the Home

Women do not take part in extrafamilial affairs. The reason is that worthy husbands and sons take care of everything for them, while unworthy ones can always find ways to hide their deeds from the women.

Many men today indulge in pleasure and gambling; some end up mortgaging their lands, and even go so far as to mortgage their houses without their wives' knowledge. Therefore, when husbands are bad, even if wives try to handle outside matters, it is of no use. Sons must have their mothers' signatures to mortgage their family properties, but there are sons who falsify papers and forge signatures, sometimes borrowing money at high interest from people who would not hesitate to bring their claim to court. Other sons sell illicit tea and salt to get money, which, if discovered by the authorities, results in fines.

Mothers have no control in such matters. Therefore, when sons are bad, it is useless for mothers to try to handle matters relating to the outside world.

For women, these are grave misfortunes, but what can they do? If husbands and sons could only remember that their wives and mothers are helpless and suddenly repent, wouldn't that be best?

Women's Sympathies Should Be Indulged

Without going overboard, people should marry their daughters with dowries appropriate to their family's wealth. Rich families should not consider their daughters outsiders but should give them a share of the property. Sometimes people have incapable sons and so have to entrust their affairs to their daughters' families; even after their deaths, their burials and sacrifices are performed by their daughters. So how can people say that daughters are not as good as sons?

Generally speaking, a woman's heart is very sympathetic. If her parents' family is wealthy and her husband's family is poor, she wants to take her parents' wealth to help her husband's family prosper. If her husband's family is wealthy but her parents' family is poor, then she wants to take from her husband's family to enable her parents to prosper. Her parents and husband should be sympathetic toward her feelings and indulge some of her wishes. When her own sons and daughters are grown and married, if either her son's family or her daughter's family is wealthy while the other

is poor, she wishes to take from the wealthy one to give to the poor one. Her sons and daughters should understand her feelings and be somewhat indulgent. But taking from the poor to make the rich richer is unacceptable, and no one should ever go along with it.

Orphaned Girls Should Have Their Marriages Arranged Early

When a widow remarries she sometimes has an orphaned daughter not yet engaged. In such cases she should try to get a respectable relative to arrange a marriage for her daughter. She should also seek to have her daughter reared in the house of her future in-laws, with the marriage to take place after the girl has grown up. If the girl were to go along with the mother to her stepfather's house, she would not be able to clear herself if she were subjected to any humiliations.

For Women Old Age Is Particularly Hard to Bear

People say that, though there may be a hundred years allotted to a person's life, only a few reach seventy, for time quickly runs out. But for those destined to be poor, old age is hard to endure. For them, until about the age of fifty, the passage of twenty years seems like only ten; but after that age, ten years can feel as long as twenty. For women who live a long life, old age is especially hard to bear, because most women must rely on others for their existence. Before a woman's marriage, a good father is even more important than a good grandfather; a good brother is even more important than a good father; a good nephew is even more important than a good brother. After her marriage, a good husband is even more important than a good father-in-law; a good son is even more important than a good husband; and a good grandson is even more important than a good son. For this reason women often enjoy comfort in their youth but find their old age difficult to endure. It would be well for their relatives to keep this in mind.

It Is Difficult for Widows to Entrust Their Financial Affairs to Others

Some wives with stupid husbands are able to manage the family's finances, calculating the outlays and receipts of money and grain, without being cheated by anyone. Of those with degenerate husbands, there are also some who are able to manage the finances with the help of their sons without ending in bankruptcy. Even among those whose husbands have died and whose sons are young, there are occasionally women able to raise and educate their sons, keep the affection of all their relatives, manage the family business, and even prosper. All of these are wise and worthy women. But the most remarkable are the women who manage a household after their husbands have died leaving them with young children. Such women could entrust their finances to their husbands' kinsmen or their own kinsmen, but not all relatives are honorable, and the honorable ones are not necessarily willing to look after other people's business.

When wives themselves can read and do arithmetic, and those they entrust with their affairs have some sense of fairness and duty with regard to food, clothing, and support, then things will usually work out all right. But in most of the rest of the cases, bankruptcy is what happens.

Beware of Future Difficulties in Taking in Female Relatives

You should take into your own house old aunts, sisters, or other female relatives whose children and grandchildren are unfilial and do not support them. However, take precautions. After a woman dies, her unfilial sons or grandsons might make outrageous accusations to the authorities, claiming that the woman died from hunger or cold or left valuables in trunks. When the authorities receive such complaints, they have to investigate and trouble is unavoidable. Thus, while the woman is alive, make it clear to the public and to the government that the woman is bringing nothing with her but herself. Generally, in performing charitable acts, it is best to make certain that they will entail no subsequent difficulties.

Before Buying a Servant Girl or Concubine, Make Sure of the Legality

When buying a female servant or concubine, inquire whether it is legal for her to be indentured or sold before closing the deal. If the girl is impoverished and has no one to rely on, then she should be brought before the authorities to give an account of her past. After guarantors have been secured and an investigation conducted, the transaction can be completed. But if she is not able to give an account of her past, then the agent who offered her for sale should be questioned. Temporarily she may be hired on a salaried basis. If she is ever recognized by her relatives, she should be returned to them.

Hired Women Should Be Sent Back When Their Period of Service Is Over

If you hire a man's wife or daughter as a servant, you should return her to her husband or father on completion of her period of service. If she comes from another district, you should send her back to it after her term is over. These practices are the most humane and are widely carried out by the gentry in the Southeast. Yet there are people who do not return their hired women to their husbands but wed them to others instead; others do not return them to their parents but marry them off themselves. Such actions are the source of many lawsuits.

How can one not have sympathy for those separated from their relatives, removed from their hometowns, who stay in service for their entire lives with neither husbands nor sons. Even in death these women's spirits are left to wander all alone. How pitiful they are!

Translated by Patricia Ebrey

39

LONGING TO RECOVER THE NORTH

In the early years of the Southern Sung, most of those who have left written record expressed in some way their anguish over the loss of North China to the Jurchen. The emperor and his court called their capital at Hangzhou a temporary resting place. Literary men dreamed of leading armies to push out the barbarians. Officials pleaded for the court to stand firm and not compromise, believing an irredentist policy a matter of loyalty and patriotism.

To express their despair or heroic ambitions, many writers turned to poetry. Below are six poems by writers who lived through these years. The first is by one of the few women to make a name for herself as a poet. She had been living in the North when the Jurchen invaded and had to flee south to safety. The second is by a man much more famous as a general than as a poet. All are written in the ci, *or song lyric style, a style that gained popularity from late Tang times on.*

To the tune, "Butterflies Love Flowers"

The long night passes slowly
With few happy thoughts.
Then I dream of the capital and see the road back to
    it.
I could report on the spring there,
On how the moon and the flowers
Reflect on each other.

Although our food and drink are very simple,
The wine is fine and the plums sour,
Matching our feelings.
Tipsy, we stick flowers in our hair
But do not laugh.
How sad that both the spring and we humans are
    growing old.

         —by Li Qingchao (1084–1151+)

To the tune, "Full River Red"

My hair bristles in my helmet.
Standing by the balcony as the rain shower stops,
I look up to the sky and loudly let Heaven know
The strength of my passions.
My accomplishments over thirty years are mere dust.
I traveled eight thousand *li* with the clouds and the
    moon,
Never taking time to rest,
For a young man's hair grows white from despair.

The humiliation of the Jingkang period
Has not yet been wiped away.
The indignation I feel as a subject
Has not yet been allayed.
Let me drive off in a chariot
To destroy their base at Helan Mountain.
My ambition as a warrior

169

Is to satisfy my hunger with the flesh of the barbar-
ians,
Then, while enjoying a rest,
Slake my thirst with the blood of the tribesmen.
Give me the chance to try again
To recover our mountains and rivers
Then report to the emperor.

—by Yue Fei (1101–1141)

To the tune, "Telling My Innermost Feelings"

In years past I traveled ten thousand *li*
In search of glory.
I fought the mounted barbarians at Liangzhou.
The passes and rivers are already disappearing like
dreams,
And dirt encrusts my old fur uniform.

Before the barbarians could be exterminated
My hair turned gray.
My tears are useless.
I never expected that in this life,
My heart would remain at Mount Tian
While my body would grow old in this region of
rivers and lakes.

—by Lu You (1125–1210)

To the tune, "Song of the Six Prefectures"

I see their forts amid the forest when I gaze toward
the Huai River.
The cloud of dust darkens the sky and the frosty
wind is bitter.
The silence of the border region rends my heart.
Recalling the events of those years,
I conclude it was Heaven's decision,
For human efforts were of no avail.
The region of the Zhu and Si Rivers, where music
had been played,
Now smells of goats and sheep.
Right across the river, cattle graze at sunset
And tents are pitched all about.
See their king hunt at night,
His cavalry's torches lighting the river.
The sad sounds of their flutes send a chill through
our hearts.

I think of the arrows that hung at my waist and my
sword in its scabbard,

Now moth-eaten or covered with dust.
What did they accomplish? How fast the time has
gone.
My heart is still passionate but my years are num-
bered.
I see how our delightful capital plays music for the
foreigners.
The beacon fires have been extinguished, the soldiers
given rest.
Envoys, with their fine hats and carriages, hurry
back and forth, unfeeling.
Yet I have heard that the old who were left behind in
the central plains
Constantly look toward the south
Hoping to see the decorated imperial chariots.
Arriving at this place makes this traveler's feelings
well up
And his tears fall like rain.

—by Zhang Xiaoxiang (1132–1169)

To the tune, "The Partridge Sky"

In my prime, beneath my flag were ten thousand
warriors.
My horseman, in brocaded uniforms, burst across
the river.
At night the northern soldiers held fast to their silver
quivers.
At dawn our archers let fly their golden arrows.

Thinking back on those events,
I sigh over my present circumstances.
The spring wind will not darken my greying beard.
I've traded my ten-thousand word treatise on mili-
tary strategy
For my neighbor's book on planting trees.

—by Xin Qiji (1140–1207)

To the tune, "Prelude to the Water Melody"

The southern forces have not been seen for a long
time,
But not because we have run out of talent.
A man of initiative, with a pair of hands,
Could get us back our myriad heroes.
Happily our envoy moves east
As relentlessly as the river.
He will bow on entering the barbarian's tent,
Then hang his head on our streets!

In the land of Yao, the region of Shun, the realm of
  Yu,
There must be a few who have felt the humiliation of
  serving under barbarians.
Our vast land now smells of goats and sheep.
Where are the souls of the heroes of long ago?
When will we get through?

Why ask about the fate of the barbarians?
The red sun will rise in the sky.

—by Chen Liang (1143–1194)

Translated by Patricia Ebrey

40

ZHU XI'S CONVERSATIONS WITH HIS DISCIPLES

The revival of Confucianism in the Song period was accomplished in large part by great teachers who gathered around them adult students intent on learning more about the wisdom of the sages and how to apply it in their lives. The students were usually expecting to attempt the civil service examinations, but the most inspiring teachers urged their disciples to set their sights on the higher goals of knowledge and self-cultivation.

Perhaps the greatest of all these teachers was Zhu Xi (1130–1200). Immensely learned in the classics, commentaries, histories, and the teachings of his predecessors, Zhu Xi managed to serve several times in office, write, compile, or edit almost a hundred books, correspond with dozens of other scholars, and still regularly teach groups of disciples, many of whom stayed with him for years at a time. Zhu Xi considered himself a follower of the Cheng brothers Cheng Hao (1032–1085) and Cheng Yi (1033–1107), and elaborated their metaphysical theories about the workings of the cosmos in terms of principle (li) and qi (vital energies, material force, psychophysical stuff). In the conversations which his disciples recorded, however, he also discussed all sorts of other issues relevant to their understanding of nature, the past, and how to conduct their lives. The selection below is only a tiny fraction of the thousands of conversations his followers recorded.

A student asked, "Do dried and withered things have principle?"

Zhu Xi responded, "Once an object exists, it has a principle. Heaven didn't invent writing brushes; it was human beings who took rabbit hairs to make them. But once there were brushes, there was a principle for them."

A student asked, "Principle is something people and animals alike get from Heaven. What about insentient things? Do they also have principle?"

"Certainly they have principle," Zhu Xi responded. "For instance, boats can only travel on water and carts can only travel on land."

*   *   *

*   *   *

A student asked, "How can we distinguish the Way from principle?"

Zhu Xi responded, "The Way is the path. Principle is the pattern."

"Is it like the grain in wood?"

Zhu Xi answered, "Yes."

The student then commented, "If that is the case, the Way and principle seem to be the same."

"The word 'Way' covers a great deal," Zhu Xi said. "Principle consists in the many veins encompassed by the Way." He added, "The Way is the whole; principle is the fine structure."

* * *

Wang Zichong asked, "When I was in Hunan, I met a master who taught people only what actions to take."

Zhu Xi responded, "If a person does not understand the moral principles, how can he take actions?"

"This teacher explained, 'Once you practice it, you will understand it.'"

"Compare this to a person walking along a road," Zhu Xi said. "If he does not see it, how can he walk on it? Lots of people today teach people how to act. They all set their own standards, then teach them to others. Naturally a good person of average disposition does not have to probe into the principles of things or study extensively. But the sage wrote the *Great Learning* to help people move into the realm of sages. When people have fully grasped the principles, they will naturally be filial in their service to their parents, respectful to their elder brothers, and worthy of their friends' trust."

* * *

A student asked, "What should I do about being confused by different theories when I read?"

Zhu Xi answered, "Start with an open mind, then read one theory. Read one view before reading another. After you have read them again and again, what is right and wrong, useful and useless, will become apparent of itself. The process can be compared to trying to discover whether a person is good or bad. You observe him wherever he goes, notice what he says or does, and then know if he is good or bad." He also said, "You simply must have an open mind," and "Wash away your old opinions to let new ideas in."

* * *

A student asked, "What can I do to attain a reverent attitude?"

Zhu Xi said, "Simply do this: on the inside, have no foolish thoughts, on the outside, have no foolish actions."

* * *

A student asked, "How can a person develop his sincerity and reverence and get rid of his desires?"

Zhu Xi responded, "These are the end-points. Sincerity requires getting rid of all sorts of falseness. Reverence requires getting rid of all sorts of laziness. Desires should be blocked."

* * *

Zhengchun said, "I'd like to survey a great many books."

"Don't do that," Zhu Xi said. "Read one book thoroughly, then read another one. If you confusedly try to advance on several fronts, you will end up with difficulties. It's like archery. If you are strong enough for a five-pint bow, use a four-pint one. You will be able to draw it all the way and still have strength left over. Students today do not measure their own strength when reading books. I worry that we cannot manage what we already have set ourselves."

* * *

A student asked whether studying for the examinations would interfere with his efforts at real learning. Zhu Xi responded, "Master Cheng said, 'Don't worry about it interfering with your efforts, worry about it robbing you of your determination.' If you spend ten days a month preparing for the examinations, you will still have twenty days to do real study. If it changes your determination, however, there is no cure."

* * *

Renfu asked about the saying, "Human goodness is the principle underlying love."

Zhu Xi said, "This saying makes sense if you think about the mind, nature, and feelings. The mind is the master of the body. A person's nature consists in humanity, righteousness, propriety, and wisdom. They find their expression in the feelings of commiseration, shame, deference, and the ability to distinguish right from wrong. Commiseration is love, the beginning of human goodness. Human goodness is the substance, while love is an aspect of its function."

* * *

A student inquired, "Human nature is just the nature of Heaven and earth. In the beginning it didn't come from somewhere else, nor does it later go back to another place. It just seems this way from the condensing or dispersing of *qi*."

Zhu Xi responded, "You're right, it doesn't return anywhere at the end. It is like the reflection of the moon in a pan of water. Without the pan of water, there would be no reflection. No one could suppose the reflection flies into the sky to return to the moon. It's also like a flower dropping and then being gone. How could you think it went somewhere and next year will be reborn on this branch?"

The student also asked, "How can we analyze popular theories about anomalies, demons, and the like?"

Zhu Xi said, "Eighty percent of what ordinary people say is nonsense, but twenty percent is accurate. In most of these cases, the person's life span was not up when he was drowned, or murdered, or fell victim to a violent illness. Since his *qi* had not been exhausted, he was able to possess people. There are also cases of people who die suddenly and their *qi* hasn't yet completely dispersed because of the richness of their original endowment. Eventually their *qi* does disperse, for essence and *qi* are combined to produce people and things. As in the phrase, "The wandering of the spirit becomes change," there

will be no more *qi*. For when people talk about immortals, they only talk about ones from recent times. The immortals of antiquity are no longer seen. The *Zuo Commentary* tells the story of Boyu wreaking revenge, but no one sees his ghost today."

The student also asked, "Mr. Xie said, 'My ancestors' spirit is my own spirit.' Do you agree?"

"The sentence puts it very well," Zhu Xi responded. "Ancestors and descendants have only one *qi*. When sincerity and reverence are fully developed, they can affect each other. It can be compared to a large tree whose seeds are on the ground. When they grow and become trees, they are in fact that large tree."

* * *

A student asked, "What should an educated man do if he is marrying an ordinary person and he wishes to perform the proper rituals but the other family disagrees?"

Zhu Xi smiled, looked at Yigang for a long time, then said, "This is a waste of effort. All that is needed is to send someone to talk it over with the other family. The ancient rituals are less trouble. Why wouldn't they be willing to practice them?"

Zhiqing said, "If there are steps in the ancient rituals that are very hard to practice, you don't have to insist on them. For instance, the part about revolving the carriage wheels three times. This doesn't mean that you have to revolve the sedan chair three times." Even the master laughed in response to this.

Yigang said, "If the customary practices don't harm moral principle very much, would it be all right to retain a small number of them?"

Zhu Xi said, "Yes."

* * *

Zhu Xi said, "When wind acts on things, it enters into all of them. Today coffins are buried in the ground. To a small extent they get blown, some even blown over."

A student asked, "If one places on object on

the ground, even a fierce wind will not necessarily be able to move it. Since the ground is so strong and solid, how could wind blow through it to move things?"

Zhu Xi answered, "I think that in the ground when wind collects together and wants to come out, its power intensifies, but when it is out on the flat land, its *qi* disperses."

The student said, "Perhaps there is no such principle."

Zhu Xi said, "In Zhenghe county, a man buried his parent at a certain place. After the burial he heard sounds from the grave from time to time. His family thought that these sounds occurred because the place was good. After a long time the family property slowly declined and the descendants became poor. They thought that the place was unfortunate so took the coffin out to look at it. They found that one side had been smashed and was ruined. The place it had been was exactly in the front part of the pit, the part formed by curved bricks, where the coffin enters."

The student said, "Perhaps water caused this."

Zhu Xi answered, "No. If water had entered, how could there have been the sound of hitting? I don't know what the explanation is."

* * *

A student asked, "What should one do if before a parent died, he or she left instructions to have Buddhists perform the services?"

Zhu Xi responded, "This is a difficult question."

The student persisted, "So should he employ them or not?"

Zhu Xi said, "There are some things the heart of a child cannot bear to do. This issue requires careful consideration."

* * *

A student asked, "What if one's mother dies and one's father is still alive and the father wants to follow customary practices with regard to mourning garments, employ Buddhist monks for services, and have the body cremated?"

Zhu Xi responded, "What do you think?"

The student responded, "One could not obey."

Zhu Xi said, "The first two are superficial matters. If it is as you say, obeying would be all right. But cremation cannot be practiced."

Yong said, "Cremation destroys the parents' remains."

Zhu Xi added, "Discussing it along with mourning garments and Buddhist services shows an inability to recognize degrees of importance."

* * *

A student asked, "When Yang forces first moved and gave birth to people and things, it seems they all were produced at once, but according to the theory [of the great ultimate], it seems they were produced in stages."

Zhu Xi responded, "We can't give the order, but there must have been stages. Shao Yong calculated back 128,000. What was it like before that? There must have been a world before the great ultimate, like last night and this morning. Yin and Yang set things in motion all at once, but before then, there must have been dimness that gradually became clear. Therefore there were these stages present in it all along."

The student also asked, "If we thus speculate about the period before the great ultimate, will the period after it be similar?"

Zhu Xi responded, "Certainly. Master Cheng said, 'Movement and quiescence have no beginning; Yin and Yang have no starting point,' which clarifies it. Today on high mountains there are rocks with oyster shells in them, showing that a low place has become a high one. Further, oysters have to live in muddy sand, but now they are in rock, so what was soft became hard. The cosmos changes; there is no constancy."

* * *

A student asked, "Recently Liao Zihui said that when he visited you this year he asked you about Master Yanping's doctrine of quiet sitting, and that you had some disagreements with it. Is that so?"

Zhu Xi responded, "This is a difficult topic.

There is no harm in someone who understands principle sitting quietly, but it is not right to insist on quiet sitting. Those who understand principle thoroughly are naturally quiet. Nowadays, people insist on quiet sitting to get out of doing things. That won't do. I once heard Master Li say that when he first heard Master Luo lecture on the *Spring and Autumn Annals* he was not impressed and wondered how much understanding Luo had attained by quiet sitting at Mount Luo-fou. I also had doubts, but now I think it works. How can a person whose mind is excited perceive principle? One must be quiet to perceive it. What is called quiet sitting simply means having nothing on one's mind. When one's mind is thus clear, principle will make itself known, and the mind will become even clearer and quieter."

* * *

A student asked, "When selfish thoughts arise, I immediately weed them out, but even though I get rid of the stems and branches, the roots remain, and when I encounter a similar stimulus, they arise again. What can I do about it?"

Zhu Xi responded, "That is just the way it is. That is why [Confucius's disciple] Zengzi said, 'In trepidation, as though standing on a precipice or on thin ice.'"

* * *

Zhu Xi asked Kuang, "How long have you been here?"

"Eighty-five days."

"Aren't you going tomorrow?"

Kuang said, "Early tomorrow I will be saying goodbye."

Zhu Xi said, "Do you have any remaining doubts?"

"Right now I have no points that need clarifying, but as I apply myself, some will surely arise, so I will write you letters to ask for your instruction."

Zhu Xi said, "Just work hard at applying yourself. The biggest fear for a student is that he will grow lax. Do not expect instant results. If today you learn something or put something into prac-

tice, that is something positive. Just do not stop. Little by little you will gain a thorough understanding. If there are points you are not clear about, think about them yourself, don't rely on others or wait until you can ask questions. If there is no one to ask, you might give up. People advance in their learning when they can rid themselves of the desire to depend on others."

* * *

Dou said his dreams were very garbled. Zhu Xi responded, "The spiritual soul and the earthly soul interact to constitute sleep. The mind is still present and can think as usual. That is how dreams result." Zhu Xi then discussed his own experiences, "When I was sick for several days, I dreamed only about explaining the *Book of Documents*. Once when serving in office I dreamed only about judging legal cases."

Dou said, "These are still daily affairs."

Zhu Xi said, "Even though these are everyday affairs, still they shouldn't appear in dreams."

* * *

Every evening when his students gathered, one of the older ones would start to chat as soon as he sat down. Zhu Xi scolded him, "Sir, you are over forty and still do not understand the books you read, yet as soon as you sit down you talk about other people's affairs. On some recent nights you gentlemen have chatted idly until ten P.M. While we are gathered together, why don't you reflect on yourself or do serious work rather than talk about trivial things?" He then sighed and sighed.

* * *

Zhu Xi had an asthma attack and for days none of his students asked him any questions. One evening he summoned them to his room. The students still did not ask any questions. Zhu Xi angrily demanded, "You gentlemen are just sitting idly. If you are not going to do anything, why don't you go home? Why did you come here from so far away?"

* * *

A student asked, "What are the differences between the Buddhist and Taoist doctrines of nonbeing?"

Zhu Xi said, "To Laozi, being existed. This can be seen from his saying, 'I want to see the subtlety of nonbeing; I want to see the results of being.' The Buddhists consider Heaven and earth to be illusory and the four elements [earth, water, fire, and wind] to be temporary combinations. Thus to them everything is nonbeing."

Translated by Patricia Ebrey

41

THE ATTRACTIONS OF THE CAPITAL

The two Song capitals, Kaifeng and Hangzhou, were not merely administrative centers; they were also flourishing commercial cities. Both were located at centers of communication—Kaifeng at the juncture of the Yellow River and the Bian Canal, Hangzhou midway between the Yangzi and the seacoast, at the other end of the canal. In these two cities, with their concentration of people and wealth, a distinctly urban style of life evolved. Numerous amenities, including a great variety in food, entertainment, and luxury goods, were available to city residents. The division of labor reached a very high level, with many workers engaged in highly specialized enterprises.

Below is a description of the city of Hangzhou written in 1235. At that time the city encompassed seven to eight square miles.

MARKETS

During the morning hours, markets extend from Tranquility Gate of the palace all the way to the north and south sides of the New Boulevard. Here we find pearl, jade, talismans, exotic plants and fruits, seasonal catches from the sea, wild game— all the rarities of the world seem to be gathered here. The food and commodity markets at the Heavenly-View Gate, River Market Place, Central Square, Ba Creek, the end of Superior Lane, Tent Place, and Universal Peace Bridge are all crowded and full of traffic.

In the evening, with the exception of the square in front of the palace, the markets are as busy as during the day. The most attractive one is at Central Square, where all sorts of exquisite artifacts, instruments, containers, and hundreds of varieties of goods are for sale. In other marketplaces, sales, auctions, and exchanges go on constantly. In the wine shops and inns business also thrives. Only after the fourth drum does the city gradually quiet down, but by the fifth drum, court officials already start preparing for audiences and merchants are getting ready for the morning market again. This cycle goes on all year round without respite.

By far the most exciting time of the year is the Lantern Festival. Rows upon rows of businesses and private residences are all richly decorated, and numerous tents are set up for various spectacles and activities. (It is impossible for me to give an exhaustive description here.) During the Longxing reign [A.D. 1163–1164], the Imperial

Temple and the Noble Ladies' Quarters were located at Central Square, opposite the present imperial dye and bleach works. Once, after performing the state sacrifice, Emperor Xiaozong [r. 1162–1189] stopped to see the lantern displays. We saw the rows of imperial attendants in front of the curtain of the emperor's carriage, and the piles of cash that they spent to buy food. They also gave out cash and gifts liberally to the onlookers, some of whom were fortunate enough to get real gold or silver pieces.

Whenever there is an imperial procession or a religious parade, the carriages form a spectacular, long wall, the tip of one touching that of another.

On the lot in front of the wall of the city building, there are always various acting troupes performing, and this usually attracts a large crowd. The same kind of activity is seen in almost any vacant lot, including those at the meat market of the Great Common, the herb market at Charcoal Bridge, the book market at the Orange Grove, the vegetable market on the east side of the city, and the rice market on the north side. There are many more interesting markets, such as the candy center at the Five Buildings, but I cannot name them all.

COMMERCIAL ESTABLISMENTS

Various businesses are designated by the word "company," which is a taxation category imposed by the government and is used for all businesses dealing in commodities, regardless of their size. Even physicians and fortunetellers are included. Other trades sometimes also borrow the word "company" for their own use, such as liquor company and food company. Some businesses are called "gatherings," such as a flower gathering, fruit gathering, dried-fish gathering. . . . Artisans sometimes call their businesses "workshops," such as comb workshop, belt workshop, gold-and-silver plating workshop. There are some businesses that use unusual names; for example, shops dealing in the "seven treasures" (gold, silver, pearl, amber, etc.) may call themselves curio com-

panies, whereas a bathhouse may be designated a fragrant-water company.

In general, the capital attracts the greatest variety of goods and has the best craftsmen. For instance, the flower company at Superior Lane does a truly excellent job of flower arrangement, and its caps, hairpins, and collars are unsurpassed in craftsmanship. Some of the most famous specialties of the capital are the sweet-bean soup at the Miscellaneous Market, the pickled dates of the Ge family, the thick soup of the Guang family at Superior Lane, the fruit at the Great Commons marketplace, the cooked meats in front of Eternal Mercy Temple, Sister Song's fish broth at Penny Pond Gate, the juicy lungs at Flowing Gold Gate, the "lamb rice" of the Zhi family at Central Square, the boots of the Peng family, the fine clothing of the Xuan family at Southern Commons, the sticky rice pastry of the Zhang family, the flutes made by Gu the Fourth, and the Qiu family's Tatar whistles at the Great Commons.

WINE SHOPS

Among the various kinds of wine shops, the tea-and-food shops sell not only wine, but also various foods to go with it. However, to get seasonal delicacies not available in these shops, one should go to the inns, for they also have a menu from which one can make selections. The pastry-and-wine shops sell pastries with duckling and goose fillings, various fixings of pig tripe, intestines and blood, fish fat and spawn; but they are rather expensive. The mansion-style inns are either decorated in the same way as officials' mansions or are actually remodeled from such mansions. The garden-style inns are often located in the suburbs, though some are also situated in town. Their decoration is usually an imitation of a studio-garden combination. Among other kinds of wine shops are the straight ones that do not sell food. There are also the small retail wine shops which sell house wine as well as wine from other stores. Instead of the common emblem—a painted branching twig—used by all other winehouses, they have bamboo fences and canvas awnings. To go drinking in such a place is called "hitting the cup," meaning that a person drinks only one cup; it is therefore not the most respectable place and is unfit for polite company.

The "luxuriant inns" have prostitutes residing in them, and the wine chambers are equipped with beds. At the gate of such an inn, on top of the red gardenia lantern, there is always a cover made of bamboo leaves. Rain or shine, this cover is always present, serving as a trademark. In other inns, the girls only keep the guests company. If a guest has other wishes, he has to go to the girl's place. . . .

The emblems of wine shops are a branching twig painted red, crimson curtains with laces of red and gold tones, and a gardenia lantern. It is said that this convention started with the visit of Emperor Guo (of the Five Dynasties) to the Pan-lou winehouse in Bianjing.

The wine chambers are usually named. If the building has several stories, they may be distinguished by the term "mountain." Thus there may be a first mountain, a second mountain, a third mountain, etc. These "mountains" are figurative heights indicating the capacity for wine. For this reason, when you go to a wine shop, refrain from going upstairs if you only intend to order a few drinks and to stay for a short time. If you do not order too many drinks, you can sit downstairs, in the area designated as "tables facing the door and the streets."

After you are seated, the waiter will bring you a few sample delicacies. He will then ask you what you would like to have and in what quantity. Only afterwards will he bring you your order. People who are unfamiliar with this custom often start eating these samples and make themselves the laughingstock of the day.

The expenses incurred on visiting an inn can vary widely. If you order food, but no drinks, it is called "having the lowly soup-and-stuff," and is quite inexpensive. If your order of wine and food falls within the range of 100–5000 cash, it is called a small order. However, if you ask for female company, then it is most likely that the girls will order the most expensive delicacies. You are well advised to appear shrewd and experienced, so as not to be robbed. One trick, for instance, in ordering wines is to give a large order, of say, ten bottles, but open them one by one. In the end, you will probably have used only five or six bottles of the best. You can then return the rest. . . .

RESTAURANTS

Most restaurants here are operated by people from the old capital, like the lamb rice shops which also serve wine. There is an art to ordering dishes: if you wish to fill yourself quickly, then you should first order the heavy items (such as bean soup, rib-and-rice, sticky-rice, etc.) and then the light ones (such as fried gizzards, tripe, and kidneys); if you prefer to enjoy the good taste of the foods before you fill yourself, then order the light dishes first and the heavy ones last.

The so-called southern style is a misnomer. These restaurants were originally established in the old capital to serve southerners who were not used to the northern diet. Now that they *are* in the South, the term southern style becomes misleading. At any rate, noodles and seafood are the specialty of these restaurants, and each has its own house menu.

There are special food shops such as meat-pie shops and vegetable-noodle shops, but these are not very formal, and therefore you should not invite your guests to eat there. The vegetarian restaurants cater to religious banquets and vegetarian dinners. The Quzhou rice shops are reputed for steamed rice and home-style food; they are good places to go to eat your fill but not suitable for elegant company.

There are also shops specializing in snacks. Depending on the season, they sell a variety of delicacies from fried meats, pastries, stewed ginger, and soy beans to pickled pig's feet. In the evening, food venders of all sorts parade the streets and alleys, supporting trays on their heads or carrying baskets on a pole, and chanting their trade songs. The residents in the capital are used to them, but visitors from other parts of the country find them a curious breed. . . .

TEAHOUSES

In large teahouses there are usually paintings and calligraphies by famous artists on display. In the old capital, only restaurants had them, to enable their patrons to while away the time as the food was being prepared, but now it is customary for teahouses as well to display paintings and the like.

The teahouses also sell salted soybean soup in the winter and plum-flower wine in the summer. During the Shaoxing reign [1131–1162], teahouses used to play the plum-flower wine tune and serve tea with a ladle just as in wine shops.

Often many young men gather in teahouses to practice singing or playing musical instruments. To give such amateur performances is called "getting posted."

A "social teahouse" is more of a community gathering place than a mere place that sells tea. Often tea drinking is but an excuse, and people are rather generous when it comes to the tips.

There is a special kind of teahouse where pimps and gigolos hang out. Another kind is occupied by people from various trades and crafts who use them as places to hire help, buy apprentices, and conduct business. These teahouses are called "trade heads."

"Water teahouses" are in fact pleasure houses, the tea being a cover. Some youths are quite willing to spend their money there, which is called "dry tea money."

Other jargon calls for explanation: A "teakettle carrier" does more than just bring wine and tea to private households; he also carries messages and functions as a social go-between. "Dirty tea" designates the kind of street vagabonds who, in the name of selling tea, actually beg for cash or gifts.

THE FOUR DEPARTMENTS AND SIX OFFICES

For the households of the noble and the wealthy there are the Four Departments and Six Offices in charge of entertainment. They manage dinner parties and keep related matters in good order. In the commercial areas of the capital, one can also find people who specialize in these matters. Thus, whenever there is occasion for an elaborate party, a middle-class household simply hires these professionals to manage everything.

The Setup Department is responsible for preparing the place for the occasion: setting up tents and awnings, banquet tables and seats; providing screens, embroidered hangings, paintings, calligraphy, and so on. The Kitchen Department is in charge of the design, purchase, and preparation of food. The Tea and Wine Department takes care of the drinking needs of the guests, offering tea and drinks, warming up wines, and opening wine bottles. It is also responsible for ushering guests to their seats and for escorting them out at the end of the feast. The Serving Department specializes in serving food and drinks and in waiting on the guests.

The Fruit Office is in charge of making decorative arrangements of various kinds of fruits, as well as supplying seasonal fruits that go well with wines. The Sweetmeats Office supplies preserved fruits and sweetmeats as appetizers. The Vegetable Office provides pickled and fresh vegetables that please the eye as well as the palate. The Oil and Candle Office is in charge of illumination, performing such duties as setting up candle holders and lanterns, snuffing candles, and lighting incense. The Perfume and Medicine Office is equipped with medicine chests and supplies sachets, exotic perfumes, and herb medicines that help sober up the guests who have had too much to drink. The Decor Office is responsible for hanging up paintings and decorations, designing and displaying flower arrangements, as well as for keeping the banquet hall clean and orderly.

If the professionals of the Four Departments and Six Offices are competent, then both the host and the guests will be much more at ease. On the other hand, if these people should make mistakes, the guests will also understand that it is not the host's fault. After the banquet, compensations and tips should be meted out in the following order: the chef first, the persons in charge of tea and wine next, the entertainers last.

ENTERTAINMENT CENTERS

The entertainment centers commonly called "tiles" are places where people gather and are just as easily dispersed. It is not clear when the term first came into use, but in the old capital the entertainment centers were places where many dissipated people—scholars as well as commoners—gathered, and where many young men were ruined.

In these centers there are schools for musicians offering thirteen different courses, among which the most significant is opera. The old music schools had such divisions as the flute department, big-drum department, stick-drum department, clapper department, balloon-guitar department, zither department, dance department, singing department, opera department, and military acts department. Each of these had a department head, above whom were school administrators, disciplinary officers, and masters of ceremonies. All were filled by appointment. The players wore loose robes of purple, scarlet, or green, with yellow aprons. The actors wore headdresses; the other musicians wore ordinary caps. There were also boys' and girls' troupes, as well as a military band; the latter gave rise to the present-day custom of the band of musicians on horseback parading behind the emperor's carriage. . . .

In each scene of an operatic performance there are four or five performers who first act out a short, wellknown piece, which is called the gorgeous piece; then they give a performance of the opera itself, which is called the second piece. . . . The opera is usually based on history and teaches a moral lesson, which may also be political criticism in disguise. . . . A miscellaneous act is a comic scene taken from an operatic performance. In the old capital, the stock characters of a miscellaneous act were the rustic villagers from Shandong or Hebei, who were the funniest country bumpkins in the eyes of the citizens of the capital. . . .

The hundred games used to be the official entertainment of the old capital. Wrestling and fighting are categorized as butting games; there are also displays of different styles of boxing techniques. The experts in kicking games feature in the ritual plucking of the golden rooster at the general pardon after an emperor's coronation. They can climb high poles, do somersaults, walk on stilts, juggle spears, do the death dance, play with swords, display horsemanship, and so on.

The various skills of the entertainers have their respective high-sounding names. Their acts include: kicking bottles, juggling plates, kicking musical stones, twirling drumsticks, kicking writing brushes, and playing ball. There are also performances with trained insects, fish or bears, fireworks, fire shows, water shows, puppet shows, and marksmanship of all kinds.

Puppet shows include string puppets, cane-top puppets, water puppets, and flesh puppets. The stories are usually fictitious and fantastic. Shadow plays originated in the old capital. At first the figures were made with white paper; later they were made ofleather and painted various colors. The stories of the shadow plays are pretty much the same as those used by the storytellers; generally speaking, they are a mixture of truth and fiction. The loyal and righteous are given a handsome appearance, wheras the wicked and treacherous are depicted asmonstrously ugly—a kind of implicit criticism that is easily understood by the people in the streets. The storytellers can be divided into four groups: those who specialize in social tales, mysteries, and miracle tales; those who deal in military adventures; those who explicate sutras by telling religious tales; and those who relate historical events. . . .

CLUBS

For men of letter, there is a unique West Lake Poetry Society. Its members include both scholars residing in the capital and visiting poets from other parts of the country; over the years, many famous poets have been associated with this society. People interested in verse riddles may join such clubs as South Studio, North Studio, or West

Studio, all of which are situated on the right bank of the Zhe River. People who like sports form various football and archery clubs.

The Upper Indian Temple has a Luminous Society, the members of which are qealthy Buddhists from the city and its suburbs. They donate incense, candles, and cash to help the temple with its expenses. The Tea Society provides free tea for the believers whenever any of the Buddhist temples holds a service. The Dharma Propagation Temple in the city has a Pruifying Society, which gathers men on the 17th day and women on the 18th day of each month for preaching and explicating sutras. At the end of each year it also holds a seven-day-and-seven-night service. In the West Lake region, a let-live campaign is launched in the fourth month of each year to return fishermen's catches to the lake. There are also numerous sutra societies associated with various temples, which hold rituals on the birthdays of various saints and deities.

Other groups include the Physical Fitness Club, Anglers' Club, Occult Club, Young Girls' Chorus, Exotic Foods Club, Plants and Fruits Club, Antique Collectors' Club, Horse Lovers' Club, and Refined Music Society.

GARDENS

The gardens within the sity limits include Ten-Thousand-Pines Ridge, Garden of Good Views, Eastern Mountains, Plum Pavillion, etc. . . . Outside of the eastern New Gate there are the Eastern Imperial Garden and Five-Willows Imperial Garden. To the west of the city is the Vista Imperial Garden. . . . To the west of the South Mountain Long Bridge there is Revels Imperial Garden; in front of the Pure Mercy Temple there is a Screen-Mountain Imperial Garden; facing the Cloud Summit Tower there is a Pearl Garden. . . . I do not know all the names of the private gardens owned by thenoble and the wealthy families. The garden next to Bao Mountain is most famous for its peach blossoms. Other gardens specialize in rare plants. . . .

BOATS

The capital is encircled by a river on the left side and by West Lake on the right; thus the most convenient way to travel is by boat. The boats for hire on West Lake vary greatly in size. Some are fifty feet long and have a capacity of more than one hundred passengers; others are twenty to thirty feet long and can take thirty to fifty passengers. All of them are exquisitely constructed, with carvings on the railings and paintings on the beams. They sail so smoothly that the passengers may forget that they are on water. These boats are for hire in all seasons and never lack patrons. They are also well equipped with everything; a tourist can get on board in the morning, drink wine, and enjoy himself; at dusk he may walk home by following a trail. It is not tiring but is rather expensive. Some wealthy families have their own pleasure boats, and these are even more exquisitely built and more luxuriously fitted out.

Dragon boat competitions are held in spring at the West Lake and in autumn at the Zhe River. The dragon boats are light and swift and make a grand spectacle. . . . In early and mid-autumn there are swimmers in the Zhe River, who, brandishing pennants and poles, display the most breath-taking skills. I believe this is a unique attraction of the capital.

SPECIALTY STORES

The commercial area of the capital extends from the old Qing River Market to the Southern Commons on the south and to the border on the north. In includes the Central Square, which is also called the Center of Five Flowers. From the north side of the Five Buildings to South Imperial Boulevard, there are more than one hundred gold, silver, and money exchanges. On the short walls in front of these stores, there are piles of gold, silver, and copper cash: these are called "the money that watches over the store." Around these exchanges there are also numerous gold and silversmiths. The pearl marts are situated between the north side of Cordial Marketplace and Southtown Marketplace. Most deals made here involve over ten thousand cash. A score of pawnshops are scattered in between, all owned by very wealthy people and dealing only in the most valuable objects.

Some famous fabric stores sell exquisite brocade and fine silk which are unsurpassed elsewhere in the country. Along the river, close to the Peaceful Ford Bridge, there are numerous fabric stores, fan shops, and lacquerware and porcelain shops. Most other cities can only boast of one special product; what makes the capital unique is that it gathers goods from all places. Furthermore, because of the large population and busy commercial traffic, there is a demand for everything. There are even shops that deal exclusively in used paper or in feathers, for instance.

WAREHOUSES

In Liu Yong's [ca. 1045] poem on Qiantang, we read that there were about ten thousand families residing here; but that was before the Yuanfeng reign [1078–1085]. Today, having been the "temporary capital" for more than a hundred years, the city has over a million households. The suburbs extend to the south, west, and north; all are densely populated and prosperous in commerce as well as in agriculture. The size of the suburbs is comparable to a small county or prefecture, and it takes several days to travel through them. This again reflects the prosperity of the capital.

In the middle of the city, enclosed by the Northern Pass Dam, is White Ocean Lake. Its water spreads over several tens of *li*. Wealthy families have built scores of warehouse complexes along this waterfront. Each of these consists of several hundred to over a thousand rooms for the storage needs of the various businesses in the capital and of traveling merchants. Because these warehouses are surrounded by water, they are not endangered by fires or thieves, and therefore they offer a special convenience. In other commercial centers such as Shashi and Huangchi of Taiping prefecture there are no such facilities.

HUSTLERS

These are the same breed of people as the retainers of Prince Mengchang.* They have no regular profession, but live off of other people by providing trivial services.

Some of these hustlers are students who failed to achieve any literary distinction. Though able to read and write, and play musical instruments and chess, they are not highly skilled in any art. They end up being a kind of guide for young men from wealthy families, accompanying them in their pleasure-seeking activities. Some also serve as guides or assistants to officials on business from other parts of the country. The lowliest of these people actually engage themselves in writing and delivering invitation cards and the like for brothels.

There are others who make their living entertaining at private parties. In the past some of these people were quite well versed in activities such as play-acting, jesting, playing musical instruments, juggling, singing, reciting poems, playing wine games, swimming, and boxing. Some who specialize in training birds are called leisure practitioners. They train hawks, eagles, pigeons, doves, quail, and cocks for fighting and gambling.

There are also professional go-betweens, nicknamed "water-treaders," whose principal targets are pleasure houses, where they flatter the wealthy young patrons, run errands for them, and help make business deals. Some gather at brothels or scenic attractions and accost the visitors. They beg for donations for "religious purposes," but in fact use the money to make a living for themselves and their families. If you pay attention to them, they will become greedy; if you ignore them, they will force themselves on you and will not stop until you give in. It requires art to deal with these people appropriately.

* A prince of the state of Qi in the third century B.C. famous for attracting retainers

THE THREE TEACHINGS

There are civil and military schools inside as well as outside the capital. Besides lineage schools, capital schools, and county schools, there are at least one or two village schools, family schools, private studios, or learning centers in every neighborhood. Often the students' recitation of texts from one school is echoed by that of another. In the years when the imperial examinations are held, the students from the capital sometimes do quite well.

Buddhist temples are numerous. There are around one hundred Zen monasteries (such as the Numinous Mystery and Great Filial Piety monasteries) and a similar number of the Vinaya Sect temples (such as the Bright Blessings and Immortality temples) and seminaries (such as the Great Dharma Propagation, Grove of Wisdom, and Source of Wisdom seminaries). There are also convents, religious societies, and various places of worship. Whenever a big monastery holds a service, these small groups also attend. Some of the masters are highly accomplished.

Daoist worship is held in the Imperial Great Unity Temple, the Eternal Happiness Temple, and various other temples, studios, and halls. The Daoist temples house monks who have abandoned the mundane world, as well as masters from all parts of the country. There have been frequent reports of miracles and epiphanies of divine beings, which other people have recorded.

Translated by Clara Yu

42

THE MUTUAL RESPONSIBILITY SYSTEM

Periodically through Chinese history, the government tried to organize people to make them easier to rule. One recurrent method was to group people into units of five or ten households, then group five or ten of these units into a superior unit, and so on, in successive levels up to the county (xian). In the Song, Wang Anshi set up such a mutual responsibility system (baojia). Ten households formed a bao, *with a head chosen from among the households heads of the* bao. *Five* bao *formed a large* bao, *also with a head, and ten large* bao *formed a general* bao. *The duties of these various* bao *were supposed to be restricted to detecting and reporting criminals, but other duties, involving tax collection and military service, tended to be added from time to time.*

Below is a notice about the functioning of the mutual responsibility system posted by Zhen Dexiu (1178–1235) while he was magistrate of Pucheng county in Fujian province. From it we can infer some of the people's uneasiness about the system as well as some of the practical difficulties the government faced in trying to enforce it. This notice is also evidence of the kind of knowledge ordinary people would have had about government policies, since certainly few of them ever read the formal regulations or edicts.

In ancient times people regarded an obligation toward a neighbor as a significant matter. They considered themselves friends whether they were in the village or elsewhere. They assisted each other in the duties of guarding their villages and they supported each other in times of illness. Our local units of today are actually derived from such ancient practices, but now very few people realize the meaning of such organizations, and neighbors often treat each other like strangers.

Recently the mutual responsibility system (*baojia*) has been reactivated by the government. This is something which pleases me very much, for not only can the mutual responsibility system provide us with protection against the unexpected, but it will promote the ancient practice of neighborly relationships among people who live in close proximity. Because of uncertainties as to how to make the division into geographical units, this system has not yet been put into effect. Nevertheless, people in the various communities have already expressed suspicion about the system out of fear that it will mean obligatory labor. I have listened attentively to the arguments of the elders and would like to point out that the practice of the mutual responsibility system will be limited primarily to dealing with thefts and negligence. For instance, if one family is robbed, it usually cannot catch the thief; whereas when the whole community is engaged in the search, the thief will have no place to hide. If a house is on fire and the family cannot extinguish it, the neighbors will offer their assistance, and the fire will certainly be put out. Military activities such as fighting against rebels from other parts of the nation will be responsibility of the militia forces, the recruited soldiers, and the national guard; our people will not be required to perform such duties.

Generally, only one man per family will be required to enlist. Poor scholars with no servants and single men who are old or physically unfit are exempt from duty. Every five days there will be roll call, just to keep a rough count of the number of people involved. Sometimes there will be a call to patrol the region, but usually it will not be necessary. These are my plans, but up to now most of our citizens have not understood them and thus have been skeptical of the program. They fail to see that the mutual responsibility system is designed to protect them, not disturb them, and that they have nothing to be apprehensive about. I have lived here six years, and all the people in this city are my neighbors. I have always wanted to meet each one of you, yet there never seemed to be an opportune occasion. I would like to hold a general assembly now, but my resources do not allow it. I will, however, make a joint sacrifice with one hundred neighboring families at our local temple in the middle of this month. I will provide all the offerings which will, after the ceremony, be shared by everyone present—scholars, farmers, artisans, or merchants—without discrimination. This will be in accord with the ancient principle of community harmony. As to the seating, however, there will be assigned areas for each group.

On that day I will explain to you the meaning of a friendly neighborhood as well as the purpose of the mutual responsibility system to dispel your doubts. I will have the gathering announced in all areas under my administration and have this notice posted on doors so that everyone will be informed of it.

Translated by Clara Yu

43

ON FARMING

A major factor in allowing the population of Song China to reach one hundred million was the increased settlement of the South and the expansion of intensive wet-field rice cultivation. Peasants' work patterns adjusted to growing two or sometimes even three successive crops on the same field, part of a general tendency toward applying more time, labor, and fertilizer to smaller pieces of land. Because intensive techniques were so productive, the government often took steps to encourage their adoption, even distributing illustrated guides.

Below are selections from a treatise on farming written by Chen Pu in 1149. It discusses both wet-field cultivation and methods used for vegetables and other crops. This treatise was aimed at those actively engaged in agriculture and enjoyed wide circulation for several centuries. This and other popular texts on agriculture are the best sources we have for what peasants may have thought of their daily work.

FINANCE AND LABOR

All those who engage in business should do so in accordance with their own capacity. They should refrain from careless investment and excessive greed, lest in the end they achieve nothing. Tradition has it, "Profit comes from a little; confusion comes from a lot." In the farming business, which is the most difficult business to manage, how can you afford not to calculate your financial and labor capacities carefully? Only when you are certain that you have sufficient funds and labor to assure success should you launch an enterprise. Anyone who covets more than he can manage is likely to fall into carelessness and irresponsibility; under such conditions, he cannot reap even one or two out of every ten portions, and success will certainly elude him. Thus, to procure more land is to increase trouble, not profit.

On the other hand, anyone who plans carefully, begins with good methods, and continues in the same way can reasonably expect success and does not have to rely on luck. The proverb says, "Owning a great deal of emptiness is less desirable than reaping from a narrow patch of land." Too true! I have the following example to prove my point. In ancient times there was a great archer, Pu Qie, who was able to draw a delicate bow and string two orioles on one arrow, high in the clouds. The reason he could achieve such dexterity in aiming was that he had more strength than needed to draw the bow. If the bow had been heavier than he could handle, he would have trembled and staggered under its weight; then how could he have gotten his game? By extension, for the farmer who is engaged in the management of fields, the secret lies not in expanding the farmland, but in balancing finance and labor. If the farmer can achieve that, he can expect prosperity and abundance.

TOPOGRAPHY

Concerning mountains, rivers, plateaus, lakes, and swamps, their altitudes differ and so their temperatures and degrees of fertility do also. Generally speaking, high lands are cold, their springs chilly, their soil cool. The tradition that "In the high mountains there is more winter," refers to the constant windy cold. Also, these areas are more prone to droughts. On the other hand, low lands are usually fertile but prone to flooding. Thus, different methods of land management are required for different terrain.

In the case of high land, choose a spot where water can converge and dig a reservoir of appropriate size. (For every ten *mu* of land, two to three *mu* should be set aside for the reservoir.) In late spring and early summer when rainfall is frequent, strengthen the embankments and deepen and widen the reservoir so that it will have enough space to contain the water. On the embankments plant mulberry and pomegranate trees on which cows can be tethered. The cows will be comfortable under the shade of the trees; the embankments will be strengthened because the cows constantly tread on them; and the mulberry trees will grow beautifully because of the nourishing water. Whenever there is a drought, the water in the reservoir can be released for irrigation, and whenever there is heavy rainfall, the crops will not be harmed by floods.

As to lowlands, because they are easily flooded, you must study their topography and build high, wide embankments surrounding the area most likely to be inundated. On the slopes of the embankments vegetables, hemp, wheat, millet, and beans can be planted. On either side you can also plant mulberry trees and raise cows. Because of convenient water and grass, the cows can be successfully raised with little effort.

For lakes and marshy swamps, use the "rape-turnip soil" system. First, bind logs together to form a base for the field. Let the base float on water but remain tied to land. Then lay the "rape-turnip soil" on the wooden platform and plant there. As the platform floats on water, it rises and falls with the water level, so the crops are never lost to floods.

PLOWING

Early and late plowing both have their advantages. For the early rice crop, as soon as the reaping is completed, immediately plow the fields and expose the stalks to glaring sunlight. Then add manure and bury the stalks to nourish the soil. Next, plant beans, wheat, and vegetables to ripen and fertilize the soil so as to minimize the next year's labor. In addition, when the harvest is good, these extra crops can add to the yearly income. For late crops, however, do not plow until spring. Because the rice stalks are soft but tough, it is necessary to wait until they have fully decayed to plow satisfactorily.

In the mountains, plateaus, and wet areas, it is usually cold. The fields here should be deeply plowed and soaked with water released from reservoirs. Throughout the winter, the water will be absorbed, and the snow and frost will freeze the soil so that it will become brittle and crumbly. At the beginning of spring, spread the fields with decayed weeds and leaves and then burn them, so that the soil will become warm enough for the seeds to sprout. In this way, cold as the freezing springs may be, they cannot harm the crop. If you fail to treat the soil this way, then the arteries of the fields, being soaked constantly by freezing springs, will be cold, and the crop will be poor.

When it is time to sow the seeds, sprinkle lime in the wet soil to root out harmful insect larvae.

THE SIX KINDS OF CROPS

There is an order to the planting of different crops. Anyone who knows the right timing and follows the order can cultivate one thing after another, and use one to assist the others. Then there will not be a day without planting, nor a month without harvest, and money will be coming in throughout the year. How can there then be any worry about cold, hunger, or lack of funds?

Plant the nettle hemp in the first month. Apply manure in intervals of ten days and by the fifth or sixth month it will be time for reaping. The women should take charge of splicing thread and weaving cloth out of the hemp.

Plant millet in the second month. It is necessary to sow the seeds sparsely and then roll cart wheels over the soil to firm it up; this will make the millet grow luxuriantly, its stalks long and its grains full. In the seventh month the millet will be harvested, easing any temporary financial difficulties.

There are two crops of oil hemp. The early crop is planted in the third month. Rake the field to spread out the seedlings. Repeat the raking process three times a month and the hemp will grow well. It can be harvested in the seventh or the eighth month.

In the fourth month plant beans. Rake as with hemp. They will be ripe by the seventh month. In mid-fifth month plant the late oil hemp. Proceed as with the early crop. The ninth month will be reaping time.

After the 7th day of the seventh month, plant radishes and cabbage.

In the eighth month, before the autumn sacrifice to the god of the earth, wheat can be planted. It is advisable to apply manure and remove weeds frequently. When wheat grows from the autumn through the spring sacrifices to the god of the earth, the harvest will double and the grains will be full and solid.

The *Book of Songs* says, "The tenth month is the time to harvest crops." You will have a large variety of crops, including millet, rice, beans, hemp, and wheat and will lack nothing needed through the year. Will you ever be concerned for want of resources?

HOUSING

The ancient kings who reigned over subjects in all four directions and took advantage of the earth in the right seasons must have had good principles. They decreed that five *mu* of land should be set aside for housing, out of which two and a half *mu* were for a cottage erected in the center of the fields.

In the period of plowing and sowing, move into this cottage to facilitate management and provide supplies for the farm workers. At the same time start a garden and plant vegetables. Along the walls, mulberry trees can be planted for the breeding of silkworms. In this manner you will live up to the system exemplified by the ancients.

When the ninth month has come, transform the vegetable garden into a harvest processing area. In the tenth month, when the harvest is done and the year's work finished, you can rest as compensation for your labor of plowing and sowing in the spring. Now move the whole family, both old and young, back to the house. For if you stay too long in the cottage in the fields, your house will become dilapidated as a result of neglect.

FERTILIZER

At the side of the farm house, erect a compost hut. Make the eaves low to prevent the wind and rain from entering it, for when the compost is exposed to the moon and the stars, it will lose its fertility. In this hut, dig a deep pit and line it with bricks to prevent leakage. Collect waste, ashes, chaff, broken stalks, and fallen leaves and burn them in the pit; then pour manure over them to make them fertile. In this way considerable quantities of compost are acquired over time. Then, whenever sowing is to be done, sieve and discard stones and tiles, mix the fine compost with the seeds, and plant them sparsely in pinches. When the seedlings have grown tall, again spinkle the compost and bank it up against the roots. These methods will ensure a double yield.

Some people say that when the soil is exhausted, grass and trees will not grow; that when the *qi* [material force] is weak, all living things will be stunted; and that after three to five years of continuous planting, the soil of any field will be exhausted. This theory is erroneous because it fails to recognize one factor: by adding new, fertile soil, enriched with compost, the land can be reinforced in strength. If this is so, where can the alleged exhaustion come from?

WEEDING

The *Book of Songs* says, "Root out the weeds. Where the weeds decay, there the grains will grow luxuriantly." The author of the *Book of Rites* also remarks, "The months of midsummer are advantageous for weeding. Weeds can fertilize the fields and improve the land." Modern farmers, ignorant of these principles, throw the weeds away. They do not know that, if mixed with soil and buried deep under the roots of rice seedlings, the weeds will eventually decay and the soil will be enriched; the harvest, as a result, will be abundant and of superior quality.

There is method to weeding. In the Zhou dynasty, Minister Ti, who was in charge of weeding, ruled that, "In the spring the weeds begin to sprout and grow, and in the summer one has to go and cut them down daily." This is to say, in the summer the weeds grow easily, therefore one should labor every day to curb their growth. "In the autumn one should hoe them with measure." This means chopping off the seeds so that they will not reach the soil. "In winter one should go and plow the fields daily." That is because the crops have now been reaped, and plowing through the roots of the weeds will expose them to snow and frost, so that they decay and do not revive the next year. Also, they can serve as fertilizer for the soil.

CONCENTRATION

If something is thought out carefully, it will succeed; if not, it will fail; this is a universal truth. It is very rare that a person works and yet gains nothing. On the other hand, there is never any harm in trying too hard.

In farming it is especially appropriate to be concerned about what you are doing. Mencius said, "Will a farmer discard his plow when he leaves his land?" Ordinary people will become idle if they have leisure and prosperity. Only those who love farming, who behave in harmony with it, who take pleasure in talking about it and think about it all the time will manage it without a moment's negligence. For these people a day's work results in a day's gain, a year's work in a year's gain. How can they escape affluence?

As to those with many interests who cannot concentrate on any one and who are incapable of being meticulous, even if they should come by some profit, they will soon lose it. For they will never understand that the transformation of the small into the big is the result of persistent effort.

To indulge in pleasure and discard work whenever the chance arises and to meet matters only when they become urgent is never the right way of doing things. Generally speaking, ordinary people take pride in having the prosperity to indulge in temporary leisure. If there should be a man who remains diligent in prosperity, everyone else will mark him as a misfit, so great is their lack of understanding!

Translated by Clara Yu

44

A MONGOL GOVERNOR

The Mongols began as one of many nomadic tribes in the area north of China proper. Their rise and rapid creation of a world empire began when Chinggis [Ghengis] (d. 1227) was declared the Khan in 1206. During the course of the next sixty years they conquered China as well as much of central and west Asia. In the process the Mongols visited great destruction on settled populations everywhere but also created the conditions for unprecedented exchange of ideas and goods across Asia. China fell to the Mongols in stages. The Xia (Tanguts) submitted in 1211. The Jin (Jurchens) fell bit by bit from 1215 to 1234. Song territory in Sichuan fell in 1252, but most of the south not until the 1270s.

The Mongol conquerors could not replace all the local administrators with their own people, but when they retained subjects of the former states they had to supervise them closely. Below is a biography of a Mongol officer given the task of supervising the prefects and magistrates of several areas in North China during the decades when the Mongols were consolidating their rule.

This biography is an epitaph meant to be inscribed on stone and buried in the grave. Such epitaphs were a well-established genre of private history-writing, usually written or commissioned by the subject's children. As such they naturally drew attention to the person's merits and were silent on his or her failings. In this case the author was a Chinese literati who put his emphasis on the qualities Chinese officials could admire in this Mongol administrator.

EPITAPH FOR THE HONORABLE MENGGU, GREAT GENERAL OF HUAIYUAN, GOVERNOR OF HUAIMENG ROUTE, AND MILITARY ADMINISTRATOR OF SEVERAL ARMIES

Emperor Taizu [Chinggis Khan] received the mandate of Heaven and subjugated all regions. When Emperor Taizong [Ogodei Khan] succeeded, he revitalized the bureaucratic system and made it more efficient and organized. At court, one minister supervised all the officials and helped the emperor rule. In the provinces, commanderies and counties received instructions from above and saw that they got carried out. Prefects and magistrates were as a rule appointed only after submitting [to the Mongols]. Still one Mongol, called the governor, was selected to supervise them. The prefects and magistrates all had to obey his orders.

The fortune of the common people and the quality of the government both were entirely dependent on the wisdom of the governor.

Zhangde, one of the ten routes, is crucial to communication between north and south. In the fourth month of 1236, the court deemed Menggu capable of handling Zhangde, so promoted him from the post of legal officer of the troops of Quduqu to be its governor. At the time, the Jin had fallen only three years earlier. The common people were not yet free of the army, the injured had not yet recovered, those who had fled had not yet returned, and the residents were not yet contented. Because regulations were lax, the soldiers took advantage of their victory to plunder. Even in cities and marketplaces, some people kept their doors closed in the daytime. As soon as Menggu arrived, he took charge. Knowing the people's grievances, he issued an order, "Those who oppress the people will be dealt with according to the law. Craftsmen, merchants, and shopkeepers, you must each go about your work with your doors open, peaceably attending to your business without fear. Farmers, you must be content with your lands and exert yourselves diligently according to the seasons. I will instruct or punish those who mistreat you." After this order was issued, the violent became obedient and no one any longer dared violate the laws. Farmers in the fields and travelers on the roads felt safe, and people began to enjoy life.

In the second month of 1238, Wang Rong, prefect of Huaizhou, rebelled. The grand preceptor and prince ordered Menggu to put down this rebellion, telling him to slaughter everyone. Menggu responded, "When the royal army suppresses rebels, those who were coerced into joining them ought to be pardoned, not to mention those who are entirely innocent." The prince approved his advice and followed it. When Wang Rong surrendered, he was executed but the region was spared. The residents, with jugs of wine and burning incense, saw Menggu off tearfully, unable to bear his leaving. Forty years later when he was put in charge of Henei, the common people were delighted with the news, saying, "We will all

survive—our parents and relatives through marriage all served him before."

In 1239 locusts destroyed all the vegetation in Xiang and Wei, so the people were short of food. Menggu reported this to the great minister Quduqu who issued five thousand piculs of army rations to save the starving. As a consequence no one had to flee or starve.

During the four years from 1240 to 1243, the great southern campaigns took place. Wherever the armies passed, the local officials complained. Menggu, through loyal and diligent preparations, was able to supply the troops without hurting the people.

In 1247 some previously pacified cities in the Huai and Han areas rose in revolt. Refugees fled north and south. Border generals and local officials joined the fray, fighting and plundering. Menggu, by establishing trust, was able to gather together more than ten thousand households and settle them down as commoners. Even children were included.

At that time the harvest failed for several years in a row, yet taxes and labor services were still exacted. Consequently, three or four of every ten houses was vacant. Menggu ordered the officials to travel around announcing that those who returned to their property would be exempt from taxes and services for three years. That year seventeen thousand households returned in response to his summons.

In the first month of 1248 Zhu Ge, a bandit from Huizhou, organized a gang and rebelled. The military officers were planning to go overboard in their response to this, but Menggu declared, "The state has honored me, enriched me, delegated control of the troops to me, and entrusted the fate of the region to me. Does it want me to pacify the bandits or become a bandit myself? There is no need to act recklessly. If the bandits are not caught or the rebellion not suppressed, I will accept the responsibility." He then personally led the troops, capturing thirty-eight bandits at Heilu Mountain, and restoring peace to the local population. By fall there were no more rebels. When the bandit Xie Zhiquan rebelled in the third month of 1249, he pacified him the same way.

General Chagan recognized Menggu's honesty and humanity. Whenever the other circuits condemned prisoners to death, he had Menggu conduct the review investigation. Innumerable times, Menggu relied on the law to redress grievances and reduce penalties. Ten years before, a peasant in Anyang had offended a noble and been ordered to turn over six young girls. Menggu ordered the noble official Alachur to marry them all out to commoners. There was a drought in the summer of 1250. After Menggu prayed for rain, moisture became adequate.

In the spring of 1262, Li Tan revolted and sent his henchmen to far away places disguised as mounted couriers. They traveled through many routes, east and west, the officials unable to recognize them. Menggu discovered them and got them to admit their treacherous conspiracy, thus defeating them. When there was a drought in 1263, Menggu prayed for rain and it rained. That year he was given the title Brilliant and August General and made governor of Zhongshan prefecture. In 1270 he was transferred and became governor of Hezhong prefecture. In the spring of 1274 he was allowed to wear the golden tiger tablet in recognition of his long and excellent service, his incorruptibility, and the repute in which he was held where he had served. He was advanced out of order to great general of Huaiyuan, governor of Huaimeng route, and military administrator of several armies. On the 29th of the second month he died of illness in the main room of his private residence at the age of seventy-one.

Menggu was a Mongol, and when young was called Mongol Baer. His father was Xibaer, his mother Lengla. He had six wives . . . , seven sons, . . . and six daughters. . . . Seven years after he was buried, Naohai and his other sons recorded Menggu's virtuous government service for an epitaph and came to ask me to write the inscription.

Alas! When I think about all the government officials of the past and present, I come to the realization that the greedy ones are invariably oppressive and the honest ones are invariably incorrupt, the connection between their virtues and their administrative behavior as automatic as shape to shadow or sound to echo. Those who are greedy are not satisfied; not satisfied, they take by force, not caring how much they harm the world. Those who are honest do not take what is not theirs, no matter how slight it might be. How would they harm others to benefit themselves? The house where Menggu lived when he governed Zhangde nearly forty years ago, and the fields from which he obtained food then, were just adequate to keep out the wind and rain and supply enough to eat. When he died there were no estates or leftover wealth to leave his sons or grandsons. Therefore they had to model themselves on him and concentrate on governing in a way that would bring peace and safety, show love for the people, and benefit all. They have no need to be ashamed even if compared to the model officials of the Han and Tang dynasties. . . .

Translated by Patricia Ebrey

45

A SCHEDULE FOR LEARNING

The behavior and outlook of members of the upper class cannot be adequately understood without some appreciation of what they experienced as students. Elementary instruction in reading and writing might require only three or four years, but those who wanted to gain mastery of the classical texts and the literary skills needed to take the civil service examinations had to continue studying much longer, often into their twenties. Some young men studied with tutors, but schools and academies were also quite common.

The content and character of such education was strongly influenced by the ideas of Zhu Xi (1130–1200), discussed above in selection 40. In the Yuan dynasty, Cheng Duanli (d. 1345) compiled a guide for students and teachers incorporating these ideas, called A Schedule for Learning. *The ministry of education had copies of it sent to teachers in all prefectures. Below are Cheng's preface and the rules for a local school established by two disciples of Zhu Xi in the thirteenth century which Cheng included in his first chapter.*

PREFACE

Nowadays, fathers and older brothers who wish to benefit their youngsters give them an education, and yet hardly two or three out of every ten of our youths actually achieve anything academically. This is not solely the fault of the youngsters and their teachers; the elders, for their lack of foresight, should also share the blame. Before the youngsters have studied and understood the nature of things, they are forced by their elders to compose essays. The teachers, though aware of the danger of such a practice, nevertheless wish to display their own talents; they are therefore willing to comply with such requests. In this way, the sequence of the learning process is confused. Instead of attaining their goals by a shortcut, the youngsters end up not getting anywhere at all. Not only are their writings worthless, but they usually do not even know one book thoroughly. Months and years go by; when they finally realize their mistakes and begin to regret them, they have become too old. Furthermore, when incorrect methods are used in the beginning, various wrong ideas are likely to stick because of the importance of first impressions. This in turn causes the students to wander on the periphery of true learning all their lives, ignorant of their own mistakes.

The sequence of teaching practiced by Confucius was as follows: first he made the students concentrate their minds on the Way; then he taught them virtues; then he made them act in accordance with the principle of humanity. Only after these principles had been incorporated in their daily lives did the students begin to study. In the *Rituals of the Zhou* the grand educator listed the six arts after the six virtues and six model behaviors, which clearly indicates the order of significance. Our present system of selecting government officials still regards personal virtue as the first criterion; next comes knowledge of the classics and the ability to govern, with writing ability as the last consideration. This is a very reasonable system. The examinations on the classics, furthermore, are based on the teachings of Master Zhu Xi, combining study of philosophy with advancement in officialdom, much to the benefit of those who devote themselves to the Way. This is what the civil service examinations of the Han, Tang, and Song dynasties lacked, and therefore scholars are now offered a rare opportunity. Unfortunately, our students fail to take advantage of this system.

Our students try to follow the teachings of Master Zhu in their study of the classics, yet they are ignorant of his method of study. Because they have no method, they tend to use flowery language to promote themselves. During the period when the teachings of Master Cheng flourished, Hu Wending lamented the wordiness of most people's writing. I fear that the same trend is returning in our time. To correct the situation, I have compiled a "Schedule for Learning," which I would like to share with my friends. This work is based on the selection of Master Zhu's method of study compiled by Fu Hanqing. I have also included other helpful theories by scholars in earlier eras.

In my humble opinion, if we wish to study the classics, to understand the nature of things, to be familiar with all political theories, to investigate our institutions, to be well versed in everthing ancient and modern, to wield language at will, and finally, to popularize our discoveries and contributions throughout the entire nation, we should follow this schedule for learning. For it is the purpose of this work to differentiate between the essential and the trivial and to retain a proper order of progress. In this manner we will not forget what we have learned thoroughly, and we will review and reflect daily on what has not yet been fully digested until it becomes a part of ourselves. Eventually, mind and reason will become one, and a profound tranquillity will be achieved amidst constant changes and movements. There will be a convergence of the self and the Way, and virtues will be reflected naturally in our discourse and writings, which will become models for our contemporaries as well as for posterity. Our method is thus not to be compared with the ordinary methods of studying one narrow subject.

Written by Cheng Duanli, in the eighth month, 1315, at the Academy for Establishing Virtue in Chizhou.

SCHOOL REGULATIONS ESTABLISHED
by Masters Cheng and Dong

All students of this school must observe closely the following regulations.

1. *Ceremonies held on the 1st and 15th of every month.* At daybreak, the student on duty for that day will sound his clappers. At the first round of the clappers, you should rise, wash your face, comb your hair, and put on proper clothing. By the second round of the clappers, you should be dressed either in ceremonial robes or in summer robes and gather in the main hall. The teachers will then lead you to the image of Confucius, to which you will bow twice. After the incense has been lit, you will make two more bows.

Afterwards, the teachers walk over to the southwestern corner, and you line up in order of your ages in the northeast. Then you pay respect to the teachers by making two bows to them, while the teachers accept the salutation, standing erect. An older student then comes forward and delivers a short greeting; this is followed by two more bows to the teachers. Afterwards, the teachers retire into a room, and you form a circle and bow to each other twice. When this is done, you go to your seats.

2. *Daily salutations held in the morning and in the evening.* On ordinary days, the student on duty sounds the clappers as described above. At the second round of the clappers you will enter the hall and line up to wait for the teachers to come out. Then the teachers and you bow to each other with hands folded in front. Next, you divide into two groups and bow to each other, after which you begin your daily studies.

At night, before bedtime, the clappers are sounded again. You must all gather to repeat the same ceremony as in the morning.

Whenever there is an assembly of students, such as at a group lecture, a dinner, or a tea, the salutations are the same as just described. For a lecture, you should wear ceremonial robes or summer robes. For all other occasions you may dress less formally.

3. *Daily behavior.* You should have a defined living area. When in a group you will be seated according to your ages. When sitting, you must straighten your backs and sit squarely in the chair. You should not squat, lean to one side, cross your legs, or dangle your feet. At night, you should always wait for the elders to go to bed first. After they are in bed, you should keep quiet. Also, you should not sleep during the day.

4. *Gait and posture.* You should walk slowly. When standing, keep your hands folded in front. Never walk or stand in front of an elder. Never turn your back on those who are your superiors in age or status. Do not step on doorsills. Do not limp. Do not lean on anything.

5. *Looking and listening.* Do not gape. Do not eavesdrop.

6. *Discourse.* Statements should always be verifiable. Keep your promises. Your manners should be serious. Do not be boisterous or playful. Do not gossip about your neighbors. Do not engage in conversations about vulgar matters.

7. *Appearance.* Be dignified and serious. Do not be insolent. Do not be rough or rude. Do not be vicious or proud. Do not reveal your joy or anger.

8. *Attire.* Do not wear unusual or extravagant clothing. Yet do not go to the other extreme and appear in clothes that are ragged, dirty, or in bad taste. Even in your private quarters you should never expose your body or take off your cap. Even in the hottest days of summer you should not take off your socks or shoes at will.

9. *Eating.* Do not fill yourself. Do not seek fancy foods. Eat at regular hours. Do not be discontent with coarse fare. Never drink unless on a holiday or unless you are ordered to do so by your elders. Never drink more than three cups or get drunk.

10. *Travel.* Unless you are called upon by your elders, ordered to run errands by your reachers, or faced by a personal emergency, you are not allowed to leave the school grounds at will. Before your departure and after your return you should report to your teacher. You must not change your reported destination, and you must return by the set time.

11. *Reading.* You should concentrate on your book and keep a dignified appearance. You should count the number of times you read an assigned piece. If, upon completion of the assigned number, you still have not memorized the piece, you should continue until you are able to recite it. On the other hand, if you have memorized the piece quickly, you should still go on to complete the assigned number of readings.

Only after a book has been thoroughly learned should you go on to another. Do not read too many things on a superficial level. Do not attempt to memorize a piece without understanding it. Read only those books which expound virtues. Do not look into useless writings.

12. *Writing.* Do not scribble. Do not write slanted or sloppy characters.

13. *Keep your desk tidy.* The assigned seats should be kept in order. Your study area should be simple but tidy. All book chests and clothing trunks should be locked up carefully.

14. *Keep the lecture halls and private rooms clean.* Each day one student is on duty. After sounding the second round of the clappers, he should sprinkle water on the floor of the lecture hall. Then, after an appropriate wait, he should sweep the floor and wipe the desks. The other

cleaning jobs should be assigned to the pages. Whenever there is cleaning to be done, they should be ordered to do it, regardless of the time of the day.

15. *Terms of address.* You should address those who are twice your age as "elder," those who are ten years older than you as "older brothers," and those who are about your age by their polite names. Never address one another as "you." The same rules should be followed in letter writing.

16. *Visits.* The following rules should be observed when a guest requests to visit the school. After the teacher is seated and the student on duty has sounded the clappers, all students, properly dressed, enter the lecture hall. After the morning salutation, the students remain standing; only when the teacher orders them to retire may they leave. If the guest should wish to speak to a student privately, he should, after seeing the teacher, approach the student at his seat. If the student finds the visitor imcompatible, he is not obliged to be congenial.

17. *Recreational.* There are rules for the playing of musical instruments, for archery, as well as for other games. You should seek recreation only at the right time. Gambling and chess games are lowly pastimes and should be avoided by our students.

18. *Servants.* Select those who are prudent, honest, and hardworking. Treat them with dignity and forbearance. When they make mistakes, scold them or report to the teacher. If they do not improve after being punished, report to the teacher to have them discharged. A student should not expel his page at will.

If you can follow the above regulations closely, you are approaching the true realm of virtue.

Translated by Clara Yu

46

A SCHOLAR-PAINTER'S DIARY

The life of upper-class men involved not only study and official service but also refined pursuits such as collecting antiques or old books and cultivation of the arts—especially poetry writing, calligraphy, or painting. For many individuals these interests totally overshadowed any philosophical, political, or economic concerns; others usually sober-minded found in them occasional outlets for creative activity and aesthetic pleasure. A large share of the informal social life of upper-class men was oriented around these refined pastimes, as they gathered to compose or criticize poetry, to view one another's treasures, or to patronize young talents. In these activities, they frequently mingled with Buddhist and Daoist clergy.

The diary of Guo Bi, from which sixteen days are given below, illustrates the kind of relationships that existed between poetry, painting, calligraphy, and connoisseurship in the social and cultural life of a group of upper-class men. Guo Bi was a scholar and artist of the early fourteenth century who painted landscapes and bamboo and was noted for his calligraphy. Diary writing does not seem to have been practiced to any appreciable extent before the Song, and for the next several centuries most diaries, like Guo Bi's, were records of trips.

1309, The sixth month, 12th day: Staying at Xinghua. Mr. Zhan Derun invited me for dinner. The guests were the same as yesterday except for Gong Zifang. Zifang is the nephew of Zizhong, and lives in Gaoyou. After dinner, I accompanied the others to Perfect Truth Daoist Monastery, where we sat under four catalpa trees to catch some breeze. I wrote twenty wine poems for Zhao Boqian.

13th day: I painted a picture of an impressive stone for Mr. Zhan. The stone was less than a foot long and six or seven inches high. Its shape was very unusual and yet no trace of a chisel could be detected. It was as though it had been carved by fairies. When I finished painting the stone, I asked Mr. Wang, the painter, to come see it. Then with my coconut cup I started drinking, and by noon I was already drunk. Yesterday I went with Gong Zifang, Zang Zixuan, and Xu Guiyan to visit Jinggong at the county school. There we ran into Mr. Zhao and Mr. Huang. All of us sat on the ground and enjoyed a chicken and a jug of wine. When finished with the wine, we went our separate ways.

14th day: Staying at Xinghua. Liu Juchuan's new wine had just matured; its taste was pure and its flavor unique. In the morning he brought over a pot, and we enjoyed several cups with Mr. Zhan. At noon Liu barbecued two birds, and we drank some wine together. Besides me, the guests included Huang Zhongwen, Li Jinggong and others. After the wine, Hu Zizhen's brother-in-law, Zang Zixuan, hired a small boat and invited Gong Zifang, Xu Shengzhi, and me to visit Lotus Flower Swamp. Zhao Boqian also came along. After a little while Mr. Zhan, his son, and Liu Juchuan also joined us in another small boat. After lingering for some time, we went to Righteous Road Monastery. The monk in charge prepared wine for us, but I cannot say very much for its taste. Next we went back to the boats and picked lotuses. By this time the sun was setting and a breeze began to blow. We made cups out of lotus leaves and drank wine from them. Those who could not hold their liquor all got drunk. Not until the moon had risen on the horizon did we return. It was a very merry day, except for the mosquitoes—they somehow spoiled the fun.

15th day: Staying at the Zhan household at Xinghua. An Dou, the county assistant, and Xing, the warden, came over. Mr. Zhan prepared wine for them and served melons. At night I sat with Mr. Zhan on the bridge. With a cool breeze blowing and the moon shining, we drank some wine and enjoyed the melons.

16th day: I made a calligraphy scroll for Mr. Zhan. At noon I drank wine.

17th day: Staying at Xinghua. It has been extremely hot every night. I perspired so much, I felt I had been rained on. The mosquitoes in Xinghua are big and ferocious. When you sit unsheltered, they swarm over to attack, and there are so many of them that you feel as if sand had been thrown at you. In the evening, Juchuan invited me to enjoy the cool breeze at the county school. Later I had a few cups of wine with Li, Zang, and Huang.

18th day: Staying at Xinghua. Hu Zizhen, Li Jinggong, Wang Shizhong, and I went to the county school and visited Huang Zhongwen in his office. The evening was unbearably hot. Mr. Zhan took a rowboat out onto the lake to get some cool air; yet he too was bothered by the mosquitoes and came back disappointed. That day, Mr. Zhan showed us an ancient bronze vessel with a horse on top and two lines of text under it: "Worthy elders—good sons and grandsons." When one strikes the bronze, it makes a sound.

19th day: Had breakfast at Hu Zizhen's. It rained in the evening, then became cooler.

20th day: Painted a picture of orchids for Wang Shizhong. I went to Original Goodness Monastery with Gong Zifang and Zang Zixuan to get some cool air. Next we stopped at Four Sages Daoist Monastery. Gong and Zang invited Xu Dongxi, Xu Shengzhi, and me, then all five of us went to visit Liu Dongan. We pooled our money to buy some wine and enjoyed the fragrance of the lotus flowers, not returning until dark. Later I went to the county seat and in the great hall I found a plaque which read: "Hall of Admiration for Fan." They say the plaque was made because Fan Zhongyan had once been magistrate here. In the evening I talked Derun into settling some business.

21st day: Staying at the Zhan residence at Xinghua. Liu Juchuan came and had lunch with me. Gong Zifang and Xu Shengzhi bought some paper and asked me to do calligraphy and bamboo drawings for them.

22nd day: I gave my writings to Zhan Derun. For my farewell dinner he had a goose cooked. The guests included Hu Zufang. Warden Xing came over. Using a poem by Wei Suzhou, I made a calligraphy scroll for Derun.

23rd day: The customs commissioner, Aban, paid me what he owed. Li Jinggong and Zhao Boqian, hearing that I was leaving, presented me with ten catties of yellow fish and brought a roll of paper to ask for samples of my drawing and calligraphy. Warden Xing requested a screen with my calligraphy and bamboo drawings. He offered me presents of two geese, some noodles, and wine cups. I took the wine cups, which were in the Lizhao style.

24th day: Everything was set for the trip and I was about to board the boat, when there was suddenly a heavy downpour. It continued all day so I had to stay another day. Xu Dongxi, who is very good at portraits, brought with him two rolls of paper to ask for one of my bamboo sketches. Hu Zizhen made me a present of his calligraphy. He also asked me for a title for Master Wen's painting of grapes and my bamboo sketches. I also painted two old trees for Mr. Zhan. Afterwards I packed.

25th day: In the morning I took leave of Mr. Zhan and his son. They gave me a coconut scoop and a square ink block for presents. They asked Wang Shizhong to accompany me to the pier in the rain. Unfortunately, the local officials had appropriated all the boats for catching locusts. I had to ask Wang Shizhong to negotiate with the county government before I was able to leave. That day, Xu Shengzhi and Gong Zifang paid eight thousand cash for the boat fare. By dinner time the three of us had arrived at Gaoyou county. We went to visit Eastern Peak Temple and left our belongings at Gong Zifang's house. In the evening I took a bath and felt refreshed. Compared to Xinghua, Gaoyou had practically no mosquitoes. I slept soundly until midnight. When I woke up my bed was filled with silvery moonlight.

26th day: In the morning, Gong Zifang and I went to Heavenly King Monastery. There we visited Abbot Hai and took a look at the newly constructed pavilions. Zifang served me breakfast. Afterwards, on our way to the county seat, we passed Zhuoying Bridge; then we went to the county school to pay our respects to Confucius. At the back of the school there was a pavilion called Love-Lotus, with a plaque written by Qian Chunfu. Further back there was Literary Journey Pavilion, which was built by Chen Maoshu and inscribed by Yan Wufeng. At the side of the pavilion

was a shrine housing statues of Sun Xinlao and Qin Taixu. Later I went with Zifang to the market to drink some tea. Returning, I passed by the gate of the painter Zhang Xinjian. When he learned that we were from the same village, he asked me to stay for a cup of tea and showed me his paintings. Next I went to Xu Shengzhi's house, but he happened to be out. At his door, I came across Master Gong Zixiang, and we talked about an encounter we had had thirteen years earlier. The two of us then went up to Westerner Buddhist Monastery, the magnificent architecture of which impressed me. Zixiang dragged me to his place for lunch. He showed me a purple bull painted by Xu Xi and a few other specimens of paintings and calligraphy. Then he brought paper and asked me to do some ten scrolls of calligraphy for him. His three sons were waiting on us; the oldest is called Lifu, the youngest Boya, but the name of the second I cannot recall. After lunch, Zixiang accompanied me back to Zifang's house. Zixiang's residence is called Heavenly Lodge. According to him, there is a "Fair Lady Well" in front of it. Xu Shengzhi came by to see me and left me a pig's head and some pastry as presents. In the evening Zifang cooked a goose and drank wine with me. Lifu brought paper, asking me for some calligraphy. Zifang's brother was also present. Zifang is the son of Yuexi. Even in the summer heat, he treats me like a guest, with extreme hospitality.

27th day: In the morning Zifang accompanied me to the outskirts of Gaoyou City to board my boat. I took breakfast in the boat. At noon I got to Zhaobo and changed boats. At that time it started raining very hard, making it impossible to get to shore. Thus, through the pouring rain I rode in a boat which was very damp and narrow. All the riders were common people, so there was no one to talk to. Fortunately, the wind was perfect, and I reached Yangzhou by dinner time. I stopped to see Sheng Maoshi. The two of us then went to a bathhouse. Afterwards, we returned to his place for some wine. Mr. Pei Junde also drank with us. At night I stayed at an inn.

Translated by Clara Yu

PART V

THE MING DYNASTY

After the Mongol empire broke apart and the Yuan dynasty collapsed, a Chinese dynasty was founded, the Ming (1368–1644). The early Ming was a period of recovery from some of the setbacks of Mongol rule, but many Yuan institutions were retained, since the forms and institutions of the Song could not be directly or fully restored. The Mongol capital at Beijing was made the Ming capital in 1421 and except for brief intervals has remained the capital of China until today. Economic revival led to a high level of commercial activity and handicraft production, but not to the innovative spirit of the early Song. Nevertheless, the Ming seems to have been one of the most prosperous periods of Chinese history. It was during these centuries that the great potential of south China came to be fully exploited. New crops such as cotton, maize, and sweet potato came to be widely cultivated, and industries such as porcelain and textiles flourished.

The Ming is generally considered the first truly despotic or autocratic Chinese dynasty (if the Yuan is considered an alien dynasty). The problems of central control of a huge, complex empire appeared pressing to the early emperors, who were intent on assuring personal control of the machinery of the bureaucracy and finding ways to keep the officials in line. The Jurchen and Mongol innovation of provincial governments, consisting of branches of the central government, was developed further as a way to cope with the difficulty of direct central control of the whole empire. The censorate, imperial guard, and eunuchs were all used to keep the emperor informed of possible wrongdoing throughout the country. The arbitrary actions of the emperors undoubtedly demeaned the status of high officials and often jeopardized their welfare, but would have had less impact on villagers, whose affairs were still left pretty much to elders and local notables.

Sources for the Ming are even more varied than for the Song. Particularly valuable are genealogies, charters, and other records of group activities which show the proclivity of peasants and townsmen to form corporate groups of various sorts, such as lineages, guilds, village associations, and secret societies. Such groups were probably common before the Ming, but they cannot be as well documented until then. The major reason for forming corporate groups seems to have been to gain protection from the casual mistreatment or exploitation of officials, large landowners, rich merchants, and other powerful people. Once one group of people had organized to protect their own interests, others would imitate them so as not to be left isolated. Indeed, by the Ming there is evidence that isolated individuals, without groups to support them, often lived precarious lives or had to put themselves under the protection of a landlord or employer who could take advantage of their weak position.

Vernacular fiction is another valuable source for the structure and content of social life and culture which becomes plentiful only in the Ming. The development of fiction in the vernacular language had begun in the Song with storytellers, and had progressed further in the Yuan, when drama flourished. During the Ming the stories that had evolved through oral and dramatic performances were written down as short stories and four long novels, *Journey to the West*, *Romance of the Three Kingdoms*, *Water Margin*, and *Jin Ping Mei*. This colloquial fiction is a valuable source for understanding Chinese civilization for two reasons. First, many stories contain realistic portrayals of social life; while often exaggerated for humorous effect, the conversations and behavior of tradesmen, servants, bullies, concubines, government clerks, teachers, and so on are colorfully portrayed and must have corresponded to social types recognized by the audience. The second value of fiction is as a repository of themes, images, and symbols with broad appeal. Much like myths and folk tales, stories of bandits, treacherous women, and docile servants could dramatize the conflicts of everyday life and resolve them in ways emotionally satisfying, even if unrealistic. The great love, from at least the Yuan period on, of stories of the outlaws in the *Water Margin* saga must be seen in this way—not as evidence that Chinese peasants and townsmen admired bandits (whom they probably considered a scourge if they were ever unfortunate enough to live within their reach), but as evidence that the flouting of authority provided symbols that helped make sense of life as people actually found it. Selections from both *Water Margin* and *Jin Ping Mei* are included in Part V.

47

PROCLAMATIONS OF THE HONGWU EMPEROR

In 1368 Zhu Yuanzhang (1328–1398) founded the Ming dynasty. He was the first commoner to become emperor in 1500 years. His origins were truly modest; after his parents died in an epidemic when he was sixteen, he became a monk and even for a while begged for his living. During the chaotic years of the fall of the Yuan dynasty, he became a rebel organizer. In 1356 his group of rebels seized Nanjing and two years later Beijing. Known by his reign title as the Hongwu Emperor, he is famous as both a conscientious and a despotic ruler. In the two proclamations below, he discusses two topics that were to worry social and political observers for the rest of imperial China: the corruption of high officials occupying positions that made extortion or acceptance of bribes all too easy; and the disruptive and dishonest activities of the assorted underlings, runners, guards, and servants who did the bidding of officials and controlled ordinary people's access to them. Hongwu's proclamations can be read as expressions of the values and thoughts of a man who rose meteorically within the Chinese social system. They also reveal much about the working of the bureaucracy and its impact on people's lives.

AN IMPERIAL EDICT RESTRAINING OFFICIALS FROM EVIL

To all civil and military officials:

I have told you to refrain from evil. Doing so would enable you to bring glory to your ancestors, your wives and children, and yourselves. With your virtue, you then could assist me in my endeavors to bring good fortune and prosperity to the people. You would establish names for yourselves in Heaven and on earth, and for thousands and thousands of years, you would be praised as worthy men.

However, after assuming your posts, how many of you really followed my instructions? Those of you in charge of money and grain have stolen them yourselves; those of you in charge of criminal laws and punishments have neglected the regulations. In this way grievances are not redressed and false charges are ignored. Those with genuine grievances have nowhere to turn; even when they merely wish to state their complaints, their words never reach the higher officials. Occasionally these unjust matters come to my attention. After I discover the truth, I capture and imprison the corrupt, villainous, and oppressive officials involved. I punish them with the death penalty or forced labor or have them flogged with bamboo sticks in order to make manifest the consequences of good or evil actions.

Those who have died from their punishments are mute. However, those who survive confuse the truth by speaking falsely. Lying to their friends and neighbors, they all say they are innocent. They complain, "The court's punishments are savage and cruel." This kind of slander is all too common. Yet I had clearly warned my officials from the beginning not to do anything wrong. Too often they have not followed my words, thereby bringing disaster upon themselves.

When a criminal commits a crime or when a good person mistakenly violates the law, he is going to be punished. Among these guilty ones there will always be some who are so afraid of being flogged or of dying that they will try to bribe the law enforcement officials with gold and silk. The law enforcement officials, for their part, place no value on bringing glory to their ancestors, their wives and children, or themselves; nor do they seek to preserve their own lives. The guilty persons, afraid of death, use money to buy their lives. The officials, not afraid of death, accept the money, thereby putting their lives in danger of the law. Yet later, when they are about to be punished or are on their way to the execution ground, they begin to tremble in fear. They look up to Heaven and they gaze down at the earth. They open their eyes wide, seeking for help in every direction. Alas, by then it is too late for them to repent their actions. It is more than too late, for they now are no longer able to preserve their lives.

For example, the former vice-president of the ministry of war, Wang Zhi, accepted a bribe of 220,000 cash for making up false reports on runaway soldiers and other matters. I questioned him face to face, "Why are you so greedy?"

He replied, "Money and profit confused my mind. They made me forget my parents and my ruler."

I then asked, "At this moment what do you think about what you did?"

"Facing punishment," he replied, "I begin to feel remorse, but it is too late."

Alas, how easily money and profit can bewitch a person! With the exception of the righteous person, the true gentleman, and the sage, no one is able to avoid the temptation of money. But is it really so difficult to reject the temptation of profit? The truth is people have not really tried.

Previously, during the final years of the Yuan dynasty, there were many ambitious men competing for power who did not treasure their sons and daughters but prized jade and silk, coveted fine horses and beautiful clothes, relished drunken singing and unrestrained pleasure, and enjoyed separating people from their parents, wives, and children. I also lived in that chaotic period. How did I avoid such snares? I was able to do so because I valued my reputation and wanted to preserve my life. Therefore I did not dare to do these evil things.

For fourteen years, while the empire was still unpacified, I fought in the cities and fields, competing with numerous heroes, yet never did I take a woman or girl improperly for my own pleasure. The only exception occurred after I conquered the city of Wuchang. I was enraged at Chen Youliang's invasion, so after I took over the city, I also took over his former concubine. Now I am suddenly suspicious of my own intentions in that case. Was it for the beauty of the woman? Or was it the manifestation of a hero's triumph? Only the wise will be able to judge.

In order to protect my reputation and to preserve my life, I have done away with music, beautiful girls, and valuable objects. Those who love such things are usually "a success in the morning, a failure in the evening." Being aware of the fallacy of such behavior, I will not indulge such foolish fancies. It is not really that hard to do away with these tempting things.

DISMISSAL OF EXCESSIVE LOCAL STAFF BECAUSE OF THEIR CRIMES

Among those with no redeeming features, the worst are the riffraff found in the prefectures of Su and Song. It is indeed a great misfortune that these ne'er- do-wells can cause such great disturbances among the cities' inhabitants. For the average town dweller there are four types of occupation. These idle riffraff engage in none of them, but just hang around, concerned only with establishing connections with the local officials. In the city and suburbs of Songjiang alone there are 1350 persons who do not engage in any actual production but busy themselves only with currying favor with local officials. In the city and suburbs of Suzhou, 1521 individuals fall into this category. Alas, those who engage in productive work are few, while those who shirk work are many!

These idlers understand neither the hardships of the farmer nor the hard labor of other occupations. They work for the local government, calling themselves the "little warden," the "straight staff," the "record staff," the "minor official," and the "tiger assistant"—six types in all, each with a different name.

Even during the farmers' busiest season these idle persons will go to the fields to make trouble and interrupt agricultural activities. When it is time to transplant rice, and the farmers, with rice sprouts in their hands, are busy with their chores, these idlers will come into the fields, clutching an official dispatch. They will drag people away from the irrigation water wheel and arrest them on the spot. They have even been known to take the rice sprouts out of a farmer's hands and arrest him right in his field. Yet when formal official matters are not really pressing, government officials are not supposed to interrupt agricultural work. Therefore, how could one interrupt the farmer as he farms with something that is really nothing?

At this time, if I were to thoroughly eradicate this riffraff, in addition to those already imprisoned, I would have to deal with no less than 2000 people from each of these two prefectures. These men take part in none of the four useful occupations. They utilize the prestige of the government to oppress the masses below. If people outside the government do not know how wicked these men are, they are going to say that I am harsh in my punishments, since they see only the severity of the law. They do not know that certain persons have used the name of the court and the government to engage in evil practices.

In the morning I punish a few; by evening others commit the same crime. I punish these in the evening and by the next morning again there are violations. Although the corpses of the first have not been removed, already others follow in their path. The harsher the punishment, the more the violations. Day and night I cannot rest. This is a situation which cannot be helped. If I enact lenient punishments, these persons will engage in still more evil practices. Then how could the people outside the government lead peaceful lives?

What a difficult situation this is! If I punish these persons, I am regarded as a tyrant. If I am lenient toward them, the law becomes ineffective, order deteriorates, and people deem me an incapable ruler. All these opinions can be discerned in the various records and memorials. To be a ruler is indeed difficult.

I have exterminated the vicious riffraff in the prefectures of Suzhou and Songjiang. Evil persons in other areas, seeing this edict, take heed. Discontinue your evil practices and you will perpetuate your good fortune and prosperity. But if you violate this edict, you will be exterminated and your family will be broken. Be cautious! Be cautious!

Translated by Lily Hwa

48

THE DRAGON BOAT RACE

The Chinese did not have a custom equivalent to making one day a week a day of rest. In busy seasons, peasants worked long hours every day; in slack seasons they would work less intensively. Festivals and holidays, however, broke up their year and gave them welcome rest. Colorful and entertaining, they were times to have fun. Festivals were also important in creating community identity, since villages or larger communities took pride in the performances they put on and often invited other communities to watch.

One of the most popular seasonal festivals in China took place on the 5th of the fifth month, which occurred sometime in June according to the Western calendar. The nature of the festival varied from place to place, but where there were rivers, boat races were traditional. The following selection is a description of the boat race as it was performed in Hunan in the late Ming. The account was written by Yang Sichang (1588–1641), a native of the area. He makes it clear that the races were not simple diversion, but occasions for the expression of intense competition, with all the hold over the audience of contemporary sporting events.

The dragon boat race originated in the old Yuan and Xiang regions as a ceremony to call back Qu Yuan.* Being north of Lake Dongting, our Wuling is part of Yuan (Changsha, south of the Lake, is in the old Xiang) and therefore the boat race flourishes here. Since we inherited it directly from the state of Chu of the Zhou dynasty it is only natural that our boat race cannot be matched by that of any other province.

The boat race is held at the center of the prefectural seat. The most distant places from which

boats still come are Yujiagang, fifteen *li* downstream, and Baishadu, thirty-five *li* upstream. On the day of the festival, flagmen and drummers on boats going to and fro make a deafening noise heard for about fifty *li*. The race course runs for about ten *li* along the southern shore from Duanjiazui to Qingcaozui and along the northern shore from Shangshigui. The river is wide there and well suited for a race course. The southern shore is covered with grass, forests, and snowy white sands. On the northern shore are high buildings with beautifully painted balconies and old city walls. The spectators gather there. . . .

The current popular belief is that the boat race

* Qu Yuan (322–295 B.C.) was the archetype of the loyal minister who lost the favor of his king through slander. In despair, he threw himself into the river to drown.

is held to avert misfortunes. At the end of the race, the boats carry sacrificial animals, wine, and paper coins and row straight downstream, where the animals and wine are cast into the water, the paper coins are burned, and spells are recited. The purpose of these acts is to make pestilence and premature death flow away with the water. This is called "sending away the mark." Then the boats row back without flags and drumbeating. They will be pulled onto land and housed in huts on the shore till the next year, as this year's races are over. About this time the people have rites performed to ward off fires. Also, those who are ill make paper boats in the same color as the dragon boat of their region and burn them at the shore. . . .

Priests of local temples are employed during the boat races in order to suppress evil influences. Sometimes people go to the mountains to invite famous priests, called "mountain teachers," who are especially skillful. The night before the race, the headman provides sacrificial animals and wine and asks the priest to perform. The priest jumps head over heels from the bow to the stern. Buckwheat is scattered and a fire is lighted. This is called "brightening the boat." Drums are beaten throughout the night to ward off the influences of opposing priests, who, if caught, might be beaten to death.

On the day of the races the priest makes an oil fire to launch the boat. He can foresee unfailingly the victory or defeat of the boat from the color and height of the flame. The god he serves is called the Immortal of Xihesa. The priest's spells include "the furious fire of the violent thunder burning Heaven." His finger charms include "arresting the front dragons," "stopping the devil-soldiers," and "moving the mountains and overturning the seas." With his trouser legs rolled up and his feet bare, he jumps seven steps and then throws water into the fire. When the fire rises again, the boat starts. Some sentences of his spell are: "The Heaven fire burns the sun. The earth fire burns the five directions. The thunder fire, executing the law, burns to death the various inauspicious things. The dragon boat taking to the water will float at will in the five lakes and four seas." The outer side of the bottom of the boat is swept with a bundle of reeds from stem to stern in order to prevent anything from being hung on the boat by an enemy. The other ceremonies, being secret, cannot be described.

The man chosen as the headman of a racing boat must be brave and have a family. Several days before, he distributes steamed cakes and pieces of paper to those who belong to his region and is repaid in money. On the top of the pieces of paper pictures of dragon boats are printed and on the bottom some sentences are written.

Supplying food and wine during the race is assigned to rich men, who are honored if they contribute generously. Others supply food because they have made a vow to do so. On the day of the races there are small boats in the river bringing food. They are decorated with two trees of paper money and colored silks, and musicians play in them. The boatmen must force in the food and wine beyond the point of satiation until nothing is left. Otherwise anything left has to be thrown into the water together with the dishes and chopsticks.

In the evening when the boats return, the people take the water in the boats, mix it with various grasses, and use it to wash their bodies. This is said to prevent bad luck and is a kind of purification.

The boatmen are all familiar with the water and are expert swimmers, but the headman, flagman, drummer, and clapper need not be able to swim, as the oarsmen are responsible for their lives. On the day of the races all wear on their heads the charms furnished by the priest and stick small reddish-yellow flags with egret feathers in the hair at their temples to ward off evil. The spectators display red or green pieces of silk, some with sentences written on them. and give them to the passing dragon boats as presents. As a boat passes by its home base, the people set off fireworks, wave their fans, and applaud. If the boat belongs to some other place, they shout ridicule at it, some of them getting angry and even throwing tiles at it. The boatmen respond by grabbing their oars or gesturing to show their willingness to fight. . . .

Each boat belongs to a distinct region, and the people of its home base quarrel with those of the others about who won and who lost. Even the children and women do not admit defeat. Most men who have moved away from where their ancestors lived are still loyal to the boat of their ancestral region. But others who have moved do not root for any boat, which makes them despised by their neighbors as cowardly. At this time, while playing chess, guessing fingers, and even when drinking, people say nothing but "victory." Sometimes they shout "dong, dong" to imitate the sound of the drums; sometimes they wave their sleeves to accompany the rowing and cry "victory! victory!" It is the custom to have this kind of enthusiasm for the races. Officials stationed within the territories of the different boats should not join the contending groups, but, in fact, they are also divided according to the popular way of thinking. . . .

The people watch the boat races from the shore. Along the northern shore from Qingpingmen to Shigui, about five or six *li*, are buildings of three or four stories in which space can be reserved by paying an advance fee of up to several hundred cash. On the day of the races, the people, carrying wine bottles and food boxes, ride on carts and horses or walk along the roads to get there by mid-morning. Tables are covered with fruit and food for sale. The best fruits are the "plums from the Han family" and the "wheat-yellow peaches"; the food includes shad and vegetables. When the start of the race is announced, everyone stops talking, laughing, or leaning against the balustrades. Attentively they watch, wondering which is their boat and whether it will meet victory or defeat. All too quickly victory is decided. Then some are so proud it seems as if their spirits could break the ceiling, and some have faces pale as death and seem not to know how to go down the stairs. . . .

The people can only rent space in buildings within their respective regions. Those who belong to the flower or the white boat do not enter the region of the black boat; those of the black or the red boat do not enter that of the flower boat. No one would do so consciously unless he wanted a fight, because sometimes terrible consequences result.

Because there are too few buildings for all the spectators, there are numerous food shelters on the southern shore and houseboats in the river. People on the southern shore can see quite clearly as the boats cross the river from the northern to the southern bank. When a boat nears a bank, if it does not belong to their region, people fling stones at it, and the men on the boat wave their oars menacingly. The spectators' boats in the river often obstruct the route of the racing boats. If a boat happens to be just in front of a racing boat and cannot get out of the way, it can be broken to pieces in seconds. . . .

The victorious boat rows with its stern forward. The men hold their oars vertically, dance, and beat gongs on the boat. When they pass a losing boat, they threaten it. Those losing try to do the same but with less spirit, or if a little further behind, they silently acknowledge defeat. At sunset the boats disperse. At the home of the headmen, feasts are prepared and the boatmen all gather to dine. At the victor's home, food and wine are especially abundant and his neighbors, relatives, and friends come to offer congratulations. The next day, the door of his house will be beautifully decorated with colored silk, and a feast and a dramatic performance will be held. Some people write sentences or short poems on the city gates to ridicule the losers, or tie up a dog or a tortoise with some grass and fruit and place them there for the same purpose. When the men of the defeated boats happen to pass by, they lower their heads and go on their way. Their relatives or friends sometimes send such things to them to make fun of them.

From the fourth month the people begin to talk enthusiastically about the boats. In the fifth month the race is held and victory and defeat are decided. Yet even by the eighth or ninth month the people are still not tired of the subject.

Translated by Patricia Ebrey

49

VILLAGE ORDINANCES

In every dynasty villages were allowed considerable self-government, and by the Ming many villages had councils that set and tried to enforce their own rules or ordinances. Well-known Confucian scholars, including Zhu Xi in the Song and Wang Yangming in the Ming, urged local literati to take leadership roles in helping villagers in these activities, seeing them as ways to promote morality and good social order.

The following three sample village ordinances come from late Ming reference books aimed at broad audiences and consequently given titles like The Complete Compilation of Everything the Gentry and Commoners Need to Know *and* The Complete Book of Practical Information Convenient for the Use of Commoners. *The sample ordinances in them provide evidence of the principles by which villages, or at least village leaders, thought their affairs should be run and show the kinds of restraints people could be placed under by decisions of their neighbors.*

PROHIBITION ORDINANCE

In the imperial court there are laws; in the village there are ordinances. Laws rule the entire nation; ordinances control only one area. Although laws and ordinances differ in scope, the matters they deal with are equally significant.

Each year we set up ordinances for our village, and yet, to our deep regret, they are denigrated by the greedy and overturned by the influential. As a result, they are rendered ineffective, customs deteriorate, and incalcuable damage is done by our people and their animals.

The problem is not that ordinances cannot be enforced; rather, it is that those in charge of the ordinances are unequal to their posts, and those who design them are incompetent. Recently we have followed the suggestion of the villages and grouped all households into separate districts, each with a fixed number of members. On the first and the fifteenth of each month, each district will prepare wine and hold a meeting to awaken the conscience of its residents. In this manner, contact between the high and low will be established, and a cycle will be formed. Anyone who violates our village ordinances will be sentenced by the public; if he thinks the sentence is unfair, he can appeal to the village assembly. However, let it be known that no cover-up, bribery, blackmail, or frame-up will be tolerated; such evil doings will be exposed by Heaven and punished by thunder. We know that even in a small group there are good members as well as bad ones; how can there be a lack of honest people among our villagers?

From now on, our ordinances will be properly enforced and the morality of our people will be restored. The village as a whole as well as each individual will profit from such a situation, and there will be peace between the high and the low, their morality and custom having been unified. Thus, what is called an "ordinance" is nothing but the means to better ourselves.

ORDINANCE PROHIBITING GAMBLING

This concerns the prohibition of gambling. Those who are farmers devote their time to their work and certainly do not gamble. It is the unemployed vagrants who have the gambling disease—a disease which is detrimental to social customs and ruins family fortunes. Unfortunately in our village the population increases daily, and proper behavior does not prevail. As a result vagrancy becomes the fashion. Among us there are homeless rovers who, lacking occupations, form gangs and occupy themselves solely with gambling. They either bet on card games or play with dice; vying to be the winner, they continue day and night, without food or sleep. They have nothing with which to support their parents or their wives and children. Thus, unlawful intents are born, and wicked schemes are hatched. In small offenses they dig holes or scale walls, using all the cunning they have to steal from others; in more serious cases they set fires and brandish weapons, stopping at nothing. If we fail to prohibit gambling, the situation will become impossible. This is why we are gathered here to enact an ordinance for the prohibition of gambling. From now on those in question should repent for their past sins and reform their souls; they should espouse duty and kindness; they should tend to their principal occupa-

tions. Should there be anyone who persists in this evil practice and fails to honor this ordinance, he will definitely be punished. The light offenders will be confined, upon the decision of our village assembly, and the serious ones will be brought to the officials for sentence.

Our purpose is clearly stated in the above, and this notice is not posted without good reason.

PROHIBITION ON TRAVEL AT NIGHT

This ordinance is drawn up by so-and-so to prohibit travel at night, for the purpose of safeguarding our village.

In ancient times, night travel was strictly prohibited, and violaters were punished without exception. Robbers and thieves were prevented from climbing walls and boring holes in houses, to the benefit of all the inhabitants of the area.

Recently, however, night wanderers, instead of resting at night, have dared to saunter around at will. Because of this we have prepared wine and called for this meeting to draw up a strict ordinance. As soon as the sun sets, no one will be allowed to walk about; not until the fifth drum will traffic be allowed to start again. We will take turns patrolling the streets, carrying a bell, and clapping the nightwatchman's rattle. He who sights a violator will sound his gong, and people in every household will come out with weapons to kill the violator on the spot. Should anyone fail to show up for roll call at the sound of the gong, he will be severely punished upon the decision of the village assembly.

We have made copies of this ordinance to be posted at various places so that night wanderers will be warned and thieves and rogues will not prevail. Duly enacted.

Translated by Clara Yu

50

COMMERCIAL ACTIVITIES

As seen in selection 14, "The Debate on Salt and Iron," early Confucian views were distrustful of the profit motive and consequently of commercial activity in general. Still, merchants thrived in almost all periods of peace, and Chinese society by Ming times was highly commercialized. The two parts of this selection show two sides of Chinese commercialization: ordinary people's buying and selling, borrowing and mortgaging; and merchants' far-flung pursuit of profit.

The first part consists of seven blank contracts taken a late Ming reference book. By the Tang dynasty, contracts were widely used in China for private transactions. In the Ming even illiterate peasants generally realized the importance of having a piece of paper to prove the original terms of an agreement. Financial agreements could be drawn up by any two individuals, but brokers or witnesses were often asked to participate. Legal experts were rarely consulted; instead people would use sample contracts (or scribes who had books of them) to ensure that the key issues had been covered, such as the stipulation that the transaction had not been coerced and the specification of responsibility if anything went wrong.

Often one of the parties in a financial transaction of the sort covered in these contracts was a small town merchant. Other merchants dealt at a much larger scale in interregional wholesale trade, and often made great fortunes. Rich merchants regularly educated their sons as scholars, and many scholars and officials in Ming times came from commercial families. Ming views of merchants and their social roles are revealed in two essays given here. The first was written by Zhang Han (1511–1593), a Ming official whose family had established its fortune through the textile industry. It shows ambivalent feelings toward merchants and commerce not atypical of the period. The second is a biography of a merchant respected for his skills in business but even more for his virtue and generosity. It was included in a collection of biographies compiled by Wang Daokun (1525–1593), a high official and writer who was the son and grandson of salt merchants.

SAMPLE CONTRACT FOR
THE SALE OF A HOUSE

The undersigned sellers, _____, unable to sustain themselves, agree to sell their part of the house with _____ rooms, together with the main structure of _____ rooms, encompassing _____ to the east, _____ to the west, _____ to the south, _____ to the north, its boundary clearly stated in the above, including the tiles on the roof and the land on which the house is constructed (for those who do not sell the land, just state: "the foundation of the house"), complete with doors and windows, all in sound condition, to the buyer, _____. This transaction is mediated by _____.

On this date, all three parties negotiated the price, which comes to _____ only. The deed and the full payment were exchanged, leaving no outstanding debts.

Before this transaction, all the sellers' relatives involved were consulted. The house has not been previously sold or mortgaged. Should any questions arise, the sellers assume full responsibility.

This transaction is completed out of the free will of the seller and the buyer; there has been no pressure from any creditor to sell the house as payment for debts. After the sale, the buyer will have full control of the property and there should be no other disputes. (In cases where only the house is for sale, then state: "The sellers will vacate the premises on the date selected by the buyer, their noncompliance or resistance being prohibited.") Should either party violate any terms of this contract, he will have to compensate the other party with an amount equivalent to half of the total sale price.

This contract is draw up as evidence of the sale.

SAMPLE CONTRACT FOR
THE MORTGAGE OF A HOUSE*

The undersigned mortgagor, _____, because of inadequate funds, agrees to mortgage his house of _____ rooms, encompassing _____ to the east, _____ to the south, _____ to the west, _____ to the north, its boundary clearly stated in the above, through a mediator to the mortgagee, _____, for _____ amount of silver, which has been received in full. The house is now available for immediate occupancy by the mortgagee.

It is agreed that the sum received will not accrue any interest and the house will not yield any rent. The mortgage will remain effective until _____ year, at which time the mortgagor will, by reimbursing the mortgagee for the sum specified above and presenting this contract as evidence, reclaim his property.

If the mortgagor is unable to pay back the mortgagee at the specified time, the latter will be entitled to continue occupancy of the house; the mortgagor will also be fined _____ amount.

It is further stated that there are no prior mortgages on the house, nor are there any questions as to its ownership. Should any such question arise, it will be the sole responsibility of the mortgagor.

This contract is drawn up as evidence of the present mortgage transaction.

SAMPLE CONTRACT FOR
THE SELLING OF CATTLE

The undersigned seller, _____, agrees to sell a water buffalo (bull/cow), its age as indicated by its teeth, its body intact, having four limbs, head and tail, to the buyer, _____, for use in ploughing. The seller, the buyer, and the mediator have agreed on the price, _____, which is to be paid in full on the same day this contract is signed. The condition of the merchandise has been examined by the buyer; the seller assumes full responsibility for its origin.

This contract is drawn up as evidence of the sale.

---

* Note the difference between this kind of mortgage and our own: In this case the owner of the house is essentially "pawning his house for a sum of money; he cannot live in the house until he repays the loan.

SAMPLE CONTRACT FOR THE PURCHASE OF A CONCUBINE

The undersigned, _____, from _____ village, has agreed to give in marriage his own daughter _____, aged ____ years, to the second party, _____, as a concubine, through the mediator, _____.

On this date the undersigned has received ____ amount as betrothal payment. He agrees to give his daughter away on the date selected by the second party. He will not dare to cause any difficulties or to extort more money from the second party. He also guarantees that the girl has not been previously betrothed, and that there is no question as to her origin. Should such questions arise, or should the girl run away, he will he held responsible. Should the girl die of unexpected circumstances, it is her fate, and not the responsibility of the second party.

This contract is drawn up as evidence os the agreement.

SAMPLE CONTRACT FOR THE SELLING OF A SON FOR ADOPTION

The undersigned, _____, from _____ county, _____ village, is unable to raise his own son _____, aged ____ years, because of poverty. After consulting his wife and relatives (uncle/brother _____ and _____, etc.), he has decided to sell the child, through a mediator, to _____ as an adopted son.

On this date the undersigned received ____ amount of money from the second party, and the transaction was completed. The second party agrees to raise the child, who will be at his disposal for marriage, will be as obedient to him as a servant, and will not avoid labor or run away. This contract is signed out of the free will of both parties, there being no prior sales, and no questions as to the origin of the child; nor is the seller forced by a creditor to sell the child as payment for debts. From now on the child belongs to his new owner; alive, he shall never return to this original family; dead, he shall not be buried in the graveyard of his original family. Should he run away or be kidnapped, only the seller and the mediator are responsible; should the child die of unexpected circumstances, it is his fate, and not the responsibility of his owner.

This contract, stamped with the palm prints of the child, is to be held by the owner as evidence of the transaction.

SAMPLE CONTRACT FOR HIRING A WORKER

The undersigned, _____, in order to support his family, agrees to work for _____ for one year as a laborer. The wages of ____ have been agreed on by both parties and are to be drawn by the employee at set intervals.

After the contract becomes effective, the hired worker will not avoid labor, but will devote himself to it. Should any unpredictable misfortune befall him, it is his fate, and not the responsibility of his master. If he should fail to work, deductions will accordingly be made from his daily wages.

This contract is drawn up as evidence of the agreement.

SAMPLE CONTRACT FOR FORMING A BUSINESS PARTNERSHIP

The undersigned, _____ and _____, having observed that partnerships bring profit and enterprise brings success, have agreed to pool their capital for profit. As witnessed by a mediator, _____, they have each contributed ____ as capital, and will cooperate sincerely in their business venture. The profit yielded will be divided between them each year to provide for their families. The capital will remain untouched to serve as the fountainhead of the business. Each individual will take care of his own personal expenses and not draw from the capital, nor should business and private expenditures be in any way mixed in bookkeeping. The two parties have taken an oath by drinking blood-wine to work together in harmony and share both profits and losses. They will not disagree, feud, or seek separate profits. The party that breaks this contract will be persecuted by gods and men alike.

This contract is drawn up in two copies as evidence of the agreement.

Translated by Clara Yu

ZHANG HAN'S ESSAY ON MERCHANTS

Money and profit are of great importance to men. They seek profit, then suffer by it, yet they cannot forget it. They exhaust their bodies and spirits, run day and night, yet they still regard what they have gained as insufficient.

Those who become merchants eat fine food and wear elegant clothes. They ride on beautifully caparisoned, double-harnessed horses—dust flying as they race through the streets and the horses' precious sweat falling like rain. Opportunistic persons attracted by their wealth offer to serve them. Pretty girls in beautiful long-sleeved dresses and delicate slippers play stringed and wind instruments for them and compete to please them.

Merchants boast that their wisdom and ability are such as to give them a free hand in affairs. They believe that they know all the possible transformations in the universe and therefore can calculate all the changes in the human world, and that the rise and fall of prices are under their command. They are confident that they will not make one mistake in a hundred in their calculations. These merchants do not know how insignificant their wisdom and ability really are. As Zhuangzi says, "Great understanding is broad and unhurried; little understanding is cramped and busy."

Because I have traveled to many places during my career as an official, I am familiar with commercial activities and business conditions in various places. The capital is located in an area with mountains at its back and a great plain stretching in front. The region is rich in millet, grain, donkeys, horses, fruit, and vegetables, and has become a center where goods from distant places are brought. Those who engage in commerce, in-

cluding the foot peddler, the cart peddler, and the shopkeeper, display not only clothing and fresh foods from the fields but also numerous luxury items such as priceless jade from Kunlun, pearls from the island of Hainan, gold from Yunnan, and coral from Vietnam. These precious items, coming from the mountains or the sea, are not found in central China. But people in remote areas and in other countries, unafraid of the dangers and difficulties of travel, transport these items step by step to the capital, making it the most prosperous place in the empire. . . .

South of the capital is the province of Henan, the center of the empire. Going from Kaifeng, its capital, to Weizhong, one can reach the Yangzi and Han rivers. Thus, Kaifeng is a great transportation center; one can travel by either boat or carriage from this spot to all other places, which makes it a favorite gathering place for merchants. The area is rich in lacquer, hemp, sackcloth, fine linen, fine gloss silk, wax, and leather. In antiquity, the Zhou dynasty had its capital here. The land is broad and flat, the people are rich and prosperous, and the customs are refined and frugal. . . .

In general, in the southeast area the greatest profits are to be had from fine gauze, thin silk, cheap silk, and sackcloth. Sanwu in particular is famous for them. My ancestors' fortunes were based solely on such textile businesses. At the present time, a great many people in Sanwu have become wealthy from the textile industry.

In the nation's northwest, profits are greatest in wool, coarse woolen serge, felt, and fur garments. Guanzhong is especially famous for these items. There is a family named Zhang in that area which has engaged in the animal-breeding business generation after generation. They claim to have ten thousand sheep. Their animal-breeding enterprise is the largest in the northwest and has made them the richest family in the area. In the surrounding areas of Yan, Zhou, Qi, and Jin, many other people have also become rich from animal breeding. From there, merchants seeking great profits go west to Sichuan and south to Guangdong. Because of the nature of the special products from the latter area—fine and second-grade pearls, gold, jade, and precious woods—profits can be five- or tenfold or more.

The profits from the tea and salt trades are especially great, but only large-scale merchants can undertake these businesses. Furthermore, there are government regulations on their distribution, which prohibit the sale of tea in the northwest and salt in the southeast. Since tea is produced primarily in the southeast, prohibiting its sale to the non-Chinese on the northern border is wise and can be enforced. Selling privately produced salt where it is manufactured is also prohibited. This law is rigidly applied to all areas where salt is produced during the Ming dynasty. Yet there are so many private salt producers there now that the regulation seems too rigid and is hard to enforce.

Profits from selling tea and the officials' income from the tea tax are usually ten to twenty percent of the original investment. By contrast, merchants' profits from selling salt and official income from the salt tax can reach seventy to eighty percent of the original invested capital. In either case, the more the invested capital, the greater the profit; the less the invested capital, the less the profit. The profits from selling tea and salt enrich the nation as well as the merchants. Skillful merchants can make great profits for themselves while the inept ones suffer losses. This is the present state of the tea and salt business.

In our Zhejiang province it appears that most of the rich gain their wealth from engaging in the salt trade. But the Jia family in Wuling became rich from selling tea and have sustained their prosperity for generations. The [ancient] *Book of Zhou* says, "If farmers do not work, there will be an insufficiency of food; if craftsmen do not work, there will be an insufficiency of tools; if merchants do not work, circulation of the three necessities will be cut off, which will cause food and materials to be insufficient."

As to the foreign trade on the northwestern frontier and the foreign sea trade in the southeast, if we compare their advantages and disadvantages with respect to our nation's wealth and the people's well-being, we will discover that they are as different as black and white. But those who are in charge of state economic matters know only the benefits of the Northwest trade, ignoring the benefits of the sea trade. How can they be so blind?

In the early years of the frontier trade, China traded sackcloth and copper cash to the foreigners. Now we use silk and gold but the foreigners repay us only with thin horses. When we exchanged sackcloth and copper cash for their thin horses, the advantage of the trade was still with China and our national wealth was not endangered. But now we give away gold and silk, and the gold, at least, will never come back to us once it flows into foreign lands. Moreover, to use the silk that China needs for people's clothing to exchange for useless, inferior horses is clearly unwise.

Foreigners are recalcitrant and their greed knows no bounds. At the present time our nation spends over one million cash yearly from our treasury on these foreigners; still we cannot rid ourselves of their demands. What is more, the greedy heart is unpredictable. If one day these foreigners break the treaties and invade our frontiers, who will be able to defend us against them? I do not think our present trade with them will ensure us a century of peace.

As to the foreigners in the southeast, their goods are useful to us just as ours are to them. To use what one has to exchange for what one does not have is what trade is all about. Moreover, these foreigners trade with China under the name of tributary contributions. That means China's authority is established and the foreigners are submissive. Even if the gifts we grant them are great and the tribute they send us is small, our expense is still less than one ten-thousandth of the benefit we gain from trading with them. Moreover, the southeast sea foreigners are more concerned with trading with China than with gaining gifts from China. Even if they send a large tribute offering only to receive small gifts in return, they will still be content. In addition, trading with them can enrich our people. So why should we refrain from the trade?

Some people may say that the southeast sea foreigners have invaded us several times so they are not the kind of people with whom we should trade. But they should realize that the southeast sea foreigners need Chinese goods and the Chinese need their goods. If we prohibit the natural flow of this merchandise, how can we prevent them from invading us? I believe that if the sea trade were opened, the trouble with foreign pirates would cease. These southeast sea foreigners are simple people, not to be compared to the unpredictable northeast sea foreigners. Moreover, China's exports in the northwest trade come from the national treasury. Whereas the northwest foreign trade ensures only harm, the sea trade provides us with only gain. How could those in charge of the government fail to realize the distinction?

Turning to the taxes levied on Chinese merchants, though these taxes are needed to fill the national treasury, excessive exploitation should be prohibited. Merchants from all areas are ordered to stop their carts and boats and have their bags and cases examined whenever they pass through a road or river checkpoint. Often the cargoes are overestimated and thus a falsely high duty is demanded. Usually merchants are taxed when they enter the checkpoint and are taxed again at the marketplace. When a piece of goods is taxed once, the merchant can still make some profit while complying with the state's regulations. But today's merchants often are stopped on the road for additional payments and also suffer extortions from the clerks. Such exploitation is hard and bitter enough but, in addition, the merchants are taxed twice. How can they avoid becoming more and more impoverished?

When I was vice-president of the Board of Public Works in Nanjing, I was also in charge of the customs duties on the upper and lower streams of the Black Dragon River. At that time I was working with the censor, Fang Keyong. I told him, "In antiquity, taxes on merchants were in the form of voluntary contributions based on official hints, not through levies. Levying taxes on merchants is a bad policy. We should tax people according to their degree of wealth or poverty. Who says we cannot have good government?" Fang agreed with me, so we lowered the taxes on the merchants some twenty percent. After the taxes were lowered, merchants became willing to stop at the checkpoints. All boats now stop when they should and the total tax income received from merchants has increased fifty percent. From this example one can see that the people can be moved by benevolent policies.

THE BIOGRAPHY OF ZHU JIEFU

Zhu Jiefu, whose formal name was Jie, started as a Confucian scholar. He was from Tunxi of Xiuning and his father, Xing, was a salt merchant who lived away from home at Wulin. Xing had taken Shaoji of Wulin as his concubine but she was barren. Later, when he returned home for his father-in-law's birthday, his primary wife became pregnant and gave birth to Jiefu. In his early childhood, Jiefu lived in Wulin with his father and went to school there. Shaoji, relying on his father's favor, did not treat him as her son. Jiefu, however, served her respectfully and worked diligently in school. At the age of fourteen, he officially registered Wulin as his native place and was designated an official student of that place. Shortly thereafter, his father died at Wulin. The concubine took the money and hid it with some of her mother's relatives and would not return to her husband's hometown. Jiefu wept day and night, saying, "However unworthy I may be, my late father was blameless." Finally the concubine arranged for the funeral and burial of Jiefu's father in his hometown. Thus, everything was done properly.

After the funeral, Jiefu was short of funds. Since for generations his family had been in commerce, he decided not to suffer just to preserve his scholar's cap. Therefore he handed in his resignation to the academic officials and devoted himself to the salt business. He thoroughly studied the laws on salt merchandising and was always able to talk about the strength and weaknesses of the law. When the envoy from the salt manufacturing division asked for his suggestions, Jiefu would respond promptly. As a result, all the other salt merchants respected him as their leader.

During the Jiajing period [1522–1567], salt affairs were handled by the central law officer, who increased the taxes suddenly, causing great inconvenience for the merchants. They gathered in Jiefu's house and asked him to serve as their negotiator. Jiefu entered the office and stated the advantages and disadvantages of the new law eloquently in thousands of words. Leaning against his couch, the central law officer listened to Jiefu's argument and finally adopted his suggestions.

At that time, the merchants suffered greatly from two scoundrels who often took them to court in the hopes of getting bribes from them. During tense moments at trials, the merchants usually turned to Jiefu as their spokesman. Being lofty and righteous, he always disclosed the scoundrels' crimes and incriminated them. The merchants thus esteemed Jiefu for his virtue and wanted to give him a hundred taels of gold as a birthday present. But he protested, "Even if my acts have not been at the lofty level of a knight-errant, I did not do them for the sake of money." Thus, the merchants respected him even more and no longer talked about giving him money.

When there was a dispute among the merchants that the officials could not resolve, Jiefu would always promptly mediate it. Even when one group would go to his house and demand his compliance with their views, he would still be able to settle the dispute by indirect and gentle persuasion. Hence, people both far and near came one ofter the other to ask him to be their arbitrator. Yet, after settling a dispute, Jiefu would always step aside and never take credit himself.

The populace in Tunxi city where Jiefu lived was militant and litigious. When he returned home for his father's funeral, slanderous rumors were spread about him, but Jiefu humbled himself and never tried to get back at the instigators. Later, when he rapidly grew rich, people became even more critical. Jiefu merely behaved with even greater deference. When the ancestral shrine fell into disrepair, Jiefu on his own sent workmen to

repair it. When members of his lineage started talking about it, he had the workmen work during the day and consulted with his relatives in the evening. Finally the whole lineage got together and shared the task with him.

Once Jiefu bought a concubine in Wulin who bore a child after only a few months. His family was about to discard the child but Jiefu upbraided them, saying, "I love my children dearly. How could I cause someone else's child to die in the gutter?" He brought the child up and educated him until he was able to support himself.

In the past many wealthy merchants in the eastern provinces had striven to associate themselves with the gentry. But for several years the merchants had been barely scraping by, limiting their access to such friendship. Yet when Jiefu was in East Yue for business he became acquainted with some members of the gentry there. He gained a reputation for his hospitality, and even when common people visited him, he always treated them very well. Some people came to rely upon Jiefu as much as if he were a relative. If he did not offer them enough, they would complain, "You stupid little rich merchant, why are you so stingy with me?"

Jiefu finally discontinued his salt business and ordered his son to pursue a different career. By that time he was already planning to retire to his hometown. Then in 1568 a central law officer who was appointed to inspect the salt business started to encourage secret informants. Soon Jiefu was arrested, an enemy having laid a trap for him. However, the official could not find any evidence against him. But then He, whose son Jiefu had once scolded, came forward to testify. Consequently, Jiefu was found guilty. When the litigation against him was completed, he was sentenced to be a frontier guard at Dinghai. The merchants said, in describing Jiefu's case, "Beating the drum, the official seized a lamb and claimed it to be a tiger; pretending to net a big fish, he actually aimed at the big bird."

When Jiefu received his sentence to enter the army, he controlled his feelings and immediately complied. His son, fearing his father would acquire a bad name, suggested that he send a petition to the emperor. Jiefu merely sighed and said, "Your father must have offended Heaven. The truth is that the central law officer is a representative of his Heavenly Majesty, not that your father is falsely charged."

The frontier general Liu had heard of Jiefu and therefore summoned him to work in his own encampment. At that time, a friend of the general's moved to Xindu upon his retirement. The general sent Jiefu to Xindu as his personal messenger but within a short time Jiefu became seriously ill. He advised his son, Zhengmin, "Your father's name has been recorded in the official labor records. Now he is about to die as a prisoner. Never let your father's example stop you from behaving righteously. Remember this." Then at the age of sixty-five, he died.

Translated by Lily Hwa

51

WHAT THE WEAVER SAID

By the Ming dynasty, textile production had become a major industry involving considerable specialization and establishment of large and small workshops, networks of brokers, and markets. Cotton cloth was woven mainly by peasants working in their homes as a means of gaining extra income. Fancy silks, however, were generally produced in workshops by weavers paid wages. Below is an account of a weaver in such a workshop written by the scholar and teacher Xu Yikui (d. ca. 1400). His purpose in recording his conversation with the weaver was to provide a moral lesson, but there is no reason to doubt his description of what he saw and heard.

When I lived in Xiangan Ward in Qiantang, I had a wealthy neighbor who employed live-in weavers. Late every evening one of them would start to sing and the rest would join in. From the sound of their voices, they seemed to be cheerful. "How happy they are!" I sighed.

One morning I walked over there and found it to be just a rickety old house. There were four or five looms in a room, arranged in a row from the north to south, and about ten workers, all of whom were laboring with both hands and feet. They looked pale and spiritless. I called one worker over and said, "From what I have seen, your work is very hard. Why are you still so happy?"

The worker replied, "Happiness is determined by the thoughts in a person's mind. If he isn't greedy, he can be happy with very little. But those who are greedy may earn a thousand strings of cash a day and still always feel unhappy. Though my job is a humble one, I can earn two hundred cash a day. The master provides me with food and clothes, so I can use my wages to support my parents, wife, and children. We are far from having delicious food, yet neither are we suffering from hunger or cold. I consider my life a normal one: I am not discontent, and the material I weave is very beautiful and highly valued by people. Thus, the master can easily sell the products and we are able to earn our wages easily. Since this is all we really want, our inner contentment naturally comes out in our voices as we sing together. We do not think of the hardship of the work.

"Not long ago, there was a weaver employed in another workshop. He earned approximately the same amount of money as we do. Yet, after working for a while, he started to complain: 'I am a more skillful weaver than anyone else, but

I still get the same wages. I am going to work for someone who will pay me twice as much.' Later on, one workshop owner did offer him double. The master examined his work and noticed that it was indeed superior, and the other weavers, after seeing his skill, also respected him highly. The master was very happy, thinking, 'This one weaver's work is better than that of ten others put together. It is well worth doubling his pay.' After working for a while, the weaver again became dissatisfied. He thought, 'I am such a superior weaver that if I leave this occupation and engage in another, I will undoubtedly be superior in that one, too. If I take employment under a high official, by playing up to him and serving him wholeheartedly, I will be able to gain great wealth and glory for myself. Why should I work in a weaving factory forever?'

"Eventually, he did take a position serving a high official. He worked among the slaves taking care of carriages and horses, and for five years did not find anything he could consider an opportunity for wealth and glory. Then one day, after another five years had passed, he provoked the official, who became infuriated and dismissed him and refused to see him ever again. By that time, the weaver had already forgotten his former trade. Moreover, people were disgusted with his arrogance and inability to be content, and no one wanted to hire him to weave. In the end he died of hunger and cold.

"I took this person as a warning. How could I fail to feel content and happy?"

This worker is indeed content, and exemplifies what Laozi meant when he said, "One who knows how to be satisfied will always be satisfied." This is why I recorded his story. At the time of our conversation, there were about ten workers present. The one who talked to me was named Yao.

Translated by Lily Hwa

52

TENANTS

From the time of the late Zhou dynasty, when free buying and selling of land became common, tenancy was a recurrent problem. Some farmers would flourish and buy more land. Others would fall into debt, have to sell their land, and work the land of others either as hired hands or as tenants paying their landlords a fixed share of the harvest or a fixed yearly sum. Tenancy was always considered a social and political evil because large landowners stood to gain too much local power. Often they would protect their tenants from tax and labor service obligations to the government, thereby attracting more tenants but also reducing the government's revenues. From the Han through the Tang, the government repeatedly tried to limit landholdings and tenancy, but after mid-Tang great variation in the size of landholdings was legally tolerated.

How did tenants see their position? Contracts are one of the few sources that can give us a clue to this question. Although contracts would usually have been composed by the master or a scribe, their content was so important to the tenant that it must often have been deeply impressed on his mind. Below are two contracts from an estate in Huizhou, in Anhui province, which date from the late Ming. In certain parts of China, including the Huizhou area, tenants were often obligated to perform nonagricultural duties for their masters, such as helping at festivals, weddings, and funerals. Such tenant-servants were acquired through contracts, and their status was often hereditary. The two contracts here show two common ways a person could become a tenant-servant: in exchange for gravesites; or to gain the right to marry the widow of another tenant-servant. After these two contracts is the brief description from a local history of an abortive revolt of tenant-servants in this area during the upheavals that accompanied the fall of the Ming.

1

The servants Hu Shengbao, Hu Zhubao, Hu Chibao, and the sons and grandsons of the four Hu branch families draw up this contract. Previously our ancestors, Hu Ang and Hu Sheng, besought from Master Hong Shou one piece of open land, the Lower Pond Hill, located in our county, for the purpose of burying our ancestors, Hu Fu and his wife. Since then, fifteen more coffins have been buried there. Each coffin occupies the space of nine paces. Kept in this cemetery was also one small coffin of the master's family and one stone tablet. Our ancestors had drawn up statements specifying that we could bury no one outside these given spaces. It stated that we could only have further burials in the master's cemetery with his permission. It is agreed that the descendants of our Hu family will observe this regulation in perpetuity; no arbitrary burial is allowed. If there are any violations of this rule, the master can present the case to the court and have us punished as violators.

Recently because of our failure to perform adequately our duty of escorting his children to school, the master expressed his intent to take our case to court. All the four branch families, realizing our weak position, pleaded for forgiveness and were willing to accept punishment. It is agreed that from now on, whenever there are marriages, funerals, or sacrifices in the master's house, we will offer our services.

The master, in consideration of the fact that we live far away from his estate and that he has enough servants on the estate, only requests us to send over two people to help with the sacrifice and cleaning during the Clear and Bright Festival [for honoring the dead]. In addition, on occasions when members of the master's family are going to school, going to the examinations, or responding to the call to serve in public office, the descendants of the four families will each dispatch one person to serve for one day. We dare not refuse the call for service. We also agree to keep watch carefully over the master's family graveyard.

After this contract is drawn up, the descendants of the four Hu families will observe the regulations in perpetuity. Should there be any violations, the master can present the case to the court and have us punished as violators.

In order to guarantee the agreements, we draw up this contract as evidence.

Dated on the 17th day of the twelfth month of 1605.
The servants who draw up the contract, Hu Shengbao, Hu Xibao, and their sons and grandsons, Hu Qi, Hu Chengming and Hu Yangui, Hu Zhubao, Hu Chu and their sons and grandsons, Hu Xisun, Hu Xialong, Hu Chibao and Hu Sheqi, Hu Ji, Hu Qibao and their sons and grandsons, Hu Shefu and Hu Shelong
The person who wrote the contract, Hu Chengming

2

Tenant Wang Mengxi draws up this contract. The resident tenant Lü San of the Old Father Temple Estate, Hu Family Mountain, passed away, leaving behind him his widow, Juxiang, nee Lin, and two sons. The elder son is Youshou; the younger one is Baoshou. They are both young and weak and unable to perform the duty of cultivating the field for the estate.

The master, considering that I have not been married, permitted me to marry the widow, Lin, to enter her family, to raise her two children, and to pay the rent to the master.

Previously Lü San had separated his property from that of Lü Xing. I will take possession of the house and lands which belonged to Lü San. Upon entering the widow's house, I will carefully serve the master, diligently cultivate the land, and earnestly raise the two children. I do not dare to come or go at will or to make trouble. Later on if I have children of my own, I will divide my earnings and the field and the house equally among all of them. If I am lazy or indolent, the master can take action against me.

In order to guarantee this agreement, I have drawn up this contract as evidence.

Dated on the 27th day of the eleventh month of 1634.

The person who drew up the contract, Wang
Mengxi [sign]
Younger cousin, Lü Xing [sign]
Roommate Lin Fahu [sign]

3

Yi county and Xiuning county were both under the jurisdiction of Huizhou. In the fourth month of 1645, before the Qing troops had arrived, the tenant-servants in these counties formed twelve stockades and demanded the return of their contracts from their masters. If their masters acted in any way against their will, they were killed and their houses burned. The tenant-servants all said: "The emperor has been replaced; our masters should now be our servants." Masters and servants began to address each as "brothers." In weddings, the bride and groom had to walk, for there were no servants to carry them. This situation bore a resemblance to the rebellion of Jiangyin, except it seemed even worse in Yi county.

When this revolt reached Xiuning, the people of good birth there were all in a quandary. They subsequently formed seventy-two societies, with the wealthy contributing food and silver to ensure local security. The county magistrate, Ouyang Xuan, was from Jiangxi. He invited the gentry of the county to a banquet, during which he made a tearful declaration that he would immediately raise troops. Jin Sheng and Huang Geng also mobilized their own troops. For this reason, the tenant-servants did not dare make any more moves.

Translated by Lily Hwa and Clara Yu

53

SHI JIN THE NINE-DRAGONED

From at least the late Song, Chinese storytellers and dramatists delighted audiences with tales of the 108 heroes and outlaws of Liangshan. Based on an actual gang active in the last decades of the Northern Song, this legend grew over the years and these bandits came to be credited with numerous feats of strength, daring, and cruelty. An episodic novel about the members of this bandit gang, called Water Margin, *developed from this long oral tradition and probably was put in its present form in the fifteenth century.*

The section of this novel given below recounts how one young man came to embark on a career that would eventually lead him to join the bandits of Liangshan. This episode provides descriptions of social customs, such as ways of treating teachers and guests. Moreover, by contrasting the docility and weakness of villagers and servants with the behavior of the hero, it suggests some reasons why Chinese peasants, townsmen, and even members of the upper class were so attracted to stories of the reckless pursuit of honor and profit.

Let us now tell about Instructor Wang Jin and his mother. After leaving the Eastern Capital to escape Minister Gao, they traveled for over a month, taking their meals on the road, stopping at night and setting out early in the morning. Finally one evening, Wang Jin, walking behind his mother's horse with the luggage on his shoulders, said to her, "Heaven has taken pity on us. We have escaped. Soon we'll be in Yan'an prefecture, where Minister Gao cannot arrest us even if he wants to."

Mother and son were so overjoyed that they went past the inn where they should have stopped. "It's so late now, and there's not a single village in sight. Where can we spend the night?" Just as they were worrying themselves with these thoughts, they caught the glimmer of a light through a patch of woods some distance away. Wang said to his mother, "We'll be all right now. We'll just go there and beg to stay for the night and be on our way again early tomorrow."

When they turned into the woods, they found a large farmhouse surrounded by a mudwall, lined by some two to three hundred willow trees. Instructor Wang went to the gate of the village and knocked. Finally, a servant came out. Setting down his load, Wang saluted the servant, who asked their purpose.

"Let me explain," Wang said. "My mother and I were so eager to go a little farther that we went beyond the last inn and found ourselves in the middle of nowhere. So, we would like to stay overnight in your village. We will pay for the lodging and leave promptly in the morning. We hope you can help us."

"Wait here a moment," said the servant, "while I ask my master. If he says so, you may stay." The servant went in, and eventually came out again to say, "Our master says to show you in."

Wang helped his mother dismount, then picked up his luggage again and entered with the servant. He led the horse to the threshing ground, set down his luggage, and tied the horse to a willow tree. Mother and son now went to the main hall to meet the master of the house.

The master was an old man of over sixty, his hair and beard completely white. He wore a warm wadded cap, a straight-cut loose robe belted by a black silk sash, and leather boots. When Wang Jin saw him, he hurried to salute. The old man stopped him, saying, "Don't stand on ceremony. You are travelers and must be exhausted. Please be seated." Wang and his mother sat after the usual preliminaries. The old man asked them, "Where are you from? Why have you arrived here late at night?"

Wang replied, "My name is Zhang. I am originally from the capital, but I lost all my money in business. Now that I have no way to make a living, I'm on my way to Yan'an prefecture to stay with relatives. Today, because we were eager to cover as much distance as possible, we missed the last inn. We hope to stay at your village overnight and will be on our way again early tomorrow morning. We will be happy to pay the standard rate for the lodgings."

"No problem," said the old man. "Who in this world can carry his own house over his head when he travels? I suppose you haven't eaten yet, have you?" Then he ordered a servant to bring food.

In no time a table was set right in the hall, and the servants brought out a tray with four kinds of vegetables and a plate of beef. They set the plates on the table, warmed some wine, and poured it into cups. The master of the house said, "In this backwater area, we do not have much to offer our guests. Please don't take offense."

Wang rose from his chair to thank him. "My mother and I have intruded on you and troubled you. We don't know how to repay you for your kindness."

"Please—no such nonsense!" the old man said. "Come, have some wine."

At his urging, mother and son drank some five or seven cups of wine. Afterwards rice was served, and they took their meal. When the dishes were cleared away, the old man showed the pair to the guest room where they would spend the night. Wang then made another request, "The horse that my mother rode—could you please take care of it, too? I will also pay for its stall and feed."

"No problem at all. I myself also have a few horses and mules. I'll just tell the servants to put your horse in the stable and feed it with the others."

Thanking him, Wang brought his luggage to the room. A servant lit the lamp and brought them hot water for washing their feet. The old man went back to his inner quarters to rest. Thanking the servant, Wang and his mother closed the door and went to bed.

The next morning, Wang and his mother did not get up. When the old man passed by the guest room, he heard the mother groaning. So he called out, "Sir, it's dawn, time to get up."

When Wang heard him, he hurried out of the room and saluted him. "I have been up for a long time," he said. "Sorry for all the trouble we caused you last night."

The old man then asked about the groaning. Wang explained, "Sir, I won't hide it from you. My mother is exhausted from riding and last night she suffered pains in her heart."

"Don't worry," said the old man, "let your mother stay a few days in my house. I have a good prescription for heart pain, and I'll send a servant to the town to fill it for her. Tell her to relax and take her time resting." Wang Jin again expressed his thanks.

But let's not go into every detail. In short, Wang and his mother stayed at the farm while she took her medication. In about a week's time, Wang felt that his mother had recovered and prepared to leave. On his way out to the stable in the back of the house to see his horse, he passed an open yard where he saw a young man practicing with a cudgel. He was naked from the waist up and tattooed all over with blue dragons. About eighteen or nineteen, his face was as bright and shiny as a silver plate.

After watching him for a while, Wang Jin inadvertently remarked, "That's very good! But you're still making mistakes and couldn't beat a real master."

This remark infuriated the young man, who shouted at Wang, "Who are you? How dare you put me down? I've studied with seven or eight famous teachers. There's no way you can beat me! I dare you to fight with me."

Hardly had he finished speaking when the old man appeared and scolded him, "Don't be rude."

"But this jerk laughed at my fencing techniques."

The old man then asked Wang if he knew martial arts. "Rather well," he replied. Then he asked who the young man was, and the old man told him he was his son. Wang said, "Since he is the young master of the house, I wouldn't mind giving him a few hints to improve his skills—that is, if he wishes to learn."

"That would be great," said the old man, who then told the youth to pay Wang Jin the obeisance due a teacher.

This the young man would have nothing to do with. Now even more angry than before, he said to his father, "Dad, don't listen to this jerk. I'll be his student only if he can win over this cudgel of mine."

"If the young master doesn't think I'm his equal," Wang Jin said, "we can spar just for fun."

Hearing this, the young man, who already occupied the center of the yard, whirled his cudgel so swiftly that it looked like a windmill. He called out to Wang Jin, "Come on, come on! I'm not a man if I'm afraid of the likes of you."

Wang Jin laughed, but did not make a move.

The old man then said to him, "Sir, since you are willing to teach my son, why don't you go ahead and try the cudgel with him?"

"I'm afraid that I may hurt him, which would be embarrassing."

"It doesn't matter," the old man said. "Even if you break his arm or leg, it is all his own fault."

"In that case, forgive me for my audacity." Saying that, Wang Jin picked a cudgel from the weapon rack. Then he went to the center of the yard and struck a pose.

The young man looked at him, then, whirling his cudgel, rushed at him. Wang turned and ran, trailing his cudgel on the ground. The young man, flourishing his cudgel, ran after him. Now, Wang suddenly turned around, raised his cudgel, and crashed down on the young man, who lifted his cudgel to meet the blow, only to find that Wang Jin had changed direction. Wang swiftly drew back the cudgel, and thrust it toward the young man's chest. With one twirl, he knocked the cudgel out of the young man's hands and threw him to the ground.

Wang dropped his own cudgel and hastened to help him get up, apologizing. The young man scrambled to his feet, then immediately pulled over a stool and forced Wang to sit on it. He knocked his head on the ground in front of Wang Jin and said, "I've wasted my time with those worthless teachers. You are now my teacher; please instruct me."

"I haven't been able to think of a way to repay all the trouble my mother and I have caused these many days. I would be glad to teach you."

Delighted, the old man told his son to get dressed, and together they took Wang Jin to the inner guest hall. There they ordered the servants to kill a sheep and prepare various wines, foods, fruits, and sweets. Wang Jin's mother was invited to join them. After the four of them were seated and the wine was served, the old man rose to make a toast. Then he said to Wang, "Sir, you are such a master of martial arts, surely you must be a head instructor in the army. My son may have eyes, but he failed to recognize a hero."

Wang Jin laughed and said, "To tell you the truth, my name is not Zhang. I am Wang Jin, Head Instructor of the eighty-thousand-man imperial army in the Eastern Capital, and I have spent my life playing with weapons. You see, the new Commander of the Imperial Army, Gao, was once given a beating by my father. When he became the commander, he sought to vent his old hatred on me. Unfortunately I was under his command and in no position to argue with him. That's why I fled with my mother in the hopes of getting a job with the commander-in-chief of Yan'an prefecture. It wasn't my plan to come here. You and your son have been very kind to us, curing my mother and looking after us for so many days. I feel very indebted to you. If your son is willing to learn, I'll do all I can to teach him. But what he has learned so far is only show, of no value in combat. I must teach him again from the beginning."

"Do you understand how wrong you were, my son? Come over and pay respect to your teacher again!"

The young man once more knocked his head on the ground before Wang Jin, while the old man told him, "Sir, for generations our family has lived here in Huayin county with Little Flower Mountain right in front of us. This village is called Shi Family Village and contains three to four hundred families, all named Shi. Since his childhood, my son has been entranced by the martial arts and unwilling to learn farm work. His mother scolded him to no avail and eventually died of anger and frustration. Unable to control him, I've had to let him do what he wants. I don't know how much money I've spent for his teachers. I even had a famous artist tattoo his arms, shoulders, and chest with nine dragons, which resulted in his being called 'Shi Jin the Nine-Dragoned' by people here in the county. Sir, now that you are here, it will be great if you can help him complete his training. I will reward you handsomely for it."

Wang Jin, now highly pleased, replied, "Rest assured, sir, I will not leave until I've taught him everything."

From the day of that banquet, Instructor Wang

and his mother stayed in the village. Every day Shi Jin would come and beg Wang to teach him the techniques of the eighteen weapons of war, and Wang taught him everything from scratch. Shi Jin's father was in the Huayin county seat serving as a village headman.

Time slipped quickly by. Within a little more than half a year Shi Jin had mastered the skills of all eighteen weapons: the lance, battle-hammer, bow, crossbow, jingal, whip, truncheon, double-edged sword, chain, hooks, axe, battle-axe, as well as the three-pronged spear, halberd, shield, cudgel, spear, and rake. With Wang putting his heart into teaching the young man, Shi Jin learned the secret techniques of each weapon. When Wang saw that he had mastered them all, he thought to himself, "Nice as it is to be here, I can't stay forever." So, one day, he said it was time to go to Yan'an. Shi Jin, however, wouldn't let him go, saying, "Don't leave. I'll take care of you and your mother till the end of your days. How about it?"

"My good brother," Wang replied, "you have been very kind, and everything is very nice here. But I'm afraid that Commander Gao will send someone to arrest me. You'd be implicated, not a very good prospect. For these reasons, I've decided to go to the commander-in-chief in Yan'an. It's on the border where people are needed. I'll be able to get a job there and settle down."

When Shi Jin and his father found that they couldn't change Wang Jin's mind, they prepared a farewell feast for him. To show their gratitude, they presented him with a platter on which lay two rolls of satin and one hundred taels of silver.

The next day Wang Jin packed his luggage and got his horse ready, and he and his mother bade their host farewell. Wang helped his mother onto the horse, and they started their journey to Yan'-an. Assigning a servant to carry Wang's luggage, Shi Jin escorted him for a distance of ten *li*, so reluctant was he to let his teacher go. Then he bowed to the ground to him, and they parted in tears. Shi Jin returned home with his servant, while Instructor Wang again shouldered his bundles and walked behind his mother's horse on their way to Guanxi.

We will now leave Wang Jin, who went to seek a career in the military, but continue our story of Shi Jin, who returned to his village.

Every day Shi did nothing but train to increase his strength. As he was in his prime and unmarried, he would get up before dawn to practice his skills and during the day would spend all his time in the back of the village riding on horseback and shooting arrows. Less than half a year had passed in this way when one day his father fell ill. He did not improve for many days, and Shi Jin sent all over for doctors to care for him, but the old man could not be cured and passed away.

For the sake of his father, Shi Jin selected the best coffin and outer casket. He engaged monks to pray for him, to hold memorial services through the forty-nine-day mourning period, and to establish merits for the old man in the next world. He also engaged Daoist priests to set up an altar and perform a dozen redemption services to ensure his passage to Heaven. Then Shi Jin selected an auspicious day and a propitious hour for the burial. All the three to four hundred families of the village joined in the funeral procession in mourning dress. They buried his father in the ancestral graveyard on the mountain west of the village. From then on, Shi Jin's family estate lacked a manager, for he would not concern himself with farm work; the only thing he enjoyed was challenging others to spar with him using various weapons.

Three or four months after the old man's death, on a very hot day in the middle of the sixth month, Shi Jin was idling away his time and pulled up a bench to sit in the shadow of the willow trees near the threshing ground. A breeze wafted through the pine grove on the other side, and Shi Jin exclaimed, "Ah, what a good, cool breeze!" Just then he saw someone peeping out from behind the trees. "What are you up to—you who are spying on my village?" shouted Shi Jin. He jumped up and went around on the other side of the trees, where he found the hunter Li Ji, nicknamed "Rabbit-lancer."

"Li Ji, what are you searching for in my village? Are you planning to rob us?"

Stepping forward, Li Ji said, "Sir, I was just going to have a drink with 'Shorty' Qiu Yilang. When I saw you there resting, I didn't dare to intrude."

"I have a question for you," Shi interposed. "You used to bring by game to sell in our village, and I paid you for it. Why have you stopped doing it? Is it because you think I don't have the money to pay you any more?"

"Sir, how dare I even dream of such a thing! The truth is that I haven't had any game to sell."

"Nonsense," said Shi Jin. "Little Flower Mountain is so big; I can't believe that there isn't a deer or rabbit on it."

"Haven't you heard?" said the hunter. "There's a band of robbers in the mountains now. They've built themselves a hideout and gathered some five to seven hundred men and over a hundred good horses. The chief is called Zhu Wu, nicknamed 'Clever Strategist,' the second in command is Chen Da, nicknamed 'Gorge-leaping Tiger,' and the third in command is Yang Zhun, 'White-speckled Snake.' These chiefs lead their men to raid people's houses. Even the Huayin county government can't handle them and is now offering a reward of three thousand strings of cash to anyone who captures them. But who dares? Since we hunters don't even dare climb the mountain to hunt for game, how can I have any for sale?"

"I've heard about these bandits," said Shi Jin, "But I didn't know they'd gotten so powerful. Sooner or later they'll bring trouble. Well, Li Ji, if you ever have any game, bring some by." Li Ji bowed and left.

As Shi Jin went back into the house, he thought, "These bandits are growing so strong. Inevitably, they'll come to our village to make trouble. In that case . . ." He then ordered the servants to butcher two fat buffalos and bring out some good home-brewed wine. After burning a stack of paper coins for the gods, he sent servants out to invite over all the three or four hundred farmers of the Shi Family Village. When they arrived, Shi Jin seated them in the main hall according to seniority. As the servants poured wine for the guests, Shi Jin told them, "I have learned that there are three great bandits on Little Flower Mountain, who have gathered five to seven hundred men and taken them looting. Having become so strong, sooner or later they will come to our village to bother us. I've especially invited you here to discuss this matter. In case they should come, we ought to be prepared. If the bamboo clappers at my house are sounded, all of you should come with arms to help me. If something happens to any of you, we'll do the same. In this way we will help each other and together we'll protect our village. If the chiefs themselves should come here, I'll take care of them."

All the people said, "Sir, we farmers all depend on you to make the decisions. When the clappers are sounded, we'll all come to help." They thanked Shi Jin for the wine, and each went back home to get his weapons ready. Shi Jin also began precautionary measures; he repaired his doors and walls, set up watch stations, and got his armor, weapons, and horses ready.

Now let's turn to the three chiefs, who were holding a conference in their hideout at Little Flower Mountain. The leader, "Clever Strategist" Zhu Wu, was from Dingyuan and could fight with a sword in each hand. Although not particularly skilled in fighting, he knew military maneuvers well and was clever at strategy. The second in command was Chen Da, from Yecheng, whose weapon was a steel lance with a white tip. The third one, Yang Chun, was from the Jieliang county of Puzhou, and he used a big, long-handled sword. At the conference, Zhu said to Chen and Yang, "I heard that the Huayin county government has offered three thousand strings of cash to anyone who captures us. I'm afraid that we'll have to put up a fight. Since we're low on both money and food, we'd better go get some. Not only are we short now, but we need to stock up provisions for a long war."

Chen Da, the "Gorge-leaping Tiger," added, "You're right. We'll go to Huayin county and ask to 'borrow some rations' from them and see what they say."

"Don't go to Huayin county," injected the "White-speckled Snake" Yang Chun. "Let's go to Pucheng county and run no risks."

Chen said, "Pucheng has very few people and not a lot of cash or food. We'll do better in Huayin. The people there have lots of money and grain."

"Elder brother, you don't understand," explained Yang. "To raid Huayin, we must pass Shi Family Village. That 'Shi Jin the Nine-Dragoned' is a tiger of a man, not to be provoked. He'll never let us pass."

"Brother, what a coward you are! If you can't even get through a mere village, how can we fight the government soldiers?"

"Elder brother, don't underestimate Shi Jin. He's really something," Yang Chun warned.

Zhu Wu concurred. "I've also heard that the man is extremely brave and capable. Let's not go that way, brother."

At this Chen Da yelled, "Shut your traps, you two! Don't tell me how great he is and how worthless we are. He's just a man and doesn't have three heads or six arms." Then he called out to his followers, "Get my horse ready! We'll attack the Shi Family Village right now. And afterwards we'll take Huayin county."

Zhu Wu and Yang Chun tried to dissuade him, but Chen Da wouldn't listen. He put on his armor and mounted his horse, selected some one hundred and fifty men, then, to the accompaniment of drums and gongs, descended the mountain heading straight for Shi Family Village.

Shi Jin was just getting his weapons and horses ready when a servant reported the bandits were coming. He ordered the bamboo clappers sounded. When the farmers all around Shi Family village heard the clappers, they gathered together, three or four hundred of them. Bearing lances and staves, they rushed over to Shi Jin's place. There they saw the young man. On his head was a flat-topped turban; on his body a vermilion mail over a blue padded silk robe; on his feet a pair of green boots; and around his waist a wide leather belt. In front and behind, he wore metal plates as shields; on his back hung a bow and a quiver of arrows; in his hand he held a three-pointed, double-edged sword with four holes on which eight large metal rings were attached. A servant led forth a fiery red horse, which Shi Jin mounted, his sword in hand. In front of him were some forty strong retainers and behind some ninety farm laborers. The farmers of the Shi clan made up the rear of this procession. Shouting and yelling, they all made straight for the crossroad north of the village.

Chen Da had led his men dashing down Little Flower Mountain and ordered them to take position. Shi Jin saw that Chen Da wore a red concave cap, a gilded iron breast plate over a red padded robe, high boots, and a woven belt seven feet long. He rode on a tall white horse and held in horizontal position a steel spear eighteen feet long. His men, who had split into two groups and stood on either side, were shouting and yelling. The two leaders then approached each other to talk.

Chen Da looked at Shi Jin and bowed from his horse. Shi addressed him in a loud voice, "You and your men kill, set fires, and rob people of their possessions. These are all capital offenses. You all have ears and ought to have heard of me! How dare you come here looking for trouble?"

Chen Da answered, "We are short of food up in our mountain hideout and are on our way to Huayin county to borrow some. We only wish to pass your village; we wouldn't dare touch even a blade of grass here. If you let us pass now, we will thank you on our return."

"Nonsense! I am the village headman and was just about to go and capture you. How dare you ask to pass through my village! If I let you go, I myself will be implicated when the county magistrate hears of it."

"Within the four seas all men are brothers," said Chen Da. "Please let us pass."

"Cut the idle talk! Even if I let you go, there is someone else who wouldn't. Ask him; if he's willing to let you pass, you may."

"My good man," asked Chen Da, "whom am I to ask?"

"Ask this sword in my hand," replied Shi Jin. "If he lets you go, so will I."

Chen Da grew very angry and said, "You've

driven me beyond endurance. Don't you be presumptuous with me!"

Shi Jin, now also incensed, flourished his sword and spurred on his horse in the direction of Chen Da, who raised his spear and charged at Shi Jin. Their horses drew near, and a long fight ensued. Finally, Shi Jin faked a mistake and allowed Chen Da to thrust the spear toward his chest. At that instant Shi suddenly turned sideways, and Chen, his spear in hand, lunged right in front of him. With great ease Shi stretched out his long arm and, with a twist of his strong waist, lifted Chen from his saddle. Then, seizing him by the woven belt he wore, Shi tossed his to the ground. Chen Da's horse galloped away like a gust of wind.

Shi ordered his servants to tie Chen up. After chasing the bandits away, Shi returned home, where he tied Chen to a pillar in the center of the courtyard. He announced that he would capture the other two leaders and then go for the reward. Then he gave everyone a round of drinks and told them to return to their homes for the time being. They all applauded him. "You're a real hero, sir!"

Let's leave this joyous drinking crowd and return to Zhu Wu and Yang Zhun, who had stayed in their mountain hideout, holding their breath. They sent out some men to find out what had happened, and these men returned with the defeated bandits leading Chen Da's riderless horse. "Bitter, bitter news!" they cried. "Brother Chen wouldn't listen to the chiefs and now has lost his life." Upon Zhu Wu's inquiry, the men reported the details of the battle and concluded, "He couldn't measure up to the invincible Shi Jin."

Zhu Wu said, "This is all because he wouldn't listen to me."

"Let's all go out there and fight to the death!" said Yang Chun.

"That won't help any," Zhu said. "If even Chen is not Shi Jin's equal, you won't have a chance. I do have a plan, but if it doesn't work, it'll be the end of both of us." Then he whispered his plan to Yang Chun, adding, "There's no other way."

"An excellent plan!" exclaimed Yang. "Let's go at once; there's no time to lose."

Back in the village, before Shi Jin's anger had abated, a servant ran in so fast that it seemed he had wings. "The bandit leaders Zhu Wu and Yang Chun have come here themselves," he reported.

"Those guys are doomed. I'll send them both to the magistrate. Bring my horse!" Shi Jin ordered. Meanwhile, the bamboo clappers sounded everywhere, and all the farmers gathered. Shi Jin mounted his horse, but before he could depart from the village gate, he saw that Zhu Wu and Yang Chun had already walked up to it. The pair of bandit chiefs dropped to their knees, four streams of tears flowing down their cheeks.

"What's going on?" Shi Jin got off his horse and shouted at them. "Why are you kneeling?"

Zhu Wu replied in tears, "The three of us were forced to become bandits because we were persecuted by the law. Whe we became blood brothers, we made a vow: 'Though we were not born on the same day, we will die on the same day.' We dare not compare our bond with that between the heroes of the Three Kingdoms, Guan Yu, Zhang Fei, and Liu Bei, but that is what we aspire to. Chen Da, my younger brother, wouldn't listen to my advice and offended you. You captured him and we have no way of convincing you to release him, so we have come here to die with him. We beg you to send all three of us to the magistrate and collect the reward. We swear that we will not even bat an eye, for we want to die at the hands of such a hero as you."

When Shi Jin heard this, these thoughts ran through his mind: "What brotherly love! If I turn these people in for a reward, all the heroes in the world will hold me in contempt for such an unworthy act. Since ancient times it has been said, 'A tiger does not eat a piece of offered meat.'" Aloud he said, "You two, come inside with me."

Zhu Wu and Yang Chun were unafraid. They followed Shi Jin into the inner hall and there again fell on their knees and asked to be tied up. Shi asked them to rise many times but they refused. As a hero naturally admires heroic qualities, Shi Jin finally said to them, "Since there is such a bond between you, I would be less than a real man if I

were to send you to the magistrate. Why don't I release Chen Da and return him to you."

"No," said Zhu Wu. "That would implicate you, which won't do. It's better for you to send us in and collect the reward."

"That I will not do," Shi Jin said. "Will you eat and drink with me?"

"We are not even afraid to die," Zhu Wu replied. "Why should we be afraid of your wine and meat?"

Very pleased with this reply, Shi released Chen and prepared wine and food for the three right in the inner hall. Zhu Wu, Yang Chun, and Chen Da thanked him for his clemency. After a few rounds of drinks, they grew warmer toward each other. When the dinner ended, the three thanked their host again and together set out for the mountain. Shi saw them off at the village gate and then returned home.

When Zhu Wu and the others arrived at their mountain hideout, they took their seats, and Zhu said, "If we hadn't used this scheme to win his sympathy, we wouldn't have emerged alive. Although we achieved our goal, we must admire Shi Jin for his sparing us on the grounds brotherly love. Let's send him some presents one of these days to thank him."

In short, on a moonless night about a fortnight later, the three bandit leaders gathered thirty taels of slim gold ingots and commanded two of their men to take the gift to Shi Family Village. When the servants reported that two men were knocking at the gate, Shi Jin quickly threw on his clothes and hurried out. "What is it?" he asked the men.

"Our three chiefs send their repeated regards. They have sent us here with a small token of their gratitude for your sparing their lives. Please do not refuse it, sir."

At first Shi Jin would not accept the gift, but when he thought of the givers' good intention, he relented. He ordered the servants to serve the messengers plenty of wine, and, before leaving, gave them some odd silver as a tip. Half a month later, Zhu Wu and his men succeeded in obtaining some large pearls in the course of their exploits, and they again sent some men on a midnight mission to present the pearls to Shi Jin, who once more accepted the gift.

Another half month passed, and Shi Jin thought to himself, "Those three men have been very respectful to me. Let me send them something in return." So, the next day he ordered a servant to send for a tailor and he himself went into town to buy three pieces of red embroidered silk, which he asked the tailor to use to make three robes. Then he selected three fat sheep to be cooked and placed in large boxes. He instructed two servants to deliver the presents. Shi Jin's head servant, named Wang Si, was quite capable in dealing with officials and had a way with words. For these reasons, the villagers all called him "Peerless Diplomat." On this occasion, Shi Jin picked him and another trusted servant for the mission. They took the boxed presents to the foot of the mountain, and, after being interrogated by Zhu Wu's men, were shown to the leaders. Zhu and the other leaders were very pleased; they accepted the silk robes, the fat sheep, and the wine. They also tipped the two messengers with ten taels of silver. After having a dozen drinks, the two returned to the village and conveyed to Shi Jin the bandit leaders' best wishes. From then on. Shi Jin and the three chiefs maintained constant contact. Wang Si was repeatedly sent to the mountain with presents, and the chiefs reciprocated with messengers bearing gold and silver for Shi Jin.

Time went by and soon it was the eighth month. Shi Jin wished to talk with the chiefs and so sent Wang Si to Little Flower Mountain with an invitation for Zhu, Chen, and Yang. He would hold a banquet on the evening of the Mid-Autumn Festival and wanted them to join him for wine and viewing the full moon.

Wang Si ran up the mountain and delivered the invitation. After reading it, Zhu Wu was delighted and the three cheifs immediately wrote a reply, promising their attendance. They rewarded Wang Si with some four or five taels of silver and let him drink a dozen cups of wine before he departed. At the foot of the mountain, however, he chanced to see one of the bandits who often brought presents to the village. The latter would not let him leave, but dragged him to a roadside wine house, where Wang Si drank another dozen cups of wine. After the two parted, Wang Si headed for his village. The wind blew down from the mountain, and, as he was walking, the wine began working on him. He staggered along, swaying with every step. Hardly had he walked ten *li* when he saw a grove of trees in front of him. Once in it, he passed out on the lush green ground.

It so happened that the "Rabbit-lancer" Li Ji was looking for rabbits at the foot of this slope. He recognized Wang Si of Shi Family Village and hurried to the grove to help him get up. That proved impossible but he caught sight of some silver showing from Wang Si's shoulder bag. Li Ji thought to himself, "He is drunk. But where did he get all this silver? Well, why shouldn't I take some?" Just as it was destined that the stars of the Dipper were to end up in one place, so Heaven provided this opportunity. Li Ji untied the shoulder bag and, with a toss of the hand, threw its contents on the ground—the letter and all! He picked up the letter and, since he could read a little, opened it. He saw the words "Zhu Wu, Chen Da, Yang Chun of Little Flower Mountain." The letter itself contained words that he did not know, but he sure knew those three names. He thought, "When will a hunter like me ever get rich? Yet the fortune-teller said that this year I would come into a large fortune. This must be it! Didn't the Huayin county government offer three thousand strings of cash to get those bandits? I can't believe this Shi Jin! The other day when I went to his village to see 'Shorty' Qiu, he said I was there on the prowl for things to steal. Who'd think he's the one who runs around with bandits!" The hunter took the silver and the letter, then went straight to Huayin county to report to the officials.

Let's now talk about Wang Si. He woke up in the middle of the night, bathed in moonlight. When he jumped up in alarm, he found himself surrounded by pine trees. He fumbled around, but the bag and the letter were both gone! A search turned up nothing but the empty bag in the grass, which made him very worried. "The silver doesn't matter," he thought, "but the letter—what am I going to do? I don't know who took it." Then a plan occurred to him and he said to himself, "If I return to the village and say I've lost the letter, Master Shi will surely become enraged and kick me out of the village. It would be better to tell him there wasn't a written reply. How is he ever to find out the truth?"

His plan formed, Wang Si sped back to the village as if he had sprouted wings on his back. By the time he arrived, it was close to daybreak. When Shi Jin saw him, he asked, "Why so late?"

The servant replied, "Thanks to you, my lord, the three chieftains would not let me go, entertaining me with drinks half the night. That's why I'm so late."

"Have you brought back a letter or reply?"

"The three chieftains wanted to write a reply, but I told them, 'My lords, since you have decided to accept the invitation, there is really no need to put it in writing. I have had quite a few cups of wine; if I should lose the letter, it would be no laughing matter.' "

Shi Jin was very pleased with this answer. "You are really capable," he said. "No wonder people call you 'Peerless Diplomat.' "

Wang Si continued, "And I did not dare to delay even a moment. I ran straight back here, without taking one minute's rest on the road."

Then Shi Jin said, "Since they are coming, let's send some people to town to get fruit and wine for the feast."

Time passed quickly, and soon it was the Mid-Autumn Festival. The weather was beautiful and Shi Jin ordered his servants to kill a fat sheep and some hundred chickens and geese for the banquet. As evening drew near, the three chiefs on Little Flower Mountain ordered most of their men to stay behind to keep watch at the hideout, picking only a few to accompany them. Each of the three carried a big sword in his hands and another hanging from his waist. They did not mount their horses but instead walked down the mountain. On arrival at Shi Family Village, Shi Jin received them, and after the usual ceremonies, brought them to the back courtyard, where a feast had been prepared. The three chiefs were shown to the

seats of honor, whereas Shi Jin himself sat across from them. As soon as the front and the back gates were barred, the drinking commenced. Servants took turns pouring the wine, while others carved and served the mutton. After they had had a couple of drinks, a bright full moon pushed itself above the eastern horizon.

Shi Jin and the three chiefs were chatting when suddenly they heard loud shouts from outside the wall and saw the glare of torches. Greatly startled, Shi Jin jumped up from his seat and said, "My three good friends, please remain seated. I'll go find out what is happening." Then he ordered the servants not to open the gates.

Pulling a ladder against the wall, he climbed up and looked out. He saw the sheriff of Huayin on horseback; behind him were two leading officers and three or four hundred soldiers. The entire village was surrounded. Shi Jin and the three chiefs thought to themselves, "We're done for!" In the light of the torches, they could see gleaming steel-pronged spears, swords, five-pointed spears, and hooks, all as thick as hemp stalks in a field. The two leading officers yelled out, "Don't let the bandits escape!" . . .

"Now, what are we to do?" asked Shi Jin.

The three chiefs knelt down to the ground and said, "Older brother, you are innocent. We don't want to involve you. You must tie us up and give us up for the reward. It wouldn't look good to get you implicated in this."

"I will do nothing of the kind," said Shi Jin. "Otherwise people will think that I have tricked you into coming here in order to turn you in for the reward, and I'll become a universal laughing-stock. No, I'll live or die with you. Please get up and stop worrying; we'll think of something. But first let me get to the bottom of things." At that he climbed the ladder again and called out, "Why do you two officers come here in the middle of the night to bother me?"

They replied, "Sir, you still won't confess? Here, this is your accuser, Li Ji."

"Li Ji," shouted Shi Jin, "why do you falsely accuse me?"

"At first I did not know what it was. I picked

up a letter from Wang Si, and read it in front of the county magistrate; then the whole matter came out."

Shi turned to Wang Si, "Didn't you say that there was no written reply? What was this letter, then?"

"I was drunk and forgot about the letter."

At this Shi Jin gave out a loud cry, "You moron! Now what are we to do?"

The officers and their men, all afraid of Shi Jin, did not dare to come in to get him. The three chiefs pointed toward the outside and said, "Just give them a reply." Shi got the message and called out, "Officers, you don't have to bother. Please step back, and I'll have them tied up and send them out to you for the reward."

The two officers, afraid as they were of Shi Jin, consented, "We don't want to make any trouble. We'll just wait for you to bring them out and then go together with you to the magistrate for the reward."

Getting off the ladder, Shi Jin came to the main hall. He first had Wang Si brought to the backyard, and, with one thrust of the sword, killed him. Then he ordered some servants to pack up all the valuables and others to light some thirty or forty torches. Meanwhile, Shi and the three chiefs put on their armor and picked their weapons from the rack. Each had a short sword hanging from his waist and a big sword in his hand. By the time they set fire to the thatched huts in the rear of the village, the servants had also packed their own belongings.

When the crowd outside saw the fire, they all ran toward the back of the village, and Shi Jin took this opportunity to set fire to the main section. Then he flung open the gates and, with a loud cry, rushed out, killing whoever was in his way. Right behind Shi were Zhu and Yang; then came Chen with the bandits and Shi's servants. They fought their way out and deceived their enemies by pretending to go one direction while actually heading in another.

Shi Jin was a true tiger no one could stop. Against the background of the fire and confusion, he hewed open a passage through his enemies and came face to face with the two leading officers and Li Ji. When Shi saw them his anger rose, just as the saying goes, "When enemies meet they recognize each other clearly." The two officers, seeing that the outlook was bad for them, turned and ran. Li Ji wanted to do likewise, but before he could, Shi Jin caught up with him. He raised his sword and, with a downward blow, cut him in two. The two officers were trapped in their flight by Chen Da and Yang Chun. Each gave a blow with his big sword, and the two lives were ended. The sheriff was so scared that he retreated at full gallop. Terrified, each of the soldiers ran for his life. Soon all had disappeared.

Shi Jin led the men, running and fighting, straight to Little Flower Mountain. Entering the hideout, they sat down, and after they had rested a moment or two, Chu Wu and the other chiefs ordered their men to kill cows and horses for a feast to celebrate the victory. We need not go into the details. A few days later, Shi thought to himself, "I was in such a hurry to save these three people, I set fire to my village. Although I salvaged the valuables, all the furniture and heavy things are lost." As he worried about his future, he decided that it was not a good idea to stay. So he spoke his mind to the three chiefs, "My teacher, Instructor Wang, is now working for the commander-in-chief of Guanxi. I had wanted to go and look for him when my father passed away. Now that I have lost everything, including my house and my fortune, I will go look for him."

Zhu Wu and the others said, "Older brother, don't leave. Stay a little longer. We can talk it over later. If you don't want to become a bandit, you can wait till the whole thing has cooled down, then we will rebuild your village for you, and you can still be a good citizen."

"I appreciate your kindness," Shi Jin said. "But my mind is made up. If I can find my teacher, I will be able to become an officer and will have a good life ahead of me."

Zhu Wu said, "Older brother, if you don't mind the small size of this hideout, you can stay and be a chief. You'll be happy here."

"I am a man with no criminal record," said Shi

Jin, "and must not bring shame to my deceased parents. Don't ever again mention the subject of my joining you as a bandit."

After a few more days' stay, Shi insisted that he had to go, despite the best efforts of Zhu and the others to make him stay. Shi Jin left all his men with the bandits. Taking only a little silver and a bundle of clothes, he entrusted the rest of his belongings to the chiefs. He put on a white brimmed fur hat with a red tassel, and under it a soft black scarf, tied under his chin with a yellow ribbon. On his body he wore a uniform of white silk belted with a sash of plum-red color. On his legs he wore black-and-white garters tied in a zig-zag pattern and on his feet hemp sandals suited for travel in the hills. At his side hung a "wild goose feather" sword.

Swinging his bundle over his shoulders, Shi Jin picked up his big sword and bade farewell to Zhu and the other chiefs. All Zhu Wu's men accompanied him down the mountain, where they parted in tears. Then Zhu Wu and the men returned to their hideout.

Translated by Clara Yu

54

FAMILY INSTRUCTIONS

As seen in earlier selections, filial piety and differentiation between men's and women's roles were central values of the Chinese family system. Other values associated with Chinese "familism" included diligence, frugality, and willingness to identify with the larger family and its long-term survival and prosperity. The "Family Instructions" below elaborate on the importance of these virtues and traits. They were included in the late Ming genealogy of the Miu lineage in Guangdong province. In Ming times, it was quite common for groups of patrilineal relatives to organize themselves as lineages, holding some land in common, conducting joint ancestral rites, perhaps building an ancestral hall or publishing a genealogy. Family disputes concerning matters such as inheritance would often be referred to the leaders of the lineage. Lineage councils would also help parents discipline unruly or disobedient children, especially grown ones. To facilitate making judgments in such cases, lineages like this one compiled rules for family behavior and advice on achieving family harmony. Traditional precepts and neo-Confucian moral values were usually emphasized, with some adjustments to fit the daily life of ordinary peasants and working people.

WORK HARD AT ONE OF THE PRINCIPAL OCCUPATIONS

1. To be filial to one's parents, to be loving to one's brothers, to be diligent and frugal—these are the first tenets of a person of good character. They must be thoroughly understood and faithfully carried out.

One's conscience should be followed like a strict teacher and insight should be sought through introspection. One should study the words and deeds of the ancients to find out their ultimate meanings. One should always remember the principles followed by the ancients, and should not become overwhelmed by current customs. For if one gives in to cruelty, pride, or extravagance, all virtues will be undermined, and nothing will be achieved.

Parents have special responsibilities. The *Book of Changes* says: "The members of a family have strict sovereigns." These "sovereigns" are the parents. Their position in a family is one of unique authority, and they should utilize their authority to dictate matters to maintain order, and to inspire respect, so that the members of the family will all be obedient. If the parents are lenient and indulgent, there will be many troubles which in turn will give rise to even more troubles. Who is to blame for all this? The elders in a family must demand discipline of themselves, following all rules and regulations to the letter, so that the younger members emulate their good behavior and exhort each other to abide by the teachings of the ancient sages. Only in this way can the family hope to last for generations. If, however, the elders of a family should find it difficult to abide by these regulations, the virtuous youngsters of the family should help them along. Because the purpose of my work is to make such work easier, I am not afraid of giving many small details. . . .

2. Those youngsters who have taken Confucian scholarship as their hereditary occupation should be sincere and hard-working, and try to achieve learning naturally while studying under a teacher. Confucianism is the only thing to follow if they wish to bring glory to their family. Those who know how to keep what they have but do not study are as useless as puppets made of clay or wood. Those who study, even if they do not succeed in the examinations, can hope to become teachers or to gain personal benefit. However, there are people who study not for learning's sake, but as a vulgar means of gaining profit. These people are better off doing nothing.

Youngsters who are incapable of concentrating on studying should devote themselves to farming; they should personally grasp the ploughs and eat the fruit of their own labor. In this way they will be able to support their families. If they fold their hands and do nothing, they will soon have to worry about hunger and cold. If, however, they realize that their forefathers also worked hard and that farming is a difficult way of life, they will not be inferior to anyone. In earlier dynasties, officials were all selected because they were filial sons, loving brothers, and diligent farmers. This was to set an example for all people to devote themselves to their professions, and to ensure that the officials were familiar with the hardships of the common

people, thereby preventing them from exploiting the commoners for their own profit.

3. Farmers should personally attend to the inspection, measurement, and management of the fields, noting the soil as well as the terrain. The early harvest as well as the grain taxes and the labor service obligations should be carefully calculated. Anyone who indulges in indolence and entrusts these matters to others will not be able to distinguish one kind of crop from another and will certainly be cheated by others. I do not believe such a person could escape bankruptcy.

4. The usual occupations of the people are farming and commerce. If one tries by every possible means to make a great profit from these occupations, it usually leads to loss of capital. Therefore it is more profitable to put one's energy into farming the land; only when the fields are too far away to be tilled by oneself should they be leased to others. One should solicit advice from old farmers as to one's own capacity in farming.

Those who do not follow the usual occupations of farming or business should be taught a skill. Being an artisan is a good way of life and will also shelter a person from hunger and cold. All in all, it is important to remember that one should work hard when young, for when youth expires one can no longer achieve anything. Many people learn this lesson only after it is too late. We should guard against this mistake.

5. Fish can be raised in ponds by supplying them with grass and manure. Vegetables need water. In empty plots one can plant fruit trees such as the pear, persimmon, peach, prune, and plum, and also beans, wheat, hemp, peas, potatoes, and melons. When harvested, these vegetables and fruits can sustain life. During their growth, one should give them constant care, nourishing them and weeding them. In this way, no labor is wasted and no fertile land is left uncultivated. On the contrary, to purchase everything needed for the morning and evening meals means the members of the family will merely sit and eat. Is this the way things should be?

6. Housewives should take full charge of the kitchen. They should make sure that the store of

firewood is sufficient, so that even if it rains several days in succession, they will not be forced to use silver or rice to pay for firewood, thereby impoverishing the family. Housewives should also closely calculate the daily grocery expenses, and make sure there is no undue extravagance. Those who simply sit and wait to be fed not only are treating themselves like pigs and dogs, but also are leading their whole households to ruin. . . .

OBSERVE THE RITUALS AND PROPRIETIES

1. Capping and wedding ceremonies should be carried out according to one's means. Funerals and burials, being important matters, should be more elaborate, but one should still be mindful of financial considerations. Any other petty formalities not found in the *Book of Rites* should be abolished.

2. Marriage arrangements should not be made final by the presenting of betrothal gifts until the boy and girl have both reached thirteen; otherwise, time might bring about changes which cause regrets.

3. For the seasonal sacrifices, the ancestral temple should be prepared in advance and the ceremonies performed at dawn in accordance with [Zhu Xi's] *Family Rituals* and our own ancestral temple regulations.

4. For burials one should make an effort to acquire solid and long-lasting objects to be placed in the coffin; but one need not worry as much about the tomb itself, which can be constructed according to one's means. The ancients entrusted their bodies to the hills and mountains, indifferent to whether their names would be remembered by posterity; their thinking was indeed profound.

5. Sacrifices at the graves should be made on Tomb Sweeping Day and at the Autumn Festival. Because the distances to different mountains vary, it is difficult to reach every grave on those days. Therefore, all branch families should be notified in advance of the order of priority: first, the founding father of our lineage; then ancestors earlier than great-great-grandfather; next, ancestors

down to each person's grandfather. Established customs should be followed in deciding how much wine and meat should be used, how many different kinds of sacrificial offerings should be presented, and how much of the yearly budget should be spent on the sacrifices. All of these should be recorded in a special "sacrifice book" in order to set standards.

6. Not celebrating one's birthday has since ancient times been regarded as an exemplary virtue. An exception is the birthdays of those who are beyond their sixty-first year, which should be celebrated by their sons and grandsons drinking to their health. But under no circumstances should birthdays become pretexts for heavy drinking. If either of one's parents has died, it is an especially unfilial act to forget him or her and indulge in drinking and feasting. Furthermore, to drink until dead-drunk not only affects one's mind but also harms one's health. The numbers of people who have been ruined by drinking should serve as a warning.

7. On reaching five, a boy should be taught to recite the primers and not be allowed to show arrogance or laziness. On reaching six, a girl should be taught [Ban Zhao's] *Admonitions for Women* and not be allowed to venture out of her chamber. If children are frequently given snacks and playfully entertained, their nature will be spoiled and they will grow up to be unruly and bad. This can be prevented if caught at an early age.

8. When inviting guests to dinner, one should serve not more than five dishes or more than two soups. Wine and rice should also be served in the right proportion.

9. When attending a funeral service, one should bring only incense and paper money, never hand towels, fruit, or wine, and should stay for only one cup of tea.

10. Gifts presented to us on the occasion of ancestor worship are to be properly compensated for by cash. If the gift box contains a pig's head, the corresponding return would be one-tenth of a tael of silver; for two geese and wine it would be three-tenths of a tael; for a lamb and wine, half a tael; a pig and wine, one tael. In addition, two-

hundredths of a tael should be placed in an envelope and presented as a token compensation for fruit and wine. Whether or not these are accepted, and whether or not another present is given in return, depends on the other party. For ceremonies held in our own village, each person should contribute two-hundredths of a tael of silver, and four people should share one table. Those who have contributed yet fail to attend the banquet will get their money back in the original envelope. This is to be stated in the village agreements and to be practiced by all.

PROHIBIT EXTRAVAGANCE

1. All our young people should wear cotton clothes and eat vegetables. Only on special occasions such as ancestor worship or dinner parties are they to be allowed to drink wine, eat meat, and temporarily put on new clothes. They are fortunate enough to be sheltered from hunger and cold; how dare they feel ashamed of their coarse clothing and coarse food! Also, they should do physical labor. As long as they are capable of carrying loads with their hands and on their backs, they have no need to hire servants. They are fortunate enough not to be ordered around by others; how dare they order other people around! They should learn to cherish every inch of cloth and every half-penny, thereby escaping poverty.

2. Among relatives, presents should not be exchanged more than twice a year, and the gifts should not cost more than one-tenth of a tael of silver. Relatives should agree to abide by the principle of frugality and refuse any gift exceeding this limit. This rule, however, does not include celebrations and funerals, for which custom should be followed.

3. Ordinarily, custom dictates the foods to be offered guests. However, relatives and friends who visit each other often can be served just a dish of fish and another of vegetables. Sima Guang once wrote:

My father was a prefect. Whenever a guest came to visit, he would always serve wine.

Sometimes there were three rounds of drinking, and sometimes five, but never were there more than seven rounds. The wine was bought from the common market. The only sweets were pears, nuts, dates, and persimmons; the only dishes were dried or hashed meats, vegetables and thick soup; the plates were either porcelain or lacquer. That was the way officials of that time entertained their guests. They met often and were courteous to each other. Though the food was cheap, their friendships were deep.

From now on, whenever a guest comes to visit, we should not have many dishes and should not force the guest to drink too much. Our aim should be to have the congenial mood last a long time, and the host and the guest enjoy it together.

4. Since our branch of the family has many members, when a visitor comes, it is difficult to have everyone present for dinner. Instead, only some members of the family will be asked to share the company of the guest. This is designed to save expense. The members will all have their turns at being invited and should not compete among themselves, lest jealousy or suspicion arise.

EXERCISE RESTRAINT

1. Our young people should know their place and observe correct manners. They are not permitted to gamble, to fight, to engage in lawsuits, or to deal in salt privately. Such unlawful acts will only lead to their own downfall.

2. If land or property is not obtained by righteous means, descendants will not be able to enjoy it. When the ancients invented characters, they put gold next to two spears to mean "money," indicating that the danger of plunder or robbery is associated with it. If money is not accumulated by good means, it will disperse like overflowing water; how could it be put to any good? The result is misfortune for oneself as well as for one's posterity. This is the meaning of the saying: "The way of Heaven detests fullness, and only the humble gain." Therefore, accumulation of great wealth

inevitably leads to great loss. How true are the words of Laozi!

A person's fortune and rank are predestined. One can only do one's best according to propriety and one's own ability; the rest is up to Heaven. If one is easily contented, then a diet of vegetables and soups provides a lifetime of joy. If one does not know one's limitations and tries to accumulate wealth by immoral and dishonest means, how can one avoid disaster? To be able to support oneself through life and not leave one's sons and grandsons in hunger and cold is enough; why should one toil so much?

3. Pride is a dangerous trait. Those who pride themselves on wealth, rank, or learning are inviting evil consequences. Even if one's accomplishments are indeed unique, there is no need to press them on anyone else. "The way of Heaven detests fullness, and only the humble gain." I have seen the truth of this saying many times.

4. Taking concubines in order to beget heirs should be a last resort, for the sons of the legal wife and the sons of the concubine are never of one mind, causing innumerable conflicts between half brothers. If the parents are in the least partial, problems will multiply, creating misfortune in later generations. Since families have been ruined because of this, it should not be taken lightly.

5. Just as diseases are caused by what goes into one's mouth, misfortunes are caused by what comes out of one's mouth. Those who are immoderate in eating and unrestrained in speaking have no one else to blame for their own ruin.

6. Most men lack resolve and listen to what their women say. As a result, blood relatives become estranged and competitiveness, suspicion, and distance arise between them. Therefore, when a wife first comes into a family, it should be made clear to her that such things are prohibited. "Start teaching one's son when he is a baby; start teaching one's daughter-in-law when she first arrives." That is to say, preventive measures should be taken early.

7. "A family's fortune can be foretold from whether its members are early risers" is a maxim of our ancient sages. Everyone, male and female,

should rise before dawn and should not go to bed until after the first drum. Never should they indulge themselves in a false sense of security and leisure, for such behavior will eventually lead them to poverty.

8. Young family members who deliberately violate family regulations should be taken to the family temple, have their offenses reported to the ancestors, and be severely punished. They should then be taught to improve themselves. Those who do not accept punishment or persist in their wrongdoings will bring harm to themselves.

9. As a preventive measure against the unpredictable, the gates should be closed at dusk, and no one should be allowed to go out. Even when there are visitors, dinner parties should end early, so that there will be no need for lighting lamps and candles. On very hot or very cold days, one should be especially considerate of the kitchen servants.

10. For generations this family has dwelt in the country, and everyone has had a set profession; therefore, our descendants should not be allowed to change their place of residence. After living in the city for three years, a person forgets everything about farming; after ten years, he does not even know his lineage. Extravagance and leisure transform people, and it is hard for anyone to remain unaffected. I once remarked that the only legitimate excuse to live in a city temporarily is to flee from bandits.

11. The inner and outer rooms, halls, doorways, and furniture should be swept and dusted every morning at dawn. Dirty doorways and courtyards and haphazardly placed furniture are sure signs of a declining family. Therefore, a schedule should be followed for cleaning them, with no excuses allowed.

12. Those in charge of cooking and kitchen work should make sure that breakfast is served before nine o'clock in the morning and dinner before five o'clock in the afternoon. Every evening the iron wok and other utensils should be washed and put away, so that the next morning, after rising at dawn, one can expect tea and breakfast to be prepared immediately and served on time. In

the kitchen no lamps are allowed in the morning or at night. This is not only to save the expense, but also to avoid harmful contamination of food. Although this is a small matter, it has a great effect on health. Furthermore, since all members of the family have their regular work to do, letting them toil all day without giving them meals at regular hours is no way to provide comfort and relief for them. If these rules are deliberately violated, the person in charge will be punished as an example to the rest.

13. On the tenth and twenty-fifth days of every month, all the members of this branch, from the honored aged members to the youngsters, should gather at dusk for a meeting. Each will give an account of what he has learned, by either calling attention to examples of good and evil, or encouraging diligence, or expounding his obligations, or pointing out tasks to be completed. Each member will take turns presenting his own opinions and listening attentively to others. He should examine himself in the matters being discussed and make efforts to improve himself. The purpose of these meetings is to encourage one another in virtue and to correct each other's mistakes.

The members of the family will take turns being the chairman of these meetings, according to schedule. If someone is unable to chair a meeting on a certain day, he should ask the next person in line to take his place. The chairman should provide tea, but never wine. The meetings may be canceled on days of ancestor worship, parties, or other such occasions, or if the weather is severe. Those who are absent from these meetings for no reason are only doing themselves harm.

There are no set rules for where the meeting should be held, but the place should be convenient for group discussions. The time of the meeting should always be early evening, for this is when people have free time. As a general precaution the meeting should never last until late at night.

14. Women from lower-class families who stop at our houses tend to gossip, create conflicts, peek into the kitchens, or induce our women to believe in prayer and fortune-telling, thereby cheating them out of their money and possessions. Consequently, one should question these women often and punish those who come for no reason, so as to put a stop to the traffic.

15. Blood relatives are as close as the branches of a tree, yet their relationships can still be differentiated according to importance and priority: Parents should be considered before brothers, and brothers should be considered before wives and children. Each person should fulfill his own duties and share with others profit and loss, joy and sorrow, life and death. In this way, the family will get along well and be blessed by Heaven. Should family members fight over property or end up treating each other like enemies, then when death or misfortune strikes they will be of even less use than strangers. If our ancestors have consciousness, they will not tolerate these unprincipled descendants who are but animals in man's clothing. Heaven responds to human vices with punishments as surely as an echo follows a sound. I hope my sons and grandsons take my words seriously.

16. To get along with patrilineal relatives, fellow villagers, and relatives through marriage, one should be gentle in speech and mild in manners. When one is opposed by others, one may remonstrate with them; but when others fall short because of their limitations, one should be tolerant. If one's youngsters or servants get into fights with others, one should look into oneself to find the blame. It is better to be wronged than to wrong others. Those who take affront and become enraged, who conceal their own shortcomings and seek to defeat others, are courting immediate misfortune. Even if the other party is unbearably unreasonable, one should contemplate the fact that the ancient sages had to endure much more. If one remains tolerant and forgiving, one will be able to curb the other party's violence.

PRESERVE THE FAMILY PROPERTY

1. The houses, fields, and ponds that have been accumulated by the family should not be divided

or sold. Violators of this rule will be severely admonished and barred from the ancestral temple.

2. Maps of the family graves should be printed. The graves are to be well taken care of and frequently repaired. The custodians of the graves should be treated well.

3. Books constitute the lifeline of a family. A record should be kept of their titles. They should be aired out at regular intervals, stored in a high chamber, and kept from being dispersed. In this way we can keep intact our ancestors' writings.

4. Paintings, maps, books, scrolls, and utensils should be stored in separate wooden cabinets. There should be a notebook in which all these are registered. Whenever an item is loaned to someone, a slip of paper with the description of the item should be temporarily pasted on the shelf. When the item is returned, it should be replaced in its original position.

5. There are many thieves in the country; therefore, one should be careful not to leave clothing and other objects about. Doors should be locked and carefully guarded. Be prepared! On noticing anything suspicious, look into it immediately and take preventive action, in order to achieve maximum security.

6. In order to cultivate the moral character of the young, one must severely punish those who are so unruly that they have no sense of righteousness or who so indulge their desires that they destroy their own health. One should also correct those who have improper hobbies, such as making too many friends and avoiding work, indulging in playing musical instruments and the game of Go, collecting art and valuables, composing music, singing, or dancing. All these hobbies destroy a person's ambition. Those who indulge in them may consider themselves free spirits; yet little do they know that these hobbies are their most harmful enemies.

7. If among patrilineal and affinal relatives and fellow villagers there are people who give importance to propriety and are respected for their learning and ability, one should frequently visit them to request advice and offer one's respects. Then, in case of emergencies in the family, one will be able to obtain help from them. Besides, receiving frequent advice is good in itself. By contrast, to make friends with the wrong sort of people and join them in evil deeds is to set a trap for oneself. If one is jealous of upright gentlemen and avoids upright discourse, misfortune will strike, the family will be ruined, lives may even be lost. Then it will be too late for regrets.

8. Scholars, farmers, artisans, and merchants all hold respectable occupations. Scholarship ranks the highest; farming is next; and then craft and business. However, it should be up to the individual to measure his ability against his aspirations as well as to find the most suitable occupation for himself. In these family instructions, I have given first place to the profession of scholarship, but have also devoted a great deal of attention to the work of farmers, artisans, and merchants. These family instructions attempt to show the correct procedures to be followed in everyday life. If one truly understands them and fulfills the duties appropriate to his way of life; if one upholds public and private obligations; if one can in good conscience invite Heaven's favor, then misfortune will stay away and bliss will enter without conscious effort on one's part. In this way, a person can face his ancestors without shame and instruct his posterity; there are no other secrets to having good and capable descendants.

Translated by Clara Yu

55

CONCUBINES

Concubinage is probably the feature of the Chinese family system most foreign to Western experience. Although it is undoubtedly true that the vast majority of Chinese men could never afford a concubine in addition to a wife, still the practice of concubinage colored Chinese life at many levels. Poor families were affected as the suppliers of daughters. They were always aware that if they could not afford to marry their daughters off, they could sell them to rich men. This step meant turning an economic liability into an asset, but most people tried to avoid it, not only because they worried about the happiness of their daughters but also because their own prestige was involved. For families of modest means, concubinage meant that if the first wife failed to produce a surviving son after perhaps ten years of marriage, a concubine might be purchased in the hope she would bear a son. In families of prosperous merchants, landlords, scholars, and officials, concubinage was an even more common part of family life. Most members of such families would have spent at least a part of their lives in large households in which one or more men had a concubine in addition to his wife.

Below are three sources that reveal various aspects of concubinage. The first concerns the way concubines were offered for sale. Probably most of the girls had entered this market after their parents turned them over to a broker for a sum of money, signing a contract giving up their rights to her. The second is a memoir written by Mao Xiang (1611–1693) recording how he ended up taking a singing girl as his concubine. As he presents it, it was the girl who pursued him, eager for a patron who would pay her debts and buy out the contract which bound her to the owner of her establishment. The writer presents his wife as rather neutral in the whole process, but certainly in many cases wives or earlier concubines were displeased when a man took a new concubine. Some of the interpersonal dynamics in a household with wives and concubines is depicted in the last piece, an episode from the novel Jin Ping Mei, *published in 1610. This novel recounts the varied adventures of Ximen Qing, a congenial but unambitious and undisciplined heir of a prosperous commercial family whose household had grown to include a wife and five concubines. In the episode included here, Lotus, the newest concubine, demonstrates the malice she could vent on her competitors.*

THE THIN HORSE MARKET

Upwards of a hundred people in Yangzhou earn a living in the "thin horse" business. If someone shows an interest in taking a concubine, a team of a broker, a drudge, and a scout stick to him like flies. Early in the morning, the teams gather to wait outside the doors of potential customers, who usually give their business to the first team to arrive. Any teams coming late have to wait for the next opportunity. The winning team then leads their customer to the broker's house. The customer is then served tea and seated to wait for the women. The broker leads out each of them, who do what the matchmaker tells them to do. After each of her short commands, the woman bows to the customer, walks forward, turns toward the light so the customer can see her face clearly, draws back her sleeves to show him her hands, glances shyly at him to show her eyes, says her age so he can hear her voice, and finally lifts her skirt to reveal whether her feet are bound. An experienced customer could figure out the size of her feet by listening to the noise she made as she entered the room. If her skirt made noise when she walked in, she had to have a pair of big feet under her skirt. As one woman finishes, another comes out, each house having at least five or six. If the customer finds a woman to his liking, he puts a gold hairpin in her hair at the temple, a procedure called "inserting the ornament." If no one satisfies him, he gives a few hundred cash to the broker or the servants.

If the first broker gets tired, others will willingly take his place. Even if a customer has the stamina to keep looking for four or five days, he cannot finish visiting all the houses. Nevertheless, after seeing fifty to sixty white-faced, red-dressed women, they all begin to look alike and he cannot decide which are pretty or ugly. It is like the difficulty of recognizing a character after writing it hundreds or thousands of times. Therefore, the customer usually chooses someone once his mind and eyes can no longer discriminate. The owner of the woman brings out a piece of red paper on which are listed the "betrothal presents," including gold jewelry and cloth. Once he agrees to the deal, he is sent home. Before he even arrives back at his lodgings, a band and a load of food and wine are already waiting there. Before long, presents he was to send are prepared and sent back with the band. Then a sedan chair and all the trimmings—colorful lanterns, happy candles, attendants, sacrificial foods—wait outside for the customer's arrangement. The cooks and the entertainer for the wedding celebration also arrive together with foods, wine, candy, tables, chairs, and tableware. Without the customer's order, the colorful sedan chair for the girl and the small sedan chair for her companion are dispatched to get the girl. The new concubine performs the bowing ceremony with music and singing and considerable clamor. The next morning before noon the laborers ask for rewards from the man, then leave to prepare another wedding for another customer in the same manner.

HOW DONG XIAOWAN BECAME MY CONCUBINE

I was rather depressed that evening, so I got a boat and went with a friend on an excursion to Tiger Hill. My plan was to send a messenger to Xiangyang the next morning and then set out for home. As our boat passed under a bridge, I saw a small building by the bank. When I asked who lived there, my friend told me that this was [the singing girl] Dong's home. I was wildly happy with memories of three years before. I insisted on the boat's stopping, wanting to see Xiaowan at once. My friend, however, restrained me, saying, "Xiaowan has been terrified by the threat of being kidnapped by a powerful man and has been seriously ill for eighteen days. Since her mother's death,* she is said to have locked her door and refrained from receiving any guests." I nevertheless insisted on going ashore.

Not until I had knocked two or three times did the door open. I found no light in the house and

---

* The "mother" here may well be the woman who managed her, rather than her natural mother.

had to grope my way upstairs. There I discovered medicine all over the table and bed.

Xiaowan, moaning, asked where I had come from and I told her I was the man she once saw beside a winding balustrade, intoxicated.

"Well, Sir," she said, recalling the incident, "I remember years ago you called at my house several times. Even though she only saw you once, my mother often spoke highly of you and considered it a great pity that I never had the chance to wait on you. Three years have passed. Mother died recently, but on seeing you now, I can hear her words in my ears. Where are you coming from this time?"

With an effort, she rose to draw aside the curtains and inspected me closely. She moved the lamp and asked me to sit on her bed. After talking awhile, I said I would go, not wanting to tire her. She, however, begged me to remain, saying, "During the past eighteen days I have had no appetite for food, nor have I been able to sleep well. My soul has been restless, dreaming almost all the time. But on seeing you, I feel as if my spirit has revived and my vigor returned." She then had her servant serve wine and food at her bedside, and kept refilling my cup herself.

Several times I expressed my desire to leave, but each time she urged me to stay. . . . The following morning, I was eager to set off on the trip home, but my friend and my servant both asked me not to be ungrateful for Xiaowan's kindness as she had had only a brief chance to talk with me the previous night. Accordingly I went to say goodbye to her. I found her, fresh from her toilet, leaning against a window upstairs quite composed. On seeing my boat approaching the bank, she hurried aboard to greet me. I told her that I had to leave immediately, but she said that she had packed up her belongings and would accompany me. I felt unable to refuse her.

We went from Hushuguan to Wuxi, and from there to Changzhou, Yixing, and Jiangyin, finally arriving at Jinjiang. All this took twenty-seven days, and twenty-seven times I asked her to go back, but she was firm in her desire to follow me. On climbing Golden Hill, she pointed to the river and swore, "My body is as constant as the direction of the Yangzi River. I am determined never to go back to Suzhou!"

On hearing her words, I turned red and reiterated my refusal, "The provincial examination is coming up soon. Because my father's recent posts have been dangerous ones, I have failed to attend to family affairs and have not been able to look after my mother on a daily basis. This is my first chance to go back and take care of things. Moreover, you have so many creditors in Suzhou and it will take a lot to redeem your singing-girl's contract in Nanjing. So please go back to Suzhou for the time being. After I have taken the examination at the end of summer, I will send word and meet you in Nanjing. At any rate, I must await the result of the examination before I even think about these matters. Insisting on it now will do neither of us any good."

She, however, still hesitated. There were dice on the table, and one of my friends said to her jokingly, "If you are ever going to get your wish [to become his concubine], they will land with the same side up." She then bowed toward the window, said a prayer, and tossed the dice. They all landed on six. All on board expressed their amazement, and I said to her, "Should Heaven really be on our side, I'm afraid we might bungle the whole thing if we proceed too hurriedly. You had better leave me temporarily, and we'll see what we can do by and by." Thus against her wishes she said goodbye, concealing her tearstained face with her hands.

I had pity for her plight but at the same time once I was on my own felt relieved of a heavy burden. Upon arrival at Taizhou, I sat for the examination. When I got home in the sixth month, my wife said to me, "Xiaowan sent her father to bring word that since her return to Suzhou, she has kept to a vegetarian diet and confined herself to her home, waiting on tiptoe for you to bring her to Nanjing as you promised. I felt awkward and gave her father ten taels of silver, asking him to tell her that I am in sympathy with her and consent to her request, but she must wait till you finish the examination."

I appreciated the way my wife had handled Xiaowan's request. I then directly proceeded to Nanjing without keeping my promise to send someone to fetch her, planning to write to her after I had finished the examination. However, scarcely had I come out of the examination hall on the morning of the 15th of the eighth month when she suddenly called at my lodgings at Peach Leaf Ferry. It turned out that after waiting in vain for news from me, she had hired a boat, setting out from Suzhou and proceeding along the river with an old woman as her companion. She met with robbers on the way, and her boat had to hide among reeds and rushes. With the rudder broken, the boat could not proceed, and she had had practically nothing to eat for three days. She arrived at Sanshan Gate of Nanjing on the 8th, but not wanting to disturb my thoughts during the examination, she delayed entering the city for two days.

Though delighted to see me, she looked and sounded rather sad as she vividly described what had happened during the hundred days of our separation, including her confinement at home on vegetarian fare, her encounter with robbers on the river, and her other experiences of a voyage fraught with danger. Now she was more insistent than ever on getting her wish. The men in my literary society from Kashan, Sungjiang, Fujian, and Henan all admired her farsightedness and sincerity and encouraged her with their verses and paintings.

When the examination was over, I thought I might pass it, so hoped I would soon be able to settle my affairs and gratify her desire to become my concubine. Unexpectedly, on the 17th I was informed that my father had arrived by boat. . . . I had not seen him for two years and was overjoyed that he had returned alive from the battlefront. Without delaying to tell Xiaowan, I immediately went to meet him. . . . Before long she set out by boat in pursuit of me from the lodging house at Peach Leaf Ferry. A storm at Swallow's Ledge nearly cost her her life. At Shierhui she came on board and stayed with me again for seven days.

When the results of the examination were announced, I found my name on the list of the not quite successful candidates. I then traveled day and night to get home, while she followed weeping, unwilling to part. I was, however, well aware that I could not by myself settle her affairs in Suzhou and that her creditors would, on discovering her departure, increase their demands. Moreover, my father's recent return and my disappointment in the exams had made it all the more difficult to gratify her desire at once. On arrival at Puchao on the outskirts of my native city, I had to put on a cold face and turn ironhearted to part from her, telling her to go back to Suzhou to set her creditors at ease and thus pave the way for our future plans.

In the tenth month, while passing Jinjiang, I went to visit Mr. Zheng, the man who had been my examiner. At that time, Liu Daxing of Fujian had arrived from the capital. During a drinking party in his boat with General Chen, my friend Prefect Liu, and myself, my servant returned from seeing Xiaowan home. He reported that on arrival at Suzhou she did not change out of her autumn clothing, saying that she intended to die of cold if I did not see my way to settle her affairs promptly. On hearing this, Liu Daxing pointed to me and said, "Pijiang, you are well known as a man of honor. Could you really betray a girl like this?"

"Surely scholars are not capable of the gallant deeds of Huang Shanke and Gu Yaya," I replied.

The prefect raised his cup, and with a gesture of excitement exclaimed, "Well, if I were given a thousand taels of silver to pay my expenses, I'd start right away today!"

General Chen at once lent me several hundred taels, and Liu Daxing helped with a present of several catties of ginseng. But how could it have been anticipated that the prefect, on arrival at Suzhou, failed to carry out his mission, and that when the creditors had kicked up a row and the matter had been brought to a deadlock, he fled to Wujiang? I had no chance to make further inquiries, as I returned home shortly afterwards.

Xiaowan was left in an awkward position, with little she could do. On hearing of her trouble,

Qian Qianyi of Changshu went to Bantang himself and brought her to his boat. He approached her creditors, from the gentry to the townsmen, and within three days managed to clear every single debt of hers, the bills redeemed piling up a foot in height. This done, he arranged a farewell banquet on a pleasure boat and entertained her at the foot of Tiger Hill. He then hired a boat and sent someone to see her to Rugao.

On the evening of the 15th of the eleventh month when I was drinking wine with my father in our Zhuocun Hall, I was suddenly informed that Xiaowan had arrived at the jetty. After reading Qian's long interesting letter, I learned how she had gotten here. I also learned that Qian had written to a pupil of his, Zhang of the ministry of rites, asking him to redeem her singing's girl's contract at once. Her minor problems at Suzhou were later settled by Mr. Zhou of the bureau of ceremonies while Mr. Li, formerly attached to that bureau, had also rendered her great assistance in Nanjing.

Ten months thereafter, her desire was gratified [and she became my concubine]. After the endless tangle of troubles and emotional pain, we had what we wanted.

THE SPITE OF LOTUS

Now that she was the favorite, Lotus became more and more intent on having her own way. She was never at peace. Suspicious of the others, she was constantly peeping from behind doors and spying through cracks. One day, in a bad mood over nothing, she upbraided her maid Plum. Plum was not the docile type who could accept criticism quietly, so to vent her anger she ran off to the kitchen, where she pounded her fists on the tables and pans. Snow, the fourth wife, watched all this and teased her, "You silly little thing. If you want a man so much, can't you look elsewhere? Why must you have your fits here?"

Angry already, Plum now lost her temper. "How dare anyone insult me!" she declared. When Snow saw fit to ignore her, Plum ran back to her mistress. She embellished the incident and told Lotus, "That one says you personally handed me over to the master so that we could keep him all to ourselves."

Plum's story did nothing to improve Lotus's bad mood. That morning she had risen earlier than usual to help Moon, the principal wife, get ready for a funeral. She had been so tired she took a nap, and was just going back to her own suite. On her way there she ran into Jade, the third wife.

"Why are you looking so worn out?" Jade asked.

"Don't ask me! I had to get up early," Lotus replied, then added, "Sister, where are you coming from?"

"I stopped at the kitchen."

"Did the one there tell you anything?"

"No, not that I can think of."

Lotus did not let on what was bothering her, but she was forming a hatred for Snow. She and Jade sat down and passed some time doing needlework. After finishing the tea and cakes Plum and Chrysanthemum set out, they decided to play a game of chess. But no sooner had their game become exciting than Ximen was announced and entered the room.

Ximen gazed in satisfaction at the two well decked-out ladies. Silk hair nets revealing curls at their temples, earrings of blue sapphire, white silken dresses with red bodices and embroidered skirts, tiny arched and pointed slippers—how exquisite their taste was! "Just like a couple of courtesans, worth at least a hundred taels of silver!" he teased.

"Courtesans, my word! You have one in your household, but she's in back, not here," Lotus bantered back.

Jade rose to withdraw, but Ximen caught her and drew her back into the room. "Where would you be going? As soon as I arrive you try to escape! Tell the truth—what have you two been doing in my absence?"

"Nothing wrong," Lotus answered. "We were both feeling low, so we started a game of chess." Lotus helped him put the chessmen back and commented that he had returned from the funeral rather early.

"Yes, there were a lot of officials there and it was terribly hot, so I made a quick exit."

When Jade asked about Moon, Ximen said she would be coming later in the sedan chair and that he had sent two servant boys to meet her. He sat down next to them and asked, "What were your stakes in this game?"

"Oh, we were just playing for the fun of it," Lotus answered.

"Then let me challenge you each to a game. Whoever loses forfeits a tael of silver to pay for a party."

"But we don't have any money with us." Lotus objected.

"Never mind. You can give me a hairpin as security."

First he played with Lotus and she lost. He began to reset the pieces for a game with Jade, but Lotus suddenly tipped over the board, causing the chessmen to fall in a jumble. Then she ran out of the room and into the garden.

Ximen chased her and found her picking flowers. "What a spoilsport! You run away because you lost, my lovable little oily-mouth," he called to her, panting.

Coyly, Lotus looked up at him. "What a villain, to pursue me just because I lost! You wouldn't dare do that to Jade!" She playfully pelted him with blossoms. Ximen went up to her and took her in his arms, then stuck out his tongue to give her a piece of candy from his mouth.

Their diversions were soon interrupted by Jade who called, "Moon has just returned. We'd better go."

Lotus broke loose from Ximen and said she would talk to him more later. Then she hurried after Jade to pay her respects to Moon.

Moon asked them, "What makes you two so merry?"

"Lotus lost a tael of silver playing chess with the master, so she will have to host a party tomorrow," Jade answered. "You must come."

Moon smiled and Lotus soon took her leave. She rejoined Ximen in the front suite and had

Plum light some incense and draw a hot bath so that later they could amuse themselves like a couple of fish.

Although Moon was Ximen's principal wife, her ill health usually kept her from fulfilling all the duties of the mistress of the house. Grace, the second wife, performed most of the social duties such as paying visits and receiving guests, and handled the household budget. Snow, the fourth wife, took charge of the servants and was the chief cook. Wherever Ximen was in the house, if he wanted something to eat or drink, he would send his request to Snow via one of the maids of the lady he was visiting.

That night Ximen stayed with Lotus. They drank some wine, took a bath, and went to bed. The next morning things started to happen. It began when

Ximen cajoled Lotus by promising that right after breakfast he would go to the temple market to buy her some pearls. But when he told Plum to fetch him breakfast (ordering lotus-seed cakes and carp soup), the girl would not budge.

Lotus intervened, "There's a person in the kitchen who says I induced Plum to yield to you so that she and I could keep you for ourselves. She called us all sorts of names. So don't make Plum go there."

"Who are you referring to?"

"I don't want to name names. Even the pots and pans have ears around here. Just send Chrysanthemum instead."

Ximen did as he was told. More than enough time passed to have cooked two breakfasts and Lotus had the table all set, but Chrysanthemum still did not return. Ximen was near to losing his patience, so Lotus sent Plum after all, telling her, "Go see where that slave is dallying. She must've taken root someplace!"

Reluctantly Plum complied and found Chrysanthemum standing in the kitchen. "You depraved slave," she scolded. "Mistress will cut you to pieces! What's keeping you? Master is out of patience! He wants to go to the market and I must bring you back with me at once."

She would have continued, but Snow interrupted, "Silly wench, you behave like some Mohammedan on a feast day! Isn't the pot made of iron? Will the soup get hot just by sitting in it? I have some gruel ready, but instead he wants cakes and soup. What kind of a worm is at work in his stomach?"

This was more than Plum could take. "Impudence! Do you think I came here for the fun of it? Are you going to get the stuff ready or not? Just wait! Master will be furious when I tell him about this!" Dragging Chrysanthemum by the ear, she turned to go.

As they left, Snow shouted, "That slave and her mistress are both too cocksure! But my time will come! "

"Maybe it will! What do I care?" Plum retorted.

Still in a huff, Plum produced Chrysanthemum before her mistress, who noticed how pale her face was. "What's the matter?" Lotus asked.

"Ask her! I found her standing in the kitchen. That person was taking forever to prepare a little breakfast! All I said was that the master was in a rush and you wanted to know what was keeping her. That kitchen woman called me a slave wench and other ugly things. She even reviled the master calling him some extravagant Mohammedan! Does she think he needs her permission before asking for something? She complained that he wouldn't eat her gruel! She seems to think the purpose of a kitchen is not cooking but cursing!"

"What did I tell you!" Lotus exclaimed. "We shouldn't have sent Plum. I knew that that one would pick a quarrel and insinuate that Plum and I had made you into our exclusive property! Oh, why do I have to endure such insults!"

Her outburst produced immediate effect: Ximen dashed into the kitchen and began kicking Snow. "You evil bag of bones! What gives you the right to curse the girl I sent to fetch some breakfast? You call her a slave? If you want to see a slave, look at the reflection in your own puddle!"

Snow knew better than to talk back to Ximen, but as soon as he left she turned to Lai Bao's wife. "What evil luck I'm having! You are my witness. You saw her prance in here like some demon! Did

I say the least thing to her? But off she goes with that little maid and tells lies to the master so that he abuses me for no fault of mine! Just wait! I'll be on the lookout! Sooner or later that impudent slave wench and her mistress will make a false move!"

Unknown to Snow, Ximen had paused to listen outside the door. Convulsed with rage, he barged back in and pummeled her. "You depraved slave, you slut! Tell me now you didn't insult her! I heard you with my own two ears!" He kept hitting her until she could not take the pain any longer, then stormed off, leaving her shrieking.

Hearing the commotion, Moon, who had just risen and was having her hair dressed, sent her maid Jewel to investigate. Jewel came back and related the whole story. "He's never wanted cakes before," Moon remarked. "But Snow should have done his bidding as quickly as possible, and certainly she shouldn't have scolded the maid over nothing."

She sent Jewel back to the kitchen to tell Snow to finish the breakfast. So, in the end, Ximen got his meal and was off to the market with one of the servant boys.

Snow could not get over how she had been mistreated. As soon as Ximen was out of the house she went to Moon's room to give her version of the incident. Little did she know Lotus had followed her and was eavesdropping outside the window to everything she told Moon and Grace. "You have no idea what this woman is capable of!" Snow ranted. "She is absolutely man-crazy and can't stand to spend even a single night alone! Even a dozen husbands wouldn't be enough for her! She got rid of her first husband by poisoning him! Just imagine what she's planning for us! She's turned our husband into some kind of beady-eyed chicken who never notices the rest of us!"

"Now, now," Moon tried to calm her, "weren't you at fault? He did send the maid for the cakes, and if you had sent her right back with them, none of this would have happened. There wasn't any call for you to provoke her."

"I was the one who got provoked! That maid

was impertinent even when she used to work for you, but you never objected when I corrected her, even the time I hit her with the back of a knife. What makes her so privileged now that she works for Lotus?"

"The fifth mistress is outside," Jewel warned as she came in.

The next moment Lotus entered. Looking straight into Snow's face, she stated, "If you know for a fact that I had poisoned my first husband, then why didn't you stop the master from bringing me here? That way you wouldn't have had to worry about me getting him all for myself. As for Plum, she doesn't belong to me. If you object to the current arrangements, let her wait on Moon again. Then I wouldn't care if you picked quarrels with her. But don't worry— there's a simple solution to everything. When the master comes back I'll ask him to write out a letter of divorce!"

"I really don't understand why you two have to squabble," Moon interjected. "If only you both talked a little less . . ."

"But Lady," Snow objected, "her mouth pours forth words like a river! No one is a match for her! If she lost her tongue she could still make the master believe anything by merely rolling her eyes! If she had her way, all of us, except perhaps you, would be driven out of here!"

For a while Moon let them hurl insults back and forth at each other. Then when Snow said, "You call me a slave, but you're the real slave," and seemed on the point of striking Lotus, Moon ordered Jewel to remove Snow from the room.

Back in her own suite, Lotus took off her clothes, removed her makeup, and mussed up her dark hair. In this disheveled condition, she threw herself on her bed and sobbed.

When Ximen returned that evening with four ounces of pearls, he found Lotus in this state, demanding a divorce. "I never cared anything about your money," she protested through her tears. "It was just that I loved you. But what do I get in return but insults? Now I'm called a husband murderer! It would be better if I didn't have a maid, since anyone who works for me has to put up with such treatment!"

Lotus's tale turned Ximen into a demon. He whirled through the house until he set down on Snow. Grabbing her hair in one hand, he thrashed her with his short stick, not stopping until Moon came to restrain him.

"Let's everyone behave," Moon said, then addressing Snow, added, "Don't upset the master."

"You culprit! You evil bag of bones!" Ximen railed at Snow. "I heard what you called them in the kitchen! Just let me catch you one more time!"

All this Snow suffered because of Lotus's spiteful scheming. There's a verse to prove it:

Lotus depended on her husband's favor
To make Snow suffer deep humiliation.
Using gratitude to accumulate hatred—
The consequences will take centuries to unfold.

Ximen returned to Lotus's room and took from his sleeve the pearls he had bought her. Lotus was no longer petulant; Ximen had taken her side and fought her battles for her. She repaid his affection tenfold and his delight in her only increased.

Translated by Patricia Ebrey

56

WIDOWS LOYAL UNTO DEATH

From early times, it was considered preferable for a widow not to remarry after her husband died. Widows who refused to remarry, even when pressured by their parents or parents-in-law, were singled out for praise and emulation in all of the collections of accounts of exemplary women, published either as independent volumes or as chapters in dynastic histories or the histories of particular localities. In the Song dynasty, the great neo-Confucian thinker Cheng Yi (1033–1107) had declared that it was better for a widow to starve to death than remarry, since personal integrity was a more important matter than life. In the Ming dynasty, this saying was often quoted and the cult of widow chastity reached extreme levels, with many young widows not merely refusing to remarry, but committing suicide. Their actions were widely celebrated, and their families were often given the right to display banners or arches proclaiming their virtue.

The following accounts of such widows are from the local history of Fuzhou in Fujian province.

Xu Sungjie, daughter of Xu Yuanyan, married Chen Boshan at the age of seventeen. When her husband was gravely ill, he told her to remarry because she had no son. At his death, she embraced him and cried bitterly. After the coffin was closed, she hanged herself to die with her husband. The official Bai Bi was impressed with her fidelity and so arranged for her burial and had a banner with the inscription "filial piety and propriety" displayed at her door.

Lin Shunde, the daughter of the prefect Lin Jin, was engaged to Sun Mengbi. When Mengbi died, she was with her father at his post. Once the announcement of her finance's death reached her, she put on mourning dress and wept to tell her parents that she wished to go to his home. Her parents packed for her and told her to behave properly. On arriving there, she performed the rituals for her first meeting with her parents-in-law, then she made an offering at her finance's coffin. After he was buried, she served her mother-in-law for the rest of her life. The local official inscribed a placard with "She hurried to the funeral of a husband she had never seen. Suffering cold and frost, she swore not to remarry." . . .

Fu Xiajie was the wife of Chen Banghuai. Her husband was taken hostage by some bandits. She supported herself by making hemp cloth. After a long time someone told her that her husband had died. She was spinning at the time. She then immediately entered her bedroom and hanged herself.

Wu Jinshun was the wife of Sun Zhen. On the first anniversary of her husband's death, she was so forlorn that she died of grief.

Zhang Zhongyu was engaged to Chen Shunwei, who died prematurely when Zhongyu was eighteen. When she learned of his death, she decided to hurry to the Chen family. Her parents tried to stop her, but she cried and said, "Once you betrothed me to the Chen family, I became a daughter-in-law of the Chen family." So, she hurried to attend her fiance's funeral and bow to her mother-in-law. Then, she cut her hair and removed her ornaments. She lived a secluded life. In the first month of the xinsi year [1461], there was a fire in her neighborhood. She leaned herself against her husband's coffin, wanting to be burned up with her husband. Suddenly a wind came and extinguished the fire. Only her house survived. On the sixth day of the sixth month of the wuzi year [1468], a large army approached. People in the county fled helter-skelter. Zhongyu remained to guard the coffin, keeping a knife with her. When the army arrived the next day, she showed the banner and the tablet from the previous official. The soldiers recognized her righteousness, and general Bai attached his order on the door so that no other soldiers would enter her house. One day she became severely ill and told her mother-in-law, "Don't let any men put their hands on me when I am shrouded after I die. Use the money in the small box that I earned by splicing and spinning to bury me with my husband." Then she died.

Sun Yinxiao was the daughter of Sun Keren and married Lin Zengqing at the age of seventeen. Lin, who made his living fishing, drowned after they had been married for only two months. Sun was determined to kill herself. After the mourning period was over, she made a sacrifice with utmost grief. That night, she dressed carefully and bound a wide girdle round the beam to hang herself. When the magistrate Xu Jiadi heard of this, he paid a visit to offer a sacrifice to her soul.

Wang Yingjie was the wife of Qiu Bianyu. She was widowed at nineteen before bearing any children. As a consequence she decided to die. Her family had long been rich and her dowry was particularly ample. She gave it all to her husband's younger brother so that in the future he could arrange for an heir to succeed to her husband. Then she ceased eating. Her mother forced her to stop, so she had no alternative but to pretend to eat and drink as usual. When her mother relaxed her vigilance, she hanged herself.

Wang Jingjie, whose family had moved to Nantai, married Fu Yan, a candidate for the examinations. Yan studied so hard that he got ill and died. When Wang learned of this, she emptied out her savings and gave it to her father-in-law to pay for her husband's funeral, asking him to do it properly. The evening after he was buried, her brother came to console her and she asked how her parents were doing. Her brother slept in another room. At dawn, when the members of the family got up, they kept shouting to her, but she did not answer. When they pried open her door, she was already dead, having hanged herself. She was solemnly facing the inside, standing up straight. She was twenty-one.

Zhang Xiujie married He Liangpeng when she was eighteen. Before a year had passed, he became critically ill. He asked her what she would do, and she pointed to Heaven and swore to follow her husband in death. Since she wished to commit suicide, the other family members had to prevent her. After several months, their only son died of measles. Zhang wept and said, "It is my fate. I had been living for him." That night she hanged herself.

Huang Yijie was engaged to Chen Rujing from Changle who lived in Lianjiang. Before they were married, he died. When she was fifteen, she heard of it and was saddened by it. As she slowly understood what it meant, streams of tears rolled down her cheeks. Without her knowledge a matchmaker arranged a new engagement. In the fifth month of the bingyin year [1506], her first fiance's mother came to call. Huang followed the courtesies appropriate to a daughter-in-law when she went out to meet her, and they both expressed their grief, not holding back. After a while she asked her mother-in-law why she had come, and she told her that she had heard of the new engagement and so had come to get the brideprice back. The girl was startled and thought, "Could this be true? Only in extremely unfortunate circumstances is a dead man's wife sold." She told her mother-in-law, "Fortunately not much has been done with it. Let me make a plan." Disoriented, for a long time she sat, not saying a word. Then she asked her mother-in-law to stay for the night and told her everything she wanted to say. She gave her the hairpins and earrings she had received as betrothal gifts, saying, "Keep these to remember your son by." At dusk, her mother-in-law took her leave, and the girl, weeping, saw her to the gate. She then took a bath, combed her hair, and changed into new clothes. Those things done, she took a knife and cut her throat. The first cut did not sever it, so she had to cut it again before she died. In the morning when her family found her body, there were traces of three cuts.

Translated by Patricia Ebrey

57

TWO PHILOSOPHERS

In the early Ming, Zhu Xi's synthesis of Confucian learning was honored by both the state and the community of Confucian scholars as the best guide to true knowledge. Zhu Xi's commentaries to the classics were the ones to study when preparing for the civil service examinations. Leading thinkers worked within the intellectual framework Zhu Xi had established and focused on tasks he had identified as important, such as self-cultivation through the "investigation of things." In mid and late Ming, however, more and more thinkers rejected key elements in Zhu Xi's philosophy, moving Confucian thought in more inner directed and individualistic directions.

Below are selections from two of the most influential Confucian thinkers of the Ming, Wang Yangming (Wang Shouren, 1472–1529) and Li Zhi (1527–1602). Wang Yangming was an official of considerable stature. In 1506, soon after passing second in the 1499 examinations, he attracted notice for protesting the imprisonment of censors who had accused a notorious eunuch of corruption. For his pains, he was beaten and exiled to the far southwest. A few years later he was recalled and later given command of a campaign to suppress banditry and rebellion in several areas in the south. As a thinker, Wang is identified with the learning of the mind, a strand of Confucianism with old roots. In Wang's formulation, the idea of innate moral knowledge is central. To discover truth, in particular to distinguish right from wrong, people should look inward; and once they know something is right, they should act on it. Thus the achievement of sagehood does not require prolonged study of the classics, and ordinary people can aspire to it.

In part because of the catalytic effect of Wang Yangming's ideas, the age in which Li Zhi lived was intellectually tumultuous, with many strands of individualistic and iconoclastic thought emerging. Li, from a commercial family in coastal Fujian, passed the provincial examinations but never went on to the next level, the jinshi. *As a consequence, he held only minor official posts over the course of his career. In 1585, at the age of fifty-nine, he retired to a Buddhist temple and devoted himself to study and writing. Like Wang Yangming, he emphasized the original goodness of the human mind, but he was more eclectic than Wang and more explicitly drew elements of Buddhism and Daoism into his discussions. Objecting to arbitrary and artificial rules, he validated expression of emotions and bodily appetites, thus opening himself to the charge of undermining the foundations of morality. He made many enemies and was eventually arrested for heterodoxy. He committed suicide in jail.*

Below are records of conversations between Wang Yangming and his disciples and letters between Li Zhi and his followers. As they reveal, in the Ming, as in the Song, new ideas were formulated, elaborated, and refined in the teacher-disciple and scholar-friend networks that gave shape to literati life.

WANG YANGMING'S CONVERSATIONS

In 1520 I want to Qianzhou and saw Wang Yangming again. I told him that recently although I was making a little headway in my studies, I was finding it hard to feel secure or happy. He responded, "The problem is that you go to your mind to seek Heavenly principles, a practice called obscuration by principle. There is a trick for what you want to do."

"Please tell me what it is."

"It is simply the extension of knowledge."

"How does one do it?" I asked.

"Take your intuitive moral knowledge as your personal standard. If you think about something, you will know it is right if it is right, wrong if it is wrong. You cannot conceal anything from your intuitive moral knowledge. Just don't try to deceive it. Honestly follow it in whatever you do. That way you will keep what is good and get rid of what is bad. What security and happiness there is in this! This is the secret of investigating things and the real way to effect the extension of knowledge. If you do not use this sure mechanism, how can you investigate things? It is only recently through personal experience that I have figured this out myself; at first I was worried that relying on intuitive moral knowledge alone would not be enough. But after having looked closely into the matter, I have found that this method is entirely flawless."

*   *   *

Once when Wang Yuzhong, Zou Shouyi, and I were attending him, Wang Yangming said,

"Each person has a sage inside of him or her, which he or she suppresses because of lack of confidence." He then looked at Wang Yuzhong and said, "You have been a sage from the start." Yuzhong rose and politely demurred. The teacher added, "This is something everyone has. Why should you demur?"

"I do not deserve your praise."

"Everyone has this, so naturally you do. Why be so polite? Politeness is not appropriate here." Yuzhong then accepted with a smile.

Wang Yangming carried the discussion further, "Intuitive moral knowledge exists in people. No matter what they do, they cannot destroy it. Even robbers know that they should not rob. If you call them robbers they are embarrassed."

Wang Yuzhong said, "Material desires can obscure the intuitive moral knowledge in a person, but not make it disappear. It is like the clouds obscuring the sun. The sun is not lost."

Wang Yangming said, "You are so smart. No one else sees it."

*   *   *

A lower-ranking official, who had for a long time been listening to discussions of our teacher's doctrines, once said, "His doctrines are excellent, but because I am so busy keeping records and taking care of legal cases, I cannot study them further."

When Wang Yangming heard of his remark, he said to him, "When did I say you should abandon your records and legal cases to take up study? Since you have official duties, you should use them as a basis for your study. That is the true investigation of things. For instance, if you are questioning a plaintiff, you should not get angry because his answers are impolite or become pleased because he uses ingratiating language. You should not hate him for his efforts to go around you and purposely punish him. Nor should you bend your principles and forgive someone because he implores you. You should not dispose of a case quickly because your own affairs are too pressing, nor let other people's criticisms or praise or plots influence your decision. These ways of responding are all selfish. All you need to know is in yourself. Carefully check for any sign that you are biased, for that would confuse your recognition of right and wrong. This is how to investigate things and extend knowledge. Real learning is to be found in every aspect of record keeping and legal cases. What is empty is study that is detached from things."

* * *

Our teacher's method of shaping people is such that a single word may have the deepest impact. One day Wang Gen came back from a stroll. Wang Yangming asked him, "What did you see on your walk?"

"I saw that the people filling the streets are all sages."

"You saw that all the people filling the streets are sages, but those people all saw you as the only sage."

On another occasion, Dong Yun returned from a stroll and said to Wang, "Today I saw something strange." When Wang Yangming asked him what it was, he answered, "I saw that all the people filling the streets are sages."

"This is always the case. Why do you call it strange?" Wang asked.

Probably Wang responded differently in these two cases because Wang Gen was not yet adjusted to the idea and Dong Yun's grasp was not secure. In each case he argued the contrary point of view to help them progress.

* * *

In 1526 when Huang Honggang, Zhang Yuanchong, Wang Ji, and I were on our way back from taking the civil service examinations, we gave lectures along the way on our teacher's doctrines. Some people believed what we said, others did not. Wang Yangming said, "When you lectured about learning, you acted like you were a sage. When the people saw a sage coming, they were scared away. How could your lectures succeed? To lecture about learning to the people you must act like a simple, uneducated person."

Translated by Patricia Ebrey

LI ZHI'S LETTERS

Letter to Zhuang Chunfu

Rizai has arrived and I have learned that [my wife's] funeral is over—this is something to be glad of. I lived with her for more than forty years and we knew each other well. As I have been living at Bianzhou a long time and the place has become like a home town to me, I naturally feel sad when I have to leave. I feel the same about leaving her, except that the affection between husband and wife is stronger. Besides the intimacy between pillows and sheets, I also had her diligence, her wise financial management, and her assistance at home. She and I respected each other and treated each other with sincerity. We also lived up to filial duty, friendship, loyalty, and obligation, and we helped others, sometimes at great cost to ourselves. We were much more truthful than the scholarly sort of today who seek only a virtuous name but not virtuous deeds. It is all the more difficult for me to be separated from her now because, besides her love and affection, I will also greatly miss her deeds, merits, good advice, and virtues.

My wife, Huang Yiren, was your mother-in-law. Her only fault was that she never listened to anyone as far as learning was concerned, which was regrettable. Were my bosom made of iron and stone, I could not but feel sorrowful. What is more, when two married people approach old age and are called back to Heaven separately, without even being able to bid farewell to each other—isn't it a most grievous thing? Ah, let it be, let it be!

After I received the sad news of her departure, I dreamed of her every night, but she was always alive and well in my dreams. Did she really come here to be with me? Or did her spirit come to me because I thought of her? I recall that she was always very prudent; seldom would she cross the threshold to enter my meditation abode. Yet, what is wrong with coming to the meditation abode once in a while? She never reached the graceful carefreeness which goes beyond the boundaries of worldly virtues.

The point is, once we recognize the fact that the soul is the only true existence, then where is the demarcation between man and woman? If, after her departure from this world, Yiren is still bound by those old behavior codes, she will never be able to reach a carefree state. The existence of the soul proves that the being itself is deathless and by nature boundless. Therefore, how can one better oneself with boundaries and limits? The very carefreeness of the soul is itself the Pure Land and the Paradise: there is no other Heavenly world.

Chunfu, you should burn this letter for the soul of your mother-in-law so that she may know my wishes. Tell her not to covet the joy of reincarnation, for, once she is placed in a woman's womb to be reborn, she will be deprived of her awareness of the other world. Tell her not to yearn to be worshiped as a Heavenly being, for once reborn in Heaven, she will instantly forget her wish of her previous life to be carefree. Once the retributions end, the karma is in turn manifested, and one is reborn into the six paths of existence with no end to it.

Judging from your mother-in-law's behavior on earth, doubtless she is now in Heaven. Let her mark my words well: although she is already in Heaven, she should remember to wait for me and meet me when my days come to an end. In this way we will be able to rely on each other through many lives, without being separated by mistake. If she temporarily entrusts her thoughts to Buddhism, it will be excellent; but even if she cannot, should she meet some old friend of mine whom I have always respected, she could also follow him while she waits for me. But do tell her that she should by no means covet rebirth.

Chunfu, be sure to burn incense and paper money for your mother-in-law. Read my letter to her three or five times. Enjoin her repeatedly in front of her image. Recite my letter to her clearly and loudly. My Yiren will receive the message.

To Zeng Jiquan

I hear that you intend to shave your hair and become a monk. You really should not do so.

You have a wife and concubines, as well as a house and land. What is more, you do not yet have a son. Now, without a son, to whom are you going to entrust your family and possessions? To desert them without a reason is not only unkind but irresponsible. If you have really transcended life and death and seen through human existence, then it is preferable to cultivate yourself at home.

I should like to ask you some hypothetical questions: Can you really hold a monk's bowl to beg for food from door to door? Or can you really fast for several days without begging for a meal from people? If you can do neither, but still have to rely on farming for a livelihood, then isn't it more practical to cultivate yourself at home?

In the beginning, when I had just started studying the Way, not only did I have a wife and family, I also was an official who had to travel tens of thousands of *li*. But I felt that my learning increased day by day. Later on, I stayed in Chu to be close to my good friends and teachers, but my wife would not stay with me; I had to let my son-in-law and my daughter accompany her home. There she had her daughter, nephew, and others waiting on her constantly. I handed over to her whatever savings I had from my offices. As I alone was away from home, I did not need to worry about her and was able to stay down here and enjoy the company of my friends. The reason why I shaved my hair was that various people at home always expected me to return and often actually traveled a thousand *li* to pressure me to return and to bother me with trivial, worldly affairs. So I shaved my hair to show them that I had no intention of returning. Also, the ignorant people down here eyed me as a heretic, so I let myself behave as such to satisfy them. And yet was my sudden decision to shave my hair based primarily on these reasons? In addition, I knew I was getting old and would not stay in this world of men for long; that was the true reason. Now you, sir, are in your prime years, the fittest time to beget children, to live, to aspire for greatness. Furthermore, you do not own too much land and your estate is not very large. This is the ideal condition in which to live—unlike those rich men who are tied down with so many financial worries that they do not have even one minute of leisure.

Now, tell me, why do you have to discard your hair in order to learn the Way? I, for one, did not get rid of mine and leave home when I started studying it. Do mark my words and bear them in mind.

On Reading the Letter to Ruowu from His Mother

Ruowu's mother wrote to him, "I am getting older year after year. I have been a widow since you were eight and have brought you up. You left me to become a monk and that was all right. But now you want to leave in another sense to go to Jingang. Even your teacher waited until his parents passed away before becoming a monk. If you want to go away, you can wait until I have died. It will not be too late then.

"You say that even when you live close to me, you have never been able to help me in any way. Yet, when I am ill or indisposed, it is convenient to have you around. That way I do not worry

about you. You also are carefree, not having to worry about me. Thus we both live with peace of mind, and where there is peace of mind there is tranquillity. Why are you set on leaving home to seek for quiet? Besides, Qin Suge, who has always been generous to you, has bought you the temple. You always think in terms of the Way; I, however, think in terms of the ways of the world. I believe that what harmonizes with the ways of the world also conforms to the Way.

"Now, even if you forget about my old age, you have an obligation to care for your two small children. Even after your teacher became a monk, he took care of his sons during the famine years. This was because he could not put them out of his mind. For should he have failed to take care of them, they would have become roving good-for-nothings and the butt of insults and ridicule.

"Now you want to cultivate sereneness of the mind, but are you going to be concerned about your children? I do not believe you can be unconcerned about them. The fact is that you are concerned, but out of fear of being ridiculed by others, you hide your feelings. Let me ask you this: which is more honest, which is better, 'concerned but refusing to be involved,' or 'concerned and involved'? The way I see it, if you take care of your children, although it may seem that you are concerned, yet because you can thus achieve peace of mind, you are actually not concerned. On the other hand, if you do not take care of them, you are seemingly unconcerned, yet because your mind feels secret pangs, you are in fact concerned. You ought to examine your own mind. If you can achieve a peaceful mind, then that is the eternal dwelling place, that is the Jingang you are looking for.

"Why do you only listen to others? To listen to others and not to examine your own mind is to be manipulated by circumstances. Once you submit to that, there will be no peace of mind for you. . . . I fear for you: You now find Longtan not quiet enough and wish to go to live in Jingang. Should you someday find Jingang not quiet enough, where else are you going to go? You always talk only of the 'Way'; I wish now to talk to you about 'mind.' If you do not believe me, ask your teacher. If what matters is the surroundings, then you should indeed go and dwell in Jingang. If what matters is the mind, however, then you have no need to go away. If your mind is not serene, then even if you should travel to the other side of the sea, you would still not find quiet, let alone in Jingang."

On reading the letter, I sighed. I congratulate you on having a mother who is a real Buddha. From morning till night you have with you a teacher of the mind. She speaks with the voice of the ocean tide and teaches the ultimate truth which can never be contradicted. In comparison, the rhetoric of our peers is neither to the point nor effective. We are like those who talk about food, acting as though we could feed people with our mere words. All we achieve is making people laugh at each other, yet we do not even feel ashamed of ourselves. In retrospect, I realize that the several pages I wrote to you were mere exaggerations which would impress the foolish but had no bearing whatsoever on the truth. I now beg you to destroy my letters so that your godly mother may not read them, lest she say that I have spent all my life expounding harmful ideas. I also wish you would circulate your mother's letter and make students of Buddhism read it from time to time, so that they will learn to study true Buddhism. As long as one studies true Buddhism, one is a real Buddha. Even if a person has never recited "Amitabha" once, Amitabha will lead him to the correct path. Why is this? Because, to study Buddhism one has to cultivate virtuous behavior and filial piety. If we can get to see Amitabha by studying false Buddhism, then what kind of Buddhism did Amitabha himself study to become what he is? I am sure he was but an ordinary man who exhibited filial virtues and benevolence.

When one gives voice to one's deepest emotions, one can penetrate a reader's heart like a spear and move him to tears. I am sure you feel the same as I. No one who ever reads your mother's letter will be able to hold back his tears.

To Liu Xiaochuan

I look forward earnestly to seeing your father and also seeing you. Do I have to invoke Heaven to testify to my sincerity?

And yet the season is still the "great cold" period of the year. How does an old man like me dare to travel? Also, since the tenth month I have been studying the *Book of Changes* with Ruhou at night. We study one hexagram per night because during the night it is quiet with no visitors or affairs interfering, only the five or six of us who take this seriously and argue and analyze until the second nightwatchman's drum. It will take us four and a half months to finish the book. A couple of the most serious-minded are guests from a thousand *li* away who came here with their families and rented nearby houses to be close to my Eternal Rewards Meditation Abode. It would not be right to desert them abruptly.

In my opinion you should come here. Take a light boat and let the river carry you conveniently down here. You will soon be listening to explications of the *Book of Changes* and be purged of your despondency. Ruhou is an unworldly man whose only concern is study. Although he seldom travels, he is no less a scholar for it. You should come here to meet him. Why are you guarding your home so stupidly, like a child or a woman? By all means, do come down here. I will be standing on tiptoe watching for you. You cannot, should not, and will not disappoint me! What's so precious about your office that you have to shut yourself up in there, watching over everything? Believe me, you will fall ill because of it. You are a man, yet you do not have the all-transcending spirit to seek for teachers and friends in the wide world. Instead you ask an old man to travel to you. How absurd! Do come down here quickly, immediately!

If you come, come by yourself. Do not bring anybody with you, for I do not like other people. Such people as Zhending and Kanggun who accompanied your uncle two years ago on the lake made me so sick that I still flinch at the thought of them. Such people are the most pitiful creatures on earth. Those who study the *Book of Changes*, on the contrary, are very refined, very diligent, and very interesting; they are where the real joy of the Way lies.

If you come, bring a lot of rice and firewood in your boat, since these things are expensive here. In the Jiao household there are more than sixty people to be fed, and yet there is not even one *mu* of land to bring in income. Hardly able to support me, how can they feed my guests? Now, remember to bring rice. The firewood you can forget.

Writing in a hurry, I have not been careful about details. Please excuse me.

Final Testament

Since spring I have been ill most of the time and I am eager to depart this world. I am glad that this will is to fall into the hands of my good friends. This is quite rare and I am very fortunate; do believe how important it is to me.

When I die, you should hurry to select a high mound outside the city. Dig a rectangular grave facing south, ten feet long, five feet wide, and only six feet deep. When the rectangle is completed according to scale, then dig another two feet five inches into the earth to make a smaller rectangle six and a half feet long and two feet five inches wide within the first rectangle. In this smaller rectangle rest my body. Spread five reed mats at the bottom of the grave and lay me on top. Who can say that this is not clean? As long as my mind is restful in there, it is paradise. Do not fall for the customary sounds and sights and thereby act against my wish. Although Ma Chenglao can afford a pompous burial for me, it is better to let me rest peacefully. This is my most important wish! Now my spirit is dispersing and in no time I will be enjoying my body's resting place.

Before setting me down in the rectangle, put my body on a board. Let me be dressed in the clothes I die in. Do not provide new clothes for me, lest my body feel ill at ease. Yet do cover my face with a piece of cloth. Put my head on a pillow as usual. Cover my whole body with a white sheet and use a footbinding strip to tie the sheet around my body, lacing it from my feet up. At the fifth drum when the temple gate is opened, have four strong men carry me out evenly to the grave.

At the grave you can then lay me down on the reed mats and take the board back to its owner. After my body is down, put twenty to thirty wooden boards across the rectangle, then another five sheets of reed mat over them. Then you can put the soil back in the grave, pounding it solid and even. Pile more soil on top of the grave so that my body's dwelling place is recognizable. Plant trees around the grave and place a tombstone in front of it with the words, "Tomb of Mr. Li Zhuowu." Each word should be four feet square. You can ask Jiao Yiyuan to write it; I believe he will not decline the request.

Those of you who wish to remain at my tomb site must do so out of sincerity. If you are indeed sincere, Master Ma will certainly see to it that you are taken care of; you will not have to worry. Those who are not concerned with me may go wherever they wish. While I was alive I never wanted any relatives to follow me; naturally after I die I will not need to be attended by them. This should be clear.

Please do not change a word of what I have written.

The 5th day of the second month,
The Will of Li Zhuowu.

Please listen to me and do what I ask of you.

Translated by Clara Yu

58

A CENSOR ACCUSES A EUNUCH

Over the centuries many officials, imbued with Confucian notions of loyalty to the throne and the responsibility of officials to speak out, courageously protested against bad officials and harmful policies. Particularly obligated in this way were the censors, for they were charged with serving as the emperor's "eyes and ears" and impeaching officials anywhere in the government who violated laws, administrative regulations, or traditional moral standards. Because censors could submit their memorials directly to the emperor, bypassing the routine channels of communication, they could accuse senior figures whose subordinates had no way to submit memorials except through them.

Below is the memorial submitted in 1624 by the censor Yang Lien (d. 1625), impeaching the eunuch Wei Zhongxian (1568–1627). Yang was a member of the Donglin Academy, a group of high-minded Confucian scholars formed in the late Ming who were committed to opposing the moral decay and political corruption of their age. Eunuch power was one of their chief targets. Like the Han and Tang dynasties before it, the Ming had not been able to curb the power of the tens of thousands of eunuchs who staffed the imperial palaces. Emperors who grew up in the palace among the eunuchs often turned to eunuchs as confidantes, giving the favored ones extraordinary access to power.

This memorial did get through to the emperor, but he did not act on it. Wei Zhongxian, moreover, had his revenge. In 1625 he obtained a forged confession implicating Yang Lien and five others. Arrested, Yang died in prison after enduring torture.

A treacherous eunuch has taken advantage of his position to act as emperor. He has seized control and disrupted the government, deceived the ruler and flouted the law. He recognizes no higher authority, turns his back on the favors the emperor has conferred on him, and interferes with the inherited institutions. I beg Your Majesty to order an investigation so that the dynasty can be saved.

When Emperor Taizu [i.e., Hongwu] first established the laws and institutions, eunuchs were not allowed to interfere in any affairs outside the palace; even within it they did nothing more than clean up. Anyone who violated these rules was punished without chance of amnesty, so the eunuchs prudently were cautious and obedient. The succeeding emperors never changed these laws. Even such arrogant and lawless eunuchs as Wang Zhen and Liu Jin were promptly executed. Thus the dynasty lasted until today.

How would anyone have expected that, with a wise ruler like Your Majesty on the throne, there would be a chief eunuch like Wei Zhongxian, a man totally uninhibited, who destroys court precedents, ignores the ruler to pursue his selfish ends, corrupts good people, ruins the emperor's reputation as a Yao or Shun, and brews unimaginable disasters? The entire court has been intimidated. No one dares denounce him by name. My responsibility really is painful. But when I was supervising secretary of the office of scrutiny for war, the previous emperor personally ordered me to help Your Majesty become a ruler like Yao and Shun. I can still hear his words. If today out of fear I also do not speak out, I will be abandoning my determination to be loyal and my responsibility to serve the state. I would also be turning my back on your kindness in bringing me back to office after retirement and would not be able to face the former emperor in Heaven.

I shall list for Your Majesty Zhongxian's twenty-four most heinous crimes. Zhongxian was originally an ordinary, unreliable sort. He had himself castrated in middle age in order to enter the palace. He is illiterate, unlike those eunuchs from the directorate of ceremonial. Your Majesty was impressed by his minor acts of service and plucked him out of obscurity to confer honors on him. . . .

Our dynastic institutions require that rescripts be delegated to the grand secretaries. This not only allows for calm deliberation and protects from interference, but it assures that someone takes the responsibility seriously. Since Zhongxian usurped power, he issues the imperial edicts. If he accurately conveys your orders, it is bad enough. If he falsifies them, who can argue with him? Recently, men have been forming groups of three or five to push their ideas in the halls of government, making it as clamorous as a noisy market. Some even go directly into the inner quarters

without formal permission. It is possible for a scrap of paper in the middle of the night to kill a person without Your Majesty or the grand secretaries knowing anything of it. The harm this causes is huge. The grand secretaries are so depressed that they ask to quit. Thus Wei Zhongxian destroys the political institutions that had lasted over two hundred years. This is his first great crime. . . .

One of your concubines, of virtuous and pure character, had gained your favor. Zhongxian was afraid she would expose his illegal behavior, so conspired with his cronies. They said she had a sudden illness to cover up his murdering her. Thus Your Majesty is not able to protect the concubines you favor. This is his eighth great crime. . . .

During the forty years that your father the former emperor was heir apparent, Wang An was unique in worrying about all the dangers he faced, protecting him from harm, never giving in to intimidation or temptation. Didn't he deserve some of the credit for your father's getting to the throne? When he died and Your Majesty succeeded, Wang An protected you, so he cannot be called disloyal. Even if he had committed some offense, Your Majesty should have explained what he had done wrong publicly for all to see. Instead Zhongxian, because of his personal hatreds, forged an imperial order and had him killed in Nanhai park. His head and body were separated, his flesh given to the dogs and pigs. This not only revealed his enmity toward Wang An, but his enmity toward all the former emperor's old servants, even his old dogs and horses. It showed him to be without the slightest fear. From that time on, which of the eunuchs was willing to be loyal or principled? I do not know how many thousands or hundreds of the rest of the eunuchs, important and unimportant alike, were slaughtered or driven away for no crime. This is his eleventh great crime. . . .

Doesn't Your Majesty remember the time when Zhongxian, against all rules, rode his horse in the palace grounds? Those who are favored too much become arrogant; those who receive too many favors grow resentful. I heard that this spring when he rode a horse in front of Your Majesty, you shot and killed the horse, but forgave Zhongxian. Despite your generosity, Zhongxian did not beg to die for his offense, but rather acted more arrogantly in Your Majesty's presence and spoke resentfully of Your Majesty when away. He is on guard morning and night, missing nothing. His trusted followers keep guard all the time. In the past traitors and bandits have struggled to wreak havoc and take over. This is in fact what Your Majesty now faces. How can you release a tiger right by your elbow? Even if Zhongxian were cut into mincemeat, it would not atone for his sins. This is his twenty-fourth great crime.

There is adequate evidence of his crimes. They are widely known and have been widely witnessed; they are not a matter of gossip. Zhongxian, guilty of these twenty-four great crimes, kills or replaces any eunuch he fears will expose his treachery. Thus those close at hand are terrified and keep silent. He expels or imprisons any of the officials he fears will expose his villainy, so the officials also all look the other way and keep silent. There are even ignorant spineless fellows eager to get rich and powerful who attach themselves to him or hang around his gate. They praise whatever he likes and criticize whatever he hates, doing whatever is needed. Thus whatever he inside wants they do outside, whatever they outside say he responds to inside. Disaster or good luck can depend on slight movements. And if per chance the evil deeds of the inner court are revealed, there is still Lady Ke to make excuses or cover up.

As a consequence, everyone in the palace recognizes the existence of Zhongxian but not of Your Majesty; everyone in the capital recognizes the existence of Zhongxian but not of Your Majesty. Even the major and minor officials and workers, by turning toward the sources of power, unconsciously show that they do not recognize the existence of Your Majesty, only of Zhongxian. Whenever they see that some matter needs urgent attention or an appointment needs to be made, they always say, "It must be discussed with the eunuch." When a matter cannot be handled or a person appointed, they just explain that the eunuch is not willing. All matters, large and small, in both the palace and the government offices, are decided by Zhongxian alone. A document may have Your Majesty's name on it, but in fact Zhongxian handled it. For instance, the other day when Zhongxian went to Zhongzhou, all matters were still directed to him using night couriers, and no rescripts were issued until he arrived. . . .

In the tenth year of the first emperor of the dynasty [1377], there was a eunuch who had been in service a long time but carelessly mentioned a governmental matter. The emperor dismissed him that very day and told his officials, "Even though we attribute the fall of the Han and Tang dynasties to the eunuchs, it was the rulers who made it possible by trusting and loving them. If in the past eunuchs had not commanded troops or participated in politics, they would not have been able to cause disorder no matter what they wanted. This eunuch has admittedly served me a long time, but I cannot overlook his mistake. Getting rid of him decisively will serve as a warning to those to come." How brilliant! A eunuch who mentioned a governmental matter became a warning for the future. What about Zhongxian who deceives his ruler, recognizes no one above him, and piles up crimes? How can he be left unpunished?

I beg Your Majesty to take courage and thunder forth. Take Zhongxian to the ancestral temple in fetters. Assemble the military and civil officials of all ranks and have the judicial officials interrogate him. Check all the precedents from previous reigns on eunuchs having contacts with the outside, usurping imperial authority, breaking dynastic laws, disrupting court business, alienating the people, and violating the trust of the ruler. Sentence him in a way that will please the gods and satisfy public indignation. . . .

If all this is done and yet Heaven does not show its pleasure, the people do not rejoice, and there is not a new era of peace within the country and at its borders, then I ask that you behead me as an offering to Zhongxian. I am well aware that once my words become known, Zhongxian's clique will detest me, but I am not afraid. If I could get rid of the one person Zhongxian and save Your Majesty's reputation as a Yao and Shun, I would fulfill the command of the former emperor and could face the spirits of all ten of the former emperors. My lifetime goal has been to serve loyally. I would not regret having to die as a way of paying back the extraordinary favors I have received during two reigns. I hope Your Majesty recognizes my passion and takes prompt action.

Translated by Patricia Ebrey

PART VI

THE QING DYNASTY

Although the Ming was overthrown by peasant rebellions of the usual sort, the next dynasty was founded not by a warlord or rebel leader but by the chieftains of the Manchus, a non-Chinese people living in the hilly forests and plains to the northeast of China proper, the large area generally called Manchuria. The Manchus had long been in contact with the Mongols and Chinese and for decades had been building up the political and military institutions needed to govern sedentary farming populations.

Like the Mongols, the Manchus were alien conquerors; yet their dynasty, the Qing (1644–1911), did not represent nearly as fundamental a break with Chinese traditions. The Manchus tried to maintain their own identity and traditions, but largely left Chinese customs and institutions alone. In fact, in many respects the eighteenth century was the apogee of Chinese civilization. Some two to three hundred million people lived peaceably in an empire even bigger than China today, stretching from Manchuria, through Mongolia, and into Central Asia and Tibet. Traditional scholarship and arts flourished under the patronage of the Qing emperors, and even in rural areas schools were common and basic literacy relatively high.

Yet during the Qing dynasty the stability of traditional Chinese civilization was being gradually undermined by the steady increase in the size of the population. By 1850 the population reached about four hundred million. This demographic growth affected many other aspects of life. By the beginning of the nineteenth century, the pressure of population on available land resources was becoming acute. All of the land which could profitably be exploited using traditional methods was already under cultivation, so any increase in food supply had to come from less and less rewarding additions of labor or marginal land. As a consequence, the prospect of widespread suffering became very real, especially in times of drought or flood. The government structure did not keep pace with the population's growth; in fact, it remained static in size during the Qing period, so that by the end of the dynasty government services and control were stretched thinner to cover two or three times as large a population as at the beginning. At the local level more authority was taken over by the gentry, especially by men who had passed the lower-level civil service examinations.

The growing importance of the "examination gentry" was a major social development of late imperial China. Since at least the Ming period, competition in the examinations had been fierce; by the nineteenth century it was brutal. Of the two million students who sat for the first, or prefectural, examination in any given year, only thirty thousand passed to become *shengyuan* (government students). Even these men had only about a one to two percent chance of rising high enough to become officials, for only fifteen hundred passed the provincial examination as *juren* (recommended men) and only five hundred the metropolitan examination as *jinshi* (presented scholars). Only the *jinshi* could count on becoming officials. The *shengyuan* and many of the *juren* remained local gentry with only unofficial responsibilities and sources of income. Those with extensive landholdings could maintain the way of life of cultivated literati, but others were often forced into marginal positions.

At the same time that these demographic and social changes were beginning to weaken the Qing government, China was confronted with a new foreign threat. China's defeat by the British in the Opium War of 1840–1842 set in action a humiliating chain of events. Westerners came to occupy privileged positions in a number of "treaty ports" along China's coast and acquired territorial rights to small parts of China such as Hong Kong. They sold manufactured goods that competed with Chinese industries. Their missionaries gained the right to try to convert Chinese to Christianity. Most troubling of all, their armies and navies repeatedly proved themselves superior to China's, raising fundamental questions about how China could strengthen herself and what, if anything, she should copy from these foreigners.

From the time of the great and devastating Taiping Rebellion (1850–1864) until the overthrow of the Qing dynasty in 1911, instability and restiveness seem to have pervaded almost all segments of Chinese society. Although the vast majority of the Chinese never saw a Westerner during this period and changed few of their habits or attitudes, by the end of the dynasty the foreign threat had come to have far-reaching effects. Intellec-

tual leaders and high officials were divided into reformers and conservatives. The gentry as a whole was demoralized, convinced that the dynasty
was on an inevitable downward slide. Peasants and townsmen in port
cities, or areas where missionaries were active or modern enterprises such
as railroads were being introduced, protested these intrusions and the
changes they were causing. At the same time, Chinese merchants and
entrepreneurs in the port cities took advantage of the new opportunities
to amass fortunes and lead the way toward new capitalist culture.

Sources for the Qing period are rich and plentiful. Genealogies, gazet-
teers, fiction, and personal memoirs all survive in greater quantity than for
earlier periods. One new kind of source seldom available before the Qing
is original documents, such as contracts, agreements, account books, and
so on, which accidentally survived into the twentieth century and then
were preserved by scholars who recognized their value to legal, institutional, and economic history. A few such documents are translated in Part
VI.

59

THE YANGZHOU MASSACRE

Few areas of China escaped unscathed during the decades of rebellion and war-fare surrounding the fall of the Ming. Sporadic uprisings began in 1628 and soon were occurring all over North China. The death toll mounted steadily, especially after a group of rebels cut the dikes of the Yellow River in 1642, thereby killing several hundred thousand people in the flood and subsequent famine. Rebels sometimes slaughtered people indiscriminately, most notably Zhang Xianzhong when he took Sichuan in 1644–46.

The Manchus entered the fray after Beijing fell to the rebel Li Zicheng and the last Ming emperor committed suicide. Invited by Ming generals to help them retake Beijing, the Manchus soon showed they intended to take the throne themselves. Some Ming generals continued to work with them, others tried to establish a successor to the Ming throne in Nanjing. These loyalist troops decided to resist the Manchus at Yangzhou, a major city on the north bank of the Yangzi River. For a week they held out, then the city fell. As retaliation for Yangzhou's resistance and as a warning to other cities, the Manchus slaughtered thousands, some say hundreds of thousands, of its residents.

The following memoir recounts what one man saw and heard during the siege and massacre. Since the Qing government naturally did not want its subjects to remember too vividly how it had conquered the land, essays like this one could not be openly published during the Qing dynasty. This one survived through manuscript copies that got to Japan. In reading this account of the devastation of Yangzhou, one might imagine that the city would never fully recover. However, its location near the juncture of the Yangzi River and the Grand Canal made it too important a city to abandon. By the end of the seventeenth century its prosperity was restored and the Kangxi emperor (r. 1662–1722) stopped there on his second and third southern tours, apparently confident that memories of the massacre had dimmed. In the eighteenth century Yangzhou even became an artistic center of considerable importance, known especially for its painters.

On the 14th of the fourth month of 1645, Commandant Shi Kefa gave up the defense of Boyanghe and retreated to Yangzhou. Ordering the city gates closed, he prepared for a siege. Up to the 24th, the city remained unconquered and our soldiers held all of the gates. My house was in the eastern part of the new city, where a general named Yang was in command. His officers and soldiers stood around like chessmen. . . .

Early in the afternoon the next day, my wife's relatives came from Guazhou to take refuge from the Earl of Xingping's fleeing soldiers. My wife, not having seen the family for a long time, was greatly cheered. By then one or two people had already told me that a large force of enemy soldiers was about to enter the city. I rushed out to ask people about it. Someone said, "They're our reinforcements from Huang Degong, Marquis of Qingnan." I noticed that the guards on the wall were still quiet and orderly but that people in the streets were getting excited. Crowds of barefoot and disheveled refugees were flocking into the city. When questioned, they were too distraught to reply. At that point dozens of mounted soldiers in confused waves came surging south looking as though they had given up all hope. Along them appeared a man who turned out to be the commandant himself. It seems he had intended to leave by the east gate but could not because the enemy soldiers outside the wall were drawing too near; he was therefore forced to cut across this part of town to reach the south gate. This is how we first learned for sure that the enemy troops would enter the city.

Just then a mounted soldier with slackened reins rode slowly north, his face upturned, wailing. Two soldiers walked in front of his horse, not willing to let go of the reins. This image is still vivid in my memory, and I wish I had learned the man's name. When the rider was still some way off, the panicky guards on the city walls began to jump, discarding their helmets and spears, some breaking their legs or even their necks. By the time I looked back at the guard tower on the city wall, it was empty.

The commandant had seen that the city wall was too narrow for the cannon to be set up there and so had ordered a platform to be erected, one side resting on the footpath on the wall and the other against the houses opposite. This way more space was available for deploying the cannon. Yet before this work could be finished, the enemy soldiers had scaled the wall, swords in hand, and begun the carnage. This caused those defending the wall to flee in such disorder that they clogged the exits. Many of them ran to the cannon platforms which had been set up and climbed on their hands and knees in an attempt to cross over to the houses behind. The platforms were not stable and collapsed as soon as the weight of the people became too great; people fell like leaves, eight or nine out of ten dashed to death. Those who reached the houses shattered the roof tiles as they trampled on them, making a noise which reverberated in all directions and sounded like the clash of swords or severe hail. The people inside the houses, in their terror and confusion, poured out by the hundreds. At the same time every room and courtyard, even bedrooms, was invaded by those who had jumped from the roofs in their frantic search for hiding places. The owners were powerless to prevent it. In my neighborhood all the doors were tightly fastened, everyone holding his or her breath.

My house backed against the city wall, and peeping through the chinks in my window, I saw the soldiers on the wall marching south then west, solemn and in step. Although the rain was beating down, it did not seem to disturb them. This reassured me because I gathered that they were well-disciplined units.

Then I heard urgent knocking at my door, which turned out to be my neighbors. They had agreed to try to placate and welcome the "royal army." As a sign of submission, they wanted to set up tables and place burning incense on them. I knew that nothing much could help, but having no other way to calm them, I tentatively agreed. Thereupon I changed my clothes and stuck out my head to watch and wait. For a long time no one came. I retreated again to the back window and found that the regiment on the wall had broken ranks; some soldiers were walking about, others standing still.

All of a sudden I saw some soldiers escorting a group of women dressed in Yangzhou fashion. This was my first real shock. Back in the house, I said to my wife, "Should things go badly when the soldiers enter the city, you may need to end your life."

"Yes," she replied, "Whatever silver we have you should keep. I think we women can stop thinking about life in this world." She gave me all the silver, unable to control her crying.

At this point a townsman came rushing in and shouted, "They've come! They've come!" I dashed out and saw a few mounted soldiers coming from the north, riding slowly with reins in hand. As soon as they reached the group who were welcoming the royal army, they lowered their heads as if to consult with each other. Each of us was looking out for himself and not talking to the others, even though we were only an arm's length apart.

As the soldiers grew nearer I discovered that they were going from door to door demanding money. They were not extravagant in their demands, however, leaving as soon as they were given a little. In cases where they failed to get any, they waved their swords about but did not strike anyone. Finally they came to my door. One mounted soldier pointed to me and yelled to another behind him, "Search the man in blue for me." But before the man had dropped his reins, I had run away. He did not try to pursue me, but remounted and rode off.

I thought to myself, "I am wearing rough clothes and look like a commoner. Why did he pick on me?" Soon my younger brother arrived, then my two older brothers. We discussed the situation and I said, "The people who live in our neighborhood are all rich merchants. It will be disastrous if they think we are rich too." I then urged my brothers to brave the rain and quickly take the women by the back route to my older brother's house. His home was situated behind Mr. He's graveyard and was surrounded by the huts of poor families. I stayed behind alone to see what was going to happen. A long time passed as I nervously waited for my eldest brother to return.

I could find "no way up to Heaven nor any door down to earth." Besides, it rained in torrents.

Finally, my eldest brother reappeared and said, "People are being killed in the streets! What are we waiting for here? It doesn't matter so much whether we live or die, as long as we brothers stay together." Immediately I gathered together our ancestral tablets and went with him to our second brother's house. There ten people in all (my one younger and two elder brothers, my elder brother's wife, a nephew, my own wife and son, my wife's younger brother and sister, and I) took refuge.

As it grew darker, we could hear soldiers butchering people outside our door. As a temporary refuge, we climbed to the roof. In the downpour we ten squatted together covered only by a rug, our tangled hair soaked through. The bitter cries, resounding through the air, pierced my ears and wrenched my soul. Not until very late that night did we have the courage to come down from the roof and start a fire to cook some rice. By then fires had broken out everywhere in the city. More than a dozen places close by were ablaze, as were innumerable ones further off. The red glow flashed like lightning or a sunset as the crackling ceaselessly thundered in our ears. We could hear the faint sounds of people being beaten. Even the wind wailed with an inexpressible bitterness.

When the rice was cooked, we stared at each other, so overcome with grief that we were unable to raise our chopsticks to eat. We were equally unable to think of a plan. My wife took the silver she had given me and divided it into four shares. Each of us brothers hid one share so that our clothes, hats, shoes, and belts were all stuffed. My wife also found a ragged coat and worn-out pair of shoes for me to change into. That done, we lay awake with our eyes wide open until dawn. During the night there seemed to be a bird in the air, twittering like a reed organ or sobbing like a child, hovering somewhere not too high above our heads. Everyone reported having heard it.

The 26th. After a while, the fires began to abate and the day gradually brightened. Once more we climbed up to the roof to hide but found that a lot of people had already sought refuge there by the rain gutters.

Without any warning a man from the building east of us began to scramble up our wall. A soldier with his sword drawn was running after him. But when he saw our group, he abandoned the chase and made directly for us. In alarm I sneaked down as fast as I could. My brothers followed immediately, none of us stopping until we had run over a hundred paces. In our escape I lost track of my wife and son and did not know whether they had been killed.

The cunning soldiers, suspecting that many people were still hidden, tried to entice them out by posting a placard promising clemency. About fifty to sixty people, half of them women, emerged. My elder brother said, "We four by ourselves will never survive if we run into these vicious soldiers, so we had better join the crowd. Since there are so many of them, escape will be easier. Even if things do not turn out well, as long as we are together, we will have no cause for regret." In our bewilderment we could think of no other way to save our lives. Thus agreed, we went to join the group.

The leaders were three Manchu soldiers. They searched my brothers and found all the silver they were carrying, but left me untouched. At that point some women appeared, two of whom called out to me. I recognized them as the concubines of my friend Mr. Zhu Shu and stopped them anxiously. They were disheveled and partly naked, their feet bare and covered with mud up to the ankles. One was holding a girl whom the soldiers hit with a whip and threw into the mud. Then we were immediately driven on. One soldier, sword in hand, took the lead; another drove us from behind with a long spear; and a third walked along on our right and left flanks alternately, making sure no one escaped. In groups of twenty or thirty we were herded along like sheep and cattle. If we faltered we were struck, and some people were even killed on the spot. The women were tied together with long chains around their necks, like a clumsy string of pearls. Stumbling at every step, they were soon covered with mud. Here and there

on the ground lay babies, trampled by people or horses. Blood and gore soaked the fields, which were filled with the sound of sobbing. We passed gutters and ponds piled high with corpses; the blood had turned the water to a deep greenish-red color and filled the ponds to the brim.

We arrived at the house of the jailer, Yao Yongyan. Entering through the back door, we passed through many rooms and found bodies everywhere. I supposed that this was where we would die. We went through several rooms until we came to the street door. We then entered the house of the Shanxi merchant, Jiao Chengwang, which had been taken over by the three soldiers. Another soldier was already there. He had seized several attractive women and was rifling their trunks for fancy silks, which he piled in a heap. Seeing the three soldiers arrive, he laughed and pushed several dozen of us into the back hall. The women he led into a side chamber.

In that room there were two square tables at which three tailors and a middle-aged woman were making clothes. The woman was a local resident. Her face was heavily made up and she was wearing brightly colored clothes. She laughed and flirted, seeming to be in high spirits. Whenever she came across anything fine, she shamelessly tried to wheedle it away from the soldiers. The soldiers often said to people, "When we conquered Korea, we captured tens of thousands of women, and yet not one of them lost her chastity. How can there be so little shame in a great country like China?"

The three soldiers stripped the women of their wet clothing all the way to their underwear, then ordered the seamstress to measure them and give them new garments. The women, thus coerced, had to expose themselves and stand naked. What shame they endured! Once they had changed, the soldiers grabbed them and forced them to join them in eating and drinking, then did whatever they pleased with them, without any regard for decency.

One soldier suddenly jumped up, his sword drawn, and cried out, "Come on, you southern Barbarians!" Several of those standing in the front had already been tied up, my eldest brother among them. Saying to me, "What alternative do we have?" he took my hand and ran forward. My younger brother also followed. The fifty-odd men who were bound were so scared that they could not move, even when the soldiers raised their swords and shouted. Right behind my eldest brother, I rushed out of the hall, but soon discovered that the slaughter was going on outside as well as inside. Outside a group of people were standing in a row awaiting their fate. At first I thought of submitting, but suddenly my heart took a leap, and, as if helped by some spirit, I sprang away quickly and returned to the back hall without attracting the attention of any of the bound men.

The western section of the building, where many old women still remained, was not a safe place for me to hide, and so I slipped out back. It was impossible for me to walk through that area, though, because it was filled with horses and camels. Trembling, I dropped to the floor and crawled under the bellies of these beasts. If the slightest thing had startled them, I would have been trampled into the mud.

After passing through several courtyards, I could locate no way out except a side alley leading to the back door. But this door was fastened tightly with an iron lock. Once more I headed out to the front along the lane, but hearing people being killed in the front panicked me. I looked back, and on the left side I saw four people in the kitchen. It seemed they had been captured and forced to do the cooking. I begged them to let me attend the fire or draw water for them so that I could save myself. But they adamantly refused, "Whenever we four are ordered to work, they call the roll. If they find more people next time, they will surely suspect some trick, and our lives will be in jeopardy." I appealed to them plaintively, but this made them even more angry and they threatened to hand me over. With this I left, more anxious than ever.

Not very far from the house I saw some steps and a platform on which a jar had been placed. I climbed up the platform, but no sooner had I touched the jar than I fell off. The jar had been empty, and I had inadvertently used too much force. Seeing no alternatives, once more I ran to the door at the end of the lane. Using both hands I shook the lock a hundred times but failed to make it move. I struck it with stones, but the sound was loud enough to reach the outer courtyard and I was afraid of being heard. So I reverted to shaking the lock, my fingers aching and bleeding. Then unexpectedly the lock turned! I pulled at it with all my strength and soon had it off. Next I tried the bolt which was made of hibiscus wood. Water-logged from the rain, it was swollen and twice as solid as the lock. I pulled on the bolt with all my might. Instead of the bolt loosening, the hinges ripped off, the door fell flat, and the wall collapsed with a sound like a thunderclap.

I leapt over it as if flying. Where such strength came from I have no idea. With all possible speed, I ran out the back door and found myself at the base of the city wall. Foot soldiers and horsemen were everywhere, making it impossible to go forward. Therefore I turned at the back door of a house to the left of the Jiaos' residence and elbowed my way in. Any place that was safe was full of people who did not want to let any more in. This house was divided, back to front, into five rooms, all of which were crowded like this. I made my way straight to the front gate. Because it was close to the street where soldiers were endlessly streaming by, it was considered a dangerous spot and deserted. Entering quickly, I found a bed with a wooden canopy. I climbed on top of it by way of the pillars and crouched to conceal myself.

Scarcely had I regained my breath when I heard the sound of my younger brother wailing, coming from the other side of the wall. Then I heard the blows of the sword. After three blows there was silence. A few moments later I heard my elder brother implore, "I have silver in the cellar at home. Release me and I will go and fetch it for you." There was one blow, then silence again. For a time my spirit was wrenched out of my body; my heart was boiling, my eyes tearless, my innards torn. No longer in control of myself, all I wanted was to die.

Later on a soldier brought a women in and

wanted her to sleep with him in the bed below me. Despite her refusal, he forced her to yield. "This is too near the street. It is not a good place to stay," the woman said. I was almost discovered, but after a time the soldier departed with the woman.

The room had a ceiling which seemed to be made of matting. It was not strong enough to sustain the weight of a man, but if I could creep across it, I could reach the beam. I climbed up by holding the rafters with both hands and resting my foot on the projecting roof pole. Inside it was pitch black, since the mat was underneath. Every time the soldiers came in they would thrust upward through the matting with their spears and, finding it empty, conclude that no one was up there. Thus I managed to end the day without encountering any more soldiers. But I have no idea how many were slaughtered underneath me. Every time a few mounted soldiers passed along the street, dozens of men and women, loudly lamenting, would be trailing behind them. As the day was cloudy, I could not judge the time. A long time passed, then mounted soldiers came less and less frequently until only the incessant weeping of the people could be heard from the outside.

I thought of my brothers, two of whom were already dead. I did not know the fate of my eldest brother or the whereabouts of my son and wife. I wanted to find them and see them again. Therefore I slowly climbed down from my hiding place by holding onto the beam and furtively made my way to the front street. The heads of the corpses in the street were piled up on each other like pillows, and as it grew dark, it was impossible to recognize them. I bent over several corpses and called out, but received no answer. To the south I saw the torches of a confused crowd approaching and quickly got out of their way. As I walked along the foot of the city wall, I constantly stumbled against dead bodies. Whenever I heard something I dropped to the ground and pretended to be a corpse myself. After a long while I reached a path. In the darkness people could not see each other and often collided. But the main street was lit by torches and was as bright as day. Walking from

seven to nine in the evening, I finally reached my elder brother's house.

I found the door closed and was afraid to knock. Then I heard my sister-in-law's voice. I knocked gently a few times, and my wife came to answer. My eldest brother had come back earlier, and both my wife and son were there. I wept with my eldest brother but did not dare to tell him of the deaths of our other brothers. My sister-in-law questioned me, but I gave her only vague replies. . . .

When dawn brought in the 29th, five days had passed since the 25th, and I was beginning to imagine that by some stroke of fortune we might be spared. But then I heard some garbled stories about a planned wholesale slaughter of the population. It seemed that over half of those who had survived so far had decided to risk their lives in an attempt to flee by climbing over the city walls with ropes, but so many were killed that the moat became as flat as a road from the corpses, and suffering reached a new height. Those who did escape had to face the bandits who at night waited stealthily in groups by the moat and robbed the refugees of their gold and silver.

With the danger so great and my eldest brother unwilling to be separated from us, we decided not to try escape. But I worried all night; our old hiding place was no longer safe, and my wife had already had to plead pregnancy to survive. Finally we decided I would hide in the dense weeds by the pond and my wife and [son] Penger would lie on top. Though the soldiers repeatedly forced them to come out of hiding, they were able to induce them to go away by offering money.

At length, however, there came a soldier of the "Wolf Men" tribe, a vicious-looking man with a head like a mouse and eyes like a hawk. He attempted to abduct my wife. She was obliged to creep forward on all fours, pleading as she had with the others, but to no avail. When he insisted that she stand up, she rolled on the ground and refused. He then beat her so savagely with the flat of his sword that the blood flowed out in streams, totally soaking her clothes. Because my wife had once admonished me, "If I am unlucky I will die no matter what; do not plead for me as a husband or you will get caught too," I acted as if I did not know she was being beaten and hid far away in the grass, convinced she was about to die. Yet the depraved soldier did not step there; he grabbed her by the hair, cursed her, struck her cruelly, and then dragged her away by the leg. There was a small path about an arrow's shot in length winding out from the field to the main street. The soldier dragged my wife along this and every few steps would hit her again. Just then they ran into a body of mounted soldiers. One of them said a few words to the soldier in Manchu. At this he dropped my wife and departed with them. Barely able to crawl back, she let out a loud sob, every part of her body injured.

Suddenly the whole city was ablaze. The thatched huts surrounding He's graveyard were quickly reduced to ashes. Only one or two houses, a little separated from the others, were fortunate enough to escape. Those hidden in the houses now were forced out by the fire, and ninety-nine in a hundred were killed as they showed themselves. Those who stayed inside, sometimes up to a hundred people in a single house, were cremated; their numbers now will never be known.

At this point it was no longer possible to hide. If caught, whether we offered money or not, we would be killed. The only recourse left was to go to the roadsides and lie among the corpses so that no one could distinguish us from the dead. My son, my wife, and I went and lay among the graves, so dirty and muddy from head to foot we did not look at all human.

As time passed the fire raged fiercer. The lofty trees around the graves caught fire; it glowed like lightning and roared like a landslide. The violence of the wind made the fire burn so brilliantly that the sun seemed to turn pale. To us it looked as though countless demons were driving hundreds and thousands of people into hell. Many times we fainted with fright, hardly sure whether we were still among the living. Then, startled by the sound of loud footsteps and terrible screams, I spotted my eldest brother some way off, standing beside a wall struggling with a soldier who had caught

him. Since he was very strong, he succeeded in throwing off the soldier and began to run away, but was instantly pursued. The soldier I recognized as the man who the previous day had abducted and then released my wife. By midday my brother had not returned and my heart began to pound.

Finally he came running, with no clothes on and his hair undone, driven along by the soldier. Out of desperation he asked me for silver to save his life. I had only one ingot left, but I took it out and offered it to the soldier. Seeing it made him so angry that he struck my brother with his sword. The latter rolled to the ground, his body bathed in blood. Penger, only five years old, pulled at the soldier and cried for him to stop. The man then wiped the blood from his sword on my son's clothes. Had he delivered one more blow, my brother would surely have died. Next the soldier grabbed me by the hair and demanded more silver, hitting me over and over again with the back of his sword. I apologized for having no more silver and said, "If you insist on silver, then I am afraid I shall die, but there are other things I can give you." Without letting go of my hair, he went with me to Mrs. Hong's house. On the steps I poured out the contents of two earthenware jars full of my wife's possessions and let the soldier take what he wanted. He grabbed all my wife's gold and pearl jewelry and the best of her clothes. Seeing the silver locket around my son's neck, he took his sword and cut it off. When he left he turned and said, "Even though I did not kill you, someone else will." I then knew it was true that the city was to be razed; our death seemed inevitable.

After leaving our son at the house, my wife and I quickly went out to look for my brother. We found that his neck had a gash an inch deep on both the front and the back, and his chest had even worse wounds. We helped him to Mrs. Hong's house, where he lay confused and half insensible to the pain. After attending to him, we went back to hide in our old place.

Our neighbors were all hidden among the rushes. Someone yelled to me, "Tomorrow the city will be razed and no one will be spared. You had better abandon your wife and flee with me." My wife also advised me to go, but I kept thinking of the danger my brother was in. How could I bear to leave him? So far I had relied on my supply of silver; now that it was gone I realized we could not survive. Brooding on this, I lost consciousness.

It took a long time before I came to my senses. I saw that fires in the city were gradually dying down, and I heard a cannon fired three times in the distance. The soldiers on patrol were decreasing in number. My wife clutched our boy as we sat together in a manure pit. . . .

Unexpectedly there appeared a handsome-looking man of less than thirty, a double-edged sword hung by his side, dressed in Manchu-style hat, red coat, and a pair of black boots. His follower, in a yellow jacket, was also very gallant in appearance. Immediately behind them were several residents of Yangzhou. The young man in red, inspecting me closely, said, "I would judge from your appearance that you are not one of these people. Tell me honestly, what class of person are you?"

I remembered that some people had obtained pardons and others had lost their lives the moment they said that they were poor scholars. So I did not dare come out at once with the truth and instead concocted a story. He pointed to my wife and son and asked who they were, and I told him the truth. "Tomorrow the prince will order that all swords be sheathed and all of you will be spared," he said and then commanded his followers to give us some clothes and an ingot of silver. He also asked me, "How many days have you been without food?"

"Five days," I replied.

"Then come with me," he commanded. Although we only half trusted him, we were afraid to disobey. He led us to a well-stocked house, full of rice, fish, and other provisions. "Treat these four people well," he said to a woman in the house and then left.

By this time night had already fallen. We learned that my wife's brother had been carried off by the soldiers. Now knowing whether he was

dead or alive, my wife was in a state of grief. A few moments later the old woman brought some boiled rice and fish for us to eat. Since we were not very far from Mrs. Hong's house, I took some food to my eldest brother, but he could not eat more than a few mouthfuls because his throat was too sore to swallow. I wiped his hair and washed his wounds, my heart rent by his condition. However, knowing of the order to end the slaughter in the city made us all feel somewhat comforted.

The next day was the last of the fifth month. Killing and pillaging continued, although not on the previous scale. Still the mansions of the rich were thoroughly looted, and almost all the teenage girls were abducted. On this day the Earl of Xingping reentered Yangzhou, and every grain of rice, every inch of silk now entered these tigers' mouths. The resulting devastation is beyond description.

The 2nd. Civil administration was established in all the prefectures and counties; proclamations were issued aimed at calming the people, and monks from each temple were ordered to burn corpses. The temples themselves were clogged with women who had taken refuge, many of whom had died of fright or starvation. The "List of Corpses Burned" records more than eight hundred thousand, and this list does not include those who jumped into wells, threw themselves into the river, hanged themselves, were burned to death inside houses, or were carried away by the soldiers.

The 3rd. Distribution of food was announced. I went with old Mrs. Hong to the Juekou Gate to get some rice. This rice, heaped as high as a mound, was part of what the commandant had stored as rations for his troops. Several thousand bushels soon disappeared. The people lined up for food had scorched hair, smashed heads, broken legs and arms, and sword cuts all over their faces which resembled streams of wax pouring down from a candle. In the struggle for rice, even friends and relatives ignored each other. The strong got some and then returned for more, while the old, weak, or severely wounded were not able to get a single ration all day long.

The 4th. As the sky was clear, the sun shone hot, and the bodies began to smell. Everywhere around us the dead were being burned; the smoke gathered like a mist, and the stench permeated the area. On the day I burned some cotton along with some bones of the dead and used the ashes as a salve for my brother's wounds. Unable to speak, he could only nod to me through silent tears.

The 5th. By now those who had remained hidden were beginning to reappear. Upon meeting one another, people would cry but were at a loss for words.

We five, although less apprehensive than before, still did not dare to stay home. Early in the morning we got up and, after eating a little food, went out to a deserted field. We dressed in the same fashion as before because of the hundreds of foragers roving about. Although they carried no swords, they intimidated people with clubs and seized their possessions. Anyone who tried to resist them was clubbed to death, and any woman they encountered was molested. At first we did not know whether they were Manchu soldiers, our own guards, or commoners-turned-bandits.

That day my brother's wounds festered, broke open, and he died. Words cannot express my grief.

When this calamity began there had been eight of us: my two elder brothers, my younger brother, my elder brother's wife, their son, my wife, my son, and myself. Now only three of us survived for sure, though the fate of my wife's brother and sister-in-law was not yet known.

From the 25th of the fourth month to the 5th of the fifth month was a period of ten days. I have described here only what I actually experienced or saw with my own eyes; I have not recorded anything I picked up from rumors or hearsay. The younger generation is now fortunate enough to enjoy the blessing of peace and has grown lax. Reading this account should wake them up.

Translated by Patricia Ebrey

60

PROVERBS ABOUT HEAVEN

Proverbs are a valuable source for understanding common assumptions and ways of thinking that people take as so obvious and well-accepted that they do not have to be argued; merely by invoking the proverb or saying, one is certain that others will understand. It is true that the repertoire of proverbs contains many that are mutually contradictory (such as two given below: "Heaven helps the good man," and "Heaven is high and the emperor far away"). In such cases, most people probably would acknowledge believing both, not as statements of universal applicability, but still as "truth."

Below are some proverbs collected in China in the nineteenth and early twentieth centuries. They occurred in everyday speech but in a variety of contexts. All of these proverbs concern Heaven, which literally means "sky." Heaven is not paradise, a place where souls go after death (such as the Pure Land of the Buddhists); rather it is closer to the Western concept of Providence or the Supreme Being.

1. The net of Heaven is large and wide but it lets nothing through.
2. All things have their root in Heaven.
3. Heaven produces and Heaven destroys.
4. The heart of the people is the heart of Heaven.
5. It is easy to oppress the people beneath you but difficult to deceive Heaven above.
6. Men can be imposed upon but not Heaven; men can be deceived but not Heaven.
7. Men's whispers sound like thunder in Heaven's ears; their secret thoughts flash like lightning before Heaven's eyes.
8. The slightest virtue, although unseen by men, is surely seen by Heaven.
9. Men see only the present; Heaven sees the future.
10. When men's desires are good, Heaven will certainly further them.
11. Heaven helps the good man.
12. To depend upon men is not as good as to depend upon Heaven.
13. A fire started by men is called a fire; a fire started by Heaven is called a calamity.
14. Men should beware of coveting riches; when riches come through covetousness, Heaven's calamities follow.
15. Those who accord with Heaven are preserved; those who rebel against Heaven perish.
16. Heaven sets the price of fuel and rice.
17. Great blessings come from Heaven; small blessings come from man.

18. Because men do not like the cold, Heaven does not cause winter to cease.
19. Man would order things thus and so but Heaven's way is never such.
20. Heaven responds to man as promptly as shadow to form or echo to voice.
21. Heaven never produces a man without providing him clothes and food.
22. For each man produced by Heaven, earth provides a grave.
23. Man depends on Heaven as a ship on her pilot.
24. It is Heaven's role to declare a man's destiny; it is man's role to shorten or lengthen his days.
25. When you have done your duty, listen to the will of Heaven.
26. Heaven and earth are the greatest; father and mother are the most honored.
27. Death and life are predetermined; riches and honors depend upon Heaven.
28. Heaven complies with the wishes of good men; happiness springs naturally in harmonious homes.
29. Heaven is high and the emperor far away.
30. Heaven does not spare truth; earth does not spare its treasures.
31. Heaven is man on a large scale; man is Heaven on a small scale.
32. Heaven never stops a man from making a living.
33. In our actions we should accord with the will of Heaven; in our words we should accord with the hearts of men.
34. If Heaven above lets fall a plum, open your mouth.

61

TAXES AND LABOR SERVICE

From early times the Chinese government imposed taxes and service obligations directly on ordinary households, not going through tax-farmers or other intermediaries. Equitable taxation was the goal, and periodic reforms were instituted to rationalize the collection of taxes and make their burdens more even. Reform of labor service obligations was also regularly undertaken from the Tang dynasty on, and generally involved efforts to commute service obligations to cash payments. However, since local officials did not always have the resources to hire workers whenever something needed to be done, time and again they would draft people to serve without pay.

The following essay reveals some of the complaints of the sorts of families who had to bear much of the burden of providing taxes and labor service. Middle income families, including the families of lower degree holders, were often heavily burdened, since they did not have the power or privileges of the highest ranking families, nor were they so poor that there was nothing the government could take from them. This essay is specifically concerned with the tax and labor service systems in Song prefecture (in the modern Shanghai area) in the seventeenth century. The author, Ye Mengzhu, relied on the recollections of old people for some of his evidence but also had personal experience with aspects of the system, having lost his post because of tax arrears in 1661.

TAXES

Our prefecture's taxes are the highest in the country. Suzhou yields more tax income than does the whole province of Jejiang. The land encompassed by Song prefecture, although only one-third the size of Suzhou, yields half as much tax income as Suzhou. From this one can see that Su and Song prefectures are the most heavily taxed in the whole southeast delta area,

and that Song prefecture's taxes are by far the highest.

I have talked with old people about how things were during the Longqing [1567–1572] and Wanli periods [1573–1620], and they all say that at that time local produce was abundant and the people were happy. Officials were not punished for their performance in tax collection, and the common people were not disturbed by tax-prodders. Today our taxes are not much higher than before, but the officials make strenuous efforts to collect them, piling one penalty on top of another for failure to pay, and, since the people are drained of all their riches, their overdue taxes never get paid. . . .

Throughout the Ming dynasty, officials considered their tax collection accomplished when they had collected eighty percent of the required amount, and the people who paid eighty percent of their taxes were considered law-abiding subjects, even those who only paid sixty to seventy percent were considered cooperative. Moreover, because peace had existed for a long time, the regulations had become routine. As there were extensive stores of grain, the tax grain to be shipped out could be reduced in quantity. There were priority expenses that had to be met, such as the salaries of government officials, the wages for workers, the expenses for schools, and the allowance for the salaried students; but other expenses could be delayed. The yearly repair of government buildings, city walls, and storage structures did not have to be done on time. The alms granaries had to be filled, but not necessarily with the first round of collected tax grain. The yearly rewards for scholars who passed the civil service examination and the traveling expenses for the new candidates could not be ignored but they did not have to be given regularly, and the traveling expenses for those on the waiting list could be deferred. The soldiers who defended our cities had to be paid; yet the seasonal display of their training and equipment could be omitted. Other such cases where the expenses might be delayed were innumerable. So, when sixty or seventy percent of the tax was collected, it was ready to be shipped. When eighty percent was collected, some revenue could even be set aside as savings. In this way, taxes were collected in installments and the revenue was spent as actual needs arose. Officials were not punished for neglecting their tax collection duties, and the people were not squeezed dry.

Beginning with this dynasty, things changed. In the fifth month of 1645, an imperial decree was issued to reduce the taxes of the southeast delta area by fifty percent. As a result, local govern-ments had to reduce all taxes that could be delayed and to cut out all but urgent expenses. It was true that, owing to the good intention of the emperor, the yearly taxes, though not quite as low in the reigns of Longqing and Wanli, were much lighter than before. And yet, when non-urgent expenses were cut, everything else was absolutely necessary, and officials could no longer balance out by appropriating funds set aside for non-urgent matters to supply immediate needs. Furthermore, much of the tax revenue was used to pay the soldiers. Since they had to be paid in full, taxes also had to be paid in full. Consequently, a local official now had to collect one hundred percent of the taxes before his duties were fulfilled, and he had to punish those who did not pay the full amount. For this reason, all local officials concentrated on their tax-collection duties and paid little attention to the welfare of the people.

As to the taxpayers, some were law-abiding, others were defiant. Their fields also varied in quality, as did their yearly harvests. . . . All these factors made it impossible to obtain a one hundred percent tax collection. Moreover, although the tax was lowered, people were accustomed to the old ways and failed to anticipate the consequent strict execution of the law, so many continued to owe taxes. As a result, many magistrates lost their posts because of their failure to collect all the taxes due. The county revenue officer usually counted the newly collected tax against the old deficit. The transfer of county officials also caused problems because the new and old magistrates evaded their responsibilities to each other. Often magistrates had to rent houses and stay near their former post because of unfinished tax business. This situation continued until the last years of Shunzhi [1644–1661], when the prefect of Jiangning was unable to solve the problem and blamed the gentry, the literati, and the government functionaries. He proposed to the throne that they be punished. The order was first applied to Wuxi county in Zhang and the Jiating county in Su, and then, in the fifth month of 1661 the new tax law was adopted in the four prefectures Su, Song, Zhang, Zhen, and the county of Liyang. It required an explanation for delayed tax payments and stipulated that the owed amount be paid up by the end of the year.

Now, while it was true that the gentry, literati, and government functionaries did owe taxes, the sum was barely ten percent of the amount owed by the common people. Besides, there were mistakes in the records when the law was first implemented. The bookkeepers, who did not comprehend the seriousness of the matter, only recorded rough figures for the taxes paid by individuals from one day to another. Sometimes a completed payment was erroneously recorded as still outstanding; other times, a small unpaid amount was mistakenly recorded as a large one. Sometimes, the name of the person who had paid up his taxes failed to show up on the record; other times, such a person's name failed to be deleted from the list of delinquents.

In its severity, the new law made no distinction based on how high one's office was or how much or how little tax one owed. All the government officials on the list of delinquents were to be dismissed from their offices and all the gentry in retirement were to be demoted in rank. Consequently, 2,171 local gentry and literati and 11,346 lower degree holders were listed as offenders and were scheduled to be dismissed or demoted. At first, it was reported that these offenders were to be extradited to the capital to be severely punished, and all hearts pounded. Then it was decided that those who could pay up before the imperial decree arrived could avoid extradition, bringing some relief. But still, hundreds were unable to pay up by that date and were released only if they managed to clear their debts before the scheduled extradition. Those people certainly would not have remained prisoners if they had had some way out.

Then officials began to collect unpaid taxes for the previous ten years, and the citizens, frightened of the devastating consequences, rushed in to pay, selling their estates at any price. Sometimes, a person would face several deadlines on one day, or would be called upon to appear before several officials. When he tried

to comply with one, he would have to ignore the others. The officers were as fierce as wolves and tigers, and the literati were treated as if they were common criminals. At such moments, the only course for many was to borrow. And yet, the monthly interest was twenty to thirty percent and one day's delay in payment would result in compounded interest. . . . Consequently, when a person borrowed ten taels of silver, he would only get nine to begin with, and this would be equivalent to little more than eight taels of pure silver. When he brought in the latter amount to the revenue office, it would be regarded as little more than seven taels. If he should fail to meet the deadline for the tax payment, then he might spend more than half of his loan just to appease the tax collectors. One month later, the officers would be out for his blood again, in packs. A person who owned one hundred *mu* could have his land, his house, his pots and pans, even his children confiscated and still be in debt for the taxes. Fettered by the law and driven by the whip, he would be too desperate to make a wise decision. That is why so many people abandoned their property and fled to other areas and still congratulated themselves on having preserved their lives. That was the saddest episode in the history of the tax system.

On the 15th day of the eleventh month of 1662 there was a rumor that all unpaid taxes had to be paid up by the end of that day and those who failed to do so would be exiled to the most desolate areas of the country. People turned panicky and fought to pay their taxes, so much so that the tax collectors were not able to handle the rush. Later it was discovered to be only a rumor, yet everyone's heart had sunk in fear. . . . At this time the emperor was young and the state was ruled by four regents who were strict and allowed no exceptions. . . . The officials Zhang Renan and Ye Fangai were demoted because they both owed one-thousandth of a tael of silver. The county student Cheng Pijie was dismissed from office because he owed 0.7 of one-thousandth of a tael. From these cases one can see the severity of the law. . . .

LABOR SERVICE

Our prefecture ranks first not only in land taxes but also in labor service. This phenomenon is not found in any other province or prefecture.

The heaviest duties used to be the "transportation of cloth" and the "northern transportation of rice." At first our county had to supply one person per year to attend to the transportation of cloth; later, the number increased to three. Their task was to buy cloth of various colors and quality with state revenue, then ship it to the capital by boat. Each year our county supplied twenty-three persons to undertake the northern transportation of rice. Their task was to select more than 13,000 piculs of fine white rice and glutinous rice and ship it to the capital for the court of imperial entertainments to use in supplying the granaries for the officials' salaries. Only the richest people were assigned such duties. In addition to the northern transportation of rice, there was also a shipment of rice to the south, to Nanjing. For this shipment two persons were assigned each year from our county. Besides these duties there was tax collection. Each year forty-eight persons were drafted for collection of the county revenue—a total of more than 200,000 taels of silver. Another thirty-eight persons were assigned to exchange the 110,000 piculs of tax rice for silver and hand it over to the transporters.

All the above duties were categorized as heavy ones and were reassigned and reviewed every five years. Light duties included expediting tax prodder and hastening tax prodder. These were reassigned and reviewed every ten years. Only landowners were assigned to them. There was also a public works superintendent responsible for the repair and maintenance of city walls, public halls, ponds, and waterways, as well as other miscellaneous duties.

When the labor service rules were first implemented, there were subsidies for transportation expenses, for loss of rice in refining, and for the cost of labor. Because these were important duties, the system was worked out in detail. But it gradually deteriorated so that, for instance, the people responsible for transportation and delivery were told to collect the taxes themselves. But this was not the worst. These people, because of their service obligations, became subject to continual extortion: at home they faced unreasonable demands from the local government headquarters; en route they were at the mercy of various local runners and lower government officials; arriving in the capital, they became victims of insatiable officials from all government departments and often were detained for a whole year without being able to obtain a discharge. Thus, those assigned to transportation and delivery suffered extremely.

As to those who served as tax collectors, many had to hire bookkeepers and accountants of their own. Others had to deal with powerful gentry and officials who protected their relatives. These relatives would underpay or pay in low-quality silver, and the tax collectors did not dare to protest. They also had to entertain and present gifts to the continually arriving local functionaries. All these expenses, plus having to make up taxes not paid, brought great suffering to the tax collectors.

Those who were assigned the task of grain exchange, on the other hand, were sometimes even able to make a profit, provided they were shrewd and encountered good times. The reason was that, for each picul of rice, the taxpayer actually had to pay another three pecks of rice to cover wastage. . . . After 1646 or 1647, however, the government tightened the rules and stipulated that tribute rice would have to be sifted and tossed against the wind before it could be submitted. Consequently, people began to select good quality rice for taxes. Before it was deposited in the granaries, there were inspectors who carefully examined its quality. If they found unhusked grains, they would punish the exchange workers. As a result, some corrupt practices were eliminated, but exchange workers could be blackmailed by the transporters. . . . This financial burden, to which were added presents for the officials and other miscellaneous expenses, amounted to a total expenditure which was often twice as much as the value of the rice. Thus, in the end no one performing grain exchange duties could escape bankruptcy and people began to fear this duty as a trap.

It was not until 1646 that Imperial Inspector Tu Guobao, sensitive to the people's distress, ordered prefectures and county governments to make detailed studies of the possible simplification of the three major labor service duties, namely, the transportation of cloth, the northern transportation of rice, and the collection of taxes. He also ordered that the prefecture and county governments take over collection and transportation. As a result, an unnecessary source of waste was eliminated as the heavy labor service duties were terminated. . . .

Originally the duty of the public works superintendent was confined to public construction. . . . Later on, however, local officials and influential gentry began to treat the public works superintendent as a private servant. If a river were located close to a gentry family's graveyard, then the family would order the public works superintendent to dredge it; if a public pond were near their residence, they would demand that the public works superintendent repair it. They would make up various excuses to persuade the local government to grant their requests, and the officials would knowingly comply, thereby establishing a system of corruption. Thus, an official might dispatch one hundred workers for a job which required only ten so that the gentry would receive payoffs from people who wished to be exempted from their assigned duty. Should there be no construction work, the official would extort twenty to thirty taels of silver from each, on the pretext that they had neglected their duties.

The miscellaneous duties also increased day by day. During the Ming dynasty there were many types of labor service but never any miscellaneous duties, which came into being only after the heavy duties were abolished. Thus, in the early years of the Shunzhi reign [1644–1661], when the government was trying to eliminate the Mao pirates, people were drafted as sailors; when troops were mobilized from other areas, people had to take care of the provisions for the horses; when warships were being built, people had to work as drillers and wood purchasers. Later, when the pirates penetrated inland, people were assigned to build bridges and to place cast iron chains and stockades along the beaches. They also had to repair forts, bonfire platforms, and patrol stations along the coast.

All the common people who were assigned duties were filled with fear and resorted to bribing their way out of the assignments. For each district, it would take from a few dozen to one or two hundred taels to get out of an assignment; yet once a person escaped one, he would immediately be assigned to some other. As a result, those who succeeded in getting out of all assignments bankrupted themselves. And those individuals who did report for their duties were subject to so many ploys that they eventually would end up paying more than those who bribed the officials. Only then would those who had bribed their way out feel that they had gotten their money's worth, and only then would the people who actually served regret that they had not offered bribes in the first place. . . .

I had a rather wealthy neighbor, Mr. Gu, who used to send his children to study under my instruction. Later he was ruined by labor service duties. He told me that in order to accommodate the runners, he once had to make twenty-four meals in one day. Between 1664 and 1665, he abandoned his estate and fled. It is not hard to discern why the people all lived in fear!

Translated by Clara Yu

62

PERMANENT PROPERTY

A steady source of income was generally a prerequisite for upper-class life, making possible lengthy education and preparation for official careers. The traditional way to assure such income was landholding, though from the Song dynasty on, many fortunes were undoubtedly amassed through commerce or industry, and in all periods family fortunes could be greatly augmented by successful government careers.

The essay below presents one man's perception of the importance of landholding to members of the upper class and discusses some of the practical difficulties involved in their lives, which combined scholarship, officeholding, and estate management. The author, Zhang Ying (1638–1708), was a prominent official who lived in an agriculturally productive area of Anhui province. He addressed this essay to his sons.

All worldly things that once were new will eventually age. A house that has stood for a long time will decay; clothes worn for a long time will become shabby. Cattle, slaves, and horses are costly when purchased, yet ten years later they are no longer the same, and after another ten years they do not even exist. Only land remains new through hundreds and thousands of years. Even if, due to negligence, the soil becomes barren, once fertilizer is applied, it becomes rich again. With cultivation desolate land becomes productive; with irrigation dry land becomes arable; with weeding neglected soil becomes fertile. Since time immemorial man has not had to worry about the land becoming worn out or ruined, nor about its running away or becoming scarce. Indeed, land is truly precious.

Nowadays the young heirs of large estates wear fancy clothes, ride strong horses, and seek pleasure to their hearts' content in song and dance. A fur garment easily costs scores of gold taels; a feast, several taels. The price of grain in our area has been low for the past decade so that now ten piculs of grain will barely pay for a feast and a hundred piculs will scarcely buy a fur garment; but the young heirs act ignorant of this. They do not wish to know that the peasants, bodies soaked and feet muddy, toil all year round to produce a hundred piculs of grain. Furthermore, with the unpredictability of floods and droughts, one year's harvest does not guarantee the next. I have heard that in Shaanxi province there is an annual famine and with each famine the price of a picul of grain goes up six or seven taels. Yet young heirs of today will sell precious grain cheaply merely to satisfy a desire for another fur garment or another feast. How can one not be deeply disturbed by these matters?

The ancients have a saying: "Use the products of the earth sparingly and you will be content." The youthful heirs should be made to observe the toil of the peasants and should be made to keep accounts when the granaries are opened for grain sale. They should observe how it takes a strong man to carry one picul of grain, and how what four or five men can carry sells for only one gold tael, a tael which can be carelessly spent, disappearing who knows where. Such experiences should make the youthful heirs less wasteful. But what hope is there? The young heirs of today live sheltered lives; well fed and warmly clothed, they do not realize that precious resources should be conserved and casually cast them away like dirt.

Those who accumulate wealth will always worry about fire, flood, or robbery, since valuables can suffer instant misfortune. Indeed, the commoner who accumulates ten taels of gold stops sleeping soundly at night. Land alone is not subject to fire, flood, or robbery, for even the most violent cannot snatch away one single inch of it. Thousands of *mu* of land may be worth ten thousand taels of gold, yet not one man is needed to stand guard. Should war or riot drive a person from his home, he may return to find his house gone, his livestock lost, his belongings vanished— but his land will always be there. The land that belonged to the Zhangs will still belong to the Zhangs; that which belonged to the Lis will still belong to the Lis. As soon as one has rooted out the weeds and tilled the soil, one will have a prosperous farm again. Indeed, nothing else under the sun is as secure as land. How can one fail to try to preserve it?

It is better to seek wealth from Heaven and earth than from other men. I have seen people lend out money for interest secured by mortagages on tillable land. In three to five years they have a return as great as the original sum lent, but the borrower, despite appearing grateful, may become contentious and resentful and may refuse to pay back the principal. I have heard of poor scholars who, having saved several dozen gold taels, lend it out in this manner, but when they become more prosperous it becomes less advantageous for them to do so (because of the enmity incurred).

The profit from land is different. Those who sow halfheartedly reap lightly; those who sow diligently reap abundantly. Some can harvest three times in four seasons, others twice in a year. The main fields can be used for rice and wheat; the side plots and border mounds for hemp, beans, peas, cotton, and so on. Every little piece of land will produce a few pennies of income. Therefore, it is worth pondering the proverb, "The land does not begrudge its treasures." In the beginning the land nourishes our grandfathers, then our fathers; soon it will nourish our sons and grandsons. It is a humble benefactor and a tireless servant. It never complains of its labor as it produces in great variety. Those who enjoy its benefits need not have scruples. Although they gain a great deal, they do not feel the discomfort brought by unjustified profit; thus they can face Heaven, earth, and the spirits of their ancestors. They have no need to scheme and they are spared the jealousy of others. Is there anything that can compare with land?

I have said that one should not sell one's land, yet everywhere in the world we see people doing just that. Even the wise frequently do so. Why? The reason is debt, and debt comes from mismanagement. Those who do not know how to budget expenses according to income will eventually become so deeply in debt that they have to resort to selling land that has been in their families for generations. Therefore we may say that unwise management leads to debt and debt leads to selling of land—which leads to poverty. To stop the process before it starts, one should begin by budgeting expenses.

A simple, long-lasting way to do this is the "regulating expenses according to income" method devised by Lu Jiushao [of the Song dynasty]. His procedure is to figure out the total income for the year, deduct taxes from it, then divide the rest into three parts. Set one part aside to provide for a year of poor harvests. Divide the remaining two parts into twelve portions and spend one portion each month. In this manner, if the crops are good every year, one is in conformity with the ancients' principle of "saving one-third of what one reaps." Should there be a poor harvest one year, then one may make up shortfalls with the previous year's savings; should there be bad harvests several years in a row, one can use the savings accumulated over many years. Only in this way can the need for contracting debts be avoided. In contrast, if each year's income is spent each year, then whenever there is a flood or drought, one will have to resort to selling land. To think that people should fail to recognize such obvious logic! . . .

Mismanagement of household economy is not the only cause of debt and land sale; other causes include indulgence in gambling, women, and extravagances—the dangers of which go without saying. The most ridiculous people of all are those who sell their land to pay for marriage expenses. For as long as there are sons and daughters there will be marriages, but they can be arranged according to one's means, with the savings from past harvests. How can one sell a generations-old resource to provide luxury and splendor for a moment? Do these people think that after the marriage they could be full without food or warm without clothing? Alas, what stupidity!

Anyone who does not want to sell his estate should carefully consider how to preserve it by making the best possible use of it. This can be done two ways, through wise selection of farm tenants and through the establishment of adequate irrigation.

An apt proverb says, "A good tenant is better than a fertile field." If tenants are idle and incompetent, the fields will deteriorate despite the owner's labor and planning. The owners of fields are like loving parents who entrust their baby to cruel servant girls, ignorant of the baby's suffering. There are three advantages to good tenants: first, they sow on time; second, they nourish the land with diligence; third, they control irrigation wisely.

The ancients said, "Timing is of utmost impor-tance in farming." He who tills the fields a month early gets an extra month's benefit; therefore, winter is the best season for ploughing and spring only second best. He who sows a day early gets a day's benefit; therefore, the late crops should be sown before the first day of autumn. As for nourishing the land, the ancients referred to manure as "that which turns a hundred *mu* into a field." They also observed, "It is not enough to fertilize only in bad years." The *Book of Songs* says, "Where weeds decay grains grow abundantly." If one is diligent, one *mu* can produce as much as two. The field does not expand, yet the tenant can have more than enough and the owner can also reap profits. To apply water wisely depends a great deal on timing. It should be collected, held, and released only at the right times. Only good, experienced farmers have such knowledge.

Inferior tenants have three shortcomings: they miss the opportune time for tilling; they are not diligent in nourishing the land; and they do not know the best methods of irrigation. If there happens to be a good year and rain falls at the right time, then even bad tenants will have a good harvest and their defects will be hidden. Yet, when there is a drought, the difference between good and bad tenants will be instantly clear. In a bad year, the landowner can get double the usual price for his grain, unless he is prevented by incompetent tenants. . . .

The estate managers often prefer bad tenants to good ones. Good tenants have prosperous households, have the self-respect not to flatter, have a simple and straightforward manner, are thrifty and will not take unreasonable orders from the managers. Bad tenants, on the other hand, are idle and insolent, will cajole the managers, and will do anything to satiate the managers' greed. Because of these differences, managers prefer bad tenants to good ones, not in the least concerned about the condition of the owner's fields. Moreover, managers welcome floods and droughts, for in such times land rent cannot be paid in full and they can tamper with the revenue. Beware of such age-old corruption and evil practices.

Wherever good tenants live, the farm houses

are tidy and neat, the gardens and yards are lush, the trees are abundant. All these are beyond the control of the land owner and his managers. Yet a good tenant can keep up everything himself. A bad one is just the opposite, making the selection of tenants a highly important task. . . .

The young heir of an estate should carefully inspect his farm twice a year, each spring and autumn. In addition, he should occasionally drop by unexpectedly. He should not merely visit. First, he should learn any boundaries of his fields which are not easy to remember. He should ask experienced tenants to point them out to him, if necessary, repeating his request a second or even a third time; usually after five or six times he will know them. Whenever he has a doubt, he should feel free to ask questions; he should not be afraid of looking silly, otherwise he will remain ignorant all his life. Second, he should observe the tenants to determine whether they save, whether they are strong, whether they are frugal, and whether they are improving the land. With these facts, he should be able to judge which are the good tenants and which the inferior. Third, he should closely inspect the irrigation system to determine the depth of the reservoirs and the strength of the embankments, so as to decide what kinds of repairs are needed. Fourth, he should investigate the state of the woods and hill land. Fifth, he should apprise himself of the fluctuations in the price of grain. These steps will give him firsthand knowledge of his estate.

If, however, a young man merely listens to his managers while sitting under the eaves of the farm house, he will gain nothing but a little rest, a meal, and a night's lodging. His eyes will not encounter the fields, nor his feet the farm paths. Meanwhile, the manager will gather the tenants around him to make a great uproar with their complaints. Some will want to borrow seed grain, others to borrow food against their rent; some will say their ponds are leaking, others that their houses are collapsing. In this way they will intimidate their master, who will be so embarrassed that he will escape at the first opportunity. He will learn nothing in response to his questions about the borders of his

fields, the diligence of his tenants, the produce of the forests, or the value of the crop. When he returns to the city and meets his friends, this one will greet him and say, "I have just come back from my farm," and that one will say, "I have just inspected my fields." And the master himself will respond, "I have just arrived from my farm. How tiresome it was!" Alas! What is the use! This is what I did myself when I was young, and I still regret it. The heir of an estate should never take its management as something vulgar or petty to be avoided, nor should he inherit title to it without taking up the responsibility. Think carefully about the business of farming and compare it with receiving handouts from others: which is nobler and which baser?

A family's wealth and esteem provide but temporary glory. What one depends on ultimately for supporting one's descendants is farming and studying. An estate should be worth two or three thousand taels of gold before its heir goes to live in the city. Why is this so? Such an estate yields a yearly income of some one hundred taels, which must cover firewood, vegetables, poultry, pork, fish, shrimp, pickled and minced food, as well as expenses incurred by invitations among relatives, social occasions, and entertainment. When the harvest is good, grain brings only a low price, and even when the harvest is poor the price is not much better. Therefore the income from his estate will barely allow the young heir to keep up with his expenses. In short, those with estates worth less than one thousand taels should definitely not live in the city. By living in the country, the heir can cultivate a few acres of land himself, doubling his yield, and making it possible to support a household of eight people. He can raise chickens and hogs in his own pens, grow vegetables in his own garden, keep fish and shrimps in his own pond, and from the adjacent mountains take firewood. In this manner he can live weeks and months without having to spend more than a few cash. Besides, living in the country, there will be fewer social occasions. Even when visitors come, it will only be necessary to treat them to chicken and rice. The women, if diligent, can weave cloth.

The heir can wear cotton clothes and ride a feeble donkey, there being no need for glamour. All these things a city dweller cannot do. Living in the country, the heir can till the land and enjoy his studies. He can also employ a teacher for his sons. Such a life is serene and simple. Not a coin in his pocket, he will not be bothered by robbers and thieves.

My father knew the art of country living very well. What he left for us did not amount to much, yet he lived better than city dwellers who had several thousand taels' worth of property. Furthermore, life among mountains and waters is lei-surely and free from money worries. What a shame it is that people should fail to see this point! If, after success in studies, one becomes a renowned official and is able to afford living in the city, then moving there is fine. If, after one or two generations, country living is again advisable, then move back. In this manner, one alternates city living and country living, farming and studying, and the family lineage will be long and prosperous, a highly desirable state of affairs.

Translated by Clara Yu

63

LAN DINGYUAN'S CASEBOOK

Magistrates, the officials in charge of counties (xian), were the only representatives of the central government most people ever encountered. Their manner of enforcing laws, conducting trials, and collecting taxes affected the lives of all residents of the county. Local political life therefore cannot be understood without considering the behavior of magistrates.

Below are two cases that Lan Dingyuan (1680–1733) included in a record of his official experiences. Lan was from a scholarly family of Fujian province and was the author of several books. He never passed even the juren examinations, yet because of his participation in a military campaign and his reputation for knowledge of the coastal area, he was introduced to the emperor. Thereafter he was appointed magistrate of Puning and Chaoyang counties in Guangdong. His description of his activities is best read as a personal account; although he did not hesitate to brag, he also could not help but reveal the values, assumptions, and prejudices that he brought with him to his post as magistrate. In the two cases here, his views on popular religious beliefs and activities are particularly relevant.

THE SPIRIT OF THE KING OF THE THREE MOUNTAINS TELLS EVERYTHING

One day Chen Agong rushed in to see me and begged me to try to discover the fate of his daughter.

He said, "My daughter, Qinniang, is married to Lin Azhong. They live in the neighboring village. She has been married for three years but has had no children. Azhong's mother is very cruel and despises my daughter for coming from a poor family. On the 13th day of the ninth month when I went to see her, I could find no trace of her. I don't know whether she has been beaten to death,

sold off as a servant, or remarried into another household."

"Does your daughter often come back to visit you?" I asked.

He replied, "She came to see me in the eighth month and went back to her husband on the 6th day of the ninth month. You can ask Wang A-sheng about this."

When I made inquiries into the case, Azhong's mother-in-law, Mrs. Xu, complained that the charges were unfair. She said, "I have been a widow for seventeen years and have one daughter-in-law. But from the time of her marriage she has visited her parents every month. In the seventh month she went home twice. On the 6th day of the eighth month she went home again. On the 17th and the 24th day of the eighth month and on the 3rd day of the ninth month we unsuccessfully asked her to come back. I have no idea why she did not come back. Then on the 13th day of the ninth month Chen Agong came bursting into my home demanding to know the fate of his daughter. I am sure Agong has evil designs and has merely hidden his daughter away, hoping to marry her to someone else."

I questioned Chen Agong. "When exactly did your daughter leave your house? Did she walk or go by sedan chair? Who accompanied her?"

He replied, "My daughter told me she wanted to return to her husband on the 6th of the ninth month. I am a poor man and could not afford to hire a sedan chair to take her home, so I sent her brother, Aju, to accompany her half way. They set out walking from my house."

I asked, "What is the distance between your two residences?"

"It is over ten *li*," he answered.

Azhong and his mother cried out, "She did not come back. You can ask the neighbors."

I asked Wang Asheng, "When and where did you see Chen Agong's daughter return to her husband's place?"

Asheng said, "I only heard about it from Aju. I did not actually see them go. A short distance from my home lies King of the Three Mountains Temple. On the 6th day of the ninth month, while I was hoeing my garden on the left side of the road, I saw Aju coming back from the temple. He told me he had been asked by his father to accompany his sister who was returning to her husband. I asked him, 'Where is your sister now?' 'Already gone,' he replied. That is what I heard, and I know nothing else of the matter."

"Is the Chen family rich or poor?" I asked.

Asheng said, "They are very poor."

"How far is it from Agong's house to the temple?"

"About three *li*."

I pressed him further, "How many *li* are there between the Lin family residence and the temple?"

"That distance is around six or seven *li*."

With anger in my voice I demanded an explanation from Agong. "Your daughter is married and your family is not rich, yet you let her come home all the time in spite of the extra expense it brings you. How is this? When her husband's family tried to get her back, you would not let her go. On the 3rd day of the ninth month her husband requested that she return home, but you refused to let her. Why then would you all of a sudden send her home of your own free will on the 6th? Now let us consider the rest of your story. You did not instruct your boy to accompany her all the way to her husband's place but had him turn back in mid-journey. What were your intentions in bringing in Asheng, who had no connection with the case? Your son said that he had just casually mentioned a word of the affair to Asheng, and yet you have cited this as your main piece of evidence. I suspect you have plotted to remarry your daughter and have caused all this commotion."

Agong cried bitterly and loudly, "Father and child are most dear to each other. Although my family is poor, we have enough vegetables and water to make a tasty meal. When my daughter's husband urged her to come home, I didn't want her to leave, but later I realized that I was doing wrong to keep her and that I should let her go back. Isn't it reasonable that I should try to do the right thing in order to make up for my previous selfishness? As for my son's returning after going only halfway, the boy is still only a youngster, and so I didn't dare let him wander too far from home. I asked him to accompany her only halfway because I figured my son-in-law's home would then be close enough for her to get there without danger. My son returned home quite soon after they departed so I scolded him because I thought perhaps he had not accompanied her even halfway. He defended himself, saying, 'I passed the temple and Uncle Asheng saw me!' Now my daughter is missing and I am under suspicion. I am certainly one who appreciates the principle that a woman must be faithful to her husband all through her life. How then could I possibly let my daughter remarry when her husband is still alive?"

I questioned Aju, a boy of ten years. He said, "I escorted my sister to the front of the temple and then returned."

I asked, "Why didn't you take her all the way to her husband's place?"

"My father ordered me to take the livestock out to pasture, so I let my sister continue on alone after going halfway."

I threatened him, saying, "Your sister was kept home to be remarried. How dare you lie to me? If you do not tell me the truth, I will cut off your fingers."

Aju was terrified. He cried but said nothing more. I tried several ways to trick him, but he always replied, "No, not so."

I then asked him, "Is there a monk at the temple?"

"No," he replied.

"Are there any beggars?"

"No."

"Is there any family around the temple?"

"No."

"Is there a tree, creek, river, or pond there?"

"No."

"Are there any neighbors around your home?"

"No, there aren't any neighbors."

I really suspected that Chen Agong had sold his daughter, but he was cunning and stubborn, and Aju was still quite young. Therefore I could not use threats of torture to break the case. Then it came to me that southerners are afraid of ghosts and spirits. I would try to bring this to bear on the case.

Calling in the plaintiff and the defendant, I said, "Since neither of you has any substantial evidence to back up your allegations, it is rather difficult for me to make a judgment in this case. But since the boy and girl passed by the temple, the spirit of the King of the Three Mountains must know the true story. You all go home for the time being, and I will send an official dispatch to ask the spirit about the matter. I will resume court tomorrow."

The next day I called Chen Agong straight into the courtroom and, pounding on the table, reviled him: "What kind of human being are you? You

have hidden away your daughter and remarried her. Then you adopted the tactics of a shyster lawyer and came running with the first accusation so as to throw your opponent off balance. Who do you think you're fooling? Even though you lie to men, you cannot deceive Heaven. You know that Heaven is but three feet above our heads and that there are gods watching us all the time! The King of the Three Mountains has told me all. Are you still obstinate enough to stick to your story? I know who it was your daughter remarried, where she got married, and how much you received for her. If you do not buy her back, I will order that you be punished under the press."

Agong was so frightened that he could not answer back. He groveled on the floor, kowtowed, and begged for forgiveness.

I said, "If you get your daughter back, I will pardon you."

He blurted out, "Yes, certainly I will. It was the extreme poverty of my family that forced me to let my daughter remarry. She is now married into the Li family of Huilai, who paid three taels for her. I will sell my cow to buy her back."

I ordered Agong to be whipped thirty strokes and then to be clapped into the wooden collar for public humiliation in town. I gave him a stern warning: "If you redeem your daughter and bring her back, I will release you. If you don't, I will leave you in the collar until you die."

Agong thereupon sent his wife, Wang, to Huilai to buy back the daughter. The Li family demanded that she pay double the original price they had given for the girl, so Wang was forced to sell her youngest daughter as well as the cow to raise the money. Hearing of these events, the greedy first husband saw an opportunity to make six taels. He told Wang that he could not accept Qinliang back because she had lost her chastity and secretly came to terms with her, releasing Qinliang from all obligations to him for six taels. After he got the money from Wang, he married another girl. Qinliang remained with the Li family and did not have to be redeemed.

While all this was going on, Agong was forced to remain in the collar for nearly two months and almost died. He moaned to his wife, "I regret that I did not sell the cow and our youngest daughter in the first place so that I could have avoided such a punishment. If I had only known that the King of the Three Mountains would tell everything! Now that the affair is finished, you must petition the magistrate to let me go."

When Wang told me what her husband said, I laughed and released him.

DEPRAVED RELIGIOUS SECTS DECEIVE PEOPLE

The people of Chaoyang believed in spirits and often talked about gods and Buddhas. The gentry regarded Da Dian [of the Tang Dynasty] as their great Buddhist master, and ladies of the gentry families joined together to go to the temples to worship the Buddha. In this way, heretical and depraved teachings developed and the so-called Latter Heaven sect became popular.

The origin of the Latter Heaven sect is unknown. Zhan Yucan and Zhou Awu first preached it in our area, claiming to have received the teaching from a white-bearded Immortal. When the former magistrate apprehended them, they ran away with their families but later returned to Chaoyang. The sect also called itself the "White Lotus" or the "White Willow." (It probably belonged to the "White Lotus Society" but found it expedient to use other names.)

Zhan Yucan's wife, Lin, was thought to be the "Miraculous Divine Lady." She claimed to possess the ability to summon wind and rain and to give orders to gods and spirits. She was the leader of the Latter Heaven sect and was assisted by her paramour, Hu Aqiu, who called himself the "Ben Peak Divine Gentleman." These two cast spells and used magic charms and waters to cure illness and to help pray for heirs. They even claimed to be able to help widows meet their deceased husbands at night.

The people of Chaoyang adored them madly; hundreds of men and women worshiped them as their masters. People from Chenghai, Jieyang, Haiyang, Huilai, and Haifeng made pilgrimages here carrying gifts of money, animals, wine, and flowers to offer in worship. On the 10th day of the second month of winter on my return from the prefectural city I was informed of these events. By this time members of the sect had already constructed a large building in the northern part of the county where they established a preaching hall and gathered several hundred followers. They hired actors for a period of two days to celebrate the opening of their church. I dispatched runners to apprehend the sect leaders, but the runners were afraid to offend the gods lest the soldiers of hell punish them. Besides, the local officials and many of the influential families favored the sect. So they all escaped.

I, therefore, went to the place myself, pushed my way into the front room, and arrested the Divine Lady. Then I went further into the house to search for her accomplices. The place was like a maze, filled with concealed rooms. Even by day one had to light a torch to get around, or one would bump into people in the dark and easily get lost. It was indeed an ideal place to hide criminals. As I proceeded on my search, above the Divine Lady's bedroom, in a dark, concealed chamber, I seized Yao Asan, Yang Guangqin, Peng Shizhang, and about a dozen other men. Similarly, above the Divine Gentleman's bedroom I found a wooden seal of the Empress Lady of the Moon, a heretical sutra, incense, a wig, and clothes, but at this time I had no idea of how they were used. I looked all around for the Divine Gentleman. Finally, the local rowdies as well as certain influential families, knowing they could no longer hide him, handed over Hu Aqiu. Through questioning him, I learned of all his occult tricks.

In fact, these charlatans had no special powers whatsoever but used incense and costumes to bewilder people. The foolish people who trembled on just hearing the names of gods and spirits were impressed when they saw that the Divine Lady had no fear of gods and goddesses. Hu Aqiu, who accompanied her, wore rouge, female clothing, and a wig. People believed Hu was the genuine Empress Lady of the Moon and never suspected he was a man.

When these pious women entered his bedroom and ascended to the upper chamber, they would be led to worship the Maitreya Buddha and to recite the charms of the *Precious Flower sutra*. Then stupefying incense was burned and the women would faint and fall asleep so the leaders of the sect could do whatever they pleased. (This incense was also called soul-bewildering incense; people who inhaled it would feel tired and want to sleep.) Later members would cast spells and give the women cold water to drink to revive them. The so-called "praying for heirs" and the "meeting with a deceased husband" occurred while the women were dreaming and asleep.

The members of the Latter Heaven sect were extremely evil; even hanging their heads out on the streets would have been insufficient punishment for their crimes. However, this had been a year of bad harvest, so the villagers already had lots of worries. Moreover, the case involved many people, including members of local gentry families. Therefore, sympathetic to the people's troubles and wanting to end the matter, I destroyed the list of those involved which the culprits had divulged during the trial.

I had Lin, the "Divine Lady," and Hu Aqiu beaten and put in the collar, placing them outside the court so that the people could scorn them, beat them, and finally kill them. As to Zhan Yucan, the man who had allowed his wife to commit such a heinous crime, and his accomplices, Yao Ashan and some ten other people, they were all beaten and put in the collar as punishment. I inquired no further into the matter so that the other accomplices could repent and start a new life. I confiscated the sect's building, destroyed the concealed rooms, and converted it into a literary academy dedicated to the worship of the five great [neo-Confucian] teachers. Thus the filthy was swept away and the clean restored.

In my leisure time, on the days of the new and the full moon, I went to the academy to lecture or discuss literature with the people of the county. Zhang Pi gave one hundred bushels of grain for the salary of a teacher, allowances for the students, and the expenses of the spring and autumn school sacrifices. As formal study developed, heretical beliefs ceased to exist. The morality and customs of the people also changed for the better. Commander Shang and Governor Yang heard about the elimination of the depraved sect and sighed in admiration: "Without the elimination of this sect, great damage would have occurred. It is a marvelous accomplishment to have gotten rid of it. The magistrate expelled the evil but refrained from seeking fame for himself. Had he not done so, many people in the area would have been put into jail and many women would have committed suicide by night. It is indeed an act of great mercy to preserve others' reputations."

Translated by Jeh-hang Lai and Lily Hwa

64

EXHORTATIONS ON CEREMONY AND DEFERENCE

In the Qing dynasty, the government mandated twice monthly public lectures in every county. On those occasions, local officials or scholars were to explain the Sacred Edict of the Kangxi emperor (Shengzu, r. 1662–1722) and the amplifications of the Yongzheng emperor (Shizong, r. 1723–1735). So that these emperors' moral exhortations would reach the uneducated, the lecturers were instructed to use the local vernacular and draw examples from everyday life. A number of officials published their lectures as guides for others. The lecture translated here, on the ninth maxim, was by an eighteenth-century salt commissioner named Wang Youpu. His task was to convince ordinary people, including merchants and soldiers, that their lives would be better if they all would be more polite. Through the arguments he marshals, he shows his faith in people's ability to cultivate the traditional virtues of ceremony and deference but also his sense that in actual life friction and conflict were pervasive.

DEMONSTRATE CEREMONY AND DEFERENCE IN ORDER TO IMPROVE POPULAR CUSTOMS

His Majesty's meaning is as follows:

In the empire there are what are called popular customs (*fengsu*). What are *feng* and *su*? A Han dynasty scholar said that the hearts of all the common people in the world contain feelings of benevolence, justice, propriety, wisdom, and sincerity. But people in the North are generally hardy, those in the South generally delicate. Where people's temperaments are fast-paced, business is executed promptly; where they are slow, work is performed more leisurely. People of one place do not understand the dialect of those in the other. All this proceeds from the fact that the climate (*fengqi*) is different in every place and men feel a certain influence from it. This is the reason for the word *feng*.

Further, what people here like, people there hate. On occasions when one is active the other is at rest. There is no fixed mode; everybody acts according to the common practices (*su*) of his locality. This is the reason for the word *su*.

Popular customs vary greatly: in some places people are kindly, in others, reserved; in some places they are extravagant and pompous, in others frugal and simple. Because the customs of every place differed, the ancient sages created ceremonial practices in order to standardize conduct. The sage [Confucius] said that to secure the ease of superiors and bring order to the people, nothing is better than ceremony (*li*). This sentence teaches us that ceremony is extremely important. Were Heaven and earth to depart from the forms of ceremony, they would no longer be Heaven and earth. Were the myriad creatures to depart from ceremonial forms, they would no longer exist. The forms of ceremony are vast and its uses are manifold. Were reason and virtue, benevolence and justice to depart from ceremony, they could no longer be true reason and virtue, benevolence and justice. Were the honorable and the mean, the noble and base, to depart from ceremony, one could no longer distinguish between them. Were the rituals for manhood, marriage, mourning, and ancestor worship to depart from ceremony, one could not conduct those rituals. In fact, if Emperor Shizong, in offering sacrifices to Heaven or to the temple of his ancestors, or in giving private feasts, were to depart from ceremony, those things could not be performed. In a word, ceremony is the root of all customs.

But when you practice ceremonial behavior, there should be no awkward stiffness; all should be natural and easy. The essence of ceremony is contained in the word "deference." The sage said that as long as ceremony and deference were used, there would be no difficulty in ruling the empire. If these two words, ceremony and deference, are sufficient to regulate the vast concerns of an empire, shouldn't it be even easier to regulate an individual or a family through them? The sage also said a ruler who wants the common people not to fight must first set an example for them of ceremonial behavior and deference. Thus it may be seen that this word, deference, is also the root of the practice of ceremony.

Were I now to speak of the details of rituals and ceremonies, you soldiers and common people probably would have difficulty learning them because they are so numerous. But you all possess the basic elements of ceremonial behavior. For example, you know that there should be filial piety towards parents, honor and respect for superiors, harmony between husband and wife, affection among brothers, honesty among friends, and mutual responsibility among those of the same lineage. This proves that internally you already possess the basic elements of ceremony and deference. Why then make a fuss about the externals? If you could really, in dealing with others, be extremely cooperative, in conducting yourselves be extremely obliging, in the family express the affection appropriate between parents and children, elder and younger brothers, in your villages maintain accord between the old and the young, the great and the small, then those habits of struggling over minor differences and getting into noisy disputes would be reformed and the tendency toward indulgent and degenerate conduct would be restrained.

If I had no desire which might induce you to compete or me to steal; if I never allowed momentary anger to get me into a fight; if I never held you in contempt because you are poor and I am rich; if you didn't try to hurt me because you are strong and I am weak; if everybody became kind, without any sign of pettiness; then this would be true ceremony and deference, and in the fullest sense there would be honor and justice.

Though everyone knows how to talk of ceremony and deference, they do not all practice it. Why don't they practice it? Because at present they only know how to use the rules of ceremony to reprove others, not how to use them to correct themselves. For example, if we are quarreling, you'll say I'm impolite and I'll say you are. One will say, "Why don't you yield to me?" And the other will reply, "You haven't yet yielded to me. Why should I yield to you?" At length the animosities become so complex that they cannot be disentangled. What gain is there in that? You should think a little and say, "Although he is without proper manners, where are my manners? Although he hasn't yielded to me, in the beginning why didn't I yield to him?" If both parties would admit part of the blame, wouldn't numerous disputes be avoided?

It is just that people love to quarrel and will not give in to others. For instance, a scholar who has a rough idea of how to compose a few verses of various kinds of poetry regards himself as the literary prodigy of the day and disdains to cast an eye on others. But if he realized that the subjects of study are inexhaustible and that the empire possesses an abundance of learned men, he would say, "The books I have read are only a fraction of what men have written and my compositions don't amount to even a spot of brightness among the whole lot." Automatically he would be modest and defer to others. He who really acts with modesty and deference is a virtuous and worthy scholar.

Farmers are also in the habit of quarreling about their fields. I say that you have encroached on the dike a little; you say that I have ploughed a furrow too many. Perhaps some animal, an ox or a sheep, has trodden down the grain, and this gives rise to a quarrel. Or perhaps one person dams up the water till it overflows his own fields, not letting it pass by and irrigate those of his neighbor, and this leads to a struggle. Craftsmen are also quick to get into violent quarrels. You want to keep me down and I want to keep you down; I try to turn your employer against you and you try to turn mine away from me. We each care for our own prosperity only, with no regard to whether the other lives or dies.

Merchants and shop owners are even worse. When you see me earning money, you become jealous; when I see you making a profit, my eyes turn red with envy. When a particular kind of trade is profitable, you want to engage in it, and so do I. When trading conditions are good in a certain place, you will conceal it from everyone else and secretly hurry there yourself. Knowing that a certain kind of goods is losing value, a merchant will trick people into taking them off his hands and afterwards go and insist on getting the payment. There are others who, beginning trade with empty hands, borrow money at high rates but are a long time in repaying their bills. This is what is called "You seek high [interest] while I seek delay [in repayment]." Others get into disputes about the scales used or the quality of coins. There are so many sources of disputes that it would be an endless task to mention all of them. To sum it up, people will not yield to each other on anything; if only they would yield, they would all become honest and generous men.

As to you soldiers living in camp, you can't avoid having rough and crude personalities. At work and at rest you use your swords and staffs and engage in combat. Everybody says that soldiers, because of their very nature, do not understand ceremony. Therefore, from now on you must try to understand the principle of yielding and ceremony. In your village try your best to show deference to others and to temper the roughness of your personalities.

Let all of you—scholars, farmers, artisans, merchants, and soldiers—take care in practicing ceremonial deference. If one place becomes good, then many places will become so, and finally the entire realm will be in excellent harmony. Won't we then have a world in perfect concord?

In an ancient book it says, "The humble gain; the self-satisfied lose." These two phrases are exceptionally apt. How do the humble gain? Humility consists of modesty and mildness. Men of the present day can't perceive their own faults at all. Therefore they perpetually quarrel, not realizing that strife is the road to the destruction of their families and their personal ruin. In every affair, great or small, retreat a step and you will certainly gain the advantage. For example, suppose a man curses me, and I let pass a couple of phrases. If he is a good man he will naturally feel sorry. If he is a bad man, on seeing that his curses have no effect, he will give up. Wouldn't this prevent a lot of trouble? Do you think that by his cursing me he will rise to greater glory, or that I by bearing with him will fall into disgrace? If I defer to him in this way, people will just praise how good I am and will all want to join me, perhaps confiding to me the secrets of their hearts or entrusting to me their money. If he is so overbearing, people will all hate and avoid him. If he runs into trouble, who will pay attention to him? Haven't I then gained the advantage?

Among the ancients there was a man named Lou Shide. He once asked his brother, "Suppose that someone spit in your face. How would you react to him?" When his brother said he would just wipe it off, Lou Shide said, "If you wipe it off, the man will hold you in even greater contempt.

Just accept it with a smile and wait until it dries of its own accord." Just think, meek Lou Shide afterwards rose to become prime minister. Isn't this evidence that "the humble gain"?

How do the self-satisfied lose? Self-satisfaction occurs when a person is impressed with his own importance. It does not refer only to property owners and officials who rely on their money and influence to deceive and humiliate others and thus invite disaster. It also refers to young men who call their elders "old fogies" and even if they are poor or feeble do not address them in a respectful manner; it also refers to young men who tell local officials and gentry, "We will not cringe before you," and arrogantly try to gain the upper hand. This emotion of self-satisfaction will inevitably lead a man to exceed what is appropriate to his station. He will undertake daring acts, bringing on calamity. This shows how "the self-satisfied lose."

The principles taught by these two sentences may be compared to an earthen vessel. When the vessel is empty (= modest) it can still gain. If it is full (= self-satisfied), you cannot put more things into it, and if you force them you may overturn the vessel or break it into pieces. From this can be seen how the humble gain and the self-satisfied lose. These principles may also be compared to a man who has some chronic disorders. Knowing that his body is weak, he will be careful in all matters, not daring to eat much food or indulge in wine or women. Consequently he may enjoy a long life. The man who doesn't have the slightest health problem, by contrast, will depend on his strength and vigor. He will eat and then go right to sleep, take off his clothes in drafty places, and show not even the least moderation in regard to wine and women. Then one day he gets an incurable illness. Aren't these accurate examples of how the humble (= cautious) gain and the self-satisfied lose?

Formerly there was a Mr. Wang Yanfang who was exceptionally ready to defer to others. Once a cattle thief, when captured, said, "I will willingly receive my punishment, but please don't inform Wang Yanfang." When Wang heard of this, he sent someone to give the thief a piece of cloth and persuade him to become good. From this incident the thief became so reformed that when he saw someone drop his sword in the road he stood guarding it till the owner came back to get it. In antiquity there also was a Mr. Guan Youan who was equally deferential. When an ox belonging to another family came and ate the young shoots of his field, he was not at all angry, but took the ox, tied him to a tree, and brought him grass to eat. Because he was so accommodating and humble, all the people of his village reformed. In a time of rebellion, the bandits didn't bother him, and those who had fled from danger came to him for protection. Just think of it: when one man knows how to yield, a whole district can be reformed, and even bandits can be influenced. Aren't ceremonial behavior and deference then real treasures?

Furthermore, if you compete over things, you don't get any more for it; if you yield, neither do you have any less. The ancients said it very well: "A person who always makes way for others on the road won't waste one hundred steps in his whole life. He who always gives in on questions of boundaries won't lose even a single section over the course of his life." Hence it can be seen that yielding and ceremony bring gain and never humiliation. Then why not yield? Emperor Shizong hopes that you all will listen to the instructions of the former Emperor Shengzu and examine yourselves by them.

If you are able to get along with others, those who are rude will imitate you and learn to get along. If you are able to manage business fairly, those who are dishonest will learn to be fair by following you. When one person takes the lead, all the rest will follow. When one family follows, then the whole village will do the same. From near to far, everywhere people will be good. At first it will take effort, but constant practice will make it easy. Men will become honest and popular customs pure and considerate. Only this would constitute full adoption of the meaning of Emperor Shizong's repeated instructions to you.

Translated by Patricia Ebrey

65

VILLAGE ORGANIZATION

Many matters of social and political importance were left to local residents to initiate themselves. Often local gentry or village elders would call residents together to make decisions or to undertake village projects. They might also approach neighboring villages to gain their cooperation for projects of mutual benefit. Should any controversy arise, however, they could always appeal to the magistrate.

The two documents below show some of the forms and mechanisms of such village and intervillage organization. The first is a water-use agreement originally recorded in 1828 and still in use in the early twentieth century. When first drawn up, the rights to water were divided among different people on a twenty-one-day cycle. Over the years, however, many people had sold their rights, and these changes were recorded by pasting new sections into the original agreement. The second document, dating from 1875, is a stone inscription recording how residents of several villages in what is now Inner Mongolia had gone about establishing a temple and attached market.

RECORD OF THE OLD SOUTH DITCH

The Old South Ditch is the lower stream of Dog-Head Spring. During the early Ming period, the water in the spring was so abundant that it often overflowed on its course north of Wu Family Estate, through Small Great-Water Village and East Great-Water Village, to the Seven-Mile River. The elders of our village (East Great-Water Village) traced the source of the spring because they wanted to dredge the area and cut an irrigation ditch to channel water first eastward, then northward, and finally back eastward so that the spring would irrigate all the fields of the villagers. How-ever, the spring gushed forth so strongly that the irrigation ditch was unable to contain it. Therefore, the village elders built a small canal south of Small Great-Water Village to channel some of the water to the Seven-Mile River and thus reduce the volume flowing into the irrigation ditch at East Great-Water Village. This small canal also made it easier to close the sluice gate while the ditch was being dredged in the spring and summer. It was at this time that the irrigation ditch was given the name Dog-Head River, and the name South Ditch fell out of use.

During the Longqing period [1567–1573], White-Berth, Big-Worthy, and other villages observed the unused water running down the canal to the Seven-Mile River and decided to tap it with irrigation ditches of their own. Our village, however, was reluctant to let them do this, so they appealed the matter to the magistrate, Di Mingshi. He went to inspect the river system himself, and, seeing all the unused water running down the canal to the Seven-Mile River, he issued an order to the elders of our village which read: "It is better to share water with neighboring villagers than to let it go to waste. And if two more ditches are built, East Great-Water Village will also enjoy the benefits of further irrigation."

The village elders did not dare to oppose the magistrate's order. So White-Berth, Big-Worthy, and the other villages constructed a stone sluice gate on the small drainage ditch south of Small Great-Water Village. They also built a circulation ditch and another ditch to the north.

Since the people of East Great-Water Village had dredged the Dog-Head River, it would have been unfair to put them on a par with the people of the other villages when it came to sharing labor and benefits. It would also have been unfair for the other villages to drain off too much water and leave East Great-Water Village without enough for irrigation. Therefore, Magistrate Di ordered the other villages to share the expenses of repairing the upper stream sluice gates and of dredging the upper reaches of Dog-Head River. He required us only to dredge the part of the river below the north ditch. Thus, we would start the work, and the other villages would finish the job.

Magistrate Di ordered that the eight villages along the circulation ditch use only forty percent of the irrigation water but permitted East Great-Water Village to use sixty percent. This made a distinction between those with the main right to the water and those with the right to the surplus. So that the two other ditches would not widen after years of use and thus drain off more than forty percent of the water, Magistrate Di ordered a stone sluice gate two feet narrower than the width of the Dog-Head River to be built on the circulation ditch. The north ditch had a rather deep bottom, thus allowing more water to flow

through it, so the magistrate ordered that stones be put on its bottom and sides, thus decreasing the flow of water to the allotted forty percent. With these precautions, he hoped that the forty–sixty ratio could be maintained and that water usage would cause no problems for later generations.

With the construction of the circulation ditch and the north ditch, the lower stream of the Dog-Head River became the southernmost irrigation ditch. For this reason it became known again as Old South Ditch. Thus the water came to be divided between East Great-Water Village and the other villages of the area.

Those villagers who were in charge of water distribution on the Old South Ditch were dubbed Old Man and Little Tithing. Those persons who had the most land had to furnish personnel for these positions—they could not decline the job. It cost five cash to use water for one day and one night. Furthermore, each person was limited to the water he could take in a given cycle of twenty days. This water usage procedure could not be altered, and it became the standard water distribution system for the Old South Ditch. Unfortunately, with the construction of the stone sluice and the placing of stones on the river bed, not as many people could take full advantage of the irrigation ditch.

Because water was distributed on a cash basis, the strong could not snatch it away from the weak. Relying on the wisdom and fairness of Magistrate Di, the villagers complied with all these regulations and the elders of the village handed down the benefits of these rules to us. Therefore, we have recorded these events on the first page of our village record so that later generations may be aware of them.

Translated by Lily Hwa

INSCRIPTION FOR THE NEWLY ERECTED TEMPLE-MARKET "OUR LADY"

We have heard that one who does a job well does it thoroughly, and one who starts something should also finish it. This is the wise teaching of the ancient sages and the rule for us to follow.

On the northeast side of the city of Tuogetuo, there are densely populated villages and extensive farmland. Whenever the field work gets heavy, hiring farmhands from distant regions becomes a problem. Those who discussed the problem in the past noted that the village of Shilideng is situated in the center of all these communities; if a temple-market could be built there, they reasoned, all people in the area would benefit. However, although this was proposed several times, nothing came of it.

In 1874, the village of Shilideng again brought up the proposal. All the people liked the idea, yet they also realized how difficult it would be to put into practice. The chairman of the meeting, Shi Ruqi, and others, volunteered to undertake the task. "Whether we succeed or not," they said, "we will do our best and not shirk our responsibilities."

The decision having been made, it was announced to all the villagers, who began collecting funds among themselves and soliciting donations from the neighboring communities, which willingly contributed to this cause. On an auspicious day in the fourth month, the land was measured and the ground broken. From then on, workers and materials gathered at the site, designers, builders, sculptors, and painters cooperated with each other, and the new temple-market was completed in a matter of months.

On the opening day of the market, hundreds of different kinds of goods were brought in from all over, and people came from all directions. The quiet village now acquired a new look. The donors were all pleased with the speedy construction, and the employers were also happy because now it was easy to hire farmhands.

Yet a construction project without a written record is like an enterprise half-finished, and an enterprise half-finished defeats all the effort already spent. We would like later generations to understand our reasons for building the temple-market, and we would like to solicit their continuous effort to maintain the place properly. They should repair the building and the walls of the temple; they should try hard to bring business to the market; they should also do their best to ensure orderly transaction of business here. It is important to appease the gods and to satisfy the people, for this will bring our village as well as the surrounding communities a good reputation.

*Composition by the Confucian scholar
Cui Peiyu of Daizhou.
Calligraphy by the Licentiate Cui Fushi of Daizhou.
Tablet erected by Committee Chairman She
Weihan and twelve others,
on an auspicious day of the fourth month
of 1875.*

Translated by Clara Yu

66

THE VILLAGE HEADMAN AND THE NEW TEACHER

Although documents such as tenancy contracts, village agreements, and legal cases provide insight into various elements in rural social, economic, and political relations, no source conveys so well the atmosphere of village life as fiction. None of the major novels centers on villagers, but they have occasional vignettes in which rural life is portrayed.

The following selection is from the long, episodic novel The Scholars, *written by Wu Jingzi (1701–1754). This book was the first and perhaps the most successful novel of social satire, and contains delightful parodies of hypocrites and pompous fools of various stations in life. The section that follows presents a realistic though undoubtedly exaggerated description of how affairs were decided in one village.*

In Xue Market, a village of Wenshang county, Shandong, there lived over a hundred families, all of whom worked on the land. At the entrance to the village was a Guanyin Temple with three halls and a dozen empty rooms. Its back door overlooked the river. Peasants from all around contributed to the upkeep of this temple, and only one monk lived there. Here the villagers would come to discuss public business.

It was the last year of the Zhenghua period of the Ming dynasty [1487], when the country was prosperous. One year, on the 8th of the first month, just after New Year, some of the villagers met in the temple to discuss the dragon lantern dance which is held on the 15th. At breakfast time the man who usually took the lead, Shen Xiangfu, walked in, followed by seven or eight others. In the main hall they bowed to Buddha, and the monk came to wish them a happy New Year. As soon as they had returned his greeting, Shen reproved him. "Monk! At New Year you should burn more incense before Buddha! Gracious Heaven! You've been pocketing money from all sides, and you ought to spend a little of it. Come here, all of you, and take a look at this lamp: it's only half filled with oil." Then he pointed to an old man who was better dressed than most. "Not to mention others, Mr. Xun alone sent you fifty catties of oil on New Year's Eve. But you are using it all for your cooking, instead of for the glory of Buddha."

The monk apologized profusely when Shen had finished. Then he fetched a pewter kettle, put in a handful of tea leaves, filled the kettle with water, boiled it over the fire, and poured out tea for them. Old Mr. Xun was the first to speak.

"How much do we each have to pay for the lantern dance in the temple this year?" he asked.

"Wait till my relative comes," said Shen. "We'll discuss it together."

As they were speaking, a man walked in. He had red-rimmed eyes, a swarthy face, and sparse, dingy whiskers. His cap was cocked to one side, his blue cloth gown was as greasy as an oil vat, and he carried a donkey switch in one hand. Making a casual gesture of greeting to the company, he plumped himself down in the seat of honour. This was Xia, the new village head for Xue Market.

Sitting there in the seat of honour, he shouted: "Monk! Take my donkey to the manger in the back yard, unsaddle it, and give it plenty of hay. After my business here I have to go to a feast with Bailiff Huang of the county yamen." Having given these orders, he hoisted one foot on to the bench, and started massaging the small of his back with his fists, saying, "I envy you farmers these days. This New Year I've got invitations from everybody in the magistrate's yamen, literally everybody! And I have to go to wish them all the season's greetings. I trot about on this donkey to the county seat and back until my head reels. And this damned beast stumbled on the road and threw me, so that my backside is still sore."

"On the third I prepared a small dinner for you," said Shen. "I suppose it was because you were so busy that you didn't come."

"You don't have to remind me," said Village Head Xia. "Since New Year, for the last seven or eight days, what free time have I had? Even if I had two mouths, I couldn't get through all the eating. Take Bailiff Huang, who's invited me today. He's a man who can talk face to face with the magistrate. And since he honors me like this, wouldn't he be offended if I didn't go?"

"I heard that Bailiff Huang had been sent out on some business for the magistrate since the beginning of the year," said Shen. "He has no brothers or sons, so who will act as host?"

"You don't understand," said Xia. "Today's feast is given by Constable Li. His own rooms are small, so he is using Bailiff Huang's house."

Eventually they started discussing the dragon lanterns. "I'm tired of managing it for you," said Village Head Xia. "I took the lead every year in the past, and everyone wrote down what contribution he would make, and then failed to pay up. Heaven knows how much I had to pay to make good the deficit. Besides, all the officials in the yamen are preparing lanterns this year, and I shall have too much to watch. What time do I have to look at the lanterns in the village? Still, since you've mentioned it, I shall make a contribution. Choose someone to be responsible. A man like Mr. Xun, who has broad lands and plenty of grain, should be asked to give more. Let each family pay its share, and you'll get the thing going." Nobody dared disagree. They immediately came down on Mr. Xun for half the money, and made up the rest among themselves. In this way they raised two or three taels of silver, keeping a record of the contributors.

The monk then brought out tea, sugar wafers, dates, melon seeds, dried beancurd, chestnuts, and assorted sweets. He spread two tables, and invited Village Head Xia to sit at the head. Then he poured out tea for them.

"The children are growing up," said Shen, "and this year we must find them a teacher. This temple can be used as a school."

The others agreed. "There are a lot of families who have sons who should be in school," said one of them. "For instance, Mr. Shen's son is Village Head Xia's son-in-law. Xia is always getting notices from the magistrate, so he needs someone who can read. But the best thing would be to find a teacher from the county seat."

"A teacher?" said the village head. "I can think of one. You know who? He's in our yamen, and he used to teach in Chief Accountant Gu's house. His name is Zhou Jin. He's over sixty. The former magistrate placed him first on the list of county candidates, but he's never yet been able to pass the prefectural examination. Mr. Gu employed him as tutor for his son for three years; and his son passed the examination last year, at the same time as Mei Jiu from our village. The day that young Gu was welcomed back from the school he wore a scholar's cap and a broad red silk sash, and rode a horse from the magistrate's stable, while all the gongs and trumpets sounded. When he reached the door of his house, I and the other yamen officials offered him wine in the street. Then Mr. Zhou was asked over. Mr. Gu toasted his son's teacher three times and invited him to sit in the seat of honour. Mr. Zhou chose as entertainment the opera about Liang Hao, who won the first place in the palace examination when he was eight, and Mr. Gu was not at all pleased. But then the opera showed how Liang Hao's pupil won the same distinction at seventeen or eighteen, so Mr. Gu learned that it was a compliment to his son. That made him feel better. If you want a teacher, I'll invite Mr. Zhou for you." All the villagers approved. When they had finished their tea, the monk brought in some beef noodles, and after eating these they went home.

The next day, sure enough, Village Head Xia spoke to Zhou Jin. His salary would be twelve taels of silver a year, and it was arranged that he should eat with the monk, whom he would pay two cents a day. It was settled that he should come after the Lantern Festival and begin teaching on the 20th.

On the 16th the villagers sent in contributions to Shen Xiangfu, who prepared a feast for the new teacher to which he also invited Mei Jiu, the new scholar of the village. Mei Jiu arrived early, wearing his new square cap, but Zhou Jin did not turn up till nearly noon. When dogs started barking outside, Shen Xiangfu went out to welcome the guest; and the villagers stared as Zhou Jin came in. He was wearing an old felt cap, a tattered grey silk gown, the right sleeve and seat of which were in shreds, and a pair of shabby red silk slippers. He had a thin, dark face and a white beard. Shen escorted him in, and only then did Mei Jiu rise slowly to greet him.

"Who is this gentleman?" asked Zhou.

They told him, "He is Mr. Mei, our village scholar."

When Zhou Jin heard this, he declared it would be presumptuous on his part to allow Mei to bow to him. And although Mei Jiu said, "Today is different," he still refused.

"You are older then he is," said the villagers. "You had better not insist."

But Mei Jiu rounded on them, "You people don't understand the rule of our school. Those who have passed the prefectural examination are considered senior to those who have not, regardless of age. But today happens to be exceptional, and Mr. Zhou must still be honored."

(Ming Dynasty scholars called all those who passed the prefectural examination "classmates," and those who only qualified for this examination "juniors." A young man in his teens who passed was considered senior to an unsuccessful candidate, even if the latter were eighty years old. It was like the case of a concubine. A woman is called "new wife" when she marries, and later "mistress"; but a concubine remains "new wife" even when her hair is white.)

Since Mei Jiu spoke like this, Zhou Jin did not insist on being polite, but let Mei Jiu bow to him. When all the others had greeted him too, they sat down. Mei and Zhou were the only two to have dates in their tea cups—all the others had plain green tea. After they had drunk their tea, two tables were laid, and Zhou Jin was invited to take the seat of honor, Mei Jiu the second place. Then the others sat down in order of seniority, and wine was poured. Zhou Jin, cup in hand, thanked the villagers and drained his cup. On each table were eight or nine dishes—pig's head, chicken, carp, tripe, liver, and other dishes. At the signal to begin, they fell to with their chopsticks, like a whirlwind scattering wisps of cloud. And half the food had gone before they noticed that Zhou Jin had not eaten a bite.

"Why aren't you eating anything?" asked Shen. "Surely we haven't offended you the very first day?" He selected some choice morsels and put them on the teacher's plate.

But Zhou Jin stopped him and said, "I must explain—I am having a long fast."

"How thoughtless we have been!" exclaimed his hosts. "May we ask why you are fasting?"

"On account of a vow I made before the shrine of Buddha when my mother was ill," said Zhou

Jin. "I have been abstaining from meat now for more than ten years."

"Your fasting reminds me of a joke I heard the other day from Mr. Gu in the county town," said Mei Jiu. "It is a one character to seven character verse about a teacher." The villagers put down their chopsticks to listen, while he recited:

A
Foolish scholar
Fasted so long,
Whiskers covered his cheeks;
Neglecting to study the classics,
He left pen and paper aside.
He'll come without being invited next year.

After this recitation he said, "A learned man like Mr. Zhou here is certainly not foolish." Then, putting his hand over his mouth to hide a smile, he added, "But he should become a scholar soon, and the description of the fasting and the whiskers is true to life." He gave a loud guffaw, and everybody laughed with him, while Zhou Jin did not know which way to look.

Shen Xiangfu hastily filled a cup with wine and said, "Mr. Mei should drink a cup of wine. Mr. Zhou was the teacher in Mr. Gu's house."

"I didn't know that," said Mei Jiu. "I should certainly drink a cup to apologize. But this joke was not against Mr. Zhou. It was about a scholar. However, this fasting is a good thing. I have an uncle who never ate meat either. But after he passed the prefectural examination his patron sent him some sacrificial meat, and my grandmother said, 'If you don't eat this, Confucius will be angry, and some terrible calamity may happen. At the very least, he will make you fall sick.' So my uncle stopped fasting. Now, Mr. Zhou, you are bound to pass the examination this autumn. Then you will be offered sacrificial meat, and I'm sure you will stop fasting."

They all said this was a lucky omen and drank a toast to congratulate Zhou Jin in advance, until the poor man's face turned a mottled red and white and he could barely stammer out his thanks as he took the wine cup. Soup was carried in from the kitchen with a big dish of dumplings and a plate of fried cakes. They assured Zhou Jin that there was no animal fat in the cakes, and pressed him to eat some. But he was afraid the soup was unclean and asked for tea instead.

While they were eating the dessert, someone asked Shen, "Where is the village head today? Why hasn't he come to welcome Mr. Zhou?"

"He has gone to a feast with Constable Li," said Shen.

"These last few years, under the new magistrate, Mr. Li has done very well," said someone else. "In one year he must make about a thousand taels of silver. But he is too fond of gambling. It's a pity he's not like Bailiff Huang. Bailiff Huang used to play too, but later he turned over a new leaf and was able to build a house just like a palace—it is very grand."

"Since your relative became the village head," said Mr. Xun to Shen Xiangfu, "he's been in luck. Another year or two, and I suppose he will be like Bailiff Huang."

"He's not doing badly," said Shen. "But it'll be several years before his dream of catching up with Bailiff Huang comes true."

With his mouth full of cake, Mr. Mei put in: "There is something in dreams." And turning to Zhou Jin he asked, "Mr. Zhou, these past years, during the examinations, what dreams have you had?"

"None at all," replied Zhou Jin.

"I was fortunate," said Mei Jiu. "Last year on New Year's Day, I dreamed that I was on a very high mountain. The sun in the sky was directly above me, but suddenly it fell down on my head! Sweating with fright, I woke up and rubbed my head, and it still seemed hot. I didn't understand then what the dream meant, but later it came true!"

By this time all the cakes were finished, and they had another round of drinks. By then it was time to light the lamps, and Mei Jiu and all the others went home, while Shen Xiangfu produced blue bedding and escorted Mr. Zhou to the temple to sleep, where he settled with the monk that the two empty rooms at the back should be used for the school.

When the day came to start school, Shen Xiangfu and the other villagers took their sons, large and small, to pay their respects to the teacher; and Zhou Jin taught them. That evening, when he opened the envelopes containing their school fees, he found there was one-tenth of a tael of silver from the Xun family with an extra eight cents for tea, while the others had given only three or four cents or a dozen cash apiece; so altogether he had not enough for one month's food. He gave what he had to the monk, however, promising to settle his account later.

The children were a wild lot. The moment Zhou Jin took his eyes off them, they would slip outside to play hopscotch or kick balls. They were up to mischief every day, yet he had to sit there patiently and teach them.

Translated by Yang Hsien-yi and Gladys Yang

67

BOAT PEOPLE

The Boat People were a minority group in Guangdong with a distinct dialect and distinct customs. Considered socially inferior by other Chinese of the area, they found it difficult to acquire educations or rise to positions of influence within the larger Chinese society. Consequently Boat People did not write books we can use to probe their values and culture; we must instead make the best use we can of accounts written by outsiders. Since any minority's world view and social situation will be strongly influenced by how they are treated by others, such sources can be very revealing. The following description of the history and customs of the Boat People is from the gazetteer of Gaoyao county published in 1826. Like most gazetteer entries, this one was composed by quoting from earlier local histories.

The origin of the Boat People (*danhu*) cannot be traced. Boats are their homes and fishing is their occupation. During the Jin dynasty [265–420], there were five thousand households of them outside of the control of the government. Since the Tang dynasty [618–906], they have paid taxes to the government. In the early years of the Hongwu period [1368–1398] of the Ming dynasty, they were registered by households, and headmen were appointed for each district. They were under the jurisdiction of the bureau of rivers and lakes and paid annual taxes in fish. During the Chongzhen period [1628–1643], the bureau of rivers and lakes of Gaoyao county was abolished and the Boat People were placed under Songtai station. Under our dynasty, they pay taxes to the local county.

The Boat People can endure cold and can dive deeply into the water. Whenever passengers in boats drop articles into the water, they always have Boat People retrieve them. The local inhabitants classify them as "Boat People" and refuse to marry them. They will not even allow them to settle on the land.

Therefore day and night they have to crowd together on their boats. The fish they catch are barely enough to feed them and none of them, male or female, have enough clothes to cover their bodies.

Every year they must pay taxes at the end of the spring and the beginning of summer. Those who live in the upstream area of Antelope Strait pay eighty-seven, while those who live in the downstream area pay ninety-four. The taxpayers are further classified as "Boat People units" or "worker units." The latter are those who are hired to fish for others while the Boat People units are independent fishing households who are responsible for sending their own taxes to the government. The worker units act not only as tenants for commoners but also as servants. As they are in extreme poverty those who monopolize the business are able to hire them for low wages. They give the tenants several years' advance salary, but such wages are insufficient to keep them from suffering cold and hunger. Thus, year after year the tenant fishermen are unable to pay the government tax.

The Boat People by nature are stupid and illiterate. They are afraid of seeing officials, so local magnates and rapacious clerks are able to exploit them continuously. The local riffraff treat the fishing boats as their own storehouses and use the fishermen's children as their sleeping mats, yet none of the fishermen dare to utter a word about it.

Translated by Lily Hwa

68

PLACARDS POSTED IN GUANGZHOU

The Opium War between China and Great Britain (1839–1842) was fought over issues of trade and diplomatic access. The Chinese were trying to suppress the importation of opium and the British were trying to expand the rights of British merchants to trade freely in China. When the British Navy showed it could take China's coastal cities easily, the Chinese had little choice but to accept British terms. In the treaties signed in 1842 and 1843 the Chinese ceded Hong Kong, opened five treaty ports, and gave British subjects in China special legal privileges.

In the Guangzhou (Canton) area, passions had been roused by the efforts of officials to suppress opium and resist the British, and it was not easy to get the population to accept the terms of the treaties. As seen in the following placards which local gentry posted, many local residents were determined not to let the foreigners enter.

1

We, the literati and righteous people of Guangzhou, including those who live on the land and on the water, those who live inside and outside the city, publish these instructions to let the barbarian merchants of all nations understand our intentions.

The injuries, deceits, cruel deeds, and evil acts of the English resident barbarians are as innumerable as the hairs of the head. Now they plot to coerce our high authorities. They have long wished to enter the city; and our superiors, from the depths of their virtue and the greatness of their benevolence, have given in and issued a proclamation granting permission to enter the city. They have not considered that the English barbarians, born and raised in noxious regions beyond the bounds of civilization, having the hearts of wolves, the visage of tigers, and the cunning of foxes, plan to take possession of our province and only desire to enter the walls so that they may spy out the land. Now having received a proclamation allowing their entrance, they will not only exercise violence and usurpation, but will insult and injure the people to an unspeakable degree.

Therefore, we, the literati and the people of Guangzhou, however small our strength, have prepared ourselves for the contest. We declare that sooner than obey the proclamation and suf-

311

fer these wild barbarians, we will act in opposition and adhere to the old regulations of our government. In public assembly, we decided to await the day they enter the city, then exterminate their odious race and burn their houses. With united hearts, we will destroy them in order to display celestial vengeance and manifest public indignation.

But we are aware that at the thirteen factories barbarian merchants of all nations are assembled together for commerce, the good and the bad mixed together. When the standard of righteousness is raised, the precious and the vile might be consumed together if they were not warned in advance. Therefore we give this special early announcement.

All the good barbarians who intend to remain in their places quietly and do not contemplate entering the city shall come to no harm if they promptly leave. As regards all the people who live in the vicinity of the factories, if they wish to guard themselves and their establishments, they should not go out of doors to protect or save the barbarians. Otherwise calamity will overtake them, and they will have no time for regrets. Be warned. Tremble. Be on your guard. These are special commands.

Posted in front of the thirteen factories on the 18th day of the twelfth month of 1845.

2

When the English barbarians started the quarrel about opium, our august sovereign, out of consideration for the people of the seas, and unwilling to make them suffer the horrors of war, consented to free trade [at the five ports]. He thereby manifested the highest degree of tender regard. All of our high provincial authorities have also in every way possible manifested their generosity. But the desires of the barbarians cannot be fathomed, and their repeated wanton deeds are already sufficient to make men's hair stand on end. Often of late they have, under the pretext of entering the city to take exercise and relaxation, hoped to get secret opportunities for spying out and usurping the land. Nothing can exceed their violent insults.

Consider how different our case is from the others. In our metropolis, Guangzhou, commercial transactions are all conducted outside the walls of the city, while the opposite is the case at Fuzhou and Ningbo. Therefore they have no real reason to enter the city. In asking to enter the city to take exercise and relaxation, they reveal their opposition to the old regulations. Moreover the city is an important site. Here are not only the offices of government, the granaries and prisons, but also the family residences of all the people. If a perverse line of action is allowed to begin, violent opposition to authority will shortly follow, which will lead on to shameless usurpation and eventually to mutual slaughter. War will recommence.

For the protection of our families and the preservation of their lives, we will firmly maintain the oaths we have taken and never swerve from our determination. If they truly keep to their intention to enter the city, every house and every family will prepare heaps of stones and bricks at their doors, and when the gong is sounded, every street and lane shall be closed to prevent their escape. If the barbarians use force and attack the gates, the people of every street will shower down their bricks and stones, and, shouting to each other from every quarter, will advance, slaughter the whole multitude, and then demolish their factories and burn up their ships, not allowing one to escape.

Notice has already been given to the people and scholars in every direction to assemble and train the righteous and valiant among them and to place guards at the important and dangerous passes, ready for all emergencies.

We, the inhabitants of the whole city, ought and must, with one heart and united strength, defend our ancestral city. Anyone who dares to oppose us, may both the gods and men dash to pieces.

This manifesto is issued by the united gentry and people of all Guangzhou.

69

INFANT PROTECTION SOCIETY

During the Age of Division and the Tang dynasty, when Buddhism flourished, monasteries undertook many charitable activities and social welfare services. In the Song, the government often took the initiative, setting up charitable hospitals, free graveyards, and granaries for famine relief. Still, from Song times on, members of the gentry took on much of the responsibility for charity and ran such organizations as free schools, orphanages, soup kitchens, and winter shelters for beggars and vagrants. By Qing times, managing such enterprises was one of the major functions upper class men fulfilled in their communities.

The following discussion of infanticide and ways to discourage it was written by You Zhi on the basis of his experience with a charitable foundation in Wuxi county in Jiangsu province. From 1843 to 1853 this foundation had supported between sixty and one hundred infants a year. You's account of this foundation reveals both the moral impulses that could lead to philanthropy and the practical and financial obstacles that had to be overcome when undertaking charitable projects.

In the cities it is customary to have orphanages where deserted children are taken in. . . . However, the countryside is extensive and travel is difficult, so poor people cannot afford to bring their children into the city. Thus, when poor families have too many children, they are often forced by practical considerations to drown the newborn infants, a practice which has already become so widespread that no one thinks it unusual. (People even give it euphemistic names such as "giving her away to be married," or "transmigrating to the body of someone else." The custom has become so deeply rooted that no one attempts to discour-

age it.) Not only are female infants drowned, at times even males are; not only do the poor drown their children, even the well-to-do do it. People follow each other's example, and the custom becomes more widespread day by day. (There is a case where one family drowned more than ten girls in a row; there are villages where scores of girls are drowned each year. We who dwell in the country witness the crime with our own eyes—a scene too brutal to be described.) As soon as the infants are born into this world, they become the victims of murder. They struggle in the water for a long time before they fall silent. On hearing their

313

cries, one is brought to the brink of tears; on talking about it, one's heart is rent with sorrow.

Alas! Who is not a parent? Who is not a child? How can anyone be so cruel? Is it that people are evil by nature? No. It is that the custom has become so prevalent that people can no longer see the cruelty in it. Yet, Heaven encourages life, and man abhors killing. Charitable people who are determined to accumulate good deeds even buy live animals just to release them! Why not save human lives! If we who live in the country, who see and hear this crime committed daily, simply look on without trying to save the infants, how can we excuse our own guilt? (This matter may not have come to the attention of the city officials and the country gentry. It is necessary to inquire about the matter from poor women in order to obtain details.) This is why we have to cry aloud for these infants and seek help from the charitable gentlemen of the entire nation.

When we look into the charitable institutions available, we find that, besides orphanages, there are foundling homes and nurseries which take in infants for temporary stays and transport them for the villagers. Yet, in the case of newborn infants, the little bodies might not be able to survive the trip. Therefore, adopting the principle of Su Dongpo, who saved infants in Huang'e, and Peng Nanyun, who wrote on saving those who were being drowned, we have formulated a way to offer subsidies of cash and rice to make it possible for parents to raise their children at home instead of sending them to orphanages.

We have formed a society named "The Infant Protection Society." Whenever there is a birth in our area, if the parents are truly too poor to raise the child themselves, our bureau will, according to regulations, provide them with cash and rice for six months so that they can care for the child for that period. Only when it is absolutely impossible for them to raise the infant at home will the society try to transport him or her to an orphanage as a life-saving measure. Our aim is to make the parents keep the infant, at first perhaps for the subsidy, and then out of love—for, as the baby grows, the parents will become more attached to

him or her day by day. Our expenses are modest, yet a great many lives can be saved. . . .

The following are the regulations of the Society, which can be adopted by anyone interested.

1. When the Society is first established, a bureau should be set up in a temple or any other public place since there is no time to construct a separate building. All members should share the duties of the bureau. A head should be elected out of those who are of means and of reliable character. Several other trustworthy and capable members should be elected as solicitors and inspectors. It is necessary that all the members work together toward a common goal, for only then can the Society achieve long-lasting results.

2. Contributions can be solicited in large lump sums or small donations, in the form of cash or grain—all depending on the local situation of the region. It can be done by calling a meeting within a clan, a village, or even a county; the more funds acquired, the better. All members have to work together to change this immoral custom and save lives.

3. As the number of people who drown their children is on the increase in rural areas, the Infant Protection Society is established to provide subsidies for the very poorest families only, to discourage them from killing their own children without having to use an orphanage. Therefore, any household that can manage to raise its infants is not eligible for support from the Society.

4. In the area served, whenever an infant is born and the parents are indeed too destitute to keep it, they should report to the bureau of the Society, accompanied by neighbors who are willing to serve as witnesses. The inspector of the bureau will then go personally to the home to examine the situation. If it is truly as reported, the Society will give the parents one peck of white rice and two hundred cash. Afterwards, they can claim the same amount each month, identifying themselves with tickets, for a total of five months. (The exact period can be lengthened or shortened according to individual needs; the amount of subsidy is also flexible.) After five months, if they

definitely cannot afford to keep the child, then the Society will provide transportation to an orphanage. (Those who can raise the child, but only with much difficulty, should be persuaded to do so. Even if the Society has to provide rice for two or three more months, whenever a life can be saved, action should be taken.)

5. Records are to be kept in the bureau. After the birth of the child, the parents must report the exact hour, day, and month of birth to the bureau as well as the name of the family, the village, and the county. The inspector then should look over the infant; record finger prints, toe prints, and the direction, location, and shape of the hair swirl on the head. Then the bureau should give out tickets on which is written the exact number of months of subsidy the parents are to receive. Two months later they should bring the child to the bureau for inspection, or the inspector should visit the family. If the infant dies from disease, the subsidy should be terminated on the day the death occurs. Should anyone fail to report the death of such an infant, the witnesses are to be held responsible.

6. In extremely destitute families, if a widow is pregnant and has no sons to continue her dead husband's family line and no other means of support then the subsidy can be increased after a meeting of the Society members (the period is either three or four years, the amount flexible). In this way, not only does the Society take care of orphans, but it actually sponsors chastity; this will be of no small aid to virtuous customs.

7. If a mother in a poor family should die immediately after childbirth and the infant, left without anyone to nurse it, faces imminent death, then the bureau, after making sure of the facts, should give an extra five hundred cash a month to provide for a wet nurse. This subsidy can be continued for three years.

8. With time, it is to be expected that corruption will occur. Once a subsidy system is started, there inevitably will be people who are capable of raising their children and yet pretend to be poor to obtain the money and rice. Therefore, the investigators must be careful; only those who are confirmed to be actually destitute should receive

the subsidy. Also, one should change people's ways of thinking by constantly and sincerely teaching them about the divine retribution which awaits those who drown infants.

9. When the Society is established, a geographic boundary must be set to facilitate inspections. If one tries to give help to whoever seeks it, then funds will not be sufficient, and it will be difficult to investigate cases because of the distances. Therefore, we tentatively set a limit of ten *li*; we are not able to provide help for those who live outside of the ten-*li* radius. When an infant is registered at the bureau, if it is winter, one coat filled with cotton and one wrapping blanket will be allotted; if it is spring or autumn, one lined gown.

10. Although the purpose of the Society is to persuade poverty-stricken families to keep their children instead of drowning them, in some cases the parents may be ashamed to accept charity or may have their minds set on drowning the infant because they already have too many children at home. In others, the parents may be in such straitened circumstances that keeping the infant is definitely impossible. In such cases, one should try hard to persuade them to find ways to solve their problems, without meddling in their private affairs.

11. Infants who are brought to the bureau should be provided with wet nurses immediately. If there is a woman with milk who is willing to be the wet nurse to pay for her own child, then one should pay her three years' salary according to regulations. Or, the first year she may get two pecks of rice a month, and only one peck each month through the rest of the two-year period. Since boys are usually adopted, the bureau should give out birth certificates to prevent future lawsuits concerning the rights to the child but should not subsidize them with money or rice.

12. Poxes are the most dangerous diseases of infants, especially smallpox, which is easily spread. Therefore, in the first and second or eighth and ninth months, one should give inoculations and tell the wet nurses to watch carefully. The bureau should provide some funds for medication and supply some medicine in cases of emergency.

13. Whenever a child is sick, it should be reported to the manager of the bureau, who will then pay a doctor to see the patient until he or she is fully recovered. If the mother of a newborn infant is ill or unable to produce milk, she should also report to the bureau and receive a subsidy for health care and medication.

14. The regulations of this Society are set for the extremely poor. We are sure that the households which are capable of raising their own children will not stoop to such meager assistance, nor would they send their children to orphanages. And yet, simply out of impatience with having too many children, or merely due to the custom of the region, some of these families may also have drowned their children. After the establishment of this Society, they will hesitate to do so. By and by the infants will all be able to escape cruel early deaths.

15. After the Society's proposal to the county government has been approved, a general notice of prohibition will be drawn up. Should anyone, despite the Society's efforts, insist on the evil practice of drowning children, he will be convicted and punished if discovered. No one should be lenient with him. Our hope is to change the customs in part by pressure from the outside but more by persuasion from the inside. This is by no means too harsh.

16. Although the Society is formed to protect infants, it also helps mothers, for in an extremely poor household, the livelihood of the family depends on weaving done by the housewife. A day without work means a day without food. In such cases, whenever the wife is in labor or cannot work, the family faces starvation. The woman who is laden with a hundred worries and has nowhere to turn will hardly be capable of returning to work as early as the second or third day after giving birth; if she does it is very possible that she will catch a cold or have other complications which may lead to critical problems. On the other hand, if she can get a small subsidy, she will be able to rest a few days, the infant can be saved, and the mother also can be nourished. This is doing two good deeds at once.

17. Although the Society will provide transportation of unwanted children to orphanages, the cases in which that is necessary should constitute less than twenty to thirty percent. At the time of the birth of the infant, either because of poverty or anger or because the mother has to nurse other people's children, the parents may not wish to keep the infant. But after four or five months the child can already laugh and play, and is very lovable. The parents are then unable to part with him or her. (Those who endeavor to keep their child can again be divided into two groups; the truly hard-pressed ones should qualify for subsidy for several more months.)

The most serious matter in this world is human life, and the greatest of all charitable deeds is the saving of human lives. Of all kinds of lifesaving, ours is the most urgent. I humbly hope that the gentlemen who are concerned about the ways of the world will advocate our purpose and spread our practices wherever they go and to whomever they meet. It does not matter whether the scale is large or small; each life we save is worth saving. Every time we establish a bureau, we will save numerous lives, which is no small matter. If these established regulations have faults, then they should be modified according to the specific local situations. It is our greatest hope that our fellow workers will do so.

Once I asked a friend from another part of the country if people there also drowned female infants. He said no, in his region there was no such custom. I expressed great admiration for the goodness of the people in that area. A few months later, I met this friend again, and he spoke to me in great alarm. "Would you believe it!" he exclaimed. "What you told me the other day was true! I'm so glad that you woke me up from my ignorance. Otherwise I would have missed a fine opportunity for doing good."

When I asked him for the details, my friend told me that when he returned home from our meeting, he asked a midwife about the drowning of female infants and found out that the custom was rather prevalent in his hometown. Upon this discovery he called town meetings and admonished the villagers; he also offered to protect infants and worked out village contracts to prohibit such practices. Since then he has been able to save five or six lives.

The above is a good example of the situation: the custom is prevalent in most places, yet people are not aware of it unless they give it special attention. We scholars tend to close our doors and devote ourselves to studying, thinking that by doing so we are concerning ourselves with the people and the universe. Little do we know that right outside our doors there are countless infants crying out to be saved from death! (People who refuse to bother about what happens outside their doors often do so on the grounds that they do not want to interfere with the affairs of others. Yet when it comes to saving lives, one should not insist on such principles. Otherwise the best opportunities to accumulate good deeds will be missed.)

Now, since the custom of drowning female infants is most prevalent in rural areas, charitable people in the cities and towns can do very little where they are. In their case, the best course is to investigate which regions have such wicked customs, then try to save the infants by expounding the principles of divine retribution. They should realize the significance of saving lives and should not be afraid of difficulties. For time does not wait for man; one's hair turns white quickly and one grows old. Once the best chance of doing good passes, it will be too late to repent. Cases of divine retribution for drowning female infants are too numerous to be fully listed. Those who want to help should print illustrated books on this subject to warn the foolish and the ignorant. Also, abortion by taking drugs often causes deaths; pictures against this practice should be printed as appendices to the books. As to children born from illicit relations, they should tell midwives that they will receive four hundred to five hundred cash as a reward if they bring such illegitimate children to the protection societies. In this way they will be able to save quite a few lives in secret.

The lives of men concern Heaven, and Heaven encourages life. Therefore, the saving of human lives is of utmost importance. If a man takes the life of another, not only will he be executed for the crime in this world, he will be punished in the other world as well. Wicked forces result from grievance; together they form the wheel of retributions, and misfortune will certainly befall the guilty. On the other hand, if a man saves a life or a score of lives, even hundreds of lives, imagine the bountiful reward he will receive! Whether it is a grown man's or a mere infant's, a life is a life; therefore, one should not let this chance to accumulate good slip by.

The custom of drowning female infants has become for many a mere habit. Although there are laws prohibiting it and books advising against it, they cannot reach the common people who are ignorant of reason and unable to read. However severe and earnest these laws and books may be, they cannot penetrate into every household and get to the people on the streets. In such cases, the only thing one can do is to compose catchy slogans and folk songs with themes of retribution and propagate them in villages and towns. When ignorant men and women hear these, they will understand them and be inspired and warned. Only then can this age-old, widespread custom be changed. If the blind minstrels that rove the countryside can be taught such songs, then they can make a living with them and at the same time can awaken the world. This is doing two good deeds at once and is the very best way to accumulate merit.

Translated by Clara Yu

70

MID-CENTURY REBELS

Over the centuries China witnessed thousands of violent uprisings. Yet no period suffered so many as the mid-nineteenth century, from 1850 to 1873, when the vast Taiping Rebellion brought in its wake the Nian Rebellion in the North, Moslem rebellions in the Southwest and Northwest, a Miao rebellion in the Southwest, secret society rebellions along the coast, and many more.

Rebellions varied considerably in their origins and organization. Some were started by bands of hungry peasants, others by well-organized secret societies that had elaborate ideologies incorporating elements from popular Buddhism and Daoism. The Taiping Rebellion even made use of some Christian beliefs. Nevertheless, virtually all rebellions that had any success also invoked the Confucian theory of the mandate of Heaven: the emperor had ceased to rule with virtue; therefore, he had lost his mandate and his subjects had the right to rebel.

Sources for the goals, organizing principles, and behavior of rebels are scarce. When rebellions failed, the documents they produced were destroyed as dangerous. The officials who suppressed the rebels wrote reports, but most of them lacked firsthand knowledge, objectivity, or sympathy. To overcome some of these shortcomings, the mid-century rebellions are probed here through three sources of differing origin. The first is a group of proclamations of the Small Sword Society, issued when they took over the city of Xiamen on the coast of Fujian, and preserved by British diplomats stationed there. The Small Sword Society was one of the secret societies that joined in the general initiative of the Taipings to take several cities in the early 1850s. These proclamations reveal typical rebel ideology—for instance, evoking the name of the Ming dynasty and the Han people as an anti-Manchu gesture. The second source is the "confessions" a group of rebels made after their capture. These rebels were members of bandit groups loosely related to the Taipings. The third source is a request for military aid sent in by members of the gentry of that same area. These two pieces, which were also preserved by British officials, can be used together to analyze the social milieu that gave rise to banditry and rebellion.

PROCLAMATIONS OF THE XIAMEN SMALL SWORD SOCIETY

1

The Grand Marshal Huang of the Ming dynasty and the Han people, in order to safeguard the lives of the commoners and merchants, proclaims martial law:

I have heard that Heaven and earth change their course of order: after a time of great prosperity, there must follow a period of chaos, and after a period of great turmoil, there must arise a general desire for peace.

The Qing dynasty has been governing China for more than two hundred years. Corruption of officials and oppression of the people clearly indicate that its mandate has come to an end. I now lead the Righteous and Benevolent Army to save the people and to punish those who have been cruel. I have ordered that my soldiers shall pillage neither the merchants nor the common people nor shall they rape women. The arrival of my armies will not cause the slightest disturbance to the people. If any soldier disobeys my orders I shall punish him in accordance with martial law, permitting no favoritism. You, the merchants and the people, should apply yourselves to your tasks and should not be frightened. I am strict in abiding by my words and enforcing my orders. You should obey them unerringly.

10th day of the fourth month, 1853

2

Concerning the safety of the people and normal business:

I, the grand marshal, have led my army to recover the southern provinces, to stabilize peace for the four classes of people, and to eliminate bad officials.

Since the emperor of the Qing government is young and ignorant, power has been concentrated in the hands of wicked advisors and officials of the prefectures and counties plunder the wealth of the people and use it to ingratiate themselves with their superiors. As a result the people are oppressed by greedy officials.

I, the grand marshal, have led the Righteous and Benevolent Army and have recovered Haicheng, Zhangzhou, Guankou, and Tongan. My army has advanced with irresistible power. If my subordinates have any unruly soldiers who rape women and create disturbances in the streets, you should report them to my officers immediately. I shall execute them and display their heads in public in accordance with the law.

All the people—merchants and commoners alike—should carry on with their work and trade as usual. Do not be afraid of my soldiers. After issuing an order I enforce it immediately and do not tolerate offenders. My orders must be obeyed.

3

In the name of the Grand Ming dynasty, Marshal Huang of the Han people proclaims:

It is well known that the way to good government is through benevolent policies; yet military strength is essential in governing a state. At this moment I have already conquered Xiamen and must now appoint capable persons to govern it. When employing capable individuals in the government one should pay special attention to their military ability. For this reason those who are able to pacify the world must exert care in choosing men.

Now the people of Xiamen come seeking to take the oaths and join our society. There are hundreds of millions of them. If I do not proclaim the rules of recruitment, I am afraid that the wrong persons will be selected, thereby causing an unnecessary waste of time and resources. With the proclamation of this edict, those of you who have obtained the righteous banners from me and who are willing to reconstruct the nation with me should be very careful in the recruitment of more members. Only the young and the strong and those with experience in the martial arts should be selected as our members. We must eliminate the very old, the very young, and the disabled. In other words, we must eliminate all those over sixty years of age and all those under sixteen. Only by following this method can we strengthen our forces. Do not transgress this order.

15th day of the fourth month, 1853

A STATEMENT OF VOLUNTARY SURRENDER BY MEMBERS OF THE GUANGXI ROVING BANDIT GROUP

We men from Guangdong—Da Liyu, Zhang Zhao, Zhang Guihe, Wen Xi—and we men from Guangxi—Tian Fang, Huang Shou, and Liang Fu—make this appeal.

We were born in a time of prosperity and were good people. We lived in towns and were taught to distinguish right from wrong. But because of continuous flooding in our area, we could not get a grain of rice to eat even if we worked hard in the fields, and we could not engage in business because we lacked the funds. As a result we all joined the bandits.

Not long ago we came to Guangxi to try to make a living. We met others who had come from our hometowns. We pitied each other because of our sad situation, and together we began to imitate outlaws in order to relieve our hungry stomachs. In other words, no one forced us to join the outlaws. We were driven to join them because we were desperate. Given the chance, we would have returned gladly to our normal way of life.

We thought constantly of our families, but we could not return to them. Indeed, we were drifting on a hungry, painful sea and knew not when we would reach the other side. We hope Your Excellency will forgive our past sins. We hope you will think of the great benevolence of our imperial house and give us a chance to start a new life.

We, humble people, Big-Headed Yang, Lo Da, Hou Jiu, Wang Liu, Lu Xiongjie, report our grievance and appeal to you. . . .

We hate the army runners who recently made heavy demands on us and disturbed our villages. They used the excuse of establishing a local militia to cause trouble for the good and honest people and create opportunities for the wicked ones. The words they used were virtuous-sounding; yet the deeds they actually perpetrated were most wicked. They allied themselves with government officials and formed cliques so that they could oppress our village and falsely reported that certain persons were connected with the bandits. This was due to personal grudges against the accused or to the fact that they wanted to obtain rewards. They burned down our houses and took all we had; they robbed us of our property and threatened our lives. Therefore we banded together to insure our own safety. Those who still remain in the village may run away someday while those who have left can hardly come back. Therefore, for each ordinary person who ran away, there was one more bandit, and the numbers of bandits became greater and greater. Since there are so many of us, we could not survive except by pillage, nor could we save our lives if we did not fight against the imperial troops that were sent out to exterminate us. As a consequence, we have offended the court and hurt the merchants.

We have always wanted to correct our behavior and to purge ourselves of our beastly nature. We would have liked to return to our homes to enjoy long and happy lives, but we have been left rambling around, wandering through unknown places because the officials did not have mercy on us. Usually after interrogating a bandit, they would kill him or at least expel him. Therefore those who sincerely wanted to correct their past sins were actually risking their lives. If we had surrendered to the officials, we also would have had to depend on their mercy. The thought of it tortures us day and night. Now, fortunately, Your Excellency has arrived in this area with a commission to pacify the people. You have loved the people like your own children; you have disciplined yourself strictly; you have worked diligently for the good of the nation and have relieved the suffering of the masses. We hope that you will understand our situation and judge fairly. We hope you will treat us leniently and extend your benevolence to us. We are willing to sell our weapons and buy cows for farming. We render all our respect and gratitude to you.

We respectfully report our situation to you.

MEMORIAL OF LI YUYING, JUREN DEGREE HOLDER, AND TAN DUANYUAN, SHENGYUAN DEGREE HOLDER, FROM WU PREFECTURE, GUANGXI PROVINCE

Our dynasty has followed the teachings of the ancient sages. As a result everyone in Rong county has lived in harmony for a long time. The population was increasing, and the resources were plentiful; even our dogs and chickens never had to fear disturbance.... However, in 1846 bandits and rebels began gathering on the east side of Liangxu and disturbed our local tranquillity. As their power grew, their influence spread. They even captured the city and took the government officials prisoner. There was no order in the city, and the rebels roamed everywhere. Gentry members were killed and captured; women were raped. Corpses were left lying all over the ground; houses were left in ashes; the farmers' fields were thick with weeds. It was sad indeed to see these things happen.... They pillaged property even at great distances from their base area and forced the people who were under their control to pay land taxes to them. They connived to force officials to send up false reports saying that loyalist forces had recaptured areas that had fallen to the rebels. The bandits used official seals and issued false edicts to the populace. It was intolerable to have these ruffians dominate the local government!

Last year we were lucky to have the governor and the governor-general decide to lead out their armies to destroy the bandits at Xunzhou. The governor then promised to transfer the army to Rong county where the local militia was trying to consolidate its positions pending the arrival of the government troops. The militia have been fighting for a long time and have become quite weary. I am afraid that, if the local militia collapses, the bandits will roam all over the county and prove very difficult for the government troops to control.

The local militia is capable of mustering ten thousand troops, all battle-tested veterans who hate the rebels. It is our opinion that, if only we could get a skilled commander, the militia would be quite effective against the rebels. Unfortunately, we have not been able to get an experienced officer to lead them. There have been constant arguments over battle plans, and the militia has never acted in unison. As a result we have often been defeated by the rebels. The prefect and governor-general appointed a pair of officers to supervise the local militia. They issued orders, gave out banners and seals, but did not come to take command personally. The local militia, therefore, has not been united and cannot contribute much to alleviating the critical situation.

Now that the governor of Guangxi province has dispatched his army to wipe out the bandits in Xunzhou, we hope that, after finishing with the bandits there, it will come immediately to Rong county to exterminate the rebels and save the people. If Your Excellency sympathizes with all that the people have suffered, please hasten to have the army come here to suppress the rebels.... We might suggest that you consolidate the militias of Teng, Pingnan, Beiliu, Chenqi, and Xinyi counties under your command so that the bandits may not escape our troops by hopping back and forth across county borders. When the government armies arrive in Rong county, have them train the local militia so that it can put up a better defense against the bandits. We would suggest also that you proclaim a general amnesty for those who were forced to join the rebels. We have confidence in the strategy of encircling bandit hideouts; we are sure they could not resist your attacks and their days would be numbered....

Huang Pengfen and Feng Weireng are two leaders well respected by the local militia. If you were to appoint them commanders, they would get cooperation and would be able to help achieve the goal of ridding our area of rebels. When your armies arrive here we would personally like to join them to take your orders and give you assistance if needed. With your great talent and ability as a high civil and military official, you will certainly save our people from their hardships. . . .

With the greatest of humility we present these opinions to you.

Translated by Jeh-hang Lai

71

THE CONDITIONS AND ACTIVITIES OF WORKERS

With the development of commerce and industry came the appearance not only of prosperous merchants and manufacturers, but also their employees. In the cities there were always many who needed work and would accept dirty, difficult, or even dangerous work for low pay. Independent craftsmen and merchants had long formed guilds, which set standards and prices and provided welfare benefits, but workers were normally kept from forming such associations. The first selection below is an example of a prohibition against organizing by workers. This one was carved in stone and preserved in the textile manufacturers' guildhall in Suzhou.

Further evidence of the lives of workers can be found in official reports of cases in which workers were particularly ill treated. The description of the condition of the miners in Hunan given below falls into this category. In this case, after receiving the report, the central government approved the provincial government decision to enact a special law severely punishing owners and foremen who captured, enslaved, or killed workers.

PERMANENT PROHIBITIONS OFFICIALLY ENGRAVED ON STONE

This bulletin is issued jointly by the three county magistrates (with ten promotions and ten commendations) of the prefecture of Suzhou in Jiangnan: Magistrate Chen of Yuanhe county, Magistrate Wu of Changzhou county, and Magistrate Wang of Wu county. The matter concerned is as follows:

In the spring of 1870, Shen Youshan, Wang Chengzhong, Sun Hong, Dai Meiting, Lü Jinshan, Zhu Peihe, and others made a report to the Changzhou county government. They identified themselves as manufacturers of Songjin textiles and said that Cao Azhuan, Gu Ting, and other textile workers had formed a union and tried to coerce them into donating money on the pretext of making offerings to the patron gods of the trade. Some time later, Shen Youshan, et al., charged that Cao Azhuan and his gang had formed another trade union under a different name to threaten and disturb people in the profession. In both cases the former magistrate of Changzhou issued prohibitions against such organizations.

Nevertheless, in the eighth month of this year, Lü Jinshan, Ning Jinshan, Shen Youshan, and Wang Chengzhong again reported that, although Cao Azhuan had died, a certain Wang Pei had taken his place and gathered a gang to create disturbances. Threatening to strike, they pasted posters all over town urging negotiation for wages, selected auspicious dates to present offerings to the patron gods, and extorted contributions from people in the business for that purpose. Our former magistrate, Wan, once more sternly prohibited such actions.

When the current magistrate came to office, Lü Jinshan, Ren Jinshan, Wang Renzhong, and Shen Youshan reported to him that Wang Pei, Ren Fu, Zhou Hong, Gu Ting, Wu Sishou and others were still blackmailing and disturbing the people. They asked that the culprits be prosecuted and petitioned for a permanent injunction against such activities to be engraved on stone tablets. After the hearing, the magistrate punished Wang Pei and obtained his written promise never again to start trade unions, set trade regulations, or collect money on any pretext. The magistrate also granted the request for a tablet permanently prohibiting such activities.

The petition of Lu Jinshan, et al., further stated:

The people in the Songjin textile business are scattered in our two neighboring counties, Wu and Yuanhe, and so are Wang Pei's followers. Consequently, we consider it necessary for tablets of prohibition to be erected in all three counties. We beg our magistrate to ask the magistrates of Yuanhe and Wu counties to cooperate, so that the troublemakers will never dare to break your rulings, and we of the textile profession need never again trouble you with such complaints.

Besides granting the petition and the request for prohibition tablets, we magistrates now exonerate all those in the Songjin textile profession. You should make note of the fact that the organization of trade unions has long been prohibited. From now on, if Wang Pei or any of his men dare to violate the law and attempt to form unions or guilds to put pressure on fellow workers, it should be reported to the government so that we can prosecute them. Let it be known that we will not be lenient toward violators of this ruling. Be advised and abide by the law.

Special bulletin issued on the nineteenth day of the eleventh month of 1878.

Translated by Clara Yu

INVESTIGATION REPORT

The magistrate's report stated:

The southeast portion of Leiyang county is rich in coal, which has attracted many entrepreneurs. Hundreds of coal pits of various sizes have been exploited for a long time, so that by now the coal veins lie under water which must be removed before mining can be started. To manage the water pumps, the mine owners hired foremen, known as "water men." To fill this post they usually picked the worst elements of the local population, men who are extremely violent and wicked. These men, allied with local gangsters, have formed a Blue Dragon Society and accumulated huge amounts of money. To trap poor people, they established gambling dens and sold opium; then they lent them money at usurious rates. Moreover, they colluded with wine shops and restaurants to raise their prices. Badly in debt, the poor people had no choice but to sell themselves to the mine. They would also sometimes capture travelers passing through and force them to work in the mine.

The foremen built near the pit dark, damp earthen cubicles which had only a single opening. Surrounded by stockades, both the entrance and exit of these cubicles were controlled by the foremen. These were known as "sealed drums." People lured, bought, tricked, or kidnapped were all incarcerated in such "drums," and were called "water toads." Their clothes and shoes were stripped off, and they were forced to work manning the water pumps in alternating shifts day and night without respite. No consideration was given to their hunger and cold. Those who looked tired had their backs whipped, and those who attempted to escape had their feet slashed. Moreover, because it is freezing in the pits and the work is extremely heavy, the weaker miners usually died within a fortnight, and the stronger ones suffered from rotten legs and swollen bellies within a couple of months. Without rest and medication, they perished helplessly. What was most pitiful was that those "water toads" who survived were still kept in the "drums" during the spring suspension in order to be used as water pumpers again the next season. They were called "pension rice."

This situation was kept hidden from the outside world. The dozens or hundreds of "water toads" who died at each mine every year were buried in the caves nearby. Not even their relatives were informed of their deaths. The local officials have strictly and repeatedly prohibited such practices. However, these mine owners and the "water men" used artful excuses to get around the law. Now we have summoned the mine owners for inquiries and have informed them of the permanent prohibition against "water men," "water toads," "sealed drums," and "pension rice," and we have received their guarantees which have been filed as documents. In addition, we are investigating secretly and carefully. If there are any more cases like these, they shall be severely prosecuted. And if there are any allied gangsters, runners, or any officials who conceal the crimes, they shall be severely punished too. We have prepared a draft regulation concerning the situation and are now presenting it to you. Please examine it and draw up a memorial.

Translated by Jane Chen

72

GENEALOGY RULES

To facilitate ancestor worship and a general reverence for forebears, from at least the Han dynasty men kept records of their ancestors' names, dates, and accomplishments. In the later dynasties more detailed genealogies came to be needed by lineages that owned property or had other privileges to confer on their members; such lineages had to have accurate lists of their current membership and the kinship relationships among them. Thus the flourishing of large lineages in the Ming and Qing dynasties led to the compilations of huge genealogies listing thousands of past and present lineage members.

Below are the rules established by the Liu lineage of Wantong in Anhui for the compilation of their genealogy. This list was included in the preface to the genealogy they published in 1870. Principles of family and lineage composition are carefully set down in these rules, which also explain which activities and accomplishments most enhance family honor and therefore deserve recognition in the genealogy.

PRINCIPLES OF THE GENEALOGY

1. Our genealogy combines the methods of Ouyang Xiu and Su Shi,* and uses charts together with biographical accounts. Its chief aim is to provide concise and clear facts about our family lineage. Lengthy details of specific cases will be given in other records.

2. The illustration of the family tree begins with our first ancestor; the first section lists the five generations from him to his great-great-grandson, the next section lists the next five gen-

---

* Two Northern Song statesmen and writers credited with creating the standard model for genealogies used during the later dynasties.

erations, and then the next five generations, and so on. Thus, starting from the outer branches, one can trace the ultimate origin of one's heritage; starting at the beginning, one can survey the development of the branches.

3. In each section of five generations, the branches and households are listed in order, beginning with the eldest son. First are listed the descendants of the oldest son, then those of the second son—that is, the second branch—and so on. In this way, the record has a clear outline and will not become confusing because of too many details given at once. This method is followed through the branches and subbranches.

4. Compiling a genealogy is different from

writing history. History is written to distinguish good governments from bad ones, and to set down rules and models for later generations; therefore, it should include both good deeds and bad ones. In compiling a genealogy, the purpose is to clarify the ancestry and development of a lineage and to deepen its virtuous and righteous tradition; therefore only good deeds are recorded.

5. Our genealogy, following the example of historical writings and our family regulations handed down from the Han and Tang dynasties, records each family member's name, polite name, order of birth, studio name, birth date, age attained, and the location and direction of his tomb. Those who are buried in one grave are recorded as "buried together."

6. If a living lineage member's name is offensive because it contains the same word as an elder member's name, he should change it. If he is dead, then when his name is recorded in the genealogy, another word with a similar pronunciation is substituted.*

7. If a member of the lineage passed a civil service examination, or was a student of the county, province, or capital colleges, or was a local elder, these facts are recorded under his name in the lineage chart. If he became an official, his title is recorded so as to make known his achievements.

8. In order to extend our respect to the families to which we are related, a wife whose father was an official is designated as "daughter of official so-and-so." If her father did not hold an office, yet was virtuous and lived to an old age, she is described as "daughter of retired scholar so-and-so." In all other cases, I simply record, "daughter of so-and-so."

9. A daughter whose name is listed in her father's biography is designated as "married (or betrothed) to so-and-so," to make clear her own family. If her husband or her sons achieve distinction of which our family can be proud, their titles of office are recorded.

10. An adopted heir who is the son of a member of our own lineage is listed under his natural father, with a note saying that he has been adopted by so-and-so. Under his adoptive father's name, it is recorded that a second, third, or fourth son of so-and-so has been adopted into this household, and that the first son of this adopted heir cannot be given in adoption to any other household. Following the established rules, those lineage members whose order of births have become confused are not listed in this genealogy. Those who become adopted heirs of families of a different surname from ours have the fact noted under their names in order to make it possible for them to resume their original name and return to our lineage.

11. The genealogy is designed to pass on the true lines of descent as well as to eliminate its false seeds. All persons of a different last name from ours, including stepsons who follow their mothers into our family, are not allowed to be heirs because they are not of the same flesh and blood. Thus there are specific prohibitions against such successions. If these are not strictly observed, the purity in our family heritage will be in jeopardy and the true purpose of compiling this genealogy will be defeated. That is the reason for the following rules. Anyone who adopts a son of a different surname from ours and thereby tinges the purity of our lineage will be dealt sixty blows of the staff. Anyone who allows his son to be adopted by a family of a different surname receives the same punishment. So does anyone who, in adopting an heir from our own family, causes confusion in generational order. Such an adopted son should then be returned to his natural father, and another heir should be chosen in his place.

12. A wife who, after her husband's death, marries again, or a wife who has been divorced by her husband, is not mentioned in her husband's biography, even though she has borne him children. This is because the relationship between the husband and the wife was terminated. Under the sons' names, however, it is mentioned that their mother was so-and-so who remarried or was divorced, since a son cannot cut his tie with his mother. Should the wife, after having remarried

---

* Avoidance of the personal names of immediate forebears was an old custom dating back to antiquity.

or having been divorced, return to the care of her sons, the record still remains the same, because the relationship cannot be restored.

13. A legal wife who died early without bearing children is recorded in the genealogy, but concubines without children are not mentioned. This is to retain the distinction between their ranks and their degrees of respectability.

14. The concubines are not in reality all the same. Those who are married with proper ceremonies are recorded as being "married," whereas those who are not are designated as being "taken in."

15. A young son of the legal wife precedes an older son of a concubine when they are listed in the biography of their father. This is to uphold the legitimate succession. In the lineage chart, however, all sons are ordered according to their age.

16. Biographies and eulogies are designed to relate facts and to praise virtue and distinction. Regardless of whether he had held an office or not, as long as a man possessed such virtues as loyalty, filial piety, integrity, or righteousness, and could be a model for his descendants, a biographical sketch is written in praise of him. Whether a woman was a legal wife or a mere concubine, her virtues of chastity, filial piety, and other womanly good deeds are included in the biography of her husband. A daughter's good deeds are also included in the biography of her father. All in all, the biographies should be truthful but inspiring. Those who did not live to fifty years of age are not entitled to a eulogy, only a biography.

17. The names of the male members of the family who indulged in sorcery, Buddhism, Daoism, debauchery, larceny, who misappropriated or sold parts of the family cemetery, or who married indiscriminately are taken off the family genealogy.

18. All the decrees of commendation and bestowment of titles from the emperors to members of our lineage are respectfully copied and recorded in this genealogy. This is not only to show respect for the emperors, but also to inspire later generations.

19. All the writings by friends and relatives about late members of our family such as prefaces, inscriptions, anecdotes, biographies, elegies, poems, or essays, including those recorded before and those written by renowned writers, are reproduced as models for our lineage.

20. Those writings, notes, poems, and essays written by our ancestors that have withstood the test of time are reproduced in memory of their literary achievements.

21. As the graves contain the body and the physical essence of our ancestors, they should be guarded by our descendants through all ages. In this genealogy, no drawings are made of these gravesites, but in the individual biographies, records of the location and direction of each tomb are kept, so that our descendants will be able to consult them and locate the tombs.

22. The decorum of language in this genealogy is as follows: those who were in office and virtuous, "passed away"; ordinary people "are no longer"; those whose date and place of death are unknown are marked "record lost"; those who had no children are described as "line stopped" instead of "terminated" to show compassion; those who had daughters only are said to have "no heir," because, although the line has stopped, the family's essence remains. Male members who died within three months of their births are not included in the category of "early death"; those who died before their eighth year are included in the category, but there is no mourning for them; therefore, these are not recorded in the genealogy. Those who died between eight and eleven years of age are designated by "lower early death," between twelve and fifteen, "middle early death," between sixteen and nineteen, "upper early death." All these three types are recorded in their fathers' biographies. Those who died after their twentieth birthday are all entitled to their own biographical sketches, for they are considered adults. If these members had no sons, they are only listed in the charts, and after five generations, the record stops, because there is no one to continue their lines. Female members who died before they were betrothed are not mentioned in this genealogy, for they did not become wives. For the

same reason, women who were betrothed to members of our lineage yet died before the marriage ceremony could take place are not listed in our family genealogy.

23. When lineage descendants move to another part of the country and settle down there, in their biographies such information is given in detail, so that they can be traced over many generations.

24. The ancestral temple is where the spirits of our ancestors stay; it is also where ancestral rites are performed by our descendants. It is important, therefore, to record the buildings, including the shrine in front, the rooms in the rear, and the surrounding buildings, as well as the land, which is measured on all four sides and recorded in detail.

25. No one should take a family with the same surname as ours for a branch of our family, regardless of its wealth or power. This is essential in preserving the purity of our lineage.

26. A list of the eldest sons in the primary line of the lineage and a list of our family regulations are appended in this genealogy.

Translated by Clara Yu

PART VII

THE EARLY TWENTIETH CENTURY

Efforts to reform the Qing government and make it strong enough to withstand the foreign threat had begun by the 1860s. After China's defeat by the Japanese in 1895 and her humiliation by joint Western and Japanese forces in the wake of the Boxer Rebellion of 1900, prospects for reform from within faded. Small groups of revolutionaries, the most famous of which was associated with Sun Yatsen (Sun Zhongshan, 1866–1925), turned to violence to overthrow the old regime. In 1911 a military uprising succeeded, and the last Manchu emperor agreed to abdicate in early 1912. The decades from then until the founding of the People's Republic of China in 1949 are referred to as the Republican period because monarchy was now repudiated and the Western theory of constitutional republican government was honored, if seldom actually practiced.

Social and political disorder marked most of this period. For a few years the new government unsuccessfully attempted to consolidate its power. Then from 1916 to 1927 China was politically fragmented with warlords and cliques of warlords ruling their own provinces or regions. In 1926–27 Jiang Jieshi (Chiang Kaishek, 1888–1975), the leader of the Nationalist Party (Goumindang), launched a "Northern Expedition," defeating some warlords and making alliances with others. He then established a Nationalist government, which lasted on the mainland until 1949 (and subsequently on the island of Taiwan). The years from 1927 to 1949, however, were almost as turbulent as those before. Not only were a number of warlords still largely independent, but the Communist Party had control of parts of the country, and after 1931 the Japanese steadily encroached on Chinese territory. From 1937 to 1945 China and Japan were engaged in full-scale war.

The early twentieth century was nevertheless a time of intense intellectual excitement and rapid social and economic change. The old order based on Confucian ideas was torn apart. The classically educated gentry lost their means of gaining office with the abolition of the civil service examinations and the collapse of the monarchy. Modern universities, started in the last years of the Qing, began to produce a new type of intellectual who was deeply concerned with China's fate and attracted to Western ideas ranging from science and democracy to communism and anarchism. Many young people went abroad to study in Japan, Europe, or America. On May 4, 1919, college students and their supporters protested Japan's imperialist advances and their own government's weakness, arousing in the process the patriotic and reformist spirit of a generation of young people. These "May Fourth" intellectuals called for reforms in the family system and the government and the redistribution of economic and political power. Scholars now began to doubt the validity of established views of Chinese history and began studying subjects such as class struggles, power politics, and folklore. Writers imitated Western forms of poetry and fiction and started writing in the vernacular rather than the classical language that had formerly been the mark of the educated man. Widely circulated periodicals brought this new language and these new ideas to literate people throughout the country.

During the early twentieth century, Western-style, capitalist enterprises began to make headway within the Chinese economy. The disruption of the European economy caused by World War I proved especially advantageous to China. A few cities, especially Shanghai, Canton, Tianjin, and Hankou, developed into industrial centers where thousands of people were employed in factories. One of the highest priorities of the Nationalist government was to strengthen the economy, and it undertook measures to modernize the banking, currency, and taxation systems, as well as to improve transportation and communication facilities. Another result of industrialization, however, was union organization and strikes. The greatest of these strikes took place in Shanghai in 1925. Banks and schools closed, 150,000 people stayed away from work, and foreign goods were boycotted in protest against the killing and injuring of strikers by the foreign-controlled International Settlement police.

The development of a small, Westernized, urban elite and urban proletariat in some ways left China more fragmented than ever before, since the vast majority of the peasants remained tied to the countryside and traditional ways of earning a living. Illiterate peasants were little affected by new Western ideas communicated through classroom lectures, magazines, and translated books. Moreover, during the Republican period the standard of living in the countryside stagnated because of the disruption and exploitation by warlords, international economic problems, and continued population growth. By 1930 the population on China had probably reached more than 500 million. The pressure on available land was intensified by the collapse of some local industries, such as silk raising and cotton weaving, due to foreign competition. The government and private philanthropic organizations made attempts to raise the level of rural education, create facilities for credit, encourage modern enterprises, form peasant associations, and so on, but gains were usually limited to small areas and short periods of time. Thus, the Nationalist government remained closely tied to the urban and Westernized sections of the population. At the same time the Communist Party, after 1935 under the leadership of Mao Zedong (1893–1976) and settled in Yan'an in Northwest China, was concentrating on land reform and winning the support of the rural population.

In Part VII selections have been chosen for two reasons: some depict aspects of the major social transformations of this brief period; others provide new kinds of evidence on traditional aspects of Chinese culture and social organization. The early twentieth century saw many new types and forms of written communication. Newspapers and magazines published articles aimed at a broader audience than most previous writing. Western influence in literature led to greater psychological realism in fiction and attempts to portray emotions not previously probed in depth. At the same time there was an upsurge of interest in the lives of the less privileged. Men began to describe the plight of factory hands, slave girls, and tenant farmers with more empathy than before. A semischolarly interest in folklore studies developed, leading to the recording of the habits and beliefs of elements of the population that educated men had hardly noticed before. Because of the abundance of these kinds of sources, many topics about which only indirect inferences could be made for earlier eras can be examined in some depth and complexity for the early twentieth century.

Nevertheless, the writing of the Republican period must also be used with care. Authors who wrote about ordinary people were more influenced by modern, Western ideas than those they were describing, creating a cultural gap between them and their subjects not totally unlike that between Westerners and Chinese (though naturally not as great). Moreover, the passions for reform and desire for change which motivated so much of the writing of the period gives even many descriptive pieces strongly polemical tones. Thus, many of these selections should be read on two levels: as depictions of the social conditions and way of life of those who still did not write much, and also as personal accounts expressing the concerns and values of the new intellectuals.

73

LIANG QICHAO ON HIS TRIP TO AMERICA

The young Liang Qichao (1873–1929) was closely associated with the reformer Kang Youwei (1858–1927). In 1898, when Kang's patron, the Guangxu emperor, was ousted by the empress dowager, Kang and Liang fled to Japan. There Liang became a prolific journalist. His writings, smuggled back into China, introduced Chinese readers to the world of ideas then current outside China.

In 1903 Liang traveled to North America, spending two months in Canada and five in the United States. Liang looked at American society with one question foremost in his mind: In what ways might America provide models for China in its quest to become strong and modern? Although in favor of democratic institutions, he did not see the American republican system as appropriate to China. He was particularly discouraged by the ways Chinese had organized themselves in Chinatowns in America. In the following excerpts from his account of his trip, Liang discusses both what he saw and what he read in the U.S. press.

NEW YORK

Uncivilized people live underground, half-civilized people live on the surface, and civilized people live above the ground. Those who live on surface usually live in one- or two-story houses. . . . Some houses in Beijing have entrances going down several stone steps, almost as if going underground. In New York, buildings of ten to twenty stories are not rare, and the tallest reaches thirty-three stories. This can truly be called above the ground. But ordinary residential buildings in big cities in America also have one or two basements, and so are both above and below ground.

Everywhere in New York the eye confronts what look like pigeon coops, spiderwebs, and centipedes; in fact these are houses, electric wires, and trolley cars.

New York's Central Park extends from 71st Street to 123d Street [in fact, 59th to 110th], with an area about equal to the International Settlement and French Concession in Shanghai. Especially on days of rest it is crowded with carriages and people jostling together. The park is in the middle of the city; if it were changed into a commercial area, the land would sell for three or four times the annual revenue of the Chinese government. From the Chinese point of view this may be called throwing away money on useless land and regrettable. The total park area in New York is 7,000 [Chinese] acres, the largest of any city in the world; London is second with 6,500 acres. Writers on city administration all agree that for a busy metropolis not to have appropriate parks is harmful to public health and morals. Now that I have come to New York, I am convinced. One day without going to the park leaves me muddled in mind and spirit.

Every day streetcars, elevated trains, subway trains, horse carriages, automobiles, and bicycles go clitter-clatter above and below, banging and booming to left and right, rumbling and ringing in front and behind. The mind is confused and the soul is shaken. People say that those who live in New York for a long time must have sharper eyes than ordinary people or else they would have to stand at intersections all day, not daring to take a step.

POVERTY

New York is the most prosperous city in the world, and also the bleakest. Let me briefly describe New York's darker side.

Anti-Oriental agitators criticize the Chinese above all for their uncleanness. From what I have seen of New York, the Chinese are not the dirtiest. In streets where Italians and Jews live, in the summer old women and young wives, boys and girls, take stools and sit outside their doors, clogging the street. Their clothing is shabby, their appearance wretched. These areas are not accessible by streetcar and even horse-drawn carriages seldom go there. Tourists are always coming to see how they live. From the outside there is building after multistoried building, but inside each building dozens of families are tenants. Over half of the apartments have no daylight or ventilation, and gas lights burn day and night. When you enter, the foul smell assaults your nose. Altogether, in New York about 230,000 people live in such conditions.

According to statistics for 1888, on Houston and Mulberry streets (where most of the people are Italians, with some Germans, Chinese, and Jews), the death rate was 35 per thousand, and 139 per thousand for children under five. In comparison, the overall death rate for New York was 26 per thousand, so the hardship of these poor people can be imagined. These rates, it is said, are due to the lack of air and light where they live. Another statistician says there are 37,000 rented apartments in New York, in which over 1,200,000 people live. Such dwellings are not only unhealthful but also harmful to morality. According to a statistician again, of the 483 people living in one building on a certain street in New York, in one year 102 people committed crimes. So great is the influence of these conditions.

"Crimson mansions reek of wine and meat, while on the road lie frozen bones. Rich and poor but a foot apart; sorrows too hard to relate." So goes Du Fu's poem [Tang dynasty]. I have witnessed such things myself in New York. According to statistics of the socialists, 70 percent of the entire national wealth of America is in the hands of 200,000 rich people, and the remaining 30 percent belongs to 79,800,000 poor. Thus the rich people in America are truly rich, and this so-called wealthy class constitutes no more than one fourhundredth of the population. It can be compared with one hundred dollars being divided among 400 people, with one person getting seventy dollars and the remaining thirty dollars being divided among 399 people, each getting a little over seven cents. How strange, how bizarre! This kind of phenomenon is seen in all civilized countries, particularly in big cities, [but] New York and London are the most notorious. The unequal distribution of wealth has reached this extreme. I look at the slums of New York and think with a sigh that socialism cannot be avoided.

J. P. MORGAN

This afternoon I went to visit Morgan. Morgan has been called the king of trusts and the Napoleon of the business world. I had no business to discuss with him, but was led by curiosity to meet this man whose magical power is the greatest in America. All his life he has only received guests and never called on others. Even presidents and prime ministers, if they need his help in their nations' financial matters, come to consult him and do not expect him to visit them. I was also told that his appointments are limited to one to five minutes each. Even extremely important problems can be decided in this briefest span of time, so far without error. His energy and acumen are truly unrivaled. I wrote a letter two days ago expressing my wish to request a five-minute conversation. At the appointed time, I went to his Wall Street office to visit him. There were scores of visitors in his receiving room, who were led to see him one by one; no one exceeded five minutes. As I had nothing to ask of him and did not want to waste his precious time, I went in and talked with him for only three minutes. He gave me a word of advice: The outcome of any venture depends on preparations made ahead of time; once it is started, its success or failure is already decided and can no longer be altered. This is the sole motto for his success in life, and I was deeply impressed.

THE INDUSTRIAL TRUST

In New York City at the turn of the century, a monster was created called the "trust." This monster was born in New York, but its power had spread to all of the United States and is speeding over the whole world. In essence, this monster, whose power far exceeds that of Alexander the Great or Napoleon, is the one and only sovereign of the twentieth-century world. For years I have wanted to find out its true nature; now in New York, I finally have the opportunity. . . .

The origins of the trust can be traced to the Oil Trust of 1882, which was the personal creation of [John D.] Rockefeller, known to the world as the petroleum king. Then in 1883, the Cotton Oil Trust was formed, in 1886 the Bread Trust, and in 1887 the Sugar Refining Trust. Their profits were conspicuous and startled all the world. Thenceforth the whole country became crazed about

trusts, until today almost 80 percent of the capital of the entire United States is under the control of trusts. The United States today is the premier capitalist nation in the world, and American capital amounts to almost half that of the entire world. Thus somewhat less than half of the world's total capital is now in the hands of this tiny number of trust barons. Alas! How strange! How amazing!

In sum, the trust is the darling of the twentieth century, and certainly cannot be destroyed by human effort, as is recognized by all of even the slightest learning. From now on, domestic trusts will grow into international trusts, and the nation that will be most severely victimized will surely be China. It is clear that we cannot look at this problem as if observing a fire from the opposite shore.

LYNCHING

Americans have an unofficial form of punishment known as "lynching" with which to treat blacks. Such a phenomenon is unimaginable among civilized countries. It started with a farmer named Lynch. Because he had been offended by a black, he suspended him from a tree to wait for the police officers to arrive, but the black man died before they came. So his name has been used for this ever since. Recently the common practice is burning people to death. Whenever a black has committed an offense a mob will be directly gathered and burn him without going through the courts.

Had I only been told about this and not been to America myself I would not have believed that such cruel and inhuman acts could be performed in broad daylight in the twentieth century. During the ten months I was in America I counted no less than ten-odd accounts of this strange business in the newspapers. At first I was shocked, but have become accustomed to reading about it and no longer consider it strange. Checking the statistics on it, there have been an average of 157 such private punishments each year since 1884. Hah! When Russia killed a hundred and some score Jews, the whole world considered it savage. But I do not know how to decide which is worse, America or Russia.

To be sure there is something despicable about the behavior of blacks. They would die nine times over without regret if they could possess a white woman's flesh. They often rape them at night in the forest and then kill them in order to silence them. Nine out of ten lynchings are for this, and it is certainly something to be angry about. Still, why does the government allow wanton lynchings to go unpunished even though there is a judiciary? The reason is none other than preconceived opinions about race. The American Declaration of Independence says that people are all born free and equal. Are blacks alone not people? Alas, I now understand what it is that is called "civilization" these days!

LIBRARIES

The various university libraries I have seen do not have people who retrieve books [from the stacks], but let students go and get them on their own. I was amazed. At the University of Chicago, I asked the head of the library whether or not books were lost this way. He answered that about two hundred volumes were lost every year, but hiring several people to supervise the books would cost more than this small number of books and, further, would inconvenience the students. So it is not done. In general, books are lost mostly during the two weeks before examinations because students steal them to prepare for examinations, and many of them are afterwards returned. In this can be seen the general level of public morality. Even a small thing like this is something Orientals could not come close to learning to do in a hundred years.

CHINESE FLAWS

From what has been discussed above, the weaknesses of the Chinese people can be listed as follows:

1. Our character is that of clansmen rather than citizens. Chinese social organization is based on family and clan as the unit rather than on the individual, what is called "regulating one's family before ruling the country." . . . In my opinion, though the power of self-government of the Aryans of the West was developed earlier, our Chinese system of local self-government was just as good. Why is it that they could form a nation-state and we could not? The answer is that what they developed was the city system of self-government, while we developed a clan system of self-government. . . . That Chinese can be clansmen but cannot be citizens, I came to believe more strongly after traveling in North America. . . .

2. We have a village mentality and not a national mentality. I heard Roosevelt's speech to the effect that the most urgent task for the American people is to get rid of the village mentality, by which he meant people's feelings of loyalty to their own town and state. From the point of view of history, however, America has been successful in exercising a republican form of government precisely because this local sentiment was there at the start, and so it cannot be completely faulted. But developed to excess it becomes an obstacle to nation building. . . . We Chinese have developed it too far. How could it be just the San Francisco Chinese? It is true everywhere at home, too. . . .

3. We can accept only despotism and cannot enjoy freedom. . . . When I look at all the societies of the world, none is so disorderly as the Chinese community in San Francisco. Why? The answer is freedom. The character of the Chinese in China is not superior to those of San Francisco, but at home they are governed by officials and restrained by fathers and elder brothers. The situation of the Chinese of Southeast Asia would seem different from those in China; but England, Holland, and France rule them harshly, ordering the breakup of assemblies of more than ten people, and taking away all freedoms. This is even more severe than inside China, and so they are docile. It is those who live in North America and Australia who enjoy the same degree of freedom under law as Westerners. In towns where there are few of them, they cannot gather into a force and their defects are not so apparent. But in San Francisco, which leads

the list of the free cities with the largest group of Chinese living in the same place, we have seen what the situation is like. . . .

With such country men, would it be possible to practice the election system? . . . To speak frankly, I have not observed the character of Chinese at home to be superior to those in San Francisco. On the contrary, I find their level of civilization far inferior to those in San Francisco. . . . Even if there are some Chinese superior to those in San Francisco, it is just a small matter of degree; their lack of qualification for enjoying freedom is just the same. . . .

Now, freedom, constitutionalism, and republicanism mean government by the majority, but the overwhelming majority of the Chinese people are like [those in San Francisco]. If we were to adopt a democratic system of government now, it would be nothing less than committing national suicide. Freedom, constitutionalism, and republicanism would be like hempen clothes in winter or furs in summer; it is not that they are not beautiful, they are just not suitable for us. We should not be bedazzled by empty glitter now; we should not yearn for beautiful dreams. To put it in a word, the Chinese people of today can only be governed autocratically; they cannot enjoy freedom. I pray and yearn, I pray only that our country can have a Guanzi, a Shang Yang,* a Lycurgus, a Cromwell alive today to carry out harsh rule, and with iron and fire to forge and temper our countrymen for twenty, thirty, even fifty years. After that we can give them the books of Rousseau and tell them about the deeds of Washington.

4. We lack lofty objectives. . . . This is the fundamental weakness of us Chinese. . . . The motives of Europeans and Americans are not all the same, but in my estimation the most important are their love of beauty, concern for social honor, and the idea of the future in their religion. These three are at the root of the development of West-

ern spiritual civilization, and are what we Chinese lack most. . . .

There are many other ways in which the Chinese character is inferior to that of Westerners; some happened to impress me so that I recorded them, but others I have forgotten. Let me now list several that I noted down, in no particular order:

Westerners work only eight hours a day and rest every Sunday. Chinese stores are open every day from seven in the morning to eleven or twelve at night, but though shopkeepers sit erect there all day, day in and day out, without rest, they still fail to get as rich as the Westerners. And the work they do is not comparable to the Westerners' in quantity. Why? In any kind of work the worst thing is to be fatigued. If people work all day, all year they are bound to be bored; when they are bored they become tired, and once they are tired everything goes to waste. Resting is essential to human life. That the Chinese lack lofty goals must be due to their lack of rest.

American schools average only 140 days of study a year, and five or six hours every day. But for the same reason as before, Westerners' studies are superior to those of the Chinese.

A small Chinese shop often employs several or more than a dozen people. In a Western shop, usually there are only one or two employees. It may be estimated that one of them does the same amount of work that it takes three of us to do. It is not that the Chinese are not diligent, they are simply not intelligent.

To rest on Sunday is wonderful. After each six days, one has renewed energy. A person's clarity of spirit depends on this. The Chinese are muddleheaded. We need not adopt their Sunday worship, but we should have a program of rest every ten days.

When more than a hundred Chinese are gathered in one place, even if they are solemn and quiet, there are bound to be four kinds of noise: the most frequent is coughing, next come yawning, sneezing, and blowing the nose. During speeches I have tried to listen unobtrusively, and these four noises are constant and ceaseless. I have

* Guanzi and Shang Yang were both political reformers of the first millennium B.C., remembered for strengthening the power of the ruler in an autocratic, non-Confucian way.

also listened in Western lecture halls and theaters; although thousands of people were there, I heard not a sound. In Oriental buses and trolleys there are always spittoons, and spitters are constantly making a mess. American vehicles seldom have spittoons, and even when they do they are hardly used. When Oriental vehicles are on a journey of more than two or three hours, more than half of the passengers doze off. In America, even on a full day's journey, no one tries to sleep. Thus can be seen the physical differences between Orientals and Westerners. . . .

On the sidewalks on both sides of the streets in San Francisco (vehicles go in the middle of the street), spitting and littering are not allowed, and violators are fined five dollars. On New York trolleys, spitting is prohibited and violators are fined five hundred dollars. Since Chinese are such messy and filthy citizens, no wonder they are despised.

When Westerners walk, their bodies are erect and their heads up. We Chinese bow at one command, stoop at a second, and prostrate ourselves at a third. The comparison should make us ashamed.

When Westerners walk their steps are always hurried; one look and you know that the city is full of people with business to do, as though they cannot get everything done. The Chinese on the other hand walk leisurely and elegantly, full of pomp and ritual—they are truly ridiculous. You can recognize a Chinese walking toward you on the street from a distance of several hundred feet, and not only from his short stature and yellow face.

Westerners walk together like a formation of geese; Chinese are like scattered ducks.

When Westerners speak, if they are addressing one person, then they speak so one person can hear; if they are addressing two people, they make two people hear; similarly with ten and with hundreds, thousands, and tens of thousands. The volume of their voices is adjusted appropriately. In China, if several people sit in a room to talk, they sound like thunder. If thousands are gathered in a lecture hall, the [speaker's] voice is like a mosquito. When Westerners converse, if A has not finished, B does not interrupt. With a group of Chinese, on the other hand, the voices are all disorderly; some famous scholars in Beijing consider interrupting to be a sign of masterfulness—this is disorderliness in the extreme. Confucius said, "Without having studied the *Book of Songs* one cannot speak; without having studied the rites, one cannot behave." My friend Xu Junmian also said, "Chinese have not learned to walk and have not learned to speak." This is no exaggeration. Though these are small matters, they reflect bigger things.

Translated by R. David Arkush and Leo O. Lee

74

RIDDING CHINA OF BAD CUSTOMS

Intellectuals concerned with China's military weakness often suspected that its roots lay deep in China's culture and social customs. In their desire to strengthen China, many campaigned to bring an end to customs which, when compared to Western customs, seemed uncivilized and debilitating. At the end of the nineteenth and the beginning of the twentieth century, three of the customs that attracted particular reformist zeal were footbinding, opium smoking, and the sale of girls as bondservants.

Footbinding began to spread in the Song dynasty and was widely practiced throughout the Ming and Qing. Girls of five to eight would have their feet tightly bound until the four small toes were turned under and the heel and arch compressed. A few scholars in the eighteenth century attacked this practice, but it was not until 1895 that the first anti-footbinding society was established in Shanghai. Soon similar societies were established in other cities. The first of the two pieces below relating to footbinding are the rules of such a society in Hunan. The second is an address by the early woman activist Qiu Jin (1875–1907), devoted both to the cause of overthrowing the Manchus and to women's liberation. She left her husband in 1903 to study in Japan, where she wore men's clothing and learned to make bombs. She returned in 1906 and the next year was executed for her role in an abortive nationalist uprising.

Opium smoking made enormous inroads into Chinese culture during the nineteenth century. By the end of the century, addiction was prevalent among all classes and opium was the largest item of interprovincial trade. In 1905 the Chinese government began a serious effort to eliminate the use of opium. Plans were made to suppress domestic production and an agreement was signed with Great Britain to end importation of opium. Retail trade was to be regulated, and addicts licensed to receive decreasing amounts of the drug. Unlicensed users were to be arrested. Local gentry organized anti-opium societies to spread propaganda against opium and support government programs. The third piece given below is an article from a 1907 Yunnan newspaper aimed at arousing support for these and even more aggressive measures.

Interest in social reform continued through the 1920s and 1930s. The last piece given here is from a 1920 issue of the popular Women's Magazine. *The author, a man, tries to convince his women readers that indenturing young girls as maids is wrong and that they should find ways to end the practice, a practice Westerners regularly likened to slavery.*

ANTI-FOOTBINDING SOCIETY OF HUNAN: RULES AND REGULATIONS ON MARRIAGE

1. The purpose of organizing this society is to provide opportunities for members to arrange marriages for their children so that girls who do not bind their feet will not become social outcasts. For this reason, society members must register the names and ages of all their children, and this information will be made available to all members in their selection of mates for their children.

2. Every member is entitled to make selections among the registered children. However, marriages with nonmembers' families are allowed if the young ladies do not have bound feet.

3. In selecting mates for their children, members must observe strict compatibility of age and generation. Furthermore, no match can be made unless both families agree to it. No member is allowed to coerce, intimidate, or use any other forms of undesirable persuasion in arranging a marriage.

4. Since society members have come from all parts of Hunan province, marriages can be arranged between families situated very far apart. The society encourages men of vision and determination to willingly send their daughters to distant places to be married.

5. A matchmaker may be engaged to arrange the marriage contract. Local customs and rituals may be followed regarding the exchange of gifts. The society suggest that frugality and simplicity be observed by all members, regardless of how wealthy they are. Furthermore, the bride's family is not allowed to demand wedding gifts from the groom.

6. Similarly, in preparing the bride's dowry, the society recommends frugality and simplicity. The groom's family should still observe all the courtesies and should not vent their dissatisfaction with the dowry by ill-treatment of the bride.

7. The marriage ceremony should be discarded because ancient rituals are no longer suitable for today. However, members are allowed to follow the commonly accepted rituals and ceremonies of the Qing dynasty because sometimes, for the sake of expediency, we have to do what others do. However, the society recommends that members be guided by frugality and simplicity.

8. The clothing worn by members' daughters should conform with the accepted style. However, their footwear should conform to the style of their brothers. There should be no exceptions, because other styles of footwear may be shocking and offensive to other society members, thus injuring the girl's chances for marriage.

9. If people want to have worthy daughters, then they must promote women's education. If men want their wives to be worthy, then they must donate money to establish local women's schools. The size of the school is determined by the amount of the contribution. By helping other people's daughters learn, one also helps one's own wife because only after women's education has been popularized can the foundations of a marriage be solid.

10. The above rules have been written one by one in a very simple and lucid style so they can be easily understood by everyone. If anyone feels he cannot follow any of them, he should not join the society. Furthermore, we urge all applicants to study these rules carefully to avoid future regrets.

AN ADDRESS TO TWO HUNDRED MILLION FELLOW COUNTRYWOMEN
by Qiu Jin

Alas! The greatest injustice in this world must be the injustice suffered by our female population of two hundred million. If a girl is lucky enough to have a good father, then her childhood is at least tolerable. But if by chance her father is an ill-tempered and unreasonable man, he may curse her birth: "What rotten luck: another useless thing." Some men go as far as killing baby girls while most hold the opinion that "girls are eventually someone else's property" and treat them with coldness and disdain. In a few years, without thinking about whether it is right or wrong, he forcibly binds his daughter's soft, white feet with white cloth so that even in her sleep she cannot find comfort and relief until the flesh becomes rotten and the bones broken. What is all this misery for? Is it just so that on the girl's wedding day friends and neighbors will compliment him, saying, "Your daughter's feet are really small"? Is that what the pain is for?

But that is not the worst of it. When the time for marriage comes, a girl's future life is placed in the hands of a couple of shameless matchmakers and a family seeking rich and powerful in-laws. A match can be made without anyone ever inquiring whether the prospective bridegroom is honest, kind, or educated. On the day of the marriage the girl is forced into a red and green bridal sedan chair, and all this time she is not allowed to breathe one word about her future. After her marriage, if the man doesn't do her any harm, she is told that she should thank Heaven for her good fortune. But if the man is bad or he ill-treats her, she is told that her marriage is retribution for some sin committed in her previous existence. If she complains at all or tries to reason with her husband, he may get angry and beat her. When other people find out they will criticize, saying, "That woman is bad; she doesn't know how to behave like a wife." What can she do? When a man dies, his wife must mourn him for three years and never remarry. But if the woman dies, her husband only needs to tie his queue with blue thread. Some men consider this to be ugly and don't even do it. In some cases, three days after his wife's death, a man will go out for some "entertainment." Sometimes, before seven weeks have passed, a new bride has already arrived at the door. When Heaven created people it never intended such injustice because if the world is without women, how can men be born? Why is there no justice for women? We constantly hear men say, "The human mind is just and we must treat people with fairness and equality." Then why do they greet women like black slaves from Africa? How did inequality and injustice reach this state?

Dear sisters, you must know that you'll get nothing if you rely upon others. You must go out and get things for yourselves. In ancient times when decadent scholars came out with such nonsense as "men are exalted, women are lowly," "a virtuous woman is one without talent," and "the husband guides the wife," ambitious and spirited women should have organized and opposed them. When the second Chen ruler popularized footbinding, women should have challenged him if they had any sense of humiliation at all. . . . Men feared that if women were educated they would become superior to men, so they did not allow us to be educated. Couldn't the women have challenged the men and refused to submit? It seems clear now that it was we women who abandoned our responsibilities to ourselves and felt content to let men do everything for us. As long as we could live in comfort and leisure, we let men make all the decisions for us. When men said we were useless, we became useless; when they said we were incapable, we stopped questioning them even when our entire female sex had reached slave status. At the same time we were insecure in our good fortune and our physical comfort, so we did everything to please men. When we heard that men like small feet, we immediately bound them just to please them, just to keep our free meal tickets. As for their forbidding us to read and write, well, that was only too good to be true. We readily agreed. Think about it, sisters, can anyone enjoy such comfort and leisure without forfeiting dearly for it? It was only natural that men, with their knowledge, wisdom, and hard work, received the right to freedom while we became their slaves. And as slaves, how can we escape repression? Whom can we blame but ourselves since we have brought this on ourselves? I feel very sad talking about this, yet I feel that there is no need for me to elaborate since all of us are in the same situation.

I hope that we all shall put aside the past and work hard for the future. Let us all put aside our former selves and be resurrected as complete human beings. Those of you who are old, do not call yourselves old and useless. If your husbands want to open schools, don't stop them; if your good sons want to study abroad, don't hold them back. Those among us who are middle-aged, don't hold back your husbands lest they lose their ambition and spirit and fail in their work. After your sons are born, send them to schools. You must do the same for your daughters and, whatever you do, don't bind their feet. As for you young girls among us, go to school if you can. If not, read and study at home. Those of you who are rich, persuade your husbands to open schools, build factories, and contribute to charitable organizations. Those of you who are poor, work hard and help your husbands. Don't be lazy, don't eat idle rice. These are what I hope for you. You must know that when a country is near destruction, women cannot rely on the men any more because they aren't even able to protect themselves. If we don't take heart now and shape up, it will be too late when China is destroyed.

Sisters, we must follow through on these ideas!

Translated by Nancy Gibbs

MY OPINIONS ON BANNING OPIUM

An examination of the historical evidence shows that the evil of opium smoking has existed in the world for several thousand years and has plagued China for four or five centuries. It is closely connected with the strength or weakness of the country. Millions of our people lose their money, destroy their bodies, and waste their time because of addiction to opium. Thus whether China will survive depends on whether efforts to eradicate opium are successful. How well our current bans on opium work thus is crucially connected to our survival.

Fortunately, last year, on the 3rd of the eighth

month, a ban on opium was decreed. Since then the governors-general of each of the provinces have for the most part been energetically enforcing the ban. . . .

Opium smoking is the enemy of all of us. We have the physical and moral strength to do something about it and we should do everything we possibly can to rid ourselves of it, treating it like a noxious substance or infectious disease. It is simply because education is underdeveloped and our people ignorant that they seek a narcotic to escape from their troubles. We are late in doing something about this. Therefore everyone in our country, high and low, must look on this task as a matter of life and death, of saving people from water or fire, and not slack off for a moment.

The present ban only involves closing opium shops and prohibiting officials, soldiers, and government underlings [from smoking opium]. Other measures have been put off for another ten years. I have not heard anything on what the government will do during these ten years to eliminate addiction or wipe away this stain. (The announcement last year was too vague to be useful.) Those discussing these issues often advocate adopting the methods that have already proved effective in Taiwan, but if these laws are issued, their success will depend entirely on the effectiveness of the government organs that administer them. It will depend on the new crop of policemen. The success of Taiwan's ban on opium resulted from the large number of lower-level administrators they had to carry it out. It is definitely difficult not to have some doubts about whether our police could carry out such a heavy responsibility. Thus for the government today to have any hope of success in getting the law banning opium enforced without opposition, it must quickly take steps to reform provincial administration.

I have further goals in this essay. Suppressing opium is definitely not something that can be accomplished without a lot of work. The government naturally should have a variety of policies. But society is also inextricably bound up with this, and social leaders should immediately do all they can to aid the government in this matter, in the ways listed below.

There have always been only two effective ways to change the people's habits, persuasion and punishment, or as the saying has it, "Warn by mentioning rewards, exhort with a show of force." Given the circumstances, the government now has to rely more on punishment than persuasion. Thus many of the tasks of the more positive approach fall to society.

Let me list the steps the government and society should take:

1. The provincial government must be quickly reformed to get rid of current inefficiencies and make possible effective enforcement.
2. The law on opium should include both persuasion and punishment. The morality of people of middling or lower abilities is shaped by outside pressures, therefore it is right to apply pressure.
3. Local self-government should be instituted to revive the people and shake up their old habits of thought.
4. Inspect all fields to prevent the cultivation of the opium poppy. But raise knowledge of agricultural science so people will know the profits to be had from other crops and be able to turn to them instead of opium as naturally as water flows downward.

The above fall under the purview of the government.

1. Those who lose their jobs because of the ban on opium should be given aid or help.
2. Many lecturing societies should be set up to teach orally those with low levels of education. Most of those in the lowest levels of society are illiterate or nearly so.
3. Public amusement centers should be set up for the relaxation of workers and craft centers to teach vocational skills. Today the majority of those who smoke opium come from the lower classes. They take to it because it is

a way to relax when extremely tired from work or because they are idle.
4. We must urgently foster in people the desire to save and avoid wasting time.

The above all fall under the purview of local society.

The poison of opium smoking is a catastrophe that did not exist in the past, thus the steps needed to ban it are also unprecedented. Our future survival and honor depend on what is done. Thus everyone in our country, high and low, must carry the program out with the utmost determination and persistence, not with the old lackadaisical attitude. This is my fervent hope.

Translated by Patricia Ebrey

ON FREEING SLAVE GIRLS

Why am I writing this essay? Because I believe that the Chinese institution of slave girls is bad. First of all, slave girls are not treated like people, but tortured as if they were animals; in fact, some are treated even worse than animals. These slave girls have no one to tell their troubles to and no place to seek help. Looking at this from a humanitarian point of view, this institution is indeed wrong. Secondly, since their masters do not treat them as human beings, the slave girls themselves never learn to behave as such. They set out to take advantage of their masters in everything they do. When they go shopping, they often lose money; when they are told to work, they are lazy and cut corners, not caring if their laziness causes inconveniences for other people; and when they cook, they purposely waste fuel, rice, oil, and salt. In the end it is the masters who lose out. For these two reasons we can agree that the institution of slave girls must be abolished.

Nowadays people who are imbued with new ideas understand these arguments, so I need say no more. But their proposals tend to be too lofty, too general in scope, too detached from reality. Although their ideas make sense, they are difficult to carry out. The ideas I have put down in this essay, however, are not merely empty talk, for they could easily be put into practice!

Why do I say that many people's ideas are too lofty and general? Nowadays people with new ideas are all talking about women's liberation, the liberation of all women. Isn't that too broad? There are already many independent women in our society who have no need to be liberated. Weaker, uneducated, and dependent women do need help and support in order to become self-reliant, but the help they need is not liberation. Women who do need liberation fall into the following three categories: (1) prostitutes, (2) concubines, and (3) slave girls. These women are virtually bound hand and foot by others. They have had their rights to freedom taken away from them, and their lives are often hard and bitter. In the name of humanity, how can we not first liberate these women whose lives are a living hell? Furthermore, if they are not liberated, not only will they themselves suffer, but many others will indirectly be made to suffer too. If we want to change our society, we must first liberate these women.

Since these three categories of people are different, our methods of liberating them should also be different. For example, it would be more difficult to liberate prostitutes and concubines, so in this essay I shall limit my discussions to how to liberate slave girls. I am not saying that prostitutes and concubines should not be liberated, nor even that their liberation can be delayed. But this essay is written for women with new ideas who I am hoping will carry out this liberation movement without help from men. In reality, it is easier for women to liberate slave girls than prostitutes and concubines, so we might as well begin with the simplest. . . .

Why should women liberate slave girls without help from men? Since both educated women and slave girls are females, women might be more sympathetic. Moreover, slave girls usually work for women, so the power to free them is in the hands of women, not men. Therefore, I suggest that this job should be done by women them-

selves. As I see it, the job can be divided into two stages: discontinuing buying slave girls, and freeing the ones already owned.

There are two ways to free slave girls. Concerning the slaves you own yourself, since you have the power to free them, do so immediately. For example, if I own a slave girl and I want to free her, I can go ahead and do so. Concerning the slaves you do not own, you must persuade others to liberate them. For example, if my mother, sister, or neighbors own any and I want them free, I must persuade the owner to free them. If they do not heed me, I must try again; if they still do not listen, I should try a third time, a fourth time. . . . Eventually I will reach my objective. These two ways are the only ways to liberate slave girls, and they can be carried out by everyone.

But what is to be done after they are given their freedom? This is indeed a great problem. In my opinion, the best course is to take them into your family as your daughters. You should send the younger girls to school to be educated, and in their after-school hours they should be taught to work around the house. They should be encouraged to do any work which they are fitted to do, which would benefit the whole family, and which would not injure their health. As for the older girls, you could arrange marriages for them, or if you keep them at home, you should teach them housework as well as the ways of the world. When they marry, you must be cautious and think of their happiness instead of the amount of money you will get. If you treat them like this, they will then treat you like real mothers and not want to be dishonest or take advantage of you. You should instruct the girls who have already acquired bad habits of cheating and not expect them to change their ways too readily. Sometimes punishment may be necessary as long as you are guided by your conscience. (In dealing with your own children, a certain amount of punishment is inevitable, but punishing them does not change the affection you feel for them.) In sum, we must treat liberated slave girls as our own daughters.

Some people have pointed out that servant girls once had parents who, because they needed money, sold them into slavery. No matter how sympathetic we feel toward them, it would be much better to return them to their natural parents without demanding that the money be returned. This idea sounds good but poses serious difficulties. First, more often than not, the parents of these slave girls have moved away and cannot be located. Second, if the parents have sold them once, can you feel assured that they would not sell them again? That would be no liberation at all. Therefore this method should only be used with extreme caution.

I have been discussing how to free servant girls and care for them after they gain their freedom. There is one more thing I must mention. I find that no matter what a thing is, if only one person does it, the majority consider it strange and opposition to it is enormous. But if the same thing is done by many people, others consider it perhaps worth doing and opposition is slight. Therefore I suggest that if women are to liberate slave girls, it would be best to organize a society. If all unite and work together then this would be a simple thing to do. The society might adopt these rules:

1. The society shall be called the Society to Free Slave Girls.
2. Members of the society must all be female.
3. The duty of each member is to free slave girls she owns and to persuade others to free ones she does not own.
4. The society has no other business.

From these rules we see how easy it would be. Organizing this society could be done with a minimum of red tape since members need only quietly assume their responsibilities. Furthermore, this type of liberation frees one girl at a time; therefore it is easier to carry out than mass liberation. Sincethe girls would continue to reside in their former masters' houses as members of the households, it would be quite easy to carry out.

Some people might say, "This is all very well and good, but what about the slave owners who are not so enlightened? Might they not refuse to free their slaves at your suggestion and maltreat them as usual anyway?"

I would answer, "I have no doubt cases like that will occur. But if four or five people out of every ten free their slaves after listening to me, I will consider my efforts to be half successful." Those who agree to this liberation with their mouths and not their hearts must be persuaded again and again; and if we can convert one or two of them, our success will increase by yet another ten to twenty percent. As for those people who cannot be persuaded, they will soon lose the respect of their peers. Everyone wants face, and I am sure they will change their minds under the pressure of public opinion. Furthermore, the society should investigate the treatment and living conditions of freed slaves and attempt to raise the girls' level of consciousness about themselves and about the world around them. If these three steps are carried out simultaneously, how can the movement not succeed?

I am writing this essay in the hopes that others might carry out my ideas. Originally I intended to launch this movement myself, but then I realized that this society to free slave girls should be organized by women themselves. Since I myself do not own any slave girls, I have none to free. My duty is to write this article and hope that modern educated women will carry this matter to its conclusion.

Translated by Nancy Gibbs

75

RURAL EDUCATION

By the nineteenth century, village schools of the type portrayed in selection 66, "The Village Headman and the New Teacher," were commonplace throughout China. Those who could possibly afford to do so sent boys to school for three or four years, generally from about age seven to age eleven, when the boys were not yet old enough to do much productive work. Within three or four years, a student could learn arithmetic and enough characters to read contracts, shop signs, and stories written in the vernacular language. And there was the added attraction that a child who showed extraordinary talent might somehow rise through the civil service examination system. After the abolition of the examinations in 1905, the curriculum of many schools was modernized to include training in science, mathematics, and foreign languages. A major motivation for the change was that those who mastered modern subjects came to have the best prospects; they might gain government scholarships for study abroad, especially in Japan, or at least find jobs in the emerging modern sectors of the coastal cities.

Below is an account written for a teacher's magazine by You Ziyi about his experiences introducing modern subjects in a small rural school in the vicinity of Shanghai in 1907–8. You was looking back on his experience after twenty years and does not hide his nostalgia for the place and time. Still, from his description something of what it must have been like to be a student or a teacher in such a school can be discerned. One can also see some of the cultural differences that had come to separate those with modern educations from those without.

The events described here took place in a coastal area east of Shanghai at the end of the Guangxu period [1875–1909]. In the fall, I was notified by the ministry of education to take a post in a private rural elementary school, one which still exists. . . . The principal was an old gentleman from the area who had once been the teacher of one of my colleagues at the ministry. Besides him, there was a teacher who had graduated from the ministry's normal school and had come to the school ahead of me. Thus, one was my senior and the other was my student; I filled in the position between them to form a complete teacher-student relationship. . . .

The school building was to the left of a temple. As a matter of fact, it had been converted from half of the temple.... More than thirty students were in the grade school, each of the four grades having only one class, while only six or seven students were in the extension school. The normal-school graduate took charge of most of the grade-school courses, and I taught one or two subjects, too. For the extension school, the principal and I took care of most of the teaching duties. The old gentleman taught courses like Chinese, history, and geography, while I taught natural science, mathematics, English, and so on. Other courses like drawing, crafts, music, and gymnastics were partly taken care of by the normal-school graduate, and partly combined with the grade-school classes.

Why did the students in a rural extension school have to learn English? At the time, I wondered about that, too. The reason was the environment. There was a need for it, since the place was no more than thirty or forty *li* away from Shanghai. Many successful figures from this area had struck it rich in Shanghai. In fact, the founder of the school had been a local poor boy before he went to Shanghai and made his fortune by working there. His first fortune came from undertaking a task for a foreigner. Therefore, local people with a little ambition, both parents and children, all wanted to go to Shanghai to pursue their careers. And they always had to know at least a few sentences of some foreign language in order to have a better chance, regardless of whether they aimed at business or industry.

At the very first English class, I asked the students about their ambitions. Almost all of them answered with some goal in Shanghai. One of the students had an interesting answer: "I will first attend the extension school. But, as soon as there's a chance, I'll leave for Shanghai. One of my relatives works as chief cook there. He is now trying to get me a job as a waiter in a big foreign restaurant. To do this, won't I have to know some foreign language?" His father owned the North-South Grocery Store in the town. The little master of a store wanted to go to Shanghai to be a waiter in a foreign restaurant—isn't the temptation of a lucky strike amazingly great? His father often came to the school to chat, and his notions were similar to his son's.

The people there respected me very much because I was sent by the ministry, wore Western-style suits, and could teach their children the language which might someday lead them to acquire a great fortune. Probably they took me as a prototype of the foreign God of Wealth. Who knows! But, in fact, the English I taught was bookish....

Surprisingly, in the first-grade class there were two girls, even though during the Qing dynasty coeducation was prohibited. These two girls were comparatively older and one of them was already engaged to a student in the extension school. (In the countryside, children could be engaged as early as three or five years of age, so being engaged at the age of fourteen or fifteen was not at all unusual.) With some flexibility the old principal admitted the female students, disregarding the regulations. Although he was old, he always encouraged girls to go to school, and, fortunately, there was no one who knew the educational regulations. As long as the head of the school was respected in the community, he could do whatever he pleased. As Heaven was high and the emperor was far away, he did not have to worry about any interference, so long as he was trusted locally. The regulations set by the emperor were not as important as the trust of the local people.

Even for the curriculum of the school, we never followed the imperial regulations. The subject most emphasized in the Qing dynasty was the classics. The old principal himself was expert in them, but he knew that such recondite philosophy was really beyond the children. Therefore, all he offered for the first grade was a course in morality. Even in the extension school, we simply applied the most plausible and practical ideas of the classics to courses like Chinese or history. The local people never criticized the school curricula or activities because they trusted the old principal.

In rural areas up to that time, farmers had never dreamed of extracurricular activities or games after class. The sound of reading was expected from a school, but noise and shouting were taken as signs of naughtiness on the part of the children. How could they be so impolite to the teacher! Should anyone hear gleeful sounds, he would assume the teacher was absent. How could a teacher indulge the students that way!

To eliminate such an ingrained prejudice was not at all an easy job. Therefore, we started with some trial games. At first, we did nothing more than bounce a small rubber ball, and we did that only after class had been dismissed. Subsequently, the students became more and more interested in this. The old principal was no less spirited, and one day he brought a rubber ball filled with rushes. We then organized soccer teams and set up a goal made with bamboo poles on the vacant lot west of the school building. Thereafter, we played soccer before and after class every day.

Parents of some of the students came to the school frequently, and the old principal always explained honestly the importance of exercise: "By nature children want to play around. If we prohibit them from playing in public, they will play secretly anyway, which might be dangerous. In addition to the regular courses, they should be allowed to play. When playing a game, they should follow the rules. Besides, there is always a teacher supervising as an umpire. . . ." These were the best reasons for our extracurricular activities. We preached in this way, and the local farmers believed what we said. . . .

The founder of the school had established a rule limiting each meal to one dish of meat or fish and one kind of vegetable. He wanted frugality to be the fundamental principle of this school, fearing that the rural children would become modern good-for-nothings after they entered a modern school. . . . Together with the boarders, we sat around one table when we ate and usually had three huge dishes of food. The one in the middle had plenty of meat or fish, while the two on each side were full of the same kinds of vegetables. Vegetables in the countryside were, of course, the cheapest and freshest food. . . . I had lived at many schools in Shanghai, Wuxi, Nanjing, Hangzhou, and Wuhu. To summarize my experiences, the food of those schools was always so terrible that I would not eat it until I had to. Sometimes I had unpleasant feelings when the matter of dining was even mentioned. But the experience of eating at this rural elementary school was so good that I still feel like talking about it now. . . .

I taught the natural sciences, which at that time was called "physics." In the extension school, this course could be handled as in the regular senior grade schools, all the methods being found in school manuals. However, there was no such course as general science or local geography and history for grade schools, so I had to invent one. First, I divided the grade school into two groups, the advanced class being the third- and fourth-grade students and the elementary class being the first- and second-graders. I taught different topics in the same course at the same time. The materials were the common phenomena observed in that area. I did not confine myself to natural sciences, but also covered the basic notions of geography and history.

The school had very few specimens or pieces of laboratory equipment. At first, I had planned to make a large-scale purchase upon arrival at the school. However, this was not only impossible but actually unnecessary. When I set out from the ministry, I had already given thought to the situation. To supplement my own reference pictures, I asked the department of natural science at the ministry for a biconvex mirror, a set of dissecting instruments, and a few wide- and narrow-necked bottles. These constituted all the apparatus I had for the teaching of natural science. According to present prices, they probably cost me less than five dollars. After arriving at the school, I made a net for catching insects and small water creatures out of three feet of wire, one thin short bamboo stick, and one yard of white cloth.

The subjects of our study were the phenomena

observed in the vicinity. How do the white lentils climb up the bamboo fences beside the river bridge? Why is the pumpkin as big as the stone plinth while its flower is as small as a cup? Why does the pumpkin not sweeten until it is dried in the sunshine? These were questions arising from agriculture. There were not very many students in the extension school, which was very convenient for both indoor study and outdoor observation. Our footprints could be found in the cotton field every day. The flowers withered, the fruit grew, the fruit split, and the cotton floss appeared. Various results of observations were reported daily. The students brought some real things to school, together with many questions. The floss came out of the cotton fruit. What is the basic function of the floss for the cotton plant itself? How do human beings make use of the floss? These were typical questions.

What are the names of the water plants, the flowers, and the weeds growing beside the embankment and around the fields? How do they grow up by themselves while the pumpkins and the cotton trees need to be planted? What is the use of the wild flowers and weeds? What harm do they do? These were also the topics of our study. The countryfolk rarely paid attention to the relations between agricultural products and weeds. By investigating them, we found that they were very significant. Thus, research on root preservation and weeding methods became our major topic for quite some time. . . .

What are the dragonflies doing on the water surface? Why did the grasshoppers in the paddy field change from green to brown when the plants dried out? How do they breathe without noses? These are sample questions of our insect study. Inspired, the students caught some insects every day and brought them to the class with all kinds of questions. What are their names? How do they live? What are their advantages and disadvantages? (Advantages and disadvantages were judged by the insects' food and way of life.) The children were mostly motivated by curiosity; real issues of human interest were not their major concern. However, life and the history of life apparently were somewhat romantic. And, to approach the true issues of human interest through the romantic questions about life was much more appropriate for the youngsters. I tried this approach, and it proved to be much more interesting than dealing directly with the issues of interest to the adult world. . . .

In the little river behind the school building there were many aquatic animals. We caught some and kept them in a wide-mouthed bottle which I had brought from the ministry. This actually became a temporary aquarium. How do the fish swim. How do they manage to dive and surface? Since human beings drown if they fall into the water, how is it that fish stay alive in the water but die without it? The school was not far from the coast, and there was a coastal town which was a major market. Our study of the life of fish reminded us of the fish market on the sea. The students thus reported many phenomena which they had been observing since they were young, many of which were totally new to me. Not only did I teach them, they also taught me a lot. . . . What they reported were the local experiences and legends, and what I taught was the scientific knowledge stated in the books. Combining these two resources, we found some conclusions which we thought were more convincing. . . .

The students told me many legends about ghosts, spirits, and immortals. Although I took them to be fiction, the students deeply believed them to be true. The elimination of superstitions was not at all an easy task to begin. I might passively argue against superstitious legends, but how could a single mouth fight against the beliefs of thousands of people? A much better way was to actively encourage the students to study science. The scientific attitude would make them suspicious of everything and motivate them to seek a thorough solution to every problem, so that they would no longer stick stubbornly to superstitions. For this reason, I did not point out that their fairy tales were nonsense. Instead, I raised some questions to arouse their suspicion about the existence of the ghosts and immortals which they believed in. Moreover, I described the phenomena of gravity, combustion, and so on. I did not get into the issue of whether there are ghosts and gods or not, leaving it to their own future judgment. If I had had a long period of time to work at this, I probably would have been able to uproot the superstitions totally.

In the quiet countryside, we met only a few acquaintances every day. Thus, it was an unusual event when, one day, a tall, thin man with a beard came to visit our school. Not used to seeing visitors from other places, the rural children gathered around him so tightly he could hardly move. After greeting the guest, the principal realized that he was an education inspector sent by the provincial government. A diligent and enthusiastic inspector, he visited a rural school as secluded as ours in spite of how difficult it was to get to. At that moment, I was about to teach general science to the grade school class, so he entered the classroom with me. Standing in the corner, he listened through the entire class. . . .

The provincial education inspector invited the teachers and principals in the vicinity of the provincial capital to attend a meeting at which he evaluated every school in detail. Having a high opinion of our school, he especially extolled me for the general science class I had taught that day, saying that it had been one of the most successful classes in the whole county. He criticized an old teacher for misinterpreting one word in class. However, that old teacher, who was also present, looked the word up in the Kangxi Dictionary right there and proved himself to have been correct. Our principal said that although the old teacher might have no idea at all about modern knowledge and new teaching techniques, he was definitely learned in the classics and could not have made a mistake in interpreting words. The provincial education inspector indeed had undervalued him. Because of that event, the meeting ended in disharmony.

One night, a special messenger came from the ministry. Not knowing what had happened, we were taken by surprise. The Shanghai daily newspaper, which was available in the countryside, had recently reported that the empress dowager and the emperor were both seriously ill. But, since the newspaper was always at least one day getting to us, we had not heard of their deaths yet. Being near Shanghai, the ministry had telephones and was always well-informed. Hence, they already knew of the deaths one after the other. Informed of the proper rites for schools, they sent a special messenger to deliver a mimeographed notice to us, telling us to suspend classes, hang a piece of white cloth, bow three times every day to the north, and weep in mourning.

Early the next morning, the food manager brought the white cloth and hung it on the front gate of the school. We announced the suspension of classes after the students had come. We then removed all the desks and chairs in the grade school classroom to make a temporary hall for the ceremony. In order for so many students to perform the kowtowing ceremony, we needed several dozen kneeling cushions. The clever old principal went to the temple and borrowed all the rush kneeling mats used for religious rites. The mats on which old ladies sat to chant the name of Buddha suddenly became our devices for mourning the death of the empress dowager and the emperor. These kneeling mats were usually used only once a year. That year, however, they were in the spotlight for the second time shortly after they had been used—they certainly were lucky! Perfunctorily we performed the ceremony three times every day: the principal led and the students followed. At first when the students were asked to weep in mourning, they would suddenly burst into naive laughter. If that had happened at a government institution, it would have been regarded as extremely rude. However, in the far-off countryside, no one cared.

With the New Year's vacation approaching, it became time for final exams. I discussed with the old principal and the other teacher the idea of purchasing some rewards for the diligent students in order to encourage studying. We agreed, and during our spare time we went downtown to buy some colorful paper, pens, ink, and such at the stationery store. We tried to make the prizes as accessible as possible: any student who had tried hard in one or two subjects would get at least some reward. On the last day of class, we gave the prizes, which made everyone beam with smiles. In addition, I told the students in the extension school to write to me on the stationery during the vacation. They kept their promises, for I did indeed receive their letters after I returned home.

Translated by Jane Chen

76

MY OLD HOME

A major achievement of the intellectuals of the Republican period was the creation of a new literary genre, the modern short story. Western literature and literary theories were the stimulus for this activity, but very quickly Chinese writers turned from derivative imitations of Western stories to ones firmly rooted in Chinese experience.

"My Old Home" was written in 1921 by Lu Xun (1881–1936), the first important fiction writer of the twentieth century and widely considered the best writer of his generation. Sent to Japan on a government scholarship, Lu Xun studied medicine and read Western literature and philosophy. Returning to China in 1909, he taught and began his career as a writer. In 1920 he was offered a position in Beijing University and visited his old home to arrange for moving his mother there. This story concerns that trip and deals with one of the major problems of the new intellectuals: the difficulty they faced in overcoming ingrained class barriers so that they could communicate effectively with ordinary people neither educated nor modern.

Braving the bitter cold, I traveled more than seven hundred miles back to the old home I had left over twenty years before.

It was late winter. As we drew near my former home the day became overcast and a cold wind blew into the cabin of our boat, while all one could see through the chinks in our bamboo awning were a few desolate villages, void of any sign of life, scattered far and near under the somber yellow sky. I could not help feeling depressed.

Ah! Surely this was not the old home I had remembered for the past twenty years?

The old home I remembered was not in the least like this. My old home was much better. But if you asked me to recall its peculiar charm or describe its beauties, I had no clear impression, no words to describe it. And now it seemed this was all there was to it. Then I rationalized the matter to myself, saying: Home was always like this, and although it has not improved, still it is not so depressing as I imagine; it is only my mood that has changed, because I am coming back to the country this time with no illusions.

This time I had come with the sole object of saying goodbye. The old house our clan had lived in for so many years had already been sold to another family, and was to change hands before the end of the year. I had to hurry there before New Year's Day to say goodbye forever to the familiar old house, and to move my family to another place where I was working, far from my old home town.

At dawn on the second day I reached the gateway of my home. Broken stems of withered grass on the roof, trembling in the wind, made very clear the reason why this old house could not avoid changing hands. Several branches of our clan had probably already moved away, so it was unusually quiet. By the time I reached the house my mother was already at the door to welcome me, and my eight-year-old nephew, Hong'er, rushed out after her.

Though mother was delighted, she was also trying to hide a certain feeling of sadness. She told me to sit down and rest and have some tea, letting the removal wait for the time being. Hong'er, who had never seen me before, stood watching me at a distance.

But finally we had to talk about the removal. I said that rooms had already been rented elsewhere, and I had bought a little furniture; in addition it would be necessary to sell all the furniture in the house in order to buy more things. Mother agreed, saying that the luggage was nearly all packed, and about half the furniture that could not easily be moved had already been sold. Only it was difficult to get people to pay up.

"You must rest for a day or two, and call on our relatives, and then we can go," said mother.

"Yes."

"Then there is Runtu. Each time he comes here he always asks after you, and wants very much to see you again. I told him the probable date of your return home, and he may be coming any time."

At this point a strange picture suddenly flashed into my mind: a golden moon suspended in a deep blue sky and beneath it the seashore, planted as far as the eye could see with jade-green watermelons, while in their midst a boy of eleven or twelve, wearing a silver necklet and grasping a steel pitchfork in his hand, was thrusting with all his might at a *zha* which dodged the blow and escaped between his legs.

This boy was Runtu. When I first met him he was just over ten—that was thirty years ago, and at that time my father was still alive and the family well off, so I was really a spoilt child. That year it was our family's turn to take charge of a big ancestral sacrifice, which came round only once in thirty years, and hence was an important one. In the first month the ancestral images were presented and offerings made, and since the sacrificial vessels were very fine and there was such a crowd of worshipers, it was necessary to guard against theft. Our family had only one part-time laborer. (In our district we divide laborers into three classes: those who work all the year for one family are called full-timers; those who are hired by the day are called dailies; and those who work at New Year, during festivals, or when rents are being collected are called part-timers.) And since there was so much to be done, he told my father that he would send for his son Runtu to look after the sacrificial vessels.

When my father gave his consent I was overjoyed, because I had long since heard of Runtu and knew that he was about my own age, born in the intercalary month, and when his horoscope was told it was found that of the five elements that of earth was lacking, so his father called him Runtu (Intercalary Earth). He could set traps and catch small birds.

I looked forward every day to New Year, for New Year would bring Runtu. At last, when the end of the year came, one day mother told me that Runtu had come, and I flew to see him. He was standing in the kitchen. He had a round, crimson face and wore a small felt cap on his head and a gleaming silver necklet round his neck, showing that his father doted on him and, fearing he might die, had made a pledge with the gods and buddhas, using the necklet as a talisman. He was very shy, and I was the only person he was not afraid of. When there was no one else there, he would talk with me, so in a few hours we were fast friends.

I don't know what we talked of then, but I remember that Runtu was in high spirits, saying that since he had come to town he had seen many new things. The next day I wanted him to catch birds.

"Can't be done," he said. "It's only possible after a heavy snowfall. On our sands, after it snows, I sweep clear a patch of ground, prop up a big threshing basket with a short stick, and scatter husks of grain beneath. When the birds come there to eat, I tug a string tied to the stick, and the birds are caught in the basket. There are all kinds: wild pheasants, woodcocks, wood pigeons, 'blue-backs.' . . ."

Accordingly I looked forward very eagerly to snow.

"Just now it is too cold," said Runtu another time, "but you must come to our place in summer. In the daytime we'll go to the seashore to look for shells, there are green ones and red ones, besides 'scare-devil' shells and 'buddha's hands.' In the evening when dad and I go to see to the watermelons, you shall come too."

"Is it to look out for thieves?"

"No. If passersby are thirsty and pick a watermelon, folk down our way don't consider it as stealing. What we have to look out for are badgers, hedgehogs, and *zha*. When under the moonlight you hear the crunching sound made by the *zha* when it bites the melons, then you take your pitchfork and creep stealthily over. . . ."

I had no idea then what this thing called *zha* was—and I am not much clearer now for that matter—but somehow I felt it was something like a small dog, and very fierce.

"Don't they bite people?"

"You have a pitchfork. You go across, and when you see it you strike. It's a very cunning creature and will rush toward you and get away between your legs. Its fur is as slippery as oil. . . ."

I had never known that all these strange things existed: at the seashore there were shells all colors of the rainbow; watermelons were exposed to such danger, yet all I had known of them before was that they were sold in the greengrocer's.

"On our shore, when the tide comes in, there are lots of jumping fish, each with two legs like a frog. . . ."

Runtu's mind was a treasure-house of such strange lore, all of it outside the ken of my former friends. They were ignorant of all these things and, while Runtu lived by the sea, they like me could see only the four corners of the sky above the high courtyard wall.

Unfortunately, a month after New Year Runtu had to go home. I burst into tears and he took refuge in the kitchen, crying and refusing to come out, until finally his father carried him off. Later he sent me by his father a packet of shells and a few very beautiful feathers, and I sent him presents once or twice, but we never saw each other again.

Now that my mother mentioned him, this childhood memory sprang into life like a flash of lightning, and I seemed to see my beautiful old home. So I answered:

"Fine! And he—how is he?"

"He? . . . He's not at all well off either," said mother. And then, looking out of the door: "Here come those people again. They say they want to buy our furniture; but actually they just want to see what they can pick up. I must go and watch them."

Mother stood up and went out. The voices of several women could be heard outside. I called Hong'er to me and started talking to him, asking him whether he could write, and whether he would be glad to leave.

"Shall we be going by train?"

"Yes, we shall go by train."

"And boat?"

"We shall take a boat first."

"Oh! Like this! With such a long moustache!" A strange shrill voice suddenly rang out.

I looked up with a start, and saw a woman of about fifty with prominent cheekbones and thin lips. With her hands on her hips, not wearing a skirt but with her trousered legs apart, she stood in front of me just like the compass in a box of geometrical instruments.

I was flabbergasted.

"Don't you know me? Why, I have held you in my arms!"

I felt even more flabbergasted. Fortunately my mother came in just then and said:

"He has been away so long, you must excuse

him for forgetting. You should remember," she said to me, "this is Mrs. Yang from across the road. . . . She has a beancurd shop."

Then, to be sure, I remembered. When I was a child there was a Mrs. Yang who used to sit nearly all day long in the beancurd shop across the road, and everybody used to call her Beancurd Beauty. She used to powder herself, and her cheekbones were not so prominent then nor her lips so thin; moreover she remained seated all the time, so that I had never noticed this resemblance to a compass. In those days people said that, thanks to her, that beancurd shop did very good business. But, probably on account of my age, she had made no impression on me, so that later I forgot her entirely. However, the Compass was extremely indignant and looked at me most contemptuously, just as one might look at a Frenchman who had never heard of Napoleon or an American who had never heard of Washington, and smiling sarcastically she said:

"You had forgotten? Naturally I am beneath your notice. . . ."

"Certainly not . . . I . . . ." I answered nervously, getting to my feet.

"Then you listen to me, Master Xun. You have grown rich, and they are too heavy to move, so you can't possibly want these old pieces of furniture any more. You had better let me take them away. Poor people like us can do with them."

"I haven't grown rich. I must sell these in order to buy. . . ."

"Oh, come now, you have been made the intendant of a circuit, how can you still say you're not rich? You have three concubines now, and whenever you go out it is in a big sedan-chair with eight bearers. Do you still say you're not rich? Hah! You can't hide anything from me."

Knowing there was nothing I could say, I remained silent.

"Come now, really, the more money people have the more miserly they get, and the more miserly they are the more money they get. . . ." remarked the Compass, turning indignantly away and walking slowly off, casually picking up a pair

of mother's gloves and stuffing them into her pocket as she went out.

After this a number of relatives in the neighborhood came to call. In the intervals between entertaining them I did some packing, and so three or four days passed.

One very cold afternoon, I sat drinking tea after lunch when I was aware of someone coming in, and turned my head to see who it was. At the first glance I gave an involuntary start, hastily stood up and went over to welcome him. The newcomer was Runtu. But although I knew at a glance that this was Runtu, it was not the Runtu I remembered. He had grown to twice his former size. His round face, once crimson, had become sallow and acquired deep lines and wrinkles; his eyes too had become like his father's, the rims swollen and red, a feature common to most peasants who work by the sea and are exposed all day to the wind from the ocean. He wore a shabby felt cap and just one very thin padded jacket, with the result that he was shivering from head to foot. He carried a paper package and a long pipe, nor was his hand the plump red hand I remembered, but coarse and clumsy and chapped, like the bark of a pine tree.

Delighted as I was, I did not know how to express myself, and could only say:

"Oh! Runtu—so it's you? . . ."

After this there were so many things I wanted to talk about, they should have poured out like a string of beads: woodcocks, jumping fish, shells, *zha*. . . . But I was tongue-tied, unable to put all I was thinking into words.

He stood there, mixed joy and sadness showing on his face. His lips moved, but not a sound did he utter. Finally, assuming a respectful attitude, he said clearly:

"Master! . . ."

I felt a shiver run through me; for I knew then what a lamentably thick wall had grown up between us. Yet I could not say anything.

He turned his head to call:

"Shuisheng, bow to the master." Then he pulled forward a boy who had been hiding behind his back, only a little paler and thinner, and he had no silver necklet.

"This is my fifth," he said. "He's not used to company, so he's shy and awkward."

Mother came downstairs with Hong'er, probably after hearing our voices.

"I got your letter some time ago, madam," said Runtu. "I was really so pleased to know the master was coming back. . . ."

"Now, why are you so polite? Weren't you playmates together in the past?" said mother gaily. "You had better still call him Brother Xun as before."

"Oh, you are really too . . . What bad manners that would be. I was a child then and didn't understand." As he was speaking Runtu motioned Shuisheng to come and bow, but the child was shy, and stood stock-still behind his father.

"So he is Shuisheng? Your fifth?" asked mother. "We are all strangers, you can't blame him for feeling shy. Hong'er had better take him out to play."

When Hong'er heard this he went over to Shuisheng, and Shuisheng went out with him, entirely at his ease. Mother asked Runtu to sit down, and after a little hesitation he did so; then leaning his long pipe against the table he handed over the paper package, saying:

"In winter there is nothing worth bringing; but these few beans we dried ourselves, if you will excuse the liberty, sir."

When I asked him how things were with him, he just shook his head.

"In a very bad way. Even my sixth can do a little work, but still we haven't enough to eat . . . and then there is no security . . . all sorts of people want money, there is no fixed rule . . . and the harvests are bad. You grow things, and when you take them to sell you always have to pay several taxes and lose money, while if you don't try to sell, the things may go bad. . . ."

He kept shaking his head; yet, although his face was lined with wrinkles, not one of them moved, just as if he were a stone statue. No doubt he felt intensely bitter, but could not express himself. After a pause he took up his pipe and began to smoke in silence.

From her chat with him, mother learned that he was busy at home and had to go back the next day; and since he had had no lunch, she told him to go to the kitchen and fry some rice for himself.

After he had gone out, mother and I both shook our heads over his hard life: many children, famines, taxes, soldiers, bandits, officials and landed gentry, all had squeezed him as dry as a mummy. Mother said that we should offer him all the things we were not going to take away, letting him choose for himself.

That afternoon, he picked out a number of things; two long tables, four chairs, an incense burner and candlesticks, and one balance. He also asked for all the ashes from the stove (in our part we cook over straw, and the ashes can be used to fertilize sandy soil), saying that when we left he would come to take them away by boat.

That night we talked again, but not of anything serious; and the next morning he went away with Shuisheng.

After another nine days it was time for us to leave. Runtu came in the morning. Shuisheng did not come with him—he had just brought a little girl of five to watch the boat. We were very busy all day, and had no time to talk. We also had quite a number of visitors, some to see us off, some to fetch things, and some to do both. It was nearly evening when we left by boat, and by that time everything in the house, however old or shabby, large or small, fine or coarse, had been cleared away.

As we set off, in the dusk, the green mountains on either side of the river became deep blue, receding toward the stern of the boat.

Hong'er and I, leaning against the cabin window, were looking out together at the indistinct scene outside, when suddenly he asked:

"Uncle, when shall we go back?"

"Go back? Do you mean that before you've left you want to go back?"

"Well, Shuisheng has invited me to his home. . . ." He opened wide his black eyes in anxious thought.

Mother and I both felt rather sad, and so Runtu's name came up again.

Mother said that ever since our family started

packing up, Mrs. Yang from the beancurd shop had come over every day, and the day before in the ash-heap she had unearthed a dozen bowls and plates, which after some discussion she insisted must have been buried there by Runtu, so that when he came to remove the ashes he could take them home at the same time. After making this discovery Mrs. Yang was very pleased with herself, and flew off taking the dog-teaser with her. (The dog-teaser is used by poultry keepers in our parts. It is a wooden cage inside which food is put, so that hens can stretch their necks in to eat but dogs can only look on furiously.) And it was a marvel, considering the size of her feet, how fast she could run.

I was leaving the old house farther and farther behind while the hills and rivers of my old home were also receding gradually ever farther in the distance. But I felt no regret. I only felt that all around me was an invisible high wall, cutting me off from my fellows, and this depressed me thoroughly. The vision of that small hero with the silver necklet among the watermelons had formerly been as clear as day, but now it suddenly blurred, adding to my depression.

Mother and Hong'er fell asleep.

I lay down, listening to the water rippling beneath the boat, and knew that I was going my way. I thought: although there is such a barrier between Runtu and myself, the children still have much in common, for wasn't Hong'er thinking of Shuisheng just now? I hope they will not be like us, that they will not allow a barrier to grow between them. But again I would not like them, because they want to be akin, all to have a treadmill existence like mine, nor to suffer like Runtu until they become stupefied, nor yet, like others, to devote all their energies to dissipation. They should have a new life, a life we have never experienced.

The access of hope made me suddenly afraid. When Runtu asked for the incense burner and candlesticks I had laughed up my sleeve at him, to think that he still worshipped idols and could not put them out of his mind. Yet what I now called hope was no more than an idol I had created myself. The only difference was that what he desired was close at hand, while what I desired was less easily realized.

As I dozed, a stretch of jade-green seashore spread itself before my eyes, and above a round golden moon hung in a deep blue sky. I thought: hope cannot be said to exist, nor can it be said not to exist. It is just like roads across the earth. For actually the earth had no roads to begin with, but when many men pass one way, a road is made.

Translated by Yang Hsien-yi and Gladys Yang

77

THE SPIRIT OF THE MAY FOURTH MOVEMENT

On May 4th, 1919 more than three thousand students from thirteen Beijing universities assembled at the Gate of Heavenly Peace to protest the Versailles Peace Conference's decision to uphold Japan's claims to parts of Shandong province that had previously been held by Germany. After some students broke through police lines to beat up the ambassador to Japan and set fire to the home of one official, the governor suppressed the demonstrators and arrested their leaders. These actions in turn set off a wave of protests around the country in support of the Beijing students and their cause. In subsequent years, the term "May Fourth Movement" came to stand for the efforts of students and other young people to take on the task of national salvation.

The account below describes the experiences of one young woman student in the days of the first wave of protests. It was written many years later by Deng Yingchao (1904–1992). A few years after the events described here she married the Communist Party activitist Zhou Enlai (1898–1976). In later years she came to play an active role in party affairs, particularly women's issues.

When the May Fourth Movement took place in 1919, I was only sixteen years old, a student at the Tianjin Women's Normal College. . . . On May 4, 1919 students in Beijing held a demonstration asking the government to refuse to sign the Versailles Peace Treaty and to punish the traitors at home. In their indignation, they burned the house at Zhaojialou and beat up Lu Zhongxiang, then Chinese envoy to Japan. The following day, when the news reached Tianjin, it aroused the indignation of students there who staged their own demonstration on May 7th. They began by organizing such patriotic societies as the Tianjin Stu-

dent Union, the Tianjin Women's Patriotic Society, and the Tianjin Association of National Salvation. We had no political theory to guide us at that time, only our strong patriotic enthusiasm. In addition to the Beijing students' requests, we demanded, "Abrogate the Twenty-One Demands!" "Boycott Japanese Goods!" and "Buy Chinese-made goods!" Furthermore, we emphatically refused to become slaves to foreign powers!

Despite the fact that it was a patriotic students' demonstration, the Northern warlord government of China resorted to force to quell the protest. The police dispersed the march with rifles fixed with bayonets and with hoses; later they resorted to rifle butts and to even arrest. However, our political awareness awakened a new spirit in us during our struggle with the government. New European ideas and culture had poured into China after World War I, and the the success of the 1917 October Revolution in Russia introduced Marxism-Leninism to China. . . . We did not yet know that to achieve our revolutionary goal, we intellectuals should unite with workers and peasants. We just had some vague idea that Lenin, the leader of the Russian revolution, wanted to liberate the oppressed workers and peasants.

What we did know intuitively was that alone we students did not have enough strength to save China from foreign powers. To awaken our compatriots, we organized many speakers' committees to spread propaganda among the people. I became the head of the speakers' group in the Tianjin Women's Patriotic Society and in the Tianjin Student Union. Frequently we gave speeches off campus. At first, we women did not dare give speeches on the street due to the feudal attitudes that then existed in China. So the female students went instead to places where people had gathered for an exhibition or a show, while the male students gave speeches in the street to passersby. There were always a lot of listeners. We told them why we should be united to save our country; that traitors in the government must be punished; and that people should have the right to freedom of assembly and association. We talked about the suffering of the Korean people after their country was conquered; and we publicly lodged our protests against the Northern warlord government that persecutes progressive students. Usually tears streamed down our cheeks when we gave our speeches and our listeners were often visibly moved.

In addition to making speeches we also visited homes in out-of-the-way places and slum areas. We went door to door to make our pleas, and some families gave us a warm welcome while others just slammed the door on us. However, nothing could discourage us. One day during summer vacation, we went to the suburbs to give speeches. On our way back to the city, we got caught in a downpour. Everybody was soaking wet, just like a drowned chicken! The next day, however, everyone was ready to go again.

We delivered handbills and published newspapers to spread our patriotic enthusiasm even further. The Student Union newspaper, for example, was run by the Tianjin Student Union and each issue sold more than twenty thousand copies—a considerable number at that time! It was originally published every three days; however, later it was increased to every day. Its editor-in-chief was Zhou Enlai. The Women's Patriotic Society also published a weekly. Both papers reported foreign and national current events, student movements across the country, student editorials, progressive articles, and cultural and art news.

The reactionary Northern warlord government, however, turned a deaf ear to us. They ultimately bowed to Japanese powers, shielded the traitors, and tried to suppress the student movement. At that time people were denied expressing their patriotic views. So what we then struggled most urgently for was freedom of assembly and association; the right to express one's political views; and freedom of the press. United under these common goals, we struggled bravely.

Various associations for national salvation in Tianjin decided to organize a general mass meeting of the residents of Tianjin on October 10, 1919. The purpose was to demand that the officials who betrayed China be punished and to call on local residents to boycott all Japanese goods. A march was scheduled at the conclusion of the meeting. Prior to the meeting, however, news spread that Yang Yide, the chief of the police department, was going to disband the meeting and if necessary use force to stop the march. We were not frightened, but got ready to fight back if fighting broke out. During the meeting, female students stood at the periphery of the group so that we could be the first to escape if the meeting were broken up by the police. We chose strong bamboo poles to carry our banners since they could be used as weapons if needed.

Shortly after we began the meeting, a group of policemen arrived, surrounded the group, and instantly pointed their rifles at us. Our meeting continued as if nothing had happened. It was not until it was time to assemble for the march that conflict occurred. The police refused to let us pass. So finally we just charged at them, shouting, "Policemen should be patriotic, too!" "Don't strike patriotic students!" The police hit with their rifle butts and many students were beaten. Some even broke their glasses. We fought back with our bamboo poles. Then some students knocked off the policemen's hats so that when they bent down to retrieve them, it gave us a means of escape.

Just at that moment, the speakers from the Tianjin Student Union arrived in the back of a truck. With them helping on the outside, we broke through the encirclement and the march began! We marched around the city until daybreak the next day. It was not until we had lodged protests against Yang Yide for his savage treatment of the students that we finally ended the demonstration. Yang's ruthlessness had so aroused our indignation, that we women broke with tradition and the next day appeared on the streets proclaiming Yang Yide's cruelty towards students to all who passed by.

After the October 10th incident, the situation worsened. In November, the Tianjin Association for National Salvation was closed down and twenty-four leaders were arrested. Soon the Tianjin Student Union was also disbanded. But we continued our progressive activities secretly and found a room in a student's home in the concession area to use as our office. A concession area was a track of land in a Chinese port or city leased to an imperialist power and put under its colonial rule.

In December of that year another confrontation occurred. That day the students gathered around the office building of the provincial government to present a petition to Governor Cao Rui, asking for the release of the arrested students and for the various national salvation associations to be allowed to resume operation. However, not only did he refuse to receive us, but he had the gates locked and posted armed guards. Our representatives, Zhou Enlai, Guo Longzhen (a woman), and Yu Fangzhou, managed to get in from a hole under the door. They were beaten once they were inside. The students became more indignant and refused to leave. At midnight, the armed guards drove the students away by brutal force, hitting students with bayonets and rifle butts and spraying them with columns of water. Many students were wounded and some had to be sent to the hospital. In this we saw clearly the ferocious face of the reactionary government and that freedom and democratic rights could not be gained without a fierce struggle.

In the following year, we shifted our priority to rescuing the arrested students. We struggled to win over public sentiment, fought against illegal arrests, and asked for public trial of our representatives. It was not until that summer, however, that all twenty-eight of those who had been arrested were finally released.

During the movement, not only were we suppressed by the reactionary government, but were suppressed by the college authorities as well. They ordered students not to leave the campus to take part in any progressive activities. On May 7, 1920, a group of us from the Women's Normal College planned to attend a meeting commemorating the May 7th Incident, the day the Japanese government sent an ultimatum to the Chinese government urging it to sign the Twenty-One Demands. When we were ready to leave, we discovered college authorities were refusing to let us. A confrontation ensued and resulted in our eventually forcing open the gate and attending the meeting.

When we returned, much to our surprise, a notice had been posted that all the students who had attended the meeting—a total of two hundred—were expelled! How enraged we were! We decided to leave the college as soon as possible. Our dedication to our patriotic duty was so strong that we were ready to sacrifice anything for the goal of national independence! Without any rest or supper we spent the night packing our luggage. When we were ready to leave en masse, luggage in hand, we again discovered that the gate had been locked.

In addition to this, they had cut off our communication with the outside world by locking up the telephone room. This time the confrontation lasted through the night and into the morning of the next day when all two hundred of us left the college. One week later, public pressure forced them to reinstate us, and we immediately returned to school.

The women's liberation movement was greatly enhanced by the May Fourth Movement; this became an important part of the movement. And slogans such as "sexual equality," "freedom of marriage," "coeducational universities," "social contacts for women," and "job opportunity for women," were all put forward. In Tianjin we merged the men's students union with the women's. Fearing that public opinion would be against it, some of the women were hesitant at first. However, the male and female activists among us took the lead and we worked together bravely to overcome all obstacles. In our work, we were equal and we respected each other. Everyone worked wholeheartedly for the goal of saving China, and we competed with each other in our efforts. Women students, particularly the more progressive ones, worked especially hard for we knew we were pioneers among Chinese women to show that women are not inferior to men. Inspired by the new ideals, the progressive men students broke down the tradition of sexual discrimination and treated us with respect. For example, each department of the student union had one male and one female in charge. In addition, women had equal say in decision making. The men and women's student union in Beijing admired us for our brilliant work and merged afterwards.

At this time cultural movements were developing rapidly and students were receptive to publications which promoted new ideas. In Beijing, for example, there were *New Youth, Young China,* and *New Tide* magazines. In Tianjin, the Student Union every week would invite a progressive professor (such as Li Dazhao) to give us an academic lecture on new literary ideas such as how to write in vernacular Chinese rather than in classical stereotyped writings. Today these things are commonplace, but then it was very new and important. As more scientific subjects and new ideas poured into China, we felt an urgency to learn, discuss, study, and understand them. Thus by the end of that summer, a small well-organized group—the Awakening Society—was established by twenty of the more progressive student activists. I was the youngest in the Society. Although I often heard other members talking about such thing as socialism or anarchism, I was too young to understand them. At that time we did not have definite political convictions, nor did we know much about Communism. We just had a vague idea that the principle of distribution in the most advantageous society was "from each according to his ability, to each according to his needs." We knew only that a revolution led by Lenin in Russia had been successful, and that the aim of that revolution was to emancipate the majority of the people who were oppressed, and to establish a classless society. How we longed for such a society! But at that time we could not learn about such a society because we could scarcely find any copy of Lenin's ideas or information about the October Revolution.

The Awakening Society existed for only a few months. We lost some members when they were arrested in the incident over the petition to the governor. Others graduated and left Tianjin. Eventually the Society ceased to exist. However, the majority of us eventually joined the Chinese Socialist Youth League established in 1920, or the Communist party established in 1921....

Translated by Liu Xiaohong

78

THE HAIFENG PEASANT ASSOCIATION

Among the many foreign ideas and ideologies to attract the attention of intellectuals in the first two decades of the twentieth century was socialism. Particularly after the success of the Bolshevik revolution in Russia in 1917, Marxism gained more and more adherents, and in 1921 the Chinese Communist Party was founded. During the 1920s the main base of support for the new Communist Party was in the cities, among urban intellectuals and unionized factory workers. However, some progress was also made in organizing peasants.

Below is an account by Peng Pai (1896–1929) of his pioneering attempts to found peasant unions in 1921–1923. Peng became interested in agrarian socialism while a student in Japan from 1918 to 1921. On his return he joined the Communist Party and began to put his ideas into practice. The account below covers the period of his initial success. He later had to flee Haifeng when the local military authorities decided to suppress the unions.

THE BEGINNING OF A PEASANT MOVEMENT

In May, 1921, I was the head of the Education Bureau of Haifeng county. Still dreaming of realizing social revolution through education, I called for all the students in the county, most of whom were children of the wealthy, to celebrate the "May First" Labor Day at the county seat. That was an event unprecedented in the history of Haifeng. Not one single worker or peasant participated in the celebration. The pupils of the First Elementary School paraded the streets, holding red banners with "join the reds" written on them. It was truly childish. The gentry class of Haifeng thought that we were now going to practice property sharing and wife sharing, and they started numerous rumors, attacking us before [the governor] Chen Jiongming. As a result, I was discharged from my duties, and, one after another, all the progressive teachers and school principals I had appointed also lost their positions.

At that time we were fighting a confusing battle with Chen Jiongming's hometown paper, the *Lu An Daily*. Along with comrade Li Chuntao and others I published a few issues of *Red Heart Weekly* as the mouthpiece of the workers and peasants. In fact, not a single worker on the streets or peasant on the farm was behind our journal or even had a hint of what we were doing. One day when I returned home, my little sister tried to prevent me from entering the house. She said, "I don't know why, but mother is crying and says she is going to kill you." First I thought she was joking, but when I went into the family hall, I saw that indeed my mother was weeping.

It turned out my seventh younger brother had gotten hold of a "Letter to Peasants" which we published in the *Red Heart Weekly* and read the essay aloud. When my mother happened to hear it, tears flowed down her cheeks. Finally she burst out into loud wails, crying, "Our ancestors must have failed to accumulate virtue, for here we have a prodigal son. Your grandfather worked hard for what we have today. If you carry on like this, our family will certainly be ruined!" I tried my best to console her, and she finally calmed down.

At that time it occurred to me that if the peasants could read this essay, they would be very happy, perhaps as happy as my wailing mother was upset. Besides, I was confident that peasants could be organized. Consequently, I abandoned the senseless war of words with the *Lu An Daily* and took up practical action in the farm villages. At the time, all my local friends were against it. They said, "Peasants are extremely disorderly. You won't be able to organize them. Plus, they are ignorant and resistant to campaigns of any kind. You'll just be wasting your energy."

My family could be considered a large landowner. Every year we would collect about one thousand piculs of grain and had over fifteen hundred peasants under our control. Since my family had less than thirty members altogether, each member had fifty peasants as slaves. Consequently, when they heard that I wanted to start a peasant movement, my relatives all hated me with a passion (except for my third elder brother and fifth younger brother). My oldest brother would have liked to kill me, as would all the others in our lineage and village. The only thing I could do was ignore them.

On a certain day in May, I started my own campaign for the peasant movement. The first place I went to was a village in Red Mountain. I was dressed in a white western-style student suit and wore a white hat. A peasant about thirty years of age was mixing manure in front of the village. When he saw me coming, he said, "Sir, how are you? Are you here to collect taxes? We are not putting on a play here."

"No, I'm not here to collect taxes for plays," I replied. "I'm here to be your friend. I know you have hardships, and I would like to talk with you."

To which the peasant said, "Yup, hardships are our destiny. So long now. We don't have the leisure to talk with you. Excuse me." And he hurried away.

After a little while, another peasant came along. He was a little over twenty and seemed more sensible. He asked me, "Sir, to which battalion do you belong? What is your rank? What is your business here?"

I replied, "I am not an official nor a military officer. I was a student, and I've come here to make friends with you."

He laughed and said, "We are useless people, unworthy of aristocrats like you. You must be kidding! Good-bye." Without a moment's hesitation, he turned and walked away. I was going to say something, but he had already gone too far to hear me. I became very distressed, especially when I recalled my friends' warning that my efforts would be a waste of energy.

When I was entering a second village, the dogs bared their teeth at me and barked fiercely. I took this demonstration of power for a sign of welcome and went straight into the village. But then I saw that all doors were locked. The villagers had all gone into town or into the fields. By the time I hurried to a third village, it was already twilight, and I was afraid that the villagers might suspect me of foul play, so I didn't go in. Instead, I headed for home.

Arriving home, I found that not one soul in my own family would talk to me. I had become an enemy. They had already eaten, and the only thing left was some rice gruel. I had a bit of the gruel and went to my room. I opened my diary and tried to record my achievements for that day, but all I could write was a big zero.

I spent all night trying to figure out methods that would work. At dawn I crawled out of my bed, had a bite of breakfast, and went back to the villages. On my way, I saw many peasants coming into the city, carrying bundles of potatoes or urine barrels on a pole over their shoulders. Whenever I met them on a narrow road, I would respectfully step aside to let them pass. Now, city folks usually would not make way for country folks. Instead, peasants who carried loads had to make way for the empty-handed city people. Thus I figured that at least some of the peasants would notice my respect towards them.

I found myself back at the village I had visited the day before. This time I encountered a peasant of forty, who asked me, "Sir, are you here to collect land rent?"

"No, no, I am here to help you collect your due. Someone owes you money, and you've forgotten it. I'm here to remind you."

"What!" the man exclaimed. "I'll be lucky not to owe others money. Who'd owe anything to me?"

"Don't you know?" I told him. "The landlords owe you a lot. Year in and year out, they sit at home and do nothing, and you work in the fields until you drop dead. In the end they are the ones who get the yields as rent. The piece of land worth at most one hundred dollars has been tilled by you for a hundred, a thousand years—and how much grain have you submitted to the landlords? We think it's really unfair. That's why I'm here to talk with you, to find out a way to get even with the landlords."

The man smiled and said, "That'll be great indeed! But we will be locked up and beaten up if we only owe them a pint or a tenth of a pint. Such is fate—those who collect rent always collect rent, and those who till the fields always till the fields. Goodday, sir. I've got to go to town."

"Big brother, what is your name?" I asked.

"My name is—uh, I live in this village. Come again when you have time."

I realized that he was unwilling to tell me his name, and decided not to press him.

There were women working in the village, but most men were out in the fields. Since it was not proper for me to talk to women, I lingered for a long while, but finally moved on to another village.

Although I went through several villages that day, the result was the same as the day before: zero. The only difference was that in my diary I wrote down a few more sentences.

That evening, two things suddenly occurred to me. First, my language was too formal and refined; much of it was lost on the peasants. I would have to translate the jargon into everyday language. Second, my appearance, physique, and clothing were all different from the peasants'. They had long been oppressed and cheated by those who looked different, and naturally suspected that I was an enemy. Also, my appearance indicated my class, and thereby alienated the peasants. I decided, therefore, to wear simpler things. I also came up with a new plan. The next day, instead of going to the villages, I would go to the crossroads where I would meet more peasants.

The next day, I went to a main road in front of Longshan Temple. This road was the principal artery for traffic between the Red Mountain, Beihu, Chi'an, and Hekou regions. Every day, countless peasants passed by and rested in front of the Temple. I took this opportunity to talk to them, explaining the reasons for their hardships and the remedies, pointing out to them the evidence of landlords' oppression and discussing the necessity for the peasants to unite. At first I was talking to only a few people, but as the listeners increased, I began giving speeches. The peasants were, however, only half credulous. On that day, four or five peasants actually talked to me, and a dozen or more listened. It was a great achievement.

THE UNITED STRUGGLE OF SIX PEOPLE

After that day, I spent two weeks at intersections, talking to the peasants who passed by or giving speeches. Those who talked to me increased to a dozen or so, and my audience now consisted of thirty or forty, a major step forward. One day, as I walked into town, I noticed something rather peculiar about how people in the stores looked at me. Then, many relatives started to come to see me, bringing food with them, and asking about my "illness." I was really puzzled. Later, a servant told me, "You'd better just stay home and rest from now on." I asked him why, and he replied, "The people out there all say you've gone mad. You ought to rest and take care of yourself." I almost died of laughter. I later discovered that it was a rumor started by the gentry, but many peasants in the villages also believed that I was insane. They seemed to be afraid of me and tried to avoid me. Nevertheless, I continued my campaign in front of Longshan Temple.

One day I gave a speech, saying that if the peasants could unite, they would be able to reduce their rent, and the landlords would be powerless. The various oppressive measures such as the three lease rules, presents to landlords, home delivery of rent, rent increases, and suspension of leases could all be eliminated. At this moment a peasant about forty years old shouted in a loud voice, "You're just shooting off your mouth! All this talk of reducing rent! As long as your family's Minghe estate keeps harassing us for rent, I won't believe a word of it."

Before I could make a reply, a young peasant beside me stood up and retorted. "You're wrong," he said. "The land you till belongs to Minghe. If Minghe reduces its rent, only you benefit. What about me? I don't till Minghe's land. The problem is not how to plead for the lowering of rents, but whether we can unite as a group. This is like a chess game; victory belongs to those who have the best strategies. If we do not have any strategy, we will eventually lose, and it will be no use begging from others. We are not talking about your personal problems, but the problems of the majority."

I was very happy to hear this and said to myself, "Here is a comrade!" After asking his name, I invited Mr. Zhang Maan to come to my place to talk that night. I expressed my joy when he arrived, and he said to me, "Often, after listening to your speech, we argue with the villagers who are still 'asleep.' They are always afraid that you are telling lies. But a few of us really believe you."

"Who are they?" I asked.

He named Lin Pei, Lin Huan, Li Laosi, and Li Sixian. "They are all good friends of mine," he added.

"Do you think we should ask them to join our discussion? Would you go get them while I prepare some tea?"

He agreed, and in a little while the tea was ready and Zhang came back with his friends, all young peasants under thirty who spoke and acted enthusiastically. After I learned their names, I started to talk about the peasant movement with them. I raised difficult problem, "Every day I go to the villages to propagate my ideas, but the peasants pay no attention to me and refuse to talk. Do you have a solution?"

Lin Pei said, "The reasons are, first, the peasants are too busy. Second, what you say is too profound; sometimes even I can't understand you. Third, you lack people you know to lead the way. The best time for us to go is around seven or eight at night, when there is a lot of free time in the villages. Then you need to make things easier to understand. And we can also lead the way for you."

When I heard what he said, I realized how smart he was. He also warned me in a very serious manner that I should never show any contempt for the gods when I talk to the peasants. This was a comment that gave me even more respect for him.

"Let's start a peasants' union now," suggested Li Laosi. "If more people join us, that's great; but even if no one joins, we'll keep it going. How does that sound?"

"Great idea," I said. "Tomorrow I'll go with two of you to the villages, and at night we'll make a public speech." They all thought that was a good plan, and it was decided that Zhang Maan and Lin Pei should go with me the next morning.

We continued our discussion for a long time. After the meeting, I wrote "Victory is in sight."

The next morning, after breakfast, my peasant friends Zhang and Lin came to get me, and we went to the villages around Red Mountain. Because of their introduction, the villagers felt close to me and talked to me sincerely. I asked them to come to the lecture that night, and they responded enthusiastically. When evening came, they had tables, chairs, and lights all prepared for me. I had an audience of sixty to seventy. Children were in front, men behind them, and women in the rear. I talked about the causes of the hardships peasants endured, the facts of landlords' exploitation, and the ways to peasants' liberation. I used the question-and-answer format, and the peasants approved of what I said. I also came to know that they could understand me. I concluded my speech by saying that the next time I would play a phonograph and give a magic show. I promised to let them know in advance.

The next day we went to other villages, and the results were equally encouraging. On the third day I announced that I would give a magic show and a lecture. When the time came, more than two hundred peasants turned up. They applauded my show and listened to my lecture. For the next week or two I used this method, which proved very successful. But I began to notice that Lin Pei and Zhang Maan appeared pensive, distressed, and listless. I thought that the landlords must have started rumors that made them worry, so I asked them what was wrong. At first they wouldn't say anything, but when I pressed, one of them said, "Our parents and brothers are very upset because we spend our time with you instead of working in the fields. My parents scolded me, saying 'You hang around with Peng Pai. Peng Pai won't starve to death, but you sure will!' This morning when I was leaving the house, my father came very close to hitting me. And it's not just my parents; my wife and my brothers are equally upset. That's why I'm dejected."

After deliberating for a long time, the three of us came up with a plan. I went and borrowed three silver dollars from a friend, and gave them to Lin Pei. When Lin returned home that day, he took the coins out of his pocket, counted them, and dropped them on the floor, making noises. Sure enough, his mother asked him where he had gotten the money. He answered, "Who'd go out there without pay? Do you think I only run around for fun? I'm doing this for money." When his mother heard this, her anger turned into joy. His brothers also stopped their criticism. His wife, of course, was only too delighted to see that her husband had money. After this act, Lin Pei turned the money over to Zhang Maan, who also did the same thing in front of his mother, with equal tri-

umph. The money was then returned to my friend. This ruse bought us about a week's time, during which Lin and Zhang could work hard. They progressed rapidly and were actually able to give speeches afterwards.

However, nothing was more difficult than asking the peasants to join the union. They would always say, "I'm all for it. When everyone else has joined, I will certainly do so." We explained to them that if everyone were to think that way, the peasants' union would not be a reality in even a thousand years. We told them that joining the union is like crossing a river. On this shore is hardship, on the other side happiness; each and every one of us is afraid of drowning, and no one dares to be the first to cross the river, but by joining the union we can cross the river together, hand in hand. We described the peasants' union as an organization of mutual assistance in which all members are as close as brothers. Some of the peasants were persuaded by our argument and agreed to join in, but when I wrote down their names in a register, others became apprehensive and hurried away. I had to stop using the register. Still we could only enlist a couple of people in a week, and after over a month's effort, we only had around thirty members.

At about this time, an accident happened in the Yunlu village of Red Mountain. The daughter-in-law of a member of our union, who was only six years old, fell into an outhouse and drowned. Thirty or forty people from her family came to Yunlu. They charged our member with murder and were determined to avenge the girl's death. The thirty members of our union held a meeting to decide on countermeasures, and we agreed to go to Yunlu to reason with the avengers. When we arrived, we asked them on what grounds they made their accusations and recorded all their names in a notebook. We bluffed them, saying, "You're all tricked." Not knowing what we had up our sleeves, they all became apprehensive because their names had been put down on paper. Then a district chief named Zhuo Mengmei came to mediate, suggesting that our friend be punished. He was driven away by the members of the union, and only barely escaped a beating. The avengers were now even more intimidated. They pleaded with us: "At least let us examine the body."

We said to them, "Go ahead, if you dare to. If you're not afraid of being put in jail, you can go right ahead and open up the coffin!" The women were all frightened when they heard the word "jail," and they pulled at the shirts of their men, wanting to go home.

Upon this we pressed even harder for them to leave. They asked us, "We came here on account of our relative. What does it have to do with you?"

"Don't you know we have formed a peasants' union?" we replied. "The union is a union for the poor. Its members are all closely united, closer than real brothers. What concerns one concerns all. Today, this friend of ours is in trouble, and we have come to help him, risking our own lives. Since you are also peasants, someday you will certainly join the union, and once you do so, we'll help you just as we've helped him. Now, why don't you go home."

Crestfallen, they left, and there was not the least bit of damage done to us. News got around, and many peasants learned that the brothers of the union were loyal to each other and were able to help each other. We also used this incident for the purpose of propaganda: "We have no power if we are not united. We will be taken advantage of if we have no power. To have power, join the peasants' union immediately." And membership gradually increased.

Not long afterwards, we found that some peasants would try to get others' land to till, and landlords would increase rent and change tenants. So the union drew up some regulations to prevent such incidents. Briefly, these regulations were:

1. Unless permission is given by the member and by the union, no one may encroach on a member's rented land.
2. Unless the member relinquishes his lease and the union gives its permission, no one may rent the land already rented to a member of the union. Violators are subject to severe punishment.

3. In case a landlord takes back his land from a member by means of increasing the rent, and as a result a member's livelihood is in danger, he may ask for help from the union, which will either persuade nearby members to allow him to till part of their land, or will introduce him to another trade.

After the regulations were publicized, there was no longer any competition for land among our members, and the landlords also were afraid to raise the rent of members of the union. At times, nonmembers would fight for the land already rented by our members, but under the advice of the union's representatives, they would usually quickly return the land to the members. Once, a landlord became annoyed and refused to lease his land to the original tenant (i.e., a member of our union). We then announced a boycott, and the landlord, fearing that his land would lie fallow, was forced to lease the land back to the member. This was another victory for us.

When the peasants rowed their boats into the cities to collect nightsoil, etc., local ruffians would force them to pay a fee of two cents to anchor their boats on the pier. If a peasant failed to comply, his rudder would be removed, and to claim his rudder, he had to pay several dollars. The peasants were all annoyed by this, and our union declared that this would have to stop. Our strategy was as follows. Whenever these ruffians passed by the villages or brought their boats by, we would charge tolls. If they refused to pay us, we would also refuse to pay the "pier fee." In this way, the pier fee was abolished without much ado.

We also discovered that peasants easily got involved in quarrels, and as a result allowed themselves to be used by the gentry class. They would file lawsuits in the courts and end up breaking up their families and losing everything they ever owned. For this reason, we sent out notices to the members of the union, telling them that any quarrels or disagreements among members should first be reported to the union. If any member should fail to report a case to the union, but instead went straight to the gentry or the courts, he would be expelled from the union even if he was in the right, and the union would use all its power to support his opponent. When a member of our union had a confrontation with a nonmember, he also had to report to the union. In negotiating with a landlord, if a member did not report to the union, the union would not be responsible for his failure.

From then on, the locus of political power moved from the hands of the gentry and the rich to the peasants' union. The police and judicial branches of the local government witnessed a decrease in "business," which made the policemen and judges resent the union. As the union was able to solve many problems for the peasants and won many victories for them, its membership increased daily.

FROM THE RED MOUNTAIN UNION TO THE HAIFENG CENTRAL UNION

By now it was September, 1922. We had about five hundred members, most of whom were from the twenty-eight villages of Red Mountain. So we set a day in September to hold the founding assembly of the peasants' union of Red Mountain. Besides the members, the principal of the high school, Li Yueting, and the principal of the elementary school, Yang Sizheng, attended the assembly and gave speeches. Huang Fenglin was elected as the head of the Red Mountain union. The meeting ended with a tea party, and the members all went home happy. This founding assembly influenced the people of the various villages, and applicants grew in number. On the average we were getting ten new members every day.

The procedure for joining the union was as follows. The applicant had to appear in person at the union headquarters and pay a membership fee of twenty cents. (Originally we had intended to have them pay a registration fee plus yearly or monthly membership dues, but we were afraid that this might be too complicated for them, so, for clarity and propaganda purposes, we decided to charge twenty cents per year. But we planned to change it when the peasants became more experienced as members of the union.) Then they would receive a

briefing and a membership card (the words were printed on a blank calling card) like this:

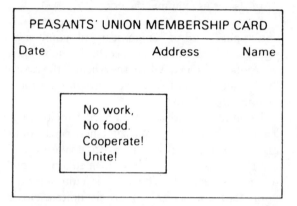

PEASANTS' UNION MEMBERSHIP CARD

Date   Address   Name

No work,
No food.
Cooperate!
Unite!

At this time the union issued manifestos and publicized its benefits. In addition, we continued our campaign efforts day and night. In October, we had an average of twenty new members every day. Following the example of Red Mountain, numerous other areas all established their own regional unions. The county seat was now surrounded on all sides by union organizations, and the time had come for us to prepare for a Haifeng central union.

A "Funeral Expenses Co-op" was formed by the union. Any member of the union could join the co-op, and we reached a total of around 150 members. The rule was that for any member who died or who lost a parent, every other member would donate two cents for funeral expenses. The first day this method was announced, a member's father died. The members each put out two cents, which came to more than thirty dollars, and they also went to attend the funeral. The member concerned was delighted. On the fifth day, another member's father died. As the members of the "Funeral Expenses Co-op" could no longer afford the two cents, the union had to advance the money, which was to be paid back by the co-op later on. On the seventh day, a member died, and the union had to advance another thirty dollars. The members of the co-op panicked: five or six people had died within the first ten days; what were they to do if the trend should continue? An assembly was held, and it was decided that the co-op would be temporarily discontinued, and that it would be resumed when the funds of the union became more sufficient.

A medical dispensary was also established. It was located on the main street of Haifeng. The doctor in charge was an enthusiast of the peasants' movement and a trained Western-style physician. Any member of the peasants' union who needed medicine could present his membership card and get a fifty percent discount. Nonmembers could also get medicine, but at the full price. All members were entitled to the free clinic operated by the doctor, whose wife also delivered babies for no charge. Any medicine used in connection with natal care was also half-priced, and usually came to twenty or thirty cents only. This brought many peasants to the dispensary for medicine and for deliveries. We also caught some nonmembers posing as members, using borrowed membership cards. We had to add several regulations on the membership card, restricting its use to members themselves. We also made up a rule that a member must pay two cents for the replacement of a lost membership card.

On the first day of January, 1923, the Haifeng central union was established. The total membership had reached 20,000. And the population within the union's jurisdiction was 100,000, a quarter of the population of the entire county. On that day, more than sixty village representatives of the union came for the assembly, the procedure of which was:

1. The chairman announced the purpose of the assembly.
2. The representatives made their reports.
3. The chairman reported on the preparation for the central union.
4. Speeches.
5. Elections.
6. Discussion of regulations.
7. Proposals.
8. Banquet.

Peng Pai was elected as the president of the union, Yang Qishan the vice-president, Lao Jingqing the treasurer, Lin Pei the manager, Zhang Maan the investigator . . . (the rest has escaped my mind). . . .

One problem that we discussed during the assembly was that membership dues might have to be increased to support the central union. We investigated other possibilities and came up with the following idea. Peasants sold their goods in the sweet-potato markets, the sugar markets, the vegetable markets, the bean markets, the rice markets, the firewood markets, the pig markets, and the hay markets, all of which were controlled by the gentry, the local landowners, and the temple priests. We figured that the sweet-potato markets alone must produce at least 500 dollars in income. If we took account of all the markets, then there would be 3000 dollars to 4000 dollars. Could we take over the rights to these markets? If we took over the markets, we would inevitably come into conflict with the gentry. So, the first thing to do was to negotiate with them. If they were stubborn, our plan was to move the sweet-potato market, and within three days, all other markets would follow suit and move to other places. The union then took action. We first made a model scale, and sent a member to the sweet-potato market to supervise the sales. The gentry protested heatedly. The union then put out notices for all the peasants of the county, ordering them to move their sweet potatoes to stands next to their neighborhood union offices and prohibiting them from selling sweet potatoes in the old market. As a result, we won the battle and took control over the sweet-potato market. The income from the market was allocated to support the dispensary. . . .

Concerning the work of the Department of Education, the peasants were afraid of the "new education" program. Whenever the subject was mentioned, fear would show up on their faces. . . . The union, however, created a new slogan, "peasant education," which meant the founding of peasant schools. Our "peasant education" program was different from the "new education" program. It aimed at teaching peasants to keep accounts so landlords could not cheat them, to write letters, to use the abacus, to write the names of various feeds and agricultural tools, and to operate the union. That was all. The peasants were all for the program. Besides, the union hired teachers for them at a low cost, provided school facilities, and did not charge the students. No wonder the peasants were happy.

Where did the funds for the schools come from? Each village where a peasant school was formed set apart a piece of land of suitable size, and this was the "school's field," rented by the school from a landlord. The seeds and manure were paid for by the union; the tilling tools, animals, and human labor were provided by the students' families, who would divide among themselves the duties of tilling and sowing. When the time came for weeding, the teacher of the school would lead the students to the "school's field," and divide them and the field into four parts. Each group of students would be responsible for a part of the field. A contest would be started, and, in no time, the fields would be pruned, while the students had learned something about farming. When the grain was ripe, the students' relatives again went out to the fields to reap the harvest. The rent was paid to the landlord, and the rest of the harvest became the teacher's salary. Within a month after this system was started, a dozen such peasant schools were founded, including night schools, all of which were under the leadership and supervision of the union's Department of Education. From then on, over 500 village children, hitherto completely deprived of an opportunity for education, attended school. . . .

At this time the Haifeng central union reached its peak of activities. The county magistrate of the time, Weng Guaiqing, who was Chen Jiongming's most trusted man, disapproved of the union, but he dared not ban it, and we were allowed more freedom to develop our programs. Also, the union had by now acquired considerable power. The slogans we used for the peasants were:

1. Reduce rent.
2. Abolish the "three lease rules."
3. Abolish presents to landlords (chickens, ducks, rice, or money).
4. Don't give bribes to the police.

The slogans we used for outsiders were:

1. Improve agriculture.
2. Increase peasants' knowledge.
3. Perform charitable deeds.

Our plan was not to reduce rent until after five years of preparation.

Soon it was the Chinese New Year of 1923. Dragon dancers and music troupes from all the villages came to celebrate, and the union organized a New Year's Festival for all peasants in Haifeng. On the 16th of the first month, the festival was held at the grass carpeted field in front of the Donglin Ancestral Temple at Qiaodong. More than 6000 members and 3000 nonmembers participated, and the banners of each village's bands, dragon dancers, and music troupes danced in the air. The sequence of the festival was (1) music, (2) the chairman announced the purpose of the festival, (3) speeches, (4) songs and music, (5) dragon dances, (6) three cheers for the peasants, (7) firecrackers. The speakers included Peng Pai, Huang Fengin, and Yang Qishan, who pointed out that before the proletarian revolution was realized, there could be no joyous New Year, for New Year's Day was a time for the exploiters to oppress us and to demand us to pay our debts. We were now united in our hardships, not in joy. However, this was an opportunity in which we might demonstrate our strength to our enemies, and awaken the spirit of revolution in ourselves. We were prepared for a battle with our enemies. This was the reason why, on the one hand, we felt weighed down by our emotions, but on the other hand elated.

On that day, we issued 2000 new membership cards, and received over 400 dollars in dues. It was the highest point in the history of the union. After that, around 100 new members would join each day, and we could hardly keep up with the work. Every day about 300 peasant friends would come to the union for information, for conversation, and to sign up as members. We were extremely busy.

But we also caught the attention of the landlords, who said, "We didn't think they would succeed. We thought all that talk was nonsense. But now, it actually has happened!" . . .

Translated by Clara Yu

79

THE DOG-MEAT GENERAL

The abolition of the monarchy and the literary civil service examination system did not put an end to abuses of power or incompetence on the part of officials. To the contrary, disorder provided leeway for the rise of warlords, many of whom were not only incompetent and corrupt, but also brutal and destructive.

Below is an account of Zhang Zongchang (1881–1932), a poor boy who, in less than thirty years, rose from juvenile delinquent to general to governor of a province. When the Nationalist Party succeeded in its Northern Expedition against the warlords in 1928, Zhang retreated to Manchuria, then to Japan. On a visit back to his native area in 1932 he was assassinated by the son of one of his earlier victims. The article below was written after his death, based on the responses a magazine received when it solicited accounts of his cruelties and oppression from its readers.

Zhang Zongchang, nicknamed "Dog-meat General" and "Lanky General," was from Yi county in Shandong. His father was a trumpet player (hired for funeral processions, etc.) and barber, and his mother was a shamaness. At the age of twelve or thirteen, Zhang started helping his father by playing the cymbals. When he was fifteen or sixteen he went with his mother to Yinkou, and worked as a servant in a gambling house, mixing with pickpockets and thieves. The gentry of the town, annoyed, drove him away. He then fled to Guandong [in Manchuria] to join the "bearded bandits." His mother stayed on at Yinkou, and lived with the proprietor of a bathhouse, then with a cobbler, then with a cloth vendor. The cloth vendor, in a fit of jealousy, killed the cob-

bler, and was sent to jail. Because of this, Zhang's mother was sent into exile. Lacking any means of transportation, she gave herself to a rickshaw puller so that he would take her back to Yi county. In this way she returned to the trumpet player. But the trumpet player was too poor to support her, so he sold her to a grain wholesaler named Jia for some millet. We all know that Zhang Zongchang had two fathers, and this is the explanation.

When the revolution started in 1911, Zhang led about one hundred "bearded bandits" from Guandong to Yantai [in Shandong] to join Commander Hu Ying's army. When Hu resisted the revolutionary forces, Zhang went to Shanghai to join the regiment commander of the revolutionary army. At that time, there was a truce between the North and the South, and the regiment commander resigned, but not before he had made Zhang, who was not only strong but also brave, the leader of his men. Zhang and his army were then reorganized by Commander Cheng Dechuan of Jiangsu. Now called "Juangfu" troops, they were sent to Fengpei and Xiaoyi to put down bandits, and were under the Division Commander Leng Yuqin. When the Second Revolution started and Leng was defeated, Zhang took over Leng's soldiers and gained even more military power. However, because Zhang was connected with Leng, his troops were soon dissolved by Feng Guozhang, the honorary title "model supervisory regiment" given him was but an empty name. From then on, Zhang made a profession of murdering his revolutionary comrades. The assassination of Shanghai's commander, Chen Qimei, was Zhang's doing. Because of this, Zhang was taken into the confidence of Feng Guozhang. When Feng was the national vice-president, he appointed Zhang as the chief of his personal guards. . . .

Zhang was very brave in battle, but he had no mind for strategy. His soldiers were mostly bandits, and therefore very valiant warriors, which by and large accounted for his success in military ventures. But he also had an advisor who assisted him in military maneuvers, the fortune-teller Tong Huagu. During the Fengtian-Zhili war, Zhang was stationed to the east of the Xifeng pass. One day, Zhang came across Tong and went up to him for advice. Tong told him that his physiognomy revealed that he would achieve great distinction. He also predicted that the next day, when the Zhili troops passed by train, the train would derail, and if Zhang would take this opportunity, he could attack them and win a big victory. The next day, Zhang stationed his troops to wait for the Zhili troops. Just as Tong had predicted, the train derailed, and Zhang routed the enemies. At the time of the battle Tong paced back and forth on top of a hill, his hair untied, his mouth uttering words of magic. After the battle, Zhang asked Tong to step down from the hill, and with utmost deference appointed him as his military advisor.

From then on, Zhang followed Tong's words to the letter where military action was concerned.

It turned out that the fortune-teller was rather shrewd. The night that he met Zhang, he hired a few peasants to remove the screws connecting the rails over a bridge, thereby causing the derailment. Because he knew Zhang could easily be fooled, he used a fairy tale as a stepping-stone to a career. At any rate, on account of Zhang's military distinctions, he was finally appointed governor of Shandong. . . .

Not long after Zhang became governor, two phrases were heard all over the cities: "Cut apart to catch light" and "listen to the telephone." The former referred to the human heads which were treated like watermelons, cut in halves to bask in the sun; the latter referred to the same, except the heads were hung from telephones poles, and from afar they seemed to be listening on the telephone. At the same time, at the train stations along the Jiaoji and Jinpu lines, people started to hear the strange expression, "My head is my passport; my ass is my ticket." This was because people were being regularly kicked, beaten up, abused in vile language, and spat in the face by the soldiers. To the sights of the city of Jinan there were also added White Russian soldiers, who were drunkards, ruffians, and rapists. Living in Shandong at this time, one could really feel the truth in the saying, "A man's life is worth less than a chicken's."

Soon after Zhang Zongchang came to his post, he unveiled his ugly nature and started his vile deeds. Under his "steel sword" policy, the once-flourishing academies disappeared, the better students fled, and the provincial assembly was silenced. On the other hand, clever people moved with the current and began buttering Zhang up. Upholding the philosophy that "In an age of chaos, don't miss the chance to loot during the fire," they went after offices. From circuit intendants and county magistrates to bureau chiefs, all positions were refilled with much pomp. Whenever these henchmen went to a local district, their first priority was to extort and exploit, so that they could repay past favors and secure future ones, whereas the people were becoming skinnier daily.

Too true was the proverb, "In the official's house, wine and meat are allowed to rot, but on the roads are the bones of those who starved to death."

Zhang Zongchang came to Shandong in June of 1925, and he fled on the 30th of April, 1928. In these three years he took a total of 350,000 dollars of the people's blood money.

Zhang Zongchang was a warmonger, by nature fond of disorder. After his arrival in Shandong, there was not even one day of peace. In the Lusu war, Zhang fought with Sun Chuanfang back and forth between Bangfu, Xuzhou, Hanzhuang, and Lincheng. In the Luyu war, he battled Jin Yune and Li Ji at Mount Tai. In the battle at Baliwa, he almost lost all his arms and men. In the battle at Nankou, he fought side by side with the Fengtian and Zhili troops against the Nationalist army, forcing them into Gansu and Shaanxi. During the Nationalists' Northern Expedition, Zhang fought like a wounded beast along the Jinpu railroad.

After each battle, the field was strewn with bodies. The loss of the soldiers required replacement, which in turn required military funds, which resulted in higher taxes. When funds were raised, more soldiers were drafted, and another war was in the making. This cycle was repeated again and again. This was the way Zhang Zongchang ruled the province of Shandong from 1925 to 1928. The white banners of recruitment flew all over the province, and young people were driven straight into their graves. In such a situation, how could the people of Shandong escape hardship and poverty?

TAXATION

During the less then four years that Zhang Zongchang ruled, there was not one day that he failed to take money from the people. Besides the regular taxes, there were special taxes and blatant extortions. Whenever he needed a sum of money, he would issue an order to several counties for them to come up with the cash. And when he spent the money, well, that was the end of that. Thus, the people of Shandong were really in deep water, and they suffered more than the rest of the nation.

The regular land taxes were eight to twenty dollars for each tael of land value. After the Northern Expedition, the Provincial Bureau of Finance released a statistics report showing that "From the day Zhang Zongchang came to Shandong till the day he left, the recorded land taxes, tributes, and special taxes that he collected amount to a sum which, if figured by regular rates of taxation, would exceed all taxes to be paid until 1939."

Below are the various types of taxes he collected:

1. One-time special land tax for military reconstruction
2. One-time special tribute rice for reconstruction
3. One-time special land tax for suppressing the Reds
4. Tribute for suppressing the Reds
5. Special land tax for military purposes
6. Supplementary land tax for military purposes
7. Supplementary tribute rice for military purposes
8. Supplementary tax for the Lidong Pass
9. Special tax for relief funds
10. Special supplementary tax for river conservancy works
11. Supplementary tax for highway works
12. Tax for barracks works
13. Military loans
14. Government bonds for reconstruction
15. Special tax on tobacco and liquor
16. Government sales special tax
17. Registration fees for establishments
18. Stamp tax for registrations
19. Registration fees for real estate
20. Tax for license to distribute paper currency
21. Stamp tax on paper currency
22. Long distance telephone fees
23. Tax on tobacco seeds
24. Fines on tobacco saplings
25. Business license fees
26. Donations for army shoes

27. Pension certificates for the families of soldiers in the First Army Corps who were killed in Jiazi war
28. Pension certificates for the families of the soldiers in the Zhilu Army Corps who were killed in the war against the Reds
29. Fees for license to examine tobacco
30. Stamp tax for license to sell tobacco
31. Donations for the construction of a living shrine for Zhang Zongchang
32. Donations for a bronze statue of Zhang Zongchang
33. Advance for firewood and straw
34. Donations for the entertainment of the officers and soldiers
35. Restaurant taxes
36. Tax on dogs
37. Tax on dwellings
38. Tax on wealthy families
39. Poll tax
40. Exclusive sales of opium by government operated stores
41. Tax on opium-pipe lighters
42. Tax on light vehicles
43. Tax on rickshaws
44. Stamp taxes
45. Tax on livestock
46. Local tax on already-taxed foreign goods
47. Tax on vegetables
48. Exclusive sales of nightsoil by government-operated "golden-juice" stores
49. Tax on prostitution houses
50. Tax on theatrical performances
51. Tax on chickens ...

FLOODING THE MARKET WITH PAPER MONEY

Zhang Zongchang issued the following paper currencies:

1. Banknotes of the Provincial Bank of Shandong
2. Military stamps
3. Co-op certificates

Altogether several tens of millions of dollars were issued, all without any reserve to back them up. When he was losing his battles on the frontiers, these forms of currency came to be regularly discounted and financial chaos resulted. Zhang's soldiers continued to use his paper money for purchases, however, without accepting a discount on the face value. If anyone objected they would use their fists, legs, and foul tongues against their opponents. For this reason, arguments and fights were frequent, and the merchants suffered. There is a story that a store refused to accept military stamps. Zhang gave orders to arrest the owner, who was beaten up and then shot.

EXTORTION FOR MILITARY EXPENSES

In order to raise funds to pay his soldiers and buy arms, Zhang Zongchang frequently "borrowed" from various banks and commercial unions. Though these were loans in name, they were extortions in fact. The Gongli Banking House, which had operated in Shandong for over a decade, went out of business because of such extortions, and its manager went into exile. . . .

BUILDING A LIVING SHRINE AND CASTING A BRONZE STATUE

To manifest his own "merits and distinctions," Zhang planned to build a living shrine and a bronze statue for himself along the Daming Lake of Jinan. The expenses were extorted from the people. He shipped a full trainload of granite from Mount Tai for the construction. But because of the rapid advance of the troops of the Northern Expedition, there was not enough time for the actual work to begin. However, the "donations" for these purposes had been collected in full. . . .

YOUTH SQUADS

Zhang Zongchang especially recruited an army of teenagers for his son, calling them "young students of war." Their arms were specially designed small foreign-made rifles, and they were given good uniforms, food, and pay. Zhang appointed his son the leader, and put several thousand such youths under his control. The youth squads were stationed at the southern barracks of the Jinan area. When they were in training, they would sing the children's song, "There is a fat little baby in our family." Consequently, they came to be known as the "Baby Squads." . . .

NOT PAYING THE TROOPS

Zhang kept all the money that he extorted from the people for his personal use, seldom paying his soldiers. Consequently, his men lost their confidence in him, and he lost many battles. In order to improve the morale, he raised some money to pay the men, but it turned out to be too little. When each soldier only got fifty cents, they said to each other, "Let's fight another fifty cents' worth of war for Zhang Zongchang."

SALVOS AGAINST HEAVEN

In the summer of 1927, there was a severe drought in Shandong. Not a drop of rain fell, and the crops were all dying. Zhang Zongchang ordered a general fast and personally went to the "Dragon King Temple" to pray for rain. But the Dragon King was apparently not impressed, and the drought continued. In a rage, Zhang slapped the Dragon King's face many times. He then went to the Zhangzhuang Arsenal and fired cannon balls into the sky for hours, so as to vent his anger at Heaven. Nevertheless, it still did not rain. . . .

STATE SALES OF OPIUM

Zhang Zongchang decreed that opium could only be sold by the state, but an opportunist opened up a store in a newly built shopping center, calling it "Opium Quitting Center." But in fact it was an opium store, and every month this person presented a gift of "state sales tax on opium" to Zhang.

EDUCATIONAL BACKGROUND

Once Zhang Zongchang held a meeting of high-ranking military officers in the governor's office, and these officers introduced themselves, one saying, "I graduated from X university," another saying, "I am attending Y university," Hard-pressed, Zhang Zongchang said, "I, Zhang Zongchang, am a graduate of the College of the Green Forest."*

DRAFTING SOLDIERS

Zhang literally dragged young people from the streets to become his soldiers so that he could send them to the frontiers, using their flesh against the cannon balls of the enemy. Many students were dragged away, and only after negotiations, were released. In order to prevent such incidents, the schools issued each student a cloth tag with his name and the school's seal printed on it. In this way the students were distinguished from the common people.

CLEARING THE STREETS

Whenever Zhang came out of his office, he would clear the streets, and all traffic was stopped. The main street in front of the governor's office was sprinkled with clean water. In front of this motorcade, he had the showy white Russian cavalry squad. Soldiers were stationed all along the streets, their rifles loaded with real bullets, their backs to the street. All precautions were taken against possible assassins. . . .

Translated by Clara Yu

---

* The Green Forest was a term for the hideout of bandits.

80

THE GENERAL STRIKE

Unionization of China's urban workers began with the May Fourth Movement in 1919 and made considerable progress in the early 1920s, aided by organizers from the young Communist Party. There were fifty major strikes in 1921 and ninety-one in 1922. The first serious violence against strikers took place on February 7, 1923, when the soldiers of the warlord Wu Peifu attacked striking railway workers and killed sixty-five. During the following two years, anti-union repression became widespread. The incident that created the greatest uproar occurred on May 30, 1925, when the English police in the International Settlement in Shanghai shot at a group of demonstrators, killing ten. A general strike was then organized, which involved 150,000 workers, merchants, and students and lasted three months. For over a year sympathizers throughout China contributed money, boycotted foreign goods, and staged strikes. In the meantime, the Communist Party had formed an alliance with the Nationalist Party to overthrow the warlords and establish a national government. Members of the Communist Party joined the Nationalist Party and tried to continue their labor union work within the framework of the alliance. For example, during the Northern Expedition, Communists aided the advance of Jiang Jieshi's army by organizing peasants and workers along the way. The alliance between the two parties was, however, fragile, since the Nationalists drew their strength from the bourgeoisie and landlords, whom the Communists opposed.

Below is an account of a strike held in Shanghai during the Northern Expedition, organized by the Communist-led General Labor Union. The account appeared in a Communist Party newspaper, Guide Weekly, *shortly after the strike. It reveals the avowed principles of the labor union movement as well as the fragility of the alliance of the Nationalists and Communists. Less than three months after it was written, Jiang Jieshi ordered an attack on the unions and a purge of Communists from the Nationalist Party. For months thereafter, Communists were hunted down and killed. Not until 1936 would there again be any semblance of cooperation between the Nationalists and the Communists.*

On February 19th the working class of Shanghai started a historic struggle which has unleashed the anger of the urban masses and launched the common people's fight for political power. A new page has been turned in the revolutionary history of China; a heroic record has been added to the history of the working class of the world.

The February 7th Movement of 1923 and the May 30th Movement of 1925 had different characteristics, a result of their historical and social causes. The heroic February 7th Incident demonstrated that the first struggles of the Chinese working class were struggles for political freedom under the rule of feudal warlords. The fierce May 30th Movement showed, in addition, that during a time of increasing nationalism, the working class was determined to revolt against imperialism. These two movements led to the Northern Expedition to eliminate the warlords. The unity formed by the Chinese working class was itself a political unity, and the principle that motivated the actions of the workers was "political power to the masses for the revolution."

Once the Northern Expedition had begun, the spirit of revolution shook every city and village. Since Shanghai is the most important city in our country, the workers there are the leaders of the entire working class, endowed with a natural responsibility in this historic, revolutionary struggle. Thus, it was among the working masses of Shanghai that the general strike broke out on February 19th. But this was no mere strike; it was a revolution. The initial stage lasted only five days; yet, since the workers went back to work, revolutionary activities have continued to increase. The following is a record of what happened in the initial stage of the revolution.

PRELUDE TO THE STRIKE

On the eve of the February 19th strike, the victorious Northern Expedition forces had claimed control of the nearby province of Jejiang. Although the actual military victory was some distance away, it struck fear in the warlords controlling Shanghai. The uncertainty of their rule provided an opportunity for the masses to take revolutionary action, thus igniting the strike. This strike was a political, not an economic one; its purpose was to overthrow the rule of warlords Sun Chuanfang and Li Baozhang, establish the political power of Shanghai's revolutionary masses (including the workers), support the Northern Expedition, and expedite the victory of the national revolutionary war. For these reasons, the workers of Shanghai rose to lead all oppressed people in their revolutionary struggle, and the general strike began. Immediately before the February 19th strike, the central organization of the workers of Shanghai, the General Labor Union, held an assembly and issued the following order:

Order for a General Strike

To all worker-friends of Shanghai: The power of the people's revolution is increasing daily! The Northern Expedition is victorious, and Sun Chuanfang's resistance has collapsed. The masses must now rise and overthrow the forces of the warlords. The General Labor Union therefore declares a general strike for the entire city of Shanghai. Its purpose is to eliminate the remaining power of the warlords and demonstrate the strength of the revolutionary masses. As soon as you receive this order, go on strike. After the strike begins, obey the orders of the General Labor Union in an organized and orderly manner. Remember, do not go back to work until you are advised to do so.

Strike in support of the Northern Expedition!

Strike to overthrow Sun Chuanfang!

Long live the people's political power!

Long live the workers' freedom!

Long live the workers' unity!

Issued by the General Labor Union of Shanghai on February 19th

When the strike began, the General Labor Union issued a manifesto and seventeen economic and political demands:

Manifesto of the General Strike

Our people's revolutionary movement has intensified since the May 30th Movement. The warlord Sun Chuanfang who controlled the Southeast has been defeated by the bravery of our revolutionary masses.

Shanghai belongs to the citizens of Shanghai, who have for decades been oppressed by the warlords. The imperialist powers have used Shanghai as their base to encroach on China and now they are continuing to menace our nationalist movement by military means. We citizens want to overthrow the dark rule of the warlords and to resist the advance of the imperialists. Ever since the May 30th Movement workers of Shanghai have been bravely struggling for our people's freedom and liberation. At this moment, the forces of Sun Chuanfang have been routed, but the imperialists are still threatening us with guns and cannons. If we do not destroy these dark, reactionary powers, our people will never see the dawn of freedom.

In order to destroy these dark, reactionary powers, the people must rise up and protest by going on strike in industry, in business, and in schools. Once the working class has begun its protest, the revolutionary masses must also take action to speed the elimination of the warlords and to assist in the victory of the Northern Expedition forces. For these reasons, this General Union now calls for all workers of Shanghai to begin demonstrating the power of the masses by organized, orderly means. We hereby declare a general strike, effective today. The following are the minimum political and economic demands we make for the workers of Shanghai:

1. Continued resistance against imperialism.
2. Elimination of the warlords' underhanded power politics.
3. Liquidation of all reactionary forces.
4. Establishment of a government that truly protects the welfare of the people.
5. Rights to hold meetings, to form associations, and to strike, as well as freedom of speech and freedom of the press.
6. Recognition of the labor union's rights to represent the workers.
7. Higher wages and a minimum wage for workers.
8. An end to inflation and protection of the livelihood of the workers.
9. An eight-hour work day.
10. Sundays and festivals are to be paid holidays, with double pay for work on those days.
11. Hiring of the unemployed. No closing of factories on the pretext of strikes.
12. An end to employers' physically or verbally abusing workers, or reducing their wages at will.
13. An end to employers' firing workers without the consent of the labor union.
14. Compensation for work-related injuries and deaths.
15. Health care plans for the workers, and half-pay when sick.
16. Equal wages for male and female workers. Improvements in the treatment of working women and children. Six weeks of maternity leave with full pay. No heavy physical labor for children.
17. Better working conditions in the factories. More doors, windows, skylights, and lavatories.

The above are the goals of the present action taken by the workers of Shanghai. We want to struggle side by side with the people of all classes in our society to destroy the remaining power of the warlords, and we hope the new government will accept these demands made by our workers.

Issued by the General Labor Union of Shanghai on February 19th

THE MASSIVE STRIKE

The strike began at 6 A.M., February 19th. . . . Tallied according to different professions, the striking workers included the entire textile industry; the entire city communications service; salespersons belonging to the Commerce Union, and those who worked in such stores as Foremost, Peace, New, and Beautiful; gold- and silversmiths; makers of tea cases; tailors of Western-style clothing; makers of canvas, incense, tea, carpets, and pig-bristle products; workers at a dozen metal and machine works; crews of the Ancient line's Guangxi, Shanxi, Guang Shuntian, Gansu, and Ningbo ships; the Sun Bright line's Mt. Lu, Fortune, and Shangyang; the Peaceful line's Prosperity; and Mt. Zhou line's Mt. Zhou; also all the workers of the Commercial, Colorful, Lovely, Chinese Merchant, Black, and Stone Presses. The total number of striking workers exceeded 150,000.

On the second day of the strike (February 20th), the number of strikers rose sharply to a total of over 275,000. Most of the increase came from those professions that had been restrained by the capitalists on the first day or had not received the order to strike. Included were 60,000 workers from the silk factories of North Sluice; 40,000 workers in the construction business; 100,000 workers from businesses such as imports, soy sauce, rice, secondhand clothes, herb medicine, and fabrics. Five hundred workers in public transportation also joined in. The number of striking textile factories in the Sandy Crossing area increased to twenty-five, which added another 15,000 workers to the strike. The dock workers of Whangpoo and Sixteen Shops also numbered 10,000. . . . All in all, in these four days, more than 360,000 workers joined in the strike, making it the biggest not only in the history of Shanghai, but in the entire nation. It demonstrated the heightening of political consciousness and the rapidly developing organization of the Shanghai working class. . . .

WHITE TERROR

On the first day of the strike, Li Baozhang, Defense Commander of Shanghai and a henchman of Sun Chuanfang, struggled to retain power by lashing out at the masses. He immediately contacted the Labor Departments of the Concessions and instituted a reign of white terror.

Within six hours of the strike, bustling, prosperous Shanghai became lifeless. All the trolleys stopped running; no ships entered or departed; the doors of post offices were bolted; department stores were closed; all factories were shut down, their sirens echoing one another but unable to call in a single worker. All these developments made the police and military patrols on the streets tremble; the ruling class, terrified and enraged, began to strike back with massacres.

Those slaughtered—our front-line soldiers—were workers handing out strike literature on the streets. The martyrs of the first day were two workers, Cai Jianxun and Shi Arong, from the metal and machine works of South City. They were arrested for distributing strike literature and were immediately beheaded. On the second day of the strike, a worker selling trolley tickets was shot at the West Gate for giving out leaflets about the strike. Two of the students who made public speeches at Cao Family Crossing were arrested and beheaded immediately. At the old West Gate, citizens who were reading strike literature were killed by the Big Sword Brigade. One head was hung from a telephone pole, and two bodies were left lying on the streets. Two workers, one from Lucky Life Iron Factory and the other from Heroic Tobacco Factory, walked past a group of policemen and annoyed them by their presence. They were arrested and shot. In addition, many people disappeared without a trace, perhaps having been murdered or arrested. The total number of casualties must have been over one hundred. . . .

THE WARLORDS' MASSACRE POLICY AND THE RIGHT WING OF THE NATIONALIST PARTY

Who were the ringleaders of the massacre? Who were the masterminds behind the white terror? The answer is the Western Hills Conference group—the right-wing faction of the Nationalist Party.

The headquarters of these rightists was situated at 44 Dragon Road in the French Concession. The recently established mad-dog *Jiangnan Evening News* was the mouthpiece of their organization. The leaders of this right-wing group were none other than those denounced by Sun Yatsen and expelled from the Nationalist Party: Zhang Ji, Zhou Lu, Xie Chi, and so on. Right after the general strike began, Zhu Zheng and company advised Li Baozhang (who held 2000 dollars' worth of stock in the *Jiangnan Evening News*) that "the only thing for you to do now is to resist the Party's forces in the front and kill workers in the rear." Thus the savage warlord Li Baozhang was assured of protection by the Nationalist Party and provided with a policy of terror against the strikers.

We are not libeling the rightists of the Nationalist Party when we say that they are responsible for the massacre. It is a fact supported by the words of the *Jiangnan Evening News*. Before the strike began, the paper had already predicted that the masses would be sacrificed. After the massacre had been carried out, the paper made a great deal of noise, accusing the Communists of sacrificing the masses. When the massacre aroused the anger of the citizens of Shanghai, the paper reported it, and at the same time advised Li Baozhang to change his "kill on sight" policy. Undoubtedly, the right-wing Nationalists are the instigators of the massacre; they are the reactionaries, the counterrevolutionaries, and therefore enemies of the people.

THE STRUGGLE FOR ARMS

The killings under the white terror naturally provoked the red terror of the revolution. An eye for an eye, a terror for a terror: this is the condition in which revolutions begin, and this was the condition for the Shanghai masses—workers and ordinary citizens alike—on February 21st, the third day of the strike.

When the time for a revolution is ripe, a general strike will directly lead to mass riots; when premature, the masses will continue their struggle for arms. When the weapons are in the hands of the warlords, white terror results; when the masses get hold of the weapons, armed revolutionary struggle explodes. This is a lesson in Marxism-Leninism, a lesson to be learned by the working class of Shanghai.

Having no weapons, the Shanghai workers had to snatch them out of their enemies' hands. The white terror that followed the strike made the working masses determined to struggle for arms. Beginning on the evening of the 21st, workers of the various regions began fighting the police and soldiers. On the 22nd, sailors who opposed the warlords' massacre policy and sympathized with the workers' movement opened unauthorized artillery fire on the Gaochangmiao Arsenal. That evening, heated battles broke out in South City and North Sluice, in which workers and citizens attempted to seize weapons. They were not completely successful because not everyone joined in and because the enemy still struggled to retain power. However, the cannonade made the enemy officers and soldiers run for shelter in the Concessions. On the 22nd, during their attacks on the defense lines and sentries of the police and military forces, workers of various regions succeeded in acquiring quite a few weapons; they also shot and killed a police captain while returning fire. Such was the first heroic effort to wrest weapons from armed enemies with our bare hands. These actions continued into the evening of the 23rd in the North Sluice and South City regions. The workers raided several police stations and were engaged in battles for hours. The stalemate came to an end when the masses retreated safely, the police not daring to chase after them. All these events show that armed revolutionary struggle has begun in Shanghai. . . .

FIGHTING FOR POLITICAL POWER

What was the purpose of the Shanghai workers' general strike and armed struggle? The rightists, who do not understand the situation of the revolution and are afraid of the power of the working class, suspect that the workers of Shanghai want to form a labor government. This is incorrect. The present aim of the Shanghai workers is to form not a labor government, but a citizens' government, a democratic government under the Republic. However, the fight of the workers is a fight for political power.

In this revolution of an oppressed people in a semicolonial state, in this revolution of Shanghai's citizens against the rule of imperialists and warlords, the struggle of the workers bred the struggle of the citizens; the revolt of the workers led to the revolt of the citizens; the political power of the workers ensured the political power of the citizens. Therefore, the slogan of the Shanghai workers was "to establish a representative government." Again, the purpose of the Shanghai workers' general strike and armed struggle was to take over political power and to lead all oppressed Shanghai citizens to form a democratic government belonging to them.

On the fourth day of the strike, when armed struggle broke out and the navymen suddenly opened artillery fire on Gaochangmiao, the unity of the armed forces and the workers in revolution was demonstrated, and the necessity and possibility for soldiers and workers to seize political power was proved. . . .

THE REVOLUTIONARY JUSTICE OF THE MASSES

In terms of history, the most significant events of the five-day general strike are the armed struggle and the beginning of the struggle for political power. Another action of the masses is worth noting, however, and that is their revolutionary justice.

On the 22nd, nearly 10,000 workers from Willow Landing gathered for a demonstration. A henchman by the nickname of "Little Trickster" had been discovered spying on the workers. As he had conspired with detectives and policemen and was responsible for the arrests of the workers' leaders, the people seized him and brought him before the dais to be judged by the masses. When the majority of the workers cried out "kill him," the chairman put the issue to a vote. A unanimous verdict was reached, and "Little Trickster" was executed on the spot.

This was a revolutionary judgment passed by the masses—terror answered with terror, counterrevolution met with revolution. By the verdict of the masses, a henchman of the industrial thieves was punished by death. Such is the law of the revolution. Certainly, the reactionaries and the counterrevolutionaries are opposed to such a verdict and call it a vicious act of the masses. But this was an eminently fair action; the enemy killed dozens of our people, we now only justly punished one. When power is in the hands of the revolutionary masses, the architect of this massacre, Li Baozhang, should also receive the same punishment.

RETURNING TO WORK IN ORDER TO ENLARGE THE STRUGGLE

Up to this point, the mass action of the general strike had developed along two correct lines; first, taking over arms for the struggle, and second, fighting for the political power of the citizens. However, because the military power of the revolution still lagged far behind, the time was not yet ripe for the revolution and the masses suffered losses. While the organized political power was still intact, on the fifth day of the strike, the Shanghai General Labor Union called for all workers to return to work at 1 P.M. the next day (February 24th) in order to prepare for an even greater struggle.

On the morning of the 24th, the order to return to work was issued:

To all our worker-friends of Shanghai:
When this Union ordered the general strike, 400,000 organized workers responded. Within a few hours, our coordinated actions shook the warlords' power, and the bustling city of Shanghai turned into a battlefield of revolution. This was the first time since the May 30th Movement that all Shanghai workers have been engaged in such a great and honorable struggle. During the five-day strike, our citizens rose in revolt and the revolutionary navymen attacked our enemies—a great symbol of the alliance of workers and soldiers. Our

strength is now known to our enemies. The Union, seeing that the struggle will be a long one, has decided not to fight alone, for fear of bearing excessive losses. For this reason, we command all our worker-friends to return to work as of 1 P.M., the 24th of this month. We must prepare for a greater struggle to come.

Long live the great strike of the workers of Shanghai!

Fight for more power!

Long live the Shanghai General Labor Union!

Issued by the Shanghai General Labor Union,
February 24th

Declaration of the End of the Strike

To all the citizens of Shanghai:

We, the working class, went on a general strike to protest tyrannical government and to show our support for the Northern Expedition. Our strike lasted five days, during which workers and citizens made great sacrifices. Now we are forced by various factors to declare a temporary end to the strike. Although the strike is halted for the moment, our struggle against the tyrannical rule of the warlords, our fight for our political power and for improvement in workers' lives will continue. During the strike, the citizens of Shanghai showed their sincere sympathy, for which we are grateful. Although we have taken the advice of businesses to return to work, we hope the revolutionary citizens of Shanghai will continue to join our fight against the dark powers, until we have completely overthrown tyranny.

Our call for returning to work is not a retreat, but a preparation for a greater struggle.

Issued by the Shanghai General Labor Union,
February 24th

THE PROCESS OF CONTINUING THE STRUGGLE

Once the order to return to work was issued, some workers went back even before noon. From noon until the next morning, more than 300,000 workers returned to their jobs. But the five-day strike had not been brought to a conclusion by any means.

All the workers and oppressed citizens of Shanghai are in the midst of a continuing struggle to gain victory. The general strike was by no means a failure. It produced results. The experience we gained and the lessons we learned during those five days—especially the solutions we found through struggle—exceeded the sum total of all lessons learned since the May 30th Movement. This is a critical moment in the history of the working class of Shanghai; it now has duties to fulfill.

The following slogans are the emerging political aims of the workers of Shanghai. They also outline the actions of the masses:

1. Down with Li Baozhang!
2. Drive out the Ji-Lu army!
3. Support the Northern Expedition!
4. Uphold the Republic!
5. Start mass uprisings; seize weapons!
6. Kill the reactionaries!
7. Avenge the dead!
8. Establish a representative government!
9. Get rid of foreign armies and reclaim the Concessions!

Translated by Clara Yu

81

FUNERAL PROCESSIONS

Funerals were important occasions in religious and social life from earliest times. Funeral processions served as great parades that entertained onlookers while symbolically reinforcing social distinctions and kinship connections. Special garments worn by the mourners revealed how closely they were related to the deceased. Also part of the processions were emblems of the rank and accomplishment of the family.

Below is an account of two funeral processions written in 1924 by Gu Jiegang (1893–1980), a prominent historian and intellectual. Unlike earlier ritual texts which merely state the rules or expectations for funerals, Gu's account gives a full description of two processions as they were actually organized. Gu's theme is the changes in funeral practices caused by the overthrow of the old gentry class with its codes of ritual and the consequent increasing importance of money in establishing social status. It should be pointed out, however, that such critiques were not new to the twentieth century. As early as the Han, writers lamented how funerals had become occasions for the display of wealth, and that those who could not afford lavish preparations felt their social status to be jeopardized.

The city of Suzhou has always been known for impressive and elaborate ceremonies, but nowadays this display of wealth and luxury has taken on a different character. In the past, the right to conduct lavish ceremonies was strictly reserved for the gentry and official classes, whereas now it has been taken over by the wealthy merchant class. Any novelty will soon become the fashion after the social elite has adopted it. Previously, elaborate ceremonies sometimes made life difficult for exalted households, but now that the class system has been overthrown, the painful task of keeping up with one's neighbors falls on everybody.

There are numerous occasions for lavish and elaborate ceremonies, the most important of which are weddings and funerals because they represent the greatest events in a person's life. A marriage celebration may be embellished to impress people, but its lavishness can never compare with a funeral. Marriages are affairs arranged by the older generation for the younger. If they are conducted with frugality, people may laugh, but they will not scold or criticize. Besides, parents often have more than one child and cannot afford to put on an elaborate show for each one. If they did not give their younger children the same lavish weddings, they would appear to be partial. Funeral ceremonies, on the other hand, are quite different because these are affairs conducted by the younger generation for their elders. If the arrangements are too simple, older relatives will make critical remarks, and sons will be accused of unfilial behavior and face the disapproval of society. Moreover, when there are many sons in a family, the responsibility and cost for one funeral can be shared by all the brothers. As more people naturally means more resources, they can be more free with their money.

The burial aspect of a funeral is not given much attention because cemeteries are located outside of the city where few onlookers are present. The most elaborate part of a funeral is the procession because it passes through city streets and avenues where spectators gather. For this reason, preparation for the funeral procession is the single greatest task for the bereaved family; it is also an important occasion for those who are eager to watch a good show. Before the procession takes place, news of it has already spread to every corner of the city: "On such and such a day, a procession from the House of _____ will pass through such and such streets." People with nothing to do wait along those city streets.

When a procession is well planned and lives up to the expectations of the crowd, there are words of praise from the spectators, such as, "This family certainly lives up to its reputation!" The sons, wearing mourning clothes and surrounded by mourning curtains, are comforted when they hear such words. However, if the procession is not outstanding or if it compares poorly with another one held that day, people ridicule it, saying things like, "Do they think this is good enough for us to watch?" Then all the preparations and all the money are wasted. Not only are their expenses and efforts in vain, but the family will long after be branded with an unfavorable reputation. When their name is mentioned, people will say, "Oh, how those sons slighted their parents!" or "That family has no face!"

In Beijing, a funeral procession of a middle-class family includes just the casket. Sons and male relatives walk ahead of it and female relatives and friends walk behind. This, after all, is the idea behind a funeral procession. People who are slightly better off hire young boys dressed in traditional costumes and musicians to lead the procession. It is believed that the dead person still has consciousness and feelings and his soul must be coaxed by the music to follow the procession. This is not an unreasonable explanation for the musicians' presence. But this kind of funeral procession is not seen in Suzhou. People here feel that it would not only cause one to lose face but also invite ridicule and criticism. Having no procession at all would almost be better. Therefore, under the cover of darkness, when everyone is sound asleep, a family hires a few coolies to carry the casket onto a boat and row it via canals to the city gate. At daybreak, when the gate opens, the casket is carried to the burial ground. This practice is called "burying the dead secretly," and is not condemned by the people of Suzhou who sympathize with families in difficulty. But those families who conduct a funeral procession through the streets must meet the current standard of extravagance. The streets of Suzhou are very narrow, so a funeral procession can cause quite a traffic jam; the longer the procession, the worse the traffic problem. But spectators do not mind it at all; they even complain when the traffic congestion is over too soon. It seems that people no longer regard funeral processions as funeral processions, but as parades in religious festivals.

In my childhood I took part in funeral processions of family friends. At that time, the processions were not long and mourning guests riding on horseback were a rare sight. Today, few guests are willing to walk; almost all of them ride horses. Furthermore, the items in a procession change constantly with new things added almost every day. How do we explain this phenomenon? In the past, the items in a procession were determined by a person's rank in office, and he could not make additions wantonly. But now that tradition has been overturned, and the people of Suzhou have been greatly influenced by the Shanghai merchants' "spirit of extravagance." And once things begin to change, they never stop.

About five or six years ago, there were two funeral processions to Suzhou from Shanghai which people have not yet forgotten. One was that of Mr. Sheng Xuanhuai, the other that of Mr. Xi Eming. Mr. Sheng was on the board of directors of Shanghai Coal and Gas Company. He owned a resort in Suzhou (the noted Liu Gardens outside of Yan Gate). After his death, his family was supposed to spend 100,000 dollars to send his casket in a boat procession to his garden here. I was not present in Suzhou at the time so I have no firsthand knowledge of just how exciting that occasion was, but according to many people, it was something never experienced before, a once-in-a-lifetime thrill. Mr. Xi was a paint manufacturer in Shanghai. After World War I broke out, the supply route for European paint was cut off; the price of paint soared sky-high, and paint manufacturers became enormously wealthy. But Mr. Xi died before he could enjoy his newfound wealth. His family felt very sorry about it and conducted a particularly lavish funeral for him, hoping his soul would rest in peace. Ever since then, elaborate and lavish processions have become a common practice in our city.

Two years ago, within three months, our family held two funerals. I still have the accounts for both processions. One was for my sister who died in Hangzhou. After her casket was settled in the funeral home there, her soul tablet was brought home to Suzhou. The other funeral was for my grandmother. The procession began at our house and ended in a funeral home two *li* away. I must declare right away that our family is not one that flaunts its wealth, but our position required us to meet the current standard of lavishness. Our two processions were rated slightly above average. After the reader has finished these accounts, I hope he does not accuse us of being too extravagant. Perhaps he can imagine the pride and joy of those rich families who can extravagantly flaunt their wealth, and at the same time the pain and anxieties of those families who are in financial difficulties but still must keep up appearances.

I. The procession for "bringing home the soul tablet" (sister)

1. oblong paper lantern, hanging from a pole
2. placard demanding silence and reverence (carried over the shoulder)
3. placard demanding people to clear the way
4. gongs
5. regimental insignia of the Manchu dynasty
6. picture of a dragon on a placard
7. placard on which is written the official rank of the deceased
8. melon-shaped paper decorations hanging from a pole
9. military band (brass instruments and drums)
10. ten embroidered banners
11. seven Daoist priests
12. *papier-mache* float to fetch the soul (all floats carried by men)
13. pavilion-shaped float made with pine needles
14. seven Buddhist monks
15. parasol made with pine needles
16. small pavilion-shaped float carrying a picture of the deceased
17. ten silk umbrellas
18. brass musicians
19. glass lantern
20. paper effigies of spirit deities
21. male relatives and friends
22. picture of a tiger on a placard
23. cymbals
24. large parasol
25. large fan
26. kerosene lantern
27. large parasol for a rider on horseback
28. Ding stallion of a high-ranking Manchu regiment (decked out with military ornament)
29. name of the lineage on a placard
30. small paper lantern
31. sedan chair carrying the soul tablet

32. accompanying sedan chairs for female mourners and guests

II. Funeral procession (grandmother)

1. a load of coins to buy passage on the road
2. horse to clear the way
3. gentleman's horse
4. six long horn players
5. stallions from Chong regiment (decked with military ornaments)
6. stallions from Biao regiment (decked with military ornaments)
7. oblong paper lantern with the lady's rank written on it
8. two pairs of yellow placards
9. nine pairs of tinfoil placards
10. six-man military band
11. umbrella for a rider on horseback
12. horse of high-ranking Manchu official
13. yellow parasol
14. a staff with feathers tied on it (the higher the rank, the more feathers)
15. dragon staff
16. palace-style fan
17. palace-style lantern
18. six swinging censers
19. yellow pavilion-shaped float carrying a large board on which is written the lady's rank, conferred by the emperor

The above completes the first part of the procession. All the items after 5 are used to set off the pavilion float (19). Since the honor was conferred by the emperor, the float is accompanied by a palace fan, palace lantern, and other paraphernalia associated with him. Items 5, 6, and 9 were associated with the office of the Manchu military governor and were originally used in military ceremonies. During the Qing dynasty an official had to hold a rank of three or higher before permission was given by the military governor to include these items to glorify the pavilion float (19) in his funeral procession. The office of the military governor is now abolished, and it would seem that his power has been taken over by the funeral directors.

20. effigies of two spirits who clear the way
21. effigies of the four guardians of the Buddhist temple
22. pavilion-shaped float carrying a soul banner
23. oblong paper lantern
24. placard demanding silence and reverence
25. Manchu regimental insignia
26. placard demanding that people clear the way
27. gongs
28. placard on which is written the official rank of the deceased
29. melon-shaped paper ornaments on a pole
30. picture of a dragon on a placard
31. embroidered banner
32. nine musicians
33. pavilion-shaped float carrying incense burner
34. silk ribbons tied to a staff
35. nine Daoist priests
36. pavilion-shaped float carrying offerings of food and drink
37. five pairs of silk-covered placards
38. eight riders on horseback (not in mourning clothes)
39. ten-man orchestra
40. picture of deceased on a large placard (to be placed at grave site)
41. silk parasol
42. nine Chan monks
43. open sedan chair
44. four placards with the word "libation" on them
45. five pairs of placards with the word "libation" written on them
46. elegiac couplets from friends (each couplet written on two long strips of white cloth tied to a bamboo pole)
47. drum player
48. pavilion-shaped float carrying elegies
49. ten paper umbrellas with "Amitabha Buddha" written on them
50. woodwind musicians in ancient costumes
51. picture of the deceased in an open sedan chair

52. male guests
53. picture of a tiger on a placard
54. cymbals
55. the titles of the deceased on a placard
56. eight riders (in mourning clothes)
57. large parasol
58. large fan
59. Western-style lantern (square glass lantern)
60. umbrella for rider
61. horse of high-ranking Manchu official
62. string musicians
63. young boy
64. young novice carrying the streamers which harbor the soul
65. glass lantern
66. sedan chair for the soul tablet, decorated with baskets of real and artificial flowers

This completes the second part of the procession. The important items are 22, 51, and 66. Effigies of the four guardians (21) were suggested by our family accountant, but my family felt that since it was something new and not widely used, we should eliminate it. Perhaps it has by now become a necessary and popular item. The guests (52) used to walk in the procession, but nowadays they no longer do so. (In recent years, many guests even ride rickshaws.)

67. numerous placards, each exhibiting an official title the deceased once held
68. decorative placard
69. managers of the procession
70. brass players
71. a strip of white cloth stretched between two bamboo poles
72. Western-style lantern (square glass lantern)
73. umbrella for rider
74. paper lantern
75. gong and wooden clappers
76. riderless horse
77. casket on a bier, carried by thirty-two people
78. white sedan chair
79. sedan chair with a white top
80. sedan chair for female relatives and guests

Of the above items, the most important is, of course, the casket (77).

Just take a look! In a funeral procession the important items should be the casket (77), sedan chair for the soul (66), and the pavilion-shaped float with the soul banner (22). In nine out of ten cases, the certificate of rank (19) is a forgery. The picture of the deceased in the sedan chair (51) must be carried back home again after the burial; therefore it does not count. The white cloth (71), white sedan chair (78), guests (52), and guest sedan chairs (80) are also necessary. They add up to seven items only. In actuality, the procession was blown up twelve times its necessary size—eighty items in all! We must attribute this "something growing out of nothing" phenomenon to the innovativeness and creativity of our citizens.

When I have some spare time, I would like very much to look into the origins of each of these items—which were the earliest in existence and which were later additions. Elderly persons have told me that years ago a funeral procession consisted of only the casket, personal honors of the deceased, and six or seven other things such as the gongs, parasols, musicians, large fan, and a brass band. They had a special term for this basic unit, but I have forgotten it. The processions I saw in my childhood consisted of this basic unit and a few additional items: the spirit to clear the way, placard demanding silence and reverence, and Buddhist monks and Daoist priests. The military band and woodwind players were added on just within the last ten years or so. Drummers were included even later. The soft and sweet sound of the woodwinds and the clamorous sounds of drums are ridiculously incompatible. The feathered staff and the dragon staff were originally used in temple ceremonies. They were carried in parades during religious holidays, festivals, and fairs, but now they are used as the vanguard for the pavilion-shaped float carrying the rank of the deceased (19). It seems things have gotten more and more out of hand. People have included stilts, floats, treasure chests, and the four professions (fisherman, woodcutter, farmer, scholar) to their processions today.

My family did not wish to flaunt its wealth and only wanted to "do the right thing"; therefore we did not include anything new. But the items we did include make me sad. I have always wanted to read the descriptions of imperial funerals written in our dynastic histories and compare them with the ones of today to find out whether the emperors of old were as extravagant in death as the commoners of today. I have not done this, but I dare to predict that the extravagance of people today far surpasses that of the emperors. They were checked by rules of ceremony, and our extravagance has been analyzed and determined by thousands of spectators.

How much did a funeral procession cost? Unfortunately I do not have an exact figure. But our family accountant made an estimate of my grandmother's funeral procession, and I have kept his figures, which are as follows:

1. labor fee for craftsmen to make placards, floats, etc. 60.00
2. material cost for placards, floats, silk, cloth, etc. 60.00
3. payment for sedan chair carriers and their meals 2.00
4. musicians playing long horns 8.00
5. Chung stallions 9.60
6. Biao stallions 6.40
7. Daoist priests 3.00
8. Chan monks 3.50
9. Buddhist monks 3.00
10. orchestra 9.00
11. drummers 7.00
12. woodwind players 6.00
13. string players 3.00
14. military band 5.00
15. manager of the funeral 35.00
16. manager of the procession 15.00
17. manager for pavilions and lanterns 15.00
18. grooms 5.00
19. forty-eight horses 48.00
20. assistants 3.00
21. [deleted in the original] 4.50
22. twenty-six hired hands to carry placards, etc. 30.00
23. rented sedan chairs 15.00
24. temporary altar on the road 3.00
25. cost of white cloth 3.00

The estimated cost was 370 dollars. If we include the other expenses of the funeral, the total cost was between four and five hundred dollars. Our house was located less than two *li* from the funeral home, yet we spent between four and five hundred dollars just to send the casket there. This indeed is too wasteful. But when you think about it, you really cannot say that it was too extravagant. The two processions of the Sheng and Xi families started from Shanghai and covered a distance that could be traveled in one and a half hours by train; yet they used more than 100,000 dollars. My family's total expense was only one-third of one percent of that. In comparison, our frugality could be considered exemplary.

At this point, my curiosity is once again aroused. I believe that families like the Shengs and Xis should make their funeral expenses accessible to the public. That would be interesting indeed! I for one would not even know how to begin planning a procession that would cost even one one-hundredth of what theirs did. Extravagance like theirs can make a person boil with rage or sigh with envy. The people who watched your funerals years ago are now dead. Your wealth probably is exhausted. Why don't you make your accounts public so students of local customs can have more research materials?

Translated by Nancy Gibbs

82

MY CHILDREN

Until the twentieth century, discussion of parent-child relations was placed within the framework of the concept of filial piety and what a child owed its parents. Twentieth-century authors were open to new views of childhood and willing to discuss their feelings toward their children with new openness. The following essay about his children was written by Zhu Ziqing (1898–1948). Zhu came from a gentry family and attended Beijing University, graduating in 1920. Thereafter he taught literature at several middle schools and universities. He also wrote poetry, criticism, essays, and sketches, which brought him considerable fame as a writer.

I am now already the father of five. Thinking of the metaphor that Ye Shengtao* likes to quote about the snail that carries a house on its back makes me feel uncomfortable. Recently one of my relatives teased me, saying, "You are getting 'skinned'!" That disturbed me even more. Ten years ago when I had just married, I read Hu Shi's *Sundry Notes*† where he says that many famous men never got married. He also quotes Bacon to the effect that whoever has taken a wife has his life "set." That startled me as if awakening me from a dream, but my family had married me off and I had had nothing to say about it. What could I do? Once I had a wife, along came five children, a heavy burden for my two shoulders; I really wonder how I can go on. Not only is my life "set" but I also worry about how the children will grow up.

Being an egotist through and through, I am not much as a husband, even less as a father. Of course, "Esteem children and grandchildren" and "Youth is the basic unit" are philosophical and ethical principles which I recognize. Once you have become a father, I know, you cannot just shut your eyes and ignore the rights of the children. Unfortunately, many of my ideas remain mere theory; in actual fact, I cope with the situation in the old-fashioned traditional way, savage in style, just like any ordinary father. Only now when I am almost middle-aged do I realize a little of my own brutality, and when I think of the corporal punishment and scolding the children have had to endure, I am at a loss to find excuses. Like touching an old scar, it still hurts to think of it.

Once, reading a translation of Arishima Takeo's "With the Young,"* I was moved to tears by his noble and deeply sincere attitude. Last year my father enquired about Ajiu, who was then still

* 1894–1988, a leading writer and editor.
† Hu Shi (1891–1962), leading philosopher and writer.

* D. 1923, Japanese author and social idealist.

with me at White Horse Lake, saying in his letter, "Since I never neglected you, I wish you would also not neglect him." I thought this remark very touching. Why am I not capable of my father's loving kindness? I will never forget how he looked after me. Human nature may really be polarized; I am certainly inconsistent, swinging back and forth like a pendulum.

You have probably read Lu Xun's "The Happy Family." Mine is indeed such a happy group. At our daily lunches and dinners, two tidal waves seem to be descending on us. First, the children keep running to and fro between the dining room and the kitchen to check on things, urging Mother or me to give out the order to serve food. The hurried patter of many little feet, accompanied by much hilarity and shouting, lasts until that order is given. Then the running and shouting resume as the order is transmitted by many mouths until it reaches the maid in the kitchen. Then back again they rush for the fight for stools: one shouts "I want to sit here"; the other complains "Brother won't let me sit"; brother retorts "Sister hit me"; whereupon I have to assume the role of peacemaker. At times, though, they become so adamant that I cannot stand it. I start shouting and, if that does not settle it, I may lose my temper, and down comes my heavy hand on someone. Then finally, after a few tears, all will find their seats and order will be restored. Next the arguments will break out about large bowls versus small bowls, red chopsticks versus black ones, rice or gruel, tea or soup, fish or meat, bean curd or carrots, with mutual accusations of dipping too often into the meat and vegetable dishes. Mother, as usual, tries to calm everyone down, but with little obvious effect. Then my rather irascible nature will not be able to stand it any longer and, of course, I will apply the old-fashioned method, thereby managing to subdue them instantly. More tears, but finally everyone will be busy with bowls and chopsticks, some wiping tears from reddened eyes. When the meal is over and they leave their seats, off they go helter-skelter, leaving behind a mess of food droppings, rice, sauce, bones, crumbs, and a jumble of chopsticks and spoons in the pattern of a colorful map.

Apart from eating, the children's main pursuit is play. The big ones come up with big ideas and the small ones with small ideas, and no one will go along with the others' wishes. Then the quarrels start again, and either the big ones bully the small ones, or the small ones manage to browbeat the big ones; anyhow, the victimized party will personally bring his or her complaint to Mother or me. Most likely I will again apply the old-fashioned method of settling the argument, but sometimes I just pay no attention. The most annoying are the fights for toys. Even if both have similar toys, one insists on the other's, and no one will give up anything he has. In a situation like this, inevitably tears will have to flow from someone's eyes. Not all of this happens every day, but a good measure of it does. If I want to read a book or write something at home, I can guarantee that my attention will be diverted several times every hour, or I will be forced to get up once or twice. On rainy days or Sundays, when most of the children are home, it has happened that I could not read even one line or write one word. I often tell my wife, "All day our home is like a battlefield with large armies in motion." This goes on not only during the daytime, but even at night when there is the commotion of babies being fed or the sick being tended to.

I was only nineteen the year I married. I was twenty-one when we had Ajiu, twenty-three when we had Acai. At that time I was like a wild horse that could not stand saddle, reins, and bridle. I knew I should not run away from it and yet, unconsciously, I tried to. Thinking back to those days, I see that I really gave the two children a hard time; my acts of violence were unpardonable. When Ajiu was only two and a half years old, we lived on the school ground at Hangzhou. Seemingly for no reason, this child was crying all the time and was also very wary of strangers. When he was not near Mother, or when he saw a stranger, he would start bawling his head off. Since many people lived around us, I could not let him disturb the whole neighborhood, but we also could not avoid having many visitors. I was most annoyed by his behavior. Once I purposely got

Mother out of the room, closed the door, put the boy on the floor and gave him a good spanking. Even now, when we talk about it, Mother finds it unpardonable. She says my hands are too harsh. After all, the child was only two and a half. In recent years I have often felt sad at the thought of that incident. Once it also happened with Acai in Taizhou. She was even smaller, just past a year, hardly able to walk, possibly because she was very much attached to her mother. I put her in a corner and let her cry and yell for three or four minutes. It made her sick for a few days, and Mother said it was really a heartless thing to do. But my sufferings were genuine too.

Once I wrote Ye Shengtao that my plight due to the children sometimes got to be unbearable and gave rise to thoughts of suicide. Although in saying this I was merely venting my anger, I really have been in this mood sometimes. Later, with more children, and having to bear my suffering for some time, I found the sharp edges of my youth had become blunted and added age had increased my rational judgment. I became more tolerant, recognizing that in the past I really had been "anything but a perfect father," as I wrote to another friend. However, I still believe that my children in their early years were much more of an annoyance than other people's. I think it may have been mainly due to our ineptness at bringing them up. Yet if we invariably scolded them and had them take all the blame for what should have been our responsibility, it was certainly a shameful cruelty on our part.

Yet I must admit there was also happiness in the true sense. As anyone will tell you, the little ones are always adorable, those captivating little mites and little darlings. Amao is now five months old. When you touch her chin or make faces, she will open her toothless mouth and give out a gurgling laugh. Her smile is like a flower unfolding. She does not like to be inside for long and if she is, she cries out loudly. Mother often says, "The little girl wants to take a walk; like a bird, she has to flit away once in a while."

Runer was three just last month; a clumsy one, he cannot yet speak well. He can only say three-or four-word sentences with no regard for grammar and a blurred pronunciation, getting every word out only with great effort. It always makes us laugh. When he wants to say *hao* [good], it comes out like *xiao* [small]. If you ask him, "Are you well?" he will reply "small" or "not small." We often make him say these words for the fun of it, and it seems he now suspects as much and has recently begun to say a correct *hao*, especially when we purposely want him to say *xiao*. He has an enamel cup which we bought for about ten cents. The maid had told him, "This is ten cents." All he remembered were two words "ten cents" and he therefore used to call his cup "ten cents," sometimes abbreviated to "cents." When that maid left, the term had to be translated for the new one. If he is embarrassed or sees a stranger, he has a way of staring openmouthed with a silly smile; we call him a silly boy in our native dialect. He is a little fatty, with short legs, funny to look at when he waddles along, and if he hurries, he is quite a sight. Sometimes he imitates me, clasping his hands behind him and walking with a swinging gait. He will then laugh at himself and also make us laugh.

His big sister Acai is over seven years old and goes to elementary school. At the table she prattles along breathlessly with stories of her schoolmates or their parents, whether anybody wants to listen or not. She always ends with a "Dad, do you know them?" or "Dad, did you know that?" Since Mother does not allow her to talk while eating, she always addresses herself to me. She is always full of questions. After the movies, she asks whether the people on the screen are real, and if so, why they don't talk. The same with photographs. Somebody must have told her that soldiers beat up people, which prompted her to ask, "Are soldiers human beings? Why do they beat people?" Recently, probably because her teacher made certain remarks, she came home and asked, "Whose side is Zhang Zuolin on?* Are Jiang Jieshi's soldiers helping us?" Endless questions of

* Zhang Zuolin (1873–1928) was the warlord in Manchuria.

this type are used to pester me every day, and often they back me into a corner for want of an answer. When she plays with Runer, they make an incongruous pair, one big and one small, and there is constant quarreling and crying. But sometimes they seem to get along. For instance, one might hide under the bed and the other try to squeeze in in pursuit. Then out they come, one after the other, from this bed to that. All one hears is their laughter, shouting and panting, as Mother would say, just like little dogs. Now in Beijing there are only these three children with us since, when we came north last year, Grandmother took Ajiu and Zhuaner back to stay at Yangzhou for the time being.

Ajiu loves books; he likes to read *Water Margin*, *The Journey to the West*, *Heroes of the Sword*, *Little Friend*, and so on. He reads whenever he has a spare moment, sitting or lying down. The only book he dislikes is *The Dream of the Red Chamber*, which, he says, has no flavor; and indeed a ten-year-old can hardly be expected to appreciate its flavor.

Last year we had to leave behind two of the children. Since Ajiu was a bigger boy and since Zhuanger had always been with Grandmother, we left them behind in Shanghai. I remember very clearly the morning of our parting. I brought Ajiu from the hotel at Two Stream Bridge to where Mother and Zhuanger were staying with some friends. Mother had told me to buy something to eat for them, so at Sima Street I went into a restaurant. Ajiu wanted some smoked fish, which I bought for him along with some cookies for Zhuanger. Then we went by streetcar to Haining Street. When we got off, I noticed an expression of apprehension and discomfort on his face. I had to hurry back to the hotel to prepare things for the journey and could say only one or two words to the children. Zhuanger looked at me silently while Ajiu turned to say something to Grandmother. I looked back once, then left, feeling myself the target of their recriminatory glances. Mother later told me that Ajiu had said behind my back, "I know Father prefers little sister and won't take me to Beijing," but this was really not doing me

justice. He also pleaded, "At summer vacation time, you must come and pick me up," which we promised to do.

Now it is already the second summer and the children are still left waiting in faraway Yangzhou. Do they hate us or miss us? Mother has never stopped longing for her two children. Often she has wept secretly, but what could I do? Just thinking of the old anonymous poem, "It's the lot of the poor to live with constant reunions and separations," saddened me no end. Zhuanger has become even more of a stranger to me, but last year when leaving White Horse Lake, she spoke up in her crude Hangzhou dialect (at that time she had never been in Yangzhou) and her especially sharp voice: "I want to go to Beijing." What did she know of Beijing? She was just repeating what she had heard from the big children. But still, remembering how she said it makes me terribly sad. It was not unusual for these two children to be separated from me, and they had also been separated from Mother once, but this time it has been too long. How can their little hearts endure such loneliness?

Most of my friends love children. Shaogu once wrote to reproach me for some of my attitudes. He said that children's noises are something to be cherished. How could anyone hate them as I had said? He said he really could not understand me. Feng Zikai* wrote an article for his *Viewing China*, which is all "amiable talk from a most kindhearted man." Ye Shengtao often talked about his worries too, such as what middle school to send the children to after they finished elementary school. He brought this topic up with me two or three times. Those friends made me feel ashamed of my own attitude. Recently, however, I have grown more aware of my responsibilities. I think, first of all, I must get all my children together. Next, I must give them strength. I have personally witnessed the case of a man who, although very fond of his children, grossly neglected them by not providing good educations for them. Not that he was spoiling them in any way; it was

---

* 1898–1975, artist and essayist.

merely that he lacked the patience to take good care of them. As a result, they will never amount to much. I think if I go on like I have, my children will be in even greater danger. I must make plans, must let them gradually know what it takes to become a good human being. But do I want them to become like me? Once at White Horse Lake where I was teaching lower middle school, I had asked Xia Mianzun this question, to be considered from the standpoint of the teacher-pupil relationship. He answered unhesitatingly, "Of course!" Recently, I came to talk with Yu Pingbo* about raising children and he had a clever answer: "In any case, do not make them worse than we are." Yes, indeed, raising them to be not worse than we are, that would do! Likeness to oneself need not be of any concern. Profession, world view, and so on—let them figure that out for themselves. Whatever they decide for themselves, they will value. Merely to guide them and help them develop themselves seems the most enlightened path to follow.

Yutong once said: "Only if we have our children graduate from universities can we say that we have fulfilled our parental duties." S. K. disagreed: "Consider also in this context your own economic ability and the children's capabilities and goals. If they graduate from middle school and cannot, or will not, go on to higher studies, let them do something else; even becoming workers, for instance, would not be improper at all." Of course, a person's social value and success do not altogether depend on his school education. By insisting that our children be university educated, we only follow our personal prejudices. I cannot decide these issues now, especially since the times are so unstable. How can one possibly foresee the future? It is a good thing the children are still small; we can wait and see what happens. All that we can do at present is to give them basic strength, breadth of mind, and good judgment. Since they are still children, it is of course too early to talk about high and far-off objectives; we should rather start out slowly from what is near at hand and basic. This, quite naturally, will proceed from the way I am. "It is up to each individual to solve for himself the mysteries of life!" Be it glory, misfortune or an undistinguished fate that awaits them, let each exert himself to the utmost of his strength. I only hope that with all these reflections I will from now on do well as a father; that would satisfy me completely. The call of the "madman" to "rescue the children"* is a frightening warning to all of us!

Translated by Ernst Wolff

---

* 1900–1990, poet and scholar.

* In Lu Xun's story "Diary of a Madman."

83

THE LIFE OF BEGGARS

For centuries beggars and street entertainers were a common feature of large cities. "The Attractions of the Capital" (selection 41) briefly described a number of hustlers and entertainers who sought money on the streets of Hangzhou in the Song dynasty. Below is a description of the beggars active in Beijing in the 1930s from a book on the social life of the area. Although the existence of hundreds or even thousands of beggars in a large city like Beijing can hardly be taken as a sign of prosperity, in this author's view the beggars themselves were not in desperate straits and their presence enlivened life in the city.

In Beijing, begging for a living is an old and time-honored profession. Born into this tradition and never having opportunities for education or employment, old and young beggars alike firmly believe that begging is their only way to make a living. "Aggressiveness in begging and strength in numbers" is the byword of the beggars of China, and Beijing is the city where their guild originated and flourished. According to older beggars, a certain emperor was once reduced to begging before he became successful. Later, as an exalted emperor, he bestowed his blessings on the beggars and granted them special permission to beg at every door, elect a leader, and establish a guild in every city. While there is no evidence to substantiate their story, the guild regards it as a trustworthy historical record because it increases its own importance. I shall now, after a careful study, present my findings about the way of life and the different styles of the beggars in Beijing.

THE LEADER OF THE BEGGARS' GUILD AND HIS POWER

There is a beggars' guild in Beijing which has all the beggars in the city under the control of its leader and his few trusted subordinates. This guild is a highly structured organization in which rank and status are closely observed and its influence is extensive. Not only must the local beggars show absolute obedience to the leader's orders, but any beggar coming from outside the city must pay a courtesy call on him in order to get permission to beg in the streets. This registration ceremony is referred to as "paying courtesy to the leader." The leader of the guild is appointed for life and lives in a fairly comfortable style. After he dies his successor is selected by the guild members from among those with the highest standing and prestige in the organization. Then the rest of the beggars are ranked approximately by age, the oldest called "Brother Number One," the next, "Brother Number Two," "Brother Number Three," and so on. Children are called "apprentices." The leader of the guild has the power to command and mediate. For example, if two beggars have been quarreling over territory, the leader mediates and they must accept his decision. When the townspeople hold weddings or birthday celebrations, the leader pays them a visit asking for donations on behalf of all the beggars. When a beggar becomes sick or dies, the leader must buy medicine and have him cared for or collect money for his burial and report his death to the authorities.

DONATIONS RECEIVED DURING CELEBRATIONS

Soliciting for donations on festive occasions has become customary for the beggars. When a household celebrates a wedding or a birthday, the leader of the beggars' guild comes and extends his congratulations, whereupon the family manager usually gives him money, ranging from forty cents to one dollar. A family holding a birthday celebration generally gives more money than one celebrating a marriage because filial sons holding a birthday celebration for their parents do not want beggars to loiter about their front door saying unlucky things. After the leader gets money, he posts a notice on the front door of the house: "This exalted household is having a celebration and our brothers are not to disturb them." Beggars who recognize this slip of paper shun the place the way small devils keep away from [the devil catcher] Master Jiang. If a family refuses to donate, a crowd of beggars soon creates disturbances at their front door and one never knows what embarrassing thing they might do next.

FORMS OF ADDRESS AND TYPES OF CRYING

When begging on the streets, the beggars must call out to different types of people with different forms of address such as, "big master," "great master," "honorable master," "madame," "your

ladyship," "young master," "sir," "young lady," "honorable proprietor," "honorable official." They must appraise a person on the spot, determine his status, and address him with the appropriate title. How to do this is a required skill for all the beggars in Beijing, one earnestly passed on from master to apprentice. Two types of beggars must also be trained to cry properly, those who cry and run about the streets, and those who beg sitting in one fixed place. Women and children must weep with correct pitch and rhythm. One often sees them crouching on the side of the road wailing and chanting with tears in their voices, touching people's hearts with their words; or one sees women wailing while walking down the streets, dragging young children behind them. When they are given money, they stop their pitiful crying and pour out their gratitude. Male beggars must shout wildly or exhibit their deformities and injuries. All these techniques must be studied and mastered. After a day of begging with them, the income gained can be quite impressive.

THE MASTERY OF SKILLS

Some beggars learn a variety of skills when they are young, such as balancing tricks, juggling, sword dancing, and magic. These skills are not taught by the guild leaders but by special masters, even professional entertainers and boxers who are looking for extra income. As long as the beggars pay for their lessons and the lessons do not interfere with begging, they are free to engage teachers for these skills. A skilled beggar makes more money than the wailing, chanting, and singing kind.

Beggars also carry a variety of utensils such as bamboo baskets and glazed bowls for holding money, rice bags and iron pots for holding food, and canes for chasing dogs away and self-defense. Sometimes people give beggars old clothes that are still in fair condition, which they then wear under the tattered jackets which show their destitution. For the skilled beggar, other items are necessary, such as musical instruments, gongs, drums, wooden clappers, theatrical swords, daggers, lances, and various equipment for animal acts.

HOSTELS FOR BEGGARS

Outside of Beijing's Chaoyang Gate, in the region south of Tianqiao, there are many hostels for beggars. Users are charged one copper cash per night and must leave in the morning. In the winter months, most of these hostels provide heat in a large room called the "fire room." Wood is burned in a hole dug in the middle of the floor which everyone sits around for warmth. The customers are old and experienced beggars who are idle during the cold weather. Among them there is usually someone who teaches "The Falling of Lotus Petals" and other traditional begging songs. Most young beggars use this opportunity to accept a master. Sometimes when the weather is so cold no one goes outside, the hostel's cook will make a large pot of porridge for all to eat. There is a charge for this, but a day's stay is only five copper cash. Male and female beggars all share the same room, and no one dares take off shoes or clothes while sleeping because they will be gone the next morning. According to my research, Beijing has nine of these hostels, an institution which does not exist in the warmer and milder south.

TRADITIONAL BEGGING SONGS

The older beggars pass on to their disciples not only skills for survival but also a variety of songs and rhymes. Lucky phrases are skillfully worked into the lyrics of begging songs. The lyrics are memorized but can be easily changed to meet different circumstances. When a beggar encounters someone who refuses to give anything, he can instantly change the lyric to mock the man and make him feel uneasy. I have jotted down some of the most common lyrics:

Well-wishing songs: "Turtle crawls to your door; your wealth will soon soar." "Madame gave me a couple of coins; madame will live a thousand years." "Old master you are most kind; this year you'll get a thousand gold pieces." "Madame took pity upon me; sons and grandsons you'll soon have."

Unpleasant verses: "If you don't give me money, I won't survive this year." "Don't give me money? I don't care! Save your money for your coffin!" "If you won't give, I won't ask. We'll see how you feel when your son dies!"

The well-wishing songs must be sung with a sad but strong voice to evoke people's sympathy and make them give voluntarily. Generally, families holding celebrations do not refuse beggars because no one wants to hear their curses at such a time.

The beggars in Beijing all refer to their profession as "living off the streets" for the obvious reason that they spend their entire lives in streets and alleys. Because of the economic decline of villages in the region in recent years, the number of beggars in Beijing has increased sharply. Everywhere one hears loud wailing and lamenting and sees strange and unusual tricks and gimmicks. I have listed them as follows:

1. *Sword slappers.* The beggars hold two long broad swords. Baring their chest, they slap the blades on it, breathe in deeply, then let out a loud grunt. This type is found most frequently during temple festivals and other holidays. A sword slapping beggar first addresses himself to a passerby, grunts, and then slaps himself with his swords. He continues to do so until his flesh is red and swollen and covered with speckles of blood. He is quite pitiful to look at.

2. *Brick slappers.* These beggars sit in the middle of the street slapping their bare chests and backs with a brick until their upper torso is covered with blood. This, too, is horrifying to see. These beggars grunt and shout just like the sword slappers. The above two types of beggars are not allowed to walk about but must remain seated in one place.

3. *Walking brick slappers.* These beggars walk down the streets while slapping a brick against

their breasts, crying, "Master, madame, have mercy on the blind and deformed." Then they let out a pathetic sigh and hit themselves with the brick. As they repeat the crying and chanting, the brick serves as a percussion instrument setting the rhythm for the melodic wailing.

4. *Street criers*. These beggars, carrying willow staffs and baskets, roam the city streets and lament. They are mostly old and weak and do not hurt themselves, but their income is much less than the types already mentioned. The last two types of beggars are allowed to walk the city streets, but they are never permitted to knock on people's doors.

5. *Head nailers*. These beggars hold a few long nails between their lips and carry bricks. Each beggar penetrates the skin of his head with a sharp nail so it stands on the top of his head. Without saying a word he begs at doors. If he is given money right away, he leaves immediately; if not, he taps the nail into his head with the brick causing a crackling noise. Usually the nail is stuck into a tumor or a wart; when it is driven in deeper, blood drips down his face, creating a horrible sight. Once he bleeds, he usually will not leave until given a generous sum of money. This type of beggar is supposed to beg on one side of the street only.

6. *Head cutters*. These beggars carry a sickle and get intoxicated before begging at doors. If not given money, one of these beggars takes the sickle between his thumb and forefinger until just a few millimeters of blade show, then passes the blade over his head until blood oozes out. He then falls to the ground and does not get up until the person gives generously.

7. *Treasure counters*. These are the most commonly seen beggars in Beijing and can be divided into three types.

a. The first holds two beef shoulder bones from which dangle bells and colored ribbons. He begs and sings while keeping time by clapping the bones together and jingling the bells.

b. The second carries a big piece of bamboo in his right hand and a small one in his left. Scraping them against each other, he sings and begs.

c. The third type wears a colorful cap with a pom-pom on top. He holds two blue ceramic bowls in his hands and knocks them against each other to make a tinkling sound as he begs and sings. Some of these beggars wear rouge and powder and look very disgusting. I have recorded some of their songs: "I've begged here and I've begged there. When you eat dinner I'll be right here." "Shopkeeper, you'll soon be rich. When you eat your dinner, you'll see me." "Shopkeeper, don't get mad; the sooner you give, the sooner I'll leave."

8. *Sack carriers*. These beggars carry cloth sacks on their backs and beg from door to door. They must address people as "uncle" and "aunt" only and not as "master" and "madame"; otherwise it is a violation of which they can be expelled from the guild.

9. *Falling lotus petals*. Two beggars, wearing colorful clothes and caps, paint their faces with rouge and powder and carry bamboo staffs with holes drilled into each segment and filled with a few copper cash. While begging, they sing and dance, swinging their arms and legs, spinning around, and jumping up and down as if they were mad. Those who do not have colorful clothes often make do with ordinary rags.

10. *Jade drummers*. These beggars have long bamboo cylinders covered with tightly stretched skin, which they strike as they sing a slow and melodious song.

11. *Frame balancers*. These beggars balance a chopstick on the tip of their nose and place a small cup on the top of the chopstick. Thus balanced, they beg from door to door.

12. *Eel threaders*. These beggars carry an iron hook and pass it through a hole previously punctured in their noses. Until paid, they continue to stand at someone's front door, pushing the hook back and forth.

13. *Nodding phoenixes*. These beggars punc-

ture a hole through the bridge of their noses and push a thick needle through it. Then they balance a small bowl on one end of the needle. Rocking and singing, they go door to door.

14. *Frozen meat.* Beggars in the North often use their children to get money. In extremely cold weather, they strip the youngsters and place them near shops and stalls to arouse sympathy from passersby and shopkeepers. These children become accustomed to such inhumane treatment; some even develop resistance to very cold weather. These beggars must remain in one fixed place.

15. *Snake charmers.* As North China is cold and harsh, only small green snakes are kept by snake charmers who carry them in bamboo cages and go from door to door to offer entertainment. These beggars are well versed in the art of handling snakes and also offer their services to capture snakes or sell snake skins and gall bladders for their restorative powers. During religious festivals, they catch water snakes and sell them to devout old ladies who later turn them loose. The next day they recapture them from the water and sell them again, turning an impressive profit.

I shall now list various ways deformed and invalid beggars can beg. They are not allowed to beg from door to door but must remain on the streets. Going down the streets, shouting pitiable cries, they try to arouse sympathy from passersby to make them give of their own free will.

16. *Sunset beggars.* Blind beggars aided by walking sticks who call out to passersby and collect money in a straw hat.

17. *Light gropers.* Blind beggars who squat on the street and grope their way around slowly while begging.

18. *One-eyed dragons.* One-eyed beggars who lean on a staff and pretend to be totally blind though actually able to see quite well.

19. *Rollers.* Beggars with totally disabled hands and feet who lie in mud rolling and howling. They are accompanied by other beggars who take care of them and collect the money. This type of beggar has the biggest income.

20. *Wall starers.* Beggars with disabled legs who pad their knees and hips with cotton and move about the street on their hands and knees.

21. *Wooden hands.* Beggars with paralyzed legs who hold two wood blocks and move about the street, dragging their bodies behind them.

22. *Moving carts.* Paralyzed beggars who lie on wooden carts pushed and dragged by two companions. Wailing and crying, they pass through the streets, and passersby can throw money into the moving cart.

23. *Rock carriers.* Male beggars who carry invalid females on their back, moaning and lamenting, through the city streets.

Translated by Nancy Gibbs

84

GENERALISSIMO JIANG ON NATIONAL IDENTITY

Among the ideas originally from the West, nationalism proved particularly potent. In the early twentieth century, Chinese intellectuals and political leaders thought that ideas of national identity and destiny then reshaping European politics could help China. Revolutionaries called for the overthrow of the Manchus on the grounds that they were alien. Sun Yatsen (1866–1925) made national self-determination one of his "Three People's Principles." China could not be strong until it rid itself of imperialist encroachments and was reconstituted as the nation of the Chinese people.

Nationalist principles as formulated by Sun were a central part of the ideology of the Nationalist Party (Guomindang), led after 1928 by Jiang Jieshi (Chiang Kai-shek, 1887–1975). During this period the gravest threat to China's national autonomy came from Japan, which occupied Manchuria in 1931 and started a full-scale invasion in 1937.

Below are two speeches in which Jiang dealt with issues of national identity. They were both delivered to meetings of high-level party committees, the first in January 1939, near the beginning of the war, and the second soon after Japan had surrendered in August 1945. In the first Jiang appeals to anti-imperialist sentiments to arouse determination to defeat Japan. In the second he considers what these principles might mean for a postwar China. If the Japanese should not rule parts of China, was it right for the Chinese to rule lands occupied by Tibetans, Mongols, or other nationalities? When were ethnic groups nationalities?

CHINA CANNOT BE CONQUERED

Comrades, this assembly meets as we enter upon the second stage in our War of Resistance. It is, therefore, an especially significant session which lays heavy responsibilities upon us. As I have repeatedly pointed out, our war may be divided into two periods. During the first period, which ended with the fall of Canton and Wuhan, we tried to wear down the enemy's strength and at the same time protect our rear so that solid foundations might be laid for the second period of protracted resistance.... We are fighting this war for our own national existence and for freedom to follow the course of national revolution laid down for us in the Three Principles of the People. We are fighting an enemy who would deny us not only our freedom but our very life, an enemy with whom we cannot compromise without bringing utter ruin upon our nation. Only resistance can preserve us from national slavery. Only resistance can save the world from the collapse of international morality and the breakdown of all guarantees of peace. Dr. Sun Yatsen devoted his life to the movement for the salvation of his country and at the same time of the world. All that he planned and achieved our enemy would throw to the winds. . . .

Japan has failed to realize the mighty power of our national resistance, the irresistible growth of our national spirit, and the true significance of our national history. The Japanese blindly hold that China can be tricked and subdued as she was by the Khitans and the Jin at the time of the Song dynasty, by the Mongols of the Yuan dynasty, and by the Manchus of the Qing dynasty. They do not understand the reasons for China's subjection in those times. They do not realize that it was the weakness of a few officials which brought about the submission of the government, a thing that should not be confused with the surrender of a whole nation. Today the Japanese cry, "Build a new order in East Asia," and expect in a short time to rule over all China. They forget that it has taken them more than forty years, a huge army, and vast expenditures to get even a tenuous hold upon our Northeastern Provinces. They refuse to take warning from past experiences, and now foolishly overstretch themselves to conquer the whole of China. Again they will fail.

Japan fails because she does not understand the characteristics of our nation, the force of the Three Principles enunciated by Dr. Sun Yatsen, the temper of our government, the signs of the times, and China's revolutionary military strategy and tactics. When Napoleon was attacking Imperial Russia, the strategy of all-front and prolonged resistance was not known. But even with his remarkable military genius and huge armies Napoleon was not able to avert defeat. How can Japan possibly succeed against republican China with its new and fervent national spirit? United against

a common enemy and under the guidance of the national government, our people have been able to carry out modern revolutionary military tactics, and no armed force can subdue us. . . .

Comrades, after eighteen months as the responsible commander-in-chief of our fighting forces, I have reached the following solemn conclusion. I commend it to your special consideration. You should instruct our people to take lessons from the annals of the Song and Ming dynasties. The fall of these two dynasties was not caused by outside enemies with a superior force, but by a dispirited and cowardly minority in the governing class and the society of the time. Today the morale of our people is excellent; the foundation of our revolution is deep and strong; and the Three Principles of the People give us a charter of liberty in harmony with the spirit of the modern age. If we do not destroy ourselves, no outside force can destroy us. . . . In more than five thousand years our nationality has never been really conquered and has most certainly never been exterminated. Furthermore, the dynastic downfalls were due to the cowardice, ignorance, lack of integrity, and selfishness of a small number of corrupt officials. The happiness and welfare of the common people did not concern them. During those despotic regimes a great gap existed between the government authorities and the common people. There were no ways by which the authorities could mobilize the power of resistance residing in the people. Yet, as a matter of fact, the spirit of the nation as a whole did not suffer from outside oppression and the people steadily opposed aggression. After an interval of two or three hundred years, the aggressors would be driven out and the nation's territory would be recovered.

Our present government, which is republican in form and revolutionary in spirit and which fights for the welfare of the nation and the people, has a far greater chance of expelling the invader. Our government is fully aware of its responsibilities and intends to complete the revolution and carry out the Three Principles of the People. It has no fear of bullying aggressors. Our resistance is a united effort of government and people. Sunzi says, "A virtuous government has the support of the people; it can command life or death from the people without exciting fear or complaint." Concord between government and people is the first essential to victory.

In our present struggle against Japan we have been able to live up to this high principle. The hearts of our people are absolutely united. Under the guidance of the government even the old and the weak, the women and the children, are conscious of the necessity of defending themselves against the enemy and of obeying implicitly the orders of the high command. Indeed, their spirit is such that they are willing to lay down their lives without a murmur. No one will barter his national birthright for slavery to Japan. The barbarism of the Japanese has everywhere aroused the spirit voiced in our ancient saying, "Prefer death to disgrace." Judging from the history of the past and the national consciousness and strong morale of our people today, China cannot be conquered.

From the geographical point of view, our country possesses natural advantages for defense. Our ancestors, two thousand years ago, took advantage of the mountainous terrain in constructing the Great Wall. From east to west our country extends through more than sixty-five degrees of longitude. From north to south it includes the climates of the frigid, temperate, and torrid zones. In any discussion of military success or failure we have always considered topography and climate of great importance. River, mountains, and deserts abound in our interior and in the west; arctic cold alternates with tropical heat. Invaders in the past have succeeded only in holding a part of our country for a limited time. They have never permanently controlled the whole of our country for a long time. Even in the Yuan and Qing dynasties, when the strongest forces attempted to conquer us, they were able to occupy only certain strategic points and the spirit of resistance among the people was not crushed. Today a nation of only seventy million people thinks it can absorb a nation of six times its population and with a far older history and civilization. What a mad dream! Topography and climate are again combining against China's invaders. No weapon in the world will be effective against this combination, reinforced by the firm determination and mighty strength of our people. Geographically, our country cannot be conquered.

China is the only nation in the Far East with an independent cultural achievement. This is borne out by history. Chinese civilization has been adopted by other peoples, but no alien civilization has ever succeeded in replacing China's own. China's civilization is imbued with a special spirit. I need not amplify this point. It is only necessary to recall the heroic behavior of our people in face of the enemy to realize the deep roots of our civilization. Japan is now trying with her mongrel civilization, of neither the East nor the West, to destroy our national spirit. But she has met with repeated failures in the occupied areas. If we are united at heart, and if we struggle with determination, the spirit of our people will be further strengthened. This resistance will infuse into our civilization a new splendor and power. Our civilization and our national national spirit can never be conquered or destroyed.

Economically we have the advantage. Modern wars usually arise out of economic conflicts and the outcome is determined by the economic strength and resources of the belligerents. China is essentially an agricultural country. Aggression descended upon us while we were in the period of national reconstruction. At first this seemed a major crisis, yet during the eighteen months of hostilities our financial structure has not been seriously injured, our currency has remained steady, and the livelihood of the people in the rear has been little affected. Owing to the excellent harvests in several provinces last year and the campaign of thrift, there are signs of plenty among our people. This is possible because we are an agricultural nation and strong in endurance, whereas industrial nations suffer more quickly from the consequences of war. . . .

Since the invasion of Manchuria in 1931 we have seen clearly that the only road upon which all mankind can march together is the road of justice and righteousness. A nation that aspires to become strong and independent cannot allow itself to be checked by temporary hardships and sacrifices. In the course of time it is bound to earn the sympathy and cooperation of other just nations. The international developments of the past seven years have fully borne out our judgment. We claim no prescience; we have only maintained the position held by our revolutionary leader, Dr. Sun Yatsen: to save our country is also to save the world. Our judgment has been guided by this principle.

Dr. Sun often said that after China had recovered her independent national status she would have a large responsibility to the world. In his addresses on nationalism and on other occasions, Dr. Sun frequently declared, "China is the pillar of the Far East and the largest country in Asia; when China is strong, her four neighbors will be safe and on cordial terms with each other, and the surrounding peoples can retain their independence and share peace and happiness." Dr. Sun pointed out also that "China has never attempted by economic weapons to oppress other peoples. China's aspirations for peace were fully evolved even at the time of the Han dynasty." We do not oppress the weak and we do not bow before tyranny. We favor mutual assistance and we seek to strengthen ourselves. Dr. Sun further observed, "China had been strong for several thousand years without affecting the existence of Korea; but Korea was annexed after Japan had been strong for only twenty years. China's traditional policy has been to aid the weak and to support the falling, to live and to let live. Our national revolution is reinforcing our own historic love of justice and peace and is hastening the advent of enduring security and happiness for all mankind. . . ."

Comrades, you must know that before our resistance began our country was regarded by the world as weaker than a third-rate power. Nevertheless, we succeeded in holding Japan, a first-class power, for more than a year and a half without being overcome. We must be ready to encounter more difficulties but we need no longer be frightened by our brutal enemy. Having entered this second period of resistance we believe that the military operations will daily turn in our favor. The only question is whether we have the strength of will to continue resistance, and whether our unity and determination will increase with every day of the struggle. . . .

NATIONAL INDEPENDENCE AND EQUALITY AMONG PEOPLES

Japan has been defeated and is surrendering. The forces of violent aggression have been completely crushed by the concerted efforts of the United Nations. At the end of the First World War, Dr. Sun Yatsen said that nations working together for the good of all would certainly succeed while individuals or nations working for their own selfish ends would inevitably fail. The truth embodied in Dr. Sun's frank words has been abundantly confirmed by the recent war with its even greater sacrifices.

At this great turning point in history, the national government should make clear to the people of China and of the whole world the main objectives in its policy of realizing national independence and completing the national revolution. . . . The aim of our national revolution is twofold. In our relations with other nations we seek national independence and freedom. Within the nation we seek equality for all ethnic groups. For fifty years we faced the ever-growing menace of Japanese aggression; national armed resistance began when we had no other alternative. Therefore the main emphasis of our national revolutionary movement was upon consolidating the strength of all our ethnic groups. We knew that we must unite in resisting foreign aggression if we were to attain national independence and freedom.

We had three most important goals and the attainment of these constituted our most urgent task. First, we had to regain our sovereign rights in the northeastern provinces and reestablish territorial and administrative integrity there. Second, we had to recover Formosa (Taiwan) and the Pescadores Islands. Third, we had to restore to Korea her independence and freedom. Should Korea not be given freedom, Formosa not be allowed to return to its mother country, and the territorial and administrative integrity of the Northeastern Provinces not be restored, all talk of national independence and freedom would be useless and the objectives of our armed resistance could not be achieved. These objectives follow the policies handed down to us by Dr. Sun Yatsen. They have been the leading aims in our armed resistance against Japan, which has meant for us the loss of millions of lives. During the war we had to unite all the ethnic groups within the nation and strive together to complete our threefold task. Only if this is done can we expect our country to be independent and make secure the political equality of all ethnic groups.

Japanese imperialism has been defeated and Japan is suing for peace. . . . We may say that the international aspect of our principle of nationalism is approaching completion. Therefore, we must formulate definite policies and take positive action to realize the domestic phase of the same principle, that is, ensure equality for all the ethnic groups within the nation and thus fulfill the entire program of our national revolution. We must also ensure the permanency of the victorious peace which we have won at the sacrifice of countless lives and enormous losses in property.

Upon the basis of Dr. Sun Yatsen's teachings, I shall now state, as a representative of the Guomindang (Nationalist Party), our policy toward carrying out the principle of nationalism and safeguarding world peace and national security. I shall first take up the nationality questions in Outer Mongolia and Tibet. Outer Mongolia and Tibet both have a long history. The ethnic groups in these two areas have always lived by themselves and are totally different from the ethnic groups inhabiting the border provinces which mix freely with other groups. Following the Guomindang reorganization in 1924, Outer Mongolia sent representatives to extend greetings and felicitations to our party. Dr. Sun Yatsen was at that time already treating them as members of a friendly neighboring country and as honored guests. Such facts are recorded in Dr. Sun Yatsen's teachings and are widely known. We have never regarded the people of Outer Mongolia as colonials or oppressed them as the Beijing government did. Ever since the inauguration of the national government we have maintained friendly relations not only with the Outer Mongolians but also with the Tibetans. Our people should realize that if we ignore the aspirations of these ethnic groups for freedom and restrain their urge for independence and self-government, it will not only be contrary to the spirit of our national revolution but will also tend to increase friction between ethnic groups and jeopardize our entire program of national reconstruction. This in turn will adversely affect world peace and security.

The ethnic group in Outer Mongolia had, in effect, declared its independence from the mother country as early as 1922 when the Beijing government was in existence. That was almost a quarter of a century ago. The world is undergoing rapid changes and this is a propitious time for renewing old friendships. Therefore, we should, in accordance with our revolutionary principles and the Guomindang's consistent policy, recognize, with bold determination and through legal procedure, the independence of Outer Mongolia and establish friendly relations with it. We must seek a satisfactory solution of this question. If we fail, happy relations between China and Mongolia will be impossible and not only our own domestic tranquillity but also the peace of the world will be seriously jeopardized.

I must here point out three fundamental points in the realization of our principle of nationalism. First, the Chinese government and people should resolve with noble, sincere, and firm determination never to imitate the way of Japan toward Korea. We should honestly aid all ethnic groups which have given evidence of their capacity for self-government and have shown a spirit of independence. We should help them achieve national independence through self-determination, freedom, and equality on the Asian continent in the bright light of total victory. For fifty years, the national revolution of the Guomindang, as it overthrew the Manchu government and resisted Japan, has been a movement not only for China's own freedom and equality, but also for the liberation and independence of Korea. From today, we shall, in this same spirit and together with all Allied nations concerned, fully respect the principle of Korean independence and equality and the position that Korea will soon attain.

Second, if frontier ethnic groups situated in regions outside the provinces have the capacity for self-government and a strong determination to attain independence, and are politically and economically ready for both, our government should, in a friendly spirit, voluntarily help them to realize their freedom and forever treat them as brotherly nations, as equals of China. We should entertain no ill will or prejudices against them because of their choice to leave the mother country. Our frontier ethnic groups should, in a friendly spirit and through legal channels, make known their wishes to the government of their mother country. In this way, they may be able to realize their aspirations. They should not defy the mother country and stir up mutual hatred.

Third, we should accord the large and small ethnic groups inside the provinces legal and political equality, and unhindered economic and religious freedom, so that a warm community spirit and friendly collaboration may develop among all the groups.

As regards the political status of Tibet, the Sixth National Guomindang Congress decided to grant it a very high degree of autonomy, to aid its political advancement, and to improve the living conditions of the Tibetans. I solemnly declare that if the Tibetans should at this time express a wish for self-government, our government would, in conformity with our sincere tradition, accord it a very high degree of autonomy. If in the future they fulfill the economic requirement for independence, the national government will, as in the case of Outer Mongolia, help them to gain that status. But Tibet must give proof that it can consolidate its independent position and protect its continuity so as not to become another Korea.

Finding a solution for the ethnic problems of Outer Mongolia and Tibet is a very great task of our national revolution. It will be a touchstone of the success of our principle of nationalism. We should be ready to assume responsibility for a solution. I hope that all the Chinese people, in accordance with our revolutionary principles and spirit of national independence, assist the government in finding an answer to these questions. For world peace and security as well as for the solidarity and reconstruction of our own nation, we must deal with the world's national questions in conformity with the spirit of the Atlantic Charter and the Three Principles of the People....

The world war that has just ended was an unprecedented conflict in human history. All the United Nations hope that this horrible war will be the last war. China has fought the longest and suffered the most. Our hope for peace is therefore the most ardent. Any measure that will strengthen our national unity and promote international peace will receive our strongest support.

In collaboration with our allies, we shall strive to bring about friendly relations between all free and independent nations, ensure the continuance of peace and prevent the reemergence of power politics. We should see to it particularly that the peoples of the world do not again suffer from inequality, the want of freedom, scarcity, and fear. If we keep this in mind, we shall see how supremely important it is that the principles of national equality and national independence be everywhere realized. The national government, guided by its own vital principles and its consistent revolutionary policy, will complete the unfinished phase of the principle of nationalism as peace dawns upon the world. This is one of our fondest hopes and I am sure our allies will understand. World peace will thus be guaranteed and our national security be made certain. Let our people with one heart and one mind strive toward this goal. National revival and reconstruction will then become a living reality and the millions of our officers and soldiers and people who gave their lives in eight years of war will rest in peace knowing that they have not sacrificed in vain, and the truth of Dr. Sun's words pronounced after the First World War will be fully verified.

PART VIII

THE PEOPLE'S REPUBLIC

The war with Japan, lasting from 1937 to 1945, produced massive social disorder. Much of east and south China was occupied and everywhere the economy was severely strained. With the defeat of the Japanese by allied forces, civil war between the Nationalist government and the Communist Red Army resumed. Although starting with only a fourth as many soldiers, in less than two years of actual fighting the Communist forces were victorious. On October 1, 1949, the establishment of the People's Republic of China was proclaimed. Under the leadership of Mao Zedong (1893–1976) and the Communist Party, the new government promptly set about reorganizing nearly all aspects of Chinese life. Foreign intervention within China was drastically curtailed, first by a Chinese alliance with the Soviet Union against the former imperialist powers, and then by the rejection of Soviet influence by the end of the 1950s.

During the initial decade of Communist leadership, profound social and economic changes were initiated. The old rural landowning elite was eliminated through a land reform program that took land from landlords to redistribute. Not only were many landlords killed, but for decades to come those classified as belonging to landlord families were subject to discrimination. The possible emergence of a new landlord class was prevented by the full collectivization of agriculture, accomplished by the end of 1956. Also during these early years, the power of the urban-based capitalists who had gained influence in the Republican period was undermined by the socialization of industry.

The socialization of agriculture and industry was intended not only to reduce social and economic inequalities but also make possible faster eco-

nomic growth, for the new leaders were as intent as the Nationalists before them to make China strong and powerful. Despite the poverty of
China's economic base, significant improvements in the living conditions
of the bulk of the population were made possible by a more equitable
distribution of the limited resources available. And measures such as improvement in the transportation of grain and increased political control of
markets mitigated the ancient scourge of famine. Social services, including
basic health care and primary education, were extended to the vast peas-
antry, who still constitute three-fourths of the population.

Very quickly the state and the Communist Party came to play larger
roles in the lives of ordinary people than any earlier government had.
What farmers would produce, where and how their children would be
educated, what they might read in books and newspapers, where they
could live or travel, all came increasingly under political control. The
appointment of state and party cadres down to the commune level facilitated this, as did enhanced political control of communications, transportation, and marketing. In addition, the government pushed repeated
campaigns to mobilize the masses both to assure popular support for new
policies being introduced and also to maximize labor power.

Many previous social cleavages and sources of diversity were overcome
in the 1950s and 1960s. Use of a standard dialect based on North Chinese
pronunciation was successfully promoted. And because class distinctions
were sharply diminished and education more widespread, the former division between elite and popular cultures significantly narrowed. In the
countryside, new collective institutions drastically limited the social significance of kinship relationships. In the 1960s and 1970s graduates of
urban high schools were sent by the million to live in the countryside, in
part to control urban unemployment but also to undermine the distinction between mental and manual laborers. Yet the difference between city
and countryside may actually have widened, as cities benefited more from
industrialization and social welfare programs, and a strict household registration system kept rural residents from moving to cities in search of a
better life. And despite Mao's intentions, the party cadres, who controlled
the government, factories, schools, and communes, became a privileged
elite.

Since 1949 the pace and even direction of change has repeatedly been
altered by shifts in political policies. The emphasis to be placed on heavy
industry, on local self-reliance, on birth control, on uprooting old habits
like forced marriages, on unmasking counterrevolutionaries have all been
influenced by political struggles. The most highly politicized period was
the Great Proletarian Cultural Revolution, initiated by Mao in 1966. It
led to a decade in which "class struggle" against revisionists and counter-

revolutionaries was continually promoted. Those previously in authority—teachers, cadres, managers—were humiliated, often brutally, and later many were sent out to the countryside for "reeducation." During this decade political considerations were promoted over economic ones even in the countryside; peasants, for instance, were not allowed to raise pigs or chickens for fear of being labeled "capitalist roaders." During these years, China was largely isolated from the outside world, maintaining good relations only with Albania.

After Mao died in 1976, and particularly after Deng Xiaoping gained ascendance from 1978 onward, the policies of the Cultural Revolution were repudiated. Agriculture was largely de-collectivized and to promote modernization of industry, foreign investment was encouraged. Contact with the outside world greatly expanded as Chinese were sent abroad to study and tourists invited to visit China. As television became commonplace, ordinary Chinese learned much more about life elsewhere and began to make new demands on their government for improvements in their standards of living and more choice in their daily lives.

In recent years many people who have left China for the West have written revealing memoirs of their experiences, writing with a candor that has generally not been possible for authors in China. No excerpts from these writings are included here, however, because they were written for outsiders, not for other Chinese. It is still important for us to read and analyze what the Chinese have written for each other, to see the assumptions they make and arguments they use. The sorts of pieces that could be published have varied from year to year, in line with political shifts. In all periods there has been a plethora of propagandistic writings, meant to instill the "revolutionary" attitudes the Party espoused by providing positive models, fictional or nonfictional. More informative, often, are accounts in the press of undesirable behavior reported so that it could be condemned. Hardest to find are first-person accounts in which people believably describe their own feelings and actions. Each of these sorts of writings must be read with a critical eye and an awareness of the political pressures on the writer. Both positive and negative examples often seem too exaggerated, too black and white. Self-criticisms, petitions, even letters to editors should often be read as tactical political acts and not simply as candid expression of inner feelings.

85

THE COMMUNIST PARTY

Founded in 1921 at a meeting of fourteen delegates from six cells, the Chinese Communist Party grew to 300,000 members by 1933, 1.2 million members by 1945, and 4.5 million members by 1949. To achieve its goal of overthrowing the existing government and establishing a socialist state, the party had to build a command structure capable of decisive leadership, a body of cadres to carry out their decisions, and an army able to fight the better-equipped Nationalists. From 1934 until his death in 1976, Mao Zedong occupied the highest leadership role in the party. Much of the credit for building the party into an effective revolutionary organization should, however, go to Liu Shaoqi (1898–1969), like Mao from Hu'nan and a member of the party since the 1920s.

The selection below is from a speech Liu gave in 1937 to representatives of party organizations then operating underground in "white" areas. In his address he stressed the importance of party members' accepting discipline and preserving secrecy. Even after the Chinese Communist Party defeated the Nationalists and shifted its central tasks to managing the state and economy, the organizational practices developed during wartime remained important.

Through the 1940s, 1950s, and 1960s, Liu Shaoqi was one of the handful of top leaders, and he served as president of the People's Republic of China from 1959 to 1968. During the Cultural Revolution, however, he was branded the chief "capitalist roader" and "China's Khrushchev" and he died from mistreatment in 1969.

While providing more favorable conditions for the party to develop and carry out its work, the establishment of Guomindang-Communist cooperation will considerably increase the possibilities for the bourgeoisie to exert its influence upon the party and undermine it from within. In order to maintain the party's independence, purity, and unity, we should (1) raise the requirements for those who wish to join the party and place them on probation for a period of time (workers may be excepted); (2) provide for intensive education of party members in political theory; (3) tighten party discipline while extending democracy within the party; (4) select party cadres carefully; and (5) pay closer attention to the right deviation of tailism. The requirements for party membership mentioned here may be less strict in party organizations working underground.

In the restoration and expansion of party organizations in some places we must depend on backbone members and cadres who are trustworthy and absolutely true to the party. On no account should these people be transferred wilfully. A clear distinction should be drawn between inner-party work and open mass work. Stricter secrecy should be enforced regarding all inner-party work and organizational matters, which should not be made known to all our comrades, particularly those working in the open. Party organs should be very small, and unnecessary organizations and official titles should be abolished. Their contacts with other quarters, especially with comrades working openly, should be established with finesse. Although this is a very difficult task, it is a most important aspect of underground work. These small, underground leading organs must be preserved even when the situation permits overt action. In cases when greater overt action becomes possible, it will suffice for the mass organizations and comrades who work in the open to take part in public activities.

With regard to the party's underground work, we should have foresight, persistence, and patience and we must not allow the slightest impetuosity or negligence because, with the situation changing, what seems unimportant today may become very important tomorrow. So, what we do today should be subordinate to what we do tomorrow. In the past, many of our comrades simply did not have a long-range perspective or patience. They were afflicted with an intolerable impetuosity and were much too negligent. Even today, they do not take into account the present circumstances and still less the future situation when assigning tasks and carrying them out. They recruit party members in public, launch revolutionary emulation drives, initiate shock campaigns, and transfer cadres and reshuffle party organizations at will. From now on, we must cease to criticize our comrades arbitrarily as "fearing death" or "vacillating," for this encourages adventurist sentiments. The hurry-scurry dis-

order in the underground organs should also be stopped.

If something goes wrong in our underground organizations, they should suspend operation. When a situation grows tense, the staff should leave the place for a while if possible. Without considerable assurance of security, no work should be embarked upon. It doesn't matter if the work is not well done. What really matters is that the organizations must under no circumstances be destroyed. We must be particularly careful to establish solid underground leading organs which will not vacillate under any storm and stress. We must take firm disciplinary measures against those comrades who violate the principles of underground work.

We shall be in a position to deal with enemy agents provided we properly coordinate our open and underground work and provided the underground organizations carry out their work in an orderly way without negligence or recklessness. Enemy agents can still sneak into our party. So in addition to carefully selecting our members, we should try to prevent these agents from doing very serious harm to us, chiefly by properly coordinating our open and underground work.

Where conditions permit, inner-party democracy should be extended. For instance, the leading organs should frequently communicate with the rank and file, ask them for criticisms of their leaders and offer guidance through discussion with them. We should not only formally adopt some democratic procedures but, much more importantly, we should advocate a democratic spirit in our work. The leading organs should carefully consider the opinions of all comrades and respect the rights they are entitled to. Leading members do not have any privileges inside the party and so must not take pride in their leading status and become conceited. They should submit to the majority, subject themselves to discipline, accept criticisms from their subordinates, listen attentively to the reports from below and make detailed explanations to the comrades concerned. They should regard themselves as ordinary people, treat other comrades as equals and brothers, and handle problems impartially. This is the democratic spirit which all our cadres should possess, the spirit in which to remold themselves and with which to educate other comrades. This is the democracy that is needed inside the party.

Instances of commandism and punitiveness still abound in the party. Our comrades, failing to solve problems thoroughly from a political angle and according to principles, have instead resorted to organizational and disciplinary measures. (Some of them are unable to solve any problem without resorting to the latter.) Moreover, they are too mechanical and absolute in their methods of leadership. This is a kind of extremely undemocratic practice. All problems should be solved from a political angle and according to principles, and only then will organizational and disciplinary measures be warranted. Discipline is necessary in the party and should be tightened, but it should not be used except as a last resort.

To tighten discipline means to heighten our comrades' sense of the need to subordinate themselves to the majority and to the party organization; it does not mean that the leading organs should make frequent use of disciplinary measures to punish our comrades. On the contrary, the more the leading organs resort to such punishment, the more obvious the poor state of our discipline is. By party discipline we do not mean that within the party comrades are forbidden to express opinions differing from those of the leading organs but that they submit themselves to the majority in action and carry out the leading organs' decisions despite differences of opinion. Such ironclad discipline in our party makes it extremely difficult for the enemy agents to undermine us. But punitiveness and commandism are aids to them.

The party's collective leadership can be established only on the basis of democracy. And it can be considered truly collective only when it incorporates the experience and the useful ideas of all the comrades. Democratic centralism and the system of individual responsibility should go hand in hand. Decisions on major issues should be made democratically, although individuals must hold the responsibility for executing these decisions. Executive organs should carry out their work in an orderly way and should be governed by discipline, while leaders should supervise and check up on this work.

The true democratic spirit is inseparable from the communist morality of selflessness; its opposite is selfishness. Conceit, ostentation, and individualistic heroism are manifestations of selfish thinking. People who think this way seek to lord it over others and are unwilling to play second fiddle; they want the right to order others about but do not want to take orders; they criticize, attack, and abuse others at will but do not allow others to criticize them; they want others to submit to their "decisions" but they themselves refuse to obey the decisions of the party organization; they consider others' violations of the principle of centralism to be breaches of discipline but deny that their own violations of the democratic principle are likewise disciplinary breaches; and they seek only their own promotion and even do so at the expense of others. These are remnants in the party of the ideology characteristic of the old society and are contrary to the spirit of democracy.

The extension of democracy in the party requires, in the first place, that our cadres should have a keen understanding of it and set an example by their own actions before they can train our comrades and the masses to practice democracy. In the past, party members and cadres were afraid to speak lest they should make mistakes and be held responsible for them. This stemmed from a lack of democracy in the party. Instead of employing persuasion and education to encourage our comrades in their work at the lower levels, we often struggle with and attack them in order to get the work done. This is not a democratic approach. It has made our comrades afraid to speak and to act for fear of setting off a struggle. Struggle is only necessary in dealing with those who persist in their mistakes and refuse to study and mend their ways. Even then, the purpose is to educate.

It was wrong to wilfully attack our comrades during ideological struggles, label them as opportunists, and dismiss them from their work because they expressed differing views. The result of this practice has been that a lot of comrades who held different views dared not express them. This only served to conceal differences on political issues and on issues of principle so that the differences could not be thrashed out. And it only led to superficial unity in the party and impaired real political and ideological unity established on principles. Instead of lessening opposition between our comrades and the leading organs, it intensified such opposition. Therefore, rather than helping the leaders, the comrades were always finding fault with them, thus giving rise to further unprincipled struggle. The seeming absence of differences of opinion is not always a good thing.

When we say that we should not attack our comrades wilfully in ideological struggles, we do not mean that we should deny the existence of divergent views on political issues and on issues of principle among our comrades. On the contrary, it is really to resolve such differences that we want our comrades to express their views fully. Most of the differences can be eliminated through persuasion and discussion. In the future, we must be particularly careful about expelling comrades because of their different views on political issues and on issues of principle. We should do so only when they violate organizational discipline and do not make amends.

All work and change depend on our cadres. Therefore, the question of the cadres is a crucial one in the party. The party's central task is to train large numbers of cadres and assign them to the various fronts. The local organizations should pay special attention to the selection of cadres for training. In his conclusion, Comrade Mao Zedong put forward the criteria for the kind of cadres we require at present. He said they must be versed in Marxism-Leninism, politically farsighted, competent in work, full of the spirit of self-sacrifice, capable of tackling problems on their own, steadfast in the midst of difficulties, loyal and devoted in serving the nation, the class, and the party, and free from selfishness and individualistic heroism. Every one of our cadres should aspire to measure up to these criteria.

To bring our present and future cadres up to these criteria will entail arduous efforts both by the party and the cadres themselves. We should not use these criteria to test them and to dismiss those who are not yet up to the criteria. It is obvious that our cadres have various shortcomings, political as well as in competence, thinking, and ideology, and some are even tainted with the bad habits of the old society. But our purpose is to remold them and raise them to the required standard, not to destroy them. This is extremely hard work, but it can be done because we are going to remold the whole of mankind. We should regularly examine our cadres, assign them appropriate jobs and tasks to which they are equal, and help them in their work. The leading organs in many places have made mistakes in this respect and should correct them.

The promotion of new cadres is an important matter at present, but they can be promoted only by stages. We should not casually boost them into very high positions, as we did in the past, for it only serves to overwhelm them. In North China, breaches in harmony and cooperation between veteran and new cadres have already cropped up. This merits our attention. Both veteran and new cadres have their own strong points as well as their shortcomings. They should learn from and respect each other, so that each can adopt the other's strong points, offset his own weaknesses, and help to improve collective leadership.

Party members who join mass organizations should set up leading party groups. But these party groups must be skillful in carrying out their work. A leading party group should absolutely accept the leadership of the party headquarters at the corresponding level and the leadership of the party groups at higher levels. The party headquarters should be prudent and considerate when giving leadership to party groups. They should discuss all matters with the comrades of the groups and should refrain from mechanically making decisions on all minor issues. This does not mean that they should not give them leadership on specific matters; rather, it means that their leadership should be dynamic.

The disorderly and unsystematic style of work of our comrades should change. They should attend to the central tasks and work in an orderly way according to the priorities at different stages. All our comrades have an ardent revolutionary spirit which, however, should be combined with a truly down-to-earth spirit, so that they can effectively push forward their work and the revolution. Once they have a clear understanding of a specific task, they should have the determination to buckle down and carry it to completion. Only with the integration of the revolutionary and the practical spirit can the addiction to empty talk be eliminated and bureaucratism be overcome.

There should be a complete change in our propaganda work, even though we have achieved a lot of successes in this respect lately. In the past, some of our comrades often failed to distinguish propaganda slogans from action slogans, inner-party education from public-oriented propaganda, slogans for the party from those for the masses, and party propaganda from the appeals of the masses. They often used such slogans as "Get armed to support the Soviet Union" and "Get armed to wage the national revolutionary war" when mobilizing the masses for action. They added to strike demands the call to "Drive the Japanese aggressors out of China." It often happened that they published articles on inner-party problems in publications distributed in general circulation, in which they declared that such and such organizations or actions were led by the party. Moreover, our propaganda has been persistently formalistic, mechanical, trivial, or exaggerated, and without due regard to facts or to its audience. Our documents, too, have always been stereotyped. All these things must be eradicated. From now on, the party's theoretical study and propaganda will take on even greater importance and should be conducted systematically through all possible public channels, such as seminars and publishing institutions. . . .

By arming our minds with Marxism-Leninism, we can overcome all our past mistakes and lead the millions of the masses to defeat Japanese imperialism and liberate China.

86

LAND REFORM

From the early 1930s until 1952, when the Communist party gained control of rural areas, it redistributed land. Each village would be visited by a team of party cadres who would organize committees of poor peasants and supervise the classification of the inhabitants into five categories: landlords (those who lived off the rents of their lands); rich peasants (those who rented out some land but worked the rest themselves); middle peasants (those who worked their own land without the help of tenants or hired hands); poor peasants (tenants and owners of small plots who also rented or worked for wages); and hired hands (those with no land who worked for wages). In periods when more radical courses were taken, not only landlords but also rich peasants and even some middle peasants would have their land confiscated and redistributed. They would also be publicly criticized and punished for their past offenses. Executions of landlords were not uncommon. During the war with Japan and after 1948, more moderate measures were generally followed both in expropriation of land and humiliation of landowners. This revolution in landholding fundamentally altered China's power structure. The landowning elite was eliminated, the source of its income and influence abolished. Much of the power landowners had previously wielded in local affairs was taken over by peasants who became local cadres and dealt with the higher levels of the state and party structure.

Changing the attitudes of deference and submission which had previously characterized most poor peasants required considerable organizational talent and skill on the part of Communist cadres. Below is a fictional and probably idealized description of how a group of peasants learned "to stand up" and assert their rights against a landlord. It is part of the novel Sun Shines over the Sanggan River, *written in 1948 by Ding Ling (pen name of Jiang Bingzhi, 1907–1985), the first prominent woman author in China. A writer since the 1920s, in 1932 Ding Ling became a member of the Communist party and in 1936, after several years imprisonment by the Nationalists, she joined the Communist base in Yan'an. She participated in land reform in several villages in North China during one of its more radical phases in 1946–47, an experience that provided her with the basis for this novel. As an example of "socialist literature," this story was meant to be edifying and help shape a new way of thinking, but it also conveys a sense of some of the social realities of the period.*

Already in the Yan'an period, Ding Ling was subject to criticism for raising issues concerning women's status in the Communist movement. During the Anti-Rightist campaign in 1957, she was more severely criticized, removed from all her posts, and sent to a remote village in Manchuria. When the Cultural Revolution broke out, she became a target of local Red Guards and spent several years in solitary confinement. Rehabilitated in 1978, she was able to travel to the United States in 1981. She died in 1985.

The nine of them swept like a gust of wind up to Landlord Jiang's door. Guo was the first one through the big gate with the others close behind. There was no one in the courtyard. From the north room came the sound of furniture being moved. Guo dashed up the steps and burst in. Jiang was standing in the middle of the room. From the way the poor tenants had come rushing in, he guessed they were after the title deeds, but he was not afraid of them. Calmly he said, "Did the Peasants' Association tell you to come? Well, ask for anything you want! I understand the situation because, remember, I've been with the Eighth Route Army too. Only be sure to get everything straight yourselves; don't let other people cheat you! Young Wang, are you here too?"

The others were speechless. Only Guo spoke up loudly, "We understand the whole situation too, Jiang! We've come to settle accounts for all these years!"

"Settle what accounts?" Jiang began indignantly. But noting the expressions on their faces and hearing steps in the courtyard, he immediately changed his tone. "You and I both know there's going to be land reform in the village. That's good! I have a fair amount of land, more than I can cultivate myself, and I told the cadres long ago that I had decided to make a gift of it. Let everyone have land to farm and food to eat! That's only fair!"

Hearing that Jiang was going to make a present of the land, Wang lost his head and demanded testily, "What about the title deeds?"

In response, Jiang opened a drawer and took out a package, saying, "I got this ready a long

time ago. I was just thinking of sending it to the Peasants' Association, but now you've come along at just the right time. There are twelve sheets here for 53.3 *mu* of land—all pretty good land, too. I'm young and can take hard work, so it doesn't hurt me to give away so much. Wang, your five *mu* are included. Take that to the Peasants' Association. If you think it's still too little, tell them Jiang says he can give some more. After all, I'm the village head. I ought to set an example for others!"

"Jiang! What are you up to . . .?" Before Guo could finish, Wang snatched the package and ran out, and the others, seeing him running away with title deeds, took off after him. The crowd outside could not imagine what had happened. As they got sight of Wang and the others rushing through the gate, Zheng hurried over and asked, "What are you doing? What's the idea?"

Wang held his hand up, unable to contain his excitement, restless as a cock after a fight, unable to speak. Another tenant next to him shouted, "We've got them! We've got the title deeds! As soon as we went in, he handed them over!" There was nervousness rather than delight in his voice. By then Comrades Wen and Yang and the others had arrived. Thinking that the tenants had been frightened and had turned back, they asked at once how things had gone. Young Wang was clutching the package firmly in childlike excitement.

"Didn't you say anything?" asked Comrade Wen. Did you just take his title deeds and leave without saying anything?"

They looked at him quizzically, wondering

what as wrong. Comrade Wen explained, "We want to settle accounts with him; we don't want him to give land away. That land is ours! What right does he have to say he'll give it away? We don't want *his* land. What we want is our *own land*. It doesn't do any good for you to run off with the title deeds without settling accounts. He'll just say we're unreasonable then, won't he?"

When the inexperienced tenants heard this, they realized, "You're right! We went to ask for what he owes us! How did he manage to shut us up so quickly? It was all the fault of that good-for-nothing boy, Wang. As soon as he ran out, everyone followed. Let's go back! Come on!"

"What about Guo? Has he gone home?" They suddenly realized he was still alone in Landlord Jiang's house. Nobody had seen him come out. "Come on!" With renewed courage, the group reversed direction and hurried back.

When Wang and the others had rushed out, leaving him behind, Guo had become anxious and called after them, "We haven't settled our scores yet. What are you running off for?" But no one had heard him. Just as he was nearing his wits' end, Jiang's wife darted in from the inner room, looked him up and down once disdainfully, then said to Jiang in her syrupy voice, "Really, what a gang of thieves! Did they take all the title deeds away?"

Guo whirled around and glared at her, saying, "Who are you calling names? Who's a thief?"

The woman's long, disheveled hair framed a small, pale face. The bridge of her nose was pinched a purple red. Her upper lip was very short, revealing a row of irregular teeth which were all the more noticeable because two of them had gold crowns. Still ignoring Guo, she walked around him as if he were so much dirt and scolded Jiang, "You idiot! You let them take all the land that you had paid for. You hadn't stolen it, had you? Couldn't you reason with them? Communizing, communizing! Well, all your property has been communized now. I suppose if they tell you to share your women, you'll do that too! Let's see how you like being a cuckold tomorrow!"

"Dammit!" yelled Jiang. "Shut your stinking mouth!" He knew it was no use giving her a wink.

Turning impatiently to Guo, he yelled, "What are you still hanging around here for? I gave away your ten *mu* of land too. Why don't you go home?"

"We haven't settled scores yet," said Guo quietly. He knew the tenants had said that they had come to settle accounts but, now that he was left all alone, he felt tongue-tied. How he detested that woman! But hit her? He could not raise his hand. Leave? He did not want to show weakness. He was not afraid of Landlord Jiang, but he felt awkward. Just then, he caught sight of Wang and the others coming back. Feeling as happy as a released prisoner, he could not help shouting, "Wang!"

Wang marched straight into the room, brushing past Guo, threw the title deeds onto a table, and bellowed, "Who wants you to give away your land? It's our land that we want, now!" Then he winked at Guo, looking very confident.

Immediately, Guo knew what to do. Drawing himself up to his full height, he said, "Okay, Jiang, we won't count earlier scores. Just since the Japanese came. You say how much that land of yours has yielded, and we won't bother with the rent reductions we were supposed to get. Let's just say I should take half the yield. In that case, you made me pay every year about a picul and a half more than I should have. Then there was the grain tax I paid for you for nine years at compound interest! How much do you think you ought to repay me? And then, there's the wages you owe me. You kept making me do this, that, and the other for you. That's got to be counted too."

A shout came from behind him: "Hey, Jiang! I didn't farm your land for five or six years for nothing either!"

By this time many other villagers, hearing the tenants were settling scores with Landlord Jiang over his rent, had come to watch the excitement. Seeing Jiang caught off guard inside, they joined the attack through the window, shouting, "The bastard! When he was ward chief he made us pay taxes and do his bidding as army porters, sending our men to Dangshan and Hongshan, and some of them never came back. We want his life in exchange!"

When the tenants saw the crowd outside, they

grew bolder. The three old ones had not meant to say anything originally, but now they joined in the shouting too. One of them cursed: "You rogue, Jiang! Do you remember New Year's Eve the year before last when you brought guards to my house and took away all my pots and pans, just because I was three pecks of rent behind? On what charge was my property confiscated? On New Year's Day we didn't even have a mouthful of gruel to eat at home. Old and young alike were crying. You heartless brute!"

Outside the shouting grew even more menacing: "Beat the dog to death! Shoot him!"

Seeing that things were going badly, his wife hid herself inside, afraid of being beaten. Jiang was in a rage but dared not act tough anymore, thinking, "Damn! Now I'm in for it. Discretion is the better part of valor." He was afraid to think, "All right, let them shoot!" But his mind was in turmoil. He thought of Landlord Zhen Wu who had been beaten by the peasants. Making up his mind, he ran inside, brought out another red package, bowed to the ground before them all and, with a glum look, entreated them, "Good masters, I've let all my neighbors down. Please be generous. I really owe too much to each of you. I can't possibly repay. The only thing to do is take the land as payment. These are my title deeds. They're all here, a hundred and twenty-seven *mu*. If you'll all be generous, I'll be a good citizen from now on. . . ."

Now that he was humbled and all the title deeds had been produced, the crowd began to subside, for they had not planned any further settlement. Reluctantly, they took the title deeds, saying: "All right, we'll work it out and see. If there's too much, we'll give some back; but if there's not enough, you'll have to think of a way to make it up. Let's go!" Those inside and those in the yard all started leaving together. The trampling of feet could be heard, interspersed with some curses which, however, were filled with satisfaction. Jiang went into the courtyard to look dejectedly after their retreating figures. He gazed at the gray sky and sighed involuntarily. Inside, his wife burst into bitter wailing.

The disposition of Landlord Jiang's land was entrusted to the nine tenants who had taken his title deeds to the Peasants' Association. This was something they had never hoped for even in their wildest dreams. The nine of them crowded into Guo's house, and the Peasants' Association sent Han to help them write an account. They did not know how to begin, feeling merely that they had to find an outlet for their pent-up emotions. Their lives during the last three days had changed too drastically, especially in the case of the three old men, one of whom said, "Ah, the day before yesterday when the Peasants' Association asked me to describe all the hardships I've had in my life, I thought, in all these scores of years, has one single good thing ever happened to me? Happiness no sooner reaches me than it turns to sorrow. That year when my wife had given birth and people came to congratulate me on being a father, I thought, 'Eh, why make all this fuss? She's lying in bed waiting for me to go and borrow some millet to make gruel.' All day I tried in vain to borrow some, so the next day I took some bedding to pawn for three pints of rice. . . . Another year I owed Landlord Jiang one picul and eight pecks for rent and he was pressing me for it. We didn't even have husks at home, but I was afraid of him—if he grew angry, he could send you off as a porter for the army. There was nothing I could do, so I sold my eldest girl. Ah, why worry about her? At least she found a way to live. I didn't cry; in fact, I felt pleased for her sake—anyhow, I had nothing to say about it. I had already stopped being human; I couldn't feel like a man. So I didn't say a word. When the Association told me to go for the title deeds, I was afraid. I'm old. Why make enemies for the young folks? But I didn't dare say I wouldn't go, so I followed along with the rest. My, who could have believed that the world really has changed! Just think, Jiang's twenty-odd acres of land are in our hands now! Who could have imagined it? I know I ought to be pleased but, strangely enough, I actually feel sad, remembering all my past troubles."

Another said, "I always used to think that I was indebted to Landlord Jiang, that I must have owed him something in an earlier life as well as in this one, making it impossible to ever pay him all back. But yesterday when everybody reckoned things up like that, why, I've cultivated his land for him for six years, paying eight piculs rent a year, while he didn't lift a finger except to use his abacus! Six eights are forty-eight piculs, plus compound interest. With that, I could have bought fifty *mu*, not fifteen! We were poor, too poor ever to rise to our feet. Our children and grandchildren had to work like animals just because the landlords lived on our rent. The more we provided them with, the tighter they held on to us. But we're not beasts after all, we're men! Why should we live like horses in harness, working without stopping until our hair is white! Now at last we see things clearly. Ah, our sons and grandsons won't be ground down like our generation!"

"We've got Jiang's land in our hands," said the third old man. "But he's still the village head. There are still people who're afraid of him, who have to obey him. This time we've got to take the job away from him! Another thing: he's not the only rich person who's exploited us. It's no good unless we overthrow them all. So, I say this is only the beginning."

"Jiang usually gives himself airs," said another. "Look how he tried to browbeat us when we went in, and then how he suddenly went soft, like wax by the fire, cringing and scraping. I think it was just because there were so many of us. There's strength in numbers, and he knows we've got powerful support with the Eighth Route Army and the Communists backing us up!" . . .

On returning to the Peasants' Association the previous day, Comrades Wen, Yang, and Zhang had talked things over with the others and decided to divide up Landlord Jiang's land first. Since, at the moment, it was not possible to hold a mass meeting to elect a committee for dividing up the land, it was decided that the tenants should make a preliminary division, to be discussed by the masses later, in order to heighten the villagers' enthusiasm and increase their confidence. Accordingly, these nine men were chosen as a temporary land division committee.

When this news spread, many villagers grew excited. Group after group went to the cooperative to lodge complaints with the Peasants' Association against Jiang, demanding to go and settle scores with him too. They asked for his property to be confiscated, saying he had no right to go on living in such a good house. It was a house he had built when he was ward chief, built with the people's sweat and blood! And why should he be allowed to store so much grain? He had a double wall full of grain. Everybody knew there was a narrow lane at the back of his house where he stored it. Why should he be allowed to keep so many clothes in his wardrobe, now that so many people had nothing to wear? They raised pandemonium, and some pushed their way into Landlord Jiang's house while he was busy pulling all the strings he could, calling on the cadres, hoping they would leave him a little more land. When the villagers saw he was out and about, they were afraid the cadres would be deceived and listen to him. Then even more of them went to find Comrades Yang and Wen and ask to have all Jiang's property moved out. Wen, who was afraid of going too far and was unthinkingly clinging to a few "policies," felt that such an act would be beyond the scope of land reform. He wanted to have nothing to do with it and even urged the villagers to hold off. But the people refused to leave, some wanting to move the things out themselves. When the militia arrived, they sneered at them, "What are you doing here? Have you come to keep an eye on us?"

Comrade Yang had a long talk with Comrade Wen and finally won his consent to have all of Jiang's movable property temporarily confiscated by the Peasants' Association. Wen realized that as matters stood, some action must be taken, so he turned the matter over to the Association.

Zheng headed the unit that pasted up notices telling of the property being sealed and giving orders to seal up all chests, containers, and unoccupied rooms, leaving only one bedroom and kitchen for Jiang to use for the time being. But crowds of people, still doubtful, followed to watch and said, "We won't touch a thing, only watch. It's all right now that the Association is taking charge. As long as you are not keeping these things for Jiang we approve."

Standing to one side, they made suggestions and supervised the work, until finally even the containers of oil and salt for daily use were all sealed up. Jiang had returned by then and, bowing repeatedly to them all, begged them not to seal up so much. His wife, her eyes red from weeping, sat sullenly on the millstone in the courtyard. Seeing her, someone suggested that the millstone be sealed up, but another answered, "They can't move it very far, so there's no need to seal it up!"

87

HU FENG AND MAO ZEDONG

In the 1930s and 1940s many intellectuals and writers were attracted to Marxism and to the Communist party, seeing in them possibilities for a new and more just society. The party, and particularly Mao Zedong, always had misgivings about the loyalty and real motives of such intellectuals. In his 1942 "Talk at the Yan'an Forum on Literature and Art," Mao established a militant tone for the party's policies toward writers and artists: they were to integrate themselves with ordinary people, and their work had to serve the needs of the revolution. Liberal notions of art for art's sake had no place in Mao's scheme.

Mao repeatedly reiterated these principles in the early 1950s, and in 1955 made an example of Hu Feng (pen name of Zhang Gufei, 1903–1985), a leading editor and literary critic. Although an avowed Marxist and a member of the League of Leftist Writers since the early 1930s, compared to Mao, Hu was a liberal who defended the freedom of the writer to express his individual feelings and thoughts. In 1954 Hu published a criticism of the stultifying effect of official requirements that writers write upbeat stories about workers and peasants and deemphasize any signs of backwardness. He wanted more autonomy for writers and more avenues for publication.

The attack on Hu was led by an old foe, Zhou Yang, and orchestrated by Mao. Hu's letters to his friends and followers were seized and used as evidence against them. Mao took a personal hand in preparing a series of People's Daily *articles that published Hu's letters and denounced him for his bourgeois values and counterrevolutionary activity. Mao's editorial comments were not attributed to him when they were first published, but the* Quotations from Chairman Mao *issued during the Cultural Revolution included quite a few passages from them, and they were also later included in Mao's* Selected Works.

The selection below consists of two parts, first some of the letters from Hu Feng to his friends that were published as evidence of his counterrevolutionary activities, then some of Mao's editorial comments. After these appeared Hu Feng was tried in secret on charges of being a counterrevolutionary and sentenced to prison, where he continued to fight, staging hunger strikes, asking for a press conference, and demanding legal counsel, until finally he suffered a nervous breakdown. He was rehabilitated in 1979.

HU FENG'S LETTERS

Chongqing, November 1,1944

To Shu Wu:

Yesterday I finished a quick reading of the book *Philosophy of Mankind* and felt as if I had fought my way through a great battle and been rewarded with some new ideas. . . .

The book seems to say much too little about individualism, which is merely touched on in conjunction with collectivism. This shows caution, yet dwelling on that topic would have been the only way in which to make the volume truly worthwhile. How criticism and censure have made their effects felt! . . .

There should be a chapter on the exalted position of the mind, too. This would bring out the independence and power of ideas and show the spirit of sacrifice. It should be the climax of the entire volume, serving as a death blow to the materialistic ideas of these rascals.

Chongqing, July 29, 1945

To Shu Wu:

The only thing that matters now is that our magazine has been completely encircled. . . . I have suffered quite a lot because of this magazine. I have thought the matter over a thousand times already. Fighting individual battles will not solve anything; eventually we shall be overwhelmed. I really do not know what to do. There seems to be only one way out; if we make concessions, then the periodical may be saved. On the other hand, if we must make concessions, then why publish it at all?

Beijing, May 30, 1949

To Lu Ling:

The world of literature and art is enshrouded by an atmosphere of great melancholy. Many seem to be in shackles, although everybody hopes for the best. Many are like the unhappy little daughters-in-law in our old Chinese family system, who are always fearful of beating that may come at any moment but who must go on living. . . . .

Beijing, January 12, 1950

To Lu Ling:

Victory will be ours, although the road may not be an easy one, and more intensive and vigorous efforts must yet be made. It is not too pessimistic to estimate that it will take five years.

As for our little magazine, let us continue to improve it. We must not see it as a major battleground in any sense; but we must remember that if we so much as cough, someone will take note of it and criticize us.

Beijing, March 15, 1950

To Shu Wu:

In Shanghai the field of literature is dominated by several big names, so we can hardly publish any books or periodicals there. Also, in Beijing the field is much too crowded. Both in Wuhan and Hunan, where the pattern set in Hong Kong is being followed, there seems to be a great deal of confusion. The Northeast, however, is free from such pressure, or at least, if pressure is there, it must be extremely weak. Besides, Tianjin is nearby, where the literary movement is prospering. With Lu Li and his associates taking charge of literary matters there, prospects for the future are indeed bright.

Shanghai, September 12, 1950

To Zhang Zhongxiao:

The circumstances are now such that many among the reading public, cut off from each other, have become blinded. First of all, with "public opinion" standardized, the average reader finds it difficult to discern what is right. Second, the great majority of readers live in organized groups in a suffocating atmosphere of pressure. Third, in matters of literature and art, the easiest way out is allegiance to "mechanism."

Yet in spite of these conditions, the seeds of opposition are found everywhere; people are clamoring for something better. This makes it difficult for the "leaders" to exert pressure, although they feel pressure itself is absolutely necessary.

What will the final outcome be? I wonder if

some signs will be visible in half a year's time. It is important that the reading public speak up, as well as those under pressure or oppression. Slowly we shall see whether a chink can be found. As it is, all the magazines are under close supervision. If this barrier cannot be torn down, we shall all die of suffocation.

Shanghai, August 24, 1950

To Geng Yong:

It is a good idea to send your letter back to them every time it is returned; this will create a problem for them. But did you change your last name last time? It would, of course, be best if you had used another name, although if you did not the last time, you should not do so now. Furthermore, in the composition of the letter you must be analytical and lucid, bearing in mind that, besides factionalism, they are also hampered by incompetence. The most important thing is that your letter possess the power to convince the readers, although in all probability, it will not be published by the journal.

Shanghai, August 22, 1951

To Zhang Zhongxiao:

I wanted to write, and so I took a look at Mao's "Talk at the Yan'an Forum on Literature and Art." After reading it I had no urge to write any more. Let me tell you a few of my views concerning that essay.

The struggle between writers and their adversaries in the creative process is indicative, I think, of the difference between genuine and false realism. Yet all he said in this regard was "Observe, practice, study, and analyze." How pacifying and simplistic!

His views on utilitarianism only serve to throttle true criticism and choke off what is new. What he says in the three sections on "exposing" and "praising" is not correct. It represents an understanding only of form and a mechanical way of looking at things. I detest ideas like "exposing" and "lauding." . . . I feel that the words should be "suffering" and "joy," "seeking" and "vain hope." I also feel that there is no room in realism for vulgar expressions of his kind.

The section that touches on Lu Xun's es-

says is not correct. Lu Xun's essays are like sharp implements for unearthing new ideas in real life. It is a misconception of Lu Xun to take them merely as "battle weapons of satire needed at the time because of domination by dark influences and consequently no freedom of speech."

Other points could also be mentioned, but these are the important ones, the ones I felt deeply to be wrong. The whole booklet may be described as nonrealism! It might have been useful in the old days at Yan'an, but it is no longer of use, in my opinion. As it is, it now is a deadly weapon. No wonder its adherents worship it like a totem. . . .

I really cannot imagine what is in the minds of those guidance experts who conceive of this booklet as embodying the most "complete" literary and art principles and who have studiously imparted this belief to others.

Shanghai, June 26, 1952

To Lu Ling:

First, in dealing with Gun Yi [apparently a code name for Zhou Yang], no matter whether he uses hard or soft tactics, our attitude toward him should be good-natured, and we should try to soften his blows. We must have respect for hard facts. We cannot risk taking the offensive haphazardly, nor should we retreat too readily. This is important. We must let him realize that, while he can use us, he cannot bully us.

Second, there are three ways open to us: (1) to hold on to that periodical and concentrate our attack on it; (2) to make known our criticisms at once; or (3) to record our views but put them aside for the moment and wait for developments. Let us wait for actual developments before deciding on anything. At one of the small group meetings you might explore how to deal with that periodical. At any rate, we should certainly be getting preparations under way.

Shanghai, May 30, 1952

To Lu Yuan:

In the reform campaign, the important thing is to speak in praise of the leadership and undertake a self-review. Except for those within the same discussion group, it would not be wise in the discussions to touch on anybody not immediately concerned. Before Liberation, each person fended for himself; since Liberation, each is supposed to work under the leader of his or her own group. There cannot be too close a relationship between any two people. . . .

If an individual must give his views at all, he should give only his impressions. . . . If we are asked what influences have affected us, we might mention the good influences, such as our desire to go among the masses to reform ourselves. In fact, have we not already asked for such an opportunity? As for the bad influences which have affected others, that is their business. . . .

Shanghai, March 17, 1952

To Lu Ling:

Dian has been told by the director that the time is ripe to discuss my case. Please verify this when Boshan comes around. If true, then there will be some fun. I rather suspect that the honorable Qiao's "indisposition" is an excuse to take time off to study my case. At the moment I am undecided whether or not to ask for a hearing to present my views in person.

Beijing, November 7, 1954

To Fang Ran and Ji Fang:

The developments here deserve watching. Today the Second Augmented Meeting of the Federation of Literary and Art Circles was held. Speaking to the assembly, I pointed out that the problems of the *Gazette* are not unique, rather that they manifest the inclinations of those in leadership positions. I cited cases to prove that from its very first and second volumes it had already shown the following trends: In outlook, it capitulated to the capitalist class and at the same time discriminated against young and revolutionary writers who did not side with it. In the field of ideology, it developed sociological concepts of the common and vulgar sort and bowed to formalism in the matter of style. I further pointed out that in the past few years it had gone steadily downhill. By saying this, I

meant to divert the meeting from the case concerning the periodical to a review of the situation as whole.

I have not finished my speech yet. At the next meeting, Xu will speak and will make his denunciation.

I had at first hoped that you people would take part in the review. But now I would like you at least to speed up the writing of your article. Be sure to paint a clear picture of persecution based on factionalism, at the same time pointedly bringing out the capitalist character of their ideology.

HU FENG'S SPEECH TO THE FEDERATION OF LITERARY AND ART CIRCLES, BEIJING, NOVEMBER 11, 1954

Armed with sociological ideas of the common and vulgar sort, the commentators and critics became arrogant. They would not look upon writers as their comrades-in-arms or as comrade-workers. They would appear at times as political tutors, at times as tactical lecturers, and, worst of all, at times as petty judges about to render their verdicts. In short, one was forced to write according to their prescribed formulas and their rules. Their attitude toward creative productions was one of extreme rigidity and cruelty. They paid no attention to the conditions of the individual writers or to the requirements of creative production, nor did they care about the real contents of their own productions or look into the matter of objectivity. Developed to the extreme, all of this subjected the writer to a formula to demarcate class status. It rendered writers practically helpless and made it imperative that even the slightest details in their works conform to the directions and distorted interpretations of the commentators and critics. . . .

The Literary Gazette has been published for five years. Why is it that only now questions are being raised about it? . . . It did not passively suppress free discussion. On the contrary, it resorted to active means, such as criticizing others to avoid being criticized or having to make a self-criticism.

During the past five years various literary reform campaigns have been undertaken: The

"Three-Anti," the "Five-Anti," and many other campaigns of ideological reform within the party. Yet all along, the *Gazette* has been remolding the general populace without reforming itself, behaving as if it had no mistakes or defects of any kind at all.

Secondly, shouldn't the *Literary Gazette* be closely attuned to the general public? Obviously it should. Yet from the very beginning, it had adopted an attitude of despising and keeping away those readers who did not side with its views, and particularly those opposed to them. It organized a correspondent's network composed of readers who favor its views and circulated among this restricted group a publication known as the "Internal Circular for Correspondents." This circular is a means by which the *Gazette* issues orders and directives to its correspondents to organize and guide attacks against other people.... The correspondents are encouraged to write letters, to convene group discussion meetings, to prepare articles, and generally to create the impression of a popular front. If they do all of these things obediently, they are rewarded. If they bring up mildly opposing views, they are criticized for being questionable in ideology. If their offenses prove to be serious, they are no longer allowed to serve as correspondents and are banished from that privileged group.

And what exactly is the result? A sense of blind obedience is fostered among the general populace with consequent adverse effects.... Some of the correspondents form a small privileged group while the *Literary Gazette* itself operates in the position of the big boss, having under its control those correspondents purporting to give it popular support.

Beijing, December 13, 1954

To Fang Ran:

I presume you have seen all of the articles and literature published. The waste involved in this matter must have been enormous.... Blinded by illusions which were too optimistic, we have tended toward adventurism without making a concrete analysis of actual condi-

tions. For this I must bear the main responsibility.

Beijing, January 26, 1955

To Ji Zhifang and Ren Min:

It has been a long time since I wrote you last. I hope you are both well. There are now new developments in the situation. Please take the things that have come to pass and those that will shortly transpire in a cool-headed manner and with silent reserve. Do no act hastily or take part in discussions since this will only make things worse. I hope you will also stop our sympathizers from doing anything. Do not write any letters or articles expressing your views. This is no time for discussions. We are under criticism and censure.

You are in the teaching profession, so it is best that you do not get involved. If it is absolutely necessary, just give a few of your criticisms of me....

Beijing, February 8, 1955

To Zhang Zhongxiao:

Do not feel sad and by all means stay calm. There are many things we must put up with. We must find renewal through forbearance, for the sake of our enterprise and more important things to come. Hence, at the coming meeting do not be hesitant. Speak out in criticism of Hu Feng and others. As for Hu, he is quite willing to write articles criticizing himself if those above wish it. It does not matter, for the masses will be able to determine how much he is in the wrong and how much he is in the right.

HU FENG'S SELF-CRITICISM

In the course of the current campaign criticizing capitalist ideology, I have begun to realize my serious errors. Their fundamental cause has been my thinking that the revolution of the bourgeoisie and its stand were synonymous with those of the working class. I glossed over the differences in principle between them. These errors have been exemplified in ideology by my confining myself to the narrow viewpoint of realism instead of adhering to political principles; by my distorting and disregarding the viewpoints of the working class; by my contradicting Marxist principles with respect to certain fundamental issues; and by my disobeying the line advocated by Chairman Mao in the fields of art and literature. They are exemplified in my way of doing things; in my attitude of refusing for a long time to undergo thought reform; in my advocating individual heroism of the sort which results in praising oneself all the time; in my giving vent to narrow factional sentiments; in my utter lack of the spirit of self-criticism; and in my tendency to deviate from the masses and collectivization. Because of my attitude of considering myself to be right all the time, I persisted in my errors and disregarded the criticisms of my comrades as well as their wishes and expectations. As a result, not only did I avoid correcting my errors but I continued in them and allowed them to grow.

MAO'S EDITORIAL COMMENTS
PUBLISHED MAY 24, 1955

In the past, it was said that they were a group of simple cultural people. This is wrong because they have worked their way into political, military, economic, cultural, and educational establishments. In the past it was said they were like a bunch of revolutionaries equipped with torches and sticks. This is wrong because most of them have serious problems. Their basic ranks are made up either of imperialist-Guomindang secret agents, or of reactionary army officers, or of renegades to the Communist party. A counter-revolutionary faction hidden within the revolutionary camp, an underground independent kingdom, has been formed with these people as the leading group.

During the period when there are still classes and class struggles at home and in the international arena, the working class and the masses of the people who have seized state power must suppress the resistance of all counterrevolutionary classes, groups, and individuals against the revolution, ban their restoration activities, and forbid all counterrevolutionary ends.

From [Hu Feng's letters] above, we can see the following: (1) Since liberation, the anti-party, anti-people conspiratorial activities of the Hu Feng clique became progressively more organized and more extensive; their attacks on the party and party-led cultural policies became fiercer. (2) Like all other counterrevolutionaries, they always adopt secret or two-faced tactics in their campaigns. (3) Because their conspiracy was exposed, the Hu Feng clique is not able to retreat under pressure, but this sort of reactionary clique whose hatred for the party, the people, and the revolution has reached such a crazy degree have not truly laid down its weapons, but is plotting to continue using two-faced tactics to preserve their strength and wait for an opportune time to stage a comeback. This is clearly demonstrated by the fact that Hu Feng uses such phrases as "By being patient you can seek a second life," or "Everything is for the cause, for the distant future" to encourage members of his clique. Like other open or hidden counterrevolutionaries, members of the counter-revolutionary Hu Feng clique put their hope in the reestablishment of a counterrevolutionary government and the overthrow of the people's revolutionary government. They see this as the opportune moment they are waiting for.

MAO'S COMMENTS PUBLISHED
JUNE 10, 1955

Those who represent the exploiting classes usually, when in a predicament, resort to the tactics of attack as a means of defense so that they can stay alive today and even flourish tomorrow. They throw in your face rumors which they have conjured up out of thin air, or they pick on a few superficialities as a means of countering the essence of a matter, or they sing the praises of one group of people to attack another, or they seize on an incident as an opportunity for "making a break-through at some point" and putting us in a difficult position. In short, they are always considering what tactics to use against us and "spying out the land" in order to employ their tactics successfully.... As members of a revolutionary party, we must be alive to these tricks of theirs and in order to defeat them must study their tactics. We must not behave like bookish scholars and oversimplify the complications of the class struggle.

MAO'S INTRODUCTION TO A SEPARATE BOOK REPRINTING THE HU FENG LETTERS

Counterrevolutionaries and those with counterrevolutionary sentiments will find much that they like in the correspondence of the Hu Feng clique. Hu Feng and his clique are indeed spokesmen for all counterrevolutionary classes, groups, and individuals, and the curses they hurl at the revolution and the tactics they use in their activities will be appreciated by all those counterrevolutionaries who can get hold of this book, for which they can derive some counterrevolutionary education about class struggle. Nevertheless, this will in no way save them from their doom. Like all the counterrevolutionary writings of their backers, the imperialists and Jiang Jieshi's Guomindang, which were directed against the Chinese people, these writings of the Hu Feng elements are records not of success but of failure. They did not save their own clique from destruction.

The masses of the people are very much in need of this material. How do counterrevolutionaries employ their double-dealing tactics? How do they succeed in deceiving us by their false appearances, while furtively doing the things we least expect? All this is unknown to thousands upon thousands of well-intentioned people. On this account, many counterrevolutionaries have wormed their way into our ranks. The eyes of our people are not keen, they are not adept at distinguishing good people from bad types. When people operate in normal conditions, we know how to tell the bad from the good, but we are not adept at seeing through those who operate in unusual conditions. The Hu Feng elements are counterrevolutionaries who put on a disguise to hide their true features and to give a false impression. But since they oppose the revolution, it is impossible for them to cover up their true features entirely. As for the leading spirits of the Hu Feng clique, they have had disputes with us on many occasions before and since Liberation. They are different in word and deed not only from Communists but also from vast numbers of nonparty revolutionaries and democrats. They were recently exposed to the full simply because we got hold of a mass of solid evidence against them. As for many of the individuals in the Hu Feng clique, they were able to deceive us because our party organizations, state organs, people's organizations, cultural and educational institutions or enterprises failed to make a strict examination of their records before admitting them. It was also because we were in a stormy period of revolution in the recent past and people of all sorts tried to get close to us as we emerged the victors; so inevitably the waters were muddied, the bad came mixed with the good, and we have not yet got around to sifting them thoroughly. Furthermore, success in spotting and clearing out bad elements depends on a combination of correct guidance from the leading organs with a high degree of political consciousness on the part of the masses, but in this regard our work in the past was not without shortcomings. These are all lessons for us.

We attach importance to the Hu Feng case because we want to use it to educate the masses of the people, and first those cadres who can read and also the intellectuals; to them we recommend this material for raising their level of political consciousness. The material is striking for its extreme sharpness and clarity. Counterrevolutionaries will naturally pay attention to it and revolutionary people even more so. If the masses of the revolutionary people learn something from this case and the material thereby increases their revolutionary ardor and their ability to discriminate, we shall have all sorts of hidden counterrevolutionaries gradually uncovered.

88

A NEW YOUNG MAN ARRIVES AT THE ORGANIZATION DEPARTMENT

From the time of victory in 1949, Mao worried that the revolutionary fervor of party members would wane, that they would lose touch with the people and become authoritarian bureaucrats. In 1956–57 he launched a campaign to expose the party to the criticism of intellectuals under the slogan "Let a Hundred Flowers Bloom." Although most intellectuals were cautious at first, once criticism started to pour forth, it soon became a torrent. At this point Mao and other party leaders abruptly changed the policy of toleration and launched an attack on the critics for harboring rightist ideology.

The following excerpt is from a story by the young writer, Wang Meng (b. 1934), published in People's Literature in 1956. During the "Hundred Flowers" period, it was widely discussed. Wang's mockery of this one sleepy and inefficient party office earned the praise of many who were troubled by bureaucratic abuses, but it also elicited considerable hostility from officials unaccustomed to this manner of criticism. During the anti-rightist phase, Wang Meng was criticized for sentimentality and despondency, traits said to be characteristic of bourgeois intellectuals with few ties to the masses. Labeled a rightist, Wang Meng was sent off to the far northwest, living in a Uighur village until he was rehabilitated in 1978. He served as minister of culture from 1986 until dismissed in 1989 after the Tiananmen crackdown.

The fourth day that Lin Zhen [the new young party member] was at the district headquarters, he went to the Donghua Gunny Sack Factory to look into the conditions of party recruitment work during the first quarter of the year. Before going, he looked over the relevant documents and read a small volume entitled "How to Carry Out an Investigation Study." He repeatedly asked Han Changxin for advice and carefully and elaborately wrote out an outline for himself. Then he mounted the bicycle supplied to him and rapidly rode out toward the gunny sack factory.

The guard at the factory entrance, as soon as he heard Lin was a party committee cadre, did not even ask him to sign his name but trustingly invited him to go on in. He walked through a large empty yard, past a huge open storage bin filled with hemp and a building which rumbled with the sound of machinery. Then, rather nervously, he knocked at the door of Wang Qingchuan, the factory director and concurrent party branch secretary. Receiving a reply of "Come in," he entered slowly, fearing that if he moved quickly he would display his lack of experience. He saw a fat-faced, thick-necked, short man playing chess with a slick-haired humpback. The short comrade lifted his head, playing with a chess piece, and after asking Lin whom he wanted to see, impatiently waved his hand and said, "Go over to the branch party office in the adjoining building and ask for Wei Heming; he's the organization committee member." Then he lowered his head once more and continued with the chess game.

Lin Zhen found the ruddy-faced Wei Heming and began questioning from his outline, "In the first quarter of the year how many persons did you recruit?"

"One and a half," Wei replied harshly and abruptly.

"What's this 'half'?"

"One person was passed, but the district committee has already delayed two months in approving him."

Lin Zhen took out a notebook and noted this down. Then he continued, "How was the recruitment work carried out? What experiences did you have?"

"The procedure was the same as before—as laid down in the party constitution."

Lin Zhen looked at the person sitting opposite him. Why were his remarks as dry as week-old bread? Wei leaned his cheek on his hand and looked away as if he were thinking of something else.

"What were the results of your recruitment work?" Lin asked.

"I just told you," Wei replied, in a manner which showed he hoped to end the discussion quickly.

Lin Zhen did not know what to ask next. He had spent a whole afternoon preparing an outline

and now after talking for five minutes he had used it all up. He was quite embarrassed.

At this moment the door was pushed open by a forceful hand. The short comrade came in and snapped at Wei, "Do you know what was in that letter that just came?"

Wei dully nodded his head. The short comrade paced back and forth and then, standing with legs apart in the middle of the floor, said, "You've got to think of a way out! The question of quality was raised last year. How is it you have to wait until the contractor writes a letter to the ministry of textiles? It is shameful if in the high tide of socialism our production cannot gradually be raised!"

Wei Heming coldly looked at the short man's face and said, "Who are you talking about?"

"I am talking about all of you!" The short man waved his hand, including Lin Zhen in his gesture.

Wei Heming was trying to keep his anger under control and looked quite frightening. His face turned even redder and standing up he asked, "And you? You don't have any responsibility?"

"Naturally I am responsible." The short comrade calmed down. "I am responsible to the higher levels. No matter how they deal with me, I've got to take it. You are responsible to me. After all, who made you production chief? Be careful. . . ." Finishing, he looked threateningly at Wei Heming and then left.

Wei sat down, opened up all the buttons on his cotton jacket and took a deep breath. When Lin Zhen asked who that man was, Wei sarcastically replied, "You don't know him? He's the factory director, Wang Qingchuan."

Then Wei told Lin in detail all about Wang Qingchuan. Originally, Wang worked in some central ministry but as punishment for some involvement with a woman, he was assigned to this factory as deputy factory manager in 1951. In 1953 the factory manager was assigned elsewhere and Wang was promoted to that position. He never did anything but run around in circles, hide in his office, sign papers, and play chess. Every month at the union meeting, the party branch meeting, and the youth league meeting he would make a speech criticizing the workers for not carrying out mass competition well, for their indifference to quality, for their economistic ideology. . . . Wei had not finished when Wang pushed open the door again. Looking at the watch on his left wrist he ordered: "Inform all responsible persons in the party, league, union, and administrative departments that there will be a meeting at 12:10 in the factory manager's office." Then, slamming the door, he left.

Wei Heming mumbled, "You see what sort of a person he is?"

Lin said, "Don't keep these complaints to yourself. Criticize him, tell the higher levels about all this. They cannot possibly condone this sort of factory manager."

Wei smiled and asked Lin, "Old Lin, you're new here, aren't you?"

"Old Lin" reddened.

Wei explained, "Criticism doesn't work. He generally does not join in such meetings; so where are you going to criticize him? If by chance he does join in and you express your views, he says, 'It's fine to put forth opinions, but you've got to have a firm grip on essentials and consider the time and place. Now we should not take up precious time put aside for discussing national tasks by giving vent to personal opinions.' Fine. So instead of taking up 'valuable time,' I went around to see him myself, and we have argued ourselves into this present situation."

"And how about informing the higher levels?"

"In 1954 I wrote letters to the ministry of textile industry and the district party headquarters. A man named Zhang from the ministry and Old Han from your office came around once to investigate. The conclusion of the investigation was that 'Bureaucratism is comparatively serious but most important is the manner of carrying out work; the tasks have been basically completed. It's only a question of shortcomings in the manner of completing them.' Afterwards Wang was criticized once, and they got hold of me to encourage the spirit of criticism from bot-

tom to top, and that was the end of it. Wang was better for about a month. Then, he got nephritis. After he was cured he said he had become sick because of his hard work, and he became as he is now."

"Tell the upper levels again."

"Hmph. I don't know how many times I've talked with Han Changxin, but Old Han doesn't take any notice. On the contrary he lectures me on respect for authority and strengthening unity. Maybe I shouldn't think this, but I'm afraid we may have to wait until Wang embezzles funds or rapes a woman before the upper levels take any notice."

When Lin left the factory and mounted his bike again, the wheels turned round much more slowly than they had on his way to the factory. He frowned deeply. The first step in his work was filled with difficulties, but he also felt a kind of challenge—this was the time to show one's fighting spirit! He thought and thought, until his bike strayed into the express lane and he was stopped and scolded by a policeman.

After finishing lunch, Lin Zhen could not wait to go off to Han Changxin to report on the situation. Han was wearily leaning on the sofa, his big form looking heavy and clumsy. He took a box of matches out of his pocket and, choosing one stick, began picking his teeth.

While Lin poured forth a disconnected account of what he had seen and heard at the Gunny Sack Factory, Han tapped his toe on the floor and kept saying, "Yes, I know." Afterwards, he patted Lin on the shoulder and cheerily said, "If you didn't understand conditions the first time out, it's not important. The next time will be better."

"But I understand the situation regarding Wang Qingchuan," said Lin, opening his notebook.

Han closed the notebook and told him, "Right, I've known about this situation for a long time. The year before last the district committee told me to settle it, so I severely criticized him, pointing out his shortcomings. We talked for at least three or four hours. . . ."

"But there weren't any results. Wei Heming said he was only better for one month."

"Even one month is something. Moreover, it certainly was not for only one month. Wei's ideology is questionable if as soon as he meets anyone he starts to tell all about his superior's faults. . . ."

"Well, was what he said true or not?"

"It's hard to say. Naturally this ought to be solved. I've talked it over with the district committee assistant secretary, Comrade Li Zongqin."

"And what did the assistant secretary think?"

"He agreed with me that the problem of Wang Qingchuan ought to be solved and can be solved. . . . Only, you shouldn't go diving into it just like that."

"Do you mean me?"

"Yes. This is the first time you've gone to a factory, and you don't understand the entire situation. Your job isn't to solve the problem of Wang; in fact, to speak frankly, a more experienced cadre is needed for his problem. Besides, it isn't that we haven't considered the affair. . . . If you go jumping into this business, you won't get out for three months. Are you completely familiar with the first quarter's summary on party building? The upper levels are anxious to receive our report!"

Lin Zhen was silent. Han patted him on the shoulder again. "Don't be upset. There are three thousand party members in our district and a hundred-and-some-odd branches. Do you think you can know all of their problems as soon as you arrive?" He yawned, the pockmarks on his tired face standing out redly. "Ahhhh—I'd better take my afternoon nap."

"Then how should I go about investigating party recruitment work again?" Lin asked hopelessly.

Then Han Changxin again rose to pat his shoulder, but Lin involuntarily moved away. Han self-confidently said, "Tomorrow we will go together; I'll help you investigate. How about that?" Then he took Lin off with him to the dormitory.

The next day, Lin Zhen was very interested to see how Han would go about investigating con-

ditions. Three years earlier when he was in the Beijing Normal School, he had gone off to observe teaching in practice. The teacher stood in front and lectured while Lin and the students listened. This time, Lin adopted the same attitude; opening his notebook, he prepared to note down carefully Han's modus operandi.

Han asked Wei Heming, "How many party members did you recruit?"

"One and a half."

"Not 'one and a half,' but two. I'm inquiring about your recruitment work, not about whether the district committee has approved them or not." Having corrected him, Han continued, "How did these two men complete their production quota?"

"Very well. One exceeded his by seven percent and the other by four percent. The factory wall newspaper shows . . ."

When he started to talk about production conditions, Wei seemed to take on a little more life, but Han interrupted him, "What shortcomings do they have?"

Wei thought for some time and then vaguely mentioned some defects. Han made him give some examples. After this Han again asked him about the party activists' completion of their quarter's production tasks, seeking figures and concrete examples. But when the manner in which advanced workers overcame difficulties and developed innovations came up, he showed no interest.

After they returned, Han quickly scribbled off a hand-written draft "Summary of Conditions Regarding Recruitment Work at the Gunny Sack Factory" whose details were as follows: ". . . During this quarter (January–March 1956) the gunny sack factory branch office basically carried through a positive and careful plan of recruiting new party members. In party building work it achieved definite results. Newly approved party members Zhu and Fan received the glorious encouragement of becoming Communist party members, strengthened their outlook as owners of their own tools, and in the first quarter exceeded their heavy production quotas by seven percent and four percent respectively. The great mass of positive workers within the party factory branch were influenced by the good example set by Zhu and Fan, and were stimulated by their decision to achieve acceptance into the party. They developed their positive attitude and creativity and magnificently completed or exceeded their production quotas for the quarter. . . ." (Below was a series of figures and concrete examples.) "This proves: 1. party building work not only does not interfere with production work, but in fact greatly stimulates it. Any work method which uses as a pretext the urgency of production work to disregard party building is mistaken. 2. . . . But at the same time it must be pointed out that party building work in the gunny sack factory still has certain shortcomings . . . such as. . . ."

Lin Zhen held the sheet of fine paper on which the "Summary of Conditions" was written and read it over and over. There was an instant when he doubted whether he had been to the gunny sack factory or whether the last time he had gone to the factory with Han he had fallen asleep. Why was it there were so many things he absolutely could not recall? He suspiciously asked Han, "What is the basis for all this?"

"Wei Heming's report that day."

"The production results were due to their party building work?" Lin began to stammer.

Han shook out the crease in his trousers and said, "Naturally."

"No, Wei didn't say that last time. They were able to raise production, but perhaps it was due to expanding competition, perhaps because the Youth League established a supervision post, but not necessarily because of the achievements of party building work. . . ."

"Naturally, I don't deny that. Various factors all worked together. You cannot split them apart metaphysically in an analysis and say this is a result of X and that is a result of Y."

"Then if we were writing a summary of rat catching work during the first quarter could we also use these figures and examples?"

Han smiled broadly at Lin's inexperience and said, "You have to be somewhat flexible. . . ."

"How do you know their production tasks were heavy?"

"Do you think there could be any factory now with light tasks?"

Lin was dumfounded. . . .

Not long afterwards, Lin Zhen was the target of severe criticism in a party small group meeting. The situation developed as follows. During one of Lin's visits to the gunny sack factory, Wei Heming told him that because the quality standard set for the quarter had not been met, Wang Qingchuan had fiercely lectured the workers. The workers had their own views on this, and Wei planned to call a discussion group together, collect these views, and pass them on to the higher authorities. Lin approved of this method and thought that in this way the "ripening of conditions" could be hastened. Three days later Wang came into the district committee in a blind rage, looking for the assistant secretary, Li Zongqin. He complained that Wei Heming—with the support of Lin Zhen—had formed a faction to carry out anti-leadership activities and moreover, that the workers in the discussion group Wei directed were all suspect because of their backgrounds. . . . And at the very end, he requested that his own resignation be accepted. Li criticized a few of Wang's shortcomings and agreed to prevent Wei from convening his discussion group again. "As for Lin Zhen," he said to Wang, "we will give him some much deserved instruction."

In the criticism meeting, Han analyzed: "Comrade Lin Zhen did not discuss the issue with the leadership but on his own responsibility agreed to Wei's calling of a discussion group. This, to begin with, is a kind of unorganized, undisciplined behavior. . . ."

Lin refused to concede and said, "Not requesting permission from the leadership was an error. But I do not understand why we not only fail to investigate spontaneously the views of the masses but on the contrary prevent the lower levels from putting forth their views!"

"Who says we won't investigate?" Han raised one leg. "We are completely in control of the situation at the gunny sack factory. . . ."

"In control but making no effort to solve the problem; that's what's so painful! The party constitution says that party members must struggle against anything that works against the interests of the party. . . ." Lin Zhen's face paled.

Experienced Liu Shiwu began to make his statement. He always made a point of entering at a discussion's most crucial point.

"Comrade Lin Zhen's enthusiasm is very praiseworthy, but for him to lecture the organization department cadres on the party constitution after having been here only a month is a little presumptuous. Lin believes that, by supporting criticism from the bottom up, he is doing a very fine thing, and his motive is no doubt very noble. But criticism from the bottom up must be initiated by the leadership. For example, let's ask Comrade Lin to think about the following: First, isn't it true that Wei Heming has a personal grudge against Wang Qingchuan? It would be very difficult to say otherwise. Then, for Wei so eagerly to call a discussion group together may have had a personal objective, couldn't it? I think that's not entirely impossible. Second, were there people in the discussion group whose backgrounds are in doubt and who may have ulterior motives? We've also got to consider that point. Third, can the convening of that kind of a meeting give the masses the impression that Wang is on the verge of being punished and thereby lead to confusion all around? And so on. As to Lin Zhen's ideological condition, I want to put forward very frankly a guess: a young man easily idealizes life; he believes life should be a certain way and then demands that it be that way. Those who do party work must consider the objective facts and whether life can be that way. Young people also easily overestimate themselves and aspire to too much. As soon as they go to a new work post they want to struggle against every shortcoming and be a 'Nastya' type of hero. This is a valuable and lofty idea but it is also a kind of vanity. . . ."

Lin Zhen wavered for a moment as if he had received a blow. He bit down tightly on his lower lip to hold in his anger and pain. Screwing up his courage, he asked again: "But what about Wang Qingchuan? . . . "

Liu Shiwu jerked his head up and interrupted, "Tomorrow I will have a talk with him. You are not the only one with principles."

89

PENG DEHUAI'S CRITIQUE OF THE GREAT LEAP FORWARD

Despite the peasant origins of most of the cadres and Red Army soldiers who won the civil war, the leaders of the Communist party began their task of rebuilding the country on the standard Marxist premise that industrialization is necessary for socialism. Thus in the early 1950s much effort was devoted to Soviet-style economic planning to concentrate available resources for the development of heavy industry. Mao was never entirely happy with the power that technical experts gained in this process, and in 1957 he proposed an alternative to the Soviet model, a Great Leap Forward. In November 1957, in Moscow, he told the leaders of the international communist movement that China would surpass Great Britain in industrial output within fifteen years. Through the concerted hard work of hundreds of millions of people laboring together, China would transform itself from a poor nation to a mighty one.

In 1958, in a wave of utopian enthusiasm, agricultural collectives were amalgamated into gigantic communes with expectations of huge increases in productivity. Throughout the country, communes, factories, schools, and other units set up "backyard steel furnaces" in order to double steel production. As workers were mobilized to work long hours on these and other large-scale projects, they spent little time at home or in normal farm work. In 1959, after the frenetic pace was relaxed, Peng Dehuai (1899–1974), the minister of defense and a military hero, offered measured criticisms of the Great Leap policies at a party meeting. Mao was affronted, vehemently countered the charges, and forced the party to choose between Peng and himself. Peng in the end was removed from his positions of authority. During the Cultural Revolution he received rough treatment at the hands of Red Guards, dying in 1974 after a lengthy period in solitary confinement.

Within a couple of years, the Great Leap proved an economic disaster, and the three years from 1960 to 1962 are known as the Three Hard Years, when millions died of the effects of malnourishment.

Dear Chairman:

This Lushan Meeting is important. In the discussions in the Northwest Group, I commented on other speakers' remarks several times. Now I am stating, specially for your reference, a number of my views that I have not expressed fully at the group meetings. I may be as straightforward as Zhang Fei, but I possess only his roughness without his tact. Therefore, please consider whether what I am about to write is worth your attention, point out whatever is wrong, and give me your instructions.

A. The Achievements of the Great Leap Forward in 1958 Are Indisputable.

According to figures verified by the State Planning Commission, total industrial and agricultural output value in 1958 increased 48.4 percent over 1957. The increase in industry was 66.1 percent, and that in agriculture and sideline production, 25 percent (it is certain that grain and cotton registered a 30 percent increase). State revenue rose 43.5 percent. Such a rate of increase is unprecedented in the world; it exceeds the established speed of socialist construction. In particular, the Great Leap Forward has basically proved the correctness of the General Line for building socialism with greater, quicker, better, and more economical results in a country like ours, hampered by a weak economic foundation and by backward technology and equipment. Not only is this a great success for China, it will also play a long-term positive role in the socialist camp.

But as we can see now, an excessive number of capital construction projects were hastily started in 1958. With part of the funds being dispersed, completion of some essential projects had to be postponed. This is a shortcoming, one caused mainly by lack of experience. Because we did not have a deep enough understanding, we came to be aware of it too late. So we continued with our Great Leap Forward in 1959 instead of putting on the brakes and slowing down our pace accord-

ingly. As a result, imbalances were not corrected in time, and new temporary difficulties cropped up. But these projects are after all needed for national construction. They will gradually—in a year or two or a little longer—bring us returns. Gaps and weak links exist in production, making it impossible to put some projects to use. Also, the serious shortage of essential reserves of certain types of supplies makes it difficult to correct in time the disproportions and the newly created imbalances. These are the difficulties confronting us. In working out the plan for 1960, we should give it more serious consideration on a practical and reliable basis. Some capital construction projects started in 1958 or in the first half of 1959 which cannot be completed must be suspended with the utmost resolution. We have to give up one thing in order to gain another. Otherwise the serious disproportions will be prolonged, and it will be impossible to extricate ourselves from our passive position in certain fields, and that would hamper our speed in the effort to catch up with or surpass Britain in the next four years. Although the state planning commission has set guidelines on the proper balance, it has difficulty in making the final decision because of various reasons.

The people's communes which emerged in rural China in 1958 have great significance. They will free the peasants in our country from poverty, and have set the right path along which we can speed up the building of socialism and march towards communism. On the issue of ownership, there was some confusion at one time, causing shortcomings and mistakes in our practical work. Though this was a serious problem, the shortcomings and mistakes have been basically corrected and the confusion basically eliminated after a series of meetings were held in Wuchang, Zhengzhou and Shanghai. The people's communes are gradually shifting to the normal course of distribution according to work.

The problem of unemployment was solved during the Great Leap Forward in 1958. The quick solution of this problem was no small matter; it was a matter of great importance to a country like ours with an enormous population and a backward economy.

In the nationwide campaign for the production of iron and steel, too many small blast furnaces were built with a waste of material, money, and manpower. This, of course, was a rather big loss. On the other hand, through the campaign we have been able to conduct a preliminary geological survey across the country, train many technicians, temper the vast numbers of cadres and raise their level. Though we paid a steep tuition (we spent over 2,000 million yuan to subsidize the effort), there were gains as well as losses in this endeavor.

Considering the above-mentioned points alone, we can say that our achievements have been really great, but we also have quite a few profound lessons to learn. It would be to our benefit to make an earnest analysis.

B. How to Review the Experience and Lessons in Our Work.

At this meeting, the participants are making many valuable suggestions in the discussions on the experience and lessons in our work last year. Our party's work will benefit greatly from these discussions. The party will be able to free itself from a passive position in some fields and take the initiative, acquire a better understanding of the laws governing the socialist economy, readjust the imbalances which always exist, and realize the correct meaning of achieving a rapid development.

In my view, some of the shortcomings and mistakes that emerged in the Great Leap Forward were unavoidable. All the revolutionary movements led by our party in the past thirty years or so have had some shortcomings accompanying their great achievements. These are the two aspects of the same question. The outstanding contradiction confronting us in construction is the tension in various fields caused by disproportions. Such a development has in essence affected the relationship between workers and peasants and between the various strata in the cities and the rural areas. Thus the contradiction takes on a po-

litical nature. It is the key link which affects our mobilization of the masses of people for continuing the leap forward.

There are many reasons for the shortcomings and mistakes in our work during the past period. The objective reason is that we are unfamiliar with socialist construction and do not have a comprehensive knowledge based on experience. We do not have a deep understanding of the law of planned and proportionate development of the socialist economy, and we have not implemented the principle of walking on two legs in various fields of work. In handling problems in economic construction, we are not as competent as we are in dealing with political problems like the shelling of Jinmen [Quemoy] and the putting down of the rebellion in Tibet. As for the objective situation, our country is in a backward state of being "poor and blank" (some of our people still do not have enough food, and last year each person was rationed six meters of cotton cloth, enough to make only a suit and two shorts) and the people are eager to change this situation. A second reason is the favorable international situation. These have been important factors contributing to our launching the Great Leap Forward. It was entirely necessary and correct for us to accelerate our construction work to try as soon as possible to put an end to poverty and backwardness and to create a more favorable international situation by taking this good opportunity and acting on the demands of the people.

A number of problems that have developed merit attention in regard to our way of thinking and style of work. The main problems are:

1. A growing tendency towards boasting and exaggeration on a fairly extensive scale. At the Beidaihe Meeting last year, the grain output was overestimated. This created a false impression and everyone thought that the food problem had been solved and that we could therefore go all out in industry. In iron and steel, production was affected with such extreme one-sided thinking that no serious study was conducted on equipment for steel making and rolling and ore crushing as well

as for coal mining and other mineral ores and for making coke, on the source of pit-props, on transportation capacity, on the expansion of the labor force, on the increase in purchasing power, on the distribution of market commodities, etc. In sum, we did not have a balanced overall plan. It was also a lack of realistic thinking that gave rise to these errors. This, I am afraid, was the cause of a series of our problems.

The exaggeration trend has become so common in various areas and departments that reports of unbelievable miracles have appeared in newspapers and magazines to bring a great loss of prestige to the party. According to what was reported, it seemed that communism was just around the corner, and this turned the heads of many comrades. Extravagance and waste grew in the wake of reports of extra-large grain and cotton harvests and a doubling of iron and steel output. As a result, the autumn harvest was done in a slipshod manner, and costs were not taken into consideration. Though we were poor, we lived as if we were rich.

What is particularly serious in all this is that it was very hard for us to get to know the real situation for a fairly long period. We did not have a clear idea of the situation even at the time of the Wuchang Meeting and the meeting of secretaries of provincial and municipal party committees held in January this year. The tendency towards boasting and exaggeration has its social cause, which is worth studying. It also has to do with our practice of fixing production quotas without corresponding measures to meet them. Though Chairman Mao reminded the party last year of the need to combine soaring enthusiasm with a scientific approach and the principle of walking on two legs, it seems that his instructions have not been grasped by most leading comrades, and I am no exception.

2. Petty-bourgeois fanaticism which makes us vulnerable to "left" errors. In the Great Leap Forward of 1958, I, like many other comrades, was misled by the achievements of the Great Leap Forward and the zeal of the mass movement. As a result, some "left" tendencies developed in our heads. We were thinking of entering a communist society in one stride, and the idea of trying to be the first to do this gained an upper hand in our minds for a time. So we banished from our minds the mass line and the working style of seeking truth from facts, which had been cultivated by the party for a long time.

In our way of thinking, we have often muddled up the relationship between strategic goals and concrete measures, between long-term principles and immediate steps, between the whole situation and part of it, and between big collectives and small collectives. The Chairman's calls such as "strive for a high yield on a smaller area and bring in a big crop," "catch up with Britain in fifteen years," etc., are long-term strategic goals. But we have not studied them carefully and have not paid enough attention to the specific current conditions so as to arrange our work on a positive, safe, and reliable basis. Because they were raised at every level, some quotas, which could only be met after several or a dozen years, became targets to be fulfilled in one year or even a few months. By so doing, we divorced ourselves from reality and lost the support of the masses. For example, the law of exchange at equal values was negated and the slogan of "giving free meals to all" was raised much too early; in some areas, state monopoly purchase and marketing of grain was abolished for a time when the slogan of "eating as much as you like" was raised on the grounds of bumper harvests of grain. Some techniques were popularized hastily even before they were tested and approved. Some economic and scientific laws were rashly neglected. All this was a "left" deviation. In the eyes of comrades showing such a deviation, everything could be done by putting politics in command. They forgot that the aim of putting politics in command was to raise political consciousness in work, guarantee the increase in the quantity of products and improvement in their quality, and bring into play the enthusiasm and creativeness of the masses to speed up our economic construction. Putting politics in command cannot replace economic laws, let alone concrete measures in economic work. We must stress both putting politics in command and taking effective measures in economic work; we should not emphasize one thing at the expense of the other. Generally, correcting "left" tendencies is more difficult than eliminating "right" conservative ideas. This has been proved in the history of our party. During the latter half of last year, there seemed to be an atmosphere in which people paid attention to combating "right" conservative ideas but ignored the "left" tendencies of subjectivism. Thanks to a series of measures adopted after the Zhengzhou meetings held last winter, some "left" tendencies have been basically corrected. This is a great victory, which has educated comrades of the whole party without affecting their enthusiasm.

By now we have got a basically clear picture of the domestic situation. Particularly because of the recent meetings, most comrades within the party basically hold the same view. The present task for the whole party is to unite and keep up the effort. In my opinion, it will be very beneficial to review in a systematic way the achievements and lessons in our work since the latter half of last year to further educate the comrades of the whole party. The aim is to make a clear distinction between right and wrong and to raise our ideological level. Generally speaking, we should not go about try-

ing to affix blame; this would be harmful to our unity and our cause. Basing ourselves on our experience and research since the latter half of last year, we can clarify some problems arising from unfamiliarity with the laws governing socialist construction. Other problems can also be grasped after a longer period of study and experiment. As for our way of thinking and work style, the profound lessons we are learning this time help us to realize the problems in them more easily. But we'll have to try very hard before they can be thoroughly rectified. Just as the Chairman has instructed us at the present meeting: "The achievements are great, the problems are many, the experience is abundant, and the future is bright." It is up to us to grasp the initiative. So long as the whole party is united and works hard, the conditions for continuing the leap forward are present. The plans for this year and next and for four more years will surely be fulfilled successfully. The aim of catching up with Britain in fifteen years can be basically achieved in four years, and we can surely surpass Britain in the output of some important products. Hence our great achievements and bright future.

With greetings,
Peng Dehuai
July 14, 1959

90

DEVELOPING AGRICULTURAL PRODUCTION

During the period when agriculture was collectivized, private ownership rights to land, tools, and draft animals were largely abolished. Except for the produce from small private plots, the income of a production team was distributed to households according to how many work points their members earned based on the number of hours they worked at tasks graded according to difficulty. A major task of local cadres was motivating the peasants in their brigade or team to work hard under this system. Enthusiasm for collective work flagged after the Great Leap Forward, but the party made concerted efforts to revive it in the following years. Below is an article from a December, 1965, People's Daily *which describes some of the strategies followed by the cadres in one brigade in south China. It was written by the party secretary of a production brigade.*

The task of guiding and stimulating agricultural production cannot be accomplished through administrative orders, nor through material incentives. The correct way is to place politics in command and begin by making a good job of ideological and political work. A review of what has happened with our brigade over the last several years will prove that the development of production depends in the last analysis on politics.

In the period from 1960 through the first half of 1961, our brigade cadres did not step up ideological and political work and did nothing to heighten the masses' class consciousness and enthusiasm for production. Instead, they kept commune members in line through various kinds of systems such as deducting work points or launching criticisms at meetings. As a result, many commune members did not know for whom they labored and displayed no initiative toward collective production. When the cadres were with them, they grudgingly forced themselves to work; when the cadres left, they relaxed. Consequently, their efficiency was very low and the quality of their work poor.

In the second half of 1961 the brigade cadres tried to promote production by means of material incentives. For instance, in order to quicken the speed of transplanting, anyone transplanting an extra 0.1 *mu* of land was given a reward of a duck's egg or twenty cents in cash. On the surface, it looked as though many commune members had become very energetic and the transplanting quotas were exceeded every day. Actually, the quality of work was very poor. Production was not properly carried out, and due to expenditures for rewards in cash and in kind, in the end less income was distributed to the commune members. Thus, it will not do to rely on systems alone, and material incentives do not work.

Beginning in 1963, the brigade cadres found themselves helpless. Following a policy of laissez-faire, they relaxed their leadership. The results in terms of production became even worse.

Then in 1965, after the socialist education movement began, our leadership nucleus was strengthened and ideological and political work stepped up. The party branch of the brigade carefully armed all party members and cadres with the thought of Mao Zedong and organized youths and commune members to study the works of Chairman Mao, telling them the histories of individual villages and families as a part of their class education. After such study, many people raised their ideological consciousness and became more enthusiastic about production. Many commune members demanded that collective production be made successful, and set the pace by working energetically.

When the early crop was grown this year, as a prominent place was given to politics, the enthusiasm of the commune members was maximized. We achieved a harvest bigger than any ever seen before in history, with the average per *mu* output 549 catties. Every household paid its debts and still had a higher income than before. There was something set aside, too, for stepping up capital construction on the farms.

The experience and lessons I have gained over the past several years have made me realize that in promoting production it is imperative to place politics in command and to start by properly carrying out political work among all the people. Commandism,* coercion, and sole dependence on material incentives do not contribute to successful production.

---

* "Commandism" refers to the behavior of cadres who give orders without paying attention to the thoughts of the masses.

91

LEI FENG, CHAIRMAN MAO'S GOOD FIGHTER

In traditional China, tales of individuals who exemplified extremely virtuous or self-sacrificing behavior formed a regular part of moral education. Young people were instructed in the tales about filial sons and steadfast women; adults enjoyed stories and plays in which characters were either paragons of virtue or totally evil. In contemporary China this method of moral instruction has continued, albeit with significant changes in the characteristics of the people to be admired.

Of the many men and women held up for emulation in the last three decades, the one who has become best known undoubtedly is Lei Feng (1939–1962). The first of many campaigns to "learn from Lei Feng" was launched by Lin Biao in 1963. Lei Feng's life had the makings of a legend. He was born into a poor peasant family in Hunan, and his childhood was a series of tragedies. When he was five, his father died, having been pressed into service as a coolie by the Japanese army. The next year his elder brother, a child laborer in a factory, died of tuberculosis. Then his younger brother perished from typhoid fever and malnutrition. His mother took a job as a servant, but hanged herself after being raped by her employer, leaving Lei Feng an orphan at the age of eight. The bitterness of Lei Feng's past intensified his enthusiasm for the social reforms introduced in the People's Republic. As a worker and soldier he was exemplary in his adherence to revolutionary attitudes and spartan living, qualities China's leaders have encouraged for their value in combating selfishness and promoting industrialization.

The following anecdotes about Lei Feng's sincerity, devotion, and good deeds come from a biography published in 1968.

When Lei Feng finished his studies in the senior primary school in 1956, a nationwide movement of agricultural collectivization was surging forward like a spring tide, and the industrialization of the country was being pushed forward on a large scale. Life with all its richness was beckoning to every young person, and many took up jobs in industry and agriculture after they left school. Like a fledgling bird Lei Feng was anxious to try his wings, so he took a job as a messenger in the local authority offices, dispatching letters and notices and helping to compile statistics, charts, and

442

forms. Whenever there was some work which he thought he could do, he would always volunteer to do it, so everyone was pleased with his work and attitude.

Later, at the age of seventeen, Lei Feng was transferred to work in the party committee office of Wangzheng county, where he began a new life. During the day he worked hard and in the evening he attended a spare-time middle school run by the county government. "The party has rescued me from the depths of misery and enabled me to lead such a comfortable life," he often thought to himself. "How shall I repay its kindness?" He provided the answer by the excellent way he worked—taking good care of public property and making himself a driving force in the office for the sale of government bonds. It was not surprising that his comrades later cited him as a model worker.

Lei Feng worked under Zhang, secretary of the county party committee, a friendly and kind man to whom he became very attached. . . . Once, when he accompanied Zhang to a meeting, he saw a screw lying on the road. Thinking it a useless thing, he kicked it away. When Zhang turned round and saw what he had done, without saying a word he bent down, picked it up and put it in his pocket. Lei Feng was surprised. "What does a party secretary want with a screw?" he wondered. Several days later Lei Feng was about to send a letter to an agricultural machinery plant when Zhang handed him the screw and told him to send it to the workers there. "Ours is a poor country," he said. "We have to work hard to build it up. A screw is a small thing but a machine can't work if it is missing one. Remember, drops of water go to make a stream and grains of rice fill a bin." Lei Feng stared at the secretary with wide-open eyes. From that time on he never squandered a single cent and deposited all his savings in the bank. . . .

In 1958 Lei Feng had begun to study Chairman Mao's writings regularly. He had made it a rule to study one hour every morning and in the evenings up to ten or eleven o'clock. Every spare moment at work in the coal yard of the Anshan Iron and Steel Company he would study Mao's *Selected Works*. After joining the army he had managed to complete volume three while boiling water for the amateur cultural troupe. Then the army leadership called on the men to "study Chairman Mao's works, follow his teachings, act in accordance with his instructions, and be his good soldiers." Lei Feng took this call to heart and wrote it down on the front covers of his copies of Chairman Mao's works. But where the authorities had asked the men to "study Chairman Mao's works," he added "every day" so that he would study them more diligently. Lei Feng's job as a driver often took him to various places, but wherever he went he always carried a satchel containing different essays by Chairman Mao, which he read at every opportunity. Soon his comrades described his satchel as a "mobile library."

About this time one of his comrades grumbled, "There's so much work to do we haven't got enough time for our personal affairs or even rest." Lei Feng did not agree, and to encourage himself to work and study even harder he wrote this passage in his diary, which he remembered from a book he had once read:

> How do you put a screw into a piece of wood which is perfectly smooth and has no holes? You use force and screw it in. Then just as a screw has to be forced and screwed in, so when you study you should bore firmly into the subject.

It was with this spirit that Lei Feng was able to complete Chairman Mao's *Selected Works*, from volume one to four. Among the many essays he read over and over were: "In Memory of Norman Bethune," "Serve the People," "Carry the Revolution Through to the End," "On Practice," and "On Contradiction." Some of the volumes were so worn that the edges of the pages were tattered and frayed, but he still kept reading them over and over again, and every time he read them he got something new out of them. As he read the essays he marked them in all kinds of ways, with lines and dots, with blue ink, and with red and blue pencil. He also made brief notes interpreting various passages. Once he came to this passage in the essay "Rectify the Party's Style of Work": "Every party member, every branch of work, every statement, and every action must proceed from the interests of the whole party; it is absolutely prohibited to violate this principle." He underlined this passage heavily with a red pencil and wrote in the margin: "Take this to heart!"

Lei Feng found an inexhaustible source of strength and wisdom in Chairman Mao's works, and he gradually came to understand the meaning of life, of revolution, and of the laws of social development. He learned how to treat one's enemy and one's comrades, and what attitude one should take toward work. He felt he could see things more and more clearly, that his vision of life was broadening, and that a big new world was opening up before him. Following the teachings of Chairman Mao, Lei Feng gradually became a dedicated proletarian fighter. This is what he wrote in his diary:

> After having studied volumes one, two, three, and four of the *Selected Works*, I feel most deeply that I know how to be a man and the purpose of my life. . . . I think one should live to make others live better.

Lei Feng studied Chairman Mao's works in three ways. He applied what he studied as he went along; he studied and applied creatively; and he used Chairman Mao's teachings to remold his ideology and guide his actions. Whenever he came across a difficult problem in his life, he would immediately turn to Chairman Mao's works to draw strength from them.

One day Lei Feng drove up to the barracks with a truckful of grain and the comrades came out to help him unload it. Among them was Old Wang who belonged to Lei Feng's squad and was known for his great strength. He could carry a sack of grain weighing more than two hundred catties and run fairly fast with it. As Lei Feng was small and unable to carry such a heavy load, he and another comrade stayed on the truck and passed the sacks down onto the shoulders of the rest of the men. When Old Wang's turn came, he leaned against the truck and teasingly said to Lei Feng,

"If you're a better man than I am, why don't you come down and carry a sack?"

Lei Feng did not reply. Then Old Wang added, "Ah, I knew all along that you didn't have the guts to compete with me. Of course not—you're so small!"

"Stop trying to needle me," Lei Feng replied calmly. "We need people to carry the sacks and we also need people to hand them down from the truck. Let's see if you can carry as much as I can move. How about that?" Lei Feng had not meant to challenge him, but his pride had been hurt by Old Wang's cutting remarks about his size.

That night he reread the essay "In Memory of Norman Bethune" by Chairman Mao until he came to this passage:

> We must all learn the spirit of absolute selflessness from him. With this spirit everyone can be very useful to the people. A man's ability may be great or small, but if he has this spirit, he is already noble-minded and pure, a man of moral integrity and above vulgar interests, a man who is of value to the people.

When he read the passage, everything seemed to fit into place and he began to see things in a new light. No longer did he have a feeling of wounded pride or a brooding sense of grievance. "Although I'm small, I'll do my best," he pledged, "to emulate Comrade Bethune's spirit of utter devotion to others without any thought of self."

A few days later the men decided to collect fodder in the mountains. Their plan was to set out after breakfast and return in the early evening, taking their lunch with them. After breakfast the thought suddenly crossed Old Wang's mind that it would be a nuisance taking lunch with him, so he ate his quickly before they set off. As soon as they were in the mountains the men set to work quickly and diligently, collecting grass and hay. At noon they sat on the mountain slope in twos and threes and began to eat their lunch. Lei Feng opened his lunch box and was about to eat when he saw Old Wang sitting by himself without any lunch. "He must have forgotten it or lost it on the way," Lei Feng thought to himself. Offering his own lunch he said, "Come on, take this." Old Wang looked at the lunch box, then at Lei Feng, shook his head, and refused to accept it. "Take it," Lei Feng said as he forced the lunch box into Old Wang's hand. "You'll be able to work better on it."

"If I take it, what are you going to do?" said Old Wang, handing it back.

"My stomach is a bit upset and I don't feel like eating," Lei Feng replied. Then he walked away pressing his hand against his stomach as if it hurt.

Holding the lunch box in his hand, Old Wang stared into space as Lei Feng slowly went away. Then he thought to himself, "Imagine, I actually said he's a small fellow and can't do anything big. I'm a big fellow all right, but I've never given my lunch away to anyone." . . .

Because Lei Feng earnestly studied Chairman Mao's writings, worked hard, remained loyal to the party and the revolutionary cause, and because he made strict demands on himself, he was given the honor of membership in the Chinese Communist Party on November 8, 1960. It was the greatest day in the twenty-two years of his life. With gratitude he wrote this in his diary:

November 8, 1960, I will never forget this day. This is the day when I had the honor of being made a member of the great Chinese Communist Party, thus realizing my highest ideal. Oh, how thrilled my heart is! It is beating wildly with joy. How great the party is! How great Chairman Mao is! Oh, Chairman Mao, it is you who have given me a new lease on life! When I was struggling in the fiery pit of hell and waiting for the dawn it was you who saved me, gave me food and clothing, and sent me to school! I finished my studies in the senior primary school, put on the red scarf, and then was given the honor of being admitted to the Communist Youth League. I took part in the nation's industrial construction and later became a soldier in the armed forces of the motherland. It was under your constant care and guidance that I, a former poor orphan, became a party member, a man with some knowledge and political consciousness.

Now that I have joined the party, I have become stronger and my vision has broadened. I am a party member and a servant of the people. For the freedom, emancipation, and happiness of mankind and the cause of the party and people, I am willing to climb the highest mountain and cross the widest river, to go through fire and water. Even at the risk of death I will remain forever loyal to the party. . . .

In Lei Feng's company there was a man named Xiao Jiao who had enlisted at the same time as he. Xiao never complained about his work or drill, and his behavior was exemplary in every way. His only flaw was that he lagged behind in his studies, being particularly backward in arithmetic, which often gave him a headache. Gradually, however, he became resigned to the situation, a fact which soon began to worry Lei Feng. Once when Lei Feng was helping him with his arithmetic, Xiao said, "I've had little education. I can't get the hang of all these things—addition, subtraction, multiplication, and division."

Trying to boost his confidence, Lei Feng told him, "Nothing is too difficult if you have the will to do it. Where there's a will, there's a way. To a revolutionary no difficulty is too great to overcome." Later he got hold of a copy of an old newspaper which carried a story describing Chairman Mao's concern for the education of soldiers. Showing it to Xiao he said, "Look, here's a story written just for you!"

"Just for me?" Xiao Jiao was puzzled.

"Listen to how really concerned Chairman Mao is about our studies!" Lei Feng said as he began to read the story, explaining it bit by bit in the hope that this would encourage his comrade. Xiao Jiao listened attentively, nodding his head from time to time. When Lei Feng had finished it, Xiao decided on the spot to buy some pencils and exercise books as soon as possible.

"You don't have to bother with those things," said Lei Feng, handing him a fountain pen and an exercise book which he had anticipated he would need.

Xiao Jiao was moved by Lei Feng's generosity but hesitated to accept the gifts. "If you give those things to me," he told Lei Feng, "what are you going to use?"

"Take them, I've got more," smiled Lei Feng. "If you want to be a part of the modernized Liberation Army, you must get an education."

Grateful to Lei Feng for his help and encouraged by the interest he had shown in him, Xiao Jiao began to study arithmetic with much more concentration and initiative. And whenever he came up against something he could not grasp, he would go to Lei Feng and ask him to explain it. Checking up on his progress, Lei Feng asked him a few days later to solve a number of arithmetical problems. Running his eye over them Xiao Jiao was sure they were easy. Then he took out his pen and got to work on them. A few minutes later he had answered all the questions correctly. Lei Feng's eyes lit up. "You've made marvelous progress," he said with a broad smile.

"But without your help I wouldn't have gotten anywhere," Xiao Jiao acknowledged. . . .

92

HOUSING IN SHANGHAI

Before 1949 most urban residents lived in rented quarters owned by relatively wealthy landlords. Thereafter, the government gradually took over more and more of the apartment houses in the big cities, starting with those owned by the largest landlords. In Shanghai, by 1966 the government had charge of eighty percent of all dwelling units. Management of publicly owned housing, therefore, had come to require a large bureaucracy in charge of apartment assignment and building maintenance. The following article suggests some of the bureaucratic problems entailed in such a task. It was published in a Shanghai newspaper in November, 1965.

BOTH MAKE CONCESSION FOR MUTUAL ADVANTAGE

The Northern Shanxi Road Housing Administration Office in Zhabei ward received a letter from resident Wu Dade of Tiantong Road. Both he and his wife were working. Wu said that besides his main home he had a room of eighteen square meters on the second floor of a house on Zhoujiazui Road in Hangjiu ward. In it he had to accommodate his elderly parents and two children. Every morning, his mother took the children by bus to his home on Tiantong Road, then sent them to school while she stayed to do household chores; in the evening, she took the children back to Zhoujiazui Road. Wu found it inconvenient to have two homes and wanted to have the whole family living together. The comrades of the housing and administration office introduced him to several families to arrange an exchange of houses,

but nothing was accomplished because no one liked his.

At that time, a Zhang family, consisting of husband and wife and five children, lived in a room of only eleven square meters at Lane 346 on Qipu Road. They found their room too small and made a request to the Northern Shanxi Road Housing Administration Office for improvement in their living conditions. The housing administration personnel noted that as Zhang was working at a factory in Hangjiu ward, if Wu Dade's room on the Zhoujiazui Road were given to him, he could save time and money in going to work and at the same time improve his living conditions. This was an unusual opportunity and both parties were taken to see the houses.

When Zhang saw the room on the second floor and noted that it faced south, was dry and spacious, had both water and power supplied, was in a quiet neighborhood and close to his factory, and had reasonable rent, he was well pleased. Yet, when he thought that his own room was small and in a noisy front partition, he was worried that the other party night not want the exchange. Wu Dade's mother also went from the back door of her son's residence to see Zhang's room about ten houses away and was satisfied with its location. Making a tour inside, she saw the room was a front partition on the ground floor that saved the trouble of climbing upstairs. Its shortcoming was that it was rather noisy and had seven square meters less space. As she looked around, she thought to herself, "The house is close to my son's and on the ground floor, too. It saves me the trouble of traveling back and forth daily and makes it easy for all members of our family to look after one another. Better take it though it is small and somewhat noisy." She immediately expressed her willingness to accept the exchange.

A month or so had elapsed but Zhang still had failed to turn up to arrange with Grandma Wu for the exchange, even though she had asked for it several times. The truth was that Zhang's wife had lived on Qipu Road for many years. Although she thought her room too small and wanted to exchange it for a larger one, she was reluctant to leave the locality if she did not have to. She also did not like the new place because she was not used to living on the upper floor and thought the staircase too narrow. Therefore the matter was left unsettled. When Zhang's factory authorities learned this, they studied the matter with Zhang and his wife and advised them not to miss this excellent chance to exchange a small home for a larger one, which would solve the problem of overcrowding, provide a quiet place to sleep, and be close to the factory. They also pointed out that the willingness of the other party to make the exchange revealed their sincere attitude and correct thinking, so Zhang should also assume a correct attitude and be willing to give something for what he was gaining. To ask for a spacious, good, convenient, quiet, and totally ideal apartment was an unrealistic goal. Taking all of this into consideration, Zhang and his wife saw that their notions had been unrealistic and decided to make the exchange.

Now the two households have what they wanted after exchanging houses with each other.

Translated by Jane Chen

93

RED GUARDS

The most turbulent period in the People's Republic's first four decades was the first three years of the Cultural Revolution. Begun by Mao Zedong in 1966, ostensibly as a campaign to produce a new socialist culture and give young people born under the new regime the experience of a revolution, the Cultural Revolution soon grew to much larger proportions than any previous campaign. The formation of the Red Guards played a key role in the course of the Cultural Revolution. Maoist leaders strongly encouraged middle school, high school, and college youth to organize themselves into Red Guard units. As Red Guards they would learn revolution and provide the Maoists with important allies in their combat with less radical leaders. In June, 1966, almost all schools and universities were closed as students devoted full time to Red Guard activities. That fall eight massive Red Guard rallies were held in Beijing, attracting, it is said, more than eight million youths.

The four selections below each take up a distinct strand in the Red Guard experience. "Long Live the Revolutionary Rebel Spirit of the Proletariat!" is a passionate manifesto demanding that young people learn revolution by practice. "Red Guards in Nanning and Liuzhou Take to the Streets to Clean Up the Four Olds" is a newspaper article describing the enthusiasm Red Guards displayed for purging China of objects and habits that they judged to reflect feudal or bourgeois influences. "March Forward Valiantly Along the Road Pointed Out by Chairman Mao" is a report issued by eleven middle school Red Guard units. It recounts the experiences of one band of young people who marched to Beijing in emulation of the Red Army's legendary march from southeast to northwest China in 1934–35. Such activities were later encouraged by the government, eager to keep Red Guard traffic from completely overwhelming China's limited rail system. Massive nationwide travel by youth was unprecedented in Chinese society and contributed to the development of national, rather than local identity among the younger generation. All three of these pieces date from the summer and fall of 1966. "Factual Account of the September 11 Bloodshed" is from a Red Guard newspaper published during the following year, in September, 1967. It shows the violence that resulted as Red Guard factions fought against each other. To overcome this violence, the army was called in and Red Guard organizations were placed under the supervision of worker and soldier "Mao Zedong Thought Pro-

paganda Teams." In late 1968 Red Guard units were disbanded and many of the former Red Guards were assigned to the countryside.

LONG LIVE THE REVOLUTIONARY REBEL SPIRIT OF THE PROLETARIAT!

Revolution is rebellion, and rebellion is the soul of Mao Zedong's thought. Daring to think, to speak, to act, to break through, and to make revolution—in a word, daring to rebel—is the most fundamental and most precious quality of proletarian revolutionaries; it is fundamental to the party spirit of the party of the proletariat! Not to rebel is revisionism, pure and simple! Revisionism has been in control of our school for seventeen years. If today we do not rise up in rebellion, when will we?

Now some of the people who were boldly opposing our rebellion have suddenly turned shy and coy, and have taken to incessant murmuring and nagging that we are too one-sided, too arrogant, too crude, and that we are going too far. All this is utter nonsense! If you are against us, please say so. Why be shy about it? Since we are bent on rebelling, the matter is no longer in your hands! Indeed we shall make the air thick with the pungent smell of gunpowder. All this talk about being "humane" and "all-sided"—let's have an end to it!

You say we are too one-sided? What kind of all-sidedness is it that suits you? It looks to us like a "two combining into one" all-sidedness, or eclecticism. You say we are too arrogant? "Arrogant" is just what we want to be. Chairman Mao says, "And those in high positions we counted as no more than the dust." We are bent on striking down not only the reactionaries in our school, but the reactionaries all over the world. Revolutionaries take it as their task to transform the world. How can we not be "arrogant"?

You say we are too crude? Crude is just what we want to be. How can we be soft and clinging towards revisionism or go in for great moderation? To be moderate toward the enemy is to be cruel to the revolution! You say we are going too far? Frankly, your "don't go too far" is reformism, it is "peaceful transition." And this is what your daydreams are about! Well, we are going to strike you down to the earth and keep you down!

There are some others who are scared to death of revolution, scared to death of rebellion. You sticklers for convention, you toadies are all curled up inside your revisionist shells. At the first whiff of rebellion, you become scared and nervous. A revolutionary is a "monkey king"* whose golden rod is might, whose supernatural powers are far-reaching and whose magic is omnipotent precisely because he has the great and invincible thought of Mao Zedong. We are wielding our "golden rods," "displaying our supernatural powers" and using our "magic" in order to turn the old world upside down, smash it to pieces, create chaos, and make a tremendous mess—and the bigger the better! We must do this to the present revisionist middle school attached to Qinghua University. Create a big rebellion, rebel to the end! We are bent on creating a tremendous proletarian uproar, and on carving out a new proletarian world!

Long live the revolutionary rebel spirit of the proletariat!

RED GUARDS IN NANNING AND LIUZHOU TAKE TO THE STREETS TO CLEAN UP THE "FOUR OLDS"

According to a *Guangxi Daily* report, on August 23, Red Guards and revolutionary teachers and

---

* The Monkey King is a famous character from the Ming novel *Journey to the West*.

students in the city of Nanning, inspired by the revolutionary spirit of revolt shown by the Red Guards in the capital, and filled with great revolutionary pride, took to the streets to post revolutionary leaflets and big-character posters and carry out oral propaganda. Using the thought of Mao Zedong as a weapon, they violently attacked all old ideas, old culture, old customs, and old habits. They demanded that Nanning be built into a great school of Mao Zedong's thought.

A group of Red Guards in the Second Middle School in Nanning climbed up to a traffic policeman's stand and, through the medium of loudspeakers, read aloud to the people their Manifesto of Revolt: "Today, the clarion call for the Great Proletarian Cultural Revolution has been sounded, and the battle between the proletariat and the bourgeoisie has begun. We must promote the fearless spirit of the proletariat—the spirit of staining our bayonets with blood—and the revolt against feudalism, capitalism, and all demons and monsters. Backed by Chairman Mao and the Party Central Committee, this revolt is sure to succeed. Let the thought of Mao Zedong shine upon every corner. . . ."

Revolutionary "young generals" of the Guangxi College of Arts formed four propaganda teams for the purpose of replacing bourgeois ideology with proletarian ideology and getting rid of the old to make way for the new. In no time they composed a revolutionary song entitled "Raise the Iron Broom of the Revolution," and sang it in the streets and shops. With revolutionary pride, they sang: "Sweep and break. Raise the iron broom of the revolution to sweep away the vestiges of feudalism, uproot the bourgeois ideology, hold aloft the red banner of the thought of Mao Zedong, establish proletarian and destroy bourgeois ideology, destroy a lot and build a lot, and construct a new socialist country." The masses around them sang with them.

Red Guards of the Guangxi Nationality College in a remote suburban area arrived in the morning at the Station for the Reception of the Masses operated according to the revolutionary rules. These Red Guards proposed to change the names of streets, places, and stores—such as People's Livelihood Road, People's Rights Road, Emperor Ridge, and White Dragon Bridge—into new names with revolutionary content. They proposed getting rid of all poisonous things in barber shops, tailor shops, and book-lending shops immediately. In shops that the Red Guards of the Nanning Ninth Middle School and revolutionary teachers and students visited, they were received warmly by the workers and employees, who were determined to respond to their revolutionary proposals.

The workers of the Handicraft Product Center of Nanning said, "We have long wanted to discard artistic products decorated with emperors, kings, generals, prime ministers, scholars, and beauties. Now that you have come to support us, we'll take immediate action." They immediately tucked away the carved standing screens and hanging screens and hung more portraits of Chairman Mao in the shop.

The workers of the New South Barber Shop at the suggestion of the Red Guards took down the pictures showing decadent bourgeois hair styles such as the "wave-type" and "big western style" and indicated that they would in future refuse to do such bizarre hair styles for their clients.

Fourteen Chinese and Western medicine shops under the Medical Company of Nanning held workers' forums one after the other and, after discussion, that same night adopted new signboards expressing revolutionary ideas.

The revolutionary masses of the city's cultural palace and museum listened to the broadcasts at eight o'clock in the morning and by nine had posted a big character poster at Prince Liu Park. They thought that the term "Prince Liu" reflected feudal bureaucratic ideas and was incompatible with the spirit of the times. They thought the name should be changed into "People's Park," so immediately wrote "People's" on a piece of paper and pasted it on top. This suggestion was warmly supported by the revolutionary masses passing by.

MARCH FORWARD VALIANTLY ALONG THE ROAD POINTED OUT BY CHAIRMAN MAO

Our long march team was made up of eight boys and three girls averaging eighteen years of age. We started out from Bengbu on September 11, and crossed Anhui, Jiangsu, Shandong, and Hebei provinces. After forty-four days of walking we had covered a thousand kilometers and arrived in Beijing to be alongside our beloved leader Chairman Mao.

Chairman Mao has said, "Our policy must be made known not only to the leaders and to the cadres but also to the broad masses." Vice Chairman Lin Biao has said, "The whole country should become a great school of Mao Zedong's thought." As Red Guards of Mao Zedong's thought, it was our glorious duty to disseminate his ideas. We decided to organize our long march team to spread propaganda and to do our bit in the great cause of turning the whole country into a great school of Mao Zedong's thought.

At the same time, we knew we had never been tested in revolutionary struggles, even though we all come from railway workers' families and have been brought up under the red flag. In the Great Proletarian Cultural Revolution we learned that young people cannot become worthy successors to the proletarian revolutionary cause if they have not tempered themselves in the storm of class struggle, integrated themselves with the workers and peasants, and remolded their world outlook. The long march, we decided, was a good way of tempering and remolding ourselves.

These were the considerations that became decisive in our determination to undertake a long march. Before we left, we spent several days studying "The Orientation of the Youth Movement," "Serve the People," "In Memory of Norman Bethune," "The Foolish Old Man Who Removed the Mountains," and some other writings by Chairman Mao. We armed ourselves with Mao Zedong's thought; his teachings unified our ideas and increased our confidence and courage.

When the day for our departure arrived, we were all very excited. We made a pledge addressed to Chairman Mao: "Our most beloved leader Chairman Mao! The brilliance of your ideas is the light that guides us in heart and mind. We are resolved to fulfill your words, 'Be resolute, fear no sacrifice, and surmount every difficulty to win victory.' We shall not falter in getting to Beijing." . . .

To make a start is always difficult. The first day we walked twenty-seven kilometers. Many of our schoolmates suffered swollen feet and had to clench their teeth with each step they took. Even when we stopped and rested, our backs and feet really ached. A few of us debated about going back home; whether to go forward or retreat became a question of revolutionary determination. It was a crucial moment. To solve the problem, we studied a passage in Chairman Mao Zedong's works in which he says, "How should we judge whether a youth is a revolutionary? . . . There can only be one criterion, namely, whether or not he is willing to integrate himself with the broad masses of workers and peasants and does so in practice."

We took this as a mirror in which to examine our own ideas and decided that the purpose of our long march was to integrate ourselves with the masses, to learn from the workers, peasants, and soldiers, and to train ourselves as proletarian revolutionary successors who can truly stand all tests. "How shall we wage revolution if we can't even pass this first test?" we asked ourselves. "No! We must keep on. To go forward means victory!" In this way we applied Mao Zedong's ideas and prevailed over the vacillating muck in our minds. We all became more confident than ever.

We all carried knapsacks as well as gongs, drums, and study material. On the average we each carried a load of about fifteen kilograms. But we plucked up our courage and kept going, though the weather was very hot. At the time our clothes, and even our knapsacks, were soaked through with our perspiration.

We sang. At any difficult moment we all sang the wonderful lines from Chairman Mao's poem: "The Red Army fears not the trials of a distant march; to them a thousand mountains, ten thousand rivers are nothing"; and we also sang: "We count the myriad leagues we have come already; if we reach not the Great Wall, we are not true men!"

Each of us had a quotation from Chairman Mao Zedong written on a placard fixed to his knapsack. The one behind read it aloud in turn, and all of us took it up in chorus. It raised our spirits and helped to shore up our determination. For Chairman Mao's words brought to mind what the old Red Army did on its 12,500-kilometer Long March. It gave us fresh energy and the will to persist. Each step we took, we told ourselves, brought us a step closer to our great leader, Chairman Mao.

Our journey from Xuzhou to Hanchuan presented us with another difficult test. That day we arrived at a small place where we had planned to eat, only to find the public mess hall closed. We could have asked the peasants to cook a meal especially for us but decided not to, since we knew that they were busy with farm work. We put on our regular propaganda performance and walked on, very thirsty and hungry. The weather was broiling. We felt almost completely exhausted. But we read aloud Chairman Mao's statement: "Give full play to our style of fighting-courage in battle, no fear of sacrifice, no fear of fatigue, and continuous fighting." We recalled that the Chinese people were hungry every day before Liberation. When the old Red Army on the 12,500-kilometer Long March crossed snow-capped mountains and marshlands, they were reduced to boiling their leather belts and digging up roots for food. They often went hungry. What did it matter if we missed our meals for one day? It was an opportunity to show our determination. Our revolutionary predecessors endured hunger for the sake of those to come. If we now tempered ourselves we could make a better contribution to the Chinese and the world revolution, so that the great masses in the world would not go hungry. This was the gist of our talk and our thoughts, and so we no longer felt hungry. In fact, we marched on with greater vigor, and, as we walked, we beat our gongs and drums and sang revolutionary songs. That day we kept our average of four propaganda performances.

On the way we met a number of leading members of various institutions. With the best of intentions, they advised us to go to Beijing by train. We must have looked tired to them. Some of them even offered us train tickets, but, in every case, we refused. We felt that come what may, we would not give up our objective halfway. We persisted northward on foot to gain and exchange revolutionary experiences.

We Red Guards are reserves of the Chinese People's Liberation Army. We knew we had to follow its example, the finest example of adherence to Chairman Mao's teachings. The army feared no trials, strictly applied the Party's policies, and maintained high discipline. We consciously tried to emulate it during our long march by applying the three main rules of discipline and the eight points for attention which Chairman Mao himself formulated for the Chinese People's Liberation Army long ago.

None of us ever bought any sweets on the way or had any food other than our regular meals. We never wasted a grain of food and took great care of public property. We washed our own clothes, did our own mending, and cut one another's hair instead of going to a barber. In short, we were very thrifty in our way of living. We made a particular effort to temper ourselves by plain living, especially in the matter of food. The more we did so, we felt, the better we could remold our ideology. Guided by Mao Zedong's thought, we overcame one difficulty after another and successfully stood the test we had set ourselves—the first real test in our lives.

Chairman Mao said, "The Long March is a manifesto, a propaganda force, and a seeding machine." On our long march, too, a fundamental task was to spread Mao Zedong's ideas. And we persisted though we were often very tired. Altogether we gave some 120 performances in over a hundred villages and small railway stops. We estimate our total audience at more than ten thousand people. We also distributed four hundred pamphlets containing the decisions of the party central committee, speeches by party leaders, and editorials of the *People's Daily* and ten thousand leaflets and posters with Mao Zedong's ideas.

Our first performances were, indeed, a test for us! Only three of us had any experience. We were afraid people would laugh at us, but we remembered Chairman Mao Zedong's words: "It is often not a matter of first learning and then doing, but of doing and then learning, for doing is itself learning." We decided we must "learn to swim by swimming," as the Chairman taught. There was plenty of enthusiasm once we arrived at our decision. We composed our items at odd rest moments and rehearsed them on the way, gradually mastering the art of putting on a show including choral singing, solo singing, ballad recital, dialogue, and singing combined with acting.

One evening we arrived at a village where the people asked us to put on a performance. It was just one kilometer from the railway station where we were to have a meal and rest. We had been walking most of the day and were very tired, and what is more, we had missed our lunch and were very hungry. What were we to do? We held a discussion and decided to give the performance. What were hunger and fatigue to us compared with the joy of meeting the people's wishes and disseminating Mao Zedong's thought!

We put down our knapsacks and performed whenever there was an audience. One day, we put on a show for three housewives. Our persistence in spreading Mao Zedong's thought insured us of a hearty welcome everywhere from the revolutionary masses. One old worker said to us very sincerely after watching us perform: "You are really good Red Guards of Chairman Mao! We of the older generation feel more assured with such good successors growing up." . . .

One young worker at a Dengxian railway station presented us with his most prized possession—a small plaster cast of Chairman Mao—together with a letter in which he wrote: "Though we are at different revolutionary posts, we are one and the same in our determination to give our very lives in defense of Chairman Mao and to carry the great proletarian cultural revolution through to the end. We shall safeguard our impregnable pro-letarian state whatever the cost. In presenting you with this likeness of our great leader Chairman Mao, I am sure it will give you infinite strength on your journey." These deeply felt words greatly moved us, and thereafter wherever we stayed, we placed the statue in the most conspicuous place. Indeed, it always gave us fresh strength. . . .

At Fengtai station near Beijing, we went to see the nationally famous engine, the "Mao Zedong Special," and had a talk with members of the crew. It was a great experience, for they are fine students of Chairman Mao's works. What they told us opened our minds and made us all the more determined to study Chairman Mao's books and work for the revolution, and especially to study the three much-read articles and use them in remolding our ideology. We decided we would devote the whole of our lives to becoming truly reliable successors to the proletarian revolutionary cause.

All along the way the workers and peasants showed great concern for our well-being. Very often a railway worker's wife would insist on doing our washing and mending. Keeping close to the railway line all along our route, we had many indications of the deep class comradeship of the workers. It brought to mind the popular verse: "Great as are Heaven and earth, they are not as great as the good brought by the party. Dear to us as our parents are, they are not as dear as Chairman Mao. Fine and good as many things are, none is as fine as socialism. Deep as the deepest ocean is, it is not as deep as class comradeship." Our hearts were linked by this class comradeship with the hearts of these people whom we had not met before.

Our forty-four-day trek gave us the chance to learn how excellent traveling on foot is as a means to gain and exchange revolutionary experience. For it tempers your proletarian ideology, steels your willpower, and helps you to revolutionize your thinking. We learned a great many things we could not get from books and also gained personal experience of many things we had read about. In particular, we have deepened our understanding of the brilliant thought of Chairman Mao.

Of course, we have taken only the very first step in the 10,000-*li* long march that lies before us, the first step along the glorious road which Chairman Mao has shown us. We need to improve our creative study and application of Chairman Mao's works and to continue to temper and remold ourselves in the furnace of the great Cultural Revolution. We must revolutionize ourselves and become young militants who are really reliable successors to the cause of the proletarian revolution, for that is what Chairman Mao expects of us.

FACTUAL ACCOUNT OF THE SEPTEMBER 11 BLOODSHED

The appalling September 11 bloodshed which shook the municipality took place after the signing of the September 1 Agreement and the announcement of the September 5 Order approved by Chairman Mao. This was not a mere accident; it was a bloody slaughter of the revolutionary rebels and revolutionary masses, instigated by the handful of bad leaders of the conservative organizations manipulated by the capitalist-roader authorities in the party. Its aims were to provoke large-scale violent struggle, to sabotage the implementation of the September 5 Order, to apply pressure on the Party Central Committee and the Guangzhou Military District Command, to interfere with the ongoing movement of supporting the army and cherishing the people, and to alter the direction of the struggle to criticize Tao Zhu [Mayor of Guangzhou]. It was a deathbed struggle waged by the bourgeois reactionaries. After this incident, the conservatives—manipulated by the capitalist-roaders in the party—cranked up the propaganda machines. They screamed "stop thief" while they themselves were the thieves. They confused right and wrong, wantonly started rumors, and vilified and attacked the revolutionary rebels in an attempt to cause trouble for other people and acquit themselves of their crimes of murder. How malicious their intentions were!

To rectify any misconceptions, we give below a comprehensive though brief account of the on-the-spot investigations of the incident made by the Red Flag Commune of Jianguo Restaurant under the Food and Drinks Section of the "Workers' Revolutionary Alliance" and by the Elementary Education Red Headquarters.

On September 11, the "Spring Thunder," "District Headquarters," "Doctrine Guards," and other conservative forces in Guangzhou gathered their men in Foshan, Shaoguan, Zhonghua, and other suburban areas to attend the so-called inauguration of the "Revolutionary Committee of Workers in the Guangzhou Area" held at Yuexiushan Stadium. A little past nine o'clock in the morning, seventy-two trucks loaded with peasants from Zhonghua arrived in Guangzhou via Zhongshan No. 5 Road. Because there were crowds of people at the junction with Beijing Road, the trucks had to move slowly. As the thirty-second truck approached the intersection, the masses discovered some weapons in it and immediately mounted the truck to investigate. There they found a pistol, a hand grenade, and a dagger. The onlooking revolutionary masses felt deep indignation at this open violation of the agreement to keep arms under bond and unanimously roared their condemnation, some of them indignantly tearing from the truck the flag of the Alliance of Poor and Lower-Middle Peasants in Areas Around Zhonghua. Seeing that their secret had been uncovered, one of the men in the truck, in order to escape being caught, pulled out a pistol and was about to shoot. Fortunately, the masses were highly vigilant and immediately ran forward to snatch it. Later when the men of the Red Garrison Headquarters and the Workers' Pickets arrived, the masses handed the man over to them, together with the arms found in the truck.

The masses did not reproach the members of the suburban peasant's alliance, but instead had friendly chats with them and carried out ideological work among them, giving them water to drink and cigarettes to smoke. The peasants came to realize that they had been deceived and that they should not have come into the city. A leader of these peasants said, "We don't know what we came here for. The higher authorities told us that we didn't have to work today and had to come here for a meeting. Each of us was given two dollars and fifteen wage points." The peasant brothers in those trucks which did not drive away were later persuaded by the army comrades to take a rest in the assembly hall of the Guangdong Provincial People's Council. The broad revolutionary masses expressed warm welcome to them for their awakening and their revolutionary refusal to take part in the violent struggle provoked by the Workers' Committee under the District Headquarters.

At about eleven o'clock in the morning, two trucks loaded with bricks and members of the Doctrine Guards and "Hong Ban Zong" of the No. 46 Middle School sped along Zongshan No. 5 Road toward the Financial Department Building. The masses on the road laughed at them, and some people threw banana peels and handbills at them, whereupon the Doctrine Guards stopped their truck and one of them threw a piece of a brick at the crowd, wounding someone. Another Doctrine Guard got down from the truck and struck out at the onlooking masses with his leather belt. The masses were indignant at this and loudly condemned the Doctrine Guards "for attempting to kill," then they quickly surrounded the trucks. Seeing this, the Doctrine Guards at once started their trucks and pressed hard on the accelerators. As the trucks pulled away from the pursuing masses, the Doctrine Guards pulled out their pistols and shot at them. They fired a few shots and wounded four men, one in the head, one in the chest, one in the hand, and one in the foot. After that, the Doctrine Guards sped towards Yuexiushan.

At noon, despite the ironclad facts that the arms of the Zhonghua suburban Poor and Lower-Middle Peasants' Alliance had been discovered and that the Doctrine Guards had shot and wounded the masses, the presidium of the "Revolutionary Committee of Workers in the Guangzhou Area" wantonly started a rumor at the meeting that the "Red Flag Faction" had amassed their men at Zhongshan No. 5 Road (actually the masses at the road junction were unorganized and

many of them were children) to sabotage their demonstration. . . . They stirred up public opinion in favor of a violent struggle and read a so-called statement of protest.

At 1:15 P.M., the Revolutionary Committee of Workers in the Guangzhou area started its parade. The parade contingents wanted to pass Jixiang Road and go westward along Zhongshan No. 5 Road, but the road was crowded, particularly at the intersection. A handful of heartless and rabid leaders of the District Headquarters ran two of their trucks into the crowds at speeds of over forty kilometers per hour. The first truck crashed into a pillar supporting the balcony of the Urban Services Bureau building. The second bumped into a trolley bus which was stopping at Zhongshan No. 5 Road. One person (a child) was killed on the spot, and two others were injured. The masses raged with indignation over these atrocities, and picking up pieces of bricks on the roadside, launched a brave counterattack. The bad leaders used machine guns, pistols, hand grenades, and other murderous weapons to start their premeditated massacre. From the time the Doctrine Guards fired their guns to the time the Central Investigation Corps and the army unit arrived at the scene, the District Headquarters and the Doctrine Guards fired more than two hundred bullets and threw four hand grenades. According to incomplete statistics, thirteen persons among the revolutionary masses were killed (nine of them died on the spot and the other four died in the hospital) and one hundred fifty-five were wounded, seventeen of them seriously. Of the wounded, seventy-three were sent to Zhongshan Hospital, forty-three to Provincial People's Hospital, thirty-six to Municipal No. 1 Hospital, eleven to Municipal Workers' Hospital, and five to Yuexiu Area Hospital. (Those sent to military hospitals are not included in the above figures.) Apart from this, countless people were injured by bricks thrown by the District Headquarters and the Doctrine Guards. In Jianguo Restaurant alone, forty-five persons who were less seriously injured came in to have their wounds dressed. Moreover, the District Headquarters and the

Doctrine Guards beat and kidnapped seven persons from among the revolutionary masses and took them away in four trucks, the license numbers of which were: 3-318, 15-1458, 15-10029, and 15-14944.

These facts have been written in blood. They cannot be reversed no matter what rumor the Spring Thunder, District Headquarters, Doctrine Guards, and other conservative organizations may start. There must be a reckoning of their crimes in sabotaging the September 5 Order and September 1 Agreement.

94

VICTIMS

*In 1926 Mao Zedong had declared that "A revolution is not a dinner party."
Even after the victory in 1949, Mao insisted, vigilance against class enemies had
to be maintained. Struggling against them was needed to mobilize the revolutionary enthusiasm of the masses. In the period of land reform millions of landlords
and their families suffered from being labeled class enemies. In the 1951 campaign against those who had been affiliated with Nationalist organizations or
served in its army, tens of thousands were executed and many more sent to labor
reform camps. During the anti-Rightist campaign of 1957, about half a million
educated people lost their jobs and often their freedom, usually because something they had said during the "Hundred Flowers" period had been construed as
anti-party. Even more educated people were singled out for persecution during
the Cultural Revolution. College professors, middle school teachers, newspaper
writers, musicians, party cadres, factory managers, and others who could be
classed as educated suffered a wide variety of brutal treatment. Men and women
were tortured, imprisoned, starved, denied medical treatment, or forced to leave
their children unsupervised when they were sent out to labor camps. Tens of
thousands were killed or committed suicide.*

*For years victims of these campaigns could not write or talk about their ex-
periences for fear that they or their children would suffer even more. After the
Cultural Revolution was discredited and blame placed on the "Gang of Four,"
(which included Mao's wife Jiang Qing), writers were encouraged to expose the
harm the "gang" had caused. Often the most effective way they found to do this
was through fiction. Below is a story, titled "Melody in Dreams," written in 1978
by Zong Pu (b. 1928), the daughter of a well-known professor of philosophy
Feng Youlan, who was the object of severe criticism in both the anti-Rightist
campaign and the Cultural Revolution.*

1

The cello music sounded through the air. It was deep and sad like the late autumn wind sweeping leaves off the ground or the grey clouds gathering in the cold winter sky. Gradually the music became thinner and thinner as if it would be lost, never to be found. Suddenly, it burst into a loud, stirring sound which seemed to express hope and desire.

"It's Murong Yuejun playing!" Many people were familiar with her music.

Murong Yuejun, a teacher of cello at a music college, was wedded to her instrument. She and her cello were as one; through it she expressed all her feelings. Today, however, she could not finish a single piece. Putting the cello aside, she walked out onto the balcony and gazed into the distance.

It was September of 1975. Strands of her white hair gleamed in the setting sun. Her attractive face belied her age of more than fifty years. She gazed down the end of the street expectantly, but no one came. She was waiting for the daughter of her close friend Liang Feng, a man she had nearly married. He had since died, but she always remembered his daughter.

At the outbreak of the Anti-Japanese War in 1937, Liang Feng and other youths had gone to the revolutionary base of Yan'an. Yuejun, however, at the time a music student at Yanjing University in Beijing, had been taken by her parents to the south. Then she had won a scholarship to study abroad and had not returned until after Liberation in 1949. After the death of her parents, she had immersed herself in teaching music.

Now it was growing dark. She went back into her room, deep in thought. During the first years after Liberation, Liang Feng had worked abroad. In the sixties he had been recalled to China to do cultural exchange work. Yuejun had heard him speak at some meetings. She had been impressed by his way of expounding the party's policies and moved by his devotion to the party. She even met his wife, a respectable comrade and good mother.

Yuejun had also met their daughter, but the girl had not left a deep impression on her, except on one unforgettable occasion. It was during the Cultural Revolution, when all sorts of bad characters emerged to slander celebrated artists and intellectuals. Yuejun, because she had studied abroad, was attacked. At a meeting, she and some others were lined up on stage. Some famous musicians were pushed to the microphone to denounce themselves as reactionaries. Suddenly three or four youngsters beat and kicked a middle-aged man onto the stage shouting, "Down with the revisionist monster Liang Feng!"

Stealing a glance at him, Yuejun was surprised to see her friend being forced to the microphone. Facing the crowd, he said, "I'm Liang Feng, a Chinese Communist!" No sooner had he said this when some thugs leapt onto the platform and punched him. Blood poured from his mouth. Then a girl's clear voice was heard shouting, "Father! Father!" There was an uproar as some protested against the beating, while others rushed to the girl and knocked her out of the hall. Though Yuejun's head was lowered, she saw the whole scene, except the girl's face. Whenever she thought of her, she felt a mixture of sadness and warmth. Now she was going to see her for the first time since the incident.

There was a voice outside. Yuejun asked, "Is that you, Pei?" A plump woman of Yuejun's age entered. She was a party member who had been party secretary of the cello section since the 1960s.

"I just popped in to see if Liang Feng's daughter was coming to see you today."

"She's supposed to, but she hasn't turned up yet."

"Do you remember . . .?" Pei looked out of the window.

"I haven't forgotten all those slanders." Yuejun's mild glance rested on her. After each criticism meeting, Pei had whispered in her ear, "Chin up! It's a test." Or, "Never mind. Don't let it upset you too much!" This had encouraged Yuejun enormously.

Pei had high blood pressure and was easily excited. Controlling herself she said, "You must teach her well, Yuejun."

"Of course. I want to, but can I supplement the musical scores and materials?"

"I think one should, but who has the authority? The harmful members of society aren't only trying to destroy the usual ones, but our whole civilization and socialism." Pei's voice quivered.

"But what can we do?" Yuejun muttered.

"Wait until . . ." Pei slapped the arm of the chair. After a while she said she was going to see her paralyzed husband in the hospital. Smiling bitterly, she left.

It was night as Yuejun gazed out of the window at the maple tree illuminated by neighboring lights. Thinking of the girl, she supposed she would not come that night. Then there was a knock at the door. Before she could answer it, a girl came in saying loudly, "Are you Aunt Yuejun? I had such trouble finding your home. I must have asked about a dozen people along the way. Your room's dark but I spotted your cello when I came in, so I guessed this must be the right place. I'm Liang Xia."

Switching on the lights, Yuejun saw that Liang Xia was a pretty girl, with her hair cut short. She was wearing a cream-colored jacket over a black woolen jersey and deep grey trousers. With large eyes, slender eyebrows, and rosy cheeks, she was smiling quizzically at Yuejun.

"So she's sizing me up too," thought Yuejun, who shook hands with her, saying, "I've been waiting for you. . . ."

2

Liang Xia was ten years old in 1966 when the Cultural Revolution began, a marked turning point in her life. Until then she had been the pride of her parents, but her happiness dissipated with the start of the Cultural Revolution. Her father, a leader in his office, was dragged one night by people who broke into their home. Then her mother was separated from her. Liang Xia, bewildered, was left alone at home, cooking meals to take to her parents. Her father liked eating noodles and flapjacks, while her mother liked sweet food. Sometimes Liang Xia herself went hungry in order to give her parents their meals. She did this

until one day a man told her not to prepare any more for her father, since he had died five days earlier.

After her parents were detained, some of their comrades invited Liang Xia to live with them, but certain people objected saying that she could only live with a relative. She had an aunt, her mother's sister, but she had refused to take Liang Xia, only allowing the girl to visit her and help her with various chores. At that time Liang Xia was in the fourth-grade. Because of her parents, she too was criticized from time to time.

In those unhappy days, Liang Xia often dreamed that she was being weighed down by a heavy stone. Unable to remove it, she would cry herself awake. But in time she became accustomed to the sneers, and she accompanied her mother to a cadre school to do manual labor in the countryside. Then her mother was transferred to work in a small town in south China, where she met a cello teacher, who had been dismissed from his school. So that Liang Xia would not idle away her time, her mother arranged for her to have cello lessons.

Just two months ago, Liang Xia's mother had died of illness. The death was particularly tragic because she had heard that shortly there would be a meeting to clear her husband's name. So Liang Xia came to Beijing and stayed with her aunt. She hoped that Yuejun could give her cello lessons. That was the reason for her visit.

"I'm sorry for being late, but I had to help my aunt with the washing up." She glanced round the room in which Yuejun had lived for many years. Against the window was a marble-topped mahogany desk left to Yuejun by her parents. In one corner stood a piano against which leaned a cello. In front of her bed was a folding screen painted with flowers and birds. Two armchairs flanked a stand and behind it was a lamp with an orange shade. The gentle light gave an atmosphere of tranquility.

"It's nice and cozy here," Liang Xia said as she followed Yuejun to the kitchen, where she took the thermos flask from her and poured herself a cup of tea. Yuejun told her that several years previously, a couple intruded into her family's home.

Dividing the room was a screen and bookcases, they lived there a few months before they moved out.

"We were driven out of our home and had to leave everything," Liang Xia said matter-of-factly. "When my parents were detained, I stayed in the attic. It seemed quite cozy at the time. But mother was ill after her release and whenever she used the stairs I had to carry her on my back."

Yuejun wondered how Liang Xia, with her delicate build, had managed that. Curious to know about her mother's illness, Yuejun nevertheless said nothing for fear of opening old wounds.

But as if she had read her thoughts, Liang Xia continued, "Mother had all sorts of complaints. I was like her doctor. I knew every medicine she took. In the end she died of pneumonia. I thought many times she would die, but she always survived. So I thought she'd recover that last time." Her tone seemed detached. Yuejun, however, was very sad.

"How many years have you been playing the cello?" Yuejun looked at her cello. "You love music, don't you?"

"No, I don't." Her reply surprised Yuejun, who stared fascinated at her thick lashes and dark eyes. "I have to learn something to get myself a job. I've been playing since I was fourteen, but I'm not interested in it. I really preferred working in the countryside, but since my mother was too ill to join me, I went with her."

Yuejun was disappointed and wondered whom Liang Xia would follow now.

The girl added, "My parents were always talking about you, so I feel as if I've known you for ages. Mother said you could help me become a musician." A flicker of hope came into her eyes veiling the indifference which seemed to say, "But it doesn't matter if you refuse."

"Why bother learning to play the cello if you don't like it?"

"To make a living, of course," Liang Xia said with a giggle.

If she had heard such a reply ten years earlier, Yuejun would have been insulted. Now nothing astonished her.

"Play me something," she said after a pause.

When Liang Xia went to get the cello, she found a curtained-off alcove that stored Yuejun's junk. Lifting the curtain, Liang Xia exclaimed, "Goodness! Why do you store all your things here, auntie? One day I'll help you sort them out." Then holding the cello she began to play.

She played the second movement of a concerto by Saint-Saëns. In spite of her poor technique, there was something in her playing which moved Yuejun. Although she failed to grasp the meaning of the music, she expressed her own feelings. She was making music.

"She has a good musical sense," Yuejun thought.

She soon finished, but the room retained the atmosphere she had created. Putting the cello aside, Liang Xia searched Yuejun's face.

"To have a feeling for the music is very important," Yuejun said warmly. "But you don't handle your bow correctly yet. Look, it should be like this," and so saying she took the bow and gave the girl her first lesson.

3

After that, Liang Xia came once a week. When she was not studying, she would chat or help Yuejun with something. She was bright and seemed to know a lot, though sometimes she was ignorant of the most common things. For example, once a colleague was discussing some classical novels with Yuejun, when Liang Xia interrupted them saying she had read many of them. It seemed she had read whatever she could lay her hands on, but there were still large gaps in her education. She would often ask simple questions like when was the Opium War and what was it about. She may have seemed self-centered, confident of how to take care of herself, because since the death of her parents no one else had. Sometimes, however, she was also eager to help others.

One day Yuejun was learning to give injections. Liang Xia offered her arm because she said she was not afraid of pain. Then she added coolly, "The trouble is, you're afraid because you haven't been beaten up enough!" She seemed to have seen through everything and scorned the glowing revolutionary jargon in the newspapers. She would say, "All lies! Even Premier Zhou was slandered as a reactionary. Who's foolish enough to swallow that!" Her only belief was that Premier Zhou would triumph over those "bastards." Yuejun hoped the same. When she referred to Jiang Qing, she called her a "she-devil" who had created so many scandals and who still tried to fool the people. "She praises a novel about vengeance, while she really intends to attack us. One day I'll take my revenge out on her!" Her words puzzled Yuejun. She spoke freely, not caring what people thought. At times Yuejun was afraid one day she would get into trouble.

Pei, a frequent visitor, soon got to know Liang Xia well enough to make her drop her flippant tone and talk seriously. One day Pei came to hear Liang Xia play. After listening to her, she asked Yuejun, "If you want to supplement your teaching materials, why not use some Western études? You're probably too timid."

Bow in hand, Liang Xia protested, "Of course she's timid, but what about you?"

"I never said I was bold," Pei smiled, "but we've each got a head on our shoulders, and we should use it to improve things."

"My head's too heavy for me. I don't like it. If you want, Aunt Pei, I'll give it to you. Then you'll be bold enough to start a revolution. Only don't get scared because you'll have to turn everything upside-down." She burst out laughing. "Revolution sounds fine but they murdered my father under that name also!"

"No, that was counterrevolution," Pei burst out. "Stop playing dumb and remember what your mother said to you. Remember those who hounded your father to death. You must think seriously about your future."

Liang Xia immediately became grave, bit her lip and stared at Pei. After a moment she lapsed into her usual flippancy and sneered, "I don't give a shit about them! What about dinner? Let's go

and make it. I'm very good in the kitchen. . . ." She laughed.

That was always how she reacted.

Once when Yuejun asked about her future plans, she answered as briefly as before, adding with raised eyebrows, "I'll fool around until my aunt throws me out, but that won't be immediately. She knows that my father's name may be cleared and that she stands to gain." Then she went to the alcove and lifting the curtain looked at it again.

Before long her aunt threw her out. It was on an early winter day, when Liang Xia should have arrived for her lesson. At sunset she still had not come. Yuejun worried about what might have happened to her.

Suddenly Liang Xia burst in, a bulky satchel over her shoulder and a string bag in her hand. With a face flushed with rage, she cried, "Sorry to keep you waiting, but I've just had a hell of a row with my aunt." Then putting her bags in a corner, she sat down, fanning herself with a handkerchief. Her eyes burned with resentment as she jeered and laughed, "It's just ridiculous!"

"Don't laugh like that," Yuejun said patting Liang Xia's shoulder. "Tell me what happened."

"My aunt said that my father's name can't be cleared because he was a reactionary and that he had killed himself to escape punishment. As for me, since I'm his daughter, there's no future for me. My staying with her has caused her a lot of trouble. Since her husband has just been promoted to be a deputy minister and their block of flats is for ministers, ordinary people like me shouldn't be living there. We're a security risk. What nonsense."

Yuejun sympathized with her and wondered what she would do next.

"I'll stay with you, if I may? Are you afraid?" she asked standing up.

Yuejun was silent. Of course she was afraid! To let Liang Xia stay with her could mean she too would be labeled as a counterrevolutionary. But how could she push her out? After all, she was Liang Feng's daughter.

Seeing Yuejun's hesitation, Liang Xia smiled

with scorn. Then she noticed that she had reached a decision. Before Yuejun could say anything, Liang Xia walked over to the curtained alcove and put her things by it. "I've thought about it before. We can put a bed here." As she spoke she began pulling out the junk. "You sit over there, auntie." She sneezed. "So much dust! I always said I'd help you with spring cleaning one day. Now my words have come true!" She laughed delightedly.

Amidst the dust, she hummed a tune as she worked. Having finished cleaning, she arranged the things in two piles of boxes and cases, on which she placed some planks for a bed. Then she made it up with sheets and a quilt lent to her by Yuejun. With a board from the kitchen she made herself a desk. Among the junk she had found a tattered scroll with a poem on it. It read,

> Coming from your old home
> You should know what is happening there;
> Leaning against the window,
> Did you see the plums in blossom?

Holding it in her hands, Liang Xia softly read it twice.

"Who wrote it?" she asked. "Both the poem and the calligraphy are good. Why don't you hang it up?"

"Wouldn't it be criticized?" Yuejun replied joking. "It was only this year that I put my screen here. Honestly I'm afraid of courting trouble."

"Well, I'm not." Examining it, Liang Xia noticed the inscription, "A poem by Wang Wei copied by Yuejun in G. city." The girl exclaimed, "So you wrote it! No wonder the calligraphy's so good." Immediately she hung it above her bed. Stepping back she gazed at it and then, clapping her hands, asked, "But where's G. city?"

"Geneva, in Switzerland." Yuejun looked at the old writing with some emotion. "I was there alone studying music and I felt very homesick. Once I listened to Dvorak's *New World Symphony* a dozen times nonstop. Whenever it reached the second movement I was deeply moved. So I wrote that poem on the scroll. What awful calligraphy!"

"There's patriotism in your words." Liang Xia gave a bitter smile. "Now even patriotism is getting criticized."

"I didn't have any clear ideas." Yuejun sat down at the table. "But I truly missed China then. My ancestors and I were born here. I was proud to be Chinese. That's why I appreciated that short poem. But if that is all wrong now, what's left?" Moodily she turned to the window. "Of course I learned Western music, but only so that I could serve my country better."

"Your country?" Liang Xia mocked. "Today that means individualism, egotism, and counter-revolutionary revisionism!" Then she laughed, "Any way you're all right as a musician. Isn't singing and acting coming into fashion?"

Yuejun did not want to comment on her sarcastic words.

At last Liang Xia had finished tidying up. "My bed's rather like a raft, isn't it?" Going over to it she said, "I'll stay on my raft. I'll be as quiet as a mouse in the day." Having climbed on her "raft," she suddenly popped her head out of the curtain and quipped, "Carefree on my raft, I don't mind whether the seasons come or go." Then she was quiet.

"Now there's no need to act like that," Yuejun laughed. Drawing back the curtain, she found that Liang Xia was lying back on her quilt, her eyes closed. On her rosy cheeks were streaks of dirt. "Get up and wash your face, Liang Xia. We'll have a lesson. Since you'll be staying here for a while, you mustn't waste your time."

On hearing her say "for a while," Liang Xia smiled faintly and glanced sadly at her.

At half past eight that evening they had a lesson. Liang Xia played first. Her technique was improving. As Yuejun was correcting her, there was a knock at the door.

A youngster in a green uniform without any insignia entered. The expression on his regular-featured face was troubled. Seeing Liang Xia sitting with the cello in her hands, he said to Yuejun, "Excuse me, are you Aunt Yuejun? I'd like to have a word with her." Then he smiled at Liang Xia.

Ignoring him, Liang Xia concentrated on her

music, but after a while she explained, "This is Mao Tou, a friend of my cousin. Let's continue our lesson."

"Mao Tou? Is that a nickname?" asked Yuejun casually, wondering about their relationship.

"Actually I don't know his real name." With this Liang Xia continued playing.

Snubbed, the young man turned to Yuejun for help. She suggested, looking at Liang Xia, that they go for a walk in the fresh air. Then she went to her desk and switched on the lamp. Pouting, Liang Xia walked out with her friend.

The next day at school, Yuejun told Pei about her decision. Pei was delighted. "I agree with you. She should live in your home." Some colleagues who sympathized with Liang Xia felt that in this way she could have an opportunity to study, as she'd become an orphan and a loafer. Those who objected said, "What if the police start making inquiries? And if Liang Xia does something illegal, Yuejun will be implicated." Yuejun was worried, but decided that if the authorities insisted that girl should leave, then she must let her go. Otherwise Liang Xia could stay as long as she liked.

Time passed, and the two of them got along well together. Liang Xia was able, diligent, and considerate. Always in high spirits, she reminded Yuejun of an elf from a dance by Grieg. But Liang Xia claimed to be a very down-to-earth sort of person. "If you were me," she argued, "you'd be just as practical."

Once, when the weather was already chilly, Yuejun bought Liang Xia some cloth for a jacket to be made at the tailor's. But Liang Xia claimed she could make it herself and went off to Pei's home where there was a sewing machine. When she came back, she seemed very melancholy.

"What's the matter?" Yuejun asked.

"Oh, nothing!" Liang Xia fidgeted with the remnants of the cloth. "Aunt Pei's husband's been paralyzed for three years, and she goes to the hospital every day to take care of him. Her high blood pressure doesn't keep her from going to the office and studying the works of Marx and Lenin either. She told me that in the Yan'an days, people trudged in straw sandals, but each step seemed all the more significant. And one of her friends used to say that everyone at that time had a strong sense of responsibility. Life was so full of hope." After a moment her face brightened and she continued, "Aunt Pei said my father helped to reclaim the wasteland and that my mother spun yarn. I'd like to live such a life, but now it seems that just playing my cello or breathing is illegal." Scissors in hand, she shredded the cloth.

Her usual apathetic and scornful expression returned, her tender heart seemed to have hardened. As Yuejun stroked her silky black hair, there was a knock at the door. Two young men with high sheepskin hats and fashionable trousers entered. Seeing them, Liang Xia sprang forward and told them to get out, banging the door shut. Yuejun did not know where Liang Xia picked up such friends. If she was home, Liang Xia would take them out, but as long as she was teaching or busy elsewhere, Yuejun was quite oblivious as to what went on in her home. As most of them were boys, she once tentatively warned Liang Xia against falling in love too early.

Hearing this, Liang Xia burst out laughing. "Don't worry! I won't be such a fool! I don't respect those boys. When I marry, my husband will be a high official!" She grinned mockingly, as if in her eyes high officials were toys for amusement. Then with forced seriousness, she added, "Or perhaps I'll be a spinster like you. By the way, why didn't you marry, auntie?"

"You tell me," Yuejun countered, trying to avoid the question.

"It isn't that you believe in being single, but that you've never met a man you loved." She was sharp.

Since her arrival, Yuejun had been strict in making her practice various pieces every day. Though she did not assign any Western musical scores, Liang Xia often played some to amuse herself. One day when Yuejun returned, she overheard Liang Xia playing a plaintive melody by Massenet. It was so melancholy that she waited till Liang Xia had finished before entering. Yuejun often wished that Liang Xia could attend a proper school, since she had real musical talent. But it all depended on when her father's name would be cleared. If that happened, then the girl would be in a better position to study.

Meanwhile Liang Xia led a seemingly carefree life. Apart from playing the cello and seeing friends, she often read some books on her "raft." One day Yuejun was shocked to find her reading a hand-written copy of an "underground" book. "Why are you reading that?" she asked.

"Why not?" Liang Xia retorted.

"The cover alone scares me."

"You wouldn't even say boo to a goose!" Liang Xia giggled. "When my parents were detained I was often criticized and beaten. Later I fought the boys back. They beat me and I punched them. I loved it!"

Not knowing what to say, Yuejun stared at her pretty, youthful face. Despite the merry, contemptuous expression, she sensed hidden apathy and misery.

"Since I'm older now, I've grown out of fighting. It bores me." Then she tried to reassure Yuejun, "Please don't worry, auntie. Since I can't play the cello all day long, I have to read once in a while too. But I can't find any good books, so I'm reading these, even though they're dirty. It's like food. When there's nothing yummy to eat you eat anything. So there!" She glanced at the cabinet where she had some good books.

"You're wrong." Yuejun tried to argue with her.

"I know." Smiling she added, "Now I just exist. If one day I can't go on like this, then I'll change my world outlook. That's how Mao Tou puts it."

"You can read what he's read, I think." Yuejun had found that Mao Tou was a thoughtful young man who had seriously studied some books on philosophy, literature, and history. Although known as a "scholar" in his factory, he refused to join any writing teams run by the authorities. His father was an old cadre who had often shown concern for Liang Xia.

Yuejun's suggestion made Liang Xia smile again. After a moment, Yuejun opened the cabi-

net to let her choose whatever books she wanted. Happily Liang Xia looked through it until she suddenly murmured, "My father had many books. However late he worked, he never went to bed withou reading a little. What a pity I was so young! I ... I hate...." Turning round she clutched hold of the cabinet, her eyes blazing. "Oh father, father!" Her voice was as clear and pained as a few years before. "I don't believe that my father, a Communist full of enthusiasm, committed suicide. They killed him, but insist that he killed himself." She did not choose a book, but stood there gazing wistfully at Yuejun. "Do you think the day I long for will come? Mother told me I must live to see it."

Yuejun could not bear to see her expression. Wanting Liang Xia to have a good cry, tears began pouring down her own face. Even if her father had killed himself, he would never have done so unless driven to it. He must have been in a desperate situation. She wanted to cry with Liang Xia, hoping the girl's tears would wash away her cynicism. Instead Liang Xia rushed to her bed, leaving on the cabinet two nicks from her nails.

4

It was 1976 and the Spring Festival was approaching. Despite the festival, everyone was grieving. Where was the spring? People were profoundly anxious about their future since the death of Premier Zhou. There was a dreadful abyss in their hearts, which could not be filled by their tears and thoughts.

Before she went to the cadre school in January to do some manual labor, Yuejun entrusted Liang Xia to Pei's care. When she heard the sad news of the premier's death, she felt desolate. Worried that something might happen to Liang Xia, she wrote asking how she was. After she had mailed the letter, Yuejun was afraid Liang Xia's reply would get her in trouble, so she quickly sent a message telling her not to answer. However, her reply did come. It said, "I'm prepared to shoulder my responsibilities now." Though cryptic, it signified that a storm was imminent.

On her return home Yuejun found Liang Xia had changed. In the past Liang Xia's laughter made Yuejun sad. Now Liang Xia expressed her suffering in another way—by remaining silent. She thought more about her responsibilities. Sometimes Yuejun told her to play her cello to find peace in the music, but thinking about Premier Zhou disturbed her playing. In the past three weeks she had suddenly matured. Her flippancy was gone. In her dark eyes was a clouded expression, as if her thoughts seemed too heavy to convey. Some of her friends stopped coming; she was in no mood to play and that was all they were good for. When Yuejun asked her where her friends were, Liang Xia blinked as if she had never known them.

She got rid of the frivolous books but she was not interested in serious literature either. To Yuejun's surprise, Liang Xia sometimes read works of Marx and Lenin. On the eve of the Spring Festival, Pei found her reading an article by Chairman Mao, a notebook by her side. Leafing through its pages, Pei was astonished to find a heading, "Crimes perpetrated by Jiang Qing." The charges listed were logical and cogent. Pei grasped Liang Xia's hand and said admiringly, "I always knew you were a smart girl, Xia!"

Liang Xia smiled a genuine smile. "I thought a long time about your advice. I shouldn't fritter away my life and youth. Especially at this time."

Most of the notes had been made by Liang Xia and some by Mao Tou. As Yuejun read them, she felt they were telling the truth. But the truth meant trouble. She searched Pei's face wanting to know what to do. Pei smiled at her. "It's correct to expose them for what they are. These notes are what we've been wanting to say ourselves."

Liang Xia told Yuejun, "I know that's the way you feel too. But you are too timid, auntie."

Yuejun sighed, "Who can we talk to?"

"We're only allowed to parrot the editorials," Pei added.

Liang Xia was silent. Her smile faded into contempt and pessimism.

Yuejun anxiously looked at the girl, while Pei warned, "It isn't just a question of daring to struggle. It's also knowing how and when to strike."

When they were having supper, Yuejun wanted to ask Liang Xia why she and Mao Tou had written the notes, but she did not press her. After a long silence, Liang Xia said while eating, "On my way to the grain shop, I overheard two old women talking. One of them said, 'Since our premier died, we have no heart to do New Year shopping.' " Then Liang Xia put down her bowl and walked away.

Suddenly there were three knocks at the door. Liang Xia immediately darted to open it and Mao Tou entered. Although he looked tense, he did not forget his manners, greeting Yuejun before turning to Liang Xia. "Let's go out," he suggested.

"What's the matter?"

"Please sit down," Yuejun urged. "It's so cold outside. Don't go out. Tell us what's happened."

Eyeing them both, he said, "My father's been arrested!"

"What?" Yuejun was dismayed.

"On what charge?" Liang Xia asked.

"They can trump up anything," he replied, trying to control his anger. Then he continued, "A few days ago, my father told me they were concocting some charge against Premier Zhou. He said as long as he was alive he'd defend him and speak out. This morning your uncle told my father that they wanted him to attend a meeting. A neighbor reported that my father was tied up and driven away in a car. He wasn't even allowed to leave a note for the family."

"I was luckier. I saw my father being dragged away," Liang Xia murmured.

"When I went to their office to see my father, the man on duty told me coldly that he was going to stand trial and couldn't receive any visitors. Then he shoved me out of the door."

Yuejun was outraged, thinking how many families had been ruined by this gang, how many young people had been deprived of their right to work and study or even live. They would not even leave the premier alone. Our great hero had left nothing of himself after his death. Even his ashes had been scattered over the mountains and rivers. Now they intended to blacken his reputation.

Liang Xia trembled with rage. She suddenly laughed aloud. Yuejun took her hand which felt cold. "Xia!" she exclaimed.

"Those monsters are about to tear off their masks!" Brushing Yuejun aside, she put one hand on the table and the other to her breast.

"Yes, I think they are going to show their true intentions soon," said Mao Tou, looking coolly at Liang Xia. "We must continue collecting materials. The day's coming when the gang will be brought to trial and condemned."

Mao Tou paced the room and then said he was going to inform his friends about his father's arrest. He left after shaking hands with Yuejun and warning her to be careful.

At the door Liang Xia suddenly cried out, "But you haven't had your supper yet!" Mao Tou shook his head and left. Yuejun knew that his mother had died of a heart attack after an intense political meeting, and now no one was left to look after him.

Mao Tou's father was an old cadre. After he had been repudiated, he had nothing to do each day but read books, see the doctor, or visit friends. But this idle life could not keep him from fighting for the truth. The flames of truth had been burning in his heart and he was ready to sacrifice himself to defend it. If Liang Feng were alive, he would do as he did, as thousands of cadres, young people, and ordinary citizens were doing.

5

Through hell or high water, time marches on. Tempered by grief, doubt, and anxiety, the people will come to see the truth.

On the eve of the Spring Festival in April, 1976, tragedy enveloped Beijing's Tiananmen Square. Only the bright wreaths overlapping each other and the loyal hearts of the people challenged the somber surroundings. Some wreaths climbed high into the sky, while others were very small. They stretched from the Monument to the People's Heroes to the avenue. It was like a great mourning ceremony, unparalleled in history, dedicated by the people to Premier Zhou. The pine trees, covered with white paper flowers of mourning, were like a bank of snow. Gaily decorated baskets hung from the lampposts. Balloons floated in the air trailing streamers inscribed with the words, "Premier Zhou Is Immortal!" The crowds in the square were like a vast moving sea. They were silent though indignant and at the end of their patience. The flames of truth in their hearts were at last about to blaze.

If the truth could be seen, Yuejun thought, it was in that square. The people were prepared to give their lives for it. She knew Liang Xia came every day to record poems and see the wreaths. Yuejun and Liang Xia were making their way to the monument in the middle of the square. They hung their basket on a pine tree. It contained pure white flowers entwined with silver paper that glistened like their tears.

Liang Xia remembered pacing in the quiet square in January after the premier's death when she heard people weeping. A middle aged woman had lurched towards the monument crying, "Oh premier, what are we going to do now? What? . . ." Her cries carried through the square and reverberated in Liang Xia's heart.

Suddenly Yuejun felt Liang Xia shudder. Looking in the same direction, she saw a streamer by the monument which read, "Even if the monsters spew out poisonous flames, the people will vanquish them!" The street lights were dim, but words seemed ablaze. This was the strength of the people! The people had begun to fight back!

Yuejun and Liang Xia walked among the crowds who were engrossed in copying poems. Some far away could not see clearly, so others who were nearer to the monument read them aloud. If some had no paper, others would tear out pages from their notebooks. People wrote leaning on others' backs. All the crowds shared one purpose and cherished a deep love for Premier Zhou.

Unexpectedly Mao Tou appeared. With a serious expression, he whispered something in Liang Xia's ear. She hurriedly pulled Yuejun away from the crowd. On their way home, Yuejun was filled with grief and anxiety. She was not afraid for herself, but very worried about Liang Xia and Mao Tou and all the other young people in the square who were reciting poems. When she arrived home, she sat down at the desk in front of a photograph of Premier Zhou as a young man. Yuejun wished she could talk to Pei who had given her this photograph, but she had been in the hospital since March because of a heart attack. She had been working too hard.

Liang Xia was busy on her "raft." After a moment she emerged and poured herself a glass of water. She looked calm and happy, though pale. "Would you like some water, auntie?" she asked. There was no answer.

Then Yuejun said looking at her, "I want to say something to you. I guess you're going to put up some posters. It's too dangerous!" She paused before adding, "You're young. You must live to see the day.... You're the only survivor in your family."

Not in the least disturbed, Liang Xia replied, "I don't want to hide anything from you. But we must speak out and let those bastards know we are still alive. As you know, I'm not afraid of anything."

Yuejun said after a pause, tears streaming down her face, "Then let me go! I'm old, but I can do it as well as you!"

"You?" Amazed, Liang Xia gazed at her kind, attractive, tear-stained face. She too began to weep, though she tried to hold back her tears.

"Xia!" Yuejun hugged her tightly. Her tears dropped on the girl's hair, while Liang Xia's wet her breast.

Liang Xia soon dried her eyes. There was no time for a good cry. It was as if she heard the bugle call. Flames of love and hatred blazed in her heart, melting it. She had thought of telling Yuejun that she had already distributed some leaflets in the trolleys and parks. Some had expressed her views, while others contained only one sentence, "Down with the White Bone Demon—Jiang Qing, the cause of all disasters!" She was sure there would not be any trouble, but still it was better not to involve Yuejun. She decided to keep her in the dark and so she changed the subject, "All right, I won't go out now. Where are you going, auntie?"

"I'm serious," Yuejun protested.

"So am I." She wiped away her tears. "You must rest. You're too excited." With this, she went to make up Yuejun's bed and quietly slipped two sleeping pills into a glass of water. Handing it to her, she persuaded Yuejun to lie down.

Soon Yuejun felt very sleepy so she lay down, while Liang Xia paced the floor, cheerfully. "You should put some more clothes on," Yuejun advised, noticing Liang Xia was wearing only one sweater. "You must take care of yourself!" Then she wondered if she was really getting old, as she was feeling so tired.

Yuejun fell asleep and was unaware that Liang Xia had tidied up the room. Before leaving she had fondled the cello and turned to gaze again and again at the screen which shielded Yuejun's bed. Finally she made up her mind and gingerly opening the door went out.

That night she did not return. Two, then three nights passed and she still did not come home.

One evening after her discharge from the hospital, Pei came to visit Yuejun. It was already summer. Through the window the stars shone. The two women sat facing each other in silence. After a while, Yuejun took a notebook out of a drawer, saying, "I found this yesterday. Xia took notes in it."

Pei was startled when she flipped through the pages to read, "I won't live under the same sky with the sworn enemy of my family and my country." She read the sentence again and again before saying confidently, "Don't be sad. I believe she'll come back one day."

Yuejun nodded, "I hope so. I know where Mao Tou is imprisoned. But I've no news about Xia."

"We'll try to locate her." The notebook was clenched tightly in Pei's hand.

Yuejun heaved a sigh, "Recently I feel as if we've been playing a piece of music interminably but it may break off any moment now."

"Don't worry. We'll end this symphony on a magnificent, triumphant note. To tell the truth, in the past half a year, we were worried about you.

Someone tried to blame Liang's mistakes on you. But we told them nothing. In the last two months, orders came from our ministry to investigate the relationship between you and Liang Xia, but we refused to do it."

Rising to her feet, Yuejun declared, "Tell them Liang Xia's my daughter. I'll adopt her as my own daughter." Her worn, sweet face brightened, and determination shone in her eyes. Pei grasped her hand firmly.

That night Yuejun dreamed that she was playing her cello at a concert. The music from the cello was splendid and triumphant. In the audience a pair of dark eyes danced to the melody. They belonged to Liang Xia.

Then suddenly it was Liang Xia and not she who was playing on stage. Her skillful playing was inspiring and encouraging. Happy tears poured down her cheeks. The stage lights shone on her white gauze and silver-threaded dress and on her glistening tears. The powerful music reverberated inside and outside the hall. She played what was in her heart and in the hearts of the people. "Father! Dear father!" Liang Xia suddenly cried out. Her voice merged with the splendid music flying to the clouds. In the clouds appeared the Monument to the People's Heroes shining like the sun and the moon, with inscriptions personally made by Chairman Mao and Premier Zhou. Among the names of heroes was Liang Feng's. Some were known to everyone, some were ordinary people, while other heroes did not have their names mentioned. But they were all heroes of China nevertheless. They devoted their entire lives to the cause of liberation and communism. Though they have all died for one reason or another, they still live in our hearts. Their contributions are immortal and they will be forever remembered.

The dream of the people will be fulfilled. The reactionaries will be smashed. This is historically inevitable.

Translated by Song Shouquan

95

THE CHANGING COURSE OF COURTSHIP

The leaders of the Communist Party inherited the attitudes of early twentieth century reformers who saw the old family system as oppressive to youth and women. In 1950 a Marriage Reform Law was enacted which prohibited parents from forcing their children to marry against their will. The government also condemned early marriage on the grounds that it deflected the energies of youth from productive work and led to too high a birth rate. Beginning in the 1950s, girls were enrolled in schools in unprecedented numbers and women were mobilized to work outside the home in large numbers. New patterns of courtship and new attitudes toward love and marriage gradually developed, reflecting both new government policies and the new social situations in which young people found themselves. The four selections below reflect some of these changes. The first comes from a handbook published in 1964 for use of rural cadres who had to advise young people. The second is from a February, 1975 Canton newspaper and is an example of the sorts of exhortation intended to promote new types of thinking that were common during the Cultural Revolution. The third is a letter written in 1978 in response to a radio show on "The Place of Love" and gives a very different view of courtship during the Cultural Revolution. The last selection, on advertising for spouses, appeared in a 1989 women's magazine.

WHAT SHOULD ONE PAY ATTENTION TO WHEN ONE FALLS IN LOVE?

We have already said that young men and women must have a correct point of view toward love when they fall in love. Here we shall talk a little about a few concrete problems to which one should attend when falling in love.

First, with regard to the problem of dating between young men and women, may young men and women date each other in public? Of course

they may. So-called friends ought to be comrades in our socialist society. Sentiment between friends is lofty, and the relationship between one and the other is equal and cooperative, full of solidarity and love. Common ideals, common interests, common lives of labor and war have bound us together tightly and have created a brand-new comradely relationship between us. This sort of comradely relationship encourages us to progress, and it advances our solidarity. It is beneficial to socialist construction and at the same time makes our lives happier and more blissful. Under such circumstances, why shouldn't young men and women court each other publicly?

But in real life there are some people who always look askance at any relationship between a man and a woman. As soon as they see a man and a woman together, they are scandalized without looking into the true circumstances. They say this and that and make all kinds of criticisms to make people feel ashamed. There are also some people whose heads are full of ridiculous formulas. As soon as a young man and woman start to see each other often, they brand them for having an "improper style" and claim that "the relationship between the sexes is impure." Because of this, some young men and women become anxious. If they love someone, they don't dare declare their love. When they start courting, they hide here and there, not daring to see people, as if they had done something disgraceful. This is a problem worthy of our attention.

How should young men and women treat others' criticisms when they fall in love?

1. We must clear away the remnants of feudal ideology in our minds and treat the relationship between the sexes correctly. When we see a man and a woman talking together, we should not be greatly surprised. We should, moreover, not gossip or interfere with them. When a man and woman meet, they should be open-minded and not be suspicious of each other. If you love another person, you must give it serious consideration. After due consideration, if you want to propose, then propose. You need not suppress it in your heart and create suffering. If you and the other person build up a proper relationship and fall in love, even if you do encounter ridicule or interference from others, you need not feel troubled by it and may disregard it. You may also explain it to them and, if necessary, make observations on the situation to the party or the League in order to request support.

2. When they fall in love, young men and women must be particularly careful to balance well the relationship between love and work. They should not forget everything else when they fall in love, but should change love into a kind of motive power to encourage themselves to work, learn, and progress better.

3. In falling in love, one should never have improper sexual relationships as a result of temporary emotional impulses. This is immoral.

In sum, as long as we treat these problems seriously, others will not "gossip." Even if some people talk nonsense, we can still stand up to it. Facts always will prove that their opinions are wrong and our actions are honest.

Second, on the problem of "unrequited love."

"Unrequited love" means that the love relationship is broken. We know that in love itself there exist two possibilities. One possibility is that it continues to develop and leads to marriage. The other possibility is that it breaks up midway, and the love relationship terminates. The process of falling in love is a process of mutual understanding and increasing friendship. After a considerable period of mutual understanding, if one side feels forced and proposes to break off the love relationship, this is normal and means that the love between the two has not matured. A proverb says, "The melon that is gathered by force is not sweet." Love is something that cannot be forced. If love is immature and thus the love relationship is broken off, it is not necessary to create trouble for oneself. But there are some young men and women who cannot treat this problem correctly. According to them, it seems that as soon as you fall in love you must get married. Otherwise you feel cheated. Because it is "unrequited love," it creates "the greatest suffering." One cannot eat or sleep; one feels dispirited at work and even loses interest in living. This is wrong in the extreme. One should have a correct attitude in dealing with "unrequited love." First, one should understand clearly his goals in life. If one has a lofty goal in life, then one's work, learning, and progress will not be affected by setbacks in love. Second, one should be philosophical. Since the other no longer loves you, you should not put something into it that is not there.

Third, on the problem of "fickleness in love."

"Fickleness in love" is a bourgeois conception of love. Its characteristic is: "Love the new and detest the old." "The other hill seems higher than this one."* It manifests itself in changeability and untrustworthiness. One loves X today and Y tomorrow. It is a very flippant attitude. This is completely different from normal love. When a young couple feels lovingly toward each other and builds up a love relationship, they should respect each other and make their love develop and strengthen without cease. If in the process of falling in love one party feels that the love is strained and that the love relationship cannot indeed be maintained, then, based on a serious and cautious attitude and after conscious consideration, it is also quite normal that the love relationship be broken off. This is beneficial to oneself, to the other person, to one's future life, and to society. But "fickleness in love" is different. Its purpose is hedonistic enjoyment. When you enjoy each other, you are "in love." When you have had enough, then "take off." When you have the money, it is "love"; when the money is all used up, "take off." Responsible to no one, enjoyment is supreme and the individual comes first. These are dutiful acts of love and ought to be vigorously opposed.

Fourth, on the problem of matchmaking by family and relatives.

Some young people are introduced to their partners by family and relatives. Is this way of doing things good? This should be analyzed concretely, for one cannot say whether it is good or bad in general. Generally speaking, it is best for young men and women to find their beloveds by themselves and to build up a love relationship through common labor and common struggle. Some people, due to limitations of various sorts, cannot help but ask others to introduce them to a partner. It is all right to do so. But if there is no mutual understanding or love toward the partner one is introduced to, then there should be a process of mutual understanding and building up of

* The "grass is always greener on the other side."

love. This process is absolutely essential. Some young people rely on the one-sided opinion of a matchmaker; they meet a few times and agree to get married right away. This way of doing things is too rash. We should say that one ought to have more contact with the person he is introduced to so as to learn to understand one another, but not rely on "love at first sight." If you hand over your "heart" after only one meeting, then it is not serious enough. "Love at first sight" often means you only see the superficial phenomena of the other's looks, clothes, manners, etc., but cannot see the other's "real heart." Some young people often give away their hearts before they see the other's. How can this be reliable? Therefore, when you ask others to introduce a partner, if you yourself are not yet familiar with the other person, then, in addition to listening to the opinions of the person who makes the introduction, you should also listen to the opinions of people familiar with that person. More important, there must be a process of mutual understanding. This, too, is the process of falling in love.

We may see from the above problems that in the question of love and marriage there exists a struggle between new and old thinking. In order to deal correctly with the problems of love and marriage, we must oppose the remnant of feudal ideology and the ideology of the bourgeoisie. We must draw a clear boundary line with these two kinds of ideology and carry out a vigorous struggle. These, then, are the problems young men and women must pay attention to in the process of falling in love.

DARE TO DO AWAY WITH OLD CUSTOMS

It was a day in the middle of October last year. The masses of people in Sixin Brigade (Niwan Commune, Doumen county) joyously ran about passing the words: "Uncle Jinxi is taking a son-in-law today."

Let's hear the story about Uncle Jinxi taking a son-in-law.

Old poor peasant Huang Jinxi's daughter

Bingcai fell in love with He Huashen of Weiguo Brigade, Baiqiao Commune, and they planned to get married. This event made Jinxi rejoice on the one hand and grieve on the other. He was happy because thanks to the good leadership of Chairman Mao and the Communist party, his whole family was free and his children had all grown up; he grieved because he had no son and his four daughters one after the other had all gotten married and left the family. He thought to himself, "How wonderful it would be if my son-in-law could come to live with me and take care of me when I get old." His daughter understood how he felt and suggested that He come to settle in her family. He consented.

When news of this spread, a small number of people still influenced by feudal ideas began to criticize. Some said, "A fine young man like him can find a wife without difficulty. Why should he have to join the family of his wife? What a shame!" When He's father heard these erroneous views, he also thought that as it had been a practice for women to marry into their husband's family since ancient times, his son would be looked down upon and meet "bad luck" if he did as planned.

He studied conscientiously the relevant writings of Chairman Mao and the ten new things of Xiaojinchuang, and came to realize that "times have changed, and men and women are equal." If women could go settle in their husbands' families, then men could also go settle in their wives' families. Revolutionary young people must take the lead to break with traditional concepts like "men are superior and women inferior." Therefore, he patiently tried to enlighten his father, saying, "As long as we act in accordance with Chairman Mao's instructions, the cadres and masses will give us support." He also said, "If it's 'unlucky' for a man to join his wife's family, what kind of 'luck' did you have when you followed the old practice and took a wife into your family before liberation?" This refreshed his father's memory of the miserable past. He's grandparents had both died of poverty and illness under the merciless oppression of the landlords. His father worked for the landlords from early childhood, and was beaten and scolded all the time. By the time he took a wife, he had neither house nor land to his name and borrowed some money to buy a ruined boat for a house. The family led a desperate existence. After Liberation, under the leadership of Chairman Mao and the Communist party, they became masters of their own and led an ever happier life. After recalling this bit of family history, He Huashen's father repudiated the doctrines of Confucius and Mencius, like "three cardinal guidances and five constant virtues" and "men are superior and women inferior," and raised his consciousness. In the end, he even supported his son's decision to settle in his bride's house.

He and Bingcai then went ahead with their wedding preparations. They both agreed to have their wedding the new way, not accepting betrothal money or presents or giving a feast. Huang Jinxi felt it was a bit niggardly not to spend a little money treating his relatives to a few drinks on this happy occasion of taking a son-in-law. Therefore, he intended to invite a few relatives and friends for a small wedding party. When Bingcai learned what her father felt, she said to him, "You said that when you got married, you didn't give any betrothal money or presents and didn't give a wedding feast. Why didn't you feel niggardly then?"

"That was before Liberation," he answered. "Then I was so poor that there wasn't a single grain of rice in my pot. How could I afford to buy presents and give a wedding feast? It's different today; we're now well-off. A wedding is a great event which justifies spending a little money."

In order to help her father raise his level of understanding, Bingcai patiently explained, "Even though we're better off today doesn't mean we can spend money at will. Indulging in extravagance and waste is an old habit of the exploiting classes, while industry and thrift are the good virtues of us poor and lower-middle peasants. We must do away with the existing habits and customs and old conventions of the exploiting classes, and erect the new style of the proletariat. If there are to be standards for weddings, then make them the standards of the proletariat." Her father agreed with this and raised his consciousness. He even gave his consent to their preparing the wedding in an economical way. On the day of the wedding, they insistently refused gifts, did not give a feast, and did not follow any of the feudal superstitious customs. After the wedding, they immediately plunged into the battle of grasping revolution and promoting production.

FROM "BEATING THE MANDARIN DUCKS" TO THE SEARCH FOR LOVE

Comrade Editors:

I am a twenty-five-year-old member of the Communist youth league, and a member of its organizational committee. In the past, because of my own ignorance and immaturity, compounded by the poisonous influence of the "Gang of Four," I developed an erroneous understanding of the place that love should take in the life of a revolutionary. I remember the time during the Cultural Revolution (I had just turned thirteen) when I went with a large group to Shanghai, where to get a taste of "revolutionary revolt" under the leadership of some high school students, we put on red armbands, and with sticks and clubs, with leather belts and portable megaphones, we went along Zhaojiabang Road "destroying the four olds." Using our sticks and clubs and belts, we chased away all the young couples who were courting beneath the light of the moon among the flowers, shouting over and over again: "Get out of here! Stinking hoodlums! Stinking perverts!" Later, as I gradually got older, I still thought that those days when I was young and "destroying the four olds" in Shanghai had been glorious, even to the point that I actually regarded love as a detestable sentimental petty-bourgeois emotion, a degenerate activity that must be strictly banished from any revolutionary enterprise. I even thought that the very word "love" was in itself the vocabulary of hoodlums, that it was a polite euphemism for sex, for lewd, degenerate, corrupt, evil behav-

ior, a word that a revolutionary would never use.

In 1975, after I was transferred from a farming village to work in a seedling nursery, our leader gave our local youth league team the important duty of preventing the boys and girls from making friends, from seeking partners, from talking about love and affection. As soon as I discovered that a young couple, while working, studying, and playing together, had fallen in love, I set about scheming in every way possible to prevent this relationship from developing further. At meetings, they would be called by name and criticized, and after the meetings they would be threatened and "cajoled," and if these methods did not work, they would then be separated like the shepherd boy and the weaving maid of Chinese legend, one to the south fields, the other to the north fields, which were some eight *li* [four kilometers] apart. Our nursery had separated as many as eight or nine couples in this way. As a cadre of the Communist youth league, with a totally incorrect understanding about love and having received no correct guidance, I not only did not realize that such actions on the part of our leader were wrong and harmful, on the contrary, I thought that he was truly revolutionary and high-minded, that he was a progressive leader who had transcended lower-class tastes and interests. For this reason, I spared no effort to follow his lead closely, to fight energetically to stamp out the sparks of "love." I arranged for "staunch elements" of the youth league to "spy on" the young boys and girls to see whether or not any had formed couples, sent "positive elements" to "investigate" whether or not any of the young people were seeing each other or having dates, to see whether or not any of their letters contained photographs or love notes . . . and then, I went immediately to the leader to report those "secrets" that most people would have difficulty discovering. I also helped the leader open the "anti-heart battle" to tear apart these "couples" and "lovers." At a conference for youth league members, in accordance with the wishes of the leader, in concert with several committee members, I falsely stated that the call of the party for late marriages and planned parenthood inferred that "late marriage means the later the better, and not to marry at all is by far the best, in perfect accord with the interests of the nation." I even suggested that "it is entirely improper for young people in their twenties to think now about individual problems. For the present, we shall not look for mates, shall not talk of love. These are demands of the present situation, demands of the times, demands of the revolution." It was as if questions of love and marriage were incompatible with, were totally irreconcilable with, revolution. Later, I also had each comrade in turn state his resolution to "refrain absolutely from seeking a mate or talking of love for ____ years." I also stressed again that this was what distinguished those who were wholeheartedly for the revolution from those who were only halfheartedly for the revolution, that this was the touchstone that distinguished the thorough revolutionary from the "half-baked" revolutionary. Under the explicit, conscious directions of our leader, and with the active encouragement and pressure from our branch committee, the great majority of the youth league comrades expressed their resolution to refrain absolutely from talking about love for five years. There were several fanatics who took the stage to swear that they would never marry, that they would be "revolutionary" monks and nuns. Neither I nor our leader made any attempt to restrain such an unrealistic attitude. On the contrary, we were delighted and were fully content to give these ignorant "foolish young people" our enthusiastic applause and encouragement. . . .

A PIONEER

One day Ding Naijun, a forty-year-old arithmetic teacher in Sichuan, had a great idea while he watched a TV advertisement. "Why can't I write an ad that will help me meet more people and have a better chance of finding a spouse?"

In January of 1981 Ding sent a letter, along with his personal advertisement, to *The Market*, a newspaper with a large circulation. The editors of the paper hesitated, but felt sympathetic to Ding's

problem and published the seventy-five word notice advertising his desire for a spouse. Ding was in luck. Within a month he received more than three hundred replies from all over China. He began correspondence with a girl from Jilin Province and they fell in love.

Since 1981 advertising for a spouse has become more and more popular. Only a week before Ding's ad, on January 1, 1981, the Marriage Law of the People's Republic of China adopted by the Fifth National People's Congress at its third session was put into effect. This revised law stipulated that men could marry at age twenty-two and women at age twenty. It was like the opening of a sluice gate. Large numbers of young people just at the legal age came to register their marriages and those who were over thirty suddenly became "elder unmarried youths."

Most of the people in this category experienced the ten-year turmoil [the Cultural Revolution]. They left school too early. After the turmoil ended, they plunged themselves into study, trying to make up for the time and education they had lost. When they realized that they should also spend some time on finding a spouse, they found meeting suitable people was more difficult than it was for the young.

By 1984, the party Central Committee was paying great attention to this issue, which had become a "social problem" by then. It called for the whole society to show concern for the marriage prospects of these people. Therefore, matchmaking services sprang up and parties were held to help people meet each other. Many newspapers and magazines published public notices written by people hoping to marry. Since people had to pay for the ads, these publications generated more income and profit, and increased their circulation as well. This is the reason that many publishing houses are eager to continue supplying this service. To attract readers, every newspaper and magazine had to make special arrangements to handle the personal advertisements of those seeking spouses. After the Wuhan *Youth News* started a special column, "Phoenix Searching for a Spouse," more and more people came to their offices. Finally, the editorial office had to set up a new reception room. A special column in *Guangdong's Family* magazine is called "Bridge of Love" and has attracted the interest of Chinese here and overseas who are seeking a spouse. The *China Marriage and Family Research Society* started a column named "Call of Love." though it is two pages long and contains forty to fifty ads in each issue it can hardly meet the large demand. *Spring Breeze*, a magazine specially for the handicapped, also opened a column of marriage ads for handicapped people. In May 1984, *Liberation Army Daily* started the column "Green Bridge of Magpies" and opened the door to personal advertising to those Chinese soldiers who wished to marry. The nationally distributed *Chinese Women Magazine* with its circulation of one million attracted many people seeking a spouse. In one issue alone there were 101 ads.

It has turned out that public matchmaking services have not been effective or successful. However, ads in magazines and newspapers keep increasing....

In July 1984, *Chinese Women Magazine* received a letter from Daling township, Ganyu county, Jiangsu province signed by "a hundred rural young men," including Sun Kenan. The letter read, "Guided by our party's policy of letting people become rich, carried out after the Third Plenary Session of the Central Committee of the Party, every family in our township has built a new house, has a deposit in the bank, and moreover has rice and white flour as food. We have high quality clothes and can watch TV or go to the cinema. We all enjoy our life very much. Our only regret is that we lack virtuous wives, to cherish our ideals and follow the same path with us. We welcome all city girls who have courage and insight to come to our rural area."

After this ad was published, many women answered. A girl from Shanghai said, "The Third Plenary Session of the Central Committee of the Party has brought about great changes to your town. I hope to go there to choose a spouse and contribute to the building of our countryside." A young woman from Ganzhou, Jiangxi province said, "I'm a university graduate and a government employee. I'd like to make friends with a young man in your area who can share my goals in life and explore the way to wealth with me." A girl waiting for her job assignment in Sichuan said, "Having failed the college admissions examination, I've been feeling low. Maybe going to the countryside where I can strive with these ambitious young people will be a turning point in my life. Marriage to an industrious and honest rural young man may provide me with a chance to live a meaningful life."

The story of one woman is a successful example of advertising for a spouse. A thirty-one-year-old woman had been one of the urban youngsters who went to the countryside during the Cultural Revolution. She returned to the city and studied at a university. As she was already a bit older than the other students, her social circle was small and it was difficult for her to find a suitable spouse. After placing a personal advertisement she received letters from two hundred men and sixty-three of these met many of her standards. Then she eliminated thirty who were too old or paid too much attention to physical appearance and another seven who were divorced and had children. One by one she met the twenty-three men who were left, but none of them could arouse her passion. Upon reflection she realized that her hope of meeting a man who was perfect in every way was unrealistic. She took another look at the letters and decided to meet a man who was a worker. Unexpectedly he was not ignorant, but an honest and humorous person with experiences similar to hers. When she was with him, she felt happy. Many warm-hearted friends came to attend their wedding....

In 1984 the women's federation attached to the Committee of Youth League in Xiong'erzhai township in the mountainous area of Pinggu county, a suburb of Beijing, placed a single ad for two hundred young men. The letter explained the economic position and spiritual state of the young people. There were 1,900 replies from twenty-eight provinces, cities, and autonomous regions. Already thirty-five of these young men are married, twenty more are planning their weddings, and the others are still corresponding with their new friends. . . .

Recently a TV station in Shanxi started showing personal ads which have proved popular. Viewers have an opportunity to appreciate the spouse-seeker's size, looks, and manner and hear the voice. Also, people can start to get responses even more quickly after a TV ad than an ad in publications.

Last year the cost of paper increased, directly influencing the price of newspapers and magazines. The force for publications including the cost for advertisers was raised, but even the additional expense has not discouraged those seeking a spouse through a personal ad. They do not complain because the ads are successful.

In the early 1980s those using ads to find a spouse generally fell into two categories: urban youths who returned to cities from the countryside where they lived during the Cultural Revolution, and urban citizens who had been sent to the countryside and were then allowed to return to cities after various policies of the party had been implemented. Over the past few years many people in these two groups found spouses, and a new group is making use of personal ads, divorcees. It is predicted that this group will have the most interest in seeking a new spouse through personal ads.

People all long for a congenial spouse and a happy marriage. It is no surprise that they now use the technology of the modern communication system to achieve their goal.

Translated by Lin Guanxing

96

THE ONE-CHILD FAMILY

With its population of over one billion already pressing the limits of its resources, China has had to confront the need to control population growth. Since the late 1970s the government has actively pursued this goal, adopting a variety of strategies to convince couples to have only one child. Young people need permission from their units to get married, then permission to have a child. Targets are set for the total numbers of births in each place, and quotas then assigned to smaller units. In the cities, the one-child family has become commonplace, but most observers report that in the countryside families who bear a girl are usually allowed to try again for a boy, so that two- or even three-child families are still common there.

The first piece below gives some of the regulations adopted by Sichuan province in 1987 to carry out central government policies on the one-child family. Fines and other economic penalties are the main means listed for fostering compliance with the regulations. The second piece, which appeared in the magazine Young Women *in 1986, discusses some of the problems created by pressure to keep families small.*

SICHUAN PROVINCIAL BIRTH-PLANNING RULES

Article 1. To practice birth planning, exercise control over the population, and improve the quality of the population so that population growth would be suited to economic and social development plans, these regulations are enacted in accordance with the People's Republic of China (PRC) Constitution, PRC Marriage Law, and relevant regulations of the state, and in connection with Sichuan's actual realities.

Article 2. Both husband and wife have the duty to practice birth planning.

Article 6. Late marriage and late births are encouraged.

Late marriage means that both men and women are married three years later than the lawful age [of 20 for women and 22 for men]. Late births mean births by women aged 24 and above.

Article 7. Births should occur in a planned manner.

Each couple is encouraged to give birth to one child.

No births must occur without marriage.

Article 8. Couples who can meet the following requirements may have a second child:

1. The first child has a nonhereditary disease and cannot become a normal laborer:
2. Marriage between an only son and an only daughter;
3. In the rural areas, the groom moves to the house of the bride, who is an only daughter, after marriage;
4. Only sons and daughters of martyrs in rural areas;
5. Disabled demobilized soldiers in rural areas with Merit Citation Class II, A;
6. Those in rural areas who were disabled while on duty and are equivalent to the disabled demobilized soldiers with Merit Citation Class II, A;
7. The person is the only one of several brothers in rural areas who is capable of having children;
8. In the rural areas, the husband or wife is the only son or daughter for two generations;
9. In the rural areas of the Pengzhou mountain counties and the mountain townships (not including the flatland, hilly land, and valleys) within the basin approved by the cities (prefectures) of the economic construction zone, families with only daughters that have labor shortages;
10. In the rural areas of the remote mountain areas in Pengzhou mountain counties, families with only sons and daughters; and
11. Both husband and wife are returned overseas Chinese who have settled down in Sichuan.

Article 9. Couples who have no children many years after marriage, but the wife has become pregnant after adopting a child, may give birth to a child.

Article 10. Those who can meet one of the following requirements may have a second child:

1. A widower or widow remarries and before the remarriage, the widower or widow has fewer than two children, while the spouse has no children; and
2. Husband or wife who remarries after a divorce and before the remarriage, one side has only one child, while the other has no children.

Article 11. For those who can meet the requirements of Articles 8, 9, and 10 and who want to bear children, both husband and wife should submit an application, which will be examined and brought into line with birth planning by the departments at the county level responsible for birth planning work. Second births should occur after an interval of four years.

Article 23. Those who refuse education and give birth to children not covered by the plan will be fined from the month the child is born. The wages or annual income of both husband and wife will be decreased by ten to twenty percent for seven years; the total sum deducted should not be less than five hundred yuan. Those who give birth to another child after the birth permiyted according to Articles 8, 9, and 10 of these regulations will be fined at a minimum of eight hundred yuan. A heavy fine will be imposed on those giving births not covered by the plan.

Regarding pregnancy not covered by the plan, both husband and wife will be imposed a fine of twenty to thirty yuan a month during the period of pregnancy. If the pregnancy is terminated, the fine imposed will be returned.

The fine imposed will be used for birth planning work only. The provincial birth planning committee and finance department will work out use and management methods.

Article 24. If those giving births not covered by the plan are cadres and staff members, apart from imposing a fine, the units where they work should also apply disciplinary sanctions according to the seriousness of the case.

Article 25. Those who have received certificates for only children and are allowed to give birth to a second child should return their certificates and will no longer get rewards and preferential treatment from the month they are allowed to give birth to a second child. Those who give birth to another child without approval, apart from the measures stipulated in Articles 23 and 24, will no longer get rewards and preferential treatment for only children and must return the certificates and health care benefits for only children.

Article 26. Regarding doctors, nurses, and working personnel in charge of birth planning work and marriage registration and state functionaries who violate these regulations, practice fraud, and accept bribes, the units where they work or the higher level competent departments should educate them through criticisms and disciplinary sanctions. If their practices constitute an offense, the judicial organs will investigate and affix the responsibility for the offense according to law.

Persons holding direct responsibility for accidents in ligation operations due to negligence will be handled according to relevant regulations.

Article 27. Regarding those who insult, threaten, and beat doctors, nurses, and working personnel in charge of birth planning work or use other methods to obstruct birth planning, the public security organs will handle the cases in light of the "PRC Regulations Concerning Public Security Management and Punishment." If the practices constitute an offense, the judicial organs will investigate and affix the responsibility for the offense according to law.

Article 28. Drowning, abandoning, selling, and maltreatment of girl babies and their mothers are prohibited. Regarding those involved in any of these practices, the units where they work or the leading organs concerned should educate them through criticisms and disciplinary sanction in light of the seriousness of the case. If their prac-

tices constitute an offense, the judicial organs will investigate and affix the responsibility for the offense according to law.

Illegal removal of intrauterine devices is prohibited. In addition to confiscating the income obtained from illegally taking out the intrauterine device, a fine of over five hundred yuan will be imposed. A heavy fine will be imposed on those who commit the offense repeatedly. The judicial organs will, according to law, investigate and affix the responsibility for injuries and deaths caused therefrom.

A PROBE INTO THE MENTALITY OF SIXTY-FIVE RURAL YOUNG WOMEN GIVING BIRTH TO BABY GIRLS
by Zhou Juhua

Last year when I was at Qidong, I heard that a village woman left her newborn baby girl by the side of the public restroom. This year I personally saw in Qiyang a resident find a girl infant at his doorstep when he opened the door in the morning. Tied to the infant was a slip of red cloth on which was written the infant's birth date and a message begging other people to adopt the child, as the father would not accept the baby girl and the mother had no choice but to abandon her. This has aroused my indignation and provoked my thinking. I felt the necessity to visit the countryside to probe into rural women's mentality regarding the bearing of baby girls in an attempt to answer the following questions:

1. What is the proportion of rural women who are unwilling to give birth to baby girls?
2. What are the causes for the unwillingness?
3. How do rural women fare both physically and mentally after giving birth to baby girls?
4. What do rural women plan to do after they give birth to baby girls?

1. Those Surveyed

The people I surveyed comprised rural women whose husbands were also parents, women who were between twenty and thirty, and whose first-born were baby girls. . . . Ye X of Liren township of Hengyang county said: "I was sterilized after the birth of two girls. My mother-in-law condemned me by saying: 'I have only one son who married a bitch like you. You have extinguished our family. Get out of here and get yourself killed; otherwise we will never turn around.' My husband abused me, beat me, and threatened to divorce me every day. He angrily reproached me: 'If I can get rid of you, you ugly woman, I'll get another woman who can bear me a son. I'll kill you if you do not clear out.' "

Peng X of Dashan township, Hengnan county, remarked: "Once you give birth to a girl, you get insults and humiliations from all sides. They call you the devil that extinguishes the family. You can hardly put up with this kind of life!"

Hu X of Changning county recounted: "Previously my husband and my parents-in-law all treated me well. After I gave birth to a girl and was lying in, my mother-in-law did not bother to take care of me even when I called her. The girl, having no milk to suck from, was always crying and made me very upset. My husband said I had caused him to lose face and he could not lift his head in front of others. When my parents came to visit me, they, too, were insulted by them. Later even my mother did not want to come. I wish I could die!" She used to be an activist in performing arts. Now she was reticent, dark, and thin.

Wen X of Yanzhou township of Changning county had this to say: "The so-called nursing home for the aged is phony. I have never seen one in my life. I'll bear a son whatever the price." When the surveyor pressed: "What if you have another girl?" she retorted in anger: "How can you say that my secondborn will still be a girl? No matter what, I'll keep on bearing children until I have a son. I'll be happy to have a boy even if I were to lose the whole family's fortune. I am willing to pay the 200 yuan of penalty [for second birth]."

Wang X of Jinqiao district, Qidong county, observed: "When I was pregnant, both my husband and my mother-in-law took good care of me. When they saw I gave birth to a girl, they were all disheartened. I also felt guilty toward my husband

and my parents-in-law and was ashamed of myself. When I saw other people explode firecrackers and make feasts to celebrate the birth of a son, I felt even more sad. I want to give birth to another child, hopefully a boy and not a girl. People will look down upon you if you give birth to a girl. What a difficult lot we women have!"

Chen X of Xiaojia village, Qiyang county, remarked: "I gave birth to three daughters, one of them deformed. Sand, no matter how good, cannot be used to build a wall, and daughters, no matter how many, cannot provide for an old mother. Nor is it easy to find a live-in son-in-law. A young man by the name of Li Min moved into the wife's home and people called him bastard. In our village there was an unmarried old man. He became sick and died in bed, and nobody knew his death until a few days later. It was horrible! Better to have a son."

Most of the rural women are afraid to have a girl at the first birth. They are afraid of the cold shoulder turned to them by their husband, parents-in-law, and others. They are also fearful of having no one to carry on the family lineage and no one to provide for them in old age. Thus they are unhappy after the birth of baby girls, their health deteriorating and their minds laden with anxieties. They are anxious to have a second birth and they pose an obstacle to the implementation of family planning.

Suggestions:

1. Leadership at all levels should pay attention to educating families with only baby girls. In particular they should educate the husbands and parents-in-law in fostering a correct attitude toward the bearing of girl infants.
2. Leadership at all levels should show concern for women giving birth to baby girls. Efforts should be made, on the one hand, to help them resolve some practical problems and, on the other hand, to help raise their understanding so that they can be freed from their anxieties.
3. Wherever conditions permit, women's schools should be set up as soon as possible.

97

ECONOMIC LIBERALIZATION AND
NEW PROBLEMS FOR WOMEN

During the period when the state actively controlled most of the economy, wo-
men's participation in school and work steadily increased. With the relaxing of
political control of the work place that characterized the 1980s, women often
indirectly suffered. Once rural families could engage in sideline businesses, they
frequently pulled girls out of school to work in rural workshops. Employers
asked to reduce their work force to become more efficient often pressured women
with children to take extended leaves. Employers able to select their own em-
ployees from among pools of middle school or college graduates frequently
passed over the women in favor of the men. Freer markets even led to renewed
traffic in women as wives.

With the more open press of the 1980s, scholars and reporters were able to
investigate and write about these emerging problems. The articles below ap-
peared in magazines and newspapers between 1985 and 1989.

REJECTION OF FEMALE COLLEGE
GRADUATES MUST BE STOPPED
by Yang Xingnan

In this day and age when the call before the nation
is to "respect knowledge and talent," it is a
strange phenomenon that many female college
graduates find it hard to be assigned jobs. Some
units openly reject women graduates; some go to
the length of giving up employment quotas allocated by the state rather than accept them. Some
send back women already assigned them.

According to this reporter's findings, when
contacting colleges for the new crop of graduates,

some units openly stated that they wanted only
males, no females. In 1983, at the Beijing Institute
of Foreign Languages, for instance, the ratio of
male and female graduates was 1:1. The majority
of the institutions or enterprises that contacted the
school for hiring, however, wanted only males.
According to statistics, of the job offers received
by Fudan University of Shanghai in 1984, seventy
work units solicited males and stated explicitly
that no females would be accepted. This was one-
third of the units that contacted them. Of these,
such units as the Filing Section of the Shanghai
Scientific Library, the Huashan Medical School of
the Ministry of Metallurgy, and the Beijing Print-

ing Institute could have provided suitable jobs for women.

Some units used various subterfuges to reject women. For instance, in 1984, one woman graduate of the Beijing Forestry Institute, a horticulture major, was assigned to work at the Diaoyutai Guest House, which had extensive grounds. After having been interviewed and approved by the personnel division of the Ministry of Foreign Affairs, she received a letter of acceptance from the Guest House. It changed its mind, however, when she reported for work. She was told that she was unsuitable due to the nature of the job. After being ignored on her several tries to talk to the personnel office of the Guest House, she went home in tears. Another ministerial department wanted a graduate for a technical research job. Wuhan University decided to give the department one of their best, a party member with an outstanding scholastic and citizenship record, but the assignee was rejected because she was a woman.

Such instances have aroused concern on the part of relevant institutions. Fudan University, for instance, submitted a special report to departments concerned in 1983 asking for speedy correction. Nevertheless, it met with the same problem in 1984. Not a few work units voluntarily cut quota numbers in order to avoid taking in women. Some twenty units refused to accept women assigned them by Wuhan University. According to the university, the problem is especially serious with ministries and departments at the central level. I was told by people at the Student Allocation and Transfer Division of the Ministry of Education that the problem is getting worse with expansion of work units' autonomous hiring rights. I found, after looking through thirty-odd summary reports on job allocation of college graduates in 1984 provided by the Education Ministry, that as many as seven institutions of higher education have written about this problem to bring it to the attention of authorities concerned.

Rejection of female college graduates is a violation of the central authorities' policy of "respecting knowledge and talent." It seriously affects the enthusiasm of women students and has already incurred the dissatisfaction of college teachers, officials, and students alike. A speedy stop must be put to it.

EMPLOYMENT OF CHILD LABOR BY FAMILY-RUN ENTERPRISES IS A PROBLEM THAT DEMANDS IMMEDIATE SOLUTION
by the All China Women's Federation

Last year, the Women's Federation of Zhejiang and other departments concerned investigated the 284 household-run enterprises in four villages and two local communities in Jinxiang township, Cangnan county, Wenzhou municipality. It was found that these enterprises employed 483 child laborers between the ages of ten and sixteen. Among them 78 were boys, constituting 16.15 percent of the total, and 405 (83.85 percent) were girls.

On the average, these child laborers worked eight to twelve hours a day as piece workers. Their average daily wage was 1.5 to 2.5 yuan. The lowest pay was 0.8 yuan; the highest, 7 yuan.

These child laborers had a low educational level. Among them were 142 illiterates, constituting 29.29 percent of the total. Some 101 had attended first or second grade in elementary school, constituting 20.91 percent; 149 had attended second, third, or fourth grade, constituting 30.85 percent; 73 had finished elementary school, constituting 15.11 percent; 18 were in junior high school, constituting 3.73 percent.

What caused more concern was that some of the work they were doing was harmful and would affect their healthy growth. These enterprises made polyester products, printed labels, plastic ware, gambling chips, and aluminum utensils. In the processes, poisonous chemicals such as methylbenzene, cyclohexanone, and rubber cement were used as solvents. Sixty-one of the child laborers (10.3 percent) were engaged in high-frequency work, including 56 girls. According to parents and local cadres, it was common among these children to feel dizzy and nauseous and suffer from chest pain, headaches, and sore throats. One girl had numbness and rheumatic pain in the joints after two years of high-frequency work. Other girls had insomnia, bleeding gums, and abnormal menstruation. After working the gilding press for two years, several girls found their eyesight deteriorating.

Jinxiang township had so many child laborers for a number of reasons.

1. The township's economy is backward, so poor parents made their children work. Cangnan is one of the five poverty-stricken counties of Zhejiang province. In Jinxiang, per capita farmland is only 0.45 *mu* [one *mu* is one-fifteenth of a hectare]. Income from farming is low, particularly for households with many children. On the other hand, a child laborer can make as much as 100 yuan a month. In Qianbao village, peasant Cai Naixiang and his family of seven tilled only three *mu* of land. Household annual income is only 200 yuan. In 1985, three of his daughters worked in township workshops and made more than 1300 yuan a year, constituting 80 percent of the family's income. Attracted by this kind of income, the peasants are willing to send their children to work as child laborers although the work is harmful to their healthy growth.

2. The township's educational facilities are backward; both educational funds and the number of teachers are limited. The attendance rate is low, the school dropout rate is high, and many school-age children do not go to school. . . .

3. The township's household-run enterprises are rapidly developing. Among the 3700 households, 80 percent have small machines of some kind, and their enterprises are either run by a single household or jointly operated by several households. The enterprises have drawn a labor force of 4000 local inhabitants and many outsiders from other townships. These immigrants work either as full-time or part-time workers and bring child laborers with them.

4. Employers like to employ child laborers because they are given lower pay than adults and they are more obedient. They say child labor is a bargain.

County departments concerned are tackling the problem of child labor in household-run enterprises. Jinxiang township has formulated regulations forbidding employment of child labor by both household-run and township-run enterprises.

Women's Work Editor's Note: The employment of child labor by household-run enterprises is a common social problem. It should draw the attention of the whole society.

Children are the future of our country and the hope of our nation. They are growing up physically and developing mentally. Our society as a whole has the obligation to be concerned with their healthy growth, and to train them to become a new generation of people with ideals, moral integrity, culture, and discipline. To let children do heavy physical labor at a tender age will not only affect their physical growth and mental development, but also deprive them of the opportunity to study so that they are unable to master advanced technology when they grow up. This is detrimental to the children themselves and to the country's future. It is particularly impermissible to let children do work that produces pollution and is harmful to their healthy growth, either physically or mentally. This is unconstitutional.

Women's federations at all levels are shouldering the heavy task of nurturing, training, and educating children to ensure their healthy growth and development. They should make serious efforts to investigate and report the problem of child labor to make sure this problem is solved at an early date.

WHEREIN LIES THE WAY OUT FOR ME?
by Li Jing

Comrade Editor:

I am a thirty-seven-year-old career woman holding a university diploma. When the upsurge of reform came, I was ready to go all out and do something big. Unexpectedly, however, I and many other women workers were sent home by our factories as if we were bits and pieces of left-over material. This has puzzled me. The reform has provided an opportunity for many people to realize their own values. Why should it single me out and cast me off? I have been thinking hard, and thinking over and over again: Wherein lies the way out for me?

What I have been through is a downward slide, so to speak, from the top of the mountain to the bottom of the valley, from exertion to dejection and lethargy. Having suffered so much in the old society, my parents loved the new society whole-heartedly.... My mother was illiterate and did not teach us any high principles. But I learned from her that honesty is the guiding principle in life and that one must work hard and rely on one's own efforts to better one's own conditions. Although my family was poor, I worked hard and achieved remarkable results in my studies. My teachers often praised me before the whole class or even the whole school, and I was awarded the title of "triple-A student" (good in health, academic record, and work) for several years running. But just as I was ready to go out to society and start a life of my own, I was struck a heavy blow. When I was not yet fifteen years old, my mother died of cancer, and a year or so later my father suffered a cerebral hemorrhage and left us. On his deathbed, my father exhorted me to "work hard for the Communist party." For many years I felt encouraged by his remark (but no longer so today). Having experienced the sorrow of bereavement, I suddenly matured. Since my elder brother and sister were serving in the army away from home, I shouldered the heavy responsibility of bringing up my younger brothers. After school, I had to wash, cook, mend and sew clothes, check my brothers' homework, and join them at play. Other children would call out "Mom!" the moment they came home from school, but my brothers would call out "Sis!" instead. Whenever one of them fell ill, I had to get up at five o'clock in the morning and queue up at the reception desk of a

hospital waiting to register him. When I graduated from high school, the school authorities, out of consideration of my special difficulties, helped assign me to work in a small collectively owned workshop.... Three years after I entered the workshop, I became secretary of the youth league branch in the workshop and was concurrently vice chairman of the trade union, deputy company commander of the militia, and member of the youth league committee of the corporation. In 1975 I was unanimously recommended by the whole workshop to study in a prestigious university. I was truly at the height of my life then....

I married a man who knew and understood me well. One year after we were married, our child was born. Since my parents had died long ago and my mother-in-law was also dead, my husband and I had to take care of the baby all by ourselves. We hired a young nurse but failed to keep her long because she thought we paid her too little and, "in accordance with the economic rules," left for good on the excuse of going home for a short visit (in fact, in the eight months she stayed with us, her pay had twice been raised, from thirty to thirty-five and then to forty yuan). Seeing that we lived in a single-story house and had to make and keep a coal fire, the second young nurse we hired left under the pretext that it was too hard a job to look after the baby. The third young nurse we hired worked for us for only a day and a half, and while we were away from home, made herself scarce, leaving the baby on the bed. I put in a request for a nurse with the March Eighth Service Company but was told to wait for six months. I could not but force myself to ask for help from the neighborhood committee and even to visit old women in search of a nurse. In the home of one old woman, I broke into tears. The old woman was very sympathetic but there was nothing she could do as she already had a baby in her care. My husband and I had no choice but to take leave by turns in order to be home and look after the baby. Later, after being rejected several times, our application for the admission of our baby to the nursery run by the factory where my husband worked was eventually discussed and approved of at a meeting of the factory authorities, and our baby was admitted to that nursery. Unfortunately, the baby was small and weak and often got sick, and we still had to ask leave from time to time. It so happened at the time that there were a few sections in the factory that were short of hands. In order to look after the baby, I had to give up my profession and ask to be transferred to an executive office where working hours were more flexible. And in that very year the upsurge of reform swept across our small factory. In order to improve management and efficiency, the factory authorities decided to ask the surplus personnel to wait for work at home on eighty percent of their pay. I was thrown into the group of people to be sent home. I could hardly believe my own ears when I heard the news. I am a university graduate and second to none in terms of my background in education and competence. Obviously, it was my baby that pinned me down. For several days I couldn't eat or sleep. I kept thinking of my former classmates in the university. Some of them had become factory directors, leaders of groups set up to solve specific problems related to production, or section chiefs; others had become university lecturers or engineers. In contrast, I was kicked out of the factory and had become a housewife in reality as well as in name. How could I face my former teachers and fellow students? How could I face those master workers who had trained and cared for me during my apprenticeship?

So I went to see the factory director and requested work. The director rejected my request politely. I then went to see the president of the trade union but also without results. I tried to discuss my problem with my women work mates only to be told: "Stay at home to look after your baby and keep eighty percent of your pay? Why, you just couldn't hope for anything better!"

In actual fact, life is far from easy and comfortable for a housewife. My monthly income is forty-five yuan less than it used to be, but now prices are high and so are the expenses for the baby. Financially, we have to count on my father-in-law for

help. But how can I bring myself to ask the old man for money? Although my husband is rather considerate, there is nothing he can do to thaw out my depression. As I now live under both financial and mental pressure, I fear very much that I will contract the so-called housewife syndrome (a twisted mentality peculiar to housewives).

Ninety percent of those waiting for work at home are mothers like myself. When we come together, we just have to pour out our grievances endlessly. Some say: "The reform has brought benefits after benefits to others but only misery to us." Some say: "Who would have imagined that the reform is only reforming women!" Still others say: "It is not workers who want to sit idle, doing nothing; it's you, the director, who cannot find enough work for us. Why in the world send us home?" But no one can answer these questions.

How do people look at us women workers who have been kicked back home by factories?

Our close friends from the old days have gradually drifted away from us. Gloating over our bad luck, our neighbors will ask casually: "Not going to work? Why, have you lost your job?" Our loving and caring parents can only provide us with a little financial assistance over a certain period of time. What about our husbands? A newly married woman did not have the courage to tell her husband the truth and every morning when she was due to go to work she would take her satchel and go to her own parents' place. When eventually her husband would learn of her secret, they would have a big row. In the case of another women worker who had already been estranged from her husband, this has led to the further escalation of the already raging "civil war," so to speak. Even when an affectionate young couple are bickering with each other, the husband cannot help saying something unpleasant, such as "You must be hopelessly stupid! Otherwise, why have they sent you back home?"

After being sent home, we have lost the understanding and respect of the public at large.

When I am calm and cool, I think: I have lost my work for the sake of my baby. But the baby is not my private property, why should I be subject to such callous treatment? Is it not often argued that competition should be among those with an equal starting point? As women, we shoulder the heavy responsibilities of bringing up children and taking charge of household affairs, and on top of that we must compete with men in our work. How can it be said that this is competition between equals? Women shoulder the important responsibility of continuing the human race. But why is their contribution not recognized and why, on the contrary, should it be taken as an excuse to eliminate women in the competition?

Comrade Editor, it is in exceedingly low spirits that I am writing this letter to you for my own sake and also for the sake of all women workers who are home and no longer working because of the double pressure under which they live. We yearn to have the understanding of society at large, to share our thoughts and feelings with people, and even more to find a way out of our present plight.

WOMEN BEING KIDNAPPED, SOLD

Quyang county in Hebei province is the setting for a brisk but highly illegal business—selling women, China's *Women's News* reported.

Five thousand women from more than ten provinces have been induced to come to the county, where they have been sold to farmers for anywhere from 50 yuan to 5000 yuan. The practice is so lucrative there are more than 1000 people engaged in the business. One built himself a five-room house from his earnings, the paper noted. Sales of women are also prevalent in other counties around Baoding, the paper said, and cited the case of Wang Guaifa, 47, who lost both his daughter, Wang Zhengcui, 17, and niece, Chen Xinxiu, 14, to kidnappers in Baoding last January 5. Wang, the two girls and Chen Xinxiu's brother, Chen Yimin, 24, had arrived at Baoding railway station on their way to Hejian county to visit Wang's son-in-law, Liu Zhandui. They stopped to ask directions and were taken by a gang of seven in two rickshaws to a nearby village where they were held for two nights and a day. The gang robbed Wang and his nephew of everything they had and left them out on a road.

After forty days, Wang begged his way to Hejian and his son-in-law informed the public security bureau in Baoding. Detectives soon found that Chen Xinxiu had been sold for 2700 yuan and Wang Zhengcui for 3000 yuan. Both were in Lianzhuang township in Xingtang county. On March 9, police from provincial, city and county public security bureaux found and freed Chen Xinxiu. But they failed to get Wang Zhengcui, who was whisked away by Zhang Guofa, the man who bought her, and by Li Changhai, who had arranged the deal, the paper said. When police eventually tracked her down they found she had been sold three times in rapid succession. She refused to leave and the villagers stopped police from taking her away.

The police investigation took two months and cost 10,000 yuan. Only one of the girls had been rescued and two traffickers in women nabbed.

98

PEASANTS IN THE CITIES

China's rural population, still about seventy-five percent of the population, benefited from the economic reforms of the 1980s that allowed them to sell for a profit whatever they produced beyond what they had contracted to produce for the state. Standards of living in the countryside rose rapidly; as farmers were able to build new houses and buy more consumer goods including, in increasing numbers, televisions. Still, when restrictions on travel and residency were eased, many rural residents, especially young men, flocked to the cities to see if they could find better paying work there.

Below is the record of an interview with one such young man conducted by a Chinese reporter who wandered around the streets of Beijing in 1984 interviewing ordinary people. It is followed by a newspaper article published in Farmers Daily *in March 1989 on the logistical problems caused by the influx of rural residents into the major cities.*

AN URBANIZED PEASANT

You guessed it, I'm not from Beijing. And don't believe that "Shanghai Tailor" sign I've got hanging up there. I'm not from Shanghai either. My hometown's Qingpu. That's a county right outside the Shanghai municipal area. It's late now and business is pretty slow, otherwise I wouldn't be talking to you this way. Usually I'm much too busy. If I didn't have this sign up, no one would give me any business. But I'm not trying to fool anybody; Qingpu's actually run by the Shanghai government.

I come from a family of farmers. We don't get grain coupons like you people in the city, so we have to grow our own food. I finished junior mid-

dle school, but it was only a rural school for us country folk. When I graduated, there weren't any college entrance examinations to take. But even if they'd had them then, hayseeds from the country like me wouldn't have a chance of passing. Both my parents are still alive. They're illiterate farmers. Qingpu's a pretty poor part of the world, you know. A few years ago there wasn't a single light bulb in the place. But because it's so close to Shanghai, nobody believes me when I tell them that. Things have gotten a lot better the last few years. A lot of people have TV sets now. My family? Sure, we have one, we've got a real fancy color TV. Both my younger sister and I learned a trade; that's a surefire way to make money. Now we've got plenty of money, but no education. I'm living here in Beijing now, but I hardly ever write letters back home. Writing letters is too much trouble.

The year I graduated was the same year that old baldy Lin Biao got himself cracked up in a runaway airplane. After graduation all of my classmates went back home to work on their family farms. Middle school kids in the countryside had no other choice. At that time they were using the workpoint system like up at Dazhai. Young people like us worked our tails off from morning till night for a paltry seven workpoints; ten was the most anybody got in one day. They didn't figure out how much each point was worth till the end of the year, so none of us knew how much money we were making. The most they ever paid was twenty-nine per day, but that was for ten points. If you want, you can figure out how much I earned. What a grind! The worst it ever got was the year they raised all that commotion about eradicating the "four pests" [rats, sparrows, flies, and mosquitoes]. That year we had to pay the production team one-point something workpoints each day out of our own pockets. It was bad enough slaving out in the fields for close to nothing. But then we had to sign IOUs for grain (actually borrowing grain from the production team or brigade before the harvest—authors' note). There was a saying going around at that time, "If the Tangshan earthquake had hit Qingpu, it would have been a hell of a good deal." There's nothing funny about that. When there's an earthquake, at least you're sure of getting some emergency grain rations.

With an empty wallet, what's the use of going into the city? You can't buy anything there. All you can do is walk around window-shopping. In those days everybody was jealous as hell of people from Shanghai. We all felt like failures, and people started saying fate had it in for us. But things are better now. What's so great about Shanghai anyway? The people there hardly have any money. They don't have color TV or decent places to live in either. But they keep on making fun of us, like we're their stupid country cousins or something. But you know what? My wallet's bulging and their salaries are so low it'd make you cry. In fact, in one day I can make as much as they get paid for two weeks' work.

I started studying tailoring the year they began the production responsibility system. At first they called it the "field responsibility system," but the two are actually the same thing. Our family, a total of seven people, had a little over two *mu* of land to work. It wasn't enough. There were too many people and not enough land. Since they divided all the land in the brigade up evenly among the households without counting how many mouths you had to feed, the more able-bodied workers in your family the less you got to eat. I wasn't stupid. I knew the new policy was to let everyone make money and get rich, but with so little land you could only earn shit. So I went out and learned how to be a tailor. My older brother stayed home and worked the fields.

The production contract system meant dividing the land up among individual families. At the beginning these plots were called "responsibility fields", but actually assigning production quotas and dividing up the land is the same thing. The idea is, the fewer people on the land the more money you can make.

Some people were pretty poor at farming and couldn't make any money at it, so they rented their fields out to others on the sly, freeing themselves to do other work. This was legalized two years ago, and now people can take on more land if they've got the manpower to work it. In addition to turning in your state grain rice quota you've got to pay a sort of land use tax to the brigade based on the amount of land you farm. Don't forget, they still own the land. Anyway, when everyone else was sweating away out there like a bunch of idiots, I went out and started learning a real skill.

Learning to be a tailor is no simple matter. The first thing you've got to do is pay someone to teach you the ropes, since nobody's going to give away their family trade secrets for nothing. I made up my mind not to improve the lot of any tailors in Qingpu in this way. I wanted to learn in Shanghai. The last few years, everyone and their uncle in Shanghai's been opening up tailoring schools. The neighborhood committees have them, the districts have them, the educated youth organizations have them and there are even privately run ones now. But I decided to keep away from those private ones. The good thing about the places run by the city government is that if you're one of those unemployed educated youths you can study for free, or at least pay half tuition. Naturally I wanted to study for free.

There's no way I was going to pass for an unemployed educated youth, but I found a way around that. I asked my uncle to write a letter of introduction for me saying that I was his son. Those schools don't really care who you are, all they want from you is a letter of introduction. You don't have to give them any photographs either. So I borrowed my cousin's name for a while. Those schools give out diplomas if you graduate, but who needs it? When I graduated I didn't even pick mine up. It had my cousin's name on it anyway, and with my picture on it, it would have looked pretty silly hanging up here, don't you think? Anyway, the only thing that matters is whether or not you're a decent tailor, and that has nothing to do with a diploma. Later on I took intermediate and advanced classes, each time switching to a different school. Getting a letter of introduction from my uncle's factory was never a problem. I was there to learn something, not to take anybody for a ride. In those days I didn't have a spare penny to my name.

But when I finished the advanced class, I felt, I needed a diploma. Why? Because I wanted to find work in north China, and that diploma was the only proof I had that I was a real Shanghai tailor. So I asked the teacher about it. He was a real bright guy. He told me, "First time I set eyes on you I knew you weren't from Shanghai. It's written all over your face." He told me to fill in the blanks on the diploma myself, which put all the responsibility on my shoulders. Worse come to worst, he could say he didn't know what was going on. When I was about to leave, I offered him a little gift in an envelope, but he wouldn't take it. He said, "If I accept this it means I've sold you a fake diploma." You don't find too many honest

guys like that in Shanghai. Most people there wouldn't give a guy from the countryside the time of day. Look here, that's the diploma I'm talking about.

I studied in Shanghai for a year altogether. Then I went back to Qingpu and spent a few months teaching my younger sister what I had learned. We practiced on newspaper instead of cloth. Who would be crazy enough to use cloth to practice making clothing? I got all the old newspaper I needed for nothing from the Party office of the brigade. You know how it is.

They did me a favor, so I owed them one. Every time I go home now there's always someone in that office waiting for me to make something for them. Is my time worth less than a pile of old newspapers? I tell you, owing people favors is a hell of a lot worse than being in debt.

The next step was for me to apply for a small-business license from the local bureau of commerce. Normally this takes a lot of sweet talk and a bit of cash under the table. Sure, you have to give them something, otherwise you'd never get your license, or they give you one marked "Valid Only in Qingpu." If I worked in Qingpu I'd starve to death! I wanted to work up north. The moment you cross the Yangzi River, the price people are willing to pay Shanghai tailors starts going up. The first time I offered that guy in the commerce bureau a gift was in 1980, but he made up a million excuses and finally refused to give me the license. That didn't stop me, though, and I made up my mind to give it a go without a license. So I spent the next seven months working in Tianjin and Harbin and ended up earning more than five thousand yuan. Without a license you can't work in the street or even rent a room in a hotel. That makes things pretty tough. Fortunately I had a distant relative in Tianjin who let me stay in his home. I paid him one hundred fifty yuan for three months—a lot more than it would have cost to stay in a little hotel. In Harbin I stayed with an old friend from Qingpu who had worked for a while at the Daqing oil field and then got transferred to Harbin. People from your hometown often turn out to be a hell of a lot nicer than your own relatives. Business was good in those days, much better than it is now. There are so many Shanghai tailors running around now, it's like everyone in Shanghai's in the business. A few years ago I got one yuan twenty for cutting out a pair of pants. Now I'm lucky if I can get sixty *fen*. But earning that five thousand yuan was a breeze. I didn't even have a license then, and I didn't have to pay any taxes either.

When I brought all that money back with me to Qingpu at New Year's, the people in my family nearly jumped out of their skins. They thought I'd committed armed robbery or something. My father didn't say much, but my mother kept asking me, "Xinna, you didn't steal that money, did you?" My sister didn't do as well as I did, though. Where she was down in Changzhou she could just make enough to feed herself. You see what I mean when I say you've got to go north to make money.

A few days after the New Year, the head of the production brigade came to see me and said, "You've been running around free as a bird for a whole year now." Then he told me I had to pay the brigade for my grain rations and a management fee of one yuan a day. He ended up squeezing three hundred and sixty yuan out of me. I didn't have a choice, you know. If I thought he might start making trouble for my family, I'd never be able to go away and work in peace. That sort of thing's no problem any more. Now I've got a contract with the production brigade. All I have to do is pay them a management fee. Then the brigade head asked me how I got my grain coupons. I told him I bought them, how else? Twenty *fen* a kilo. But that's better now too. You can trade rice for grain coupons at the state grain stores. Grain coupons are almost totally useless anyway. They're bound to do away with them sooner or later just like they did away with cotton rationing. Finally he asked me to take his son along with me and teach him the ropes. Not me, boy! What was in it for me? I had to ease my way out of that one pretty carefully. Had I done it any other way, I would have gotten into a heap of trouble.

After talking it over with my parents, I decided it would be better to spend a thousand yuan for a license rather than keep on doing business on the sly. But then it turned out I got my license without having to spend a penny. At that time the central government came out with a new policy. Fortunately for me, it was not out of the hands of the guy I'd been dealing with in the local bureau of commerce, and everything went fine. I have to pay taxes now, a five percent commercial tax and a two percent management fee. They call that progressive taxation; the more you earn the higher the rate you pay. I was in the seven-percent bracket. The very lowest anybody has to pay is five percent. The people in the bureau are a bunch of clever monkeys. They can pretty well figure out how much business you're doing. Of course, the amount I report each month is totally up to me. But I never evaded any taxes. If they fine you that's one thing. But if they take away your license that's the end. That new policy is a good one. The more money I make, the bigger my contribution to society. That actually makes a lot of sense. In addition to the business tax and management fee for the local bureau of commerce, and the management fee and reserve fund contribution for the production brigade, I've got to pay a daily management fee to the people who run the peddlers' market where I set up my stand. It's higher in the city than in the countryside, naturally, but you can't make any money in the countryside.

The last two years, I've worked in nearly twenty different places, both big cities and little towns. Even though I can make any style of clothing you can think of, I've been earning less recently. The reason is that there are too many people in business now. If things stay the way they are, though, I can pull in about three hundred a month, no problem. That's more than a college professor earns. The most I ever earned in a month was twelve hundred yuan.

There have been some hard times too. Last November when I was in Chongqing there was hardly any work to do. Remember that anti-pollution campaign? (The campaign to combat spiritual pollution, though it was not a political campaign—authors' note). At that time the people in charge of the market wouldn't let us make any so-called weird fashions. Actually there was nothing weird about the clothes we were making. All the patterns came out of books and magazines they sell in bookstores. Maybe they were a little different from that tired-out stuff they've been selling in the state-run stores for years. But if they weren't a little different, people wouldn't come to me. Let them try to find stuff like that in the state-run stores. When I heard that they weren't making such a big fuss about weird fashions in Beijing, I decided to come here. What I heard turned out to be true. Whenever one of those campaigns hits a small town, the officials blow things way out of proportion. Those people never watch television, so they don't know what's really going on. I was staying in a hotel where they had a TV and watched it every night. Sure enough, when they showed Hu Yaobang meeting a bunch of foreigners he was wearing a good old Western suit. I've been in Beijing for about six months now. When I go back to Qingpu this time, I'm going to have to write a self-criticism, since I didn't pay my taxes last year. They're going to charge me a late fee too. I don't care, business is good in Beijing. I've got it all figured out already.

I never send any of my money home through the post office, since if you do it that way everyone in the production brigade and the post office knows exactly how much you've got. They say things like, "He's sending so many yuan home this time." Also, there's a charge for sending cash through the post office, ten yuan per thousand. What a waste! I deposit what I earn in the bank every three or four days. I've got a regular savings account. I've also got it worked out so that I'm the only one who can take money out of the account, even if I lose my passbook. Another good thing is that you can earn interest on your money this way. The people in the bank keep calling me a millionaire. What's the matter with being rich? I made my money with my own hands thanks to the government's policy. The thing is, though, if you've got the skills but there's no policy to protect you, they'll attack you sooner or later for being one of those "four baddies" [landlords, rich peasants, counterrevolutionaries, and bad elements], or a

member of the "new bourgeoisie." On the other hand, with a good policy and no skills, there's no way you're going to make it through either. What good is a person with no skills? Even if the government forced you to get rich, you'd never make it.

Sure there are a lot of people out there getting rich in slippery ways. I've never been in an airplane, or on a sleeper train for that matter. I always buy the cheapest hard-seat tickets. It's not worth throwing away a few days income on a single night's sleep. Even if I were rolling in money I'd never travel that way. There are too many better ways to spend your money. I'm still single and I don't have girlfriends. That doesn't bother me, though. If you've got money, a skill, and enough energy to keep yourself going, it's no trouble finding a decent wife.

I'm all in favor of the government's new policies. If Deng Xiaoping wanted a suit made, I'd do it for him for free. But he'd have to promise me that they won't fool around with those policies. I'm just kidding, of course. What does a big shot like Deng Xiaoping need me for? Hey, don't record that, alright? Rewind the tape. I know how to work a tape recorder like that, I've got one at home. It's better and a hell of a lot bigger than the one you're using. It's made in Japan.

I bought government bonds for a thousand yuan. You see, the government is starting to borrow cash from the people now. I'm willing to do that since there's a pretty good chance they're going to pay me back. In Shanghai, whole work units buy bonds and split the cost evenly among the workers. That's a pretty piss-poor way to do it.

This is the first time I ever heard the term "urbanized peasant." There are a lot of urbanized peasants out there who are a lot richer than I am. They make good money cultivating mushrooms and raising chickens. They can earn a lot more than I do without ever having to leave home. Some of those families can earn ten thousand yuan a year. But there are also quite a number of people worse off than I am. Since they're totally unskilled, there's nothing anybody can do to help them. There are also people who get rich one day and lose it all the next. They buy clothing in Guangzhou or Shanghai, or even in Shenzhen, and sell it up in the northeast. Some do real well at it. But others lose their shirts at it. It's a pretty chancy business. Better to make your money with your own hands, I say. When someone else gets rich, I don't never turn green with envy about it. People have told me that I should get into selling clothes as well. No way! I don't think anyone who goes into business can beat the state at it. Can you beat their set-up? Can you beat their prices? I really believe what Chairman Mao said: "Ample food and clothing through self-reliance." You call peddling clothing in the northeast self-reliance? Don't laugh. This is what I believe and nobody's going to make me change my mind. Commodity circulation? That's just buying and selling. You can't really call that work. You know, if you write about me in the newspapers everyone in Qingpu's going to make fun of me. They'll say, "He's no ten-thousand-a-year household, what's his name doing in the paper?" Actually, my family earned more than ten thousand yuan last year. But since on the books I don't live with them any more, they didn't count my income in. Families that earn ten thousand yuan get a prize of a coupon to buy a Phoenix bike. Doesn't bother me. You can buy one of those on the black market pretty easily now for about forty yuan over the regular price. Who's going to ride it? Everyone I know who rides a bike has a Phoenix already.

No, I don't have any plans worked out for the future. I can hardly write in the first place, so what good is a plan going to do me? I wasted nine years in school already. But I can get by using the northern dialect now. I've learned to use *nin*, the polite form of "you," as everybody else does in Beijing.

I plan to keep moving around like this for another couple of years and then open a little shop of my own somewhere and settle down. Maybe I'll earn a bit less that way, but who cares? I'll have a wife and child to take care of by then. Everything will be all right so long as I can keep my capital. It's going to take me another couple of years to put enough in the bank. I need twenty

thousand at least. With any less than that, the interest isn't enough to support a family.

Translated by Don. J. Cohen

THE RURAL EMPLOYMENT CRISIS AND THE OUTFLOW OF LABOR
by Wang Tai, Liu Jiajun, and Wang Yuqi

Guangzhou was reporting an emergency: Some one million workers had poured in like a flood. The peak number of workers gathering at the Guangzhou railway station square reached 30,000. Wuhan was reporting an emergency: One hundred thousand Sichuan workers had surged forward—waiting for railroad tickets, or squeezing their way into trains to head southward! Zhengzhou was reporting an emergency: There was a sharp increase in travelers at the Zhengzhou railway station. The train heading northward was seriously overloaded—so much so that it could not leave on time! Beijing was reporting an emergency: The Beijing railway station was filled with pressing crowds. The daily number of incoming and outgoing travelers reached 230,000. That of transit passengers reached a record 42,000, seventy percent of them being outgoing workers! . . .

After arriving at their destinations, some workers became wanderers living in the streets because they could not immediately find work. Some were reduced to begging, or forced to pick up garbage and discards to eke out a living. Their plight is very sad. Urban transport, catering and sanitation facilities, and social order were affected by the wave of workers. Many people were dumbfounded. As if they faced a great disaster, they cried for interception, control, and repatriation. It was only a short time ago when peasants' entry into cities was hailed as a big achievement in the rural reform. Peasants entering cities were treated as a force not to be overlooked in urban construction. All of a sudden, these incoming peasants had became a source of trouble to cities.

On the 28th of the first month of the lunar year (5 March), the General Office of the State Council issued an urgent notice calling on various areas and departments to strictly control workers or large concentrated groups. With administrative intervention from various areas and departments, and with the passage of time the wave of outgoing workers is subsiding. But the problem thus exposed and the effects of it will cause people to think seriously. . . .

In the second half of last year, in an effort to rectify the economic order, improve the economic environment, and reduce the scale of capital construction, large numbers of projects were suspended or delayed. Some peasant construction teams had to return to the countryside. According to estimates by relevant departments, the peasants forced to return to the countryside due to curtailed capital construction numbered five million people. Unlike general peasants, they had worked in cities for several years. They had become familiar with their work and been under the influence of urban civilization. They had acquired a new concept of employment. If we should send them back to the fields and to areas where they originally lived, they would really be put in an embarrassing position. Moreover, they were originally surplus workers, having nothing to do at home. Therefore, although cities had no longer needed them, they still pinned their hopes on cities. After the Spring Festival they habitually headed for cities as a matter of course. In addition, after this portion of workers and other peasants working in cities returned to the countryside, they consciously or unconsciously gave their folks the impression that "the city is a good place to make money." "The outside world is quite exciting." Surplus rural workers who had not entered the city before also surfaced under their inspiration. These two groups of people coming in and out of cities merged to form a still larger contingent and an overwhelming deluge. They first headed toward Guangdong, which had opened up relatively early and enjoyed a relatively brisk commodity economy. This was also understandable.

Our country is now in a period of the new system replacing the old one. Every new policy or measure introduced gives rise to a series of prob-

lems. This is nothing strange. The problem is that in regard to policy formulation and work arrangements, how much consideration has been given to what the peasants and those workers who had first entered the city to engage in construction projects will do after being sent back, and what would be done for them? Governments at various levels and relevant departments should take this into account. . . .

In the last few days of the first lunar month, we made a round of the Beijing railway station, and the labor market. We visited some workers, with large or small packages horizontally or vertically placed on their backs. From what they said, we gathered that they had not traveled blindly. Instead, they had well-defined goals and concrete recruiting units in mind. After getting off the train, some immediately changed to the city public bus, heading for the unit that had signed work contracts with them. Some were waiting temporarily at the railway station as transit passengers.

In a big hall of the Yongdingmen railway station, a group of thirty-odd young workers were sitting on their luggage talking and laughing. On being asked, they said that they had hailed from Fuhu town, Nanbu county, Sichuan province. They were traveling in transit to work for a brick making factory in Jiamusi city of Heilongjiang. At the Beijing railway station, we saw a worker team of more than eighty people. Striking up a conversation with them, we learned that they had come from Huaiyin county, Jiangsu province. Soon a large bus sent up by a certain unit picked them up. It was the unit that had signed work contracts with them.

There were also some peasants staying behind at the railway station and at the labor market. At the well known Jianguomen Labor Market in Beijing, we noted several hundred peasants leaning against a cement wall, waiting to be hired. But relatively few employers came forward. It was basically a seller's market. After a few days with no work, some people were downcast and financially hard up. These people might be considered "blindly motivated." Their plight called for attention. But given the freedom of buying and selling labor, a certain degree of risk taking is needed. We, therefore, cannot call all the peasants that enter the city "blindly motivated" job seekers.

We must allow a rational and purposeful circulation of labor and cut irrational and blind circulation to a minimum. We must also solve the problem of food, shelter, and transportation confronting mobile people, and protect the legitimate interests between labor and capital. This is a matter that the government and the relevant departments should put on the work agenda and start tackling. Moreover, the outgoing workers are basically circulating on their own. Concerning labor markets, most areas have either taken a laissez-faire attitude, or imposed a ban. When relevant officials are sometimes asked about this matter, they prove to be total strangers. At the Yongdingmen railway station, a young fellow from Inner Mongolia had still not found a job. We asked why he did not go home. He said: "What should I do after going home? It is little or nothing that I have been through. I would not starve after all."

Another man beside him said: "The pay for one month's work in the city is what I got working six months in my hometown. Everyone wants to leave." It seems that their "blindness" is only relative. On the contrary, there seems to be absolute "soberness." Since cities provide better employment opportunities than the countryside and a colorful life and since restrictions on the scope of activity for peasants have been lifted, with them given the freedom to find full scope for their abilities, then peasant entry into cities will be a trend that can hardly be resisted. This requires that in making decisions on economic and social development, we must not only consider an urban population of 200 million but also take note of a rural population of 800 million. . . .

Relevant data in investigations shows that at present, our country's total rural labor force—about 400 million strong—has around 220 million surplus workers. According to estimates based on the investigations by the World Bank, there would be an annual increase of 10 million people in China's labor force from 1980 to 2000. Of the existing number of workers, some 50 percent are not fully employed, and 30 percent are relatively superfluous. There are large numbers of unemployed people due to seasonal, structural, hidden, mobile, and stagnation related factors. A great surplus of workers has become a big social problem.

To counter the pressure of the "wave of workers" in the first lunar month, a decisive control of rural workers blindly breaking out and leaving elsewhere, and moving out in large concentrations is undoubtedly necessary. But where will more than 200 million surplus rural workers go after all? How do we arrange for their employment? This fundamental problem calls for a creative answer. A makeshift measure is not a long-term policy.

According to statistics, from 1978 to 1986, the number of surplus workers in agriculture absorbed by nonagricultural industries in the countryside reached 44 million. Meanwhile, several tens of millions of mobile peasants entered cities to fill some jobs. So far, our countryside has transferred about 80 million rural workers, who left the fields but not their hometowns, or who left both the fields and their hometowns. But relevant experts consider that for those surplus rural workers who have not been transferred away and those likely to be added, employment opportunities in the countryside alone can hardly be enough. Our countryside is greatly restricted by resources. The level of development of productive forces is relatively low. No matter how fast the pace of development of nonagricultural industries, the growth of employment opportunities cannot bring about the miracle of sudden growth, as appeared years ago. Nor is it possible to make the growth of employment opportunities exceed the increase in the number of workers. Therefore, simultaneously with the local absorption of rural surplus workers, a switchover to a bigger world has become an inevitable trend. . . .

99

POSTERS CALLING FOR DEMOCRACY

The educated elite in China have traditionally recognized a moral obligation to point out the errors or abuses of the government, even when doing so hurt their personal chances for political advancement or even placed their lives in jeopardy. In the early twentieth century, students staged protests against Japanese imperialism. Two generations later, as the Cultural Revolution faded, students again staged protests against government policies: at Tiananmen Square in 1976, Democracy Wall in 1978, at Hefei in 1986, and throughout the country in late April to early June, 1989. Each time a popular way to make known dangerous views was to post a "big character" poster.

The demonstrations staged in the spring of 1989 reflected the growing frustrations of students and the relative tolerance of the government in the early stages of the movement. Five posters placed by students on walls at their campuses are given below. The first three appeared on the same day, April 24, 1989, as student unions and boycotts of classes were getting organized. Three days later about 100,000 students marched from their campuses to downtown Beijing, met along the way by large crowds of supportive citizens. Shortly afterwards smaller groups of students staged a hunger strike in Tiananmen Square, surrounded by thousands of supporters. The fourth poster dates from that period. The last poster given here was posted May 26, a few days after martial law was declared and the first efforts made to get the students to leave the Square. A few days later, on June 4, the military violently dispersed the remaining students, killing several hundred.

A Memorial and Testament to the Privileged Class

The privileged class, "officials of the people,"
  you live a life to make the immortals envious;
Opening up, reform—what good opportunities—
  if you don't make money now, then you never will.
Children of officials violate the law and run wild,
  but the law barely touches them.

Although their sons and daughters are idiots,
  they can still choose between Beijing and Qinghua universities.*
These privileged accompany foreign guests, eating and drinking for free,

  * [Footnote in original] An unwritten regulation stipulates that sons and daughters of officials with the rank of vice premier and above can enter universities without taking the national comprehensive examination.

And what's more, they receive a "subsidy" of hundreds of yuan.*
Not bothering to separate official business from private affairs,
they ride gratis in airplanes and cars.
Everyone has a "special purchasing card,"
which buys them high-quality products at low
prices.†
Chartered planes and trains deliver gifts,
delicacies from every land, fresh year round. . . .
The whole family happily resides in Zhongnanhai,
their palatial second homes and villas scattered
from the mountains to the sea.
Luxurious gleaming buildings, clubs, and hotels—
the people can only look and sigh!
Well-known and clandestine "pleasure nests"—
ordinary folks cannot even approach them in their
lifetime.
A cluster of "public servants" for private masters,
cooks, doctors, bodyguards;
"Staff workers" line up in front and back,
beautiful ladies, "courtesans," await them on
both sides.
"Limited-distribution movies" with sex and violence,
only within the palaces are they not prohibited. . . .
The mighty Mercedes Benz moves through the staring red traffic light.‡
Tourists and travelers are driven out from parks and
beaches,
only because some senior official has entered the
park to play.
During their lives they enjoy to the hilt days of honor
and glory,
after death, they ascend to Babaoshan cemetery.**

Posted at Beijing Normal University, April 24

* [Footnote in original] It has been discovered that the
monthly subsidies of senior officials who host foreign guests is
over a thousand yuan.
† [Footnote in original] "Special purchasing cards" not
only allow one to buy scarce and desirable goods but also to
purchase them at prices several times lower than at ordinary
city markets. For example, hairtail fish of the highest quality
costs only 0.60 yuan a half kilogram in Zhongnanhai.
‡ [Footnote in original] The Mercedes Benz is the most luxurious in the world. When senior officials travel through a
city, the police open up a lane for them and they do not need
to stop at red lights.
** Babaoshan cemetery in the western outskirts of Beijing
is the burial place for China's top miliary and political leaders.

A Letter to Citizens of Beijing

Citizens of the capital:

We are students of Beijing Aeronautics Institute. Our sacred mission is to uphold the people's interests. We have no choice under the
current circumstances. Under circumstances
that have pushed our patience beyond its limits, we feel compelled by sadness and fury to
declare: a class boycott will commence on
April 24.
Our action is by no means an action of
blind impulse; we have a feasible program,
clear and definite objectives, and a well-
disciplined and powerful organization. We
will not accept the control or manipulation of
any person, nor will we stoop to compromise.
We have no selfish motives or hidden ambitions. Our actions these last few days sprang
from our patriotic hearts, from our pure and
loyal love for our great motherland. We do not
"desire to plunge the world into chaos" [as has
been alleged], nor are we a "small handful" of
bad people with ulterior motives. All we want
is to do our best to push forward the process of
reform and democratization, to try to obtain
for the people the most practical benefits possible.
Citizens, our interests are now closely
bound together. We swear to stand with the
people to the death, to struggle to the very
end!
We ask for all the citizens of Beijing to give
us their support! We are one with the people!
Down with bureaucracy! Down with BU-
REAUCRATS!
Long live China! Long live the people!

—Beijing Aeronautics Institute Students'
Federation, April 24, 1989

—Please understand and trust us! Please extend your hands in support!

Posted at Beijing Aeronautics Institute

Proclamation of Ph.D. Students

1. Because at present universities throughout the country still lack a united organization,
we propose that [Beijing] students immediately
establish a telephone and telegram network,

with specified communication times and locations, with universities in each of the major cities in China; and that from May 4 on, students at universities throughout the country unify their actions, organizations, slogans, and objectives.

2. Because the student movement is currently still a "campus movement," and has yet to attain widespread understanding and support from all sectors of society, we propose that [Beijing] students: (1) draft and print large quantities of literature making clear our positions and the goals we are fighting for; (2) set up "democracy walls" outside the gates of their schools; and (3) form a large number of "special action groups" to distribute and post leaflets and organize public speeches at all train stations, theaters, hotels, and main commercial districts.

3. Because at present the student movement lacks powerful media of its own, we propose that: (1) the student autonomous committee at each university take over the school broadcasting station; (2) all universities publish and issue "student movement bulletins" of their own, which will facilitate communication among schools; and (3) all universities establish news release centers, hold on-the-spot press conferences, and report to the Chinese and foreign press, as well as to all sectors of society, the progress of the student movement.

4. Since during the student movement the personal safety and interests of the students have been seriously endangered, we propose that all universities join together to form a "lawyers' working group" that will immediately bring a lawsuit over: (1) certain distorted news reports regarding the "April 20th Incident" [in which students were beaten by police]; and (2) deliberate injury of students by certain police officers. This "lawyers' working group" should act to protect the legal rights of the students during the student movement.

5. Because the class boycotts at some schools are not doing well, and the students' actions are not unified, we propose that students: (1) reinforce the pickets at their universities and seal off classrooms; and (2) organize on-campus meetings for public speeches and reports [on student activities] in order to strengthen solidarity.

Long live the students!

Posted at People's University, April 24, 1989

After All, What Are We Fighting For?

. . . If we were to ignore the issue of freedom of speech and freedom of the press, all of our [other] goals would be nothing but wishful thinking. The government's distorted news reports and wanton slander, the [Beijing Municipality's] "Ten Articles" on public demonstrations, endless propaganda, and the reorganization of the Shanghai *World Economic Herald*—these are hardly isolated events. There is only one reason for all of them: the government will not allow the people to speak the truth. Recently, the Beijing Municipal Party Committee stated openly that it would put the [local] media under its control in order to turn around the government's present defensive situation. What a shameless warlord manner this is! It is obvious that media control is the only way they see for rescuing themselves: one after another, citizens are already moving to the other side. To win the hearts of the people, the government must conduct a thorough reform, but this is impossible for them to do at the present time. Therefore, the only recourse is to deceive and poison people's minds. The government fears most that students will take to the streets to distribute handbills, make speeches, and establish ties with workers and other citizens.

The government is making a last-ditch effort. Thus, we must focus on the critical point: taking the tools of public opinion presently controlled by them and making them the people's, for the people to use. . . . The downfall of many governments has occurred after they had lost control over the tools of public opinion, or, when prevailing public opinion was made known early on. The mass media has become the most effective weapon for people all over the world; unfortunately, up to the very present, we still cannot take advantage of it, and many people do not even appreciate its significance. This kind of misguidedness in our movement may very well lead to our defeat.

And after we are defeated, the government will use the media to retaliate.

At the end of 1986, while we were struggling to realize true democracy and freedom, rights granted us under the Constitution, the Beijing municipal government hastily adopted the "Ten Articles on Demonstrations." Its purpose was obvious: to restrict the freedom of citizens. Under the Ten Articles, all demonstrations must be registered in advance, and actual demonstration is not permitted until approval has been given by the authorities. This [set of regulations] is the object of universal ridicule! Freedom of demonstration and other rights are granted by the Constitution. But now they cannot be exercised until they are approved by some aristocrats. In addition, as long as these aristocrats think a demonstration "may have some adverse impact" [on social order, production, etc.], they can always withhold approval. What an idea, this "may have some adverse impact"! Someone's subjective mind (intent on protecting its own interests and privileges) sets an unchallengeable standard that determines whether the people can exercise their own rights! A sad fact this is indeed! . . .

It is said that the Law on the Press will be promulgated at the end of this year [1989]. Based on the current situation, can we imagine what kind of law governing the press this will be? The Ten Articles have taught us a lesson already. Are there any people who can guarantee that the new press law will not become the shackles of "freedom of the press"? . . . Let me ask: how much freedom for the press can such a regulation bring? Thinking about this is enough to send chills down one's spine.

It is not hard for all to comprehend that press reform is the most appropriate breakthrough point for political reform. Public opinion functions as both a constructive and supervisory force. It is not for no reason that Western nations call the public press the "fourth power [estate]." . . . Allowing people to speak the truth is the most fundamental feature of political reform. In the truth spoken by the people, we will be able to find an inexhaustible source of prosperity for our motherland and for the revitalization of our nation. . . . Let us unceasingly continue our struggle for this

objective until the people can truly speak frankly and without restraint!

An undergraduate student, May 1, 1989

Communist Party Members, Stand Up— An Appeal to All Party Members

At present, the patriotic Democracy Movement has entered an extremely tense stage: the hunger strike of several thousand classmates in Tiananmen has already entered its seventh day, yet the leaders of our government still have not given a definite reply to the reasonable demands of our classmates. As members of the Chinese Communist Party, we believe that the attitude of the government is not wise. It is mistaken. From April 15 on, we too have been participants in the patriotic Democracy Movement. We have seen how the erroneous judgment [and attitude] of the government regarding this patriotic Democracy Movement have severely damaged the image of the party and party members. We feel deeply grieved by this.

We very much cherish the designation of being members of the Communist party. We became members of the party for the cause of communism, which the Communist party pioneered. Although we only have a few years of party standing, the education we have received in the party has taught us the value of the title of "party member." At Zhazedong [the infamous prison of the Guomindang that was in Chongqing], Communist party members were courageous and dauntless in the face of cruel torture inflicted on them by the reactionary faction. Communist party members [have a tradition of] taking the lead. Lei Feng, who [always] served the people, was a Communist party member; Zhang Zhixin, who never wavered from the truth, was also a Communist party member. The honor of the Communist party for which the older generation traded their lives and blood has been sullied today by their [opposition to] democratization and [to the installation of a] rule of law. Since April 20, we have been under considerable pressure [to support the party line], so that we have only been able to join the ranks of the protestors in our individual capacity. When we think about our party oath, about the duties and responsibilities of a party member, speaking from our consciences, we can only feel ashamed when we face the broad mass of our classmates. What the true party member stands up for is the truth, not the personal "face" of some individual leaders. To [certain] individual government leaders who have the status of Communist party membership, we say: you are not true Communist party members; the image of the Communist party is not meant to be monopolized by a few individuals, but belongs to every one of us Communist party members.

We [now] appeal:

1. To protect the honor of the Communist party and its members, all party members must stand forth and unequivocally participate as a party member [rather than as an individual], and in the name of the school's party branch, in this patriotic Democracy Movement. The interest of the people is paramount.

2. At present the movement has already reached an extremely critical moment. Party members must lead the way by their own example; must assist the students' autonomous unions in schools in organizing classmates; must maintain cool heads; and must work to avoid any unnecessary harm to our classmates.

—*Graduate Students in the Class of 1986*
Materials Department;
All party Members in the party Branch
[of the Materials Department]

Posted at Beijing Science
and Technology University, May 26, 1989

100

DEFENDING CHINA'S SOCIALIST DEMOCRACY

The aftermath of the Tiananmen protests included not only arrests, trials, and sentencing of hundreds of participants, but also concerted efforts to reeducate those who had been attracted to the ideas espoused by the protesters. Political study was stepped up at universities, research institutes, and other cultural organs, and articles appeared in the press designed to restore confidence in the superiority of China's political system. The following article appeared in People's Daily *in March 1990. It was titled, "Bourgeois and Socialist Democracies Compared."*

A small number of people who obstinately stick to bourgeois liberalization have made major efforts to advocate bourgeois democracy and distort China's socialist democracy in an evil attempt to overthrow the CPC leadership and sabotage the socialist People's Republic of China. In their minds, the capitalist system is more democratic than the socialist system instead of the other way round, and only with the establishment of the capitalist system can there be genuine democracy. These bourgeois liberal fallacies must be exposed and criticized. . . .

In a class society, democracy bears a class nature. Since mankind entered class society, there has never been equality between the ruling class and the classes that are ruled, or in the distribution of rights. Democracy is equal power distribution in the possessing class. The classes that are ruled can only obtain a part of democratic rights that serve the power distribution in the ruling class. In this sense, all forms of freedom, democ-

racy, and human rights are abstract and practiced on conditions that the fundamental interests of the possessing class should be protected or left unharmed. This is class democracy, class freedom, and class human rights.

A small number of people who obstinately hold to bourgeois liberalization, including Fang Lizhi and Wang Ruowang, have made energetic efforts to beautify American democracy. They asserted that this democracy "is genuine democracy for the entire people." In their opinions, exploitation of the majority by the capital-possessing minority has been over long ago. They said Marx wished to proletarianize the capitalists and turn them into self-supporting laborers, but Western society has capitalized the proletarians. Some Americans in power have also asserted that "America is the beacon of the world."

Is it true that the American bourgeoisie are so kind-hearted, "do not exploit," "do not exercise dictatorship," and have become the "beacon of

501

world democracy"? Is it true that the American proletarians have mixed with the bosses of financial groups, enjoy the right of equal distribution and possession, and have equal democratic rights? The answer is negative.

In the present-day world, capital is still characterized by exploitation, oppression, and dictator. This is a historical definition provided for capital by the law governing human history. Similarly, the United States, where "capitalists are the personalization of capital," cannot exclude itself from this definition.

In the United States capitalists still dominate everything. A look at the nature of American democracy will make it easy to draw a conclusion that corresponds to historical facts.

First, U.S. democratic elections are actually the trials of capital and wealth.

As everyone is aware, U.S. elections are the "elections of money." Each U.S. presidential election costs about $1 billion. During their presidential campaign, Reagan and Carter spent $45 million each. Even the expenditures for the election of a senator are as high as $500,000. At least $500,000 to $600,000 are required for the election of a state senator. Undoubtedly, only the rich can afford such huge expenditures, whereas the American workers and other laborers, even the middle class, do not dare to inquire about the elections. Statistics suggest that the per capita assets of U.S. senators amount to $5 million, and seventeen percent of them have assets worth over $5 million. No wonder the American working people call the U.S. Congress the "club of the rich." According to relevant statistics compiled by the U.S. authorities, people in power in the United States control fifty percent of the assets in the industrial, transportation, and telecommunications field, in public enterprises, and in banks, but these people account for only three percent of the country's population. Since the end of World War II, nine U.S. presidents and vice-presidents have been either members of monopoly capital groups or supported by huge financial organizations; they are representatives of these organizations.

True, the American people do enjoy universal suffrage at present. Again, the government waived restrictions on the property of voters and on women and black people. Democratic as all this looks, it cannot prove that the democracy practiced in the United States is no sham. I should like to ask: What benefits can laborers, women, and black people gain from such a universal direct election, which is held under the influence of the "contest of property and capital"? In the history of the United States, which worker has been elected as president? How many workers have been elected as congressmen or congresswomen? . . .

With regard to human rights, the world monopoly capital has also made every possible endeavor to advertise to the whole world that it is the one that truly "respects" and "safeguards" human rights. Nonetheless, out of its own class interests, the monopoly capital has not only trampled upon human rights at home but has also frequently acted as the world military police by sending troops to directly interfere with the internal affairs of other countries and practice power politics in the whole world. For instance, the United States recently invaded Panama and carried out wanton and indiscriminate bombings and killings in Panama. The United States seriously violated basic norms governing international relations. Comrade Deng Xiaoping once laid bare the true nature of the bourgeois human rights. Comrade Deng Xiaoping sharply pointed out: "What are human rights? How many people now enjoy human rights? Do human rights mean the rights of the majority of the people or the rights of the minority of the people or the rights of the people of the whole country? The so called human rights as advocated by the Western countries fundamentally differ from the human rights we are talking about. On this question, our views do differ." Andrew Young, former U.S. ambassador to the United Nations, once said: In the United States, "a lot of people have been imprisoned because they are poor, not because they are bad." In so saying, Andrew Young gave a true picture of the human rights situation in the United States.

THE SOCIALIST DEMOCRACY IS THE PEOPLE'S DEMOCRACY ENJOYED BY THE MAJORITY OF THE PEOPLE

The socialist democracy means the democratic rights enjoyed by the broad masses of the workers, peasants, intellectuals, and all the people who love their socialist motherland.

The nature of the socialist democracy is that people act as the masters of their country. The socialist state system is the state system under which laborers and citizens are allowed to manage the state, administer the society, and act as the masters of their country in the history of mankind for the first time. It is because of this reason that the socialist country is the most advanced democratic country in the history of mankind. "The proletarian democracy is a million times more democratic than any types of bourgeois democracy" (*Selected Works of Lenin*, Volume 3, page 634).

During the period when turmoil and the counterrevolutionary rebellion broke out in Beijing, a handful of people who stubbornly adhered to the stand of bourgeois liberalization flaunted the banner of "Striving for Democracy" in an attempt to confuse and poison people's minds. These people denounce our country as a despotic state in which there is no democracy to speak of. This is an out-and-out distortion of the realities in our country. What is true is that since the founding of the New China, the CPC and the People's Government have made unremitting efforts to build the socialist democracy in China. Although China's socialist democratic system is still far from perfect, China has after all established a comprehensive democratic system under which people can participate in the administration and management of the state.

The PRC Constitution stipulates in explicit terms that all powers in the People's Republic of China belong to the people. The organs through which people exercise state power in a unified way are the National People's Congress and the local people's congresses at various levels. The National People's Congress is the supreme state organ which formulates and ratifies the constitution and the laws, elects and removes from office the state president, vice-president, elects the Central Military Commission, elects the president of the Supreme People's Court and the procurator general of the Supreme People's Procuratorate, and, in accordance with the relevant procedures, appoints the premier and vice-premier of the State Council, the state councilors, and ministers, and examines and ratifies the national economic and social development plans, the state budget, and so on. This is the basic socialist democratic system instituted in our country.

The CPC-led Multiparty Cooperation and Political Consultation System has remained an important channel for the evolution of socialist democracy in China. The CPPCC has remained an important political and organizational form through which the CPC-led Multiparty Cooperation and Political Consultation System has been realized in China. Over the past few decades, the CPPCC committees at all levels, the various democratic parties, people's organizations, and public figures of all nationalities and all walks of life have played an important role in making China's state decision-making process more scientific and more democratic and in promoting the building of socialist modernization in China. . . .

There is no denying the fact that our country is still at the initial stage of socialism and our country's socialist people's democratic system and socialist legal system are still in a historical process of establishment, improvement, development, and perfection. Nevertheless, it is also an undeniable basic fact that the Chinese people have already become the masters of their country and are currently enjoying wide-ranging and real democratic rights. Take the citizens' right to vote, for example; our country instituted the universal suffrage system as early as 1953. Since then, the Chinese people have been able to elect their own deputies, hold people's congresses at all levels, form people's governments at all levels, and exercise the state power. Since 1979, China has several times revised her electoral law and instituted the system under which the electorate can directly elect their deputies to the people's congresses at county and township levels. The revised PRC "Electoral Law" stipulates that apart from the fact that political parties or people's organizations can either jointly or individually nominate candidates for the people's congress elections held at various levels, the voters or the deputies can also jointly nominate candidates for the people's congress elections held at various levels. In the revised "Electoral Law," the election system under which equal numbers of candidates run for an equal number of deputy seats has been substituted with the election system under which more candidates run for fewer seats, thus gradually enlarging the citizens' right to vote.

Given the basic realities in China, the building of socialist democracy in China can only be a gradual and accumulated process. Since the founding of the PRC, we have done a lot of work, made much headway, and achieved marked results in building the people's democratic system. However, as a comprehensive system, our country's people's democratic system has yet to be fur-

ther developed and perfected. In his speech addressed to a Beijing rally in celebration of the fortieth anniversary of the founding the PRC, comrade Jiang Zemin pointed out that it is necessary to make continued efforts to improve and perfect our country's people's congress system and CPC-led Multiparty Cooperation and Political Consultation System, establish and perfect a democratic decision-making and supervision procedure and system, expand the existing links and channels of dialogue between the CPC and the broad masses of the people, raise the citizens' consciousness in participation in the political and state affairs, and guarantee the full realization of both the will and the interests of the broad masses of the people in the state life and social life. This is the orientation for building socialist democracy in our country at the current stage. In this analysis, those who blindly worship the democratic system of the Western countries and try to transplant the parliamentary system and multiparty system of the Western countries to China are doomed to failure.

GLOSSARY

Amitabha Buddhism. The school of Buddhism that stressed salvation in the Pure Land, a paradise ruled over by the Amitabha Buddha. While on earth the Amitabha Buddha had promised entry into his paradise to those who sincerely called on his name.

Analects (*Lunyu*). The record of the sayings of Confucius, one of the Thirteen Classics. See "Confucian Teachings," selection 6.

bodhisattva. A being who has reached the point at which enlightenment or Buddhahood can be achieved but decides to stay in the world to help others achieve salvation.

Book of Changes (*Yijing*). One of the Five Classics, dating from the Zhou dynasty. A divination manual. See "Hexagrams," selection 3.

Book of Documents (*Shujing*). A collection of purported speeches, pronouncements, and court debates dating from the Zhou dynasty. One of the Five Classics. See "The Metal Bound Box," selection 2.

Book of Rites (*Liji*). A collection of late Zhou and early Han texts on ritual, government, and ethics. One of the Five Classics.

Book of Songs (*Shijing*). A collection of 305 poems, dating from the Zhou dynasty which became one of the Five Classics. See "Songs and Poems," selection 4.

Boxer Rebellion (1900). Anti-foreign uprising in northeast China. The Boxers were a xenophobic, mystic society, which sought to drive the foreigners from China and to restore the glory of the Qing dynasty. In the summer of 1900 they besieged the foreign legations' compound in Beijing, but the siege was broken by an international relief force and the rebellion suppressed.

Buddha. Means "the Enlightened." Buddhahood may be claimed by anyone who has achieved enlightenment, but "the Buddha" usually refers to the Prince Siddhartha of the Guatama clan (ca. 563–483 B.C.)

in northern India. According to tradition, he tried and rejected first a life of luxury and then a life of poverty and in 528 B.C. achieved enlightenment and began to teach. See "Buddhist Doctrines and Practices," selection 22.

cash. A copper coin, the smallest unit of currency.

catty. Unit of weight, equal to about 1.3 pounds or .6 kilograms.

Cheng brothers. Cheng Hao (1032–1085) and Cheng Yi (1033–1107). Early neo-Confucian philosophers who helped develop the metaphysical concepts of *li* ("principle") and *qi* ("material force").

concubines. Women of lower legal and social status than wives, who were, however, fully recognized mates. They were brought in to the man's home in part to produce heirs and their children were fully legitimate. See "Concubines," selection 55.

Confucius (traditional dates 551–479 B.C.). Classical philosopher, one of the most influential thinkers in Chinese history. He was born in the state of Lu (in modern Shandong) and assumed the life of the itinerant scholar-official, trying to influence the policies of the great lords of the various classical states. Although he never met with great success in the political sphere, he propagated a philosophy of life that was to be highly influential throughout subsequent Chinese history. See "Confucian Teachings," selection 6.

Cultural Revolution. A political campaign launched by Mao Zedong in 1966 as the "Great Proletarian Cultural Revolution," ostensibly to combat elitism and revisionism. It led to the mobilization of Red Guards, the closing of schools, the destruction of many monuments, and the purging of thousands of cadres. The most intense struggles occurred in the years 1966–1969, but the aftereffects lasted until Mao died in 1976. See "Red Guards," selection 93.

Daoism. A classical school of philosophy identified

with Laozi (traditional dates 604–521 B.C.) and Zhuangai (369–286 B.C.). Main strand of thought is the search for harmony with the Dao ("Way"), which is total, natural, spontaneous, nameless, and eternal. Everything that exists or happens does so because of the Dao. Daoists stress the relativity of values and the smallness of human endeavors within the working of the universe. The term popular or religious Daoism is used for the indigenous religion of the Chinese which incorporated ancient beliefs in a wide variety of ghosts, spirits, and demons with belief in immortals and the divinity of Daoist sages. After Buddhism was introduced to China, the Daoist religion developed an elaborate system of clergy and temples. See "Daoist Teachings," selection 7 and "Precepts of the Perfect Truth Daoist Sect," selection 34.

Duke of Zhou. Early statesman and philosopher who served as regent for his royal nephew the second Zhou King. Admired by Confucius, the Duke of Zhou is credited with consolidating the power of the newly founded dynasty.

examination system. The system of recruiting men for office through written and oral examinations of candidates. Most highly developed in the Song and subsequent dynasties.

filial piety. Obedience, respect, and caring for one's parents and grandparents, or in the case of married daughters, parents-in-law.

Five Agents. A component of Chinese cosmological correlative thinking developed during the late classical period. The Five Agents are wood, fire, earth, metal, and water. They are in constant interaction, overtaking and suppressing each other in a fixed progression. Illness, the change of seasons, the change of weather, and even the change of dynasties were explained in terms of these agents.

Five Classics. The *Book of Songs*, the *Book of Documents*, the *Book of Changes*, the *Spring and Autumn Annals*, and the *Book of Rites*. All were revered by the Confucians as preserving the most ancient truths.

Gang of Four. Term for four militant leaders of the Cultural Revolution officially blamed for its excesses. Their leader was Jiang Qing, Mao's wife. The others were Zhang Chunquiao, Wang Hongwen, and Yao Wenyuan.

geomancy. The "science" of locating favorable sites for houses, graves, and so on, according to the vital forces and "veins" of the earth.

gongsheng. "Senior student." A middle-level degree holder, sometimes eligible to hold office.

governor. Head of a province, the largest subdivision of the empire.

Guanyin. A bodhisattva (Buddha-to-be) noted for compassion. Usually conceived of as a female.

Guomindang. The political party founded in 1912 by Sun Yatsen and later led by Jiang Jieshi. The Guomindang or Nationalist party enjoyed early success but was plagued with defections and shifting alliances. When the People's Republic of China was officially established in Beijing in 1949, the Guomindang reestablished itself in Taiwan where it continues to exist as the ruling party of the Republic of China.

hexagrams. Graphs of six lines, some broken, some unbroken. Each of the sixty-four possible hexagrams had a name and the *Book of Changes* offered interpretations of its meaning. See "Hexagrams," selection 3.

International Settlement. Area of Shanghai in which foreigners enjoyed many privileges of self-government and immunity from Chinese law (extra-territoriality). The Shanghai International Settlement became extremely important both as a point of foreign influence and trade in China and as a refuge for Chinese seeking to avoid their own country's law.

Jiang Jieshi (1888–1975). Military and political leader of the Nationalist (Guomindang) party after the death of Sun Yatsen. After leading the Northern Expedition, he set up a Nationalistic government in 1928 and fought against warlords, the Japanese, and the Communists for the control of China for the next twenty years. President of the Guomindang government on Taiwan from 1949 until his death twenty-six years later.

Jie (traditional r. 1818–1766 B.C.). Last ruler of the legendary Xia dynasty whose evil ways were said to have caused the downfall of that dynasty.

jinshi. "Presented scholar." Beginning as one of a number of examination degrees offered during the Sui and Tang dynasties, from the Song onwards it was the highest and most prestigious degree. During the Ming and Qing dynasties candidates who had passed the *juren* or provincial level examination could take the examination for the *jinshi*, offered every third year in the capital. Those who became *jinshi* could normally expect to receive an official appointment, although delays sometimes amounted to years.

Jurchen. A non-Han people, probably related to the later Manchus, who overthrew the Khitans to establish the Jin dynasty (1115–1234). The Jurchens were conquered in turn by the Mongols who established the Yuan dynasty in 1279.

juren. "Recommended man." A provincial-level degree-holder eligible to hold office and take the capital examination.

Kangxi Emperor (1662–1722). The second and probably the greatest of the Qing emperors. He strove to reconcile the Manchu conquerors and their Chinese subjects. The final military conquest of all China by the Manchus was achieved under him.

karma. An Indian belief that became widespread in China through Buddhism. Through karma, all actions, good or bad, bring reward or retribution in this life or a subsequent one.

kowtow. "To knock the head," a ceremony of one or more kneelings or bowings with the head striking the floor. The kowtow was performed as a sign of respect for one's superiors, especially for the emperor and for the elders and ancestors of one's family.

Laozi (traditional dates 604–531 B.C.). According to tradition, the author of the text of the same name and thus a founder of Daoism as a school of philosophy. See "Daoist Teachings," selection 7.

Legalism. Classical philosophical school and important strand in Chinese intellectual history. The Legalists held that the law should be strict and universal in its application. Rather than relying on education and the good will of men in governing the state, the Legalists looked to bureaucratic regulations and rewards and punishments. Legalism became the official ideology of the Qin dynasty (221–206 B.C.). See "Legalist Teachings," selection 8.

li. A unit of length equal to about 1/3 of a mile.

Long March. Heroic march of the Communist Party and Red Army from their besieged headquarters in Kiangsi province to a new base in Yan'an, taking over two years and covering 6000 miles.

magistrate. Head of a county, the lowest unit of local government staffed by representatives of the central government.

Manchus. A tribe of the Jurchen group, originally from the northeast part of present-day China. By the mid-sixteenth century, they were developing state institutions, and in 1644 they invaded China and established the Qing dynasty, which lasted to 1911.

Mandate of Heaven. The theory that an emperor lacking in virtue has forfeited his right to the throne and that the mandate is then awarded by Heaven to the conqueror who establishes the next dynasty.

May Fourth Movement. Large-scale protest movement of students and intellectuals, begun in Beijing on May 4, 1919 over the agreements at Versailles giving the old German concession in Shandong province not to China but to Japan. In a broader sense the May Fourth Movement came to represent a general movement among educated Chinese to chart new courses for China's development, especially in the intellectual and cultural sphere. See "The Spirit of the May Fourth Movement," selection 77.

Mencius (Mengzi, ca. 372–289 B.C.). Classical philosopher and successor to Confucius. Like Confucius, his attempts to influence the rulers of his time were largely unsuccessful, but his speeches (preserved in the *Mencius*) charted new direction in Confucianism. See "Confucian Teachings," selection 6.

Mongols. Generic term for a number of Inner Asian tribes that were united by Chinggis Khan in 1206. Through a series of rapid military conquests, they established a great Eurasian empire. China was subjugated by the Mongols in stages, completed by Khublai Khan in 1279. After the collapse of their dynasty in China (the Yuan), the Mongols proved a military threat to China for several centuries but were never able to reassert their supremacy.

mu. Unit of area, equal to about .16 acres or 600 square meters.

neo-Confucianism. The form of Confucianism dominant in the Sung dynasty (960–1279) and later. See "Zhu Xi's Conversations with His Disciples," selection 40, and "Two Philosophers," selection 57.

picul. Unit of weight, equal to about 133 pounds or 60 kilograms.

prefect. Head of a prefecture, the unit above a county and below a circuit or province.

Pure Land. The paradise of the Amitabha Buddhists.

qi. Vital energy, material force, ether, breath. A term used both in philosophy and in scientific thinking.

Qianlong Emperor (r. 1736–1795). Fourth Qing Emperor who presided over the dynasty at the height of its power. While an able administrator and skillful leader in war, he is also known as a connoisseur of literature, painting, porcelain, and other arts.

runner. An underling of a magistrate or prefect who carried messages, arrested criminals, collected taxes, and performed other assorted duties.

shengyuan. Government student. A lower-level degree holder eligible to take the provincial level examination.

Shun (legendary reign ca. 2255–2206 B.C.). One of the legendary sage emperors of the golden age of antiquity. He was held up as an example of a self-made man of humble origin who achieved greatness as a wise ruler.

string of cash. A unit of currency, nominally a thousand copper coins strung through the holes in their centers, but generally short a hundred or more cash.

Sun Yatsen (1866–1925). Leader of the Chinese republican revolution and founder of the Nationalist party. Educated in medicine in Hong Kong, he became an anti-Manchu activist and helped to overthrow the Qing dynasty.

tael. An ingot of silver weighing an ounce, regularly used as money in Ming and Qing times.

Taiping Rebellion (1850–1864). Huge upheaval in south and central China during the mid-nineteenth century, led by the mentally unbalanced Hong Xiuquan. Taiping ideology incorporated elements of Christianity, utopian Confucianism, and mystical Daoism.

Tatars. See MONGOLS.

The Way (Dao). An important philosophical term in both Confucianism and Daoism. In both it referred to the cosmic order, but in Confucianism this was a human-centered moral order, in Daoism, the natural order.

Thirteen Classics. Besides the Five Classics, the Thirteen Classics also included the *Book of Etiquette and Ritual*, the *Rituals of the Zhou*, the *Guliang*, *Gongyang*, and *Zuo* commentaries to the *Spring and Autumn Annals*, the *Analects*, the *Mencius*, the *Erya*, and the *Classic of Filial Piety*. This list of the classics gained favor in the Song dynasty.

Three Principles of the People. The basis of Guomindang ideology, formulated by Sun Yatsen. They are nationalism, democracy, and the people's livelihood.

Warring States Period (484–221 B.C.). The last of the three periods of the Zhou dynasty characterized by serious fighting among the feudal states leading to the extinction of the dynasty and the rise of Qin.

Xiongnu. A nomadic people of the steppes north of China who frequently invaded during the Han dynasty. The Xiongnu are often identified with the Huns who invaded the Roman Empire in the fifth century A.D.

yamen. The headquarters of a local official. The yamen was a walled area that contained buildings for the conduct of official business and also served as the residence for the official and his immediate family and staff.

Yan'an. A city in Shaanxi province which became Mao's headquarters shortly after the completion of the Long March and remained so during World War II.

Yellow Emperor. One of the ancient mythical culture heroes. Associated with Daoism and medicine.

Yin and Yang. Components of Chinese cosmological thinking. Yin is the female, or passive principle, Yang the male, or assertive one. These are complementary principles. Although in nature one rises as the other wanes, no creature, force, or object is purely composed of one in the absence of the other.

Zhu Xi (1130–1200). One of the greatest of the neo-Confucian philosophers and author of many commentaries on the Confucian classics. His configuration of Confucianism became the official orthodoxy during the Ming (1368–1644) and Qing (1644–1911) periods. See "Zhu Xi's Conversations with His Disciples," selection 40.

Zhuangzi (369–286 B.C.). Traditionally considered to be the second of the great classical Daoist philosophers after Laozi. His writings, consisting of philosophical essays and humorous though pointed anecdotes, have been preserved in a book called the *Zhuangzi*. See "Daoist Teachings," selection 7.

Zuo Chronicle. One of the Thirteen Classics. A historical account presented as a commentary to the *Spring and Autumn Annals*. See "The Battle Between Jin and Chu," selection 5.

SUGGESTIONS FOR FURTHER READING

Books in English about China and Chinese civilization now number in the thousands with especially good coverage of the modern period. There are both an extensive monographic literature and many fine books aimed at a general audience. The following suggestions are limited to widely available books, especially paperbacks, and to the topics covered in this sourcebook.

Historical Overviews

Elvin, Mark. *The Pattern of the Chinese Past*. Stanford: Stanford University Press, 1973.

Fairbank, John F. *China: A New History*. Cambridge, Mass.: Harvard University Press, 1992.

Fairbank, John K., and Edwin O. Reischauer. *China: Tradition and Transformation*. Rev. ed. Boston: Houghton Mifflin, 1989.

Gernet, Jacques. *A History of Chinese Civilization*. Cambridge, Mass.: Cambridge University Press, 1989.

Hucker, Charles O. *China's Imperial Past: An Introduction to Chinese History and Culture*. Stanford: Stanford University Press, 1975.

Loewe, Michael. *The Pride That Was China*, Sidgwick and Jackson Great Civilization Series. New York: St. Martin's Press, 1990.

Meisner, Maurice. *Mao's China and After: A History of the People's Republic*. New York: Free Press, 1986.

Ropp, Paul S., ed. *Heritage of China: Contemporary Perspectives on Chinese Civilization*. Berkeley: University of California Press, 1990.

Schirokaur, Conrad. *A Brief History of Chinese Civilization*. New York: Harcourt Brace Jovanovich, 1991.

Sheridan, James E. *China in Disintegration: The Republican Era in Chinese History, 1912–1949*. New York: Free Press, 1975.

Spence, Jonathan D. *The Search for Modern China*. New York: W. W. Norton, 1990.

Twitchett, Denis, and John K. Fairbank, eds. *Cambridge History of China*. Cambridge, Mass.: Cambridge University Press, 1978–.

Wakeman, Frederic, Jr. *The Fall of Imperial China*. New York: Free Press, 1975.

Religion, Cosmology, and Popular Culture

Ahern, Emily M. *The Cult of the Dead in a Chinese Village*. Stanford: Stanford University Press, 1973.

Brokaw, Cynthia J. *The Ledgers of Merit and Demerit: Social Change and Moral Order in Later Imperial China*. Princeton: Princeton University Press, 1991.

Chang, K. C. *Art, Myth, and Ritual: The Path to Political Authority in Ancient China*. Cambridge, Mass.: Harvard University Press, 1983.

Ch'en, Kenneth K. S. *The Chinese Transformation of Buddhism*. Princeton: Princeton University Press, 1973.

Eberhard, Wolfram. *Guilt and Sin in Traditional China*. Berkeley: University of California Press, 1967.

Hansen, Valerie. *Changing Gods in Medieval China,*

1127–1276. Princeton: Princeton University Press, 1990.

Henderson, John B. *The Development and Decline of Chinese Cosmology.* New York: Columbia University Press, 1984.

Johnson, David, Andrew J. Nathan, and Evelyn S. Rawski, eds. *Popular Culture in Later Imperial China.* Berkeley: University of California Press, 1985.

Jordan, David K. *Gods, Ghosts, and Ancestors: The Folk Religion of a Taiwanese Village.* Berkeley: University of California Press, 1972.

Kaltenmark, Max. *Lao Tzu and Taoism.* Stanford: Stanford University Press, 1969.

Kuhn, Philip A. *Soul Stealers: The Chinese Sorcery Scare of 1768.* Cambridge, Mass.: Harvard University Press, 1990.

Loewe, Michael. *Chinese Ideas of Life and Death: Faith, Myth and Reason in the Han Period (202 B.C.–A.D. 220).* London: George Allen and Unwin, 1982.

Naquin, Susan, and Chün-fang Yü, eds. *Pilgrims and Sacred Sites in China.* Berkeley: University of California Press, 1992.

Overmyer, Daniel L. *Folk Buddhist Religion: Dissenting Sects in Late Traditional China.* Cambridge, Mass.: Harvard University Press, 1976.

———. *Religions of China: The World as a Living System.* New York: Harper and Row, 1986.

Smith, Richard J. *Fortune-Tellers and Philosophers: Divination in Traditional Chinese Society.* Boulder: Westview Press, 1991.

Teiser, Stephen F. *The Ghost Festival in Medieval China.* Princeton: Princeton University Press, 1988.

Thompson, Laurence G. *Chinese Religion: An Introduction.* 2d ed. Encino, Cal.: Dickenson Publishing, 1975.

Watson, James L., and Evelyn S. Rawski, eds. *Death Rituals in Late Imperial and Modern China.* Berkeley: University of California Press, 1988.

Weller, Robert P. *Unities and Diversities in Chinese Religion.* Seattle: University of Washington Press, 1987.

Wolf, Arthur P., ed. *Religion and Ritual in Chinese Society.* Stanford: Stanford University Press, 1974.

Wright, Arthur F. *Buddhism in Chinese History.* Stanford: Stanford University Press, 1959.

Yang, C. K. *Religion in Chinese Society: A Study of Contemporary Social Functions of Religion and Some of Their Historical Factors.* Berkeley: University of California Press, 1970.

Confucianism and Philosophy

Black, Alison Harley. *Man and Nature in the Philosophy of Wang Fu-chih.* Seattle: University of Washington Press, 1989.

Bol, Peter K. *"This Culture of Ours" Intellectual Transitions in T'ang and Sung China.* Stanford: Stanford University Press, 1992.

deBary, Wm. Theodore, ed. *Self and Society in Ming Thought.* New York: Columbia University Press, 1970.

———, and John W. Chaffee, eds. *Neo-Confucian Education: The Formative Stage.* Berkeley: University of California Press, 1989.

Ebrey, Patricia Buckley. *Confucianism and Family Rituals in Imperial China: A Social History of Writing About Rites.* Princeton: Princeton University Press, 1991.

Elman, Benjamin A. *From Philosophy to Philology: Intellectual and Social Aspects of Change in Late Imperial China.* Cambridge, Mass.: Council on East Asian Studies, Harvard University, 1984.

Fingarette, Herbert. *Confucius—the Secular as Sacred.* New York: Harper and Row, 1972.

Fung Yu-lan. *A History of Chinese Philosophy,* 2 vols., trans. Derk Bodde. Princeton: Princeton University Press, 1952.

Graham, A. C. *Disputes of the Tao.* LaSalle, Ill.: Open Court, 1989.

Hall, David L., and Roger T. Ames. *Thinking Through Confucius.* Albany: State University of New York Press, 1987.

Hsiao, Kung-chuan. *A History of Chinese Political Thought, Vol. One: From the Beginning to the Sixth Century A.D.,* trans. F. W. Mote. Princeton: Princeton University Press, 1979.

Lewis, Mark Edward. *Sanctioned Violence in Early China.* Albany: State University of New York Press, 1990.

Metzger, Thomas A. *Escape from Predicament: Neo-Confucianism and China's Evolving Political Culture.* New York: Columbia University Press, 1977.

Mote, Frederick W. *Intellectual Foundations of China.* New York: Alfred A. Knopf, 1971.

Nivison, David S., and Arthur F. Wright, eds. *Confucianism in Action.* Stanford: Stanford University Press, 1959.

Schwartz, Benjamin I. *The World of Thought in Ancient China.* Cambridge, Mass.: Harvard University Press, 1985.

Tu Wei-ming. *Confucian Thought: Selfhood as Creative Transformation.* Albany: State University of New York Press, 1985.

Weber, Max. *The Religion of China: Confucianism and Taoism.* New York: Free Press, 1968.

Wright, Arthur F., ed. *The Confucian Persuasion.* Stanford: Stanford University Press, 1960.

———, and Denis Twitchett, eds. *Confucian Personalities.* Stanford: Stanford University Press, 1960.

Wu, Pei-yi. *The Confucian's Progress: Autobiographical Writings in Traditional China.* Princeton: Princeton University Press, 1990.

Family, Kinship, and Women

Baker, Hugh D. R. *Chinese Family and Kinship.* New York: Columbia University Press, 1979.

Ebrey, Patricia Buckley. *Family and Property in Sung China: Yüan Ts'ai's Precepts for Social Life.* Princeton: Princeton University Press, 1984.

———, and James L. Watson, eds. *Kinship Organization in Imperial China, 1000–1940,* Berkeley: University of California Press, 1986.

Freedman, Maurice. *Lineage Organization in Southeastern China.* London: Atheone Press, 1958.

———, ed. *Family and Kinship in Chinese Society.* Stanford: Stanford University Press, 1970.

Hsu, Francis L. K. *Under the Ancestor's Shadow: Kinship, Personality and Social Mobility in China.* 2d ed. Stanford: Stanford University Press, 1971.

Pruit, Ida, from the story told her by Ning Lao T'ai-t'ai. *A Daughter of Han: The Autobiography of a Chinese Working Woman.* Stanford: Stanford University Press, 1967 (originally published 1945).

Waltner, Ann. *Getting an Heir: Adoption and the Construction of Kinship in Late Imperial China.* Honolulu: University of Hawaii Press, 1990.

Watson, Rubie S., and Patricia Buckley Ebrey, eds. *Marriage and Inequality in Chinese Society.* Berkeley: University of California Press, 1991.

Wolf, Arthur P., and Chieh-shan Huang. *Marriage and Adoption in China, 1845–1945.* Stanford: Stanford University Press, 1980.

Wolf, Margery. *Women and the Family in Rural Taiwan.* Stanford: Stanford University Press, 1972.

Wolf, Margery, and Witke, Roxane, eds. *Women in Chinese Society.* Stanford: Stanford University Press, 1975.

Traditional Social and Economic Organization

Chesneaux, Jean, ed. *Popular Movements and Secret Societies in China, 1840–1950.* Stanford: Stanford University Press, 1972.

Eastman, Lloyd E. *Family, Fields, and Ancestors: Constancy and Change in China's Social and Economic History, 1550–1949.* New York: Oxford University Press, 1988.

Fei, Hsiao-tung, and Chang Chih-i. *Earthbound China: A Study of Rural Economy in Yunnan.* Chicago: University of Chicago Press, 1945.

Gamble, Sidney D. *Ting Hsien: A North China Rural Community.* New York: Institute of Pacific Relations, 1954.

Huang, Philip C. C. *The Peasant Economy and Social Change in North China.* Stanford: Stanford University Press, 1985.

———. *The Peasant Family and Rural Development in the Yangzi Delta, 1350–1988.* Stanford: Stanford University Press, 1990.

Kuhn, Philip A. *Rebellion and Its Enemies in Late Imperial China: Militarization and Social Structure, 1796–1864.* Cambridge, Mass.: Harvard University Press, 1970.

Meskill, Johanna Menzel. *A Chinese Pioneer Family: The Lins of Wu-feng, Taiwan, 1729–1895.* Princeton: Princeton University Press, 1978.

Myers, Ramon H. *The Chinese Peasant Economy: Agricultural Development in Hopei and Shantung, 1890–1949.* Cambridge, Mass.: Harvard University Press, 1970.

Naquin, Susan. *Millenarian Rebellion in China: The Eight Trigrams Uprising of 1813.* New Haven: Yale University Press, 1976.

———, and Evelyn S. Rawski. *Chinese Society in the Eighteenth Century.* New Haven: Yale University Press, 1987.

Perkins, Dwight H. *Agricultural Development in China, 1368–1968.* Chicago: Aldine, 1969.

Rawski, Evelyn Sakakida. *Education and Popular Literacy in Ch'ing China.* Ann Arbor: University of Michigan Press, 1978.

Rowe, William T. *Hankow: Commerce and Society in a Chinese City, 1796–1889.* Stanford: Stanford University Press, 1984.

———. *Hankow: Conflict and Community in a Chinese City, 1796–1895.* Stanford: Stanford University Press, 1989.

Skinner, G. William, ed. *The City in Late Tradi-*

tional China. Stanford: Stanford University Press, 1977.

Yang, Martin C. A *Chinese Village: Taitou, Shantung Province*. New York: Columbia University Press, 1945.

Traditional Elites

Beattie, Hilary J. *Land and Lineage in China: A Study of T'ung-Ch'eng County, Anhwei, in the Ming and Ch'ing Dyrnsties*. Cambridge, Mass.: Cambridge University Press, 1979.

Chaffee, John W. *The Thorny Gates of Learning in Sung China: A Social History of Examinations*. Cambridge: Cambridge University Press, 1985.

Chang, Chung-li. *The Chinese Gentry: Studies on Their Role in Nineteenth-Century Chinese Society*. Seattle: University of Washington Press, 1955.

Dardess, John W. *Confucianism and Autocracy: Professional Elites in the Founding of the Ming Dynasty*. Berkeley: University of California Press, 1983.

Ebrey, Patricia Buckley. *The Aristocratic Families of Early Imperial China: A Case Study of the Po-ling Ts'ui Family*. Cambridge: Cambridge University Press, 1978.

Fei, Hsiao-t'ung. *China's Gentry: Essays in Rural-Urban Relations*. Chicago: University of Chicago Press, 1953.

Ho, Ping-ti. *The Ladder of Success in Imperial China: Aspects of Social Mobility, 1368–1911*. New York: John Wiley, 1964 (originally published 1962).

Hung, William. *Tu Fu: China's Greatest Poet*. Cambridge, Mass.: Harvard University Press, 1952.

Hymes, Robert P. *Statesman and Gentlemen: The Elite of Fu-chou, Chiang-hsi in Northern and Southern Sung*. Cambridge: Cambridge University Press, 1986.

Liu, James T. C. *Ou-yang Hsiu: An Eleventh-Century Neo-Confucianist*. Stanford: Stanford University Press, 1967.

Waley, Arthur. *The Life and Times of Po Chu-i, 772–846 A.D.*. London: George Allen & Unwin, 1949.

———. *Yuan Mei, Eighteenth Century Chinese Poet*. New York: Grove Press, 1956.

Traditional Government

Bodde, Derk, and Clarence Morris. *Law in Imperial China, Exemplfied by 190 Ch'ing Dynasty Cases,*

with Historical, Social, and Juridical Commentaries. Cambridge, Mass.: Harvard University Press, 1967.

Ch'u, T'ung-tsu. *Law and Society in Traditional China*. Paris: Mouton, 1961.

———. *Local Government in China Under the Ch'ing*. Stanford: Stanford University Press, 1962.

Crossley, Pamela Kyle. *Orphan Warriors: Three Manchu Generations and the End of the Qing World*. Princeton: Princeton University Press, 1990.

Hsiao, Kung-chuan. *Rural China: Imperial Control in the Nineteenth Century*. Seattle: University of Washington Press, 1960.

Huang, Ray. *1587, A Year of No Significance: The Ming Dynasty in Decline*. New Haven: Yale University Press, 1981.

Johnson, Wallace. *The T'ang Code: General Principles*. Princeton: Princeton University Press, 1979.

Kahn, Harold L. *Monarchy in the Emperor's Eyes: Image and Reality in the Ch'ien-lung Reign*. Cambridge, Mass.: Harvard University Press, 1971.

Perdue, Peter C. *Exhausting the Earth: State and Peasant in Hunan, 1500–1850*. Cambridge, Mass.: Harvard University Press, 1987.

Spence, Jonathan D. *Emperor of China: Self-Portrait of K'ang-hsi*. New York: Knopf, 1974.

———. *Ts'ao Yin and the K'ang-hsi Emperor: Bondservant and Master*. New Haven: Yale University Press, 1988.

van der Sprenkel, S. *Legal Institutions in Manchu China*. London: Athlone Press, 1962.

Wakeman, Frederic, Jr., and Carolyn Gant, eds. *Conflict and Control in Late Imperial China*. Berkeley: University of California Press, 1975.

Will, Pierre-Etienne. *Bureaucracy and Famine in Eighteenth-Century China*. Trans. Elborg Forster. Stanford: Stanford University Press, 1990.

Zelin, Madeline. *The Magistrate's Tael: Rationalizing Fiscal Reform in Eighteenth-Century Ch'ing China*. Berkeley: University of California Press, 1984.

Modern Elites and Modern Revolutions

Chen, Yung-fa. *Making Revolution: The Communist Movement in Eastern and Central China, 1937–1945*. Berkeley: University of California Press, 1986.

Chang Hao. *Chinese Intellectuals in Crisis: Search for Order and Meaning (1890–1911)*. Berkeley: University of California Press, 1987.

Chow, Tse-tsung. *The May Fourth Movement: Intellectual Revolution in Modern China.* Stanford: Stanford University Press, 1967 (originally published 1960).

Croll, Elisabeth. *Feminism and Socialism in China.* London: Routledge and Kegan Paul, 1978.

Eastman, Lloyd E. *The Abortive Revolution: China Under Nationalist Rule, 1927–1937.* Cambridge, Mass.: Harvard University Press, 1974.

Esherick, Joseph W. *Reform and Revolution in China: The 1911 Revolution in Hunan and Hubei.* Berkeley: University of California Press, 1976.

———. *The Origins of the Boxer Uprising.* Berkeley: University of California Press, 1987.

———, and Mary Backus Rankin, eds. *Chinese Local Elites and Patterns of Dominance.* Berkeley: University of California Press, 1990.

Grieder, Jerome B. *Intellectuals and the State in Modern China.* New York: Free Press,

Hofheinz, Roy, Jr. *The Broken Wave: The Chinese Communist Peasant Movement, 1922–1928.* Cambridge, Mass.: Harvard University Press, 1977.

Johnson, Chalmers A. *Peasant Nationalism and Communist Power: The Emergence of Revolutionary China, 1937–1945.* Stanford: Stanford University Press, 1962.

Lee, Leo Ou-fan. *The Romantic Generation of Modern Chinese Writers.* Cambridge, Mass.: Harvard University Press, 1973.

Levenson, Joseph R. *Liang Ch'i-ch'ao and the Mind of Modern China.* Berkeley: University of California Press, 1967 (originally published 1953).

Nathan, Andrew J. *Chinese Democracy.* Berkeley: University of California Press, 1985.

Perry, Elizabeth J. *Rebels and Revolutionaries in North China, 1845-1945.* Stanford: Stanford University Press, 1980.

Rankin, Mary Backus. *Early Chinese Revolutionaries: Radical Intellectuals in Shanghai and Chekiang, 1902–1911.* Cambridge, Mass.: Harvard University Press, 1971.

Schiffrin, Harold Z. *Sun Yat-sen and the Origins of the Chinese Revolution.* Berkeley: University of California Press, 1970.

Schram, Stuart. *Mao Tse-tung.* Baltimore: Penguin, 1966.

Schwartz, Benjamin. *In Search of Wealth and Power: Yen Fu and the West.* Cambridge, Mass.: Harvard University Press, 1964.

Schwarcz, Vera. *The Chinese Enlightment: Intellectuals and the Legacy of the May Fourth Movement of 1919.* Berkeley: University of California Press, 1986.

Spence, Jonathan D. *The Gate of Heavenly Peace: The Chinese and Their Revolution, 1895-1980.* New York: The Viking Press, 1981.

Snow, Edgar. *Red Star Over China.* New York: Modern Library, 1938.

Wasserstrom, Jeffrey N. *Student Protests in Twentieth-Century China: The View from Shanghai.* Stanford: Stanford University Press, 1991.

Wright, Mary Clabaugh, ed. *China in Revolution: The First Phase, 1900–1913.* New Haven: Yale University Press, 1968.

State and Society in the PRC

Bannister, Judith. *China's Changing Population.* Stanford: Stanford University Press, 1987.

Belden, Jack. *China Shakes the World.* New York: Monthly Review Press, 1970 (originally published 1949).

Bennett, Gordon A., and Ronald N. Montaperto. *Red Guard.* New York: Viking Press, 1972.

Burns, John P. *Political Participation in Rural China.* Berkeley: University of California Press, 1988.

Chan, Anita, Richard Madsen, and Jonathan Unger. *Chen Village: The Recent History of a Peasant Community in Mao's China.* Berkeley: University of California Press, 1984.

Chang, Jung. *Wild Swans: Three Daughters of China.* New York: Simon and Schuster, 1991.

Davis-Friedmann, Deborah. *Long Lives: Chinese Elderly and the Communist Revolution.* Rev. ed. Stanford: Stanford University Press, 1991.

Frolic, B. Michael. *Mao's People: Sixteen Portraits of Life in Revolutionary China.* Cambridge, Mass.: Harvard University Press, 1980.

Gao Yuan. *Born Red: A Chronicle of the Cultural Revolution.* Stanford: Stanford University Press, 1987.

Goldman, Merle. *Literary Dissent in Communist China.* Cambridge, Mass.: Harvard University Press, 1967.

Hinton, Willima. *Fanshen: A Documentary of Revolution in a Chinese Village.* New York: Monthly Review Press, 1966.

Honig, Emily and Gail Hershatter. *Personal Voices: Chinese Women in the 1980's.* Stanford: Stanford University Press, 1988.

Huang, Shu-min. *The Spiral Road: Change in a Chinese Village Through the Eyes of a Communist Party Leader.* Boulder: Westview Press, 1989.

Lull, James. *China Turned On: Television, Reform, and Resistance* London: Routledge, 1991.

Madsen, Richard. *Morality and Power in a Chinese Village.* Berkeley: University of California Press, 1984.

Myrdal, Jan. *Report from a Chinese Village.* New York: New American Library, 1965.

Parish, William, and Martin Whyte. *Village and Family in Contemporary China.* Chicago: University of Chicago Press, 1978.

Oi, Jean C. *State and Peasant in Contemporary China: The Political Economy of Village Government.* Berkeley: University of California Press, 1989.

Schell, Orville. *Discos and Democracy: China in the Throes of Reform.* New York: Anchor Books, 1989.

Shue, Vivienne. *Peasant China in Transition: The Dynamics of the Development Toward Socialism, 1949–1956.* Berkeley: University of California Press, 1980.

Sui, Helen F. *Agents and Victims in South China: Accomplices in Rural Revolution.* New Haven: Yale University Press, 1989.

Thurston, Anne F. *Enemies of the People: The Ordeal of the Intellectuals in China's Great Cultural Revolution.* Cambridge, Mass.: Harvard University Press, 1988.

Vogel, Ezra. *Canton Under Communism: Programs in a Provincial Capital, 1949–1968.* Cambridge, Mass.: Harvard University Press, 1969 (paperback: Harper Torchbooks).

———. *One Step Ahead in China: Guangdong Under Reform.* Cambridge, Mass.: Harvard University Press, 1989.

Walder, Andrew G. *Communist Neo-Traditionalism: Work and Authority in Chinese Industry.* Berkeley: University of California Press, 1986.

Wolf, Margery. *Revolution Postponed: Women in Contemporary China.* Stanford: Stanford University Press, 1985.

ORIGINAL SOURCES

1. Guo Moruo, ed., Hu Houxuan, ed.-in-chief, *Jiagu-wen heji*, 13 vols. (N.p.: Zhonghua shuju, 1978–82), nos. 6647, 6409, 6473, 11497, 9950, 13646, 14002, 12883, 776, 14206, 6459, 838, 14198, 10084, 12616, 37380, 39393. The inscriptions translated here are treated more fully in David N. Keightley, "Shang Oracle-Bone Inscriptions," in Edward L. Shaughnessy, ed., *Paleographic Sources of Early China* (Hong Kong: Chinese University Press, 1993).

2. *Shangshu* (Sibu beiyao ed.), 7:7b–10a. This book is also available in complete translation. See James Legge, trans., *The Chinese Classics* (Hong Kong: Hong Kong University Press, 1961 [reprint of 1893–95 ed.]), III, or Bernhard Karlgren, trans., "The Book of Documents," *Bulletin of the Museum of Far Eastern Antiquities* 22 (1950):1–81.

3. *Zhouyi* (Shisanjing zhushu ed.), 111a–28a. This book is also available in complete translation. See Richard Wilhelm, trans., *The I Ching or Book of Changes* (Princeton: Princeton University Press, 1967).

4. *Shijing*, Mao numbers 76, 153, 178, and 234. For complete translations, see Arthur Waley, trans., *The Book of Songs* (London: George Allen and Unwin, 1937), or Bernard Karlgren, *The Book of Odes* (Stockholm: Museum of Far Eastern Antiquities, 1950).

5. *Chunqiu jing zhuan jijie* (Sibu beiyao ed.), 11/8b–12a. The *Zuo Chronicle* is translated in the notes of Legge's translation of the *Spring and Autumn Annals* in *The Chinese Classics*, V.

6. Part 1, *Lunyu*, 2.3, 3.19, 12.7, 12.19, 13.2, 13.13, 13.15, 14.44, 15.5, 15:31, 1:14, 2:13, 12:4, 16:18, 16:7, 4:16, 15:17, 5:15, 16:10, 13:25, 13:23, 14:24, 15:20, 15:18, 15:19, 15:22, 13:26. 19:9, 1:8, 19:21, 17:24, 14:28, 2:12, 17:6, 12:2, 12:3, 1:3, 13:27, 6:21, 3:3, 4:1, 15:34, 4:5, 15:8, 15:35, 7:29, 15:9, 4:3, 4:7, 14:5, 14:7, 2:7, 1:11, 19:18, 2:5, 4:19, 4:21, 4:18, 13:18. For a complete translation of this book, see Arthur Waley, trans., *The Analects of Confucius* (London: George Allen and Unwin, 1938), or D. C. Lau, *The Analects* (New York: Penguin Books, 1979). Part 2, *Mengzi* 1A:1, 1A:6, 1B:2, 1B:12, 1B:8, 5B:9, 6B:10, 2A:6, 6A:2. For a full translation, see D. C. Lau, *Mencius* (New York: Penguin Books, 1970). Part 3, Wang Xianqian, *Xunzi jijie* (Taibei: Shijie shuju, 1978), 11:205, 207–8, 211, 13:231, 249–50, 289–90, 291, 299–300. For translations of lengthy parts of *Xunzi*, see John Knoblock, *Xunzi: A Translation and Study of the Complete Works*, 2 vols. to date (Stanford: Stanford University Press, 1988, 1990), or Burton Watson, trans., *Basic Writings of Mo Tzu, Hsün Tzu, and Han Fei Tzu* (New York: Columbia University Press, 1967).

7. Part 1, Jiang Xichang, *Laozi jiaogu* (Taibei: Dongsheng chubanshe, 1980), pp. 2–26, 33–48, 214–19, 235–39, 396–400, 459–63. For complete translations, see D. C. Lau, trans., *Tao Te Ching* (Hong Kong: Chinese University Press, 1982) or Victor H. Mair, trans. (New York: Bantam Books, 1990). Part 2, *Zhuangzi* (Baizi quanshu ed.) 1 (1:2a) 2 (1:3a, 4a–b), 3 (1:5a), 4 (1:7b), 7 (1:12b), 13 (2:10a–b), 18 (2:16b–17a), 32 (3:19a). For lengthy translations, see A. C. Graham, trans., *Chuang Tzu: The Inner Chapters* (London: George Allen and Unwin, 1981) or Burton Watson, trans., *The Complete Works of Chuang Tzu* (New York: Columbia University Press, 1968).

8. Part 1, *Shangzi* (Baizi quanshu ed.) 1:1a–b. Part 2, *Han Feizi* (Baizi quanshu ed.) 17 (5:2b), 52 (20:2a–b); 48 (18:1a–b); 50 (19:5b–6a). Complete translations are available for both these books. See J.J.L. Duyvendak, trans., *The Book of Lord Shang* (London: Probsthain, 1928) and W. K. Liao, *The Complete Works of Han Fei Tzu*, 2 vols. (London: Probsthain, 1939 and 1959).

9. *Zhanguo ce* (Shanghai: Shanghai guji chubanshe, 1978), 18:579–99, 27:993–999. For a full translation, see J. I. Crump, Jr., *Chan-Kuo Ts'e* (Oxford: Clarendon Press, 1970).

10. *Yili zhengzhu* (Taibei, 1972 reprint), juan 3. See also the complete translation by John Steele, *The I-li* (London: Probsthain, 1917).

11. Shuihudi Qinmu zhujian hengli xiaozu, ed., *Shuihudi Qinmu zhujian* (Beijing: Wenwu, 1978.), 49–53, 67–68, 76–80, 84–90, 93–94, 150–54, 173, 181, 201–2, 204–5, 223. A thorough, scholarly translation of these texts is available, A. F. P. Hulsewé, *Remnants of Ch'in Law* (Leiden: E. J. Brill, 1985), and was relied on here.

12. *Shiji* (Beijing: Zhonghua shuju, 1962), 116:2991, 123:3160, 110:2879, 2890–92. Much of this history is translated in Burton Watson, trans., *Records of the Grand Historian of China*, 2 vols. (New York: Columbia University Press, 1961).

13. Dong Zhongshu, *Chunqiu fanlu zhu* (Taibei: Shijie shuju, 1962), 6:13a, 13:1b–2a, 11:6b–7a (pp. 135, 262–63, 290–3).

14. Huan Kuan, *Yantie lun jiaozhu* (Taibei: Shijie shuju ed., 1970), 1:1–11. See also the complete translation by Esson M. Gale, *Discourses on Salt and Iron* (Leiden: E. J. Brill, 1931) and *Journal of the North China Branch of the Royal Asiatic Society* 65 (1934):73–110.

15. *Xiaojing* (Shisanjing zhushu ed.). The couplets from the *Book of Songs* which end many of the sections have been omitted. For another translation of this work, see Mary Leslie Makra, trans., *The Hsiao Ching* (New York: St. John's University Press, 1961).

16. Wang Fu, *Qianfu lun* (Congshu jicheng ed.) 8:195–208. Lengthy excerpts (but not this section) of Wang Fu's work are translated in Margaret J. Pearson, *Wang Fu and the Comments of a Recluse* (Tempe, Ariz.: Center for Asian Studies, 1989).

17. Part 1, Liu Xiang, *Lienü zhuan* (Taibei, 1971 reprint of Ming illustrated edition), 3:33b–35a. Part 2, Fan Ye, *Hou-Han shu* (Beijing: Zhonghua shuju, 1963), 28B:1003–4 commentary. Part 3, *Nüjie* (*Gujin tushu jicheng* ed., ce 395) The *Lienü zhuan* has been translated by Albert R. O'Hara, *The Position of Woman in Early China, According to the Lieh Nü Chuan, "The Biographies of Chinese Women,"* (Washington, D.C.: Catholic University, 1945). The *Nüjie* is translated in full in Nancy Lee Swann, *Pan Chao: Foremost Woman Scholar of China* (New York: Century, 1932).

18. *Huangdi neijing suwen*, 5, in *Daozang* (Taibei: Yiwen yinshuguan reprint.) This book has been translated by Ilza Veith, *The Yellow Emperor's Classic of Internal Medicine* (Baltimore: Williams and Wilkins, 1949).

19. Yan Kejun, ed. *Quan Hou-Han wen*, in *Quan Shanggu Qin-Han Sanguo Liuchao wen* (Taibei: Shijie shuju reprint), 75:3a–b; 98:2a–b; 102:4b–5b.

20. Part 1, *Hou-Han shu* (Beijing: Zhonghua shuju, 1963), 71:2299–2300. Part 2, Chen Shou, *Sanguo zhi* (Bejing: Zhonghua shuju), 8:264 commentary. Part 3, Chang Ju, *Huayang guozhi* (Congshu jicheng ed.), 2:16–17.

21. Ge Hong, *Baopuzi* (Sibu beiyao ed.), 50:2a–8a. Another translation of this piece is found in James Ware, *Alchemy, Medicine, and Religion in China of A.D. 320* (Cambridge: MIT University Press, 1966), pp. 6–21.

22. Part 1 from *Weishu* (Beijing: Zhonghua shuju, 1974). Full translations of this text are found in James R. Ware, "Wei Shou on Buddhism," *T'oung Pao* 30 (1933), 100–81 and Leon Hurvitz, "Wei Shou, Treatise on Buddhism and Taoism," in *Yünkang, the Buddhist Cave-Temples of the Fifth Century A.D. in North China*, vol. 16 supplement (Kyoto: Jimbunkagaku kenkyūjo, 1956). Part 2, *Dazangjing*, vol. 50, p. 351, 394–95. Part 3, Stein 4528, 4366, 1910, 3935, 1177. Texts reproduced in Lionel Giles, "Dated Chinese Manuscripts in the Stein Collection," *Bulletin of the School of Oriental and African Languages* 7 (1935): 820, 826, 830; 9 (1937): 8, 1044. Part 4, Pelliot 3821. Text reproduced in Jao Tsung-yi and Paul Demieville, *Airs de Touen-houang* (Paris: Editions du Centre National de la Recherche Scientifique, 1971), plates 68–69.

23. Gan Bao, *Soushen ji* (Beijing: Zhonghua shuju, 1979), 194–95, 203–4, 210–11.

24. Part 1, Fan Xiangyong, *Loyang jielan ji jiaozhu* (Shanghai: Shanghai guji chubanshe, 1958), 2:117–18. Part 2, Yan Zhitui, *Yanshi jiaxun jijie* (Taibei: Wenming shuju, 1982), 60–62, 85, 87, 91, 100–2, 259. Complete translations of both these books are available. See W. F. J. Jenner, *Memories of Loyang: Yang Hsüan-chih and the Lost Capital (493–534)* (Oxford: Clarendon Press, 1981) and Teng Ssu-yü, *Family Instructions for the Yen Clan (Yen-shih chia-hsün), by Yen Chih-t'ui* (Leiden: E. J. Brill, 1968).

25. Tang Taizong, *Difan* (Congshu jicheng ed.), 1:1a–4:43.

26. *Tanglü shuyi* (Guoxue jiben congshu ed.) 19:63–20:70, 13:112–113.

27. *Jiu-Tang shu* (Beijing: Zhonghua shuju, 1975) 79:2723–26.

28. *Quan Tang shi* (Beijing: Zhonghua shuju, 1960), 87:962, 890:10050; Zheng Chuhui, *Minghuang zalu* (Tangdai congshu ed.) 8a–9a. These and other related pieces are translated with copious notes in Paul W. Kroll, "The Dancing Horses of T'ang," *T'oung Pao* 67 (1981), 240–68.

29. Part 1, Ikeda On, *Chūgoku kodai sekichō kenkyū* (Tokyo, 1979), pp. 195–196, 198. Part 2, Niida Noboru, *Tōsō hōritsu bunsho no kenkyū* (Tokyo: Daian, 1967 reprint of 1937 ed.), plate 4. Part 3, Dunhuang wenwu yanjiusuo ziliao shi, "Cong yijian nubei maimai wenshu kan Tangdai di jieji yanpo," *Wenwu*, 1972:12, 68–71. Part 4 and 5, Niida Noboru, *Chūgoku hōseishi kenkyū: dorei, nōdohō, kazoku, sonrakuhō* (Tokyo: Tokyo daigaku Tōyō bunka kenkyūjō, 1962), pp. 30–31, 570–576.

30. Wang Dingbao, *Tang zhiyan* (Taibei: Shijie shuju ed.), 3:29–30, 40; 4:47; 8:87, 89; 9:94, 95; 11:125

31. Ono Katsutoshi, *Nittō guhō junrei kōki no kenkyu* (Tokyo: Suzuki gakujutsu zaidan, 1969), 2:418–5:81. For a complete translation of this diary, see *Ennin's Diary: Record of a Pilgrimage to China in Search of the Law*, trans. Edwin O. Reischauer (New York: Ronald Press, 1955).

32. E. I. Kychanov, " 'Krupinki zolota na ladoni'—posobie dlia izucheniia tangutskoi pis'mennosti," *Zhanry i stili literatur Kitaia i Korei* (Moscow, 1969), 213–22; E. I. Kychanov, *Vnov' cobrannye dragotsennye parnye izrecheniia* (Moscow: Nauka, 1974), pp. 8, 33, 351, 158, 31, 43, 132, 146, 152, 155, 172, 245, 256, 261, 277, 278, 290, 313, 337, 349; *Songshi* (Beijing: Zhonghua shuju, 1977), 485:13995–96 and *Xu zizhi tongjian changbian* (Taibei: Shijie shuju, 1961), 123:2a; Gule Maocai, *Fan Han heshi zhang zhong shu* (Yinchuan: Ningxia renmin chubanshe, 1989), preface.

33. *Taishang ganying bian jian zhu* (Kyoto: Chūmon, 1970 ed.). This book has been translated several times, including James Webster, *The Kan Ying Pien, Book of Rewards and Punishments* (Shanghai: Presbyterian Mission Press, 1918).

34. "Chongyang lijiao shiwu lun," in *Daozang* (Taibei: Yiwen yinshuguan reprint).

35. *Sima Wenzheng gong chuanjiaji* (Guoxue jiben congshu ed.), 42:543–45, 60:719–25; *Wang Linchuan quanji* (Taibei: Shijie shuju, 1966), 463–64.

36. Fan Zhongyan, *Fan Wenzheng gong ji* (Sibu congkan ed.), Addendum, lb–3b. These rules plus all of the amendments have been translated by Denis Twitchett in his "Documents of Clan Administration, I," *Asia Major* 8 (1960):1–35.

37. Reproduced by permission of Princeton University Press from *Chu Hsi's Family Rituals: A Twelfth-Century Manual for the Performance of Cappings, Weddings, Funerals, and Ancestral Rites*, trans. Patricia Buckley Ebrey (Princeton: Princeton University Press, 1991), pp. 155–66.

38. Part 1, Hong Mai, *Yijian zhi* (Beijing: Zhonghua shuju, 1981), pp. 746–47, 484–85, 1554–55. Part 2, Yuan Cai, *Yuan shi shifan* (Congshu jicheng ed.), 1:17–21, 3:55–56. Yuan Cai's book has been translated in full by Patricia Buckley Ebrey in *Family and Property in Sung China: Yüan Ts'ai's "Precepts for Social Life"* (Princeton: Princeton University Press, 1984).

39. Gong Baoan, *Songci sanbai shou jinyi* (Xi'an: Shanxi renmin chubanshe, 1988), 238, 257, 267–68, 273, 348, 369.

40. *Zhuzi yulei* (Beijing: Zhonghua shuju, 1986), 4:61, 6:99, 9:152, 11:180, 12:211, 213, 13:246, 20:464, 63:1551–52, 89:2274–75, 2287, 2281, 103:2602, 113:2753, 2748, 114:2768, 121:2946, 2947, 126:3012.

41. "Duzheng jisheng," in *Dongjing menghua lu, wai si zhong* (Shanghai: Zhonghua shuju, 1962), pp. 91–101.

42. Zhen Dexiu, *Zhen Xishan ji* (Congshu jicheng ed.), 7:114–115.

43. Chen Pu, *Nongshu* (Congshu jicheng ed.), pp. 1–10.

44. Hu Zhiyu, *Zishan daquanji* (Siku quanshu ed.) 15:19a–22b.

45. Cheng Duanli, *Dushu fennian richeng* (Tanggui caotang congshu, 1864), preface, la–12b.

46. Guo Bi, *Yunshan riji*, in Zhu Wen and Ruan Wuming, ed., *Song Yuan di riji xuan* (Hong Kong: Taipingyang, 1957), pp. 112–115.

47. Ming Taizu, *Da gao*, (*Huang Ming zhishu* ed.), 1:43 (pp. 45–46), 2:74 (pp. 217–220).

48. Yang Sichang, "Wuling jingdu lüe," (*Shuofu xu* ed.), la–13b. This essay is also translated in full by Chao Wei-pang, "The Dragon Boat Race in Wuling, Hunan," *Folklore Studies* 2 (1943): 1–18.

49. Quoted in Niida, *Chūgoku hōseishi kenkyū: dorei, nōdohō, kazoku, sonrakuhō*, (Tokyo: Tokyo daigaku Tōyō bunka kenkyūjo, 1962), pp. 763, 773, 781–782.

50. Part 1 quoted in Niida, *Chūgoku hōseishi kenkyū: dorei, nōdohō, kazoku, sonrakuhō*, pp. 806–811. Part 2, Zhang Han, *Songchuang meng yu* (1896

ed.) 4:16b–24a. Part 3, Wang Daokun, *Taihan fumo* (1633 ed.), 13:21a–23b, 30a–33a.

51. Xu Yikui, *Shifeng gao*, in *Wulin wangzhe yizhu* (1894 ed.), 2:3a–4a.

52. Fu Yiling, "Mingdai Huizhou zhuangpu wenyue jicun," *Wenwu*, 1960:2: 11–13; Ji Liuqi, *Mingji nanlüe* (Taiwan wenxian congkan ed.), 9:266.

53. *Shuihu zhuan* (Taibei, 1972 ed.), 1:18–2:30. This novel has been translated in full by Pearl S. Buck, *All Men Are Brothers* (New York: John Day, 1933).

54. Quoted in Taga Akigoro, *Sōfuku no kenkyū* (Tokyo: Tōyō bunko, 1960), pp. 604–608.

55. Part 1, *Taoan mengyi* (Biji xiaoshuo daguan ed.), 5:12b–14a. Part 2, Mao Xiang, *Yingmeian yiyu* (Taibei: Shijie shuju, 1959), pp. 4–6. For a complete translation, see *The Reminiscences of Tung Hsiao-wan*, by Mao P'i-chiang, trans. Pan Tze-yen (Shanghai: The Commercial Press, 1931), pp. 16–29. Part 3, *Jin Ping Mei cihua* (Tokyo: Daian, 1963 reprint of Ming, Wanli ed.), juan 2 (round 11), pp. 229–241. This novel has been translated in full by Clement Egerton, *The Golden Lotus*, I–IV (London: Routledge, 1939).

56. *Fuzhou fuzhi* (1754 ed.) 68:17b–23b.

57. Part 1, Chen Rungjie, *Wang Yangming Quanxilu xiangzhu jiping* (Taibei: Xuesheng shuju, 1983), pp. 291, 292–93, 297, 357. For a full translation, see *Instructions for Practical Living and Other Neo-Confucian Writings by Wang Yang-ming*, trans. by Wing-tsit Chan (New York: Columbia University Press, 1963). Part 2, Li Zhi, *Fenshu xufenshu* (Beijing: Zhonghua shuju, 1975), pp. 29–31, 45–46, 52–53, 140–141, 101–102.

58. Yang Lien, *Yang Dahong xiansheng wenji* (Congshu jicheng ed.), 1–7.

59. Wang Xiuchu, *Yangzhou shiri ji* (Shanghai: Shanghai shudian, 1982), pp. 229–68.

60. Retranslated from the texts collected by W. Scarborough, *A Collection of Chinese Proverbs* (Changsha, 1926), and Cifford H. Plopper, *Chinese Religion Seen Through the Proverb* (Shanghai, 1926).

61. Ye Mengzhu, *Yue shi bian*, 6:1a–5a, 12a–19a, in *Shanghai zhanggu congshu* (Shanghai: Zhonghua shuju, 1936).

62. Zhang Ying, *Hengchan suoyan* (Congshu jicheng ed.), pp. 1–9. This essay is translated in full in Hilary J. Beattie, *Land and Lineage in China* (Cambridge: Cambridge University Press, 1979), pp. 140–151.

63. Lan Dingyuan, *Luzhou gong'an* (1881 ed.), 2:11a–14a, 1:14a–16b.

64. Wang Youpu, *Shengyu guangxun yan*, 9, in *Wang Jieshan xiansheng quanji*.

65. Part 1, Chūgoku nōson kankō chōsa kankōkai, *Chūgoku nōson kankō chōsa* (Tokyo: Iwanami shoten, 1958), 6:268. Part 2, Imahori Seiji, "Shindai ni okeru sonraku kyōdotai," *Rekishi kyōiku*. 13:9 (1965), 38–51 (document, p. 50).

66. From Wu Jingzi, *The Scholars*, trans. by Yang Hsien-yi and Gladys Yang (Beijing: Foreign Languages Press, 1957), with the romanization converted from Wade-Giles to pinyin.

67. *Gaoyang xianzhi* (1826 ed.), 21:36a–b.

68. Translation adapted from that in *China Repository* 15 (1846):46–51.

69. Wu Yun, *Deyi lu* (Taibei: Huawen shuju, 1969 reprint of 1869 ed.), 2:1a–6a.

70. Sasaki Masaya, *Shinmatsu no himitu kessha, shiryō hen* (Tokyo: Kindai Chūgoku kenkyū i-inkai, 1967), pp. 246–248, 1–2, 17–19.

71. Jiangsusheng Bowuguan, *Jiangsusheng Ming Qing yilai beike ziliao xuanji* (Beijing: Sanlian shudian, 1959), pp. 14–15; *Yangwu yundong* (Shanghai: Renmin chubanshe, 1957), pp. 404–406.

72. Quoted in Makino Tatsumi, *Kinsei Chūgoku sōzoku kenkyū* (Tokyo: Ocha-no-mizu shobo, 1949), pp. 71–73.

73. R. David Arkush and Leo O. Lee, trans. and ed., *Land Without Ghosts: Chinese Impressions of America from the Mid-Nineteenth Century to the Present*. (Berkeley: University of California Press, 1989), pp. 84–95. Reproduced with permission of the publisher.

74. Part 1 and 2, Li Youning and Zhang Yufa, *Jindai Zhongguo nüquan yundong shiliao, 1842–1911* (Taibei: Zhuanji wenxue she, 1975), pp. 577–580, 423–424. Part 3, *Yunnan zazhi*, July 7, 1907, quoted in *Yunnan zazhi xuanji* (Beijing: Kexue chubanshe, 1958). Part 4, Hu Huaican, "Shifang beinü yi," *Funü zazhi* 6 (Jan. 1920): 1–4.

75. Yu Ziyi, "Ershi nian qian xiangcun xuexiao shenghuoli di wo," *Jiaoyu zazhi* 19 (Dec. 20, 1927): 30533–30545.

76. From *Selected Stories of Lu Hsun*, trans. by Yang Hsien-i and Gladys Yang (Peking: Foreign Languages Press, 1960), with romanization converted into pinyin.

77. Adapted from the translation by Liu Xiaohong in *Women of China*, May 1989, pp. 40–43.

78. *Diyi ci guonei geming zhanzheng shiqi di nongmin yundong* (Zhongguo xiandaishi ziliao congkan, Beijing, 1953), pp. 51–70. Peng Pai's report has been translated in full by Donald Holoch, *Seeds of Peas-*

ant Revolution: Report on the Haifeng Peasant Movement (Ithaca: Cornell University China–Japan Program, 1973).

79. Gong Yao et al., "Huoguo yangmin tanwu canbao zhi Zhang Zongchang," *Yijing* 6 (May 20, 1936): 316–320.

80. *Diyi ci guonei geming zhanzheng shiqi di gongren yundong* (Zhongguo xiandaishiziliao congkan, Beijing, 1954), pp. 450–466.

81. Gu Jiegang, "Liangge chubin di daozizhang," reprinted in Gu Jiegang and Liu Wanzhang, *Su Yue di hunsang* (Zhongshan daxue minsu congshu, 1928–29), pp. 30–43.

82. Zhu Ziqing, *Zhu Ziqing wenji* (Beijing: Kaiming shudian, 1959), pp. 197–204.

83. Liu Xu, "Beiping di qigai shenghuo," reprinted in Li Jiarui, ed., *Beiping fengsu leicheng* (Shanghai: Commercial Press, 1939), pp. 405–408.

84. Trans. adapted from *President Chiang Kai-shek's Selected Speeches and Messages, 1937–1945* (Taipei: China Cultural Service, n.d.), pp. 84–105, 262–70.

85. Trans. adapted from *Selected Works of Liu Shaoqi*, vol. 1 (Beijing: Foreign Languages Press, 1984), pp. 74–81.

86. Adapted from Ting Ling, *The Sun Shines over the Sangkan River*, trans. by Yang Hsien-yi and Gladys Yang (Beijing: Foreign Languages Press, 1954), pp. 203–217.

87. *Renmin ribao*, May 13, 1955; May 24, 1955; June 10, 1955; *Selected Works of Mao Tsetung*, Volume 5 (Peking: Foreign Languages Press, 1977), pp. 176–78; *Current Background* 897 (Dec. 10, 1969): 14, 15, 32.

88. Wang Meng, "Zuzhibu xinlai di qingnian ren," *Renmin wenxue*, Sept. 1956. Trans. adapted from *Current Background* 459 (June 28, 1957): 1–32.

89. Trans. adapted from *Memoirs of a Chinese Marshal— The Autobiographical Notes of Peng Dehuai (1898–1974)*, trans. Zheng Longpu (Beijing: Foriegn Languages Press, 1984), pp. 510–20.

90. *Renmin ribao*, Dec. 14, 1965. Trans. adapted from *Selections from the China Mainland Press* (hereafter *SCMP*) 3609 (Jan. 4, 1966).

91. Trans. adapted from Chen Kuangsheng, *Lei Feng, Chairman Mao's Good Fighter* (Beijing: Foreign Languages Press, 1968), pp. 14–16, 60–64, 71, 75–76.

92. *Xinmin wanbao* (Nov. 2, 1965). Trans. adapted from *Union Research Service* 43 (Apr. 12, 1966): 57–59.

93. Part 1, New China News Agency release, Nov. 11, 1966, quoting *Hongqi*; trans. adapted from *SCMP* 3822 (Nov. 17, 1966): 27–28. Part 2, *Yangcheng wanbao*, Aug. 25, 1966; trans. adapted from *SCMP* 3774 (Sept. 6, 1966): 19–20. Part 3, New China News Agency release, Nov. 19, 1966; trans. adapted from *SCMP* 3827 (Nov. 25, 1966): 19–23. Part 4, *Dongfang hong*, Sept. 21, 1967; trans. adapted from *SCMP* 4087 (Dec. 27, 1967): 1–3.

94. Translation adapted from Liu Xinwu, Wang Meng, and Others, *Prize-Winning Stories from China 1978–79* (Beijing: Foreign Languages Press, 1981).

95. Part 1, "The Correct Handling of Love, Marriage, and Family Problems," *Chinese Sociology and Anthropology* 1:3 (Spring 1969): 17–21; reprinted by permission of M. E. Sharpe, Inc. Part 2, *Nanfang ribao* Feb. 8, 1975; trans. adapted from *Union Research Service* 79 (May 13, 1975): 148–51. Part 3, "Come, Let Us Talk of Love," *Chinese Sociology and Anthropology*, Winter 1981–82, pp. 7–10, reproduced by permission of M. E. Sharpe, Inc. Part 4, *Women of China*, Nov. 1989, pp. 1–5.

96. Part 1, *Sichuan Daily*, July 4, 1987, trans. adapted from JPRS Report-China September 8, 1987. Part 2, *Nü qingnian* 7 (1986): 29–30, trans. from *Chinese Sociology and Anthropology* 20:3 (Spring 1988), pp. 93 and 98–100, reproduced by permission of M. E. Sharpe, Inc.

97. Part 1, *Zhongguo funü bao*, Feb. 27, 1985, p. 1; translation from *Chinese Sociology and Anthropology* 20 (Fall 1987): 65–66. Part 2, *Funü gongzuo* 4 (1987): 9–10; trans. from *Chinese Sociology and Anthropology* 21:3 (Spring 1989): 41–44. Part 3, *Zhongguo funü*, January 1988, pp. 6–7; translation from *Chinese Education* 25:1 (Spring 1992): 70–74. The last three reproduced by permission of M. E. Sharpe, Inc. Part 4, *China Daily*, June 1, 1989.

98. Part 1, *Chinese Literature*, Spring 1986, pp. 35–43. Part 2, *Federal Broadcast Information Service-China*, March 24, 1989, pp. 55–57.

99. Han Minzhu, ed. *Cries for Democracy: Writings and Speeches from the 1989 Chinese Democracy Movement* (Princeton: Princeton University Press, 1990), pp. 41–42, 75–76, 82–83, 105–7, 234–36. Reproduced by permission of the publisher.

100. *Renmin ribao* March 2, 1990, p. 6; trans. adapted from *Federal Broadcast Information Service-China*, March 8, 1990, pp. 24–28.

INDEX

For broad topics, see Contents According to Topics, *pp. xv–xvii.*